W9-CNC-787

Emotions in Health and Illness
Theoretical and Research Foundations

Mind and Medicine

Series Editors

Leonard S. Zegans, M.D.
Robert S. Wallerstein, M.D.
Lydia Temoshok, Ph.D.

Emotions in Health and Illness
Theoretical and Research Foundations

Editors

Lydia Temoshok, Ph.D.

Assistant Professor of Medical Psychology
Department of Psychiatry
University of California
School of Medicine
San Francisco, California

Craig Van Dyke, M.D.

Associate Professor
Department of Psychiatry
University of California
School of Medicine
Chief, Consultation-Liaison Unit
Veterans Administration Medical Center
San Francisco, California

Leonard S. Zegans, M.D.

Professor and Director of
Education and Professional Standards
Department of Psychiatry
University of California
School of Medicine
San Francisco, California

Grune & Stratton
A Subsidiary of Harcourt Brace Jovanovich, Publishers
New York   London
Paris   San Diego   San Francisco   São Paulo
Sydney   Tokyo   Toronto

Library of Congress Cataloging in Publication Data
Main entry under title:

Emotions in health and illness

(Mind and medicine)
Papers presented at a conference held in
San Francisco Feb. 13–14, 1982.
Bibliography
Includes index.
1. Medicine and psychology—Congresses. 2. Emotions
—Physiological aspects—Congresses. 3. Medicine,
Psychosomatic—Congresses. I. Temoshok, Lydia.
II. Van Dyke, Craig. III. Zegans, Leonard S.
IV. Series. [DNLM: 1. Emotions—Physiology. 2. Stress,
Psychological. 3. Psychophysiologic disorders. WL103E54]
R726.5.E46 1983   616.08   83-12724
ISBN 0-8089-1581-9

Grune & Stratton, Inc.
111 Fifth Avenue
New York, NY 10003

Distributed in the United Kingdom by
Grune & Stratton, Inc. (London) Ltd.
24/28 Oval Road, London NW 1

Library of Congress Catalog Number   83-12724
International Standard Book Number   0-8089-1581-9

Printed in the United States of America

Contents

We wish to express our appreciation to all those who helped in bringing this book, and the San Francisco conference on which it was based, to reality. We would particularly like to thank Aveleen Blumenstock, Pat McClelland, Marc Zegans, and our editor at Grune & Stratton. We also are grateful to our many colleagues at the Department of Psychiatry and the University of California at San Francisco Medical School, whose advice, support, and encouragement made this project possible.

Introduction

No concept is more intriguing or puzzling than the relationship between mind and body. For many centuries, questions about psyche and soma were reserved for philosophers and theologians. Then, in the nineteenth century, medicine and the behavioral sciences awoke to the realization, long known to the poets, that our wishes, fears, conflicts, and other emotions can profoundly alter the workings of our bodies. Early in the twentieth century, the psychosomatic movement attempted to understand such illnesses as asthma and ulcerative colitis from a psychodynamic perspective. Later, new conceptual systems arose to take into account our greater understanding of the workings of the human mind and body. A whole new field—*behavioral medicine*—introduced such interventions as biofeedback and behavior modification, which are now being used along with traditional psychotherapies and pharmacotherapies to treat patients with physical disorders. Current research is examining how stress, coping, emotion, and cognition affect physiological responses as well as the initiation and course of many diseases. These investigations are changing our concept of mind–body systems, of disease, and of the ways in which physicians work with their patients.

The *Mind and Medicine* series is intended to guide health professionals, students, and interested nonspecialists through the thicket of data, theory, and techniques flourishing in the interface between medicine and the behavioral and social sciences. The aim of this series is to present original work in new and challenging areas and to suggest how it may be applied to prevention, diagnosis, treatment, and rehabilitation. The first two volumes explore the roles emotions play in health and illness. This volume is concerned with current theory and research, while the second volume will consider clinical applications. Later volumes will discuss the developmental and interpersonal consequences of impairments of perception, communication, cognition, and movement, as well as the assessment and treatment of patients with these disorders. We intend to highlight other new perspectives and insights on the relationships between mind and medicine. We look forward to such future developments, for which we hope to provide context, clarification, and commentary.

Leonard S. Zegans, M.D.
Lydia Temoshok, Ph.D.
Robert S. Wallerstein, M.D.

Preface

Emotions are boundary phenomena in that they are both of the mind and of the body. These boundary characteristics make emotion a likely candidate to bridge the mind-body gap. We often think we can control our emotions, yet at times we sense that they possess us. Thus, emotion is a particularly appropriate subject for our initial consideration in the *Mind and Medicine* series.

The first volume in the series presents the theoretical and research foundations for the role of emotions in health and illness. In putting together this volume, we selected different dimensions of this topic: the contexts of psychosomatic and behavioral medicine; studies on stress; research on physiological concomitants and consequences of emotion; and theoretical perspectives.

Part I discusses the historical boundaries of the field. Robert Wallerstein introduces the field of psychosomatic medicine by tracing its history from the 1930s to the current period of dramatic conceptual change. Stephen Weiss then elaborates on the unique contributions of the behavioral medicine perspective to the prevention and control of chronic diseases and the promotion of health. Peter Knapp follows with an example of how the perspectives of psychosomatic and behavioral medicine may be combined. In his model of human emotions, external expressive behaviors, felt experiences of self, and physiological manifestations interact and contribute to a variety of disorders.

In Part II, Frances Cohen provides a context for understanding stress and emotion by summarizing a number of studies that focus on the relationships of stress, emotion, and behavior to the etiology of physical disease. Craig Van Dyke and I. Charles Kaufman relate psychological changes during separation and bereavement to changes in the functioning of the endocrine and immune systems. Depression is connected to the perception of health in Myrna Weissman's report of a landmark epidemiological study of psychiatric and physical disorders. Theodore Dembroski and his colleagues cite evidence suggesting that excessive response of the sympathetic nervous system to environmental challenges may be the connection between type A behavior and coronary heart disease. Similarly, Margaret Appel, Kenneth Holroyd, and Larry Gorkin discuss the role of anger and its management in relation to coronary heart disease, chronic headaches, cancer, and aging.

Part III focuses on the physiological dimension. Enoch Callaway raises critical questions about the manner in which emotions may be related to psychiatric and physical disorders. Jonathan Mueller discusses the role of neural structures in emotions. He focuses on altered behavior in relation to hemispheric specialization, acquired language disorders, temporal lobe epilepsy, and dementia. Richard Davidson presents research which suggests that impaired interhemispheric communication may contribute to decreased emotional responsiveness. Investigations documenting the biological impact of behavioral conditioning on modulating the immune response are summarized by Robert Ader, who has done seminal work in this new area. Philip Berger discusses research strategies that can better define the role of endorphins and other endogenous opiates in both normal behavior and in physical and mental disorders. George Solomon and Alfred Amkraut discuss hormones—their effects on the body's immune system, their potential contributions to a variety of physical and mental disorders, and their other ties to emotions.

In Part IV, Bruce Heller sets the stage for a discussion of some theoretical perspectives on emotion by emphasizing that an adequate model of emotion must be able to integrate and account for data across biological, psychological, and sociocultural domains. George Mandler outlines a cognitive approach to linking informational and representational features to underlying physiological mechanisms, and applies this approach to an understanding of stress and its management. A multidimensional theory of emotion, adaptation, and maladaptive transformation is proposed by Lydia Temoshok to address observed and postulated relations between stress and psychological and somatic disorders. In the last chapter, Leonard Zegans concludes that evidence and speculation point to emotion as the link between psychological meanings and organic responses.

Contributors

Robert Ader, Ph.D.   Professor of Psychiatry and Psychology, Division of Behavioral and Psychosocial Medicine, Department of Psychiatry, University of Rochester School of Medicine and Dentistry, Rochester, New York

Alfred A. Amkraut, Ph.D.   Senior Research Scientist, Alza Research, Palo Alto, California

Margaret A. Appel, Ph.D.   Associate Professor of Psychology, Department of Psychology, Ohio University, Athens, Onio

Philip A. Berger, M.D.   Associate Professor of Psychiatry, Stanford University School of Medicine; Director, Stanford Mental Health Clinical Research Center, Palo Alto Veterans Administration Medical Center, Palo Alto, California

James C. Buell, M.D.   Assistant Professor, Department of Preventative and Stress Medicine, University of Nebraska Medical Center, Omaha, Nebraska

Enoch Callaway, M.D.   Professor of Psychiatry, Department of Psychiatry, University of California, San Francisco, California

Frances Cohen, Ph.D.   Assistant Professor of Medical Psychology, Graduate Group in Psychology, University of California, San Francisco, California

Richard J. Davidson, Ph.D.   Associate Professor of Psychology, State University of New York, Purchase, New York

Theodore M. Dembroski, Ph.D.   Professor of Psychiatry; Director, Stress and Cardiovascular Research Center, Eckerd College, St. Petersburg, Florida

Robert S. Eliot, M. D.   Professor and Chairman, Department of Preventative and Stress Medicine, University of Nebraska Medical Center, Omaha, Nebraska

Larry Gorkin, Ph.D.   Department of Psychology, Ohio University, Athens, Ohio.

Bruce W. Heller, Ph.D.   Assistant Professor of Clinical Psychology, Department of Psychiatry; Director of Training, Center on Deafness, University of California, San Francisco, California

Kenneth A. Holroyd, Ph.D.   Associate Professor of Psychology, University of Ohio, Athens, Ohio

Charles E. Holzer, III, Ph.D.   Assistant Professor of Psychiatry and Sociology, Depression Research Unit, Yale University School of Medicine, New Haven, Connecticut

I. Charles Kaufman, M.D. Professor of Psychiatry, Department of Psychiatry; Chief, Psychiatry Service, Veterans Administration Medical Center, University of California, San Francisco, California

Peter H. Knapp, M.D. Professor and Director, Psychosomatic Services, Boston University School of Medicine, Boston, Massachusetts

Philip J. Leaf, Ph.D. Assistant Professor of Psychiatry and Sociology, Depression Research Unit, Yale University School of Medicine, New Haven, Connecticut

James M. MacDougall, Ph.D. Professor of Psychiatry; Associate Director, Stress and Cardiovascular Research Center, Eckerd College, St. Petersburg, Florida

George Mandler, Ph.D. Professor and Director, Center for Human Information Processing, University of California, San Diego, California

Jerome K. Myers, Ph.D. Professor and Chairman, Department of Sociology, Yale University School of Medicine, New Haven, Connecticut

Jonathan Mueller, M.D. Assistant Professor of Psychiatry, Department of Psychiatry, University of California, San Francisco, California

Helen Orvaschel, Ph.D. Assistant Professor, Department of Psychiatry, Yale University School of Medicine, New Haven, Connecticut

George F. Solomon, M.D. Professor and Vice Chairman, Department of Psychiatry, University of California, San Francisco, California

Lydia Temoshok, Ph.D. Assistant Professor of Medical Psychology, Department of Psychiatry, University of California, San Francisco, California

Gary L. Tischler, M.D. Professor, Department of Psychiatry and Institute for Social and Policy Studies; Director Yale Psychiatric Institute, Yale University School of Medicine, New Haven, Connecticut

Craig Van Dyke, M.D. Associate Professor of Psychiatry, Department of Psychiatry; Chief, Consultation-Liaison Unit, Veterans Administration Medical Center, University of California, San Francisco, California

Robert S. Wallerstein, M.D. Professor and Chairman, Department of Psychiatry, University of California, San Francisco, California

Stephen M. Weiss, Ph.D. Chief, Behavioral Medicine Branch, Division of Heart and Vascular Diseases; National Heart, Lung and Blood Institute, National Institutes of Health, Bethesda, Maryland

Myrna M. Weissman, Ph.D. Professor of Psychiatry and Epidemiology, Depression Research Unit, Yale University of Medicine, New Haven, Connecticut

Leonard S. Zegans, M.D. Professor and Director of Education and Professional Standards, Department of Psychiatry, University of California, San Francisco, California

Emotions in Health and Illness
Theoretical and Research Foundations

PART I

The Territory: Psychosomatic and Behavioral Medicine

Historical Perspective

Robert S. Wallerstein

It is for me a happy occasion indeed to introduce the inauguration of the University of California at San Francisco symposium series entitled *Mind and Medicine.*

This special pleasure is due to my own particular training: my entrance into psychiatry and psychoanalysis in the early post–World War II years from prior training in internal medicine, a once common and honored, but now rare, entry into a psychiatric and psychoanalytic career. Three years in medical residency and some years on an internal medicine service in an army general hospital preceded my own fateful switch into three more years of psychiatric residency at the Menninger School of Psychiatry, from which I finally emerged in 1951. Out of that lengthy apprenticeship in these two disciplines—internal medicine and psychiatry—the powers that be at the Menninger Clinic assumed that the staff position to which I was presumably most suited and logically would be most interested in was on the Psychosomatic Service. As this service was leaderless at the time, I became its chief, as my first professional position in psychiatry.

Thus began my original immersion in the field then called "psychosomatic medicine." It was a very different field than it is today, existing uneasily at the interface of somatic and psychological medicine. Internal medicine was on the threshold of becoming a truly academic discipline, planted firmly in the biological basic science laboratories, while psychiatry was in its first flush of its capture by the psychoanalytic idea and psychodynamic concepts. One of the first giants of psychosomatic medicine was Flanders Dunbar, a professor of medicine and of psychiatry at Columbia University College of Physicians and Surgeons in New York. In her book, *Emotions and Bodily Changes: A Survey of Literature on Psychosomatic Interrelationships*, published first in 1935 and with new editions in 1938 and 1946, Dunbar sought to write a comprehensive compendium of all the scientific knowledge that existed in this new psychosomatic field. By the time of the third edition there were already 2400 references cited, and Dunbar seemed proud that she had lived up to her intent of still being able to encompass the whole of the field within the covers of one book. Further, she had been instrumental in founding both the American Psychosomatic Society and its official journal, *Psychosomatic Medicine*, of which she was the first editor-in-chief. In fact, the journal, started in 1938, was intended originally as a sort of looseleaf supplement to Dunbar's book, a kind of annual update so that by first reading the book and then following the journal carefully, one would indeed be *au courant* on the totality of development in this field.

Much, very much, has happened in the four decades since then, and the field has long since transcended one author, one book, one journal, and one point of view. To give some historical perspective to the *Mind and Medicine* series on which we are embarking, it is worthwhile to briefly explore a necessarily overly schematized and overly simplified comparison between the field then and now.

In its early days the field of psychosomatic medicine was dominated by psychoanalytic thinking. In another volume, *Psychosomatic Diagnosis*, Dunbar elaborated the concept of the personality profile in relation to specific so-called psychosomatic afflictions: hypertensive cardiovascular disease, rheumatic disease, cardiac arrhythmias, and diabetes. Alongside Dunbar were Franz Alexander and his many colleagues, who in several books elaborated the concept of the core nuclear conflict around certain physiological functions such as intaking, eliminating, and holding in, which were then specifically linked to the psychological meanings and conflict structures that they were held to represent. These in turn were then applied to a whole range of psychosomatic disorders, including the so-called "big seven": peptic ulcer, ulcerative colitis, bronchial asthma, essential hypertension, diabetes, neuroder-matitis, and rheumatoid arthritis. Also working in this domain were Felix Deutsch, who conceptualized the psychosomatic unit, as well as others, including Maurice Levine, Mo Kaufman, Sydney Margolin, and others.

What held all of these people—and the field—together was a shared psychoanalytic perspective (Harold Wolff being at the time a singular exception to the prevailing viewpoint) and a shared conviction that the fullest psychological exploration of the psychic conflict structure of psychosomatic sufferers would unlock the doors to the understanding of their psyches and to the psychogenesis of their somatic disorders, as well as to the amelioration, if not the total cure, of their somatic disease. In addi-tion to the remarkable psychotherapeutic optimism that characterized that era, the most striking ele-ment was a one-sided or one-directional psycho-genetic perspective, marked by all the psychological and psychodynamic sophistication of the time, but marked also (for the most part) by simplemindedness of concept and measurement on the side of the con-comitant physiological and somatic inquiry and understanding.

The intervening history is long and complicated, but it can be readily enough traced through atten-tion to *Psychosomatic Medicine*, which, if it hasn't remained the only journal of its kind, has persisted as a bellwether of the field, a constantly revealing cross-sectional picture of where the field stands at any given time. In the interest of space constraints, I will briefly summarize the trends of the intervening years as I have discerned them:

- Certainly the therapeutic optimism, or rather over-optimism, that so characterized the excited beginnings of the field vanished into the crucible of difficult clinical psychotherapeutic experience with desperately ill people.
- As studies in the field burgeoned beyond the ori-ginal nucleus of psychoanalytic pioneers and pro-liferated widely across institutions and differing disciplines, it seemed to me that in centers of the highest psychological and psychodynamic sophis-tication and expertise, physiological studies of the same population were often far below state-of-the-art. Correspondingly, in those centers where biological methods and instrumentation (whether biophysical, biochemical, or physio-logical) were most advanced, the psychological/psychiatric studies were often naive and vastly oversimplified the complexity of mental function-

ing. In other words, comparable expertise and sophistication were by and large not being mounted simultaneously in the somatic and psychological realms in relation to the same population under study. This has always seemed to me to be clearly to the detriment of the field.
- There also appeared to be a long period during the clinical heyday of the central psychothera-peutic enterprise in psychiatry during which interest in the psychosomatic area languished, becoming the property of clinical and laboratory investigators and largely withdrawn from the arena of clinical application where it had fallen so far short of delivery on the overinflated thera-peutic expectations with which the enterprise had been launched.

But in the 1970s and 1980s, all of that has once again dramatically changed. Once again a rebirth of the old psychosomatic enterprise is taking place, but today it is far more complexly based and soundly conceptualized. Psychiatry as a whole has of course changed dramatically in recent years. It has grown in scope and diversity along all the dimensions of its underlying scientific bases—the biological, the psychological, and the social. A now popular catch-word for the biological aspect of its growth is the "remedicalization of psychiatry." The shift in perspective captured in that phrase has been powered by a literal explosion of new biological knowledge in our field—knowledge of brain-behavior relationships in the domain of mental and emotional disorders, as well as neural, hormonal, and immune mechanisms across the whole of the interface between disturbed physiological and psychological functioning. Along with develop-ments in all the various facets of neurobiology, neurophysiology, and neurochemistry (and inciden-tally, of course, in our understanding of genetics and the influence of inborn genetic loading upon subse-quent behavioral disorders) have been corollary applications in the directly clinical realm and in the steady growth of psychopharmacology within psy-chiatry, the varieties of psychoactive drugs, which are so large a part of the learning experience and the therapeutic armamentarium of today's psychiatrist.

This new growth in the biological realm of psychiatry has sparked the recent great revival of clinical psychiatric interest in the old psychosomatic domain, now under a variety of related rubrics: the psychiatric consultation-liaison activity and service, the health psychology focus, the behavioral medi-cine clinic and concept, and others. All of this activity is now being re-addressed in a much different manner from before; it is now simultaneously a complexly integrated biobehavioral research enterprise and a many-sided biopsychosocial clinical enterprise in hospital wards and clinics. My chief point here is that what essentially marks the difference between the psychosomatics of yesterday and today is that today the field is at last really able—and this series should amply attest to this—to approach the interface between mind and medicine with expertise, with sophistication, with rigor, with insightful questions, and with far more adequate methods simultaneously on both sides of the biological-psychological equation than we have ever heretofore been equipped to do.

It is this widespread possibility for simultaneous sophistication in the biological and the psychological realms of inquiry that makes the current era one of such excitement and promise. I hope very much that this volume, *Emotions in Health and Illness: Theoretical and Research Foundations*, the first in the *Mind and Medicine* series, will be seen as the beginning of an adequate response to that promise.

REFERENCES

Dunbar F (1935): *Emotions and Bodily Changes*. New York, Hoeber.

Dunbar F (1943): *Psychosomatic Diagnosis*. New York, Hoeber.

2

Health and Illness:
The Behavioral Medicine Perspective

Stephen M. Weiss

The tremendous advances in biomedicine over the past 60 years have resulted in a major shift in research emphasis in recent years from the acute infectious diseases to chronic illness. Most of the major viral and bacterial diseases have been conquered or controlled in the United States ("Healthy People," 1979). Chronic diseases (cardiovascular, pulmonary, neoplastic, and cerebrovascular, among others) have become the major source of health concern. Cardiovascular disease, the nation's number one killer, has become a special target for biomedical research. The consequent reallocation of resources and manpower has also resulted in a rethinking of approach, a refocusing of perspective. The search for the pathogenic agent (e.g., a virus, organ dysfunction, or biochemical substrate), so successful in combating the acute infectious diseases, has failed with such health concerns as hypertension, coronary heart disease, and stroke. Clearly, a more comprehensive approach to disease prevention and control is needed in order to comprehend the multifaceted nature of these serious health problems.

The impetus for the creation of another perspective comes from several sources. The U.S. Department of Health, Education and Welfare "Forward Plan for Health" (1977–1981); the Canadian LaLonde Report (LaLonde, 1974); and the congressional "Investigation of the National Institutes of Health" (1976), all identified the need for expanded research on the role of behavioral and life style factors in the prevention and control of chronic disease.

The birth of behavioral medicine can be formally dated to the Yale Conference on Behavioral Medicine in 1977 (Schwartz & Weiss, 1977), but the gestation period extends back perhaps 5,000 years. Homer, Plato, and Aristotle voiced remarkably similar speculations on the relationship between mind

and body. In more recent times, such luminaries as Sir William Osler, Claude Bernard, and Walter Cannon, among others, have continued this effort toward a more comprehensive understanding of health and illness. The labor pains can be dated to the past 40 years, which witnessed the development of psychosomatic medicine, in which psychiatry attempted, through psychoanalytic theory, to establish yet another perspective on the mind-body linkage (Leigh & Reiser, 1977).

This progression of theory, concept, and ideology was regarded with a jaundiced eye by many of the leading biomedical theorists in each era, albeit perhaps less so with each succeeding generation of scientific thought. The weakest link in all of these speculations, however, remained the difficulty in putting such concepts into operation through scientific research, theories, and methods acceptable to all of the relevant scientific communities. Within the past 10 years, new breakthroughs on the theoretical, conceptual, and technological levels (e.g., biofeedback; the role of the central nervous system in autonomic system mediation; physiological response to environmental stressors; computers, microprocessors, and monitoring devices) have dramatized the necessity for reconceptualizing the nature of biological and behavioral interrelationships.

Most early attempts by biomedical and behavioral researchers to address common problems independently met with less than gratifying results. Too often, more questions were raised than answered. Too often, a lack of understanding among behavioral and biomedical scientists resulted in serious, disqualifying errors or omissions that invalidated research findings.

A synthetic perspective was needed to resolve some of the inconsistencies and incongruities resulting from this state of affairs. It became increasingly obvious that to pursue successfully a multifaceted approach to chronic illness, those with the collective expertise necessary to address the various dimensions of the problems at hand would have to develop better collaborative relationships and become more familiar with each other's languages, concepts, and perspectives. Only in this way could they adequately develop a model of the combination of "real-life" circumstances that might impinge on the organism such that the interactive efforts might result in a product whose whole would be greater than the sum of its parts (von Bertalanfy, 1968). It has been the search for this unifying principle among behavioral and biomedical scientists working on problems of mutual concern that has spawned the concept of "behavioral medicine."

As a reflection of the dynamic growth and development of the field, the definition of behavioral medicine developed by the participants during the Yale conference on Behavioral Medicine in 1977 has already been superceded by a second-generation definition, promulgated and adopted at the organizational meeting of the Academy of Behavioral Medicine Research in 1978:

Yale Conference Definition: Behavioral Medicine is the field concerned with the development of behavioral-science knowledge and techniques relevant to the understanding of physical health and illness and the application of that knowledge and these techniques to prevention, diagnosis, treatment, and rehabilitation. Psychosis, neurosis, and substance abuse are included only insofar as they contribute to physical disorders as an end point (Schwartz & Weiss, 1977).

Academy of Behavior Medicine Research Definition: Behavioral Medicine is the interdisciplinary field concerned with the development and integration of behavioral and biomedical science knowledge and techniques relevant to the understanding of health and illness and the application of this knowledge and these techniques to prevention, diagnosis, treatment, and rehabilitation (Schwartz & Weiss, 1978).

This shift in emphasis from "behavioral science in biomedicine" to an "integration of biomedical and behavioral sciences" established the truly unique facet of this new field—the biobehavioral perspective—which calls for a pooling of talent across many disciplines to capitalize on the synergistic and catalytic potential inherent in such collaborative research efforts. Given the major differences in perspective and concept that had traditionally separated the various disciplines, interactive efforts sought to use these differences as a means of stimulating ideas. It encouraged participants to foresake traditional channels of conceptualization and instead to focus upon the potential inherent in multifactorial approaches. The concept of transculturation borrowed from anthropology—in which the blending of Culture 1 and Culture 2, produces not Cultures 1 and 2, but Culture 3—perhaps best illustrates this phenomenon.

COMPONENTS OF THE HEALTH-ILLNESS PARADIGM

Let us now consider the various components of the heath–illness paradigm from the perspective of behavioral medicine. These include etiology and diagnosis, treatment and rehabilitation, and prevention and health promotion.

Etiology and Diagnosis

Etiology and diagnosis of disease have been cornerstones of research and practice throughout the history of the healing arts. Scientists and clinicians concerned with mind–body interaction have traditionally devoted much effort toward understanding psychological impact on physiological status. The development of psychosomatic medicine based upon psychoanalytic theory, was the most recent attempt to establish such a theoretical framework. Although psychosomatic medicine caught the attention of the biomedical community in the 1950s and 1960s, the empirical nature of its observations was not sufficiently compelling to maintain interest into the 1970s, particularly in the absence of treatment strategies considered effective by the attending physician.

Several factors coalesced in the early 1970s, giving impetus to a reconceptualization of mind-body linkages. The behavioral and social sciences, through their increasing familiarity with and interest in health and illness issues, were becoming involved in health research. Major advances in instrumentation and data processing created exciting opportunities for psychophysiological measurement. Breakthroughs in the neurosciences provided new understanding of the interrelationships between the central and peripheral nervous systems and their mediating effect on bodily processes. "Lifestyle," including the long-term effects of our attempts to cope with our environment (subsumed under the rubric of "stress"), was targeted as one of the major factors in the development and progression of chronic disease.

All of these issues contain the common element of human behavior—either action or reaction—which is measurable topographically and/or physiologically. However, rather than confining our analysis to the relationship of behavioral and environmental factors to the development and progression of disease, the biobehavioral perspective requires an analysis of all of the factors that may contribute to the condition in question, and how these factors interact in synergistic, catalytic, or inhibitory fashion. Assessing each variable independently might result in inconsistent or contradictory findings because one is liable to miss what may be the essential ingredient of the clinical event, the interaction between two or more variables. Thus, the genetic, nutritional, constitutional, biochemical, physiological, behavioral, and sociocultural variables must be recognized for their relative contributions to the complete picture of the condition in question.

Two examples from recent work in the area of hypertension research nicely illustrate the point. Salt has been implicated in the development and maintenance of high blood pressure in research studies conducted over the past 20 years (Dahl, 1972, 1977). Recent epidemiological evidence has suggested that societies which have low-salt diets have lower blood pressures than high-salt societies (Freis, 1975). It has been concluded by many, therefore, that salt is the primary cause of high blood pressure. However, major inconsistencies have been noted in other studies, which found only modest relationships between salt and blood pressure. This inconsistency of results concerning salt may be due to a problem of perspective rather than substance.

The persistent belief that stress causes hypertension has also been plagued with inconsistent results, which again suggest the desirability of "casting a wider net." Recent studies by Anderson (1982) graphically demonstrated the *interactive* effect of salt and stress on blood pressure. When each variable was examined in isolation from the other, the effect on blood pressure was moderate. When animals were placed under stress with salt loading, however, the interaction of the two variables produced a *synergistic* effect, causing an alarming incidence of stroke among the experimental animals subjected to this procedure. A similar finding was noted by Friedman and Iwai (1976), who, through systematic variation of genetic factors, demonstrated their facilitative or inhibitory effect on blood pressure elevation. Henry and Stephens (1979) work with caffeine and stress also demonstrated the synergistic effect of multiple factors providing a result not otherwise apparent from independent assessment of single factors.

To state, or even to imply, that stress causes disease or that disease causes stress may obscure more than it clarifies. Rephrasing the question to address the role of behavioral and environmental factors both singly and in combination with other potential etiological agents in the development, progression, and maintenance of disease may provide the necessary ingredients for understanding these diseases from such a perspective. Page (1960) referred to the etiological "mosaic" of hypertension. Looking at any one color in a multi-hued mosaic without recognizing its relationship to the others involved will result in meaningless images without cohesion or pattern.

Treatment and Rehabilitation

Let us continue with the hypertension example. The diagnosis of hypertension should alert the health care provider to consider a broad range of issues ultimately linked to treatment choices. The measurement of blood pressure under standard resting conditions has been the "marker" for diagnosis and clinical treatment. But what are we really measuring? What is the basis for health provider practice?

We have no direct evidence that high blood pressure in humans causes heart disease per se. As a chronic process, the apparently damaging effect to arterial walls takes place over a period of years such that it would prove impossible to directly attribute such damage to this insidious process. Based upon highly compelling epidemiological evidence, however, we can hypothesize that the pathogenic process may be hemodynamic or atherogenic, or both. We also know that lowering of blood pressure can reduce the morbidity and mortality associated with coronary heart disease and stroke (Hypertension Detection and Follow-up Program, 1979). From this perspective, the lowering of blood pressure would appear to be a highly desirable goal. However, if we are to adopt a biobehavioral perspective we must consider whether we have considered all of the relevant information concerning blood pressure.

Recognizing the natural lability of blood pressure, traditional studies have attempted to reduce variability by adopting a standardized measurement procedure (three separate occasions in the clinic, with the patient in a seated, relaxed position). In our natural surroundings, however, we constantly act upon or react to our environment; yet we have little information on blood pressure behavior under those conditions. Given that resting blood pressures are but a very indirect measure of a dynamic condition, might not the assessment of the *variability* of blood pressure under naturalistic conditions provide us with a better understanding of the patterns of blood pressure regulation?

Until recently, the lack of appropriate instrumentation made such studies infeasible. However, advances in ambulatory monitoring, data processing, and telemetry now permit us to ask the complex questions related to *patterns* of blood pressure variability. Answers to these questions will resolve many issues related to etiology as well, and permit consideration of a broad array of individually tailored programs of blood pressure reduction.

A recent study by Surwit et al. (1982) demonstrated the usefulness of identifying daily life occurrences that produce significant blood pressure elevations. Patients were given training in relaxation techniques and instructed to practice those procedures when life events occurred which had been associated with blood pressure elevations during the initial monitoring. Subsequent periodic monitoring and standard blood pressure measurements revealed significant reductions in pressure (from hypertensive to normotensive). Thus, the biobehavioral perspective has motivated the assessment and characterization of an essentially unexplored, yet potentially critical dimension of the highly complex issues related to the development and control of high blood pressure.

Parenthetically, a similar line of reasoning concerning the dynamic nature of blood pressure resulted in creative investigations into differential blood pressure reactivity among individuals characterized by the Type A and Type B behavior patterns. Several studies on the Type A behavior pattern had found no correlation between Type A behavior and blood pressure. Dembroski and his associates (1977, 1979) noted similar results on baseline measures, but found significantly elevated blood pressure among Type A subjects under conditions of social challenge. Thus, the reactivity of blood pressure to environmental stimuli became the critical variable differentiating those exhibiting "coronary-prone" behavior from others not so characterized. Such findings support the speculation that the variability dimension could conceivably be the most important factor relating coronary heart disease and stroke to blood pressure; traditional assessment techniques provide only a vague, indirect marker of this potentially critical variable. Obviously, addi-

tional research is needed to improve our understanding of this issue.

One further illustration of the biobehavioral perspective in the treatment of hypertension bears mentioning. Traditional biomedical approaches have primarily focused upon the reduction of blood pressure by pharmacological means. However, long-term compliance rates (e.g., taking a minimum of 80 percent of the prescribed medication over a 5-year period) are exceptionally low, resulting in questionable maintenance of control (Sackett & Snow, 1979). As lifetime pharmacological regimens leave much to be desired in their own right, various nonpharmacological therapies, particularly biofeedback and relaxation techniques, have been studied as potential alternatives to drug therapies. The results of these studies have generally demonstrated statistical rather than clinical significance in blood pressure reduction with these techniques.

However, several investigators almost simultaneously decided to rephrase the question. Rather than considering pharmacological *versus* behavioral therapies, they sought to determine what might be the most efficacious *combination* of biomedical and behavioral approaches in both reducing *and maintaining* blood pressure at normotensive levels. Patel (1975), Patel & North, (1975), Green et al. (1979), and others have successfully demonstrated significant reductions in blood pressure, by beginning with pharmacological therapies, and then phasing in behavioral therapies, as a means of maintaining lowered blood pressure while gradually reducing and, in many cases, totally eliminating pharmacological therapy. Most patients have been able to maintain normotensive blood pressure levels following this biobehavioral approach with a minimum of two-thirds reduction of medication. Compliance rates with this "combination" approach have been notably high; the unpleasant side effects of antihypertensive medication appear to be powerful motivators when the goal is to reduce or eliminate dependence on these agents for blood pressure maintenance.

One further benefit was noted in a recent study by Patel et al. (1981) concerning combination approaches to blood pressure reduction at the worksite. In addition to the standard blood pressure measurements, indices of smoking, serum cholesterol, and weight were also periodically obtained. The treatment procedures not only succeeded in producing significant blood pressure reductions, but also affected smoking and serum cholesterol in the desired direction. The serum cholesterol finding was particularly interesting, inasmuch as no weight changes were noted, suggesting that changes in diet probably did *not* occur in either the experimental or control groups. Thus, the biobehavioral treatment program may have general as well as specific health-enhancing characteristics that should be pursued in future research.

Disease Prevention and Health Promotion

The ultimate goal of our efforts concerning health is not to treat disease, to diagnose disorders, or even to understand them; our ultimate goal is to *prevent* disease from occurring in the first place. In order to understand how we may prevent disease, however, we must recognize the factors associated with its occurrence and, if possible, the underlying mechanisms of its action.

When we use the term "prevention," we really mean *delay*. We are primarily concerned with the *premature* morbidity and mortality associated with the major chronic diseases. Today, heart disease, stroke, cancer, and accidents account for two-thirds of all deaths in the United States and for nearly 75 percent of all years lost from premature death ("Healthy People," 1979).

The prevention of chronic disease may be the only way in which we can ultimately place a rein on the current unacceptable escalation of health costs. Total health costs in 1950 amounted to $10 billion. By 1970 they had escalated to $70 billion. The current expenditure rate, well in excess of $325 billion (or nearly 10 percent of the gross national product), clearly demonstrates the need to bring these costs under control. We cannot deny the most advanced treatment strategies to those in need. Therefore, only through prevention strategies can we arrive at a long-term, morally and ethically acceptable solution to this problem.

Epidemiological studies have been particularly helpful in identifying "markers" and patterns of behavior associated with increased probability of disease (e.g., Belloc & Breslow, 1972; Keys et al., 1971; Rosenman et al. 1975). The term "probability" is important to keep in mind, as there is no assurance that any given individual will or will not remain healthy by following certain regimens or engaging in certain behaviors. From infancy on we constantly make decisions based upon probability

estimates, whether or not we consciously think in such terms. Risk factors for disease are just a set of probability statements concerning the likelihood of one's contracting a given condition.

Coronary heart disease remains the number one cause of morbidity and mortality among Americans, accounting for nearly 50 percent of the total mortality in the United States each year. A total of 183,000 premature deaths and 570,000 disability cases are produced by heart disease and stroke each year at an annual cost exceeding $40 billion (Farquhar, 1978).

The three most common risk factors—smoking, hypertension, and elevated serum cholesterol—have obvious health behavior correlates. A vast literature on smoking prevention, cessation, and cessation maintenance has developed over the past 20 years ("Smoking and Health," 1979). The efforts to date on smoking cessation have been quite encouraging: the majority of people who have attempted to stop smoking are able to do so. Unfortunately, the recidivism rate is appalling. Only about 30 percent of those who quit successfully maintain smoking cessation at a 1 year follow-up (Orleans, 1980).

Several health behavior correlates pertain to the problem of elevated blood pressure. Behavioral and environmental factors may significantly contribute to the development of hypertension (Eliot & Buell, 1981). Significant effort has been devoted to developing treatment approaches to reduce blood pressure (Shapiro et al., 1977). Compliance with medical regimens has been a nettlesome issue for the biomedical community and long-term maintenance of blood pressure regulation by pharmacological means has been characterized by a variety of both short-term and long-term problems ("Patient Compliance," 1980). It may be that the treatment of hypertension should be divided into two rather distinct categories: the *lowering* of blood pressure, and the *maintaining* of lowered blood pressure. The procedures employed with the former problem might not be most appropriate for the latter. In fact, several preliminary studies suggest that blood pressure may be most efficaciously lowered pharmacologically, but be better maintained at a lower level by nonpharmacological means (Green et al., 1979).

The experimental and epidemiological evidence indicating a relationship between elevated serum cholesterol and coronary heart disease suggests that dietary modification may be a major prevention strategy, at least for those hypercholesterolemic individuals identified to be at high risk for heart disease. However, this pattern is not clear-cut in persons not identified as being at high risk. Considerable research on the genetic, developmental, constitutional, and environmental factors involved is necessary to better delineate the parameters of this relationship.

These three risk factors, however, account for only approximately 50 percent of the variance associated with coronary heart disease. Thus, we must continue to explore other avenues for additional factors that may contribute to the prevalance of disease. Obesity, sedentary lifestyle, and stress factors are the so-called "secondary" risk factors that are also being considered. Substances such as alcohol, salt, and caffeine may also play some role as indirect contributors to the problem. The evidence implicating these factors has been detailed in other publications and need not be repeated here. Suffice it to say that lifestyle, behavioral, and environmental variables play a key role in the nature, intensity, duration and magnitude of these health hazards.

A MODEL OF HEALTH ENHANCEMENT PLANNING

Risk-reducing behavior is oriented toward disease prevention. Health promotion strategies focus upon health maintenance. The common factors that bind these conceptually oblique constructs concern health behavior in its various stages and contexts. Given the many interrelated factors that play some role in health behavior, we need to consider some means of systematically addressing these stages and contexts. Such a model might address three major sets of variables: (1) health behavior variables, (2) intrapersonal, interpersonal, and environmental variables, and (3) major situational variables.

As can be seen in Figure 2-1, health behavior can be subdivided into health behavior development, health behavior change, and health behavior maintenance.

Health behavior development is the actual acquiring of behavior and/or skills related to particular practices that may be considered as either enhancing or detracting from one's health status. This component concerns primarly the developmental years, although in some cases it would also apply to adults, for example in acquiring the habit of wearing seatbelts. Health behavior change is primarily concerned with shifting from one behavior pattern to another or ceasing health-destructive behavior patterns. Changing one's dietary patterns, stopping

smoking, and shifting from a sedentary lifestyle to a more active lifestyle might be examples of such behavior.

Health behavior maintenance requires particular attention because of the chronicity and perhaps automaticity which we attempt to instill in this component of health behavior, as compared to the more acute objectives involved in health behavior development and health behavior change. For example, in acquiring a skill or changing a habit one can identify the target behaviors desired and specify when they have been achieved at a given level of proficiency. The "maintenance" factor, however, involves indefinite periodic assessment of a given behavior pattern; one can only describe relative success in terms of continued longevity of that pattern. The factors involved in maintaining a given behavior pattern may be quite different than those related to the acquiring or changing of a given behavior pattern.

There are three functional levels at which each of these health behavior variables must be considered. As noted in Figure 2-1, the *intrapersonal* level is concerned with values, self-concept, personality characteristics, and other similar factors. It is related to show how individuals perceive themselves in terms of their personal effectiveness, competence, and worth. The *interpersonal* level involves all forms of relationships with family, friends, colleagues, superiors, subordinants, etc. This also includes the quality of the relationship—competitive, cooperative, helpful, social, or loving. The *environmental* level includes all of the settings and factors that affect the daily milieu of the individual. In addition to environments such as work, home, social, and cultural, other factors such as climate and political or legal circumstances may affect behavior in definable and predictable ways.

By observing the interplay between health behavior variables and functional levels, we can recognize a variety of situational factors that may also determine specific strategies in the planning of health promotion programs. For example, an individual's relations with his or her family might affect intrapersonal values in terms of health behavior development. Interpersonal or environmental factors at the school or worksite could be used to promote health behavior change or health behavior maintenance.

Thus, through the various permutations of these three sets of variables, we can explore systematically the development of all the relevant facets of a health promotion strategy. Such a model would minimize

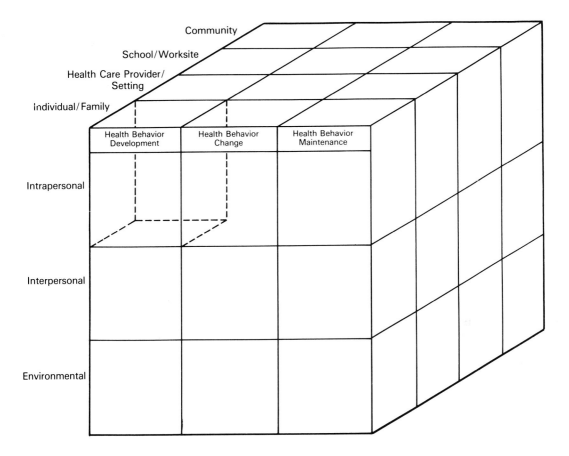

Figure 2-1. Health enhancement planning model.

some of the present confusion and diffusion of many current health promotion efforts. It would also assist in identifying gaps in program planning and would provide a step-by-step approach to health promotion activities by targeting various aspects of the problem in a manner consistent with resources available to the planning group.

CONCLUSIONS

The field of behavioral medicine encompasses the entire health–illness spectrum, from basic scientific exploration of brain–body mechanism issues to public health strategies for disease prevention and health promotion at the community level. This breadth requires extensive collaborative efforts between biomedical and behavioral scientists at the basic, clinical, and public health levels. They must combine their talents to achieve a biobehavioral perspective on the multilayered problems that affect the prevention and control of chronic disease and the promotion and maintenance of health. To make adequate use of the extraordinary diversity of talent available to behavioral medicine, a conceptual framework is needed that can simultaneously and systematically explore the various levels of human and biological function in an integrated and comprehensive fashion. This multifactorial approach requires the creative use of techniques of analysis as well as the most sophisticated electronic measurement aids available. It is perhaps for these very reasons that behavioral medicine has emerged as a distinct entity from its predecessors and is very much a product of our times—it is a combination of disciplines that are coming of age and employs sophisticated state-of-the-art technology in the pursuit of its goals.

REFERENCES

Anderson DE (1982): Behavioral hypertension mediated by salt intake. Smith O, Galosy R, & Weiss SM (Eds.). In *Circulation, Neurobiology and Behavior*. New York, Elsevier.

Belloc NB, & Breslow L (1972): Relationship of physical health status and health practices. Prev Med 1:409–421.

Dahl LK (1972): Salt and hypertension. Am J Clin Nutr 25:231–241.

Dahl LK (1977): Salt intake and hypertension. Genest J, Koiw E, & Kuchel O (Eds.). In *Hypertension*. New York, McGraw Hill.

Dembroski TM, MacDougall JM, & Shields JM (1977): Physiologic reactions to social challenge in persons evidencing the Type A coronary-prone behavior pattern. J Hum Stress 3:2–9.

Dembroski TM, MacDougall JM, Herd JA, & Shields JL (1979): Effect of level of challenge on pressure and heart rate responses in Type A and B subjects. J Appl Soc Psychol 9:209–228.

Eliot R, & Buell J (1981): Environmental and behavioral influences in the major cardiovascular disorders. Weiss SM, Herd JA, & Fox BH (Eds.). In *Perspectives on Behavioral Medicine*. New York, Academic Press.

Farquhar J (1978): *The American Way of Life Need Not Be Hazardous to Your Health*. New York, Norton.

Forward plan for health (1977-1981). DHEW Publ. No. OS 76-50024.

Freis ED (1975): Salt volume and prevention of hypertension. Circulation 53(4):589–595.

Friedman R, & Iwai J (1976): Genetic predisposition and stress-induced hypertension. Science 193:161–162.

Green EE, Green AM, & Norris PA (1979): Preliminary observations on a new non-drug method for control of hypertension. J S Carolina Med Assoc. 75:575–582.

Healthy people: The surgeon general's report on health promotion and disease prevention (1979). DHEW, USPHS Publ. No. 79-55071.

Henry JP, & Stephens PM (1979): Caffeine as an intensifier of stress-induced hormonal and pathophysiologic changes in mice. Pharmacol Biochem Behav 13:719–722.

Investigation of the National Institutes of Health (1976): U.S. Congress House Committee on Interstate and Foreign Commerce, Subcommittee on Health and the Environment. 94th Congress, 2nd Session.

Keys A, Taylor ML, Blackburn M, Brozek J, Anderson JT, & Simonson E (1971): Mortality and coronary heart disease among men studied for 23 years. Arch Intern Med 128:201–214.

LaLonde M (1974): A new perspective on the health of Canadians: A working document. Ottowa, Ontario, Canada, Ministry of Health and Welfare.

Leigh H, & Reiser MF (1977): Major trends in psychosomatic medicine–The psychiatrist's evolving role in medicine. Ann Intern Med 87:233–239.

Orleans C (1980): Quitting smoking: Overview and critical issues. In: *Smoking and Behavior*. Washington, D.C., National Academy of Sciences.

Page IH (1960): Bock KD (Ed.). In *Essential Hypertension*. Springer, Berlin, p. 1.

Patel C (1975): 12 month follow-up of yoga and biofeedback in the management of hypertension. Lancet 1:62–64.

Patel C, & North WRS (1975): Randomized controlled trial of yoga and biofeedback in management of hypertension. Lancet 2:93–95.

Patel C, Marmot MG, & Terry DJ (1981): Controlled trial of biofeedback-aided behavioral methods in reducing mild hypertension. Br Med J 282:2005–2008.

Patient compliance to prescribed antihypertensive medication regimens (1980). A report to the National Heart, Lung and Blood Institute. DHHS, USPHS, NIH Publ. No. 81-2102.

Rosenman RH, Brand RJ, Jenkins CD, Friedman M, Straus R, & Wurm M (1975): Coronary heart disease in the western collaborative group study: Final follow-up experience of 8-1/2 years. JAMA 233:872–877.

Sackett DL, & Snow JS (1979): The magnitude of compliance and noncompliance. Haynes RB, Taylor DW, & Sackett DL (Eds.). In *Compliance in Health Care*. Baltimore, Johns Hopkins University Press.

Schwartz GE, & Weiss SM (1977): Proceedings of the Yale Conference on Behavioral Medicine. DHEW, USPHS, NIH, Publ. No. 78-1424.

Schwartz GE, & Weiss SM (1978): Yale Conference on Behavioral Medicine: A proposed definition and statement of goals. J Behav Med 1:3–12.

Shapiro AD, Schwartz GE, Ferguson DC, Redman DP, & Weiss SM (1977): Behavioral methods in the treatment of hypertension: A review of their clinical status. Ann Intern Med 86:626–636.

Smoking and health: A report of the Surgeon General (1979). DHEW, USPHS Publ. No. 284-109/6619.

Surwit RS, Williams RB Jr, & Shapiro D (1982): *Behavioral Approaches to Cardiovascular Disease*. New York, Academic Press.

von Bertalanfy L (1968): *General Systems Theory*, New York, Braziller. Hypertension detection and follow-up program cooperative group (1979): Five-year findings of the hypertension detection and follow-up program. I. Reduction in mortality of persons with high blood pressure, including mild hypertension. JAMA 242:2562–2571.

3

Emotions and Bodily Changes: A Reassessment

Peter H. Knapp

Emotion was originally a touchstone in the psychosomatic area, which tested phenomena from psychological and physiological spheres and assessed their relevance to medical disorders. Dunbar's landmark monograph in 1946 implied as much by its title, *Emotions and Bodily Changes*. Less than half a century later, Weiner (1977) surveyed the field and devoted his study primarily to six major "classical" diseases. He pointed out that these may be heterogeneous, and that psychological contributions to them may be in the form of predisposing, precipitating, or sustaining factors. His careful work makes sparing reference to the border zone of feelings and his index does not include the word "emotion." (Nor its companion term, "affect," which in this chapter is used synonymously with "emotion.")

With the passage of time a number of additional concepts emerged, aiming at both simplicity and precision. Sick role, illness behavior, "stress," life style, psychoimmunology, life change, bereavement, alexithymia, behavioral medicine, genetic transmission—these have become recent foci of attention. Novel language and new areas of inquiry have not, however, vitiated old intuitions—that the faces and lives of patients suffering from a wide variety of psychosomatic or behavioral disorders reveal crucial facets which can only be called emotional.

Clarification may come from a reassessment that divides the realm of emotions into three overlapping areas: expressive phenomena; physiological manifestations; and emotion as an aspect of self-experience.

This work was supported in part by USPHS Grant 5P01-MH 26183-07.

EXPRESSIVE PHENOMENA

Phenomenological Classifications of Emotion

Darwin postulated in 1872 that expression, especially in the human face, could be traced to adaptive behaviors of animal forebears. For example, teeth are bared, the better with which to bite. His notion gained impetus in the middle of this century as interest in communication intensified.

The most striking approach to emotion per se was that of Tomkins (1962, 1963). The first of his brilliant volumes started by distinguishing *drives*, which he saw as signals giving relatively specific information about bodily states and needs, from *affects*, which he saw as less specific amplifying systems; these were the true motivators of human actions. Affects themselves he saw as primarily expressive, having as their principal site the face: "affect is primarily facial behavior" (1962, p. 205). He originally listed eight basic affects, then expanded the list (in 1970) to nine. His classification is compared with four others—those of Shand (1914), Plutchik (1962, 1980), Dahl and Stengel (1978), and Knapp (1981)—in Table 3-1. There is overlap, particularly among the states of joy, anger, fear, sorrow, and disgust, yet no classifications are identical. In fact, as did Tomkins, other authors changed their groupings slightly over time.

There have been attempts to validate some of these classifications of "basic emotions." For example, Tomkins' call for a program of verification by high-speed motion picture photography has been pursued. In particular, Ekman and his colleagues (1972), in thorough and convincing cross-cultural

Table 3-1   Basic Emotions: Five Views

Tomkins (1962, 1970)	Shand (1914)	Plutchik (1962, 1980)	Dahl & Stengel (1978)	Knapp (1981)
Excitement		Anticipation		Excitement
Surprise*	Curiosity*	Surprise	Surprise	
Joy	Joy	Joy	Joy	Elation
		Acceptance	Contentment	Euphoria
			Love	Lust
Anger	Anger	Anger	Anger	Anger
Fear	Fear	Fear	Fear	Fear
			Anxiety	
Distress	Sorrow	Sorrow	Depression	Sorrow
Disgust	Disgust	Disgust		Disgust
Shame				Shame
Contempt				
				Torpor

*Solid underlining for identity of terms
†Dotted underlining for near identity of terms

studies, have demonstrated that Tomkins' basic categories exist in a wide variety of ethnic groups and can be recognized by observers from diverse backgrounds. Developmental studies by Demos (1982), Izard (1971), and others have shown that these expressive categories are revealed early in infancy. Joy, sorrow, anger, and fear have inborn expressive patterning; long before speech they constitute a universal system of communication.

Sources of Expressive Phenomena

The study of body movement (Birdwhistell, 1963; Condon & Sander, 1974; Scheflen, 1966), lexical manifestations (McQuown, 1958; Pittenger & Smith, 1957), and acoustic phenomena (Ostwald, 1963, 1964) joined with anthropology in the new discipline, christened with Pierce's old name, *semiotics* (Sebeok et al., 1964). Its scope went beyond emotions but included them, as well as their ramifications into attitudes and styles.

Semiotics illuminates important cultural variations in medical care. Experiences of bodily processes, interpretations of illness, and expectations of caregivers in the rural United States are vastly different from those described in the Ladino-Mestizo Indians (Fabrega & Manning, 1973) or their cultural kin in the Hispanic clinics of urban American centers.

The study of expressive patterns is throwing light on general role patterns of patients and caregivers and transactions between them: illness behavior and the sick role; the mask of denial covering anxiety in foolhardy noncompliance; and the affects in patient and physician that flicker beneath the surface of their conventional interchanges.

We are only beginning to explore the many ways in which social conflict reverberates with specific psychological, and finally physiological, disturbance (Engel, 1977). How does the closing of a factory lead to individual instances of arthritis, hypertension, and gout (Cobb, 1976)? What is it in the impoverished city area, studied by Jenkins et al., (1977), that leads to a death rate from almost 30 different diseases nearly twice that seen in a nearby statistically comparable upperclass neighborhood?

These questions highlight the role of social forces and take us beyond the observable surface. They also outstrip the explanatory power of Tomkins' theory, which by focusing on what is visible, especially in the face, tends to lump together disparate states. Surprise is usually transient and related to sudden activation; sorrow may last a lifetime. The emphasis on facial expression enables this approach to capture momentary change, but it is not as able to deal with more ideational, sustained, and especially "secret" components of emotion. Guilt is an example. It is not among the basic emotions listed in Table 3-1. Frequently subtle, generally invisible, and often silent, guilt may be among the most powerful affective forces, capable of initiating or sustaining important physiological concomitants. The study of what can be seen provides only limited information about the physiological processes involved in emotion.

PHYSIOLOGICAL MANIFESTATIONS OF EMOTION

Physiology, broadly construed to include neurophysiology, neuroendocrinology, pathophysiology, and immunology, is tangible, enduring, and has comprised the mainstream of psychosomatic research. Cannon (1929) was the explorer who staked out a continent. He clarified the fundamental bipolarity of the autonomic nervous system and related endocrine responses, and sketched their role in adaptation. The nature of central nervous and endocrine components was further elaborated by Hess (1957), Hess and Akers (1955), and Selye (1970), and later by many other workers, such as MacLean (1949, 1972), and Mason and his colleagues (1961, 1968) in their elegant demonstrations of the balanced equilibrium that characterizes limbic brain and neuroendocrine organization. The parallel terms used by three pioneers are shown in Table 3-2 which also schematizes (for later reference) subdivisions within each of the major neuroendocrine systems.

The recognition of autonomic nervous system bipolarity served as a linch pin for the first great psychosomatic attempt at generalization, that of Alexander and his colleagues (1950). In a series of studies of seven chronic diseases of unknown etiology, they developed a model in which emotions were chronically mobilized but blocked from release in action, and therefore set up neuroendocrine

Table 3-2   Visceral Core Processes

Author	E Processes	F Processes
Cannon (1929)	Housekeeping	Fight–flight
Hess (1957)	Trophotrophic	Ergotrophic
Seyle (1970)	Anabolic	Catabolic
Current Model:	Intaking—Erotic	Agonistic
	Eliminative—Craving	Fearful "freezing" "fleeing"

reverberations. They postulated a circular and cyclic aspect of human emotions; blockage occurred at different points under different circumstances for particular diseases. Thus, predominantly active striving led to vascular disorder, especially hypertension, as well as arthritis and thyrotoxicosis; passive striving led to asthma, neurodermatitis, peptic ulcer, and ulcerative colitis—the so called "classical seven" disorders.

Their predictions received a degree of confirmation. This derived partly from their celebrated specificity study, involving controlled, blind judgements of edited interview typescripts which showed statistically significant, although not unfailing, success in detecting postulated patterns of emotional conflict (Alexander et al., 1968). Additional partial corroboration came from other investigators using simpler testing methods: for example, Weiner et al. (1957) in their classical prospective study of peptic ulcer formation in army recruits, or Moos and Solomon (1965) in their examination of women with rheumatoid arthritis and their sisters.

Most important was the heuristic value of the work of Alexander's group; it sharpened focus on the psychophysiology of emotion. Meanwhile information began to grow about the complex nature of both outer threat-meeting, or "F" processes, as they are called here, and inner need-meeting, or "E" processes.

Outer Threat-Meeting (F) Processes

The sympathetic nervous system is essentially monolithic, as Cannon (1929) observed; but it has shown to have its own brand of specialization. The advent of receptor neuropharmacology has revealed at least two major components, governed respectively by alpha—and beta—adrenergic receptors. Each of these has a network of enzymatic regulators and feedback loops, permitting fine-tuned release and reuptake, and at times blocking, of neurohumeral activation. As a result, it has enormous adaptive flexibility. In a number of organ systems—the lungs are a prime example (Anthracite et al., 1971)—some animal species have been found to have alpha receptors, which reinforce parasympathetic responses.

It is not clear how this new, more elaborated version of the sympathetic nervous system relates to the two psychophysiological constellations associated with sympathetic activity, the F processes of flight and fight. These processes underlie the emotions of fear and anger, which are associated with different motoric urges: fear propels the subject away from, while anger propels the subject toward the inciting object (Plutchik, 1962). The two emotions are accompanied by different cardiovascular patterns, as shown in the experiments by Schwartz et al. (1978, 1981), using imagery, exercise, and emotions. The neuroendocrine differences, however, are unclear. The traditional view that epinephrine is more involved in fear, and norepinephrine in anger (Schildkraut & Kety, 1967) is outdated but has not been replaced.

Animal studies have made important contributions to our understanding of the role of physiology in stress-related disorders. For example, the studies of Henry and his group (1967, 1971) demonstrated that crowding in mice colonies leads to sustained elevations of blood pressure along with vascular and enzymatic disturbances mimicking human hypertensive cardiovascular disease. It is far from clear, however, what relevance these observed behavioral manifestations have to human emotions.

Over time, both fear and anger are elusive, shifting entities. Anxiety as a trait has been reported by a wide range of patients with psychosomatic symptoms; yet other individuals seemingly exude anxiety for years and remain free from any obvious psychophysiological sequelae. Discrepant findings extend into the therapeutic sphere. Anxiolytic or other psychotropic drugs have been of little help in treating major psychosomatic syndromes. A further problem arises from the fact that some anxiety reactions are characterized not by "flight" but by "freezing," at times leading to the full fledged state of "conservation withdrawal" described by Engel (1954).

It is essential to understand how these emotions are "bound" or psychologically contained, and at what physiological cost. To do so involves observing how they interact with each other, often in what seems to be a vicious positive feedback cycle perpetually threatening to escape control. It also involves observing how they interact with other emotional components such as parasympathetically related states, which may include powerful cardioinhibitory activity (Knapp, 1967).

These features are crucial when we consider human disease. Reich et al. (1981) studied 117 instances of acute, life-threatening ventricular arrhythmias using independent interviews by a psychiatrist and a psychologist. They found that 25 patients had suffered acute emotional disturbances in the 24 hours before attacks; "Eighteen patients had two or more arrhythmic episodes preceded by psychological

disturbances... In 17 instances, the predominant affect...was anger."

Anger, especially when it is mobilized but prevented from full expression, is associated with acute elevations of blood pressure. The popular belief has been confirmed by numerous clinical experiments, such as that by Reiser et al. (1955), in which army recruits were irritated either in the permissive climate of peers or in the intimidating setting of officers, Harburg's (1973) investigation of ethnically stratified groups who were subjected to varying degrees of social threat, and Brod's (1959) study of arithmetical performance under a barrage of criticism.

The causal relationship between rage and sustained clinical hypertension is less clear. Ostfeld (1973), acknowledging the plausibility of the general hypothesis, commented skeptically on the lack of solid evidence linking the family of hypertensive disorders to any well-defined emotional patterns. Therapeutically, diuretics and salt restriction are by far the most efficacious and economical approaches to a majority of blood pressure elevations. For many resistive cases, however, the next line of treatment is through central or peripheral sympatholytic agents. Careful review of the literature suggests that a substantial reduction of diastolic blood pressure may be attained by various relaxation techniques, some of them supplemented by biofeedback (Frumkin et al., 1978).

It would seem premature to dismiss the role in hypertension of sympathetic activation and the emotions associated with it. Part of the problem may be attributed to techniques of assessing emotional factors over time. Jenkins et al. (1982), studying air traffic controllers, in whom hypertension was surprisingly prevalent, found that hypertensives showed a surface picture, derived from a number of self-report and peer assessment measures, of significantly less overt anger, dissatisfaction, and hostile attitudes than normotensive peers. The authors suspected that the hypertensives were in some way "encapsulated," highly defended against anger.

Given the complexity of such psychological concepts, it is no wonder that efforts have been made to simplify them. One such attempt was the introduction of the term "stress," which defines a kind of indiscriminate stimulus to physiological activation. Most often, it refers to an external threat or challenge which mobilizes sympathetic nervous and auxiliary endocrine responses. Unfortunately, use of the term blurs important distinctions between differing emotional patterns, even within the F system. It provokes confusion when it is extended to other types of challenge, such as separation and loss, which evoke quite different reactions. Use of a convenient term cannot replace careful specification of the nature of challenges, and particularly of the forms of conflict between various emotional elements.

Closely related to the current interest in stress is the research on life style. The most prominently studied style is the type A behavior pattern: a constellation of hard-driving, work-pressured, time urgent, impatient, and irritable behaviors directed at mastery of outer threats. By now, Type A characteristics, quantitatively assessed both by the original approach of Friedman and Rosenman (1959, 1975) and by Jenkins' (1971) activity survey, are well established cardiac risk factors. As often occurs, broad early generalizations have led to refinements and qualifications. Within the huge aggregate of persons showing Type A features, subtypes have begun to emerge: Type A individuals who are angry may be prone to angina (Jenkins et al., 1978); if hard working and job dissatisfied, they may be prone to coronary disease; if happy, they may be those maximally free of illness.

It is worth noting that in their air traffic controller study, Jenkins et al., (1982) found no correlation between hypertension and Type A behavior. We still have much to learn about F processes—their physiology, their relationship to more sustained endocrine and metabolic changes, and their relationship to emotions as they crystallize into attitudes, traits, and patterns of defense.

Inner Need-Meeting (E) Processes

The parasympathetic nervous system, unlike the sympathetic, is descrete and specialized. It serves a wide variety of organ systems and functions associated with sensuous contact with the environment, reproduction, intake, and elimination. It is linked in various ways to emotion and is implicated in a wide variety of disorders, including but extending beyond the "classical seven" psychosomatic disorders described by Alexander and his group.

In Table 3-2 the distinction is made between processes mobilizing for erotic contact and intake, and those mobilizing for elimination. The two processes are in rhythmic interplay. They respond to two major sets of stimuli, deficit and surfeit respectively. Each set of responses characterizes a broad array of emotional disturbances.

In the widest sense, deficit contributes to appetite disorders. Obesity, upper gastrointestinal disorders, and a number of sexual-reproductive disturbances may share common elements of craving and need, leading to conflictual hidden wishes that weave their way into pathophysiology and possibly into behavioral traits as well (Mirsky, 1957). There is a complex interplay between longing and rage, and the ways in which both are distorted and overlaid by defensive and compensatory personality structures.

In discussing surfeit responses, it may be instructive to touch upon many of the problems posed by the study of eliminative bowel disorders. In particular, the widespread inflammatory derangements in ulcerative colitis and Crohn's disease have led to contradictory findings. A number of clinical groups have uniformly found patients with ulcerative colitis to be severely disturbed (Engel, 1955; Lindemann, 1950; Mushatt, 1951; Sperling 1949). In the most carefully studied series, roughly one-fourth of the patients had overt psychotic features (Daniels et al., 1962; O'Conner et al., 1964). However, the study by Feldman and his colleagues (1967) comparing ulcerative colitis patients with random hospital admissions for other conditions found no differences between the groups. Possible flaws in that study include lack of "depth," and/or experience of the interviewers, failure to rule out massive denial and pseudonormality; until it has been controverted, however, the matter remains moot. A general complaint is that the field needs reliable instruments to assess deep emotional disturbances that are accompanied by minimal conscious distress and no overt disruption of behavior.

Allergic-immunological disorders, as a last broad group involving E processes, are considered here in more depth. Best known are those that represent responses to extrinsic, or as they may be called, "non-self," aspects of the world that have gained entry to the body or threaten to do so.

Urticaria and angioedema and a large number of skin disorders show specific patterns of response to foreign agents, usually in individuals with a greater or lesser degree of genetic predisposition. The literature is replete with clinical examples of modulation of this responsiveness by fantasy and emotion. These reveal a strong suggestion of a relationship between urges to weep and skin symptoms. Lacrimation is predominantly a parasympathetic function. The hypnotic experiments by Kepecs et al., (1951), showing intensification of "weeping" into experimentally induced cantherides blisters, represent an experimental inroad into this area, which needs replication and extension.

As an anecdotal example, a man with severe, at times life-threatening angioedema, developed a huge wheal across his entire anterior abdomen upon hearing that his wife was pregnant. Many months later, after his mother died suddenly, he developed a wheal localized to his right cheek, which, he recalled, was where she used to kiss him each night at bedtime.

The most classical allergic disorder is bronchial asthma, about which there is a huge literature. Even taking into consideration the heterogeneity of asthma patients, we can find abundant evidence that emotional factors influence patients' responses to the disorder, and that they may also significantly predispose, precipitate, and sustain the clinical syndrome. Rather than reviewing the extensive literature, let us consider one piece of animal evidence. Gold et al. (1972) showed the amplifying power of the vagus nerve in experimentally induced asthma in dogs. They experimentally increased airway resistance in one lung of an animal, separated from the other, by unilateral introduction of foreign protein to which the animal had been sensitized. The airway response was markedly attenuated by blocking the vagus nerve. Removing the block restored the original experimental allergic response. Of greatest interest is the fact that although the two lungs were separated, the vagal augmentation could also be seen in the opposite lung. Blocking of the ascending vagus on the afflicted side led to attenuation of the response on the opposite side, providing strong evidence of ascending and central, then descending activity, implicated in the allergic response. Gold et al. suggested that we must replace the old, purely allergic model of asthma with a complementary model that includes reflex vagal augmentation.

There is extensive evidence suggesting that a chain of sympathetic–parasympathetic forces plays a continuous role in regulating bronchiolar tone and airway resistance, extending from limbic systems to intracellular adenosine 5-monophosphate and quanosine 5-monophosphate; this literature has been reviewed elsewhere (Knapp et al., 1976).

Another important immunological frontier is concerned with reactions not to foreign, "non-self" agents, but to parts of the self. These autoimmune disorders now comprise a wide territory: this includes the well-known entities of rheumatoid disorders and systemic lupus erythematosis; certain rare disorders, such as pemphigus and paroxysmal cold hemoglobinemia; possibly some bowel and endo-

crine disorders, such as thyrotoxicosis and diabetes mellitus; and possibly some central nervous system disorders, especially multiple sclerosis and myasthenia gravis. This is not to imply, however, that we have proof that these disorders involve disturbed emotion, although scattered evidence points in that direction for some of them.

One of the most active research areas is concerned with immunoregulation. A picture is emerging of a highly organized system for the production and deployment of antibody and phagocytic activity. Under appropriate conditions, organisms can become sensitized to their own products. The general view of immunoregulation at present depends upon the concept of T lymphocytes as regulators in a state of "balance between helper and suppressor forces [which] can be shifted by a variety of internal or external events...including endocrine functions and viral infections" (Rose, 1981). Ader and Cohen (1975) demonstrated the conditioning of an immunosuppressive response, a finding now confirmed by others (Rogers & Reich et al., 1976: Ader, this volume, Chapter 11).

The possible range of psychoimmunology extends beyond the *hyper*reactivity of allergic and autoimmune disorders. *Hypo*reactivity may also occur: an inadequate response to nonself or external agents, which may result in heightened susceptibility to infection (Hinkle et al., 1962; Mason et al., 1967). Most visionary, and potentially most revolutionary, is the possibility that hyporeactivity to aspects of self could lower the surveillance activity necessary as internal protection against malignancy. These four possibilities, as suggested by Melnuchuck (personal communication), are shown in Table 3.3

Toward a New Physiology of Emotion

This discussion has extended beyond emotions per se, and also beyond the original models of Cannon and Selye, moving toward the new physiology of emotion called for by Engel in 1954. The search for new models cannot discard old facts. A new view must take account of F and E systems, along with their interactions. These processes also transact with two other broad systems. One is the hedonic. Intensified painful or pleasurable evaluation is intrinsic to experiences we label emotional. As argued elsewhere (Knapp, 1981), both pleasure and pain are two fold: positive pain (immutably linked to sympathetic nervous activation, such that anxiety itself may be regarded as learned anticipation of pain), and dysphoric pain, or the absence of pleasure (itself still fur-

Table 3-3 Immune Response Disorders and Disease

		Response	
	Stimulus	Hyperreactive	Hyporeactive
Stimulus	Extrinsic (nonself)	Alergic	Infectious
	Intrinsic (self)	Autoimmune	Malignant?

Adapted from Melnechuk T., Personal communication.

ther subdivided, as already indicated, into the dysphoria of deficit and of surfeit). Pleasure similarly can be positive, sensuous pleasure, libidinal in the widest sense; or it can be analgesic, the absence of pain, the primordial element in soothing.

The final system (or systems) to be considered, involve generalized activation and deactivation. At times, particularly in the case of activation, these have been virtually equated with emotion. Their role is ambiguous: we know that there is feedback between pleasure and pain and activation. Switching from activation to deactivation may occur (e.g., as already mentioned, "freezing" in situations of anxiety). The switching may involve generalized or selective aspects. More specific and of considerable interest is a set of "inhibitory" phenomena that are associated with vagal stimulation. This seems to be part of the interplay between sympathetic and parasympathetic systems, which effectively serves as a brake upon F processes and activation. Elsewhere, its relationship to eliminative processes has been indicated and the notion has been advanced that E processes serve a wide need for "purging and curbing" (Knapp, 1967).

Switching may be relatively sudden, as when we see appetite yield to satiety, or the discharge of sexual excitation lead to torpor. It may be gradual, as in change from acute distress to retreat, apathy, and apparent hopelessness. This is most beautifully documented by Kaufman and Rosenblum (1967) in their studies of infant monkeys separated from their mothers.

A set of core processes that are crucial to the generation of emotions are shown in Figure 3-1. The figure is intended to convey the predominant interactions between primary pain (P−) and F processes, and that between primary pleasure (P+) and E processes. It also attempts to indicate that both expressive and hedonic elements interact with systems of generalized activation and deactivation (for futher discussion see Knapp 1981). The evidence presented thus far hints that some relationships exist between these core elements and certain diseases. F processes appear to be related to some cardiovascular disorders and to much of what is usually intended by the term "stress." E processes appear to be related to numerous ingestive, metabolic, eliminative, and possibly immunological disorders.

EMOTION AS AN ASPECT OF SELF-EXPERIENCE

The neuropsychological core of emotion, with its automatic connection to bodily processes, does not yet constitute all of emotion. In this section, some of the additional elements necessary for emotional experience are discussed as well as inner feedback relationships between these emotional features, and outer feedback between the emotional self and others.

The Surrounding Matrix

We may conceive of the core (Fig. 3-1) as surrounded by a matrix of fantasies, developmentally primitive ideation, and imagery. The core interacts with this matrix to generate feelings linked to emotionally charged personal memories and compelling anticipations. Together, these constitute emotional experience. They also sustain it. We nurse our wrath with fantasy to keep it warm. In Figure 3-2 a somewhat arbitrary array of emotions is shown, which overlaps with similar arrays postulated by others (Table 3-1).

Primitive fantasy and imagery assess and evaluate the impact of ongoing experience and contribute to intentions or plans about dealing with these exigencies. They are primitive in the sense that they use the earliest type of ideation, namely, nondiscursive symbolism (Langer's 1948 phrase). Thus, we form global, holistic images of the world around us as good or bad, threatening or safe, as well as global images of ourselves. The latter include a vague awareness of the very bodily changes incited by these images. It may be this characteristic of emotional experience that gives the nondominant cerebral hemisphere an advantage of apprehending emotional manifestations (Wapner et al., 1981). Emotion as a totality involves widely distributed bodily processes and certainly is not simply "localized" in the right hemisphere.

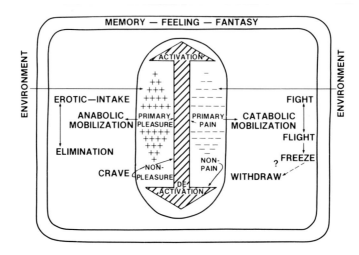

Figure 3-1. Neuropsychological core of emotions. + = Primary Pleasure − = Primary Pain

These aspects are important when we consider ways of assessing emotion. Conscious self-report by checklist or questionnaire can yield essential quantitative data. Its power, particularly in a predictive study, is shown by the striking success of Shekelle and his collaborators (1981) in predicting 17-year risk of death from cancer among 2,020 middle-aged men on the basis of their Minnesota Multiphasic Personality Inventory (MMPI) scores on the Depression scale. For other purposes, however, it may be useful to look at derivative reflections of emotion and at their reverberations within and between persons.

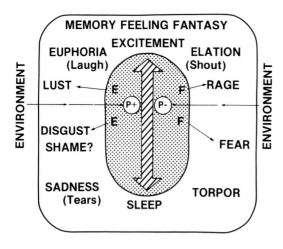

Figure 3-2. Neuropsychological core plus "feeling layer."
P+ = Primary Pleasure P− = Primary Pain.

Feedback Within the Self

Another effort to model some aspects of emotion appears in Figure 3-3. It shows an individual matching perceptions of the outside world against past experience to form evaluations. These, in turn, strike hedonic chords, and the hedonic quality automatically triggers expressive urges. Anticipations and plans follow. In a quasi-reflexive way, the core also activates bodily expression, as well as inner visceral preparations for action. Both outer and inner bodily changes are, to a varying extent, reapperceived and become a part of the continuous feedback which is the essence of emotional experience.

The program of audiovisual study, called for by Tomkins (1962), pioneered by Haggard and Isaacs (1966), and pursued by Ekman et al. (1972) may tell us much about the interplay among facial and bodily gesture, verbal nuances, and their underlying sources, all largely out of awareness. It seems necessary to assume that the distinctive labeling of consciousness—crucial though it may be for certain decisions and actions—only emerges from the core by way of ingrained patterns of expression, fantasy, and imagery.

Individuals try to avoid the self-confrontation involved in full awareness of conflictual core elements. They try to replace "unsafe" urges by safe ones. Thus, the study of psychosomatic emotional correlates has increasingly scrutinized defensive strategies and their relative success or lack of it, reflected in defensive "strain" (Knapp et al., 1970).

Often the choice made among strategic evils is to focus attention on the physiological manifestations

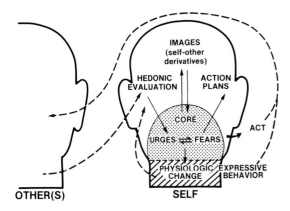

Figure 3-3. Self–other and emotional transactions.

of an urge, such as the anabolic or frankly parasympathetic precursors of felt experience—for example, the wheeze in asthma (which itself may be replacing a more dangerous urge to attack or fight). Intensified pathophysiological aspects of this sort express crude symbolic meanings of their own, for instance, "love me, care for me, I cannot hurt you." Above all, they serve to disguise ideational components.

Thus, we often see selective, escalating accentuation of bodily changes. They may extend through time and assume a prominent role in the manifest organization of the self. This conceptualization bears on the provocative term *alexithymia*, coined by Sifneos (1973; see also Marty & de M'uzan, 1963); it refers to the absence ("*a*") of words (*lex*) for emotion (*thymos*). Some have seen this as a marker for psychosomatic (and possibly some other) patients and have even postualted failure of transmission in mid-brain limbic pathways, so that it is irreversible and beyond the reach of psychotherapy. The account I have proposed is simpler. It suggests that defensive operations, particularly denial, repression, displacement, and reaction formation, fit the clinical facts better. From my own experience, such patients under appropriate psychotherapeutic circumstances reveal abundant fantasy and emotions, though these are often terrifying in their primitivity.

The Emotional Self and Others

In Figure 3-3 wider feedback loops are also shown linking the individual by means of his or her expressive behavior and acts, to the world. At the emotional level, the individual is always part of a field of key others, who induce habitual expectations and

become objects of intentions in his or her inner world. Kohut's (1977) concept of self object, as a figure who is necessary to "complete" the self, has perhaps a more general aspect: "No man is an island." Human beings are completed emotionally by the personal world around them. We must ask the following: how symbolically refined is this self–other world, as opposed to inflexible and concrete; how stable is the interpersonal emotional equilibrium, including a positively valued image of the self and confidence in its survival without dependence on the continuous presence of another?

These considerations are important when we consider life change. The early methods of Holmes and Rahe (1967), who used a social metric to measure the impact of the changes that occur in individual lives, have become more sophisticated. Horowitz et al. (1977) and Hurst et al. (1978) are among those who have assessed not merely the events but their subjective impact. Rogentine and his colleagues (1979) were highly successful in predicting relapse in patients with Stage I and II malignant melanoma from the patients' subjective ratings of the amount of adjustment needed to cope with their illness; those who rated this as low, that is, denied the implications of the diagnosis, were at markedly higher risk.

We are developing ways of assessing emotional meanings. These invariably extend to the interpersonal world, as shown by the growing number of reports about the role of bereavement and loss in a wide range of disorders (Jacobs & Ostfeld, 1977). The consequences are far more than simple sadness. Loss removes a crucial other and leads to disruption of habitual patterns of expectation so strong as to constitute bonds; in so doing it disorganizes the total emotional field. Undoubtedly, effects result from the interaction between relatively fixed biological patterns and learned emotional factors, as has been true in Hofer and Reiser's (1969) studies on the psychosomatic consequences in rat pups of experimental separation early in life.

Such deeply rooted attachment to the world of others is important for more than the study of loss. It is the raison d'être of "life style;" the challenges it provides are central to the meaning of stress; and, of course, it is essential to psychotherapy.

Emotions and Therapy

Implicit in initial psychosomatic discoveries, stimulated by psychoanalysis, were early models of emotion, such as the cathartic. Alexander's (1950) first hypothesis had this connotation. The prescription for therapy was simple: "discharge" dammed up affect. At times this was successful; explosions of feeling led to symptomatic relief, presumably by readjustment of emotional equilibria, which included the relationship to the therapist. More often, gains were slower, stalemated by resistance. Psychoanalysis itself, trying to work through resistances, ran into the dangers of regressive intensification of physiological disorders.

The search for other methods, particularly stimulated by behavioral approaches, endeavored to bypass the complexities of "inner" life, including emotions, and to concentrate on overt behavior, especially the symptomatic; thus was behavioral medicine born. Impatient with psychoanalytic ideology, it substituted its own. A discussion of the additional complexities, scientific and sociological, which accompanied efforts at simplification is beyond the scope of this chapter. Instead, some of the newer, as well as some of the older approaches to therapy are examined in the light of a broader view of emotional factors predisposing, precipitating, and sustaining medical disorders.

In Table 3-4 the field of emotion is represented in yet another manner, as a series of levels. These are progressively more removed from the core as we move upward, and more removed from conscious awareness as we move downward. Continuous feedback between the levels is taken for granted. The variety of psychosomatic dysfunctions represent derangements in such a complex cybernetic organization.

Efforts to ameliorate these dysfunctions have been directed at all these levels. The lists of techniques, and their corresponding aims are schematic and provisional. The clearest contrast is between insight-imparting techniques, at the top, and biofeedback, at the bottom. The former has as its manifest goal the understanding of motivationally powerful relationships; its deeper purpose is to extend this understanding and its effects into levels ordinarily

out of awareness. Biofeedback aims primarily to extend volitional control by providing specific physiological information ordinarily not available.

Intermediate approaches focus specifically on such aspects as imagery, inner or outer, endeavoring to capitalize on their privileged access to core emotional urges and feelings. These approaches are combined in various ways with efforts to promote general relaxation. A wide variety of behavior modification and supportive approaches have ramifications throughout many of these levels. Hypnotic therapy, for example, may include behavioral modification, trancelike meditation, or direct suggestion.

Hypnosis epitomizes two major problems that exist in this panoply of therapies. First, although it is among the oldest, its ability to influence established physiological processes is still in question. A similar lack of conclusive evidence plagues other approaches. Second, how do we determine the level of action of *any* therapy? Our contention is that motivational change originates in the core, but that the core operates through higher layers to effect constant adaptation to the world. By the same token, relationship changes in the world affect the core. If insight is efficacious, to what extent is it because of specific insightful content and to what extent because of nonspecific factors, such as a protecting, helping relationship emanating inwardly and influencing the core? The placebo problem has been taken very seriously in psychotherapy research for the past two decades. As Malan (1973) pointed out, the psychosomatic area is a superb proving ground in which to test some of the crucial questions facing such research.

CONCLUDING COMMENTS

For the ancients the soul had both psychological and physiological properties: "The biological soul was seen as the substrate of psychophysiological phenomena" (McMahon, 1976, p. 179). Galen's

Table 3-4   Therapies Directed at the Various Levels of Emotion

Methods	Levels*	Aims
Insight	Public interactions	Promote understanding
Support and suggestion	Values and concerns	Alter relationships
Meditative imagery, relaxation	Private imagery	Expand awareness
Behavior modification	Core conflict	Desensitize, reward
Biofeedback	Body change	Extend voluntary control

*Levels progress downward from conscious awareness to the neuropsychological core of emotions.

humors, when unbalanced, fostered corresponding images. Now, after four centuries of Cartesian dualism, we may be returning to such a view, prodded by Engel (1977) and buttressed by 50 years of accumulated psychosomatic facts. Even genetic programs at the cellular level are no longer seen as immutable scripts but rather as flexible guarantors of adaptation (Potter, 1981). Their flexibility may depend on enzymatic and hormonal influences, themselves affected by the history of the organism and its transactions with the surrounding world.

Emotions represent an interface between what we can capture in words and the biological tides that nourish and move us. As their role in bodily changes continues to unfold, they will endure as critical factors in medicine.

REFERENCES

Ader R, & Cohen N (1975): Behaviorally conditioned immunosuppression. Psychosom Med 37:333.

Alexander F (1950) *Psychosomatic Medicine: Its Principles and Applications*. New York, Norton.

Alexander F, French TM, & Pollock G (Eds.) (1968): *Psychosomatic Specificity: Experimental Study and Results*, vol. I. Chicago, University of Chicago Press.

Anthracite RF, Vachon L, & Knapp PH (1971): Alpha-adrenergic receptors in the human lung. Psychosom Med 33:481.

Birdwhistell RL (1963): The kinesic level in the investigation of the emotions. Knapp P (Ed.). In *Expression of the Emotions of Man*. New York, International Universities Press, 1963.

Brod J Fencl V, Hejl Z, & Jirka J (1959): Circulatory changes underlying blood pressure changes during acute emotional stress (mental arithmetic) in normotensive and hypertensive subjects. Clin Sci 18:269.

Cannon WB (1929): *Bodily Changes in Pain, Hunger, Fear and Rage*. New York, Appleton.

Cobb S (1976): Social support as a moderator of life stress: Presidential address. Psychosom Med 38:300.

Condon WS, & Sander LW (1974): Neonate movement is synchronized with adult speech: Interactional participation and language acquisition. Science 183:99–101.

Dahl H (1978): A new psychoanalytic model of motivation: Emotion as appetites and message. Psychoanal Contemporary Thought 1:373–408.

Dahl H, & Stengel B (1978): A classification of emotion works: A modification and formal test of de Rivera's decision theory of emotion. Psychoanal Contemporary Thought 1:269–312.

Daniels GE, O'Connor JF, Karush A, Moses L et al. (1962): Three decades in the observation and treatment of ulcerative colitis. Psychosom Med 24:85–93.

Darwin C (1872): *The Expression of Emotions in Man and Animal*. New York, Philosophical Library, 1955.

Demos V (1982): Affect in early infancy: Physiology or psychology? Psychoanal Inquiry 4:533–574.

Dunbar H (1946): *Emotions and Bodily Changes* (ed. 3). New York, Columbia University Press.

Ekman P, Friesen WV, & Ellsworth P (1972): *Emotion in the Human Face*. New York, Pergamon Press.

Engel GL (1954): Selection of clinical material in psychosomatic medicine: The need for a new physiology. Psychosom Med 16:368.

Engel GL (1955): Studies of ulcerative colitis III. The nature of the psychologic processes. Am J Med 19:231.

Engel G (1977): The need for a new medical model: A challenge for biomedicine. Science 196:129.

Fabrega H, & Manning PK (1973): An integrated theory of disease: Ladino Mestizo views of disease in the Chiapas Highlands. Psychosom Med 35:223.

Feldman F, Cantor D, Solls S, & Bachrach W (1967): Psychiatric study of a consecutive series of 34 patients with ulcerative colitis. Br Med J 3:14.

Friedman M, Byers SD, Diamont J, & Rosenman RN (1975): Plasma catecholamine responses of coronary-prone subjects (Type A) to a specific challenge. Metabolism 24:205–210.

Friedman M, & Rosenman RN (1959): Association of specific overt behavior pattern with blood and cardiovascular patterns. JAMA 169:1286.

Frumkin K, Nathan RJ, Prout MF, & Cohen MC (1978): Nonpharmacologic control of essential hypertension in man: A Psychosom Med 40:294–320.

Gold WM, Kessler GR, & Yu DYC (1972): Role of vagus nerve in experimental asthma in allergic dogs. J Appl Psysiol 33:719.

Haggard E, & Isaacs KS (1966): Micromomentary facial expressions as indicators of ego mechanisms in psychotherapy Gottshalk LA, & Auerbach AH (Eds.) In *Methods of Research in Psychotherapy*. New York, Appleton-Century Crofts.

Harburg E (1973): Socio-ecological stress, suppressed hostility, skin color, and black–white male blood pressure. Psychosom Med 35:276.

Henry JP, Meehan JP, & Stephens PM (1967): The use of psychosocial stimuli to induce prolonged systolic hypertension in mice. Psychosom Med 29:408.

Henry JP, Stephens PM, Axelrod J, & Mueller RA (1971): Effect of psychosocial stimulation on the enzymes involved in the biosynthesis and metabolism of noradrenaline and adrenaline. Psychosom Med 33:227.

Hess WR (1957): *The Functional Organization of the Hypothalamus*. New York, Grune Stratton.

Hess WR, & Akers K (1955): Experimental data on the role of the hypothalamus in mechanisms of emotional behavior. Arch Neurol Psychiatry 73:127–129.

Hinkle LE Jr., Christenson WN (1962): Observations on the role of nasal adaptive reactions, emotions and life stimulations in the genesis of minor respiratory emotions. Psychosom Med 24:515–516 (Abstract).

Hofer M, & Reiser MF (1969): The development of cardiac rate regulation in preweanling rats. Psychosom Med 31:372–388.

Holmes PH, & Rahe R (1967): The Social Readjustment Rating Scale. J Pshchosom Res 71:213.

Horowitz M, Schaeffer C, Hiroto D, Wilner et al. (1977): Life event questionnaire for measuring presumptive stress. Psychosom Med 39:413.

Hurst MW, Jenkins CD, & Rose RM (1978): The assessment of life change stress: A comparative psychological inquiry. Psychosom Med 40:141.

Izard CE (1971): *The Face of Emotion*. New York, Appleton-Century-Crofts.

Jacobs S, & Ostfeld AM (1977): An epidemiologic review of the mortality of bereavement. Psychosom Med 39:344.

Jenkins CD (1971): Psychological and social precursors of coronary disease. N Engl J Med 284:244, 307.

Jenkins CD, Hurst MW, Rose RM, Anderson L, & Kreger B (1982): Biomedical and psychosocial predictors of hypertension in air traffic controllers. Spielberger CD, Sarason IG, & Defares PB (Eds.): In *Stress and Anxiety*, Vol 9. New York, McGraw-Hill-Halsted.

Jenkins CD, Tuthill RW, Tannenbaum SI, & Kirby CR (1977): Zones of excess death in Massachusetts. Ne J Med 296:1354.

Jenkins CD, Zyzanski SJ, & Rosenman RN (1978): Coronary prone behavior: One pattern or several. Psychosom Med 40:25.

Kaufman EC (1973): Mother infant separation in monkeys: An experimental model. Scott JP, & Senay E C (Eds): In *Separation and Depression: Clinical and Research Aspects*. Washington DC. American Association for the Advancement of Science Publ. No. 94.

Kaufman IC, & Rosenblum LA (1967): The reaction to separation in infant monkeys. Anaclitic depression and conservation withdrawal. Psychosom Med 24:648–675.

Kepecs JG, Robin M, & Brunner MJ (1951): Relationship between certain emotional states and exudation into the skin. Psychosom Med 13:10–17.

Knapp PH (1967): Purging and curbing: An inquiry into disgust, satiety and shame. J Nerv Ment Dis 144:514–534.

Knapp PH (1981): Core processes in the organization of emotions. J Am Acad Psychoanal 9:415–434.

Knapp PH, Mathe AA, & Vachon L (1976): Psychosomatic aspects of bronchial asthma. Weiss EB, & Segal MS (Eds.): In *Bronchial Asthma: Mechanisms and Therapuetics*. Boston, Little, Brown.

Knapp PH, Mushatt C, & Nemetz SJ, Constantine H, & Friedman S (1970): The context of reported asthma during psychoanalysis. Psychosom Med 32:167.

Kohut H (1977): *The Restoration of the Self*. New York International Universities Press.

Langer SK (1948): *Philosophy in a New Key*. New York, Mentor Books.

Lindemann E (1945): Psychiatric problems in conservative treatment of ulcerative colitis. Arch Neurol Psychiatry 53:322.

Lindemann E (1950): Modifications in the course of ulcerative coilities in relationship to changes in life situations and reactive patterns, life stress and bodily disease. Assoc Res Nerv Ment Dis Proc 29:706.

Lown B, DeSilva RA, Reich P, & Murawski BJ (1980): Psychophysiologic factors in sudden cardiac death Am J Psychiatry 127:1325–1335.

MacLean PD (1949): Psychosomatic disease and the visceral brain: Recent developments of the Papez theory of emotion. Psychosom Med 11:338–353.

MacLean PD (1972): *A Triune Concept of the Brain and Behavior* (The Clarence M Hincks Memorial Lecture). Toronto, University of Toronto Press.

Malan D (1973): The outcome problem in psychotherapy research. Arch Gen Psychiatry 29:719–731.

Marty P, & de M'Uzan M (1963): La pensée opératoire. Rev Fr Psychoanal [Suppl.] 27:134.

Mason JW (1968): Organization of psychoendocrine mechanisms, II. Psychosom Med (5) part II.

Mason JW, Brady JV, Polish E, Bauer JA et al. (1961): Patterns of corticosteroid and pepsinogen change related to emotional stress in the monkey. Science, 133:1596.

Mason JW, Buescher EL (1967): Pre-illness hormonal changes in army recruits with acute respiratory infections (Abstract). Psychosom Med 29:545.

McMahon CE (1976): The role of imagination in the disease process. Psychol Med 6:179–184.

McQuown NA (1958): Linguistic transcription and specification of psychiatric interview materials. Psychiatry 20:79–86.

Melzack R, & Wall P (1965): Pain mechanisms: A new theory. Science 150:971–979.

Mirsky IA (1957): Psychosomatic approach to the etiology of clinical disorders. Psychosom Med 19:434.

Moos RH, & Solomon GF (1965): Psychologic comparison between women with rheumatoid arthritis and their non-arthritic sisters. I. Personality tests and interview rating data. II. Content analysis of interviews. Psychosom Med 27:135–164.

Mushatt C (1951): Psychological aspects of non-specific ulcerative colitis. Wittkower E, & Cleghorn R (Eds.). In *Recent Developments in Psychosomatic Medicine*. New York, International Universities Press.

O'Connor JF, Daniels G, Flood C, Karush A, et al. (1964): An evaluation of the effective uses of psychotherapy in the treatment of ulcerative colitis. Ann Int Med 60:587–601.

Ostfeld AM (1973): Editorial: What's the payoff in hypertension research? Psychosom Med 25:1–3.

Ostwald PF (1963): *Soundmaking: The Acoustic Communication of Emotion*. Springfield, Ill., Thomas.

Ostwald PF (1964): How the patient communicates about disease to the doctor. Sebeok TA, Hayes AS, & Bateson C (Eds.). In *Approaches to Semiotics*, Chap. 1, pp. 11–34. The Hague, Mouton.

Pittenger RE, & Smith HL (1957): A basis for some contributions of linguistics to psychiatry. Psychiatry 20:61–78.

Plutchik R (1980): *Emotion: A psycho-evolutionary synthesis.* New York, Harper & Row.

Plutchik R (1980): *Emotion: A psycho evolutionary synthesis.* New York, Harper & Row.

Potter Van R (1981): Physiologic adaptation at the adaptive level: The frontier where research on differentiation and malignancy meet. Perspect Biol Med 24:525–542.

Reich P, DeSilva RA, Lown B, & Murawski B (1981): Acute psychological disturbance preceding life threatening ventricular arrhythmias. JAMA 246:233–235.

Reiser MF, Reeves RR, & Armington J (1955): Effect of variations in laboratory procedure and experiments upon the ballistocardiogram, blood pressure and heart rate in healthy young men. Psychosom Med 17:185–199.

Rogentine GN, VanKammen DP, Fox BH, Dolhert JP, & Rosenblatt E et al. (1979): Psychological factors in the prognosis of malignant melanoma: A prospective study. Psychosom Med 41:647–655.

Rogers MP, Reich P, Strom TB, & Carpenter CB (1976): Behaviorally conditioned immunosuppression: Replication of recent study. Psychosom Med 36:47.

Rose NR (1981): Autoimmune disease. Sci Am 244(2): 80–103.

Scheflen AE (1966): Systems and psychosomatics. Psychosom Med 28:297–304.

Schildkraut JJ, & Kety SS (1967): Biogenic amines and emotion. Science 156:21–30.

Schmale AH (1973): Adaptive role of depression in health and disease. Scott JP, Senay EC (Eds.). In *Separation and Depression: Clinical and Research Aspects*, Washington, D.C., American Association for the Advancement of Science, Publ. No. 94.

Schwartz GE, Davidson RJ, Goleman DG (1978): Patterning of cognitive and somatic processes in the self regulation of anxiety: Effects of meditation versus exercise. Psychosom Med 40:321–328.

Schwartz GE, Weinberger DA, & Singer JA (1981): Cardiovascular differentiation of happiness, sadness, anger and fear following imagery and exercise. Psychosom Med 43:343–364.

Sebeok TA, Hays AS, & Bateson MC (1964): *Approaches to Semiotics.* The Hague Mouton.

Selye H (1970): *The Physiology and Pathology of Exposure to Illness.* Montreal Acts.

Shekelle RB, Raynor WJ, Ostfied AM, & Garron DC et al. (1981): Psychological depression and 17 year risk of death from cancer. Psychosom Med 43:117–125.

Sifneos PE (1973): The prevalence of alexithymic characteristics in psychosomatic patients. Psychother Psychosom 22:255–262.

Shand A (1914): *The Foundations of Character.* London, Macmillan.

Sperling M (1949): The role of the mother in psychosomatic disorders in children. Psychosom Med 11:377.

Tomkins SS (1962): *Affect, Imagery, Consciousness,* vol I: The Positive Affects. New York, Springer.

Tomkins SS (1963): *Affect, Imagery, Consciousness,* vol. II; *The Negative Affects.* New York, Springer.

Tomkins SS (1970): Affects on the primary motivational system. Arnold M (Ed.): In *Feelings and Emotions,* chap 6, pp. 101–110. New York, Academic Press.

Wapner W, Hamby S, & Gardner H (1981): The role of the right hemisphere in the apprehension of complex linguistic materials. Brain Language 14:15–33.

Weiner H (1977): *Psychobiology and Human Disease.* New York, Elsevier.

Weiner HM, Thaler NE, Reiser F & Mirsky IA (1957): Etiology of duodenal ulcer. Psychosom Med 19:1–10.

PART II

Stress and Emotion

4

Stress, Emotion, and Illness

Frances Cohen

In order to understand the role of stress and emotion in disease, it is useful to examine what stress is and what other factors need to be considered in evaluating these links. The word "stress" has been used in three different ways, to refer to (1) an aversive stimulus, (2) a specific response (physiological or psychological), or (3) a transaction between the person and the environment. It is useful to specify each of these separately. Thus stressors (or stress events) can be distinguished from a psychological state of stress (Lazarus & Launier, 1978), and from stress responses on physiological, psychological, or social levels.

THE RUBRIC OF STRESS

Types of Stressors

Stressors include not only life events that involve change—the type measured by the Holmes and Rahe (1967) Schedule of Recent Experience—but also continuing negative environmental conditions and situations in which no change occurs. The latter can involve situations of monotony (Frankenhaeuser, 1976) as well as situations in which differences exist between expectations and actualities (Coover et al., 1971).

It is useful to distinguish four types of stress events, based primarily on their duration (Cohen et al., 1982): (1) acute, time-limited events (e.g., awaiting a medical examination); (2) stress event sequences, in which a particular event initiates a series of stress events that occur over an extended period of time (e.g., bereavement); (3) chronic intermittent stressors (e.g., situations that occur and reoccur periodically such as conflicts with in-laws); and (4) chronic stress situations (e.g., chronic disability). In stress event sequences and chronic stress conditions,

stress reactions may occur over a considerable period of time. Future research efforts must try to distinguish the psychological and physiological effects of each of these types of stressors. Most laboratory research focuses on acute, time-limited stressors and measures short-term autonomic nervous system or hormonal changes. However, we do not know if this type of short-term mobilization has long-term health consequences or whether chronic changes in autonomic nervous system and hormonal responses are necessary before disease outcomes are likely. Some hormones such as cortisol rarely show chronic elevations, suggesting that the person may reach an equilibrium in which constant coping efforts are not required. We do not know if different coping strategies are effective for dealing with acute as compared to chronic stressors.

Types of Stress Responses

Stress responses can occur on physiological, psychological, or social levels. From a physiological standpoint, changes in autonomic nervous system, hormonal, immunological, and neuroregulatory reactions may occur. For example, heart rate, cortisol level, effectiveness of T cells, and central nervous system norepinephrine level may show alterations. Psychologically, changes can be seen in negatively toned affect, motor–behavioral reactions (expressive and instrumental), and alterations in adaptive performance (Lazarus, 1966). On a social level, outcomes include antisocial behavior, difficulties in meeting role requirements, and so forth. (See Elliott and Eisdorfer, 1982, and Lazarus and Folkman, in press, for a fuller discussion of the ways of examining stress responses.)

Although many physiological systems respond to stressors, they do not do so in a simple, straightforward manner. First, not all indicators within each physiological system respond in a similar fashion. For example, Mason (1974) demonstrated different hormonal response profiles in rhesus monkeys exposed to different noxious stimuli. Mason (1968) suggested that evaluations of the neuroendocrine response to stressors should focus not on the secretion of any one hormone, but rather on the relative overall balance among hormones. Similarly, some researchers have argued against studying just one neurotransmitter or one component of the immune response (e.g., Rogers et al., 1979).

Second, the physiological effects of stressors are not always negative. There is a considerable body of laboratory research that suggests that certain types of stressors can lead to increased resistance to some diseases and decreased resistance to others (Ader & Grota, 1973). The type of effect also depends on specifics of the stressor experience, such as the type of stressor, its acuteness or chronicity, its timing, and the species of animal studied (Ader, 1974; Friedman & Glasgow, 1966; La Barba, 1970).

Third, an important issue concerns the relationship between acute stress responses and long-term disease outcomes. The fact that behavioral stimuli can produce acute physiological changes does not mean that they necessarily lead to permanent changes in a person's health. For example, there is a normal fluctuation in most physiological systems, related to time of day, sleep, diet, etc. We do not know at what point variations may be pathological. It may be, for example, that the magnitude of changes found in normal daily immunological patterns is greater than the change occurring in response to stressful stimuli (Rogers et al., 1979). More research must be directed toward exploring the relationship between short-term physiological reactions and long-term health consequences (Elliott & Eisdorfer, 1982).

Finally, it is important to remember that increased physiological activation can have positive consequences. For example, Frankenhaeuser (1975, 1976) suggested that people who habitually secrete high levels of epinephrine have higher IQ, higher scores on ego strength, and are rated happier than those with low levels of epinephrine. Frankenhaeuser (1976) and Gal and Lazarus (1975) cautioned about considering the magnitude of the physiological response as the best measure of adaptive outcome. More useful may be the time it takes for a measure to return to baseline levels, since successful adaptation may involve both effective mobilization and demobilization of physiological systems.

Stress as a Growth Enhancing Process

Although most researchers assume that stress is a negative experience, there is an increasing interest in the role that stress plays in normal personality development. Stress events are inevitable during the life cycle and may be necessary to help develop competencies and self-esteem and to build skills needed later in life. Whether a stressful event leads to growth, crisis, or trauma is a function of a number of factors such as: the pervasiveness and duration of the event, its timing, available personal resources, the surrounding environment (including social supports, the opportunities available to act on the environment, and the meaning of the experience (Benner et al. 1980).

Furthermore, some people seek what appear to be stressful encounters, such as sky-diving, race-car driving, or highly pressured work environments (Klausner, 1968; Opton, 1969). Stress seeking may be a way to build skills and feelings of mastery or to relieve boredom. Systematic studies are needed to explore the positive effects of stress.

MEDIATING VARIABLES

Person, Environmental and Process Factors

There is a growing consensus among stress researchers that in order to understand the relationship between stress and illness outcomes, the factors that modify or mediate the relationship must be elucidated (e.g., Elliott & Eisdorfer, 1982). Although stressors may produce transient physiological and psychological changes, most stress events are not followed by long-term adverse health consequences. A stressor may produce an extreme reaction in one person and no reaction in another, or the same stressor may produce variable reactions in the same individual at different time periods. This suggests that mediating factors play a role in amplifying or reducing reactions to potential stressors. It is important to consider the different types of modifiers that may be involved. Modifiers can be categorized as person factors, environmental factors, and process factors that result from the individual's interactions with the environment (Cohen et al., 1982).

Person factors include (1) personality variables, (2) personal resources, (3) temperament, (4) past history, (5) sociodemographic variables, (6) genetic variables (biological predispositions to illness), and (7) biological variables that are not genetically transmitted. The differences in cardiovascular reactivity described by Dembroski et al. (Chapter 7) would be an example of a person factor of biological or genetic origin.

Environmental factors include (1) interpersonal factors such as social support, (2) physical setting, (3) organizational factors, (4) social characteristics of the neighborhood population (human aggregate), (5) social climate (Moos, 1976, 1979), (6) cultural factors, and (7) other environmental stressors. For example, there is a large body of literature that suggests that social supports buffer individuals from the potentially negative efforts of stressors, and that those who have social supports may live longer and have a lower incidence of physical illness (e.g., Berkman & Syme, 1979; Cobb, 1976; Dimsdale et. al., 1979; Kaplan et al., 1977).

Process factors include (1) cognitive appraisal, and (2) coping. These result from the interaction of the individual with the environment and may occur only during a specific interaction. The way in which an individual appraises and copes with a situation influences psychological and physiological reactions to stressors (see reviews by Cohen & Lazarus, 1979, 1983; Lazarus et al., 1970). Van Dyke and Kaufman (Chapter 5) describe how differences in the social structure of an animal colony influence the animal's appraisal of a separation, ability to cope, and subsequent emotional and physiological reactions.

A review of this literature is beyond the scope of this chapter. Previous reviews suggest that psychosocial variables are important modifiers of the relationship between stress and disease, but that fuller understanding of their role awaits a clearer conceptual framework (one that can, for example, distinguish internal resources from external resources such as social supports) and better assessment techniques (Cohen, 1979; Cohen et al., 1982). The interaction of biological predispositions and psychosocial variables needs further study, since adverse health consequences may result only when both are present simultanesouly (Alexander, 1950; Elliott & Eisdorfer, 1982; Hinkle, 1974; Weiner, 1977), a point discussed by Dembroski et al. (Chapter 7).

Illness-Related Factors

Weissman et al. (Chapter 6) and Appel et al. (Chapter 8) review the evidence that anger and depression are linked to the etiology of somatic disease. The expression of emotion has also been linked to recovery from illness and recovery from surgery (e.g., Cohen & Lazarus, 1979, 1983). Although one might surmise that the expression of negative emotions will have negative effects on illness outcomes, studies show that the adaptiveness of being emotionally expressive varies with the type of illness and the outcome examined. As discussed by Appel et al., more frequent expression of hostility and other negative affects and reduced inhibition are associated with increased survival rates from cancer (Blumberg et al., 1954; Derogatis et al., 1979; Klopfer, 1957; Rogentine et al., 1979; Stavraky et al., 1968; cf. Krasnoff, 1959). Similarly, Calden et al., (1960) found that non-conforming and recalcitrant patients had faster recovery from tuberculosis than those who were cooperative (cf. Cuadra, 1953).

A different pattern emerges, however, in the case of patients with irreversible diffuse obstructive pulmonary syndromes. Emotional expressiveness is associated with increased respiratory symptoms and physiological decompensation (Dudley et al., 1969). Furthermore, both asthma and tuberculosis patients who are emotionally labile require longer hospitalization and more treatment with steroid drugs (for the asthma patients) following hospital discharge (Dirks et al., 1977a; Dirks et al., 1977b, Kinsman et al., 1977).

These few studies suggest that the expression of emotion can have different consequences depending on the situation. In some cases it can directly exacerbate symptoms and hasten degeneration. In other cases it may draw the physician's attention to patients' symptoms, which could result in more frequent hospitalization and drug treatment, and also increased survival, as the disease process could be treated before the pathology progressed. Thus, depending on the outcome considered (hospitalization, drug treatment, or survival), different conclusions would be drawn about the adaptiveness of emotional expression.

CLINICAL IMPLICATIONS

The chapters in Part II suggest that stress, emotion, and behavioral factors may affect health outcomes but how the stressor is appraised, the ways in which individuals cope, and their emotional reactions, resources, environment, and biological predispositions may all play a significant mediating role. These findings imply that in selecting preventive measures we should not focus exclusively on trying to eliminate stressors. Although people can learn to avoid some stressors, they will probably need to learn to adapt to other, ubiquitous stressors. It is important to consider interventions that alter mediating factors. For example, programs can developed to improve coping skills, achieve better utilization of social supports, build individual competencies, or reduce a person's anxiety. Intervention programs that are set up to affect several factors simultaneously may be most effective.

It is also important to remember that stressors can produce effects in several domains of functioning, and that interventions may have more wide-ranging effects than anticipated. For example, although Type A behavior may increase the risk of coronary heart disease, it may also boost feelings of self-esteem and engender community respect. Thus, interventions that alter this behavior may have negative social or personal consequences. The positive and negative effects of interventions that affect life style must be carefully considered. The appropriateness of a particular intervention may also depend on the type of illness the person has and the nature of the surrounding physical and social environment.

By understanding how psychosocial variables influence health and illness, we will be better able to help people attain and maintain healthy life patterns and cope with problems more effectively. The burgeoning research in this area should lead to a more solid knowledge base in the future from which to develop systematic interventions.

REFERENCES

Ader R (1974): The role of developmental factors in susceptibility to disease. Int J Psychiatry Med 5:367–376.

Ader R, & Grota LJ (1973): Adrenocortical mediation of the effects of early life experiences. Prog Brain Res 39:395–405.

Alexander F (1950): *Psychosomatic Medicine*. New York, Norton.

Benner P, Roskies E, & Lazarus RS (1980): Stress and coping under extreme conditions. Dimsdale JE (Ed.). In *Survivors, Victims, and Perpetrators: Essay on the Nazi Holocaust*, Washington, D.C., Hemisphere, pp. 219–258.

Berkman LF, & Syme SL (1979): Social networks, host resistance, and mortality: A nine-year follow-up study of Alameda County residents. Am J Epidemiol 109:186–204.

Blumberg EM, West PM, & Ellis EW (1954): A possible relationship between psychological factors and human cancer. Psychosom Med 16:277–286.

Calden G, Dupertuis CW, Hokanson JE, & Lewis WC (1960): Psychosomatic factors in the rate of recovery from tuberculosis. Psychosom Med 22:345–355.

Cobb S (1976): Social support as a moderator of life stress. Psychosom Med 38:300–314.

Cohen F (1979): Personality, stress, and the development of physical illness. Stone GC, Cohen F, Adler NE et al. In *Health Psychology—A Handbook*, pp. 77–111.

Cohen F, & Lazarus RS (1979): Coping with the stresses of illness. Stone GC, Cohen F, Adler NE, et al. In *Health Psychology—A Handbook*. San Francisco, Jossey-Bass, pp. 217–254.

Cohen F, & Lazerus RS (1983): Coping and adaptation in health and illness. Mechanic D. In *Handbook of Health, Health Care, and the Health Professions*. New York, Free Press, pp. 608–635.

Cohen F, Horowitz MJ, Lazarus RS, Moos RH, Robins LN, Rose RM, & Rutter M (1982): Panel on psychosocial assets and modifiers of stress. Elliott CR, & Eisdorfer C (Eds.), In *Stress and Human Health*, New York, Springer, pp. 147–188.

Coover GD, Goldman L, & Levine S (1971): Plasma corticosterone increases produced by extinction of operant behavior in rats. Physiol Behav 6:261–263.

Cuadra CA (1953): *A psychometric investigation of control factors in psychological adjustment*. Unpublished doctoral dissertation, Berkeley, University of California.

Derogatis LR, Abeloff MD, & Melisaratos N (1979): Psychological coping mechanisms and survival time in metastatic breast cancer. JAMA 242:1504–1508.

Dimsdale JE, Eckenrode J, Haggerty RJ, Kaplan BH, Cohen F, & Dornbusch S (1979): The role of social supports in medical care. Soc Psychiatry 14:175–180.

Dirks JF, Jones NF, & Kinsman RA (1977a): Panic-fear: A personality dimension related to intractability in asthma. Psychosom Med 29:120–126.

Dirks JF, Kinsman RA, Jones NF, Spector, SL, Davidson PT, & Evans NW (1977b): Panic-fear: A personality dimension related to length of hospitalization in respiratory illness. J Asthma Res 14:61–71.

Dudley DL, Verhey JW, Masuda M, & Martin CJ (1969): Long-term adjustment, prognosis, and death in irreversible diffuse obstructive pulmonary syndromes. Psychosom Med 31:310–325.

Elliott GR, & Eisdorfer C (Eds.) (1982): *Stress and Human Health*. New York, Springer.

Frankenhaeuser M (1975): Sympathetic-adrenomedullary activity, behavior, and the psychosocial environment. Venables RH, Cristie MJ (Eds.). In *Research in Psychophysiology*, New York, Wiley, pp. 71–94.

Frankenhaeuser M (1976): The role of peripheral catecholamines in adaption to understimulation and overstimulation. Serban G (Ed.). In *Psychopathology of Human Adaptation*. New York, Plenum Press, pp. 173–191.

Friedman SB, & Glasgow LA (1966): Psychologic factors and resistance to infectious disease. Pediatr Clin North Am 13:315–335.

Gal R, & Lazarus RS (1975): The role of activity in anticipating and confronting stressful situations. J Hum Stress 1(4):4–20.

Hinkle LE Jr. (1974): The effect of exposure to culture change, social change, and changes in interpersonal relationships on health. Dohrenwend BS, & Dohrenwend BP

(Eds.). In *Stressful Life Events: Their Nature and Effects*, New York, Wiley, pp. 9–44.

Holmes TH, & Rahe RH (1967): *Schedule of Recent Experience*. Seattle, University of Washington, School of Medicine.

Kaplan BH, Cassel JC, & Gore S (1977): Social support and health. Med Care 15(5):[Suppl]47–58.

Kinsman RA, Dahlem NW, Spector S, & Staudenmayer H (1977): Observations on subjective symptomatology, coping behavior, and medical decisions in asthma. Psychosom Med 39:102–119.

Klausner SZ (1968): *Why Man Takes Chances: Studies in Stress-Seeking*. New York, Anchor Books.

Klopfer B (1957): Psychological variables in human cancer. J Proj Techniques 21:291–295.

Krasnoff A (1959): Psychological variables in human cancer: A cross-validational study. Psychosom Med 21:291–295.

La Barba RC (1970): Experiential and environmental factors in cancer: A review of research with animals. Psychosom Med 32:259–276.

Lazarus RS (1966): *Psychological Stress and the Coping Process*. New York, McGraw-Hill.

Lazarus RS, Averill JR, & Opton EM Jr. (1970): Toward a cognitive theory of emotion. Arnold M (Ed.), In *Feelings and Emotions*. New York, Academic Press, pp. 207–231.

Lazarus RS, & Folkman S (in press): Coping and adaptation. Gentry WD (Ed.), In *The Handbook of Behavioral Medicine*. New York, Guilford Press.

Lazarus RS, & Launier R (1978): Stress-related transactions between person and environment. Pervin LA, &

Lewis M (Eds.). In *Perspectives in Interactional Psychology*, New York, Plenum Press, pp. 287–327.

Mason JW (1968): Over-all hormonal balance as a key to endocrine organization. Psychosom Med 30:791–808.

Mason JW (1974): Specificity in organization of neuroendocrine response profiles. Seeman P, & Brown GM (Eds.). In *Frontiers in Neurology and Neuroscience Research*. Toronto, University of Toronto, pp. 68–80.

Moos RH (1976): *The Human Context: Environmental Determinants of Behavior*. New York, Wiley-Interscience.

Moos RH (1979): Social-ecological perspectives on health. Stone GC, Cohen F, Adler NE et al. (Eds.). In *Health Psychology—A Handbook*. San Francisco, Jossey-Bass, pp. 523–547.

Opton EM Jr. (1969): *Why do people like stress?* Paper presented at the Western Psychological Convention, Vancouver.

Rogentine GN, van Kammen DP, Fox, BH, Docherty JP, Rosenblatt JE, Boyd SC, & Bunney WE (1979): Psychological factors in the prognosis of malignant melanoma: A prospective study. Psychosom Med 41:147–164.

Rogers MP, Dubey D, & Reich P (1979): The influence of the psyche and brain on immunity and disease susceptibility: A critical review. Psychosom Med 41:147–164.

Stavraky KM, et al. (1968): Psychological factors in the outcome of human cancer. J Psychosom Res 12:251–259.

Weiner H (1977): *Psychobiology and Human Disease*. New York, American Elsevier.

5

Psychobiology of Bereavement

Craig Van Dyke   *I. Charles Kaufman*

"My wife was sick for two months before she died. After a month she no longer heard me when I spoke to her and I knew she would die. Before she died she told me to be sure and take care of our children and I told her not to worry about it, for I would. Finally one morning at about ten o'clock she died. I cried and cried. She stayed on the mat in the house for three days and people brought all sorts of gifts, cloth and lavalavas. Then we buried her there. After that for three months I just stayed in the house, I above and she below the ground. Finally her mother came to me and told me I must get out and walk around for if I just stayed there every day all day I would be sick too and would die. So I went out of the house and worked again . . . ."

This poignant description of a man from the Central Caroline Islands in the middle of the Pacific Ocean (Gladwin & Sarason, 1953) attests to loss being an inevitable theme of the human experience and the reaction to it (grief, mourning, the danger of morbidity and mortality, and finally, recovery) a universal phenomenon (Rosenblatt et al., 1976). As such, we may suppose that both biological and psychological mechanisms have evolved for coping with and adapting to loss. We may also suppose that, as with responses to stress generally, the mechanisms may succeed, not suffice, or even increase the risk of illness or death. Our knowledge of the details of the response to loss are still incompletely understood, especially in regard to the biological systems involved.

The most difficult loss to adapt to is the death of a close relative. Since Lindemann's (1944) classic description of the symptomatology of acute grief in individuals who lost close relatives in the Coconut Grove fire, there have been a number of studies examining the bereavement experience.[1] In most studies, the psychological aspects of bereavement so closely resemble the phenomenology of melancholia,

that grief for many years has represented the best model for understanding depressive illness. Furthermore, the bereaved are in fact at increased risk of developing depressive illness (Parkes, 1972). [We are referring here to bereavement being an immediate precipitant of depression.[2] There is no clear understanding, however, of the difference between the grieving state and depressive illness. In fact, concepts such as pathological or delayed grief were developed in an attempt to bridge the gulf between grief and depression (Lindemann, 1944). While these concepts have a certain clinical utility, they also add to the semantic confusion since there is no agreement on even such basic issues as the usual duration of the mourning process.

The physiological aspects of grief and mourning are even less well studied and understood, even though object loss is believed to be the most potent life change that precedes physical morbidity (Holmes & Rahe, 1967). Bereaved populations are more likely to develop somatic illness than non-bereaved populations (Lindemann, 1944; Parkes, 1964, 1970); and even more impressively, they have increased mortality rates (reviewed by Jacobs & Ostfeld, 1977).

---

[1]We define *bereavement* as the loss by death of a person who is very close and important, usually a close relative. We define *grief* as the state of mental suffering associated with bereavement. We define *mourning* as the work dealing with bereavement, i.e., the process of painful but necessary separation from the no longer existent object. We view grief and mourning from a psychobiological perspective, including the physiological adaptive mechanisms.

[2]However, there is also substantial evidence that early loss of a parent is associated with an increased vulnerability to depression in later life (Bowlby, 1951; Brown, 1961; Caplan and Douglas, 1969; Birtchnell, 1970; Heinicke, 1973).

However, it is not known when and how the bereaved develop somatic illness, nor what mechanisms are responsible for the increased mortality. Not only has the basic physiology of the bereaved state not been well described, there have been few attempts to correlate the psychological factors with physiological measures, although the psychobiological complexity and clinical intensity of grief led Engel (1961) to suggest that it resembles a disease and corresponds to other states that are defined as pathological (e.g., mental illness, alcoholism).

As a severe stress, bereavement might be expected to produce a reaction comparable to that produced by other severe stresses. Grief and mourning, however, clearly present features that are distinguishable from other stress responses; although it is not yet known what is unique about bereavement as a stress, nor what mechanisms are activated in response. Finally, we lack a firm understanding of the natural history of bereavement and, to our knowledge, there has been only one systematic, longitudinal study of the psychobiology of the bereavement reaction through all the stages of the process, i.e., both before and after the death of a key person (Friedman et al., 1963; Hofer et al., 1972a, 1972b; Wolff et al., 1964a, Wolf et al., 1964b).

This chapter reviews our knowledge of the psychobiology[3] of bereavement. A theoretical model is presented that contrasts bereavement with severe depression and with other forms of severe stress that do not involve actual loss.

BEREAVEMENT AND DEPRESSION

Anticipatory Grief and Mourning

When there is awareness that a close loved one is going to die, grieving may commence prior to the actual loss. Unlike grief proper (i.e., grief after the loss has occurred), which tends to decrease in intensity with time, anticipatory grief tends to increase as death of the loved one approaches, and is complicated by the need to deal with the physical and emotional presence of the person who is dying (Aldrich, 1974). From an adaptive point of view, anticipatory grief may allow the survivor to prepare emotionally for the loss (Gerber, 1974); the work of mourning may be so effective that emotional involvement ceases before the actual loss occurs (Lindemann,

---

[3]The study of mental life and behavior in relation to other biological processes (Webster's New Collegiate Dictionary, 1979).

1944). In contrast, the anticipatory period may be marked by denial and false hope so that the blow at the time of death is in no way softened (Aldrich, 1974; Parkes, 1972; Silverman, 1974).

Clayton and her colleagues (1973) examined the relationship between the length of a spouse's terminal illness and the adjustment of the survivor. They found that the duration of illness was unrelated to the prevalence of symptoms in the survivors. However, this issue remains controversial since other studies suggest that, whereas sudden death does not lead to poorer outcome, prolonged fatal illnesses are associated with more upset and disturbance in the survivors (Gerber et al., 1975; Maddison & Viola, 1968; Schwab et al., 1975).

Grief Proper and Mourning

The symptoms of acute grief were well outlined by Lindemann (1944) in his classic description. He noted somatic distress occuring in waves lasting from 20 to 60 minutes. Included were feelings of choking, shortness of breath, emptiness in the stomach, sighing, lack of muscular strength, and excruciating subjective distress described as mental pain. Mere mention of the deceased could set off these waves. This syndrome also involved intense preoccupation with the image of the deceased, a sense of unreality, and emotional distance from others. The survivor might search for the deceased in a crowd or almost perceive his or her presence in a room. The bereaved might also be preoccupied with guilt feelings over prior failures in the relationship with the deceased; minor difficulties from the past might be blown out of proportion. Not uncommonly, the survivor might become angry or irritable with those who were trying to be kind and sympathetic. Finally, the grieving individual might become disorganized or go through the motions of everyday activities in a hollow fashion. The bereaved was frequently astonished to find how much of his or her daily routine was in some fashion related to or made meaningful by the deceased.

Bowly (1961) described three phases in mourning (in his terminology, *mourning* represents the psychological response to the loss, and *grief* the subjective state). In the first phase, *protest*, the survivor behaves as if the deceased is still present. Maximal efforts are made to rejoin or recover the lost object, with resultant anxiety, anger, and grief upon failure or in response to the idea that the survivor should accept the loss. Anger at the deceased is viewed by Bowlby as a vestige of a previously adaptive emotion that served to limit or prevent the other person from leaving or separating. Phase 2, *despair*, is characterized by the realization that the deceased is no longer alive. Energy and behavior that previously focused on a reunion is now without focus, and the bereaved is disorganized, anxious, and despairing. Phase 3, *detachment*, represents a reworking of the situation so that feelings about the lost object are muted, and the bereaved is able to invest emotionally in new objects or relationships. Despite this resolution, there is a feeling that the deceased still exists; however, the behavior no longer reflects this, except in such areas as pursuit of goals that were shared with the deceased.

Parkes (1970, 1972) described three phases of bereavement reaction in widows. In the first phase, the widows experienced periods of *numbness* interposed with periods of *anxiety and panic*; this lasted from a few hours to a few days. It was followed by a phase of *pining and protest*, in which the widow yearned for her dead husband and behaved in a fashion designed either to reunite with him or to avoid the futile search. The widow was restless, bitter, tearful, and preoccupied with thoughts of the deceased. The next phase was *disorganization*, in which the widow was aimless and apathetic, with loss of normal goal-directed behavior. Although the most intense reactions to the death of a close relative may resolve in 4–8 weeks (Lindemann, 1944), Parkes (1970) believed that the full mourning process required 1–2 years. However, in that anniversary reactions can occur as long as 20 or more years after the loss (Bornstein & Clayton, 1972), mourning lasts much longer than the 1–2 years postulated by Parkes (1970). In a sense, the individual is permanently changed by the death of a close relative.

Pathological Grief and Mourning

Freud (1917) and Abraham (1927) described pathological grief reactions characterized by episodes of panic, hostility toward the self, lowered self-esteem, and regression. In essence, pathological grief involves a severe and prolonged reaction with maladaptive behavior. Lindemann (1944) pointed out that grief reactions could also be delayed or distorted. In the former, grieving is put off because of the necessity to perform critical tasks or to maintain the spirits or morale of others. It may begin spontaneously at some later date, or in response to a serendipitous event such as mention of the deceased's name or on the anniversary of the deceased's birthday or death. Parkes (1970) felt that grief

cannot be postponed indefinitely and that the more complete the repression of feelings, the more dramatic and intense they are when finally released.

Distorted grief reactions represent a subtle form of pathology, involving hostility focused on a single individual or issue, severe alteration of behavior or relationships, and self-destructive behavior. Identification with the deceased may take the form of a similar gait, manner of speech, or characteristic gesture, and in extreme cases may involve adopting a symptom from the deceased's terminal illness (Engel, 1959).

Separation in Children

Maternal separation represents for children an analogous situation to the death of a close relative for adults. However, the child's response is in part determined by age and level of development. For example, prolonged separation of infants from the mother at age 3 months results in a profound arrest of physical and mental development, a syndrome which Spitz (1945) called *hospitalism*. Spitz (1946) also described the syndrome of *anaclitic depression* in 6–10 month old infants separated from their mothers. By definition, the syndrome is presumed to result from the infant's dependence on the mother. These infants develop tearfulness, anxiety, then psychomotor slowing, withdrawal, dejection, stupor, insomnia, anorexia, weight loss, and retardation in growth and development. The strong resemblance to adult depressive illness is clear.

Engel and Reichsman (1956), in a study of a child (Monica) with a gastric fistula who was not bereft but was mother deprived, described symptoms that they thought comparable to anaclitic depression. Of further relevance was the theoretical construction that developed from that study. They were struck by the fact that in the presence of a stranger Monica would abruptly turn away and even fall asleep, while showing profound reduction in the secretion of hydrochloric acid by the stomach. They saw this behavior as a manifestation of a primary regulatory process for organismic homeostasis, designed to conserve resources in the face of possible depletion. This biological response pattern was ultimately labeled *conservation–withdrawal*.

After finding a variety of other comparable manifestations and noting that these usually followed a response pattern of active engagement in stressful situations, Engel (1962) concluded that the central nervous system is organized from birth to mediate two opposite patterns of response to a mounting need. The first, *flight–fight*, involves activity and environmental engagement to avoid danger or control sources of supply. The second, *conservation-withdrawal*, is activated when the high energy expenditures of the flight–fight reaction threaten exhaustion; it is characterized by relative immobility, quiescence, and unresponsiveness to environmental input. Engel found neurophysiological support for his theory in Hess' (1957) demonstration of separate ergotropic and trophotropic zones in the diencephalon and mesencephalon underlying the two patterns of response. The ergotropic system mediates arousal, wakefulness, and increased muscular tone, and involves activation of the sympathetic nervous system, whereas the trophotropic system mediates the opposite effects and involves activation of the parasympathetic nervous system. Gellhorn (1970) independently provided evidence of reciprocal systems that activate and inactivate the organism in relation to both environmental and internal fluctuations. Engel postulated further that flight–fight and conservation–withdrawal are the respective biological anlagen of anxiety and depression.

Psychological Theories of Grief and Depression

Freud (1917) noted the phenomenological similarity between depression and grief and examined the psychological processes in both states. The pain of grief he considered to be "the actual reaction to loss of object." Freud viewed identification with the lost object as an important mechanism to help control feelings of loss and as a way to preserve the object forever. He described the extended process of mourning as the painful but necessary psychological separation, under the influence of reality testing, from the no longer existent object. Because he found evidence that depression followed object loss or its symbolic equivalent, Freud thought that depression is modeled on grief and mourning. However, in depression, he believed that there is significant hostility to the lost object that, through identification, is redirected toward the self. Choosing a somewhat different emphasis, Bowlby (1961) suggested that persistent searching for the permanently lost object is the major motivation in pathological mourning. In contrast to these formulations, Horowitz and his co-workers (1980) postulated that pathological grief represents a reemergence of self-denigrating images and role relationship models that were kept submerged by the living relationship with the deceased.

While clinicians generally agree with many of these ideas, empirical studies have failed to support the universal role of hostility in depression (Gershon et al., 1968; Klerman & Gershon, 1970; Weissman et al., 1971). More recent psychoanalytic formulations of depression have emphasized feelings of helplessness and lowered self-esteem (Bibring, 1953; Engel & Schmale, 1972; Kaufman, 1977). Bibring's (1953) phrase, "the ego's shocking awareness of its helplessness in regard to its aspirations," captures the essence of this construct. Beck (1967) hypothesized that depression results from a cognitive style that views everything negatively. From this cognitive set arise feelings of helplessness, hopelessness, and depression. Quite similar is the learned helplessness model of depression (Seligman, 1975), based on animal experiments in which exposure to inescapable shock impaired later ability to escape when the shock was avoidable.

Distinguishing between grief and depressive illness remains a difficult and confusing task. Clayton and her colleagues examined depression in a bereaved population (Bornstein et al., 1973; Briscoe & Smith, 1975; Clayton et al., 1971, 1972; Clayton et al., 1974). Using Research Diagnostic Criteria for a primary affective disorder, they found that depression was common in widowhood. In their sample of 109 randomly selected bereaved spouses, 35 percent were depressed at 1 month, 25 percent at 4 months, and 17 percent at 1 year following the death of their spouses; 45 percent were depressed at some point during the year. These authors thought that depression in widowhood was symptomatically very similar to depression in nonbereaved individuals, differing only in that the bereaved define and accept this as a normal reaction, whereas depressed patients view their depression as abnormal, leading them to define themselves as patients and to seek help. The authors found that crying, depressed mood, and sleep disturbance were the cardinal symptoms of bereavement reaction. Other frequent symptoms included anorexia or weight loss, difficulty concentrating or poor memory, and loss of interest in social relationships and current events. Guilt feelings were usually restricted to regret over minor omissions. Thoughts of suicide or fears of losing one's mind were uncommon, although the bereaved often talked of wishing they were dead.

These investigators also noted that the depression of widowhood differed from a primary affective disorder in that it was not more common in women than men, it was not associated with a positive family history of psychiatric illness nor with affective disorder in first-degree relatives, and it was not more common in those previously treated for depression. The last finding implies that a prior history of affective disorder does not necessarily increase the risk of depression following conjugal bereavement. Finally, these authors strongly emphasized that 65 percent of the conjugally bereaved did not manifest signs of depression 1 month after the death of the spouse. *The Diagnostic and Statistical Manual of Mental Disorders* (DSM-III; American Psychiatric Association, 1980) echoes many of these points. It distinguishes uncomplicated bereavement from major depression in that the latter is characterized by morbid preoccupation with worthlessness, prolonged and marked functional impairment, and marked psychomotor retardation.

Biology of Bereavement and Depression

In the first major investigation of the psychobiology of bereavement, Mason and his colleagues (Friedman et al., 1963; Wolff et al., 1964a, Wolff et al., 1964b) examined the coping skills and urinary 17-hydroxycorticosteroid (17-OHCS) excretion rates of parents of fatally ill children. They determined that each parent had a characteristic 17-OHCS level that tended to remain within a narrow range throughout the child's illness. Somewhat unexpectedly, this level did not increase dramatically at the time of acute distress, including the death of the child. The authors thought that low 17-OHCS excretion rates were a function of effective coping, especially the use of denial, while high excretion rates reflected ineffective coping. There was also a sex difference in excretion rates, with fathers having an average level of 7.1 mg/24 hr and mothers 5.0 mg/24 hrs.

Following their initial study, these investigators performed a predictive study in which independent assessment of the effectiveness of the parents' coping was used to estimate their 17-OHCS excretion rates. Effectiveness of coping was based on the parent's level of distress during an interview and on whether the parent's behavior outside the interview situation was disrupted (e.g., at home or work). This predictive study verified the earlier hypothesis that low 17-OHCS levels reflected effective coping, and high levels ineffective coping.

As a follow-up study, these investigators (Hofer et al., 1972a, 1972b) reexamined many of the parents 6 and 24 months after the death of the child. There was a tendency for those who excreted high 17-OHCS levels prior to the death of the child to have low values after the child's death. Low excretors before the death of the child had the opposite pattern. Anticipatory mourning in the group of parents who were high excretors prior to their child's demise did not explain these findings. High excretors in the period after the death of the child were more symptomatic and more involved in active mourning than those parents who were low 17-OHCS excretors.

In another major examination of physiological alterations in the bereaved, Bartrop and co-workers (1977) compared the immunological and endocrinological function of 26 unexpectedly bereaved spouses with that of an equal number of nonbereaved spouses who were matched for age, sex, and race. The investigators noted that lymphocytes from the bereaved group demonstrated a reduce in vitro response to mitogens (phytohemagglutinin and concanavalin A) 6 weeks after the death. There were no other differences betweeen the groups in other immune measures or in endocrinological function, but the frequency of sampling was quite limited. These findings are of particular interest since they imply that the mechanism responsible for the decreased response to mitogens was not increased plasma cortisol secondary to stress. These authors did not report the psychological state of the bereaved. In a study comparing immune functions before and after death of spouse, Schleifer and co-workers (1980) also found a decreased lymphocyte response to mitogens in the conjugally bereaved.

The biology of depression has been studied much more extensively than the biology of bereavement (Akiskal & McKinney, 1975). Much of this work has focused on abnormalities in biogenic amines as possible etiologies for depressive illness and as a means of establishing subtypes of depression (reviewed by Sweeney & Mass, 1978). While the treatment of depression has benefitted greatly from drugs that influence biogenic amines, the role of the amines in the etiology of depression remains unclear.

Other lines of research in depression have focused on identifying biological markers for either the state or trait of depression. One of the most promising lines of investigation is the endocrinology of depression. Depressive illness is characterized by markedly increased levels of plasma cortisol throughout the day and night, with blunting of normal circadian fluctuation in cortisol secretion (Ettigi & Brown, 1977; Hoagland et al., 1946; Sachar, 1975). Furthermore, approximately 50 percent of patients with melancholic (endogenous) depression fail to show the normal suppression of plasma cortisol following administration of the synthetic steriod dexamethasone (Brown & Shuey, 1980; Carroll et al., 1981; Schlesser et al., 1980). Among psychiatric patients, escape from dexamethasone supression appears to be specific for patients with melancholia. The only possible exception is the very recent evidence suggesting that some patients with dementia also fail to show suppression (Spar & Gerner, 1982); however, it remains to be established that these are not cases of depressive pseudodementia (Caine, 1981). The promise of this test is that it not only provides a biological marker to assist in establishing the diagnosis of melancholia, but it also correlates with response to treatment; that is, successful treatment is associated with a return to normal suppression of plasma cortisol by dexamethasone.

Prange and his associates have established that approximately one-fourth of the patients with primary depression have a blunted thyrotropin (TSH) response to thyrotropin-releasing hormone (TRH) (reviewed by Loosen & Prange, 1982). Unlike the dexamethasone suppression test, which appears to be specific for endogenous depression, the blunted TSH response is also found in patients with mania, anorexia nervosa, and alcoholism. Since the blunted response is not observed in patients with schizophrenia, however, it does not appear to be a nonspecific effect of mental illness.

Extein and his associates (1981) administered both the dexamethasone suppression test and the TRH test to patients with unipolar depression. Using a more liberal criterion for blunting of the TSH response, they demonstrated that 64 percent of their patients had an abnormal TSH response and 50 percent failed to suppress after dexamethasone. These two findings did not appear associated, since only 30 percent of their patients were abnormal on both tests. For some patients the blunted TSH response reverted to normal when the depression cleared, while for others the abnormal TSH response persisted long after recovery. In the latter instance, the blunting of the TSH response may represent a trait marker for increased vulnerability to depression.

Another area of investigation in the search for a biological marker of depression is the study of sleep. It has long been evident that most untreated depressed patients have reduced total sleep time because of awakenings during the night and early in the morning (Hawkins, 1977). Polygraphic studies have been employed in an attempt to refine our understanding of the sleep abnormalities in depression. To date,

there are three sleep findings in depression: increased eye movement density, i.e., amount of eye movement per rapid eye movement (REM) period (Vogel, 1981); a reduction in stage 4 sleep i.e., sleep characterized by high-voltage slow waves on the electroencephalogram (EEG) (Hawkins, 1977); and shortened REM latency i.e., decreased amount of sleep prior to the first REM period (Kupfer & Foster 1978; Kupfer et al., 1978). The shortened REM latency may correlate with the severity of the depression, and it returns to normal upon recovery. These findings are of great interest as possible biological markers in depression. However, the specificity and sensitivity for each of these remain to be determined. For example, 40 percent of schizophrenic patients also have reduced levels of stage 4 sleep (Feinberg & Hiatt, 1978).

Mortality of Bereavement

A number of studies have demonstrated that the death of a loved one is a precipitatory event for many somatic diseases (Lindemann, 1944; Marris, 1958; Morillo & Gardner, 1979; Parkes, 1964, 1970). There is now evidence that conjugal bereavement is associated with excess mortality (reviewed by Jacobs & Ostfeld, 1977). Perhaps best known is the longitudinal study by Rees and Lutkin (1967), who followed 903 survivors of 371 individuals who died in a semirural area of Wales. This sample was compared to a population of 878 close relatives of 371 individuals who were matched with the deceased for age, sex, and marital status. In the first year, there was a sevenfold increase in mortality in the bereaved group as compared to the control population. The increased risk for mortality diminished over the next 3 years. The risk was greatest for spouses and for males, with older widowers having the greatest risk of all. Although one longitudinal series has failed to document increased mortality rates in bereaved populations (Bornstein et al., 1973; Clayton et al., 1971, 1972), the best total information available indicates that conjugal bereavement is associated with an approximate two fold increase in mortality, and that this effect occurs within the first 2 years of bereavement. The risk is greater for men; it is confined to the first 6 months after the death of the spouse. For women the greatest risk is during the second year (Helsing et al., 1981; Jacobs & Ostfeld, 1977).

The cause of increased mortality in the bereaved is not clear. The most obvious possibility is suicide, and there is evidence that the widowed have increased rates of suicide (Durkheim, 1951; MacMahon & Pugh, 1965). However, this does not fully account for the excess mortality. Other causes of death include accidents, infectious diseases, heart diseases, cancer, and the sequelae of alcoholism. Although evidence is lacking, it is possible that excess mortality in conjugal bereavement occurs because unhealthy individuals select spouses who are also unhealthy, or because spouses share an unhealthy environment (Jacobs & Ostfeld, 1977). An illuminating recent finding is that widowed males who remarry enjoy greater longevity than do those who do not remarry (Helsing et al., 1981). This may reflect the effects of diminished social isolation, improved health maintenance, or a reversal of physiological changes associated with bereavement. On the other hand, healthy males may simply be more likely to remarry than unhealthy males. The salutary effect of remarriage was not demonstrated for women; however, this study also failed to find excess mortality in widowed females.

Animal Models of Separation

Rat Pups

Hofer and his colleagues (Hofer, 1971, 1975; Hofer & Weiner, 1971a, 1971b; Stone et al., 1976) demonstrated that maternal separation in 10–14 day-old rat pups resulted in behavioral and physiological disturbances with subsequent failure to develop and shortened survival. In an elegant series of experiments, they were able to tease apart certain components of the interaction with the mother. The physical presence of the mother reverses many of the behavioral alterations produced by separation while the milk she provides helps regulate the pup's heart rate. Maintenance of the pup's body temperature is regulated by physical contact with the mother, and without this the caloric expenditure of the pup is devoted to maintenance of body temperature rather than growth and development. In a sense, the rat pup is dependent upon the mother for regulation of its internal milieu. By analogy, bereavement in humans might be conceptualized as the loss of another person who was important in maintaining and regulating the individual's psychological and physiological processes (Kaufman & Rosenblum, 1967; Weiner, 1982).

Infant Monkeys

Numerous investigators have studied depression using an animal model, the separated infant monkey under a variety of conditions (see review by Suomi, 1976). Kaufman and co-workers studied the reaction to separation from the mother in young macaques of two species (e.g., Kaufman, 1973, 1974, 1977; Kaufman & Rosenblum, 1967, 1969). The separations were carried out in group-living animals, with the 5-month-old infant remaining with the group in its home pen where it had been born and raised, while the mother was removed to a distant site. Pigtail (*Macaca nemestrina*) infants showed severe initial agitation, during which they were ignored or rebuffed by the remaining pigtail mothers; after 24 hours, they showed a severe depressive response—collapsed, hunched posture, the face of grief (Darwin, 1872), slowness of movement or immobility, absence of play, general social withdrawal, and crying vocalizations—comparable phenomenologically to the anaclitic depression of separated human infants described by Spitz (1946). A few of the infant monkeys died, but the great majority ultimately recovered normal function within 1 month. Bonnet (*Macaca radiata*) infants showed the same initial agitation, but they were comforted or adopted by the remaining bonnet mothers and never showed the severe depressive response.

The difference in reaction was explained by the social support that was provided to bereft bonnets based on a rather different social structure. Repeated studies and reexamination of the original data, however, demonstrated that bonnet infants also showed a depressive reaction to separation, but it was never extensive, the only manifestation being diminished play. This led Kaufman (unpublished data) to suggest that psychologically there are two kinds of bereavement depression, "coping depression" and "helpless depression." In his view, the essence of the bereavement experience is affective, namely pain, sadness, and longing which result from the loss of the loved object and the concomitant difficulty in carrying out the usual behavioral patterns of daily life that depend so much on the close relationship to the object. The rest of the clinical picture depends upon the individual's cognitive representation of his or her total situation and its motivational consequences. To pigtail infants, who have a very dependent relationship with the mother and are provided no social support, the situation appears beyond their capacity to cope, and helplessness is experienced, leading to total collapse and withdrawal, i.e., helpless depression. To bonnets, who are less dependent on the mother and receive social support, the situation appears manageable despite the painful sadness, and they cope, persisting in a semblance of their usual patterns of behavior except for play, i.e., coping depression.

In a subsequent study, Kaufman and Stynes (1978) were able to induce helpless depression in bonnets also, by rearing infants in a mixed species group and removing not only the mother but all other bonnet mothers. When left in the pen with pigtails, the bonnet infants tried very hard to secure comforting from pigtail mothers, but when this effort failed, the situation was perceived as unmanageable, and they also showed collapse and withdrawal.

In trying further to understand the reaction to separation, Kaufman was struck by the succession of phases as stages of adaptive response and found merit in Engel's idea that there are two biological response systems available for dealing with mounting stress: the flight–fight and conservation–withdrawal systems (Kaufman, 1977; Kaufman & Rosenblum, 1967). The monkey's initial reaction of agitation is seen as based on flight–fight and the subsequent depression as based on conservation–withdrawal.

Working with Kaufman, Reite developed a telemetry system for studying physiological variables in the freely moving monkey infants. This led to the demonstration that agitation was accompanied by hyperthermia and tachycardia, whereas during the subsequent depressive response, hypothermia, bradycardia, frequent episodes of cardiac arrhythmia, and marked sleep disturbances were found (notably a marked diminution of stage REM) (Reite et al., 1974; Seiler et al., 1979). Reite and co-workers (1981) later showed that an 11-day separation of a pair of pigtail monkey infants that had been raised together as peers led to diminished response of their lymphocytes to the mitogens phytohemagglutinin and concanavalin A. This effect was most pronounced at the end of the separation and during the early phases of reunion.

Using much briefer separations (less than 24 hours, thus corresponding to the agitation phase in macaques), Levine and co-workers (Coe et al., in press) demonstrated in squirrel monkeys marked increases in plasma cortisol in both the separated mother and infant. Overall, these physiological findings are consistent with the hypothesized physiology of first flight–fight and then conservation–withdrawal, and some are comparable to changes found in human bereavement and clinical depression.

BEREAVEMENT AND STRESS

In the discussion thus far the emphasis has been on the close relationship of the bereaved state to depression. However, the death of a loved one also represents perhaps the most potent of all stressful events. While a comprehensive review of the current knowledge of stress and coping is not our goal (for a review see Cohen, 1981), it is worthwhile to consider those areas that have particular relevance to bereavement. For example, Horowitz and co-workers (Horowitz 1974, 1976; Krupnick & Horowitz, 1981) pointed out the phenomenological similiarity between the responses to bereavement and those to other traumatic life events. Their *stress response syndrome* is characterized by an initial stunned daze that is interrupted occasionally by intense emotions. Following this, there may be a period of relative denial and numbness that eventually begins to alternate with periods of intensive and intrusive thoughts and imagery, strong emotions, and compulsive behavior. Common themes include sadness, discomfort about personal vulnerability, anxiety over the event recurring, anger at fate or at those who were spared, and self-depreciating feelings such as guilt, shame, and self-disgust. Finally, resolution ensues, when less intense emotions are accompanied by increased recognition and acceptance of the meaning of the event.

Research on the physiology of stress has centered on the sympathetic–adrenal medullary system (i.e., secretion of the catecholamines, epinephrine, and norepinephrine), the hypothalamic–pituitary–adrenal cortical system (i.e., secretion of corticosteroids), and more recently, the immune system. This work was pioneered by Cannon and his associates (1929, 1932), who demonstrated that the sympathetic–adrenal medullary system prepared animals in emergent and threatening situations to respond in a flight–fight manner, and by Selye (1956), who described a three-stage reaction to stress, the *"general adaptation syndrome,"* and indicated the important role of the hypothalamic-pituitary-adrenal cortical system.

Over the ensuing years there has been an intensive investigation of responses to stress. In humans the emerging picture is that of adrenal cortical activation in novel and unfamiliar situations, with rapid adaptation as control and mastery of the situation are gained. Adrenal cortical responses are more pronounced when active coping is required (Gal & Lazarus, 1975; Miller et al., 1970; Rahe et al., 1974; Rubin et al., 1969). Mason (1971, 1975) emphasized the psychological meaning of the stressful stimulus and the role of the central nervous system in the activation of the adrenal cortex. Mason (1968, 1975) also postulated that the neuroendocrine response to stress is integrated and is organized in a cata-bolic–anabolic sequence. Initial increases of the catabolic hormones–cortisol, growth hormone, epinephrine, and norepinephrine—serve the pur-pose of mobilizing energy stores, particularly glucose, as preparation for the flight–fight response. After resolution or mastery of the stressful situation, increases in the anabolic sex steriods and insulin lead to restoration of protein and glycogen stores.

The immune system has been a recent focus of study since stress can alter susceptibility to disease, usually through a decrease in host resistance, but sometimes through an increase (reviewed by Rogers et al., 1979; Solomon, 1981; see also Solomon and Amkraut, this volume, Chapter 13). Since stress influences numerous hormones and neurotransmit-ters, which in turn influence the immune system, the mediating mechanisms are unclear. The plethora of stress paradigms—exposure to temperature extremes, noise, electric shock, overcrowding, restraint, etc.—tends to confuse the picture further. However, it is increasingly clear that the ability to cope and control greatly influences the physiological response to stress. Lack of control leads to much greater effects, e.g., decreased tumor rejection (Visintainer et al., 1982). This suggests the influence of a state of helplessness on the production of disease. Never-theless, at present, the ways in which stress influences health and disease are unclear, since the response to experimental stress varies greatly depend-ing upon species, age, environmental conditions, and prior exposure, as well as upon the intensity, duration, chronicity, and controllability of the stress (see reviews by Borysenko & Borysenko, 1982; Lock, 1982; Monjan, 1981; Sklar & Anisman, 1981).

One of the most exciting recent developments in all of biology was the discovery of the endorphin and enkephalin systems (reviewed by Krieger & Martin, 1981a, 1981b). This discovery holds promise for major breakthroughs in our understanding of the physiology of stress. What is presently known is that adrenocorticotropin (ACTH) and B-endorphin originate from a common precursor(pro-opiocortin), that they share a common hypothalamic releasing factor, and that in rodents they are both released from the anterior pituitary in response to stress

(Guillemin et al., 1977; Mains et al., 1977; Roberts & Herbert, 1977; Vale et al., 1981). As one example of its role in stress, activation of this endogenous opiate system plays a major part in the stress-induced analgesia found in rodents who become helpless after inescapable shock (Grau et al., 1981), apparently through its regulation of corticosterone (MacLennan et al., 1982). This illustrates the com-plexity of the relations among the brain, neuropep-tides, and hormones, and indicates a protective aspect of a state of helplessness.

DISCUSSION AND HYPOTHESIS

There are close similarities between depression and the reactions to bereavement and stress. These three states are so closely intertwined that it becomes difficult to unravel them. For instance, almost all stressful situations involve loss, be it imagined, threatened, or real. On the other hand, bereavement, especially following the death of a child or spouse, is clearly a severe stress. Bereave-ment may be the prototype of all stressful situations, and grief and mourning the prototypic stress response syndrome. The responses to stress that have been termed flight–fight and conserva-tion–withdrawal may well represent the respective anlagen for anxiety and depression (Engel, 1962). In addition, grief and mourning so closely resemble depression that the two conditions may be phenom-enologically indistinguishable.

These considerations raise critical questions: (1) Is the response to bereavement unique or is it identical to responses after other stressful events? (2) What is the difference between grief and depression? What psychological and biological markers can distinguish these two conditions? (3) What is the basic phy-siology of the bereavement reaction? What is its rela-tionship to the psychology of bereavement? (4) What psychobiological mechanisms predispose the bereav-ed to increase physical morbidity and mortality?

Obviously, we are not in a position to answer the questions definitively. However, we do believe that the response to bereavement is unique. This is based on the fundamental importance of attachment for the survival of both the individual infant and the human species. Finally, since bereavement has been a universal experience since social life began and a meaningful experience sine the emergence of per-sonal relationships, it is a reasonable assumption that selection has favored the development of mechanisms that deal with this particular stress, i.e., that humans are prepared to cope with bereavement.

We hypothesize that the reaction to bereavement is phasic, that each phase is adaptive, and that the phases differ both psychologically and physiologically. The first phase (based on flight–fight) is an alarm reaction characterized by anxious affects, a response to the uncertainty and danger posed by the loss. The second phase (based on conservation–withdrawal) is a response to the realization of the loss and features disengagement, conservation of resources, diminished reactivity, and depressive affects. It is here that the risks of morbidity are the greatest. The third phase is recovery, with reengagement, reactivity, and the return of normal functioning.

We believe that loss is a unique form of severe stress and that the reaction to bereavement differs from that of other severe stresses (without loss), specifically in the second phase ushered in by the realization of loss.

The reaction to bereavement and clinical depression are both based on conservation–withdrawal, a purely biological response system, which, early in life, is elaborated in response to repeated brief object losses into a depressive organismic reaction state which includes psychological aspects and social referents. This depressive state is adaptive, and is neither pathological nor the manifestation of a disease per se. Its later manifestations vary, depending upon life experience, further development, and the specifics surrounding its activation. It is the core of normal unhappiness, the reaction to bereavement, and clinical depression.

In endogenous depression, we believe that there are genetically determined biological abnormalities whose nature is yet unclear, but which involve hypothalamic–pituitary–adrenal disinhibition, a blunted TSH response to TRH, and distrubances in sleep. Accordingly, despite the great similarity, there is a difference between the bereavement reaction and endogenous depression.

In line with these thoughts, certain physiological measures might differentiate bereaved individuals from those who are either severely stressed (without loss) or have an endogenous depression. Specifically, we hypothesize the following: (1) Bereavement, endogenous depression, and stress (without loss) will show comparable cardiac and adrenocortical responses; that is, all three conditions are stressful. (2) Grief and endogenous depression, but not the stress response (without loss) are psychobiological elaborations of a conservation–withdrawal biological

response and thus will show comparable immunological alterations (as measured by natural killer cell activity and lymphocyte response to mitogens). The critical difference between bereavement and other severe stress is the actual loss, realization of which activates the conservation–withdrawal biological response system, so that the immunological changes in the bereaved population will occur when the realization sets in. (3) Endogenous depression, but not grief or stress without loss, is based on biological abnormalities that involve pituitary–adrenal disinhibition (manifested by an abnormal dexamethasone supression test), a blunted TSH response to TRH, and sleep disturbances (manifested by increased eye movement density, reduced Stage 4 sleep, and shortened REM latency).

Bereavement is a natural and inevitable aspect of life. As such, it represents an ideal model for understanding and clarifying the intervening psychological and physiological variables between a stressful event and the development of illness (either medical or psychological) or death. Because of its frequent severity and long duration, the reaction to bereavement also presents the opportunity to understanding the individual's efforts to adapt to loss over time.

REFERENCES

Abraham K (1927): A short study on the development of the libido. In *Selected Papers on Psychoanalysis*. London, Hogarth Press.

Akiskal, HS, & McKinney WT (1975): Overview of recent research in depression. Arch Gen Psychiatry 32:285–305.

Aldrich CK (1974): Some dynamics of anticipatory grief. Schoenberg B, Carr AC, Kutscher AH, Peretz D, & Goldberg, I (Eds.). In *Anticipatory Grief*, New York, Columbia University Press, pp. 3–9.

Bartrop, RW, Lazarus, L, Luckhurst, E, Kiloh LG (1977): Depressed lymphocyte function after bereavement. *Lancet* 1 834–836.

Beck, A (1967): *Depression: Clinical, Experimental and Theoretical Aspects*. New York, Harper & Row.

Bibring, E (1953): The mechanism of depression. Greenacre P (Ed.). In *Affective Disorders*, New York, International Universities Press, pp. 13–48.

Birtchnell J (1970): Depression in relation to early and recent parent death. Br J Psychiatry 116:229–306.

Bornstein, PE, & Clayton PJ (1972): The anniversary reaction. Dis Nerv Syst 33:470–472.

Bornstein PE, Clayton PJ, Halikas JA, Maurice WL, & Robbins E (1973): The depression of a widowhood after thirteen months. Br J Psychiatry 122:561–566.

Borysenko M, & Borysenko J (1982): Stress, behavior and immunity. Gen Hosp Psychiatry 4:59–67.

Bowlby J (1951): Maternal care and mental health W.H.O. Monogr. Ser. No. 2.

Bowlby J (1961): Process of mourning. Int J Psychoanal 42:317–340.

Brisco, CW, & Smith, JB (1975): Depression in bereavement and divorce. Arch Gen Psychiatry 32:439–443.

Brown F (1961): Depression and childhood bereavement. J Ment Sci 107:754–777.

Brown WA, & Shuey I (1980): Response to dexamethasone and subtype of depression. Arch Gen Psychiatry 37:747–751.

Caine, ED (1981): Pseudodementia. Arch Gen Psychiatry 38:1359–1364.

Cannon WB (1929): *Bodily Changes in Pain, Hunger, Fear, and Rage.* Boston, Branford.

Cannon WB (1932): *The Wisdom of the Body.* New York, Norton.

Caplan MG, & Douglas VI (1969): Incidence of parental loss in children with depressed mood. J Child Psychol Psychiatry 10:225–232.

Carroll, BJ, Feinberg M, Greder JF, Tarika J, Albala AA, Hasket RF, James NM, Kronfol Z, Lohr N, Steiner M, de Vignl JP, & Young E (1981): A specific laboratory test for the diagnosis of melancholia. Arch Gen Psychiatry 38:15–22.

Clayton PJ, Halikes JA, Maurice WL (1971): The bereavement of the widowed. Dis Nerv Syst 32:597–604.

Clayton PJ, Halikes JA, & Maurice WL (1972): The depression of widowhood. Br J Psychiatry 120:71–77.

Clayton PJ, Halikes JA, Maurice WL, & Robbins E (1973): Anticipatory grief and widowhood. Br J Psychiatry 122:47–51.

Clayton PJ, Herjanie M, Murphy GE, & Woodruff R (1974): Mourning and depression: Their similarities and differences. Can Psychiatr Assoc J 19:309–312.

Coe CL, Weiner SG, & Levine S (in press): Psychoendocrine responses of mother and infant monkeys to disturbance and separation. Rosenblum LA, & Moltz H (Eds.). In *Symbiosis in Parent–Young Interactions.* New York, Plenum Press.

Cohen F (1981): Stress and bodily illness. Psychiatr Clin North Am 4:269–286.

Darwin C (1872): *The Expression of the Emotions in Man and Animals.* New York, Philosophical Library, 1955.

American Psychiatric Association (1980): *Diagnostic and Statistical Manual of Mental Disorders* (ed. 3). Author, Washington, D.C.

Durkheim E (1951): *Suicide: A Study in Sociology.* Glencoe, Ill. Free Press.

Engel G (1959): Psychogenic pain and the pain prone patient. Am J Med 26:899–918.

Engel G (1961): Is grief a disease? Pschosom Med 23:18–22.

Engel G (1962): *Psychological Development in Health and Disease.* Philadelphia, Saunders.

Engel G, & Reichsman F (1956): Spontaneous and experimentally induced depressions in an infant with a gastric fistula. J Am Psychoanal Assoc 4:428–456.

Engel, GL, & Schmale AH (1972): Conservation-withdrawal, a primary regulatory process for organismic homeostasis. In *Physiology, Emotions, and Psychosomatic Illness,* (Ciba Foundation Symposium 8). Amsterdam, Elsevier, pp. 57–85.

Ettigi PG, & Brown GM (1977): Psychoneuroendocrinology of affective disorders: An overview. Am J Psychiatry 134:493–501.

Extein I, Pottash ALC, & Gold MS (1981): Relationship of TRH test and dexamethasone suppression test abnormalities in unipolar depression. Psychiatry Res 4:49–53.

Feinberg I, & Hiatt JF (1978): Sleep patterns in schizophrenia: A selected review. Williams RL, & Karasan I (Eds.). In *Sleep Disorders: Diagnosis and Treatment.* New York, Wiley, pp. 205–231.

Freud S (1917): *Mourning and Melancholia* (Standard ed.), vol. 14. London, Hogarth Press, 1963, pp. 243–258.

Friedman, SB, Mason JW & Hamburg DA (1963): Urinary 17-hydroxycorticosteroid levels in parents of children with neoplastic disease. Psychosom Med 25:364–376.

Gal R, & Lazarus RS (1975): The role of activity in anticipating and confronting stressful situations. J Hum Stress 1:4–20.

Gellhorn E (1970): The emotions and the ergotropic and trophotropic systems. Psychol Forsch 34:48–94.

Gerber I (1974): Anticipatory bereavement. Schoenberg B, Carr AC, Kutscher AH, Peretz D, & Goldberg I (Eds.). In *Anticipatory Grief.* New York, Columbia University Press, pp. 26–30.

Gerber I, Rusalem R, Hannon N, et al., (1975): Anticipatory grief and aged widows and widowers. J Gerontol 30:225–229.

Gershon ES, Cromer M, & Klerman GL (1968): Hostility and Depression Psychiatry. 31:224–235.

Gladwin T, & Sarason SB (1953): *Truk: Man in Paradise.* New York, Viking Fund Publications in Anthropology 20, p. 158

Grau JW, Hyson RL, Maier SF, Madden J, & Barchas JD (1981): Long-term stress induced analgesia and activation of the opiate system. Science 213:1409–1411.

Guillemin R, Vargo T, Rossier J, Minck S, Ling N, Rivier C, Vale W, & Bloom F (1977): B-Endorphin and adrenocorticotropin are secreted concomitantly by the pituitary gland. Science 197:1367–1369.

Hawkins DR (1977): Depression and sleep research: Basic science and clinical perspective. Usdin G (Ed.). In *Depression: Clinical Biological, Psychological Perspectives.* New York, Brunner Maze, pp. 198–234.

Heinicke C (1973): Parental deprivation in early childhood. Scott J, & Senay E (Eds.). In *Separation and Depression: Clinical and Research Aspects.* Washington, D.C., American Association for the Advancement of Science.

Helsing KJ, Szklo M, & Comstock GW (1981): Factors associated with mortality after widowhood. Am J Public Health 71:802–809.

Hess WR (1957): *The Functional Organization of the Diencephalon.* New York, Grune & Stratton.

Hoagland H, Malamud W, Kaufman IC, & Pincus G (1946): Changes in the electroencephalogram and in the excretion of 17-ketosteroids accompanying electro-shock therapy of agitated depression. Psychosom Med 8:246–251.

Hofer MA (1971): Cardiac rate regulated by nutritional factor in young rats. Science 172:1039–1041.

Hofer MA (1975): Studies on how early maternal separation produces behavioral change in young rats. Psychosom Med 37:245–264.

Hofer MA, & Weiner H (1971a): The development and mechanisms of cardiorespiratory responses to maternal deprivation in rat pups. Psychosom Med 33:303–362.

Hofer MA, & Weiner H (1971b): Physiological and behavioral regulation by nutritional intake during early development of the laboratory rat. Psychosom Med 33:468.

Hofer, MA, Wolff CT, Friedman JB, & Mason JW (1972a): A psychoendocrine study of bereavement, I. 17-Hydroxycorticosteroid excretion rates of parents following death of their children from leukemia. Psychosom Med 34:481–491.

Hofer MA, Wolff CT, Friedman SB, & Mason JW (1972b): A psychoendocrine study of bereavement, II. Observations on the process of mourning in relation to adrenocortical function. Psychosom Med 34:492–504.

Holmes TH, & Rahe RH (1967): The social readjustment rating scale. J Psychosom Res 11:213–218.

Horowitz M (1974): Stress response syndromes. Arch Gen Psychiatry 31:768–781.

Horowitz M (1976): *Stress Response Syndromes*. New York, Aronson.

Horowitz MJ, Wilner N, Marmar C, & Krupnick J (1980): Pathological grief and the activation of latent self-images. Am J Psychiatry 137:1157–1162.

Jacobs S, & Ostfeld A (1977): An epidemiological review of the mortality of bereavement. Psychosom Med 39:344–357.

Kaufman IC (1973): Mother–infant separation in monkeys: An experimental model. Scott P, & Senay EC (Eds.). In *Separation and Depression*. Washington, D.C., American Association for the Advancement of Science Publ. No. 194, pp. 33–52.

Kaufman IC (1974): Mother–infant relationships in monkeys and humans: A reply to professor Hinde. White NF (Ed.). In *Ethology and Psychiatry*. Toronto, University of Toronto Press, pp. 47–68, 239–240.

Kaufman IC (1977): Developmental considerations of anxiety and depression: Psychobiological studies in monkeys. Shapiro T (Ed.). In *Psychoanalysis and Contemporary Science*. International Universities Press, pp. 317–363.

Kaufman IC, & Rosenblum LA (1967): The reaction to separation in infant monkeys: Anaclitic depression and conservation withdrawal. Psychosom Med 29:648–675.

Kaufman IC, & Rosenblum LA (1969): Effects of separation from mother on the emotional behavior of infant monkeys. Ann NY Acad Sci 159:681–695.

Kaufman, IC, & Stynes AJ (1978): Depression can be induced in a bonnet macaque infant. Psychosom Med 40:71–75.

Klerman GL, & Gershon ES (1970): Imipramine effects upon hostility in depression. J Nerv Ment Dis 150:127–132.

Krieger DT, & Martin JB (1981a): Brain peptides (Part I). N Engl J Med 304:876–885.

Krieger DT, & Martin JB (1981b): Brain peptides (Part II). N Engl J Med 304:944–951.

Krupnick JL, & Horowitz MJ (1981): Stress response syndromes. Arch Gen Psychiatry 38:428–438.

Kupfer DJ, & Foster FG (1978): EEG sleep and depression. Willimas RL, & Karacan I (Eds.). In *Sleep Disorders: Diagnosis and Treatment*. New York, Wiley, pp. 163–204.

Kupfer DJ, Foster FG, Coble P, McPartland RJ, & Ulrich RF (1978): The application of EEG sleep for the differential diagnosis of affective disorders. Am J Psychiatry 135:69–74.

Lindemann E (1944): Symptomatology and management of acute grief. Am J Psychiatry 101:141–149.

Locke SF (1982): Stress, adaptation, and immunity. Gen Hosp Psychiatry 4:49–58.

Loosen PT, & Prange AJ (1982): Serum thyrotropin response to thyrotropin-releasing hormone in psychiatric patients: A review. Am J Psychiatry 139:405–416.

MacLennan AJ, Drugan RC, Hyson RL, Maier SF Madden J, & Barchas JD (1982): Corticosterone: A critical factor in an opioid form of stress-induced analgesia. Science 215:1530–1532.

MacMahon B, & Pugh TF (1965): Suicide in the widowed. Am J Epidemiol 81:23–31.

Maddison D, & Viola A (1968): The health of widows in the year following bereavement. J Psychosom Res 12:297–306.

Mains RE, Eipper BA, Ling N (1977): Common precursor to corticotropins and endorphins. Proc Natl Acad Sci USA 74:3014–3018.

Marris P (1958): *Widows and Their Families*. London, Routledge and Kegan Paul.

Mason JW (1968): Over-all hormonal balance as a key to endocrine organization. Psychosom Med 30:791–808.

Mason JW (1971): A re-evaluation of the concept of "non-specificity" in stress theory. J Psychiatr Res 8:323–333.

Mason JW (1975): Emotions as reflected in patterns of endocrine integration. Levi L (Ed.). In *Emotions: Their Parameters and Measurement*. New York, Raven Press, pp. 48–81.

Miller RG, Rubin RT, Clark BR, Crawford WR, & Arthur RJ (1970): The stress of aircraft carrier landings. I. Corticosteroid responses in naval aviators. Psychosom Med 32:518–588.

Monjan AA (1981): Stress and immunological competence. Adler, R (Ed.). In *Psychoneuroimmunology*. New York, Academic Press.

Morillo E, & Gardner LI (1979): Bereavement as an antecedant factor in thyrotoxicosis of childhood: Four case studies with survey of possible metabolic pathways. Psychosom Med 41:545–555.

Parkes CM (1964): Effects of bereavement on physical and mental health: A study of the medical records of widows. Br Med J 2:274–279.

Parkes CM (1970): The first year of bereavement. Psychiatry 33:444–467.

Parkes CM (1972): *Bereavement*. New York, International Universities Press.

Rahe RH, Rubin RT, & Arthur RJ (1974): The three investigators study: Serum uric acid, cholesterol and cortisol variability during stresses of everyday life. Psychosom Med 36:258–268.

Rees WD, & Lutkin SG (1967): Mortality of bereavement. Br Med J 4:13–16.

Reite ML, Harbeck R, & Hoffman A (1981): Altered cellular immune response following peer separation. Life Sci 29:1133–1136.

Reite ML, Kaufman IC, Pauley JD, & Stynes AJ (1974): Depression in infant monkeys: Physiological correlates. Psychosom Med 36:363–367.

Roberts JL, & Herbert E (1977): Characterization of a common precursor to corticotropin and B-lipotropin: Identification of B-lipotropin peptides and their arrangement relative to corticotropin in the precursor synthesized in a cell-free system. Proc Natl Acad Sci USA 74:5300–5304.

Rogers MP, Dubey D, & Reich P (1979): The influence of the psyche and the brain on immunity and disease susceptibility: A critical review. Psychosom Med 41:147–164.

Rosenblatt, PC, Walsh RP, & Jackson D (1976): *Grief and Mourning in Cross-Cultural Perspective*. New Haven, Conn., HRAF Press.

Rubin RT, Rahe, RH, Arthur RJ, & Clark BR (1969): Adrenal cortical activity changes during underwater demolition team training. Psychosom Med 31:553–564.

Sachar EJ (1975): Endocrine factors in depressive illness. Flach FF, & Draghi SC (Eds.). In *The Nature and Treatment of Depression*. New York, Wiley, pp. 397–411.

Schleiffer S, Keller S, McKegney P, & Stein M (1980): Bereavement and lymphocyte function. Abstract presented at the annual meeting of the American Psychiatric Association, San Francisco, Calif.

Schlesser MA, Winokur G, & Sherman BM (1980): Hypothalamic-pituitary adrenal axis activity in depressive illness. Arch Gen Psychiatry 37:737–743.

Schwab JJ, Chalmers JM, Conroy SJ et al. (1975): Studies in grief: A preliminary report. Schoenberg B, Gerber I, Wiener A et al. (Eds.). In *Bereavement: Its Psychosocial Aspects*. New York, University Press, pp. 78–87.

Seiler C, Cullen JJ, Zimmerman J, Reite M (1979): Cardiac arrythmias in infant pigtail monkeys following maternal separation. Psychophysiology 16:130–135.

Seligman MEP (1975): *Helplessness*. San Francisco, Freeman.

Selye H (1956): *The Stress of Life*. New York, McGraw-Hill.

Silverman PR (1974): Anticipatory grief from the perspective of widowhood. Schoenberg B, Carr AC, Kutscher AH, Peretz D, & Goldberg I (Eds.). In *Anticipatory Grief*. New York, Columbia University Press, pp. 320–330.

Sklar LS, & Anisman H (1981): Stress and cancer. Psychol Bull 89:369–406.

Solomon GF (1981): Psychoneuroendocrinological effects on the immune response. Ann Rev Med 35:155–184.

Spar JE, & Gerner R (1982): Does the dexamethasone suppression test distinguish dementia from depression? Am J Psychiatry 139:238–240.

Spitz RA (1945): Hospitalism: An inquiry into the genesis of psychiatric conditions in early childhood. Psychoanal Study Child. 1:53–74.

Spitz RA (1946): Anaclitic depression. Psychoanal Study Child 2:313–342.

Stone EA, Bonnet KA, & Hofer MA (1976): Survival and development of maternally deprived rats: Role of temperature. Psychosom Med 38:242–249.

Suomi SJ(1976): Factors affecting responses to social separation in rhesus monkeys. Serban G, & Kling A (Eds.). In *Animal Models in Human Psychobiology*. New York, Plenum Press, pp. 2–26.

Sweeney DR, & Maas JW (1978): Specificity of depressive diseases. Ann Rev Med 29:219–229.

Vale, W, Spiess J, Rivier C, & Rivier J (1981): Characterization of a 41-residue ovine hypothalamic peptide that stimulates secretion of corticotropin and B-endorphin. Science 213:1394–1397.

Visintainer MA, Volpicelli JK, & Seligman MEP (1982): Tumor rejection in rats after inescapable or escapable shock. Science 216:437–439.

Vogel GW (1981): The relationship between endogenous depression and REM sleep. Psychiatry Ann 11:21–26.

Webster's New Collegiate Dictionary (1979): Springfield Mass., Merriam.

Weiner H (1982): *Plenary address*. Presented at annual meeting of the American Psychosomatic Society, Denver Colo.

Weissman MM, Klerman GL, & Paykel ES (1971): Clinical evaluation of hostility in depression. Am J Psychiatry 128:261–266.

Wolff, CT, Friedman SB, Hofer MA, & Mason JW (1964a): Relationship between psychological defenses and mean urinary 17-hydroxycorticosteroid excretion rates. Psychosom Med 26:576–591.

Wolff CT, Hofer MA, & Mason JW (1964b): Relationship between psychological defenses and mean urinary 17-hydroxycorticosteroid excretion rates. Psychosom Med 26:592–609.

6

Depression and Perception of Health in an Urban Community

Myrna M. Weissman
Gary L. Tischler
Charles E. Holzer

Jerome K. Myers
Helen Orvaschel
Philip J. Leaf

Depression is the most common psychiatric disorder in the community (Weissman & Myers, 1978; Klerman, 1978). Depressives are frequent users of medical facilities of all kinds; they perceive that their emotional condition takes its toll on health, and depression is the clinical disorder most often associated with increased risk of physical illness. For these reasons, depression is a suitable subject for an epidemiological study of the association between a psychiatric disorder and physical disorders.

There are several reasons an epidemiological approach is appropriate for the study of such an association. Epidemiology is the study of variations in the distribution of specific disorders in populations, and the factors that influence that distribution. Epidemiological studies can generate three types of information about a disorder: rates (prevalence and incidence); variations of these rates by person, time, and place; and variations of risk factors that increase the probability of developing the disorder. Such information can generate new ideas about etiology, pathogenesis, treatment, and prevention. Applied to the study of emotions and illness, the epidemiological approach can provide information on the rates of disturbed emotional and physical states, independent of who seeks treatment.

In a search for the possible relationship between mental and physical illness, the epidemiological approach can provide unbiased estimates of their rates, independently of and in association with each other. This approach is particularly important in studying depression because there is a well-documented tendency for persons with depression, as well as for persons with any two disorders, to be frequent users of health care facilities (Weissman et al., 1981). If the clinical approach were used, there might be an overestimation of the rates of depression among the physically ill because of the tendency of depressives to have a higher utilization rate than nondepressives. Therefore, studies of probability samples of a population, including treated and untreated persons, are required in order to obtain an accurate estimate of possible associations.

The Epidemiologic Catchment Area Program is a series of five epidemiological research studies performed by independent research teams in collaboration with staff members of the Division of Biometry and Epidemiology (DBE) of the National Institute of Mental Health (NIMH). The NIMH Principal Collaborators are Darrel A. Regier, Ben Z. Locke, and William W. Eaton; the NIMH Project Officer is Carl A. Taube. The Principal Investigators and Co-investigators from the five sites are Yale University, U01 MH 34224—Jerome K. Myers, Myrna M. Weissman, and Gary Tischler; Johns Hopkins University, U01 MH 33870—Morton Kramer, Ernest Gruenberg, and Sam Shapiro; Washington University, St. Louis, U01 MH 33883—Lee N. Robins, John Helzer, and Jack Croughan; Duke University, U01 MH 35386—Dan Blazer and Linda George; University of California, Los Angeles, U01 MH 35865—Richard Hough, Marvin Karno, Javier Escobar, M. Audrey Burnam, and Dianne M. Timbers.

OVERVIEW OF ASSOCIATIONS BETWEEN DEPRESSION AND PHYSICAL ILLNESS

While the nature of the association between depression and physical illness has not been clarified, several reasonable pathways have been suggested (Kathol & Petty, 1981; Heine, 1970). Physical illness may lead to depression: Patients with a serious physical illness, such as myocardial infarction or cancer, may become depressed as a natural reaction to the possibility of physical limitations, loss of function, disability, and death. Medications used to treat some physical illnesses, e.g., hypertension or arthritis can produce depression as a side effect. On the other hand, depression may lead to physical illness and increased mortality: The depressed person may lose interest in self-maintenances such as weight control and exercise, may drink, smoke, self-medicate, or become accident prone. Furthermore, the pathological changes of some diseases (e.g., Parkinson's disease, encephalitis, or systemic lupus erythematosis) may produce depression.

The symptoms of depression, particularly sleep disturbance and anorexia may increase the risk of physical problems. Other symptoms of depression (fatigue, vague bodily complaints) overlap with symptoms of physical illness and can lead to misdiagnosis and excessive or inappropriate medical procedures that can have iatrogenic effects on health (Barquero Vazquez et al., 1981; Houpt et al., 1979; Mathew et al., 1981). Whatever the pathways or combination of pathways may be, a review of the current data about depression and physical illness serves to demonstrate the existence and power of the association and the need for the comprehensive epidemiological study described later.

Interaction of Depression and Medical Illness

A number of studies have identified depression among persons seeking treatment for nonpsychiatric problems in clinics (Hoeper et al., 1980; Kathol & Petty, 1981; Nielson & Williams, 1980; Weissman et al., 1981), in general practice settings (Bebbington, 1978), or in hospitals (Lipowski, 1979; Regier et al., 1982). Without exception, all of these studies reported a high rate of depression, either as a symptom or a syndrome, in medical patients. For example, one review of studies conducted in Great Britain and the

United States, which dealt specifically with depressive disorders in general practice settings, found that 300–1,000/100,000 of the adult general population under study had reported depressive symptoms to their general practitioners (Bebbington, 1978). In terms of prevalence rates for medical inpatients, approximately 20–24 percent were found to be depressed (Lipowski, 1979). A study of a private medical practice group in Washington, D.C. reported a 12 percent current prevalence of mild depression and a 12 percent current prevalence of moderate or severe depression (Nielson & Williams, 1980). Five studies recently reviewed by Kathol and Petty (1981) examined the prevalence of dysphoria in patients with medical illnesses. Whereas all of the studies had major methodological problems, they nevertheless documented a reasonably high rate of depression in medical patients, ranging up to 32 percent.

Medical problems in depressed patients represent the other side of the coin. According to a review by Kathol and Petty (1981), two studies examined the frequency of medical illness in psychiatric outpatients and three in hospitalized populations. In most of these studies, the data are presented in such a way that it is not possible to determine prevalence rates of medical illness in depressives. The best study (Hall et al., 1980) included a medical assessment of 100 psychiatric inpatients and found that 29 percent were depressed; of these patients, 12 (41 percent) had medical disorders that either caused or exacerbated the depression.

Of considerable public health interest is whether or not depression is a risk factor for subsequent physical illnesses. Obtaining such information requires a prospective design. The few prospective studies reviewed by Goldberg et al. (1979) showed an increase in mortality overall, and in hypertension specifically. In one study, Goldberg found no relationship between depressed mood and subsequent physical illness. However, this study examined only depressed mood, rather than clinical depression, and it has been documented that there is not a strong relationship between depressed mood, as measured by self report symptoms scales, and the syndrome of depression, as measured by diagnostic assessment instruments (Myers & Weisman, 1980).

Studies of the association between mortality and depression have demonstrated an excessive mortality among depressed patients in comparision to other psychiatric patients, suggesting a possible excess of physical disorders. This excessive mortality has been shown to be more specific for depression than for all other psychiatric disorders (Coryell, 1981) but not for persons with depressive mood, independent of the clinical syndrome (Weissman et al., in press).

Utilization of Health Facilities by Depressed Persons

It has been documented that depressed persons frequently utilize health care facilities. Weissman et al. (1981) found a high prevalence of depression in a study of more than 500 subjects drawn from a community survey. Only about one-third of the persons with a current major depression received treatment specifically for their depression; the remaining two-thirds, who did not receive treatment, were high utilizers of nonpsychiatric physicians, i.e., made more than six visits per year to their physicians. Only 29 percent of persons with other psychiatric disorders, and 27 percent of those with no psychiatric disorder made more than six visits per year.

The most extensive analysis of utilization of health care facilities by persons with mental and physical disorders, and of the association between physical and mental disorders, has recently been published by Hankin et al. (1982) and Regier et al. (1982). This group of investigators studied four comprehensive health care programs in Maryland, Wisconsin, and Massachusetts, which provided all ambulatory physical health and mental health services to their enrolled or geographically defined populations. The study covered a 1-year period (1975). Because of the large number of persons (over 111,000) represented across the four sites and the geographical diversity of the sites (which allows for the examination of consistency in findings), the study deserves special attention. The following general findings are relevant to this discussion: (1) Persons with DSM-II (American Psychiatric Association, 1968) mental disorders seek care three times more frequently than those with no mental disorders (Hankin et al., 1982); (2) Persons with mental disorders visit general medical departments almost 1½-2 times as frequently as patients without such diagnoses (Hankin et al., 1982); (3) Patients with mental disorders, as compared to those without, are more likely to have other physical illnesses (classifiable by the International Classification of Diseases).

The explication of these differences requires some qualification. Hankin et al. (1982) noted that "...the differences between the two groups in all four programs was found in the 'signs, symptoms, and ill-defined conditions' category. Patients with a mental disorder were consistently found to have a diagnosis in this category more than 1½ times as frequently as patients without mental disorders" (p. 229). In a companion paper Regier et al. (1982) reported that, "...the general medical staff tends to identify and treat the neurotic disorders in which symptoms of anxiety and depression predominate...a mental disorder diagnosis was consistently associated with more frequent general medical department visits than was found for other patients" (p. 222).

A review of the data across the four sites shows that, of those persons who visited a nonmental health department, 4.0–43.4 percent had a DSM-II diagnosis of "neurosis," and 0.01–0.06 percent had a DSM-II diagnosis of "affective psychosis." The specific physical disorders of persons with depressive disorders were not presented. Regier et al. (1982) also found that patients who had a mental disorder and received treatment for it in the mental health sector had lower general medical utilization.

Design for Study of Associations

The ideal study to determine the association between specific physical disorders and depression, or any psychiatric disorder, should be based on a community sample; should include a comprehensive physical examination of each subject; and should include a comprehensive psychiatric assessment. This design would avoid diagnostic unreliability as well as spurious associations resulting from the possible tendency of persons with two disorders to be overrepresented in the health care sector. Unfortunately, such a study would present many practical and economic obstacles. An alternative is to glean information relevant to the issue from a variety of sources and to look for consistent findings.

The data that are available, particularly those based on studies of depression in the medically ill and on utilization patterns, suggest an association between physical illness and depression. The study to be presented has some, but not all, of the design features of the ideal study for examining this issue: it is community based and systematically assesses mental disorders; it does not, however, include an assessment of physical disorders on the basis of individual examinations. This limitation is partially compensated for in that subjects' perception of their physical illnesses is assessed by their response to direct inquiries about the presence of a limited number of physical disorders, some of which have high prevalence in the general population.

GOALS AND METHODS OF THE EPIDEMIOLOGICAL STUDY

The data to be presented derive from the Yale Epidemiologic Catchment Area (ECA) study, which is part of a National Institute of Mental Health (NIMH) sponsored program in epidemiological research. As part of the NIMH program, a number of similar epidemiologic catchment area (ECA) studies have been established (Eaton et al., 1981). These studies will operate for a minimum of 5 years and encompass an area at least as large as that covered by a comprehensive community mental health center.

The primary objectives of the multisite longitudinal study are to provide the following information: (1) the prevalence and incidence of specific psychiatric disorders in the community by means of appropriate surveys in households and institutional settings; (2) estimates of the number of people in need of treatment, the number of people in treatment, where services are received and when treatment is first initiated, and if not in treatment, the reasons for not seeking and/or receiving treatment; (3) the concomitant risk factors associated with or causative of newly developed mental disorders, including estimates of other nonpsychiatric disorders.

The catchment area must have at least 200,000 inhabitants and have boundaries which coincide with one or more contiguous comprehensive comunity mental health center catchment areas. Yale University in New Haven, Connecticut, received the first such grant, followed by Johns Hopkins in Baltimore, Maryland, and Washington University in St. Louis, Missouri, and subsequently by Duke University in Durham, North Carolina, and the University of California in Los Angeles.

The Yale ECA consists of the New Haven Standard Metropolitan Statistical Area of nearly one-half million population (427,000 in 1970). The ECA study is a 3-year survey of this area. There are three field periods, with an initial interview and two subsequent interviews of a household member at 6-month intervals. In the first interview wave of the study, begun in July 1980, we contacted a systematic probability community sample of 4,000 adults (18 years of age and older) in order to complete at least 3,000 interviews, as well as an additional sample of nearly 2,700 persons (65 years of age and older) to complete 2,000 such interviews.

Sampling was based upon electric meter listings, supplemented by City Directory and telephone directory information. One household in 31 was selected by the community sample, and one person from each household, 18 years of age or older, was selected at random (according to the Kish grid method) for inclusion in the sample.

In addition to the household sample, we have begun to interview an institutional sample of about 400, consisting primarily of persons in nursing homes, prisons, and inpatient mental facilities. There will be a 1-year reinterview for the institutional sample, in contrast to the two 6-month reinterviews of the community and elderly samples.

A personal interview (averaging about 70 minutes in length) was conducted for each respondent in the study. The material in the interview schedule included specific questions on psychiatric diagnosis and mental status, general health status and functional disability, sociodemographic characteristics, barriers to care and stigma attached to mental illness, utilization of general medical, mental health, and human service facilities, and role performance activities. The interviews were conducted by survey research interviewers who received 6 days of formal training.

The Diagnostic Interview Schedule (DIS)

The psychiatric diagnoses derive from information collected on the NIMH Diagnostic Interview Schedual (DIS) (Version 2), which is an adaptation of the Schedule for Affective Disorders and Schizophrenia and the Renard interviews developed for use in general population studies. The DIS currently is used in all of the ECA studies. The history, characteristics and validity of the DIS have been described by Robins et al. (1981). Briefly, the DIS is a highly structured interview designed for use by lay interviewers in epidemiological studies; it is capable of generating computer diagnoses according to some DSM-III, Feighner et al. (1972), or Research Diagnostic Criteria. It is possible to make diagnoses by all three systems with a single interview because they all address diagnoses from a descriptive rather than an etiological perspective.

The DIS elicits the elements of a diagnosis, including symptoms, their severity, frequency, distribution over time, and whether or not they can be explained by physical illness, drug or alcohol use, or another psychiatric diagnosis. The questions and the probes are structured and precoded so that, after editing, answers can be entered directly into the computer. Diagnoses can be generated both currently (last 2 weeks, 1 month, 6 months, 1 year) and over a lifetime. The DIS takes 45 minutes to 1 hour to administer and is relatively economical because it does not require a clinician, external data, extraneous coders, or a lengthy training program.

The DSM-III

The data in this paper are limited to the DSM-III diagnoses generated from the DIS. The DSM-III disorders included major depression, bipolar disorder, alcohol abuse, drug abuse, schizophrenia, agoraphobia, simple phobia, panic disorder, obsessive compulsive disorder, somatization, anorexia nervosa, antisocial personality, and cognitive deficit. The DSM-III criteria for major depression are shown in Table 6-1.

After considerable deliberation by a scientific advisory group, the DSM-III diagnoses selected for inclusion in the DIS were: major mental disorders in terms of prevalence and/or morbidity, and disorders that are of research interest and have some evidence of validity in terms of treatment response, family, and/or follow-up studies.

Data on physical illness and utilization were obtained by direct questioning of the subject. For physical illnesses the subject was questioned about self-perception of health and specific current physical disorders, including hardening of the arteries, hypertension, myocardial infarction, stroke, Parkinson's disease or general neurological problems, cancer, epilepsy, and severe head injury. For utilization, sub-

jects were questioned about their current number of visits to physicians and/or treatment facilities.

The rates under consideration are preliminary and they cover the 6-month period prior to interview. They are based on the first wave of interviews and include only persons in the community household sample, not those in the institution sample. The data are as yet unweighted for nonresponders and design, and exclude interviews of informants. DSM-III exclusion criteria are not included in arriving at a diagnosis. We expect that there will be slight changes in future analyses but that the basic thrust of the findings will not change.

RESULTS OF THE EPIDEMIOLOGICAL STUDY

The majority of the 3,017 respondents were female, under 45 years of age, white, and had fewer than 13 years of formal education (Table 6-2). Of the total sample, 15.1 percent (14.0 percent of the 1,272 males and 16.0 percent of the 1,745 females) had a current disorder; that is, an episode that occurred at some time within 6 months of the study interview and that met any of the DSM-III criteria as established by the DIS for the 13 diagnoses included in the study. The 6-month prevalence rate was 3.9 percent for major depressive episode and 11.2 percent for other current psychiatric disorders; 84.9 percent of the respondents had no current psychiatric disorder.

Table 6-1   Criteria for Major Depressive Episode DSM-III

1. Dysphoric mood or loss of interest or pleasure
2. At least 4 of the following symptoms present nearly everyday for at least 2 weeks:
   Poor appetite, weight loss
   Insomnia or hypersomnia
   Agitation or retardation
   Loss of interest
   Loss of energy
   Feeling worthless
   Diminished ability to think or concentrate
   Recurrent thoughts of death
3. Absence of mood, incongruent delusions or hallucinations
4. Not superimposed on schizophrenia
5. Not due to organic mental disorder or bereavement

Adapted from American Psychiatric Association (1980): *Diagnostic and Statistical Manual for Mental Disorders* (ed. 3). Washington, D.C.

Table 6-2   Characteristics of 3,017 Respondents

Characteristic	No.	Percent
Sex		
Male	1,272	42
Female	1,745	58
Age		
18–29	805	27
30–44	845	28
45–64	783	26
65–74	366	12
75+	205	7
Race*		
White	2,560	85
Black	342	11
Hispanic	63	2
Other	49	2
Education*		
0–8	375	12
9–12	1,324	43
13+	1,315	45

*Numbers do not add up to 3,017 because some data are missing.

The overall utilization of treatment facilities (private physician, clinic, or emergency room) for any reason during the past 6 months, is shown in Table 6-3. There was a higher percentage of respondents (10 percent) with a current depression who made 13 or more visits during the 6-month period, as compared with 6 percent of those with other psychiatric disorders and only 2 percent of those with no psychiatric disorder. Only 26 percent of the depressives, as compared with 38 percent of persons with other psychiatric disorders and 42 percent of those with no psychiatric disorder, received no treatment in the past 6 months. In general, respondents with a major depression made the most visits, averaging 5.0 in 6 months, as compared with 3.1 for subjects with other psychiatric disorders and 1.9 for those with no disorder.

The rates of utilization were examined separately by sex (not shown in Table 6-3) because there were more women than men among the depressives, and because it is well known that women, in general, use more treatment services. The results, however, did not change. Both male and female depressives, as compared with the other respondent groups, had increased utilization of services. Furthermore, 53 percent of the depressives did not see themselves as getting treatment for an emotional problem; this finding suggests that the multiple visits by depressives were not viewed as seeking help specifically for depression. Nevertheless, when only those who received no treatment for emotional problems were considered (Table 6-3), depressives still were much

more likely to make multiple visits than were the other respondents. In addition, respondents with a major depressive episode were more likely to perceive their physical and their emotional health as poor. (Table 6-4).

When we examined subjects' perception of whether they had a limited number of physical illnesses, respondents with a major depressive episode were not consistently more likely to report having or receiving treatment for any specific physical disorder (Table 6-5). Only neurological disorders were significantly more frequent in depressives.

IMPLICATIONS OF THE STUDY AND FUTURE DIRECTIONS

Based on an epidemiological approach, our findings indicate that depressed persons, as compared to those with other or with no psychiatric disorders, perceived themselves in poorer physical and emotional health, and made more visits to health care facilities.

Before discussing the implications of these findings, however, the limitations of this study must be emphasized. In particular, the data we reported covers only a 6-month period. We did not include persons living in institutions who may be more physically ill, nor data on nonresponders from informant interviews. Moreover, as noted before, the measure of physical illness was by self-report rather than by actual physical examination, and not all

Table 6-3 Current Psychiatric Diagnosis During Past 6 Months

Number of Visits	Major Depressive Episode (%)	Other Psychiatric Disorder (%)	No Psychiatric Disorder (%)
Total sample*			
0	26	38	42
1–2	38	35	39
3–12	26	21	17
13 +	10	6	2
N	118	339	2,560
X	5.0	3.1	1.9
No treatment group†			
0	30	41	44
1–2	43	38	39
3–12	21	18	16
13 +	6	4	1
N	63	274	2,394
X	3.0	2.5	1.7

*$x^2 = 63$; df=6; p<0.001.
†$x^2 = 20.4$; df=6; p<0.0023.

Table 6-4 Perception of Health by Current Psychiatric Diagnosis

Rating	Major Depressive Episode (%) (N=118)	Other Psychiatric Disorder (%) (N=339)	No Psychiatric Disorder (%) (N=2560)
Physical health*			
Excellent–Good	68	72	85
Fair	18	21	12
Poor	14	7	3
Emotional health†			
Excellent–good	39	73	89
Fair	43	22	10
Poor	18	5	1

*$x^2 = 294.7$; df=4; p<0.001.
†$x^2 = 76.2$; df=4; p<0.001.

physical illnesses were included. In the absence of physical examinations we cannot say anything about undiagnosed illness, nor about subjects who did not report their physical problems or were unaware of them. We therefore might have underestimated physical illness. The data on subsequent physical health will be available when the ECA study is completed, which will enable us to determine if the current depression has an impact on subsequent physical health, at least over a 1-year period.

Clinical Implications

While the data we presented do have limitations, the results tend to confirm other observations (Barquero Vazquez et al., 1981; Hankin et al., 1982; Hoeper et al., 1980; Regier et al 1982; Weissman et al., 1981) on the high utilization of health care facilities by depressed persons. These findings highlight the fact that major affective disorders impose a burden upon the health care system. Other studies have elaborated upon the nature of the burden imposed by demonstrating that depressed patients are often unrecognized, undiagnosed, and may make unnecessary visits and have unnecessary treatments once they enter the health care system. These observations have possible implications for the screening, diagnosis, and treatment of depressed patients. The depressed patients' perception of their physical and emotional state, as well as their psychological distress and discomfort, seem to be factors in their increased utilization of treatment facilities.

Moreover, while depressed patients are in the health care system, they do not receive treatment for their depression. The depressives made frequent visits to health care facilities during the 6 months; yet, more than one-half of the depressed respondents did not see themselves as receiving treatment for their emotional problem. It has been well documented that depression has a high morbidity and a potential mortality. Fortunately, now there are a variety of efficacious treatments, both psychological

Table 6-5 Physical Disorder During Past 6 Months By Current Psychiatric Diagnosis

Disorder	Major Depressive Episode (%) (N=118)	Other Psychiatric Disorder (%) (N=339)	No Psychiatric Disorder (%) (N=2560)	x^2	p
Hardening of arteries	0	3.8	2.2	6.5	<0.04
Hypertension	9.3	14.5	14.5	2.4	<0.29
Myocardial infarction	2.5	3.5	3.1	0.33	<0.85
Stroke	0.9	1.5	0.8	1.45	<0.48
Neurological disorder	2.5	1.8	0.6	11.06	<0.01
Cancer	2.5	2.1	1.4	1.71	<0.42
Convulsions	0.9	1.5	0.7	2.2	<0.32
Head injury	0.9	2.7	0.5	19.79	<0.001
Any of above	16.1	21.5	18.4	2.4	<0.29

and pharmacological, that can alleviate the condition. If the depression is detected, the condition may be reversed, averting much personal suffering and financial cost.

Nonpsychiatric physicians and nonphysicians who are seeing depressed patients in primary care need to direct more attention toward detecting this emotional state. Better training of nonpsychiatric physicians and nonphysicians in the detection, treatment, and appropriate referral of persons with depression may improve care. The new systematic diagnostic approaches to psychiatric disorders undoubtedly will become a standard part of undergraduate medical training, but they could well be emphasized for all physicians and nonphysicians in medical care settings through continuing medical education. Psychiatrists and other mental health professionals might profit from increased training experiences in general medical settings to sensitize them to the problems and issues of mental health care in the general sector.

Research Implications

There are several research questions suggested by the data. Epidemiological studies might provide answers to the problems of access and barriers to psychiatric treatment, which might explain why depressed people are such frequent users of the general health care system. The final results of the ECA study should provide data in this area.

Information on the natural history of untreated depression would also be helpful. Do untreated depressives turn to friends, family, or self-help groups, and is the mere act of going to the physician and receiving attention sufficient? Do their conditions improve or do the patients go on to have mild chronicity and later hospitilization? Finally, several studies have suggested the value of using self-administered tests to screen for depression in general medical clinics. The possible impact of these instruments on the treatment of depression and the reduction of utilization of general medical services requires testing in a randomized, controlled clinical trial.

The current study demonstrated that depression and attendance at medical clinics are associated. The emotional state of depression may lead to demands for care and attention from the health care systems but not necessarily to immediate physical impairment. Long-term follow-up of the subsequent physical health of depressed persons is necessary to determine if depression takes a long-term toll on

physical health and, especially, if the depressed person who does not get appropriate treatment specifically for the depression may be prone to increased physical disorder and mortality.

At this time, it is unclear which specific physical disorders, if any, are overrepresented among depressives. However, we agree with Hankin et al. (1982) that mental health specialists as well as general medical professionals must be attentive to both the physical and mental health needs of their patients.

REFERENCES

American Psychiatric Association (1968): *Dianostic and Statistical Manual of Mental Disorders* (ed. 2). Washington, D.C.

American Psychiatric Association (1980): *Diagnostic and Statistical Manual of Mental Disorders* (ed. 3). Washington, D.C.

Barquero Vazquez JL, Munoz PE, & Jourequi Madoz V (1981): The interaction between physical illness and neurotic morbidity in the community. Br J Psychiatry 139:328–335.

Bebbington P (1978): The epidemiology of depressive disorders. Cult Med Psychiatry 2:297–341.

Coryell W (1981): Diagnosis-specific mortality: Primary unipolar depression and Briquet's syndrome (somatization disorder). Arch Gen Psychiatry 38:939–942.

Eaton W, Regier D, Locke BZ, & Taube CA (1981): The epidemiologic catchment area program of the national institute of mental health. Public Health 96:319–323.

Goldberg, EL, Comstock GW, & Hornstra R (1979): Depressed mood and subsequent physical illness. Am J Psychiatry 136:530–534.

Hall RCW, Gardner ER, Stickney SK, LeCann AF, & Popkin MK (1980): Physical illness manifesting as psychiatric disease, Part 2 (Analysis of a state hospital inpatient population). Arch Gen Psychiatry 37:989–995.

Hankin JR, Steinwachs DM, Regier DA, Burns BJ, Goldberg ID, & Hoeper EW (1982): Use of general medical care services by persons with mental disorders. Arch Gen Psychiatry 39:225–231.

Heine B (1970): Approaches to the etiology and treatment of psychosomatic disorder: Psycho-genesis of hypertension. Proc R Soc Med 63:1267–1270.

Hoeper EW, Nyca GR, Regier DA, Goldberg ID, Jacobson A, & Hankin J (1980): Diagnosis of mental disorder in adults and increased use of health services in four outpatient settings. Am J Psychiatry 137:207–210.

Houpt J, Orleans C, & George LK (1979): *The Importance of Mental Health Services to General Health Care.* Cambridge, Ballinger.

Kathol RC, & Petty F (1981): Relationship of depression to medical illness: A critical review. J Affect Dis 3:111–121.

Klerman GL (1978): Affective disorders. Nicholi AM (Ed.). In *Harvard Guide to Modern Psychiatry*. Cambridge, Harvard University Press, pp. 253–281.

Lipowski, ZJ (1979): Psychiatric illness among medical patients. Lancet 1:478–479.

Mathew RJ, Weinman ML, & Mirabi M (1981): Physical symptoms to depression. Br J Psychiatry 139:293–296.

Myers JK, & Weissman MM (1980): Use of a self-report scale to detect depression in a community sample. Am J Psychiatry 137:1081–1084.

Nielsen AC III, & Williams TA (1980): Depression in ambulatory medical patients: Prevalence of self-report questionnaire and recognition by nonpsychiatric physicians. Arch Gen Psychiatry 37:999–1004.

Regier DA, Goldberg ID, Burns BJ, Hankin J, Hoeper EW, & Nycz R (1982): Specialist/generalist division of responsibility for patients with mental disorders. Arch Gen Psychiatry 39:219–224.

Robbins LN, Helzer JE, Croughan J, & Ratcliff KS, NIMH (1981): Diagnostic interview schedule: Its history, characteristics and validity. Arch Gen Psychiatry 38:381–389.

Weissman MM, & Myers JK (1978): Affective disorders in a U.S. urban community. Arch Gen Psychiatry 35:1304–1311.

Weissman MM, Myers JK, & Thompson WD (1981): Depression and its treatment in a U.S. urban community: 1975–76. Arch Gen Psychiatry 38:417–421.

Weissman MM, Myers JK, Thompson WD, & Belanger A (in press): Depressive symptoms as a risk factor for mortality and major depression. Erlenmeyer-Kimling L, Dohrenwend B, & Miller N (Eds.). In *Life Span Research on the Prediction of Psychopathology*. New York, Columbia University Press.

7

Stress, Emotions, Behavior, and Cardiovascular Disease

Theodore M. Dembroski
Robert S. Eliot

James M. MacDougall
James C. Buell

More individuals in Western societies die of cardiovascular-related diseases than of any other cause. In addition to the lethal effects (approximately 400,000 deaths a year in the United States alone), these diseases inflict enormous economic, social, and psychological damage. In spite of immense biomedical and epidemiological research, the etiology of coronary heart disease (CHD) remains mysterious. For example, inspection of the leading risk factors for CHD (i.e., elevated levels of serum cholesterol, blood pressure, and cigarette smoking) shows that the best combination of these factors does not predict the emergence of most new cases of CHD (Jenkins, 1976; Keys, 1970); nor can these factors, along with genetic considerations, changes in diet, exercise, diagnostic techniques, and age structure of the population explain the dramatic increase in CHD during the 20th century, or the recently reported declines in CHD-related deaths (Corday & Corday, 1975; Gordon & Thom, 1975; Michaels, 1966; Rosen 1978a, 1983; White, 1974). In fact, traditional factors uncovered through epidemiological studies in the United States often are associated with quite different rates of incidence and prevalence of CHD in other cultures (Keys, 1970; Kozarevic et al., 1976).

In the face of such findings many investigators have expanded their scope of interest to include behavioral components as possible etiological factors

Preparation of this manuscript was supported by Grant HL22809 awarded to the first two authors by the National Heart, Lung, and Blood Institute, and by research grant AG120 from the American Heart Association, Florida affiliate.

in CHD. Within this framework, there is a growing acceptance of the view that CHD is an outgrowth of intricate interactions of environmental, psychological, behavioral, physiological, pathophysiological, and genetic factors. Moreover, there is an increased realization that environmental and behavioral factors are closely interwoven into the fabric of the traditional risk factors. In this context, the concept of coronary-prone behavior is receiving increased attention as an important area of risk factor exploration.

CORONARY-PRONE BEHAVIOR

For purposes of discussion, coronary-prone behavior can be usefully divided into two general headings. The first category includes those behaviors associated with the traditional risk factors. Examples include dietary habits, cigarette smoking, and sedentary life style; also included under this heading are compliance and noncompliance behaviors having implications for the control of existing disease states, such as failure to maintain pharmacological regimens for hypertension control. The attention accorded the above behaviors is emphasized by the immense public and private resources that have been devoted to mass media and other intervention programs designed to alter these behaviors in a manner that significantly reduces traditional risk factors (Farquhar, 1978; MRFIT, 1976). The second category of coronary-prone behaviors falls under the general heading of "stress." It is this type of coronary-prone behavior and its related pathways that is the focus of the present chapter.

Historical Observations

The role of stress-related factors in the etiology of CHD has been acknowledged by practicing physicians for hundreds of years. According to Plutarch, when the physician Erasistratos suspected that "love" sickness had stricken Antiochus, the son of King Seleukos of Syria (third century B.C.), he ordered all of the women in the court one by one to parade by the bed of Antiochus. Erasistratos monitored the heart rate of the patient; he observed an acceleration and irregularity of the pulse when the prince's young stepmother, Stratonike, came near. Upon Erasistratos' recommendation, the 70-year-old king divorced his young wife in order that Antiochus could marry her, and the prince enjoyed a speedy recovery (Schmidt, 1983).

A few hundred years later, at the time of Christ, Celsus (30 a.d.) also recognized a relationship between behavior and the cardiovascular system when he stated that, "fear and anger and any other state of the mind may often be apt to excite the pulse" (cited in Buell & Eliot, 1979).

Similarly in 1628, William Harvey pointed out that: "Every affection of the mind that is attended with either pain or pleasure, hope or fear, is the cause of an agitation whose influence extends to the heart" (quoted in Jenkins, 1971). Not long afterward, John Hunter (1729-1793), a specialist in cardiovascular pathology, observed an association between his emotional state and angina attacks when he stated: "My life is at the mercy of any rascal who chooses to put me in a passion." It seemed, however, that Dr. Hunter possessed a firey temper, which often generated severe interpersonal conflict. It was during such a violent encounter with colleagues at a faculty meeting that Dr. Hunter died suddenly. Sir Willam Osler described the event: "In silent rage and in the next room he gave a deep groan and fell down dead" (cited in Debakey & Gotto, 1977). Later, Osler (1892) attributed CHD to "the high pressure at which men live and the habit of working the machine to its capacity." According to Osler the coronary patient was "not the delicate, neurotic person...but the robust, the vigorous in mind and body, the keen and ambitious man, the indicator of whose engine is always at full speed ahead." A number of well-known psychiatrists in the 1930s and 1940s generally agreed with Osler, including Arlow (1945), Dunbar (1943), Gildea (1949), Menninger and Menninger (1936), and Kemple (1945).

Defining the Type A Coronary-Prone Behavior Pattern

Despite the long history of rather consistent but anecdotal observations concerning the association between behavior and CHD, it was not until the 1950s that a coherent conceptual definition and a reliable operational definition of a coronary-prone behavior pattern were established. Interestingly, the latter breakthrough did not have its roots in the behavioral science community, but emerged from the pioneering efforts and keen insights of the cardiologists Friedman and Rosenman (1959). They defined the Type A coronary-prone behavior pattern as "an action-emotion complex that can be observed in any person who is aggressively involved in a chronic incessant struggle to achieve more and more in less and less time, and if required to do so, against the opposing efforts of other things or other persons." (Friedman & Rosenman, 1974). In reviewing the works of Rosenman and Friedman, Jenkins (1971) attempted to capture the various characteristics attributed to the Type A individual over the years: "*extremes* of competitiveness, striving for achievement, aggressiveness (sometimes stringently repressed), haste, impatience, restlessness, hyperalertness, explosiveness of speech, tenseness of facial musculature, and feelings of being under the pressure of time and under the challenge of responsibility," in addition to such a deep commitment to a vocation "that other aspects of their lives are relatively neglected. Not all aspects of this syndrome or pattern need be present for a person to be classified as possessing it. The pattern is neither a personality trait nor a standard reaction to a challenging situation, but rather the reaction of a characterologically predisposed person to a situation which challenges him. Different kinds of situations evoke maximal reaction from different persons."

In attempting to devise a measurement procedure or operational definition of Type A, Rosenman and Friedman (1974) devised a structured interview (SI) in which questions about the respondent's hard-driving behavior, aggressiveness, impatience, time urgency, etc. were asked in a somewhat challenging manner. They adopted this strategy because their extensive clinical experience with coronary patients had suggested that questions administered in such a fashion often evoked vigorous and explosive speech stylistics in coronary-prone individuals, whether the answer happened to contain Type A content or not. Thus, the primary criteria for designating individuals as Type A rested largely upon the manner in which a subject answered a question, rather than the actual content of the answer itself (Rosenman, 1978b).

Armed with a conceptual and operational definition of the Type A pattern, Friedman and Rosenman first launched a series of prevalence studies, which revealed that Type A stylistics were much more likely to be observed in coronary patients than in other individuals (Rosenman & Friedman, 1961). These studies served as the foundation for launching a major prospective study called the Western Collaborative Group Study (WCGS) under the direction of Rosenman and his associates (1964). The results of this incidence study established the Type A pattern as an independent risk factor for CHD, having a magnitude roughly equivalent to that of each of the traditional risk factors (Brand, 1978; Rosenman et al., 1964; Rosenman et al., 1975). Parallel research by other investigators also has linked Type A behaviors to the prevalence, incidence, and recurrence of CHD (Haynes et al., 1980; Jenkins, 1978). With some exceptions (Dimsdale et al., 1980), the Type A pattern has also been associated with arteriographically documented severity of atherosclerosis (Blumenthal et al., 1978; Frank et al., 1978; Friedman et al., 1968; Williams et al., 1980), and perhaps the progression of the atherosclerotic process (Krantz et al., 1979).

After critically reviewing the evidence in this area, a distinguished panel of scientists under the sponsorship of the National Heart, Lung, and Blood Institute recently concluded that the Type A pattern in fact is a risk factor for CHD, "over and above that imposed by age, systolic blood pressure, serum cholesterol, and smoking and appears to be of the same order of magnitude as the relative risk associated with any of these factors." (Cooper et al., 1981).

Assessment of Type A Behavior

During the 1960s and 1970s research was heavily focused on establishing an epidemiological link between Type A behavior and CHD. Since Type A is now recognized as a risk factor for CHD, it appears that one of the most important avenues of research in the 1980s will address the question of how behavior is translated into CHD. We already know that it is not through the traditional risk factors, at least as presently assessed in epidemiological studies. It seems, therefore that we must turn our

attention to nontraditional pathways and/or measure traditional risk factors in nontraditional ways in order to determine the mechanisms associated with Type A that could excite pathophysiological processes. It is important first to ask a fundamental question: What is Type A? To address this issue, one must carefully examine both the conceptual and operational definitions of Type A.

For a moment, review the attributes included in the Jenkins (1971) definition of Type A quoted earlier. Even a cursory examination reveals clearly that the Type A pattern is a multidimensional construct. A fundamental question then is: Which characteristics of the many included in the conceptual definition of Type A are associated with CHD and which are simply benign correlates?

In attempting to answer this question, Jenkins (1966) in a small-scale study of subjects in the WCGS (25 cases vs. 50 controls) reported that a sense of time urgency, job promotions, and past achievements were most characteristic of those events and behaviors that manifest silent myocardial infarction. This study was one of the first to demonstrate how reanalyses of data available from the WCGS can contribute to further refinement of the concept of coronary-prone behavior. In this context, coronary-prone behavior is distinguished from Type A behavior in that not all of the attributes contained in the multidimensional Type A construct may be related to CHD, that some characteristics may be associated with different manifestations of CHD, and that other behavioral factors associated with CHD and not presently considered as part of Type A may be uncovered in future research.

Another pioneering study pursuing the latter approach was conducted by Matthews et al., (1977), in which a subset of interviews from the WCGS (63 cases vs. 124 controls) were reanalyzed to determine which components of Type A were related to the incidence of CHD and which were not. The results showed, for example, that speed of activity, achievements, and job involvement were not related to clinically overt manifestations of CHD, while the attributes of potential for hostility, explosive and vigorous voice stylistics, competitiveness, impatience, and irritability successfully discriminated case from controls.

Based upon the promising results of the Matthews et al. (1977) study, we recognized the need for the development of a scoring key for component analyses of the SI (Dembroski, 1978). Our system yielded the following scales:

1. A global 4-point designation identical to that developed by Rosenman and associates:

    A_1—fully developed pattern
    A_2—incompletely developed pattern
    X—intermediate amount of both types
    B—general absence of type A attributes

2. A 5-point rating of each of the follwowing voice stylistics:

    loud and explosive
    rapid and accelerated
    response latency

3. A 5-point rating of the subject's propensity to the following display:

    potential for hostility
    verbal competitiveness

4. A 5-point rating of content items subsequently clustered as scale scores under four categories:

    competitive drive
    hostility
    speed of activity
    impatience.

Interrater reliability of the above components generally has been quite good for both stylistics and content. The hostility component has been the most difficult to score, but as mentioned above, it appears to be one of the more potent predictors of CHD, as well as cardiovacular reactivity to challenging maneuvers in the laboratory setting. In addition, the component scoring approach allows the application of factor analyses to determine the structure of the Type A pattern and permits a comparison of components derived from the SI with scores obtained from paper-and-pencil assessment devices which purport to measure the Type A pattern, e.g., the Jenkins Activity Scale (JAS; Jenkins et al., 1971).

With the latter issues in mind, we recently collaborated with Matthews in a study of the factor structure of the Type A pattern as assessed by component scoring of the SI (Matthews et al., 1982). Two samples of subjects were used. The first contained coronary patients and aged-matched controls; the second consisted of male college students. Despite differences in disease status, geographical location, and age, the factor structure for the two samples was remarkably similar. Moreover, the data clearly showed that the clinical ratings of voice stylistics, hostility, and verbal competitiveness are the real crux of Type A (Matthews et al., 1982). Correlational analysis showed plainly that reports of pressured drive, anger, and competitiveness are only weakly related to the final SI-defined Type A, while the clinical ratings factor accounts for the vast majority of variance (see Chesney et al., 1981; MacDougall et al., 1979; Scherwitz et al., 1977; Schucker & Jacobs, 1977). Thus, the unique variance associated with SI scoring of Type A is clearly contributed by the clinical ratings.

Additional analyses showed that the Type A scores on the JAS, a purely self-reported instrument, correlated weakly with clinical ratings, but was rather strongly related to the SI-derived *content-based* factor of pressured drive. The latter finding explains why there is only about 65 percent agreement between the SI and JAS in designating subjects Type A or B. Finally, in both samples, agreement between the SI and JAS was much stronger when only JAS-defined Type A subjects were considered. When subjects scored Type B on the JAS, however, there was only chance agreement between the two assessment procedures.

The two major instruments used to assess the Type A pattern therefore share only a slim margin of overlap and cannot be used interchangeably as if each were assessing the same construct (MacDougall et al., 1979; Matthews et al., 1982). Evidence suggests that the SI, relative to the JAS, is a better predictor of the incidence of CHD, angiographically documented severity of atherosclerosis, and cardiovascular response to laboratory-based challenges (Blumenthal et al., 1978; Brand et al., 1978; Dembroski et al., 1978, 1979ab; Williams et al., 1980). In some instances, however, the JAS may be a better predictor of other end points (Krantz et al., 1979). Thus, future research should employ both instruments to determine differential relationships to end points.

In any case, it is clear that component analysis of the SI is quite feasible and may offer a means of identifying which attributes of the Type A pattern are most closely associated with CHD. Reanalysis of data in the WCGS is essential to this aim. However, this approach is only a first step in the process of attempting to understand how the Type A pattern is translated into CHD.

From a purely behavioral standpoint, further research will be necessary to determine which components of Type A, in interaction with other psychosocial factors, may increase risk of CHD. Such factors include status incongruity, social support, depression, recent life changes, work stress, exhaustion, anxiety, symptom distress, etc. The search for interactions of this sort is absolutely essential if we are to improve the specificity value of the Type A construct. Moreover, there is a recent disconserting tendancy for researchers to find a large majority of subjects in their samples to be classified as Type A (see Matthews, 1982). The challenge before us, then, is to be more precise about which particular Type A subjects (and Type B subjects for that matter) are at risk. However, when and if combinations of psychosocial factors in interaction with specific components of the Type A pattern do show heightened risks for CHD, the task of isolating physiological processes related to pathophysiological mechanisms will still remain.

PSYCHOPHYSIOLOGICAL STUDIES OF TYPE A PATTERN

Very early in their program of research into the Type A pattern, Friedman and Rosenman began an anlysis of differences between Type A and B subjects in biochemical processes potentially related to CHD. The intent of this research was twofold: to amass additional indirect evidence linking Type A to CHD, and to begin to understand the mechanisms through which the Type A pattern might be associated with the increased risk of CHD. These studies revealed a rather consistent pattern of A–B differences, with *extreme* Type A persons evidencing the following: elevations in serum lipids and triglycerides (Friedman & Rosenman, 1959; Friedman et al., 1964; Friedman et al., 1970); higher resting levels of ACTH (Friedman et al., 1972); reduced secretions of 17-hydroxycorticosteroids in reaction to ACTH injection (Friedman et al., 1969); faster blood clotting times (Friedman & Rosenman, 1959); and elevations in urinary and serum catecholamines under challenging circumstances (Friedman et al., 1960; Friedman et al., 1975). These results suggested that extreme Type A individuals are prone to show elevations in a number of physiological parameters that are indicative of excessive psychosocial or environmental stress.

A reasonable hypothesis derived from this research is that the Type A person is at a greater risk for CHD by virtue of these potentially pathophysiological processes, which presumably arise through excessively stressful interactions with the environment. Such a hypothesis is consistent with a large body of animal research, which shows that situational stress is capable of producing predictable changes in the pituitary–adrenal and sympathetic autonomic nervous system axes, with subsequent damage to the cardiovascular system (Henry, 1983; Herd, 1978, 1983; Schneiderman, 1978, 1983).

Granting for the moment the working hypothesis that such pathophysiological reactions constitute the linkage between the Type A behavior pattern and the development of CHD and/or the triggering of clinical CHD events, it becomes important to analyze the mechanisms by which Type A is itself linked to these physiological and pathophysiological processes. There appear to be at least four plausible possibilities, none of which is mutually exclusive:

1. Type A persons, by virtue of their more involved and aggressive reactions to the demands of normal daily existence, tend to protract their contact with stressful situations and thus experience quantitatively larger amounts of environmental and psychosocial stress.
2. Type A persons, by virtue of their more involved and aggressive reactions, engage more frequently in unnecessary stressful behaviors and/or alter the physical and social environment in ways that create more stress for themselves.
3. Type A persons, by virtue of their particular constellation of behavioral and psychological characteristics, respond physiologically to normal stressors to a greater degree than do their Type B counterparts.
4. Both the Type A behavior pattern and the observed pathophysiological responses that accompany it are themselves consequences of other, as yet unidentified processes of psychological and/or constitutional nature (Cooper et al., 1981).

Before examining the data relevant to these alternatives, a caveat is in order. As noted above, it is our increasing belief that a significant discrepancy exists in the conceptual and operational definitions of the Type A pattern. Once again, it is emphasized that self-reports of competitiveness, aggressiveness, time urgency, and the like simply do not correlate well with the major interview assessment criteria of loud, rapid, explosive, and accelerated speech, which primarily were used to type individuals as A or B in the WCGS. Given the apparent fact that there are multiple, virtually independent dimensions to the Type A construct, it is entirely possible that different aspects of the pattern may confer pathophysiological risk through different mechanisms.

It is also important to note a fundamental assumption underlying much of the following psychophysiological research. This work was undertaken in an attempt to discover the person and situation variables that mediate the heightened stress responses of the Type A individual. Inherent in this research is the assumption that the commonly employed noninvasive measures of blood pressure and heart rate used in psychophysiological studies can index a person's tendency to show the more pathological pituitary–adrenal and sympathetic autonomic nervous system reactions which have been linked to cardiovascular damage in animal research. Such an assumption is probably reasonable in cases where relatively large hemodynamic changes are observed, but becomes questionable when the cardiovascular reactions are small in magnitude and can reflect the operation of a variety of mechanisms, some of which cannot be reasonably called pathological in nature.

The first of these alternatives, that Type A persons tend to protract their contact with stressful situations, thus experiencing quantitatively greater levels of stress, is well-documented from a behavioral standpoint. Several studies employing the JAS to identify Type A individuals have revealed, for instance, that Type A subjects, compared with Type B subjects, persevere in the face of fatigue (Carver et al., 1981; Weidner & Matthews, 1978), task distraction (Glass, 1977; Matthews & Brunson, 1979), and initial task failure (Glass, 1977). Unfortunately, while it is reasonable to hypothesize, based on this research, that Type A subjects may expose themselves in this way to greater amounts of stress, there was no attempt in these studies to actually measure the physiological costs incurred. It may be, for example, that Type A persons are well-habituated to these stressors and actually suffer little additional physiological stress and strain.

Another problem lies in the fact that there is a dearth of published data available to show that SI-defined Type A subjects behave in a manner similar to those typed using the JAS. Limited unpublished research from our laboratory has found only minor differences between SI-defined Type A and B subjects in task persistence (MacDougall & Dembroski, unpublished data) and actual achievement activities in college (Dembroski et al., unpublished data, 1983). Until these issues are resolved, it remains unclear whether behaviors of this type constitute a mechanism through which the Type A pattern engenders physiological stress.

The second alternative, that Type A individuals engage more frequently in unnecessarily stressful activities and/or act to increase the stressfulness of the environment, appears equally well established, at least for JAS-defined Type A subjects. Such subjects have been found to set higher performance goals for themselves (Snow, 1978), behave more irritably and aggressively when frustrated (Carver & Glass, 1978; Glass et al., 1974; Van Egeren, 1979a), respond to challenges with excessive effort and emotional intensity (Burnam et al., 1975; Carver et al., 1976), and avoid working cooperatively on difficult tasks (Dembroski & MacDougall, 1978). Whether these behavioral tendencies are accompanied by exaggerated autonomic reactions is again, not clear. In the Carver et al. (1976) study, JAS-defined Type A subjects expended slightly greater metabolic energy in walking a treadmill than did Type B subjects; while in the study by Van Egeren (1979b), the Type A individuals showed greater digital vasoconstriction along with their more aggressive interaction style. None of these studies, however, has persuasively demonstrated significant autonomic nervous system or pituitary–adrenal reactions between the types as a result of such behavioral differences. Moreover, as noted above, all of the studies employed the JAS to assess Type A behavior. To our knowledge, comparable behavioral and physiological data are not available for SI-defined Type A and Type B subjects.

The third possibility, that Type A individuals react physiologically and psychologically to a given level of environmental demand to a greater extent than do Type B individuals, has attracted much greater experimental attention. Beginning with a demonstration study by Friedman et al. (1975), a voluminous body of literature has emerged demonstrating that when faced with a variety of psychosocial and performance challenges, Type A persons are likely to show greater blood pressure and (to a lesser degree) heart rate elevations than Type B individuals (e.g., Dembroski et al., 1979a, b; MacDougall et al., 1981; Manuck et al., 1978). Limited evidence also suggests that such reactions are accompanied by elevations in circulatory catecholamines (Contrada et al., 1982; Glass et al., 1980), which have been linked in both animal and human research to myocardial damage (Baroldi et al., 1979; Eliot & Buell, 1983).

Occasionally in these studies, the greater levels of physiological reactivity are accompanied by self-reports of greater task involvement on the part of the Type A subjects, and by superior task performance (Contrada et al., 1982; MacDougall et al., 1981), but it is not clear whether greater involvement or effort actually mediates the observed physiological differences. It is noteworthy that the Type A–Type B differences in reactivity noted in studies of this type have been obtained using both the SI and JAS to classify subjects, although there is some evidence that the SI is a better predictor of such reactivity than is the JAS (Corse et al., in press; Dembroski et al., 1979a; MacDougall et al., 1981).

In addition to demonstrating Type A–Type B differences in physiological reactivity to common tasks, several studies have sought to identify those aspects of the Type A pattern that mediate the exaggerated reactivity. Although several possible factors have been suggested, including excessive involvement with self (Scherwitz et al., 1978), sensitivity to threats to control (Contrada et al., 1982), and cognitive complexity (Streufert et al., 1979), at the present time, the most firmly established component appears to be a tendency toward irritability and hostility. Studies in our laboratory (Dembroski et al., 1978; Dembroski et al., 1979a; MacDougall et al., 1981) have consistently found potential for hostility to be moderately correlated with SI-defined Type A pattern and to be one of the strongest predictors of cardiovascular reactivity to performance challenge for both men and women. This finding is of particular interest since, as mentioned earlier, Matthews et al., (1977) found potential for hostility and irritability to be one of the best predictors of CHD incidence in a reanalysis of WCGS data, and Williams et al., (1980) were able to link MMPI measures of hostility to severity of artherosclerosis.

A related issue concerns the nature of the environmental stressors that elicit the differential reactivity of the Type A subjects. Based on a thorough review of the literature, Matthews (1982) suggested that such differences are likely to be observed when tasks are frustrating, difficult, moderately competitive in nature, or demanding of slow, careful responses. Tasks at either extreme, either very undemanding or extremely demanding, are likely to yield smaller or no Type A–Type B differences. Such results argue that the difference between the types lies not in absolute potential for exaggerated reactivity, but, rather, in a lowered threshold in the Type A subjects for showing such reactions under certain circumstances.

The fourth alternative, that Type A behaviors and physiological hyperreactivity are both consequences of some more fundamental factor, has only recently been examined. In exploring this issue it is important to emphasize again that the preferred assessment technique for Type A, the SI, relies almost exclusively on verbal stylistics and clinical judgements of hostility for classifying subjects as Type A or Type B, and that trait and/or behavioral

characteristics of drive, speed of activity, competitiveness, and the like correlate rather poorly with such stylistic-based determinations. An intriguing possibility, originally suggested by Goldband et al., (1979), is that the vocal mannerisms that form the core of the operational definition of Type A may themselves reflect an underlying hyperreactivity to environmental challenge. Viewed in this manner, both the explosive, rapid voice modulation and the heightened cardiovascular responses may be seen as manifestations of more general biobehavioral reactivity to situational stress. Such a conception would not, of course, preclude the operation of the other mechanisms suggested above, mediated by other behavioral characteristics ascribed to Type A individuals.

The empirical support for this alternative is presently quite limited, but still suggestive. Studies by Kahn et al. (1980) and Krantz et al. (1983) reveal that Type A patients show larger blood pressure reactions to the physiological stress of surgery, even while under general anesthesia. This would suggest that the exaggerated reactivity of Type A individuals is not necessarily mediated by conscious cognitive or emotional responses. A second and somewhat more direct bit of evidence comes from studies by Krantz et al., (1983) and Schmeider et al., (1982) and which suggest that the pharmacological blockade of beta-adrenergic receptors is capable of reducing Type A speech stylistics without affecting the Type A content of the SI, while (in the Krantz et al., study) simultaneously reducing the magnitude of autonomic nervous system reactivity to stress. Since beta-blocking drugs are not tranquilizers or depressants per se, the clear implication of these studies is that the speech stylistics that define the Type A pattern are themselves derivative in part of excessive central and/or peripheral nervous system arousability. If these findings can be replicated in other samples and extended to environmental stressors other than the SI, then a considerable revision would be required in our thinking concerning possible relationships between Type A behavior, physiological reactivity, and CHD.

In summary, at the present time considerable research suggests that Type A persons are statistically more prone than their Type B counterparts to evidence exaggerated levels of pituitary–adrenal and sympathetic autonomic nervous system activity. Furthermore, a plausible case can be made that these pathophysiological processes mediate the link between the behavior pattern and increased risk of CHD. Through the use of noninvasive psychophysiological techniques, investigators have sought to determine the behavioral and psychological mechanisms that might account for these differences. Of the four possible classes of mechanisms described earlier, only one has received extensive attention, and there is no clear articulation of the psychological mechanisms involved. We believe that before significant additional progress can be achieved, investigators must come to a more precise understanding of the behavioral and psychological nature of the Type A pattern. An obvious first step in this process is to bring the conceptual and operational definitions of Type A into better agreement, and to recognize that the resulting construct is likely to comprise only one aspect of a larger class of behaviors which might be called "coronary prone." Very likely, each of these types of coronary-prone behavior has its own etiology and its own mechanisms through which it may confer risk.

PSYCHOPHYSIOLOGICAL ASSESSMENT BEYOND TYPE A

Evidence Supporting the Usefulness of Psychophysiological Assessment

Although there appears to be a statistical tendency for challenge-induced exaggerated cardiovascular response (or "hot" reactivity) to be more characteristic of Type A then Type B individuals, our research has revealed that some Type B subjects also show hot reactivity, and moreover some (even behaviorally strong) Type A subjects simply do not respond with excessive physiological arousal when challenged. Indeed, under some circumstances groups of both types show excessive levels of cardiovascular response during highly involving activity (Glass et al., 1980). We suggested in the past that psychophysiological maneuvers might be developed to identify individuals prone to show large levels of challenge-induced cardiovascular reactivity and that identification of these hot reactors, regardless of the Type A or B dimension might prove to be a better strategy for identifying those with coronary-prone tendencies (Dembroski et al., 1977; MacDougall et al., 1979). In short, psychophysiological responses may be a more superior index of future development of CHD than the purely behavioral assessment procedures, such as those used in the Type A approach.

Several convergent lines of evidence support this conclusion. Keys et al. (1971) reported that the diastolic blood pressure reaction to the cold pressor test was the best available predictor of future emergence of CHD during the course of a 23-year incidence

study. "Hot" reactivity also has been associated with coronary patients more than matched controls in prevalence studies (Dembroski et al., 1978; Sime et al., 1980). This reactivity is particularly pronounced when coronary patients are not on medication (Corse et al., in press). In their air traffic controller study, Rose et al. (1978) reported that normotensives who showed hot physiological reactivity while monitoring aircraft were significantly more likely than others to develop sustained hypertension. Evidence also suggests that borderline hypertensives are more physiologically reactive when challenged than are their normotensive counterparts, and, in this connection, there is a growing body of research showing that normotensives with a family history of cardiovascular diseases are more hyperreactive to challenge than normotensives without such a family history. (Falkner et al., 1979; Julius & Cottier, in press; Light & Obrist, 1980; Remington et al., 1960).

Normontensive black children are more physiologically reactive than age and body weight-matched normotensive white children, a factor that may play a role in the higher incidence of hypertension in American blacks (Alpert et al., 1981). Similarly, a program of research by Frankenhauser (in press) and co-workers found consistently that males are more physiologically reactive than females under a variety of stressful conditions, which may, in part, be related in a significant fashion to the well-known sex difference in CHD. In short, not only has challenge-induced physiological hyperreactivity been linked to the Type A pattern, it has also been linked to the incidence and prevalence of clinically manifest CHD and hypertension, family history of cardiovascular disease, race, and sex. In addition, there is a large body of animal research that shows a relationship between stress-induced hyperreactivity and various manifestations of CHD and sudden death (Schneiderman, 1978, 1983).

The optimal strategy may be to focus research attention on the detection of the hot physiological reactor in order to determine the degree to which this individual physiological variable is a risk factor for CHD and other diseases as well (Dembroski et al., 1981). What is needed is a prospective study of the ability of individual differences in physiological reactivity to predict the incidence of both minor and chronic disease.

Pilot Study of "Hot" Reactivity

In setting the groundwork for such a study, our research team is addressing a number of issues in a programmatic manner both in the laboratory and field settings. Such pilot work is essential before an expensive prospective study is launched. A brief overview of one of our ongoing studies will serve to illustrate some of the many facets involved in the reactivity issue. At present, we are examining the top 30 managers of the Western Electric Company based in Omaha, Nebraska. We gave subjects questionnaires designed to assess a variety of behavioral, psychological, and environmental variables relevant to both work and home settings. For all subjects we had access to a complete medical history and examination, in which levels of serum cholesterol, cortisol, and other variables were measured.

Psychophysiological procedures were used at rest and during the Type A interview, a history quiz, a competitive television game, and a mental arithmetic task, to measure cardiovascular function, including electrocardiogram (ECG), blood pressure/heart rate (BP/HR), and cardiac output (CO) and total systemic resistance (TSR) through impedance cardiography techniques. In order to explore whether laboratory-based reactions are associated with physiological responses during real-life work activity, we assessed on-the-job BP and ECG reactions every 15 minutes by means of an automated ambulatory BP/ECG monitor. At each cuff inflation, a subject also described activities and emotional states in a rating-scale diary that was kept throughout the workday. Stability of responses was examined by retest 6 months later.

Data analysis is still incomplete, but several interesting findings have already emerged:

1. The psychophysiological testing revealed large individual differences in cardiovascular reactivity, which do not correlate very well with reported levels of stress, anxiety, and other emotions.

2. BP/HR values at baseline, values during test activity, and change scores (i.e., test levels minus baseline values) were fairly stable at retest. In other words, a "hot" reactor (high change scores) is likely to stay a hot reactor 6 months later. Moreover, the change scores are not predicted by baseline cardiovascular values.

3. We observed previously unsuspected multiple premature ventricular contractions, both during psychophysiological testing and ambulatory monitoring.

4. We uncovered different patterns of cardiovascular reactivity. Three basic patterns of BP elevations emerged: (a) BP↑, CO↑, TSR↓; (b) BP↑, CO↓, TSR↑; (c) BP↑, CO↓ (or no change). TSR . Five subjects were categorized in the third group. Two already had overt cardiovascular disease and one had suffered clinical complications. Within an 8-month period after testing, two others developed cardiovascular events of sufficient gravity for one to be admitted to the intensive care unit and the other to require heavy medication for arrhythmias. In addition, a hot reactor in group (b) developed ventricular tachycardia and was admitted to the intensive care unit and subsequently underwent double coronary artery bypass grafting. It is emphasized that the subjects who developed complications within 8 months after testing showed normal ECGs and no abnormalities in their annual routine medical history and physical examination before we started our procedures. Moreover, during testing these subjects did not report emotions that were different from those reported by other subjects.

5. Reports of emotional states and cardiovascular responses during the working day interact in an interesting fashion. Although physical activity is the variable most closely associated with cardiovascular changes, within subject correlations between reported emotion and physiological arousal are also large, but correlations between the variables for the group tend to be insignificant. In other words, if two individuals report that they feel maximally stressed at a given point in time, we can be confident in predicting that the BP of both will be elevated above their normal resting levels; however, the reports of emotion cannot tell us how high the BP, CO, TSR, etc. of each individual is. For example, for the same reported emotion, one subject might show a systolic BP increase of 6 mm Hg above his resting level, while another might be elevated 60 mm Hg over his respective baseline value. In other words, psychophysiological testing is the only way to detect the hot reactor. Once the hot reactor is identified, however, his reports of emotional arousal can be used as a reliable indicator that his BP is highly elevated.

In summary, the early data from our research and this pilot study are encouraging with regard to the feasibility of a large prospective study in which the degree that hot reactivity is a risk factor can be more definitely determined. In our view, hot reactivity represents a new and objective clue to the likelihood of future cardiovascular disease.

REFERENCES

Alpert BS, Dover EV, Booker DL, Martin AM, Strong WB (1981): Blood pressure response to dynamic exercise in healthy children—Blacks vs. white. J Pediatr 99:556.

Arlow JA (1945): Identification mechanisms in coronary occlusion. Psychosom Med 7:195–209.

Baroldi G, Falizi G, & Mariani F (1979): Sudden coronary death. A postmortem study in 208 selected cases compared to 97 "control" subjects. Am Heart J 98:20–31.

Blumenthal JA, Williams R, Kong Y, Schanber S, & Thompson L (1978): Type A behavior pattern and coronary arteriosclerosis. Circulation 58:634–639.

Brand RJ (1978): Coronary-prone behavior as an independent risk factor for coronary heart disease. Dembroski TM, Weiss SM, Shields JL, Haynes SG, & Feinleib M (Eds.). In *Coronary-Prone Behavior*. New York, Springer-Verlag.

Brand RJ, Rosenman RH, Jenkins CD, Sholtz RI, & Zyzanski SJ (1978): Comparison of CHD prediction in the WCGS: SI *vs.* JAS. Paper presented at the American Heart Association conference, Orlando, March.

Buell JC, & Eliot RS (1979): Stress and cardiovascular disease. Mod Concepts Cardiovasc Dis 4:19–24.

Burnam MA, Pennebaker JW, & Glass DC (1975): Time consciousness, achievement striving and the Type A coronary-prone behavior pattern. J Abnorm Psychol 84:76–79.

Carver CS, Coleman AE, & Glass DC (1976): The coronary-prone behavior pattern and the suppression of fatigue on a treadmill test. J Pers Soc Psychol 33:460–466.

Carver CS, Degregorio E, & Gillis R (1981): Challenge and Type A behavior among intercollegiate football players. J Sport Psychol 3:140–148.

Carver CS, & Glass DC (1978): Coronary-prone behavior pattern and interpersonal aggression. J Pers Soc Psychol 36:361–366.

Chesney MA, Black GW, Chadwick JH, & Rosenman RH (1981): Psychological correlates of the Type A behavior pattern. J Behav Med 4:217–230.

Contrada RJ, Glass DC, Krakoff LR, Krantz DS, Kehoe K, Isecke W, Collins C, & Elting E (1982): Effects of control over aversive stimulation and Type A behavior on cardiovascular and plasma catecholamine responses. Psychophysiology 19:408–419.

Cooper T, Detre T, & Weiss SM (1981): Coronary-prone behavior and coronary heart disease: A critical review. Circulation 63:1199–1215.

Corday E, & Corday SR (1975): Prevention of heart disease by control of risk factors; the time has come to face the facts. Am J Cardiol 35:330–333.

Corse CD, Manuck SB, Cantwell JD, Giordani B, & Matthews KA (in press): Coronary-prone behavior pattern and cardiovascular response in persons with and without coronary heart disease. Psychosom Med

DeBakey M, & Gotto A (1977): *The Living Heart.* New York, Charter Books.

Dembroski TM (1978): Reliability and validity of methods used to assess coronary-prone behavior. Dembroski TM, Feinleib M, Haynes SG, Shields JL, Weiss SM (Eds.). In *Coronary-Prone Behavior*. New York, Springer-Verlag.

Dembroski TM, MacDougall JM, & Shields JL (1977): Physiologic reactions to social challenge in persons evidencing the Type A coronary-prone behavior pattern. J Hum Stress 3:2–10.

Dembroski TM, & MacDougall JM (1978): Stress effects on affiliation preferences among subjects possessing Type A coronary-prone behavior pattern. J Pers Soc Psychol 36:23–33.

Dembroski TM, MacDougall JM, Shields JL, Pettito J, & Lushene R (1978): Components of the Type A coronary-prone behavior pattern and cardiovascular responses to psychomotor performance challenge. J Behav Med 1:159–176.

Dembroski TM, MacDougall JM, Herd JA, & Shields JL (1979a): Effect of level of challenge on pressure and heart rate responses in Type A and B subjects. J Appl Soc psychol 9:209–228.

Dembroski TM, MacDougall JM, & Lushene R (1979b): Interpersonal interaction and cardiovascular response in Type A subjects and coronary patients. J Hum Stress 5:28–36.

Dembroski TM, MacDougall JM, Slaats S, Eliot RS, & Buell JC (1981): Challenge-induced cardiovascular response as a predictor of minor illnesses. J Hum Stress 7:2–5.

Dimsdale JE, Hackett TP, Hutter AM, & Block PC (1980): The risk of Type A mediated coronary artery disease in different populations. Psychosom Med 42:55–62.

Dunbar HF (1943): *Psychosomatic Diagnosis.* New York, Hoeber.

Eliot RS, & Buell JC (1983): Role of the central nervous system in sudden cardiac death. Dembroski TM, Schmidt TM, & Blumchen G (Eds.). In *Biobehavioral Bases of Coronary Heart Disease*. New York, Karger.

Falkner B, Onesti G, Angelokos ET, Fernandes M, & Langman C (1979): Cardiovascular response to mental stress in normal adolescents with hypertensive parents. Hemodynamics of mental stress in adolescents. Hypertension 1:23–30.

Farquhar JW (1978): The community-based model of life style intervention trials. Am J Epidemiol 108:103–111.

Frank KA, Heller DS, Kornfeld DS, Sporn AA, & Weiss MB (1978): Type A behavior pattern and coronary angiographic findings. JAMA 240:761–763.

Frankenhaeuser M (1983): The sympathetic-adrenal and pituitary-adrenal response to challenge: Comparison between the sexes. Dembroski TM, Schmidt G, & Blumchen G (Eds.). In *Biobehavioral Bases of Coronary Heart Disease*. New York, Karger.

Friedman M, & Rosenman RH (1959): Association of specific overt behavior pattern with blood and cardiovascular findings. JAMA 169:1286–1296.

Friedman M, & Rosenman RH (1974): *Type A Behavior and Your Heart.* New York, Knopf.

Friedman M, St. George S, Byers SO, & Rosenman RH (1960): Laceration of catecholamines, 17-ketosteroids, 17-hydroxycorticoids, and 5-hydroxyindole in men exhibiting a particular behavior pattern (A) associated with high incidence of clinical coronary artery disease. J Clin Invest 39:758–764.

Friedman M, Rosenman RH, & Byers SO (1964): Serum lipids and conjunctival circulation after fat ingestion in men exhibiting Type A behavior pattern. Circulation 29:874–886.

Friedman M, Rosenman RH, Strauss R, Wurm M, & Kositchek R (1968): The relationship of behavior pattern to the state of the coronary vasculature. A study of 51 autopsy subjects. Am J Med 44:525–538.

Friedman M, Rosenman RH, & St. George S (1969): Adrenal response to excess corticotropin in coronary-prone men. Proc Soc Exp Biol Med 131:1305–1307.

Friedman M, Byers So, Rosenman RH, & Elevitch FR (1970): Coronary-prone individuals (Type A behavior pattern): Some biochemical characteristics. JAMA 212:1030–1037.

Friedman M, Byers So, Diamant J, & Rosenman RH (1975): Plasma ACTH and cortisol concentration of coronary-prone subjects (Type A) to a specific challenge. Metabolism 24:205–210.

Gildea E (1949): Special features of personality which are common to certain psychosomatic disorders. Psychosom Med 11:273.

Glass DC (1977): *Behavior Patterns, Stress and Coronary Disease.* Hillsdale, N.J., Erlbaum.

Glass DC, Krakoff LR, Contrada R, Hilton WF, Kehoe K, Mannucci EG, Collins C, Snow S, & Elting E (1980): Effect of harassment and competition upon cardiovascular and plasma catecholamine responses in Type A and Type B individuals. Psychophysiology 17:453–463.

Glass DC, Snyder MI, & Hollis J (1974): Time urgency and the Type A coronary-prone behavior pattern. J Appl Soc Psychol 4:125–140.

Goldband S, Katkin ES, & Morell MA (1979): *Stress and Anxiety.* Washington, D.C., Hemisphere.

Gordon T, & Thom T (1975): The recent decrease in CHD mortality. Prev Med 4:115–125.

Harvey W (1968): *Three Hundred Years of Psychiatry 1535–1860.* London, Oxford University Press.

Haynes SG, Feinleib M, & Kannel WB (1980): The relationship of psychosocial factors to coronary heart disease in the Framingham study. Am J Epidemol 111:37–58.

Henry JP (1983): In *Biobehavioral Bases of Coronary Heart Disease.* Dembroski TM, Schmidt TH, & Blumchen G (Eds.). New York, Karger.

Herd JA (1978): In *Coronary-Prone Behavior.* Dembroski TM, Feinleib M, Haynes SG, Shields JL, & Weiss SM (Eds.). New York, Springer-Verlag.

Herd JA (1983): Physiological basis for behavioral influences in arteriosclerosis. In *Biobehavioral Bases of Coronary Heart Disease.* Dembroski TM, Schmidt TH, & Blumchen G (Eds.). New York, Karger.

Jenkins CD (1966): Components of the coronary-prone behavior pattern—Their relation to silent myocardial infarction and blood lipids. J Chronic Dis 19:599–609.

Jenkins CD (1971): Psychologic and social precursors of coronary disease. N Engl J Med 284:244–255, 307–317.

Jenkins CD (1976): Recent evidence supporting physiologic and social risk factors for coronary disease. N Engl J Med 294:987–994, 1033–1038.

Jenkins CD (1978): Behavioral risk factors in coronary artery disease. Annu Rev Med 29:543–562.

Jenkins CD, Zyzanski SJ, & Rosenman RH (1971): Progress toward validation of a computer scored test for the Type A coronary prone behavior pattern. Psychosom Med 33:193–202.

Julius S, & Cottier C (in press): In *Biobehavioral Bases of Coronary Heart Disease.* Dembroski TM, Schmidt TH, & Blumchen G (Eds.). New York, Karger.

Kahn JP, Kornfeld DS, Frank KA, Heller SS, & Hoar PF (1980): Type A behavior and blood pressure during coronary artery bypass surgery. Psychosom Med 42:407–414.

Kemple C (1945): Rorschach and psychosomatic diagnosis: Personality traits of patients with rheumatic disease, hypertensive cardiovascular disease, coronary occulsion, and fracture. Psychosom Med 7:85–89.

Keys A (1970): Coronary heart disease in seven countries: XIII, Multiple variables. Circulation 42:138–144.

Keys A, Taylor HL, Blackburn H, Brozek J, Anderson T, & Simonson E (1971): Mortality and coronary heart disease among men studied for 23 years. Arch Intern Med 128:201–214.

Kozarevic D, Pirk B, Dawber TR, Gordon T, & Zukel W (1976): The Yugoslavia cardiovascular disease study—1. The incidence of coronary heart disease by area. J Chronic Dis 29:405–414.

Krantz DS, Durel LA, Davia JE, Schaffer RT, Arabian JM, Dembroski TM, & MacDougall JM (1983): Propranolol medication among coronary patients: Relationship to Type A behavior and cardiovascular response. Hum Stress 8:4–12.

Krantz DS, Sanmarco ME, Selvester RH, & Matthews KA (1979): Psychological correlates of progression of atherosclerosis in men. Psychosom Med 41:467–475.

Light KC, & Obrist PA (1980): Cardiovascular reactivity to behavioral stress in young males with and without marginally elevated casual systolic pressures. Hypertension 2:802–808.

MacDougall JM, Dembroski TM, & Musante L (1979): The structured interview and questionnaire methods of assessing coronary prone behavior in male and female college students. J Behav Med 2:71–83.

MacDougall JM, Dembroski TM, & Krantz DS (1981): Effects of types of challenge on pressure and heart rate responses in Type A and B women. Psychophysiology 18:1–9.

Manuck SB, Craft SA, & Gold KJ (1978): Coronary-prone behavior pattern and cardiovascular response. Psychophysiology 15:403, 411.

Matthews K (1982): Psychological prospectives on the Type A behavior pattern. Psych Bull 91:293–323.

Matthews KA, & Brunson BI (1979): Allocation of attention and the Type A coronary-prone behavior pattern. J Pers Soc Psychol 37:2081–2090.

Matthews KA, Glass DC, Rosenman RH, & Bortner RW (1977): Competitive drive, pattern A and coronary heart disease: A further analysis of some data from the

Western Collaborative Group Study. J Chronic Dis 30:489–498.

Matthews K, Krantz D, Dembroski T, MacDougall JM (1982): Unique and common variance in structured interview and JAS measures of the Type A behavior pattern. J Bus Soc Psy 2:303–313.

Menninger KA, & Menninger WC (1936): Psychoanalytic observations in cardiac disorders. Am Heart J 11:10–21.

Michaels L (1966): Aetiology of coronary artery disease: An historical approach. Br Heart J 28:258–264.

MRFIT Collaborating Investigators (1976): The Multiple Risk Factor Intervention Trial (MRFIT)—A national study of primary prevention of coronary heart disease. JAMA 235:825.

Osler W (1892): *Lectures on Agnia Pectoris, and Allied States*. New York, Appleton.

Remington RD, Lambarth B, Moser M, & Hoobler SW (1960): Circulatory reactions of normative and hypertensive subjects and of the children of normal and hypertensive parents. Am Heart J 59:58.

Rose RM, Jenkins CD, & Hurst MW (1978): *Air traffic controller health change study*. Report to Federal Aviation Administration.

Rosenman RH (1978a): In *Coronary-Prone Behavior*. Dembroski TM, Feinlieb M, Haynes SG, Shields JL, & Weiss SM (Eds.). New York, Springer-Verlag.

Rosenman RH (1978b): The role of Type A behavior pattern in iaescemic heart disease: Modifications of its effects by beta blocking agents. Br J Clin Pract 32:[Suppl 1] 58–65.

Rosenman RH (1983): Current status of risk factors and the Type A behavior pattern in the pathogenesis of iaescemic heart disease. Dembroski TM, Schmidt TH, & Blumchen G (Eds.). In *Biobehavioral Bases of Coronary Heart Disease*. New York, Karger.

Rosenman RH, Brand RJ, Jenkins Cd, Friedman M, Straus R, & Wurm M (1975): Coronary heart disease in the Western Collaborative Group Study: Final follow-up experience of 8½ years. JAMA 233:872–877.

Rosenman RH, & Friedman M (1961): Association of specific behavior pattern in women with blood and cardiovascular findings. Circulation 24:1173–1184.

Rosenman RH, Friedman M, Straus R, Wurm M, Kositchek R, Hahn W, & Werthessen NT (1964): A productive study of coronary heart disease: The Western Collaborative Group Study. JAMA 189:15–22.

Rosenman RH, & Friedman M (1974): Neurogenic factors in pathogenesis of coronary heart disease. Med Clin North Am 58:268–279.

Scherwitz L, Berton K, & Leventhal H (1977): Type A behavior, self involvement, and cardiovascular response. Psychosom Med 39:229–240.

Scherwitz L, Berton K, & Leventhal H (1978): Type A assessment in the behavior pattern interview. Psychosom Med 40:593–609.

Schmeider R, Friedrich G, Neus H, & Ruddel H (1982): Effect of beta blockers on Type A coronary-prone behavior. Paper presented at the annual meeting of the Psychosomatic Society, Denver, March.

Schmidt TH (1983): Cardiovascular reactions and cardiovascular risks. Dembroski TM, Schmidt TH, & Blumchen G (Eds.). In *Biobehavioral Bases of Coronary Heart Diseases*. New York, Karger.

Schneiderman N (1978): Animal models relating behavioral stress and cardiovascular pathology. Dembroski TM, Feinlieb M, Haynes SG, Shields JL, Weiss SM (Eds.). In *Coronary-Prone Behavior*. New York, Springer-Verlag.

Schneiderman N (1983): Behavior, autonomic function and animal models of cardiovascular pathology. Dembroski TM, Schmidt TH, Blumchen G (Eds.). In *Biobehavioral Bases of Coronary Heart Disease*. New York, Karger.

Schuker B, & Jacobs DR (1977): Assessment of behavioral risk for coronary disease by voice characteristics. Psychosom Med 39:219–228.

Sime WE, Buell JC, & Eliot RS (1980): Cardiovascular responses to emotional stress (quiz #3 interview) in postmyocardial infarction patients and matched control subjects. J Hum Stress 6:39–46.

Snow B (1978): Level of aspiration in coronary prone and non-coronary prone adults. J Pers Soc Psychol Bull 4:416–419.

Streufert S, Streufert S, Dembroski T, & MacDougall J (1979): Complexity, coronary and physiological response. Eiser J, Grunberg M, & Oborne D (Eds.). In *Research in Psychology and Medicine*. London, Academic Press.

Van Egeren LF (1979a): Social interactions, communications, and the coronary-prone behavior pattern: A psychophysiological study. Psychosom Med 41:2–18.

Van Egeren LF (1979b): Cardiovascular changes during social competition in a mixed-motive game. J Pers Soc Psychol 37:858–864.

Weidner G, & Matthews KA (1978): Reported physical symptoms elicited by unpredictable events and the Type A coronary-prone behavior pattern. J Pers Soc Psychol 36:1213–1220.

White PD (1974): The historical background of angina reports. Mod Concepts Cardiovasc Dis 43:109.

Williams R, Haney T, Lee K, Kong Y, Blumenthal JA, & Whalen RE (1980): Type A behavior, hostility, and coronary atherosclerosis. Psychosom Med 42:539–549.

8

Anger and the Etiology and Progression of Physical Illness

Margret A. Appel
Larry Gorkin

Kenneth A. Holroyd

The suggestion that emotion plays a role in both the etiology and course of physical illness is neither new nor radical. Medical researchers and practitioners alike readily acknowledge the importance of mind–body relationships, at least in theory. Indeed, there has been a resurgence of interest in the role of emotional factors in illness, stimulated by the finding that standard physical risk factors identify only a minority of individuals who succumb to particular disorders and account for a disappointingly small proportion of the variance in the course of illness. The situation is improved little by the addition of nonspecific stress factors to predictive models.

Although the role of emotion in illness is generally acknowledged, the suggestion that particular emotions may differentially contribute to or influence disease states is less readily accepted. This lack of acceptance is, in part, the result of efforts to create a distance from psychodynamic formulations that associated specific emotions or conflicts with particular disorders. While the psychosomatic specificity formulations that dominated the field in the 1940s and 1950s generally failed to receive empirical support, there has been renewed interest in certain elements of these formulations, such as the role of emotional regulation in hypertension.

Another reason for the controversy concerning the role of specific emotions in illness is the widespread acceptance of concepts that general activation or arousal underlies all emotions in preference to theories positing specific physiological patterning for different emotions. We are encouraged to revive the specificity model by recent data suggesting at least some degree of physiological patterning for both emotions and the coping behaviors occasioned by those emotions (Holroyd,

1979; Holroyd & Lazarus, 1982; Mason, 1975). It should be noted that the generality and specificity positions are not mutually exclusive (Lazarus, 1977). Both generality and specificity are involved in the sequences of psychological and physiological changes that eventuate in somatic illness, although specificity notions provide a broader range of factors to account for variations in illness in different individuals and under different environmental conditions.

In this chapter we review evidence concerning the relationship of anger to illness. Following a general discussion of how emotion influences and is influenced by illness, we discuss the measurement of anger variables, the physiological changes associated with anger, and data implicating anger in the etiology and progression of specific physical disorders. Our goal is to demonstrate that anger may have particular relevance for certain disorders and that it is premature to dismiss it as a significant variable in the onset and course of illness: To this end, we have not provided an exhaustive critical review of the area, but rather, have been somewhat selective in the literature we chose to cite.

THE ROLE OF EMOTION IN ILLNESS

Attempts to investigate the role of specific emotions such as anger in health and illness have been plagued by at least two types of problems: the failure to keep in mind the various distinct pathways through which emotion can influence health and illness, and the tendency to treat emotions such as anger as unidimensional entities. Possible pathways for emotional influence on illness are discussed in this section, whereas issues in the measurement of anger are covered in the next section.

Emotions such as anger may contribute to illness through a number of pathways that vary in the directness of their influence (Fox, 1978; Holroyd, 1979; Holroyd et al., 1982; McFarland & Cobb, 1967; Steptoe, 1981). At the most direct level, emotion functions as an etiological factor in the progressive development of the disorder (e.g., hypertension) or in the precipitation of an acute crisis (e.g., sudden cardiac death). Neuroendocrine, immunological, and other physiological concomitants of emotion can disrupt homeostatic or protective mechanisms, triggering symptoms or damaging tissue in susceptible individuals. To date, attention has been focused primarily on such direct influences of emotion on illness.

Other less direct pathways may, however, be of more importance. Thus, emotions may stimulate coping efforts that more indirectly contribute to illness. This is most obviously the case when smoking, drinking, and overeating serve to manage or regulate emotion and at the same time expose individuals to physical risk factors for disease. Certain ways of coping with or managing emotion may also have interpersonal consequences that tax or strain interpersonal relationships and disrupt social support systems, thereby indirectly increasing vulnerability. Finally, psychological processes involved in the regulation of emotion may have their own physiological consequences that contribute to illness. We too rarely take account of these less direct pathways, preferring in much of our research and theorizing to focus instead on the more direct pathways associating the physiological concomitants of emotion with illness.

There has also been a tendency to emphasize the deleterious consequences of emotion. It is important to keep in mind that emotion may have beneficial effects. Thus, high prevalence of a particular emotion in a patient group may reflect not a pathogenic influence of the emotion on the development of illness, but the differential effect of the emotion on survival: those exhibiting the pattern of emotional responding are more likely to survive while those without it are more likely to die (McFarland & Cobb, 1967). Anger, for example, may have positive consequences when it mobilizes the patient to cope actively and thus serves as an antidote to hopelessness and depression, or when it results in the patient receiving more attention or better medical care than

would be received if he or she were more passive and less troublesome.

It also must be kept in mind that emotion may have no influence on the etiology or course of illness but may be a consequence of changes in health. For example, when metastatic and hormonal changes in cancer patients produce emotional and behavioral changes similar to those sometimes hypothesized to play a causal role in the disorder, we run the risk of making incorrect causal inferences about the role of emotion in illness (Fox, 1978). Finally, rather than one causing the other, the disease and emotional responses may co-occur because both result from the same innate biochemical, hormonal, and physiological patterns (Review Panel on Coronary-prone Behavior and Coronary Heart Disease, 1981; Thomas, 1976).

Some of the problems involved in elucidating the role of emotion in illness are currently being addressed. Attempts are being made to study patterns identified by retrospective research using prospective designs. The interaction of psychological and physiological variables in emotion is also being investigated with increasing sophistication. However, as the present review of the role of anger in illness illustrates, most of the research in this area is still at a fledgling stage.

ASSESSMENT OF ANGER

The relationship of anger and illness has been assessed by a variety of methods including self-report, interview, projective techniques, laboratory manipulations, and imaginal procedures. A review of measures of anger is beyond the scope of this chapter; instead, some general issues are raised that are often inadequately addressed in this literature.

Attempts to clarify the role of anger in the development and course of physical illness have been hindered by a lack of consensus concerning acceptable methods to assess anger arousal and management. It is unclear whether the focus should be on measures of the arousal of anger per se, on other relevant constructs (e.g., hostility, resentment, irritability), on the management and regulation of anger (e.g., repression, denial, suppression), or on the consequences of anger (e.g., aggression, guilt, physiological reactivity). Since investigators have tended to assess different variables, findings cannot be easily compared or integrated across studies.

Studies have most frequently relied on psychological tests, particularly self-report, to assess the anger variables hypothesized to play a role in illness. This reliance on psychological tests has led to a more one-dimensional view of anger than is warranted. Researchers have either looked at only one measure or have been limited in the scope of anger management variables they can investigate. In one of the few studies that looked at the dimensions of anger tapped by different anger measures, Biaggio (1980) identified five factors in four commonly used trait anger scales: willingness to experience and express anger; overt anger expression; attitude set of resentment, mistrust, and guilt; anger-provoking incidents; and negativism. In a factor analysis focusing specifically on anger measures used in hypertension research, Stauder et al. (1983) identified four factors. Despite this range of factors, certain more elusive anger management processes, such as suppression and denial, did not emerge as factors in either study. In general, neither self-report nor projective measures have proven particularly useful in assessing such processes.

The difficulties inherent in attempts to measure such management processes as suppression and denial are illustrated by the problem of how to interpret a low score on a self-report anger scale. The low score could reflect either truly low anger or defensive anger denial. A solution frequently proposed for this problem is to covary social desirability effects from self-report assessments in order to obtain an accurate reading of the subject's anger. However, evidence that differences in questionnaire-assessed social desirability may predict differences in actual anger management style (Conn & Crowne, 1964; Novaco, 1975) suggests that such covariation may yield misleading results. In these studies, high social desirability was associated with less behavioral expression of hostile feelings than was low social desirability; hence, it is not clear whether social desirability should be treated as a confounding variable or as a useful index of a particular style of anger management.

Structured interviews and laboratory tasks that actually evoke anger are more promising assessment procedures than are standard psychological tests. The structured interview has shown its superiority over self-report in the identification of the Type A risk factor for coronary heart disease (Jenkins et al., 1974; Rosenman et al., 1976). The superiority of the interview appears to reflect its relative advantage in tapping certain relevant stylistics (e.g., vigorous, explosive responses and displays of irritability) following interpersonal confrontation. In addition, individuals who are poor at self-appraisal or who use denial may be classified more accurately by the structured interview. Thus, the interview may be a more useful discriminator than self-report for some behavioral tendencies and for some populations.

Laboratory manipulations designed to engender anger also offer the advantage of tapping reactive characteristics to provocation. In addition, an even broader range of response variables, including physiological variables, can be more easily assessed in the laboratory than in the usual stress interview situation. Monitoring responses in several systems gives the investigator the opportunity to note relationships among systems. Relationships between self-report and behavior and between either of these variables and physiological responding may be particularly useful in providing clues to important regulatory processes not easily assessed by standard psychological tests. Certain anger management styles will be associated with concordance among response systems, whereas other styles will be associated with discordance among systems. Concordance may be associated with the truly low anger person who shows little arousal in terms of self-report, behavioral signs, and physiological responses. Response discordance may be used to index anger denial and suppression. A high anger denier might be expected to exhibit relatively high levels of physiological arousal during provocation but to report little anger and to show few or no behavioral signs of anger. On the other hand, anger suppression might be an appropriate classification for subjects who report high levels of anger and show high physiological arousal but exhibit no behavioral signs of anger. A similar classification system has been used successfully to study denial as a coping style in Type A individuals (Pittner & Houston, 1980).

In conclusion, the successful identification of psychological processes involved in illness requires assessment methods that can tap not only the arousal of emotion, but also the psychological mechanisms involved in the expression and regulation of emotion. We are particularly optimistic about the use of discrepancies between variables in different response classes to identify such processes. Interviews and laboratory tasks that actually evoke anger and allow the assessor to note discordance between verbal and nonverbal behavior or between these variables and physiological responding are more promising than standard psychological tests or self-report measures.

PHYSIOLOGICAL CORRELATES OF ANGER

Experimental Manipulations

Experimental manipulations designed to engender anger result in physiological changes indicative of increased arousal. A variety of frustration and harassment procedures have been found to produce increases in heart rate, blood pressure, peripheral vasoconstriction, skin conductance, muscle tension, and respiration rate (Ax, 1953; Erdmann & Van Lindern, 1980; Frodi, 1978; Funkenstein et al., 1954; Schachter, 1957; Van Egeren et al., 1978).

Psychological factors also influence physiological recovery. When subjects are given the opportunity to aggress against the frustrator, cardiovascular arousal decreases more rapidly than if they are not allowed to make a counterresponse (Hokanson & Burgess, 1962b; Hokanson & Shelter, 1961; Van Egeren et al., 1978). Aggression against a high-status frustrator or against a person other than the frustrator, however, does not lead to rapid decreases of arousal (Hokanson & Burgess, 1962a; Hokanson et al., 1963). Furthermore, smaller drops in cardiovascular responses occur when subjects have greater uncertainty about the consequences of interpersonal behavior (Van Egeren et al,, 1978). The latter studies are particularly germane to theories of hypertension that posit that continued inhibition or inappropriate expression of anger can contribute to the development of hypertension in genetically susceptible individuals.

Individual differences determine physiological reactivity to anger provocation. For example, Type A individuals show greater cardiovascular and catecholamine responses to harassment than Type B individuals (Glass et al., 1980). Compared to low-guilt individuals, high-guilt subjects show greater cardiovascular responses to provocation (Emerick et al., 1982) and less decrease or slight increases after aggressing towards a frustrator (Gambaro & Rabin, 1969; Schill, 1972). Differential physiological responses may also be associated with sex differences in coping with anger, depending on the type of provocation and the range of aggressive and reflective responses allowed (Frodi, 1978; Hokanson & Edelman, 1966).

Physiological Patterning

A central question is whether physiological changes associated with emotion reflect only a general activation dimension or whether specific emotions are associated with distinct physiological patterns. In general, hypotheses proposing specific physiological patterns have been in disfavor (e.g., Schachter & Singer, 1962). However, some evidence suggestive of physiological patterning has been found, particularly for anger versus fear. For example, early studies by Ax (1953), Schachter (1957), and others suggested that anger is likely to result in larger increases in diastolic than in systolic blood pressure, whereas fear and anxiety are likely to result in larger increases in systolic blood pressure. The results of these physiological patterning studies, together with data on blood pressure reactions to mecholyl, led Funkenstein (1955, 1956) to propose that anger directed outward is activated by norepinephrine and anxiety or anger directed inward is activated by epinephrine.

Recent studies have replicated the finding of greater diastolic blood pressures in anger than in fear induction (Schwartz et al., 1981; Weerts & Roberts, 1976). In addition, subjects who received orciprenaline, a beta-stimulant that has cardiovascular effects similar to epinephrine, reacted with anxiety and not anger to a situation in which subjects otherwise reacted only with anger (Erdmann & Van Lindern, 1980). Such results are consistent with the hypothesis that anger is associated with norepinephrine, whereas anxiety is associated with epinephrine. Furthermore, since the two catecholamines produce different cardiovascular effects, they may have differential implications for the development of cardiovascular disease (Henry & Meehan, 1981). Norepinephrine is associated with increases in cardiac output, blood pressure, and peripheral resistance, whereas epinephrine increases cardiac output but has a biphasic effect on blood pressure (partly due to vasodilation in the muscles), and less effect on peripheral resistance. Because they are associated with changes in both the myocardium and the peripheral vasculature, norepinephrine-produced cardiovascular changes may be more significant for the development of hypertension. Myocardial effects associated with either epinephrine or norepinephrine may be implicated in the development of coronary heart disease.

Attempts to differentiate anger from fear or anxiety on a physiological basis may be less significant for illness than differentiation of anger from other emotions such as depression. Depression has been implicated in the etiology or mortality of a number of disorders including coronary heart disease and cancer (e.g., Glass, 1977; Shekelle et al., 1981). Whereas anger is associated with norepinephrine and activity of the sympathetic–adrenal medullary system, depression is associated with corticosteroids and activity of the pituitary–adrenal cortical system (Henry & Stephens, 1977).

In an attempt to relate such emotion-produced hormonal changes to illness, Henry and Meehan (1981) speculated that the development of hypertension is related to activation of the norepinephrine branch of the sympathetic–adrenal medullary system, whereas coronary heart disease is related to activation of the adrenal cortical system and the epinephrine branch of the adrenal medulla, and disorders resulting from an altered immune response to adrenal cortical changes. Although the physiological mechanisms are probably much more complex, several lines of evidence presented in the following sections provide suggestive support for adrenal-mediated relationships between psychological factors and illness.

ESSENTIAL HYPERTENSION

The hypothesis that anger plays a role in the etiology of hypertension has been most closely associated with Alexander (1939, 1950). Alexander proposed that conflicts over the expression of anger lead to inhibition of aggressive and assertive tendencies by the individual at risk for hypertension. Because hostile impulses are frequently stimulated, suppression or denial of anger results in chronic tension. This tension is expressed somatically by physiological changes that eventuate in permanent hypertension. When hostile impulses are not vented or resolved constructively, the individual may be vulnerable to losing control and expressing anger inappropriately or excessively, creating additional discord in his or her social environment. Associated with the inhibition of hostility, Alexander also postulated a general inhibition of expressiveness, decreased effectiveness and efficiency, and high levels of anxiety.

In its most general sense, the hypothesis states that hypertensives will have problems with the experience and expression of anger and that these problems may manifest themselves at either extreme of the anger continuum. A series of interview studies conducted between the 1930s and 1960s provided

more consistent support for suppressed hostility than for any of the other psychological factors that had been hypothesized to be significant in the etiology of hypertension (Glock & Lennard, 1957). However, these studies have serious methodological flaws that limit their acceptability (Cochrane, 1971; Davies, 1971; Glock & Lennard, 1957; Scotch & Geiger, 1963).

Comparisons of Hypertensives and Normotensives

Anger problems have been identified in some hypertensives using self-report inventories. Compared to normotensives, hypertensives score higher on the Anger subscale of the Cornell Medical Index (Kidson, 1973), the Acting-out Hostility subscale of the Hostility and Direction of Hostility Questionnaire (Mann, 1977), and the Resentment and Anger Arousal factors of Baer's Brief Hypertension Instrument (Baer et al., 1979). High-renin hypertensives score higher on the Resentment, Verbal Aggression, and Irritability subscales of the Buss-Durkee Personality Inventory and are more likely to be classified in the Suppressed Hostility category by Harburg's Anger-in, Anger-out Scale (Esler et al., 1977). On the basis of their findings, Esler et al. described the overall personality profile associated with neurogenic hypertension as "one of controlled, guilt-prone, submissive persons with a high level of unexpressed anger" (p. 409).

Additional support for the anger hypothesis comes from laboratory studies that have found behaviors and traits indicative of anger problems. Diagnosed hypertensives have been found to use more gaze aversion during conflictual family role plays (Baer et al., 1980), to show more ineffective and inappropriate assertive behaviors and greater difficulty in emotional control in role plays (Kalis et al., 1957), to be more guarded and less self-disclosing in interviews (Handkins & Munz, 1978; Harris & Forsyth, 1973), and to express less negative affect when criticized (Matarazzo, 1954).

In one of the few studies that also monitored physiological activity, Sapira et al (1971) assessed reactions of hypertensives and normotensives to two types of filmed doctor–patient interaction. One doctor was relaxed and warm, whereas the other was rude and disinterested. Unlike the normotensives, who clearly differentiated the two doctors, the hypertensives denied seeing any differences between them. This effect was particularly apparent when the postfilm interviewer was the person who played the doctor in the films. Physiological data indicated that the hypertensives were more aroused than the normotensives, especially when they were denying role differences to the doctor-interviewer. Although Sapira et al. interpreted their results as indicating that hypertensives protectively misperceive or misinterpret potentially noxious stimuli, the data also can be interpreted as support for greater interpersonal sensitivity as well as greater appeasement and lack of assertiveness in interpersonal encounters.

The previous studies found differences in anger and associated characteristics in diagnosed hypertensives compared to normotensives. The observed differences may have etiological significance or they may have occurred for other reasons. Since hypertension is largely asymptomatic and many cases go undiscovered, there may be personality differences between hypertensives who seek medical treatment and those who do not. The personality characteristics may also be the result of hypertension or secondary to other factors associated with hypertension and its treatment. In order to determine whether psychological factors influence the development and course of hypertension, they must be shown to exist prior to the onset of the disorder. One approach to this task has been to study relationships between anger and blood pressure levels. Another strategy is to demonstrate relationships between anger and physiological precursors of hypertension other than blood pressure.

Relationships of Anger to Blood Pressure Levels

An example of the first approach is found in epidemiological studies examining the relationship between coping styles and blood pressure (Harburg et al., 1973; Harburg et al., 1979). Harburg et al. (1973) categorized white and black males on the basis of their responses to items concerning unjust treatment. The relationship of coping style to blood pressure varied somewhat by respondents' race and whether they lived in high- or low-stress areas. However, men who showed a suppressed hostility pattern generally had higher blood pressure (adjusted for age, weight, and other factors) and a greater incidence of hypertension. In a subsequent study using a different coding system, Harburg et al. (1979) found that resentment (defined by either showing anger or internalizing it) was associated with high blood pressure, whereas reflective problem solving was associated with lower blood pressure.

Two groups of researchers have assessed behavioral reactions of groups of normotensives differing in blood pressure levels. Harburg et al. (1964) found that high blood pressure males yielded more frequently during arguments in an experimental compromise task where they were paired with low blood pressure males who disagreed with them. Harris et al. (1953) found that, compared to low blood pressure subjects, women with high blood pressure were rated as less effective, less well-controlled and organized, more impulsive, and making a less favorable impression in a role play situation. In interviews conducted 4 years later, the women with high blood pressures were rated as hostile, having a low threshold for perceiving hostility in others, and behaving in ways to provoke anger in others (Harris & Forsyth, 1973; Kalis et al., 1961).

Precursors to Hypertension

Three lines of evidence suggest that cardiovascular reactivity can be a precursor to essential hypertension in genetically susceptible individuals. First, such reactivity has been observed in the early stages of the disorder (Kaplan, 1979). Second, cardiovascular reactivity can be an index of transient fluctuations in sympathetic activity that are precursors to hypertension (Kaplan, 1979; Obrist, 1981). Third, cardiovascular reactivity is associated with other variables that indicate a risk for hypertension, such as family history (Obrist, 1981). For this reason, we have examined the relationship between anger inhibition and cardiovascular reactivity in our laboratory.

In one study (Holroyd & Gorkin, in press) we found that both anger inhibition and family history of essential hypertension were associated with blood pressure and heart rate reactivity during anger-arousing role plays. In a second study (Emerick et al., 1982) we observed high and low hostility–guilt subjects who had either positive or negative family histories of hypertension. The subjects were monitored in an anger-arousing competitive task in which they were arbitrarily shocked by a confederate. High hostility–guilt was associated with less self-reported anger and less behavioral retaliation toward the confederate. Despite this calm exterior, high hostility–guilt subjects showed greater cardiovascular reactivity to the task than low hostility–guilt subjects (Fig. 8-1). Moreover, cardiovascular reactivity was greater for positive family history subjects than negative family history subjects. Thus, anger inhibition and family history both contributed to cardiovascular response. The family his-

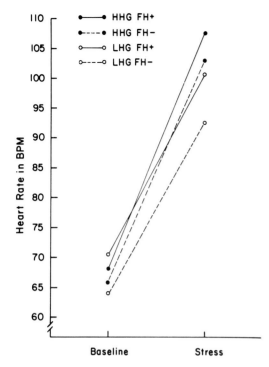

Figure 8-1. Mean heart rate in beats per minute (BPM) during nonstress day baseline and competitive reaction time task for high (HHG) and low (LHG) hostility–guilt subjects with positive (FH+) or negative (FH−) family histories of hypertension. (Adapted from Emerick KJ, Holroyd KA, Appel MA, Hursey KG, & Egrood JS, 1982: *Family history of essential hypertension and anger inhibition as determinants of cardiovascular reactivity to provocation.* Paper presented at the meeting of the Society of Behavioral Medicine, Chicago, March.)

tory effect has recently been replicated for heart rate and diastolic blood pressure reactivity in a study in which subjects competed with a harassing and deceitful confederate (Gorkin et al., 1983).

The results of these three studies together with those cited in the previous section agree with the research on established hypertensives in showing relationships between anger management and both blood pressure level and cardiovascular reactivity. By suggesting that such relationships predate the onset of established hypertension, the studies provide data suggestive of an etiological role.

Prospective Studies

Further support for the role of anger management in hypertension comes from two studies that followed subjects longitudinally. In a 5-year pro-

spective study of male Israeli civil service workers (Kahn et al., 1972), the only psychological factor that predicted incidence of hypertension was suppression of feelings in conflictual situations. Suppression was indicated by responses of brooding, keeping to self, and restraining from retaliation.

In a 20-year prospective study, McClelland (1979) found that inhibited power motive measured in males in their 30s predicted elevated blood pressure and hypertension. The men's motive patterns in their early 30s contributed more to variance in the age 50 blood pressures than did age 20 blood pressures. Individuals with the inhibited power motive pattern have a high need for power combined with a strong tendency to inhibit direct expression of this need by aggressive actions. Thus, inhibited power motive has some conceptual similarity to suppressed anger.

The previously cited studies provide a considerable body of converging evidence from different disciplines concerning the possible relationship of anger to essential hypertension. Using diverse measurement procedures, the research has implicated a variety of related variables including anger suppression, guilt proneness, resentment, behavioral inhibition, avoidance of conflict, and inappropriate assertiveness. However, a lack of consensus in assessment methods limits the conclusions that can be drawn from this body of research. For example, while almost all of the studies assessed anger inhibition, no two studies used the same assessment instrument. A factor analysis of the seven measures used in these studies revealed four distinct factors: negative emotional arousal, aggression/assertiveness, resentful versus reflective coping, and inhibited power motivation (Stauder et al., 1983). These results suggest that at least four dimensions of anger management have been assessed in the hypertension research. Studies are now needed to assess more precisely the specific anger management variables relevant for essential hypertension. This will probably require the development of assessment procedures designed specifically for this purpose. We have suggested that structured interview methods and confrontive laboratory situations may be particularly suited to the assessment of individual differences in the self-regulation of anger.

Studies in this area should also take account of moderator variables influencing the relationship between anger management variables and essential hypertension. For example, Esler et al. (1977) found that only essential hypertensives with high renin levels exhibited significant anger suppression, suggesting that anger management problems may be a contributing factor only in certain subgroups of hypertensives. Similarly, Harburg et al. (1973, 1979) found that residence in high- versus low-stress areas affected the relationship between style of anger management and blood pressure.

CORONARY HEART DISEASE

To date, the most successful attempt to relate an affective and behavioral pattern to disease is the identification of the Type A pattern for coronary heart disease. On the basis of clinical impressions, Friedman and Rosenman (1974; Rosenman, 1978) delineated a set of behavioral characteristics found in cardiac patients. A standardized stress interview was developed to discriminate individuals who show these characteristics (Type A) from those who do not (Type B). A landmark epidemiological study, the Western Collaborative Group Study (WCGS), determined that Type A men had twice the incidence of coronary disease as Type B men during an 8½-year prospective study period (Rosenman et al., 1975; Rosenman et al., 1976). The relationship with Type A persisted even when the standard coronary risk factors were statistically controlled.

WCGS participants were also administered the Jenkins Activity Survey (JAS), a questionnaire designed to assess Type A. JAS scores showed significant but not substantial associations with initial development of coronary heart disease. The association was somewhat higher for recurrent infarction (Jenkins et al., 1974; Jenkins et al., 1976). An increased risk of coronary heart disease for men with the Type A pattern was found also in the Framingham study (Haynes et al., 1980), and the relationship was extended to include women.

The Type A pattern comprises three major characteristics: competitive striving for achievement; sense of time urgency; and aggressiveness and hostility (Glass, 1977). Research on the Type A pattern is reviewed at length in Chapter 7 in this volume. Only a brief discussion of studies that relate specifically to the aggressiveness and hostility component is presented here.

Hostility and aggressiveness have received less attention in the Type A research literature than other variables such as time pressure and challenge. Although frequently mentioned as characteristic of Type A individuals, factor analytic studies of Type A measures have not identified separate aggression–hostility factors. However, items indicative of hostility and aggression load heavily on other

factors. For example, in a factor analysis of the WCGS interview data, "potential for hostility" loaded on the Competitive Drive factor and was more reliably associated with coronary heart disease than any other item on the factor (Matthews et al., 1977). A further testament to the significance of aggressiveness in Type A comes from a recent survey of research scientists studying coronary-prone behavior (Herman et al., 1981). The only two adjectives endorsed by 100 percent of the raters as characteristic of Type A individuals were "hurried" and "aggressive." Several other adjectives related to aggressiveness were endorsed by 90 percent or more of the raters: hostile, irritable, assertive, and dominant.

Laboratory data indicating greater aggressiveness in individuals classified as Type A have been presented by Glass (1977; Glass et al., 1980). Glass (1977) found that Type A individuals are not uniformly more aggressive than Type B subjects, but that hostility and aggression are elicited when Type A subjects are confronted with an appropriately challenging situation. Type A individuals delivered higher levels of shock to a confederate who harassed them than to a nonharassing confederate; whereas Type B subjects showed no differences in shock delivery to the two types of confederates. In Type A individuals cardiovascular and catecholamine activity also responded selectively to situational demands (Glass et al., 1980). Type A and Type B subjects showed similar cardiovascular and catecholamine increases in an engaging competition situation with a nonharassing opponent. However, when competing with a harassing opponent, the Type A subjects showed even greater increases in physiological activity, whereas Type B subjects reacted no more to the harassing opponent than to the nonharassing opponent. Thus, Type A individuals reacted to provocation with both increased aggressive behavior and increased physiological arousal.

Type A appears to be the most robust psychological measure related to coronary heart disease. However, the preeminence of total Type A has been challenged by recent findings. Dembroski et al. (1978) found hostility to be the component of the Type A interview that was most strongly associated with cardiovascular reactivity during a series of laboratory tasks. In fact, it is unclear from an inspection of their results whether the total Type A interview was more strongly associated with cardiovascular reactivity than the hostility component alone.

Williams et al. (1980) found that both hostility measured with a subscale of the MMPI and Type A as determined by interview were related to the presence of atherosclerosis in their patients. However, MMPI-assessed hostility was found to be more strongly related to atherosclerosis than the total Type A pattern. High scorers on the hostility scale were differentiated from low scorers by greater willingness "to endorse items suggesting a view of others as being inconsiderate, immoral, selfish, and deserving to be punished or hurt" (p. 544). These results are reminiscent of prospective data gathered by Ostfeld et al. (1964) which indicated that men who later developed coronary heart disease tended to be more suspicious about the motives of other people. This hostility–suspiciousness dimension deserves further investigation both in terms of its relationship to total Type A and as a predictor of coronary heart disease in its own right.

The major focus of coronary heart disease studies has been on expression of aggressiveness and hostility rather than suppression, although the latter has also received some attention. The degree of suppression proposed has varied from thinly veiled aggression to repression. One suggestion is that Type A individuals may suppress direct expression of hostility and aggressiveness and show it instead in a tendency to challenge or compete with others and by rancorous and contentious speech (Friedman & Rosenman, 1974; Glass, 1977). However, this suggestion remains an interesting speculation. In the Framingham studies, Haynes et al. (1980) assessed reaction to anger in terms of anger kept in, anger taken out on others, and discussion of anger with others. Suppressed hostility was a significant predictor of coronary heart disease among white-collar men and working women, independently of Framingham Type A and standard risk factors. Repressed hostility assessed with modified MMPI scales has also been associated with the presence of coronary heart disease and with an increased physiological risk for coronary heart disease (Kantor & Robertson, 1977). Clearly, the dimensions of anger management relevant to coronary heart disease must be specified more precisely than has been done to date.

Type A, in general, and aggressiveness–hostility, in particular, may affect coronary disease by at least two mechanisms (Glass, 1977; Henry & Meehan, 1981; Steptoe, 1981). One mechanism is similar to that proposed for hypertension, namely, increased sympathetically mediated physiological hyperreactivity associated with emotional reactions and behavioral coping responses. However, Glass (1977) has argued that what is important for coronary

heart disease is not hyperreactivity alone, but the repetitive alternation of hyperreactivity and hyporeactivity. He suggests that although Type A individuals initially respond to challenge with hyperreactivity, they are particularly prone to react with hyporeactivity if their coping efforts fail. Hyporeactivity would be expected to result in a different pattern of physiological responses than hyperreactivity. Specifically, hyporeactivity is associated with enhanced pituitary–adrenal cortical activity, whereas hyperreactivity is related to enhanced sympathetic–adrenal medullary activity. It may be that this combination of high adrenal medullary and high adrenal cortical activity is especially harmful in the development of cardiac disorders (Steptoe, 1981). The identification of a sequence or pattern of physiological activity that functioned specifically as a precursor to coronary heart disease would be of particular scientific and clinical value. It would not only contribute to our understanding of the pathogenesis of this disorder but might significantly enhance our ability to identify individuals at risk.

CANCER

Fox (1978) suggested that at least two types of personality are at greater risk to develop cancer: "extraverted, nonneurotic people" and "yielding, compliant, eager to please, 'good' people" (p. 106). For the first group, the greater risk appears to be mainly due to physical life style variables such as eating, drinking, and smoking rather than to extraversion per se. It is the second group that is of concern in the present discussion. The literature implies that behind the "good" exterior is a disgruntled, agitated person who has difficulty expressing emotion.

Anger has been studied sporadically in the cancer literature and the results have been mixed (e.g., Kissen, 1963; Thomas, 1976). Some of this inconsistency may be due to variability in types and sites of cancer (Fox, 1978; Sklar & Anisman, 1981). Psychological factors may, for example, be more significant to the extent that tumor induction and development are influenced by neuroendocrine and immunological functioning. Development of some tumors appears to be facilitated by catecholamine depletion and immunosuppression, whereas tumor inhibition may occur with increases in catecholamine activity (Sklar & Anisman, 1981). Neuroendocrine and immunological factors interact in complex ways and their effects may also vary depending on time of measurement and on the specific physiological functions being measured (Rogers et al., 1979).

Several recent studies on the relation between anger and cancer have focused on breast cancer. Greer and Morris (1975) found that women who were later diagnosed as having breast cancer differed from women with benign breast disease in their expression of anger. The women with breast cancer were rated as exhibiting greater degrees of both anger suppression and extreme anger expression in interview assessments. Although both patterns were found, anger suppression was more common. The finding of less expression of anger in women with breast cancer was confirmed in a second study by the same group of researchers (Morris et al. 1981). Patients who habitually suppressed anger had significantly higher levels of serum immunoglobulin A than patients who were able to express anger (Pettingale et al., 1977). Serum immunoglobulin A correlates positively with metastatic spread of breast cancer, providing suggestive data for a pathogenic role of anger suppression in this type of cancer.

Emotional expression is also related to cancer morbidity and mortality. Greer et al. (1979) found that women who responded to breast cancer with stoical acceptance or feelings of helplessness and hopelessness had poorer outcome over 5 years than women who reacted with denial or "fighting spirit." The same results were found after an additional 3 years of follow-up (Greer, 1981). Derogatis et al. (1979) also found that psychological factors were related to outcome in their prospective study of women with breast cancer. Although the differences between means tended to be small, long-term survivors had significantly higher scores on several negative affect dimensions, including self-reported hostility, alienation, guilt, and depression, than did short-term survivors. The treating oncologists rated the long-term survivors as less well-adjusted and as possessing more negative attitudes toward their illness and its treatment. Interviewer ratings also indicated poorer attitudes toward the physician in long-term survivors. Derogatis et al. characterized the difference between the two groups in terms of coping style. The long-term survivors were distressed and communicated their distress, whereas the short-term survivors were less able to communicate negative feelings.

These studies raise interesting questions concerning the role of anger in the course of breast cancer. Greer et al. (1979) reported no significant amounts of anger in their patients' reactions to the illness and also did not find that habitual anger expression style was associated with outcome. Derogatis et al. (1979) did find significant amounts of anger concerning the illness in some of their patients. A major factor accounting for the differences in anger reports between the two studies may be the difference in time of assessment. Reactions to cancer were assessed by Greer et al. shortly after masectomy; at this time the promise of successful treatment may arouse hope and mitigate angry reactions. On the other hand, Derogatis et al. assessed their patients after recurrence of the cancer when survival becomes more problematic. We might expect more anger at this time. Greer et al.'s finding that habitual anger expression was not related to outcome raises the possibility that the significant factor for outcome is illness-related anger rather than a more general anger expression style. Unfortunately, Greer et al. focused on the influence of psychological factors on outcome measures and did not report whether the patient's style of coping with illness was related to coping styles exhibited prior to illness.

Studies by both groups of investigators indicate that an active response to illness is associated with a more positive outcome for breast cancer than is a passive, hopeless response. This finding may apply to other cancers as well. For example, Shekelle et al. (1981) found that depression measured by the MMPI was associated with a twofold increase in cancer mortality over a 17-year prospective period. This result occurred independently of site and type of cancer and of various risk factors including age, smoking, alcohol use, and family history of cancer. An important factor in the relationship between depression and cancer mortality appears to be hopelessness (Bieliauskas & Garron, 1982). Anger is one antidote to the development of feelings of hopelessness, and, at times, may be a positive adaptive response in the cancer patient.

AGING

Beneficial effects of anger on survival have been reported for aging populations. One group of researchers (Lieberman, 1971, 1975; Tobin, 1980; Tobin and Lieberman, 1976; Turner et al., 1972) found that the single most powerful predictor of morbidity and mortality for aged individuals undergoing the stress of relocation was the dimension of passivity–aggressivity. More negative outcomes were associated with passivity, an effect which Tobin (1980) interpreted as due to passivity either facilitating biological disintegration or heightening stress.

Thus, passivity may lead to biological deterioration by hindering mobilization of internal resources required for survival; or passivity may heighten the experience of stress when a passive reaction is incongruent with environmental adaptive demands.

Aggressive behavior had the opposite effect on survival. The individuals who were most likely to survive were those who were "aggressive, irritating, narcissistic, and demanding.... Being a good guy—having qualities associated with passive acceptance—was a trait...found in old people most likely not to survive the crises of environmental change" (Lieberman, 1975, p. 155). Individuals who displayed more aggressive characteristics were more likely to realistically appraise threat and less likely to deny its emotional impact, which facilitated adaptation and maintenance of self-image. Similar results were reported by Aldrich and Mendkoff (1963). Patients who showed an overtly angry or philosophical response to relocation had the lowest mortality rates, whereas patients who were depressed or used denial had the highest death rates.

The Framingham study (Haynes et al., 1980) has provided additional data relevant to the relationship of psychological factors to survival in aging. In contrast to the association between Type A and coronary heart disease found in white-collar men under 65, Type B behavior was associated with myocardial infarction in blue-collar workers over 65 years of age. Haynes et al. suggested that this apparent reversal may reflect either selective survival or a health consequence of retirement. Further research is needed to determine whether the results reflect a true age-related reversal of Type A and Type B effects on coronary heart disease or whether they are an artifact of differential survival rates or of differential stresses associated with work roles.

The findings that emerge most clearly from the aging research concern the relationship of the passivity–aggressivity dimension to morbidity and mortality when the elderly experience the stress of relocation. A question raised by this research is whether aggressivity becomes a survival asset only within a period relatively close to death or whether it is an asset at all ages. Gutmann (1977) suggested that the ability to externalize anger may have general survival value at any age and across populations. He cited cross-cultural data on aging, as well as observations of individuals in Japanese and Nazi prison camps, to support his thesis. Passivity, depression, and withdrawal were associated with the development of physical illness and death, whereas vigilance, externalization of anger, and activity were associated with survival. The needling of withdrawn individuals to arouse anger even appeared to be useful as a lifesaving measure in the Japanese prison camps (Nardini, 1952).

CONCLUSIONS

We have reviewed evidence concerning the relationship of anger to essential hypertension, coronary heart disease, breast cancer, and mortality in the aged. While a considerable body of evidence suggests that anger and related variables play a role in illness, the evidence also indicates that the relationship between anger and the pathogenesis and progression of disease is not likely to be a simple one. Thus research on hypertension and cancer has focused on the pathogenic effects of anger *suppression* on cardiovascular and immune function, at the same time that research on coronary heart disease has focused on similar pathogenic effects of anger *expression*. Alternately, anger expression was associated with benefits for breast cancer victims and the relocated elderly, effects that may be mediated by the social consequences of this behavior.

These findings appear to be somewhat contradictory. They may, however, be reconciled by assuming that either extreme of anger expression may be pathogenic for illness, depending on the levels of anger involved and the appropriateness of anger to the actual threat to the individual. Anger may be pathogenic when it is excessive or occurs in a wide variety of situations independent of the actual threat they pose. This appears to be the case for Type A individuals. When individuals react with moderate levels of anger to situations realistically perceived as threatening, as in the case of cancer recurrence, the effect may be beneficial. Thus, while Derogatis et al.'s (1979) long-term cancer survivors had higher anger scores than short-term survivors, the absolute levels of anger were not high. This suggests that rather than being incapacitated by their anger, these patients were able to use their anger to combat feelings of hopelessness and to obtain responsive medical treatment.

The levels and types of anger that facilitate survival are likely to be those that lead to activity and to assertiveness in getting one's needs met without disrupting needed social relationships. Increased susceptibility to disease is more likely to occur when anger leaves interpersonal conflict situations unresolved or disrupts social support systems. Thus, the arousal of anger is likely to be less important in illness than the ways in which the individual manages anger.

The variety of descriptors and defining operations for anger and anger-related variables in the research makes simple conclusions about the effects of anger premature. Individual investigators have tended to focus on limited aspects of anger arousal and management, often ignoring the variables studied by their colleagues. Research is needed to address the relationship of the various types of anger measures to one another and to illness. This requires closer attention to defining operations and the use of more multidimensional assessment than has been the case in much of the existing research. In this regard, we are more optimistic about comparisons across multiple response systems when individuals are exposed to anger-provoking interviews and laboratory situations than we are about the information provided by standard psychological tests.

Research also needs to be addressed to the different pathways by which psychological processes affect illness. This requires better control of known physical risk factors and more attention to the demands the social environment makes on the individual, as well as the responses of the environment to the individual's coping efforts. Although we have emphasized that the disruption of social relationships may frequently be more important than physiological arousal per se, more research is needed to clarify the physiological mechanisms underlying pathogenic influences.

REFERENCES

Aldrich CK, & Mendkoff E (1963): Relocation of the aged and disabled: A mortality study. J Am Geriatr Soc 11:185–194.

Alexander F (1939): Emotional factors in essential hypertension. Psychosom Med 1:173–179.

Alexander F (1950): *Psychosomatic Medicine*. New York, Norton.

Ax AF (1953): The physiological differentiation between fear and anger in humans. Psychosom Med 15:433–442.

Baer PE, Collins FH, Bourianoff GG, & Ketchel MF (1979): Assessing personality factors in essential hypertension with a brief self-report instrument. Psychosom Med 41:321–330.

Baer PE, Vincent JP, Williams BJ, Bourianoff GG, & Bartlett PC (1980): Behavioral response to induced conflict in families with a hypertensive father. Hypertension [Suppl. I] 2:I-70-I-77.

Biaggio MK (1980): Assessment of anger arousal. J Pers Assess 44:289–298.

Bieliauskas LA, & Garron DC (1982): Psychological depression and cancer. Gen Hosp Psychiatry 4:187–195.

Cochrane R (1971): High blood pressure as a psychosomatic disorder: A selective review. Br J Soc Clin Psychol 10:61–72.

Conn L, & Crowne DP (1964): Instigation to aggression, emotional arousal, and defensive emulation. J Pers 32:163–179.

Davies MH (1971): Is high blood pressure a psychosomatic disorder?: A critical review of the evidence. J Chronic Dis 24:239–258.

Dembroski TM, MacDougall JM, Shields JL, Petitto J, & Lushene R (1978): Components of the Type A coronary-prone behavior pattern and cardiovascular responses to psychomotor performance challenge. J Behav Med 1:159–176.

Derogatis LR, Abeloff MD, & Melisaratos N (1979): Psychological coping mechanisms and survival time in metastatic breast cancer. JAMA 242:1504–1508.

Emerick KJ, Holroyd KA, Appel MA, Hursey KG, & Ergood JS (1982): Family history of essential hypertension and anger inhibition as determinants of cardiovascular reactivity to provocation. Paper presented at the meeting of the Society of Behavioral Medicine, Chicago, March.

Erdmann G, & Van Lindern B (1980): The effects of beta-adrenergic stimulation and beta-adrenergic blockade on emotional reactions. Psychophysiology 17:332–338.

Esler M, Julius S, Yueiffer A, Randall O, Harburg E, Gardiner H, & DeQuattro V (1977): Mild high-renin hypertension: Neurogenic human hypertension? N Engl J Med 296: 405–411.

Fox BH (1978): Premorbid psychological factors as related to cancer incidence. J Behav Med 1: 45–133.

Friedman M, & Rosenman R (1974): *Type A Behavior and Your Heart*. New York, Knopf.

Frodi A (1978): Experiential and physiological responses associated with anger and aggression in women and men. J Res Pers 12: 335–349.

Funkenstein DH (1955): The physiology of fear and anger. Sci Am 192(5): 74–80.

Funkenstein DH: Nor-epinepherine-like and epinepherine-like substances in relation to human behavior. J Nerv Ment Dis 124: 58–68.

Funkenstein DH, King SH, & Drolette M (1954): The direction of anger during a laboratory stress-inducing situation. Psychosom Med 16: 404–413.

Gambaro S, & Rabin AI (1969): Diastolic blood pressure responses following direct and displaced aggression after anger arousal in high- and low-guilt subjects. J Pers Soc Psychol 12:87–94.

Glass DC (1977): *Behavior Patterns, Stress, and Coronary Disease*. New York, Erlbaum.

Glass DC, Krakoff LR, Contrada R, Hilton WF, Kehoe K, Mannucci EG, Collins C, Snow B, & Elting E (1980): Effect of harassment and competition upon cardiovascular and plasma catecholamine responses in Type A and Type B individuals. Psychophysiology 17:453–463.

Glock CY, & Lennard HL (1957): Psychologic factors in hypertension: An interpretive review. J Chronic Dis 5: 174–185.

Gorkin L, Appel MA, Holroyd KA, Stauder LJ, Saab PG, & Upole VK (1983): Family history of hypertension as a determinant of cardiovascular, behavioral, and self-report responding during anger provocation. Paper presented at the meeting of the Society of Behavioral Medicine, Baltimore, March.

Greer S (1981): Psychological response to breast cancer and eight-year outcome. Paper presented at the meeting of the American Psychological Association, Los Angeles, August.

Greer S, & Morris T (1975): Psychological attributes of women who develop breast cancer: A controlled study. J Psychosom Res 19: 147–153.

Greer S, Morris T, & Pettingale KW (1979): Psychological response to breast cancer: Effect on outcome. Lancet 2: 785–787.

Gutmann D (1977): The cross-cultural perspective: Notes toward a comparative psychology of aging. Birren JE, & Schaie KW (Eds.). In Handbook of the Psychology of Aging. New York, Van Nostrand Reinhold.

Handkins RE, & Munz DC (1978): Essential hypertension and self-disclosure. J Clin Psychol 34: 870–875.

Harburg E, Blakelock EH, & Roeper PJ (1979): Resentful and reflective coping with arbitrary authority and blood pressure: Detroit. Psychosom Med 41: 189–202.

Harburg E, Erfurt JC, Hauenstein LS, Chape C, Schull WJ, & Schork MA (1973): Socio-ecological stress, suppressed hostility, skin color, and black–white male blood pressure: Detroit. Psychosom Med 35: 276–296.

Harburg E, Julius F, McGinn NF, McLeod J, & Hoobler SW (1964): Personality traits and behavioral patterns associated with systolic blood pressure levels in college males. J Chronic Dis 17: 405–414.

Harris RE, & Forsyth RP (1973): Personality and emotional stress in essential hypertension in man. Onesti G, Kim KE, & Moyer JH (Eds.). In Hypertension: Mechanisms and Management. New York, Grune & Stratton.

Harris RE, Sokolow M, Carpenter LG, Freedman M, & Hunt SP (1953): Response to psychologic stress in persons who are potentially hypertensive. Circulation 7: 874–879.

Haynes SG, Feinleib M, & Kannel WB (1980): The relation of psychosocial factors to coronary heart disease in the Framingham Study: III. 8-year incidence of coronary heart disease. Am J Epidemiol 111: 37–58.

Henry JP, & Meehan JP (1981): Psychosocial stimuli, physiological specificity, and cardiovascular disease. Weiner H, Hofer MA, & Stunkard AJ (Eds.). In Brain, Behavior, and Bodily Disease. New York, Raven Press.

Henry JP, & Stephens PM (1977): Stress, Health, and the Social Environment. New York, Springer.

Herman S, Blumenthal JA, Black GM, & Chesney MA (1981): Self-ratings of Type A (coronary prone) adults: Do Type A's know they are Type A's? Psychosom Med 43: 405–413.

Hokanson JE, & Burgess M (1962a): The effects of status, type of frustration, and aggression on vascular processes. J Abnorm Soc Psychol 65: 232–237.

Hokanson JE, & Burgess M (1962b): The effects of three types of aggression on vascular processes. J Abnorm Soc Psychol 64: 446–449.

Hokanson JE, Burgess M, & Cohen MF (1963): The effect of displaced aggression on systolic blood pressure. J Abnorm Soc Psychol 67: 214–218.

Hokanson JE, & Edelman R (1966): The effects of three social responses on vascular processes. J Pers Soc Psychol 3: 442–447.

Hokanson JE, & Shelter S (1961): The effect of overt aggression on physiological arousal. J Abnorm Soc Psychol 63: 446–448.

Holroyd KA (1979): Stress, coping, and the treatment of stress-related illness. McNamara JR (Ed.). In Behavioral Approaches in Medicine: Application and Analysis. New York, Plenum Press.

Holroyd KA, Appel MA, & Andrasik F (1982): A cognitive-behavioral approach to psychophysiological disorders. Meichenbaum DH, & Jaremko ME (Eds.). In Stress Prevention and Management: A Cognitive-Behavioral Approach. New York, Plenum Press.

Holroyd KA, & Gorkin L (in press): Young adults at risk for essential hypertension: Effects of family history and anger management in determining responses to interpersonal conflict. J Psychosom Res.

Holroyd KA, & Lazarus RA (1982): Stress, coping and somatic adaptation. Goldberger L, & Breznitz S (Eds.). In Handbook of Stress. New York, Free Press.

Jenkins CD, Rosenman RH, & Zyzanski SJ (1974): Prediction of clinical coronary heart disease by a test for the coronary-prone behavior pattern. N Engl J Med 290: 1271–1275.

Jenkins CD, Zyzanski SJ, & Rosenman RH (1976): Risk of new myocardial infarction in middle aged men with manifest coronary heart disease. Circulation 53: 342–347.

Kahn HA, Medalie JA, Neufeld HN, Riss E, & Goldbourt V (1972): The incidence of hypertension and associated factors: The Israeli ischemic heart disease study. Am Heart J 84: 171–182.

Kalis BL, Harris RE, Bennett LF, & Sokolow M (1961): Personality and life history factors in persons who are potentially hypertensive. J Nerv Ment Dis 132: 457–468.

Kalis BL, Harris RE, Sokolow M, & Carpenter LG (1957): Response to psychological stress in patients with essential hypertension. Am Heart J 53: 572–578.

Kantor S, & Robertson AJ (1977): Repressed hostility and coronary heart disease: Reappraisal of a relationship in terms of a meaning-focused approach to psychological measurement. Soc Sci Med 11: 625–634.

Kaplan N (1979): The Goldblatt Memorial Lecture, Part II: The role of the kidney in hypertension. Hypertension 1: 456–461.

Kidson MA (1973): Personality and hypertension. J Psychosom Res 17: 35–43.

Kissen D (1963): Personality characteristics in males conducive to lung cancer. Br J Med Psychol 36: 27–36.

Lazarus RS (1977): Cognitive and coping processes in emotion. Monat A, & Lazarus RS (Eds.). In *Stress and Coping*. New York, Columbia University Press.

Lieberman MA (1971): Some issues in studying psychological predictors of survival. Palmore E, & Jeffers FC (Eds.). In *Prediction of Life Span*. Lexington, Mass., Heath.

Leiberman MA (1975): Adaptive processes in late life. Datan N, & Ginsberg LH (Eds.). In *Life-Span Developmental Psychology: Normative Life Crises*. New York, Academic Press.

Mann AH (1977): Psychiatric morbidity and hostility in hypertension. Psychol Med 7: 653–659.

Mason JW (1975): Emotions as reflected in patterns of endocrine integration. Levi L (Ed.). In *Emotions—Their Parameters and Measurement*. New York, Raven Press.

Matarazzo D (1954): An experimental study of aggression in the hypertensive patient. J Pers 22: 423–447.

Matthews KA, Glass DC, Rosenman RH, & Bortner RW (1977): Competitive drive, pattern A, and coronary heart disease: A further analysis of some data from the Western Collaborative Group Study. J Chronic Dis 30: 489–498.

McClelland DC (1979): Inhibited power motivation and high blood pressure in men. J Abnorm Psychol 88: 182–190.

McFarland DV, & Cobb S (1967): Causal interpretations from cross sectional data: An examination of the stochastic processes involved in the relation between a personal characteristic and coronary heart disease: J Chronic Dis 20: 393–406.

Morris T, Greer S, Pettingale KW, & Watson M (1981): Patterns of expression of anger and their psychological correlates in women with breast cancer. J Psychosom Res 25: 111–117.

Nardini J (1952): Survival factors in American prisoners of war of the Japanese. Am J Psychiatry 109: 241–248.

Novaco RW (1975): *Anger Control: The Development and Evaluation of an Experimental Treatment*. Lexington, Mass., Heath.

Obrist PA (1981): *Cardiovascular Psychophysiology: A Perspective*. New York, Plenum Press.

Ostfeld AM, Lebovits BZ, Shekelle RB, & Paul O (1964): A prospective study of the relationship between personality and coronary heart disease. J Chronic Dis 17: 265–276.

Pettingale KW, Greer S, & Tee DE (1977): Serum IgA and emotional expression in breast cancer patients. J Psychosom Res 21: 395–399.

Pittner MS, & Houston BK (1980): Response to stress, cognitive coping strategies, and the Type A behavior pattern. J Pers Soc Psychol 39: 147–157.

Review Panel on Coronary-prone Behavior and Coronary Heart Disease (1981): Coronary-prone behavior and coronary heart disease: A critical review. Circulation 63: 1199–1215.

Rogers MP, Dubey D, & Reich P (1979): The influence of the psyche and the brain on immunity and susceptibility: A critical review. Psychosom Med 41: 147–164.

Rosenman RH (1978): The interview method of assessment of the coronary-prone behavior pattern. Dembroski TM, Weiss SM, Shields JL, Haynes SG, & Feinleib M (Eds.). In *Coronary-Prone Behavior*. New York, Springer, Verlag.

Rosenman RH, Brand RJ, Jenkins CD, Friedman M, Straus R, & Wurm M (1975): Coronary heart disease in the Western Collaborative Group Study: Final follow-up experience of 8½ years. JAMA 233:872–877.

Rosenman RH, Brand RJ, Sholtz RI, & Friedman M (1976): Multivariate prediction of coronary heart disease during 8½ year follow-up in the Western Collaborative Group Study. Am J Cardiol 37:903–910.

Sapira JD, Scheib ET, Moriarity R, & Shapiro AP (1971): Differences in perception between hypertensive and normotensive populations. Psychosom Med 33: 239–250.

Schachter J (1957): Pain, fear, and anger in hypertensives and normotensives: A psychophysiological study. Psychosom Med 19: 17–29.

Schachter S, & Singer J (1962): Cognitive, social, and physiological determinants of emotional state. Psychol Rev 69: 379–399.

Schill TR (1972): Aggression and blood pressure responses of high- and low-guilt subjects following frustration. J Consult Clin Psychol 38: 461.

Schwartz GE, Weinberger DA, & Singer JA (1981): Cardiovascular differentiation of happiness, sadness, anger, and fear following imagery and exercise. Psychosom Med 43: 343–364.

Scotch N, & Geiger HJ (1963): The epidemiology of essential hypertension: II. Psychological and sociocultural factors in etiology. J Chronic Dis 16: 1183–1213.

Shekelle RB, Raynor WJ, Ostfeld AM, Garron DC, Bieliauskas LA, Liu SC, Maliza C, & Paul O (1981): Psychological depression and 17-year risk of death from cancer. Psychosom Med 43: 117–125.

Sklar LS, & Anisman H (1981): Stress and cancer. Psychol Bull 89: 369–406.

Stauder LJ, Holroyd KA, Appel MA, Gorkin L, Upole VK, & Saab PG (1983): Anger and essential hypertension: A factor analysis of measures used in recent research. Paper presented at the meeting of the Society of Behavioral Medicine, Baltimore, March.

Steptoe A (1981): *Psychological Factors in Cardiovascular Disorders*. London, Academic Press.

Thomas CB (1976): Precursors of premature disease and death: The predictive potential of habits and family attitudes. Ann Intern Med 85: 653–658.

Tobin SS (1980): Institutionalization of the aged. Datan N, & Lohmann N (Eds.). In *Transitions of Aging*. New York, Academic Press.

Tobin SS, & Lieberman MA (1976): *Last Home for the Aged: Critical Implications of Institutionalization*. San Francisco, Jossey-Bass.

Turner BF, Tobin SS, & Lieberman MA (1972): Personality traits as predictors of institutional adaptation among the aged. J Gerontol 27: 61–68.

Van Egeren LF, Abelson JL, & Thornton DW (1978): Cardiovascular consequences of expressing anger in a mutually-dependent relationship. J Psychosom Res 22: 537–548.

Weerts TC, & Roberts R (1976): The physiological effects of imagining anger-provoking and fear-provoking scenes. Psychophysiology 13: 174 (Abstract).

Williams RB Jr., Haney TL, Lee KL, Kong Y, Blumenthal JA, & Whalen RE (1980): Type A behavior, hostility, and coronary atherosclerosis. Psychosom Med 42: 539–549.

PART III

The Physiological Dimension

9

A New Approach to the Study of Physiology and Emotion

Enoch Callaway

"Abjure the Why and Seek the How"—*The Kasidah* by Sir Richard Burton

These chapters in Part III provide us with a feast of How. They consider how endorphins influence psychological processes, how psychological processes interact with the immune system, and how light in the environment interacts with the neurophysiology of the brain. This preoccupation with *how* is a sign that psychiatry and psychology are coming of age, and these chapters are a contribution to that still evolving pattern of thought. Most clinicians need the continuing support of such papers as we try to relinquish our traditional preoccupation with *why*.

Unlike many of the other branches of modern medicine, the practice of psychological medicine retains many characteristics of ordinary social behavior. Physical examinations and surgical procedures are clearly set apart from customary social interchange. By contrast, psychotherapy has been referred to as the "rent-a-friend" business. Perhaps the common social preoccupation with *why* has something to do with the reason psychiatry has for so long been fixated at the *why* stage of intellectual development.

As humans, we are fascinated by questions of motivation, responsibility and free will. All these points of view raise questions of *why*. This preoccupation is most useful for our inner dialogue. One needs to be as clear as possible about one's intentions. We must continually ask ouselves why we take a particular action. Immediate goals must be evaluated on their own merit and also considered in the light of higher goals. These considerations naturally lead us to ask ourselves why.

This inner dialogue often spills over into conversations with those who seem at times to be extensions of ourselves. That, in itself, may be a poor practice. When I say to my wife, "Why did you forget to buy my favorite breakfast cereal?" I might more honestly have said, "I'm unhappy that you didn't buy what I wanted."

This way of thinking is even more inappropriate when it spills over into professional relationships. What use is it for the teacher to ask the hyperactive boy why he is so disruptive in class? What use is it for the psychotherapist to ask a neurotic patient why a repeated piece of disruptive behavior persists in recurring?

When I first began to study psychotherapy, our teacher required us to take detailed notes of everything we said. He claimed that we might remember what the patient said, but we were almost certain to forget some of our own remarks. We were regularly scolded for using the word *why*, as being generally an uninformative line of inquiry. Instead, we were encouraged to ask for details of what was said and felt. Such details could lead to more useful inquiry into how symptoms developed.

Today I am not sure I would go so far as to outlaw the use of *why* in psychotherapy. For example, it is often useful to consider mutual ultimate goals with a patient. The question, "Why are we working together?" often needs to be raised explicitly. In general, however, psychotherapists would, for the most part, do well to avoid the use of *why*.

There are many ways to defend the assertion that *how* is more intellectually mature and more useful than *why*. At the simplest level, *why* tends to be passive and past tense. People who believe that control lies in the hands of others usually end up wondering why their lives take the courses they do. *How* tends to be active and future tense. The active person considers how things work so that a choice of actions can be made responsibly. Often *why* is guilt provoking and actually unanswerable. The parent who asks the child, "Why did you soil yourself?" would no doubt be astounded if the child launched into a learned discussion of the multiple determinants for such an act. The question is obviously not intended to elicit information but rather to provoke shame. *How* is the question of science. If I think I know how something works, I can test that idea against action in the real world. Ideas about how things work are affirmable. Having decided on a *how*, we can learn whether or not it works.

This volume deals with the scientific foundations of clinical practice, but these chapters have a clinical utility far beyond any clinically relevant details that they may contain. That added value comes from directing our thoughts to the *how* of things. Not long ago, I was presenting some of our work on hyperactive children to a professional audience. Our data show that by using a relatively simple computer analysis, the EEGs of hyperactive children can be reliably distinguished from those of age-matched normal children. For example, hyperactive children have lower power in the EEG over the frequencies from 13 to 24 Hz than do normal children of the same age. Using this simple EEG power spectral measure, we correctly classified all of the hyperactive children in our group and all but one of the normals. Hyperactives also respond to treatment with stimulant medication by becoming calmer and less disruptive in the classroom and by performing more adequately on laboratory tests. A professional in my audience rhetorically inquired; "This confirms my suspicions about why these kids are disruptive. The cause is physiological, so requiring the families of hyperactive children to go for psychological help is a rip-off. Doesn't the fact that drugs help these children prove that hyperactivity is not psychological?"

I wish I knew an answer to such a question that would really be helpful to the questioner. How does one tactfully say that a question reflects a confused point of view? The best I could do at the moment was to point out that stimulants also improve the performance of normal children, so a response to a stimulant does not set the hyperactive children apart from the normals. Furthermore, the behavior of the hyperactive child is very much a function of the surroundings. In the one-to-one relationship we provide in the laboratory, most of them are quite well behaved. Finally, behavior modification procedures can improve the classroom performance of these children. All of this is, again, quite compatible with evidence that genetic factors play a role in the hyperactivity of some children. The point is, if we

ask how the hyperactive behavior is initiated and maintained, and how we can help the child, we can be useful. If we are trapped by musing over *why*, we are likely to become confused and useless.

Researchers who study EEGs have contributed more than their share of *why*-type speculations. For example, over the ages of 7 to 12 years, when hyperactive children are likely to come for treatment, the beta power of normals is increasing. Since hyperactives have low beta power, they have EEGs which in that respect resemble the EEGs of younger children. Such observations have stimulated speculations that hyperactivity is due to maturational lag. This explanation of why children become hyperactive does not help much. Even worse, it does not fit much of the data. For example, even with respect to other EEG studies, there are ways in which hyperactives seem to lead rather than lag normals in maturation.

If we can understand how EEG beta power is controlled by the brain, we may learn about how hyperactivity comes about. If, on the other hand, we find the child with hyperactive behavior but with normal beta power, we might wonder how this hyperactivity came to be and perhaps examine the school and family situation more closely in such cases.

As these chapters show, it takes an enormous volume of empirical observations to support the *how* habit. In earlier times, psychiatry boasted of the highest theory/fact ratio in medicine. Some investigators seem to retain this old habit of valuing theory more than observations.

A psychiatrist, distinguished for his inquiries into the psychogenic aspects of schizophrenia, was very upset by evidence for a genetic basis for this disorder. He is reported to have remarked that he did not believe the data on a genetic basis for schizophrenia, but even if the data were not false, he felt they should be suppressed. He believed that the demonstration of a genetic basis for schizophrenia would deal a staggering blow to the studies of psychogenic factors and of psychological treatment in that disorder. He was afraid that evidence for a genetic factor in schizophrenia would explain "why people develop the disorder." An organic explanation would then demand an organic approach so that the cause of the disorder could be treated. That sort of irrational fear is particularly bizarre in light of the history of psychological approaches to schizophrenia. Freida Fromm-Reichman was the most gifted pioneer in the psychotherapy of schizophrenia. She borrowed much of her approach from her teacher, Kurt Goldstein, who developed his approaches working with grossly brain-damaged patients. *How* should modify our notions of *why*, and not vice versa.

We need to be on guard against confused thinking and we can take hope from the type of work pre-sented here. A new generation of investigators is developing and it appears that questions of *how* come naturally to their mind. In these chapters the authors present fascinating observations and con-ceptualizations and stimulate further thought on the questions of *how*.

10

Neuroanatomic Correlates of Emotion

Jonathan Mueller

"Love of an idea is love of God."—Frank Lloyd Wright
"Every world is a prejudice."—F. W. Nietzsche

It could be argued that since the introduction of lithium (Cade, 1949) and chlorpromazine (Delay & Deniker, 1952) in the late 1940s and early 1950s, the major advances in psychiatry have been pharmacologic. Current literature suggests the likelihood that neuromodulatory roles will be discovered for myriad neuropeptides in the near future (Snyder, 1980). Parallel to this, training in psychopharmacology has become a central focus of modern psychiatric residencies.

By contrast, a psychiatric resident's knowledge of neuroanatomy is likely to reflect what he or she recalls from the first year of medical school. Such a student of behavior may be able to talk comfortably about mechanisms for the reuptake of neurotransmitters, but probably has little idea as to where the relevant receptors are located or what pathways lead to them. Thus, while an immense technology attains to ever greater sophistication in psychopharmacology and neurophysiology, a curious "black box" view of the brain persists in psychiatry.

In 1965 Geschwind, returning to work of German neurologists such as Wernicke and Liepmann, proposed the utility of conceptualizing disturbances of higher cortical function in terms of altered connections between cortical regions more or less specialized in function. In 1966 Luria's *Higher Cortical Functions in Man* became available in the United States. Together with Geschwind's work, it brought behavioral disorders secondary to brain lesions to the attention of American neurologists.

Over the past 15 years researchers in behavioral neurology have attempted to understand alterations in cognitive and affective functioning with reference to the brain as a structured organ. Numerous texts of neuropsychology reflect the growth of this area (e.g., Pincus & Tucker, 1974; Benson & Blumer, 1975; Lezak, 1976; Hécaen & Albert, 1978; Walsh, 1978; Benson, 1979; Heilman, 1979; Lishman, 1978; & Dimond 1980). Behavior following destructive brain lesions reflects compensatory function of non-damaged brain rather than "direct" effects of the lesion (Kiernan, 1981). Thus, localization of a lesion that produces loss of a function in no way localizes that function. However, correlations between localized pathology and altered behavior do allow us to infer the necessity of specific areas for particular behaviors. Moreover, one can localize to a network or circuit as well as to a discrete area (Gevins et al., 1981; Mesulam, 1981; Valzelli, 1980). The question is no longer whether one localizes, but what one localizes. Knowledge of brain–behavior relationships is growing rapidly, yet it is unclear to what degree psychiatrists will venture into the area which Freud contemplated with such vision when he wrote his *Project for a Scientific Psychology* in 1895.

SEPTOHYPOTHALAMO-MESENCEPHALIC CONTINUUM

An appreciation of the anatomy underlying emotion requires knowledge of three different levels, or hierarchies, of neural structures and the manner in which they are connected. MacLean (1969) coined the neologism "triune" to refer to three brains essentially functioning as one. For MacLean this triune brain consists, from outside-in, of the neomammalian brain (or neocortex), the paleomammalian brain (visceral brain or limbic system), and the reptilian brain (core-brain neuraxis or R-complex—composed of brain stem and basal ganglia) (Fig. 10-1).

The author wishes to thank Drs. W.J.H. Nauta, D.F. Benson, D. Bear, and J.W. Langston for their helpful comments and suggestions.

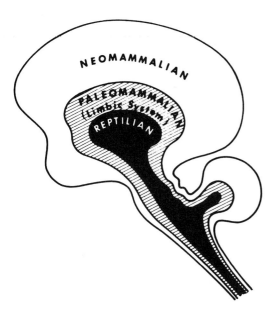

Figure 10-1. MacLean's triune brain. (From the Journal of Nervous and Mental Disease 144:p. 377 (1967). The Williams and Wilkins Co., Baltimore.)

The innermost of these three, the R-complex, is the most phylogenetically primitive portion of the human brain. Coursing through this R-complex is the reticular formation, a network comprised of connecting interneurons that extends from the lower medulla up through the rest of the brain stem (pons and midbrain) in a "central core" distribution (Moruzzi & Magoun, 1949) (Fig. 10-2). The reticular activating system is of central importance both to autonomic arousal and to maintenance of diffuse and specific cortical arousal as reflected in EEG activation. Midline and intralaminar nuclei of the thalamus appear to serve as intermediaries between the midbrain reticular activating system and cortical arousal. Because of the density of neural connections extending forward from the midbrain over the hypothalamus, and because the most anterior extension of the reticular network appears to lie in an area known as the septal region, Nauta (1958) coined the term "septo-hypothalamo-mesencephalic continuum" (SHM continuum) to refer to the totality of this central core of multiple neural tracts (Fig. 10-3).

At the front of this SHM continuum lies the septal region, a group of nuclei situated beneath the rostrum of the corpus callosum, in front of the anterior commissure, and mesial to the head of the caudate nucleus of the basal ganglia (Fig. 10-4). Since the work of Olds (1960) and Heath (1972), this area has been recognized as a "reward center." Animals with electrodes in the septal region will press a bar repeatedly to deliver current to this area of their brains. These animals will cross an electrified grid to press the bar and will also neglect food and water, pushing the bar to the point of exhaustion. Humans report a sense of sexual pleasure following septal stimulation (Heath, 1972).

In 1973 Stevens suggested that a portion of the septal complex might function as a gate or filter for the modulation of limbic inputs to the hypothalamus and prefrontal regions. Citing the work of Raisman (1969) and Moore et al. (1971) (who demonstrated sprouting of medial forebrain bundle noradrenergic terminals into the septal region following destruction of two other sources of septal afferents, the hippocampus and the amygdala), Stevens suggested that impaired septal functioning in schizophrenia might lead to limbic flooding of frontal areas (eruption of primary process thinking) and of hypothalamic discharge pathways (autonomic and behavioral dyscontrol). The resemblance of this hypothesis to speculations regarding the emergence of psychiatric disturbances in patients with temporal lobe epilepsy is considered later in the discussion of the limbic system.

Sandwiched between the septal-preoptic region and the midbrain is the hypothalamic component of this continuum (Fig. 10-5)—a group of nuclei that form the floor and anterior inferior walls of the third ventricle. The hypothalamus lies above the pituitary, below the thalamus, and behind the optic chiasm; its posterior components are the mammillary nuclei. Functionally, the hypothalamus regulates endocrine output (via the pituitary) and exerts a profound effect on the visceral autonomic nervous system. The hypothalamus is known to regulate multiple homeostatic mechanisms, and appears to play a role in the initiation and maintenance of immunologic defenses (Stein et al., 1981).

Since the work of Bard (1928), the hypothalamus has been known to regulate not only fluid balance and body temperature, but also basic drive states (fight, flight, feeding, and sexual behavior). Bard demonstrated that the "sham rage" evoked by trivial stimuli in cats deprived of their neocortical mantle depends on the posterior hypothalamus. This can be correlated with the observation that the posterior hypothalamus appears to be predominantly noradrenergic; the anterior hypothalamus is mainly cholinergic. *Irritative* lesions in the lateral hypothalamus have reliably produced rage attacks

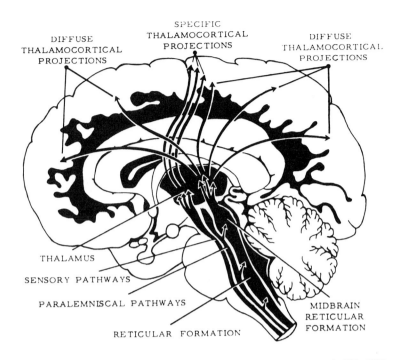

Figure 10-2. Ascending reticular activating system. (From Himwich HE, 1965: Anatomy and physiology of the emotions and their relation to psychoactive drugs. Marks J, & Pare CMB (Eds.). In *The Scientific Basis of Drug Therapy in Psychiatry*. Pergamon Press, Oxford.)

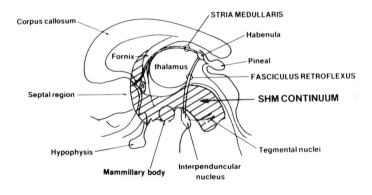

Figure 10-3. Septohypothalamomesencephalic (SHM) continuum.

and hyperphagia, while *destructive* lesions more medially (ventromedial nucleus) have produced a similar picture (Reeves & Plum, 1969). These observations suggest that the ventral medial hypothalamic region constitutes a type of "satiety center" or checking mechanism for the appetitive behavior

associated with lateral hypothalamic activity (Anand & Brobeck, 1951; for a critical discussion of the concept of hypothalamic "centers" see Grossman, 1980).

Other than the olfactory inputs, direct sensory inputs to the hypothalamus were not known until

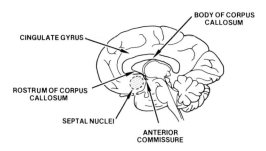

Figure 10-4. Septal region.

Moore (1973) demonstrated that direct retino-hypothalamic fibers (as suspected by Cajal) do exist. Such connections assume relevance with regard to circadian rhythms and the entrainment of endogenous self-sufficient oscillators. Nauta (1973) demonstrated two distinct frontal inputs to the SHM continuum: the first arises in the caudal portion of the orbital frontal cortex and distributes to the anterior continuum (septum and lateral hypothalamus); the second arises from the dorsal prefrontal convexity (Brodmann's areas 9 and 46), and travels to the posterior continuum (dorsal and lateral hypothalamus, as well as midbrain tegmentum). This arrangement suggests the possibility that frontal regions could monitor and/or exert control over visceral motor and neuroendocrine functions—that is, over the internal milieu (see the section on Sensorilimbic and Frontolimbic Connections for the possible relevance of these pathways to higher decision-making processes).

The third element of the SHM continuum, the midbrain, is of special importance to psychiatrists since it is the origin of two major dopaminergic pathways (Fig. 10-6). One of these pathways arises in the ventral midbrain (ventral-tegmental area of Tsai; area A10 in the system of Dahlstrom and Fuxe, 1964, or Nauta's, 1968, limbic midbrain area) and travels to the septum, olfactory cortex, amygdala, and frontocingulate region. These fibers are known collectively as the mesolimbic and mesocortical dopaminergic pathways. Neuroleptic agents appear to exert their psychotropic effects via dopaminergic blockade in the regions to which these fibers project (Glowinski, 1981). On the other hand, the unwanted side effects of neuroleptics (parkinsonian symptomatology and tardive dyskinesia) are presumed to result from dopaminergic blockade and denervation supersensitivity in the nigrostriatal dopaminergic pathway, which originates in the midbrain substantia nigra and travels to the caudate and putamen (neostriatum).

In addition to these dopaminergic projections, noradrenergic and serotonergic pathways originating in more posterior regions of the brain stem also pass through the SHM continuum. Noradrenergic pathways arise from the region of the locus ceruleus in the caudal pons, and travel to the diffuse areas of the forebrain. Serotonergic fibers arise from the midline raphe nuclei, which extend from the caudal midbrain to the medulla, and project in an over-

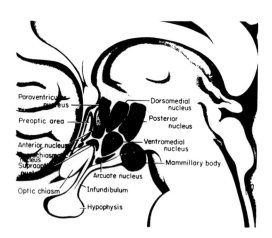

Figure 10-5. Medial hypothalamus. (From Carpenter MB, 1976: *Human Neuroanatomy* (ed. 7). p. 479. Copyright 1976, Williams & Wilkins, Baltimore.)

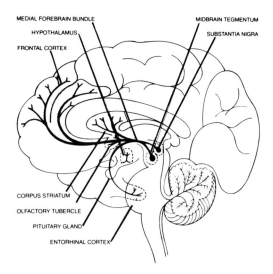

Figure 10-6. Dopaminergic pathways. (From Iverson LI, 1979: The chemistry of the brain. Sci Am 241: 134–149.)

lapping fashion with their noradrenergic counterparts to wide areas of the cortex. The totality of these dopaminergic, noradrenergic, and serotonergic pathways is known as the medial forebrain bundle. Because the medial forebrain bundle conducts in both rostral and caudal directions, it serves as a major efferent and afferent system for the hypothalamus, connecting it both to more rostral regions associated with olfaction (piriform cortex and cortex of the olfactory tubercle), and to lower brainstem structures such as the nucleus of the solitary tract and the dorsal motor nucleus of the vagus (Nauta & Domesick 1981).

In summary, the SHM continuum is strategically placed to govern endocrine and neural activities. It entertains extensive *intrinsic* connections via the following: (1) short interneurons of the reticular network; (2) the numerous pathways of the medial forebrain bundle; (3) the mammillotegmental track; and (4) the route over the dorsal thalamus via the habenular nuclei composed of stria medullaris and fasciculus retroflexus. By extension, the SHM continuum exerts powerful *upward* influences on limbic and higher cortical regions via the ascending reticular network and the neurotransmitter pathways of the medial forebrain bundle. Finally, in reciprocity with its upward influences on "higher" circuits, the SHM continuum is itself subject to *downward* effects from two major circuits: the medial and the basolateral limbic circuits.

LIMBIC CIRCUITRY

Brodal (1981, p. 690) has expressed repeated concern that the term "limbic" has become something of a runaway concept, recruiting and usurping increasingly vast stretches of cortical matter. In his words, "The 'limbic system' appears to be on its way to including all brain regions and functions. As this process continues, the value of the term as a useful concept is correspondingly reduced." While Brodal suggests abandoning the terms "limbic lobe" and "limbic system," they have become firmly entrenched and are unlikely to vanish.

The limbic system can be conceptualized as mediating between the extracorporeal sensory world, which achieves representation in the association cortex, and visceral, primitive internal drive states represented in the hypothalamus. It appears that sensory experience achieves meaning or attains permanence in memory only to the extent that it is

paired, however indirectly, with the experience of pleasure or pain at a core-brain or "visceral" level. Those structures that have been implicated in the pathology of memory (specifically, the hippocampi, fornices, mammillary bodies, dorsomedial thalamic nuclei) are also part of the brain's emotional circuitry.

In 1664, Thomas Willis, whose name is eponymously attached to the circle of blood vessels that connect the anterior (supplied by the internal carotid arteries) and posterior (vertebrobasilar) circulation, referred to the rim of the cortex surrounding the brainstem as a "cerebri limbus." Two centuries later, while viewing the mesial surface of the vertebrate brain, Broca (1878) spoke of "the great limbic lobe," thereby referring to the cingulate gyrus superiorly and the hippocampus inferiorly, joined by the "olfactory lobe" situated beneath the genu or anterior-most portion of the corpus callosum (Fig. 10-7). The term "limbic" referred to the rimming or hemlike fashion in which these structures surround the foramen of Monro–the passage from each of the lateral ventricles to the midline slitlike third ventricle. Because these prominent mesial structures were assumed to be intimately involved in olfaction, this anatomical ensemble came to be referred to as the rhinencephalon (olfactory or "nose brain") (Turner, 1890). In 1901, however, Cajal rejected this assumption, stating that although centrifugal or descending pathways pass near the olfactory centers, they have only "neighborly" relations with them. Almost 16 years before Moruzzi and Magoun (1949) presented their work on the reticular activating system, Herrick (1933) proposed that the olfactory system could function as part of a nonspecific cortical arousal system.

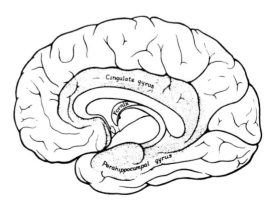

Figure 10-7. Broca's "great limbic lobe"

In 1937, Papez asked whether emotion arises magically or is the outcome of a physiologic processes dependent on an anatomic substrate. Papez extended Broca's notion of a limbic lobe to include not only the cingulate gyrus and hippocampus, but also their connections with hypothalamic and anterior thalamic nuclei (Fig. 10-8). The circuitry he proposed provided a "reverberating path" whereby impulses that arose in the hypothalamus could travel to the cortex and back again. Papez felt the flow of impulses followed an orderly path: "The hypothalamus, the anterior thalamic nuclei, the gyrus cinguli, the hippocampus and their interconnections constitute a harmonious mechanism which may elaborate the functions of central emotion..."; specifically, from mammillary bodies (posterior hypothalamus) via mammillothalamic tract (of Vicq d'Azyr) to anterior thalamic nucleus, thence to cingulate gyrus, and via retrosplenial cortex to hippocampus, whence forniceal fibers arch forward to attain the mammillary bodies (Fig. 10-9). The fibers of the fornix are known to arise from both the hippocampus proper and from its subicular portion

and constitute a bidirectional, largely cholinergic, pathway. In addition to those fibers reaching the mammillary bodies of the hypothalamus via the columns of the fornices, the fornix also gives off precommissural fibers to the septal region (Nauta, 1958), as well as postcommissural fibers that travel directly to the anterior thalamus (bypassing the hypothalamus) and to the midbrain.

Papez had stressed the importance of structures on the mesial surface of the brain, however, Yakovlev (1948) suggested that three neocortical regions might play a major role in motivation and behavior: the temporal pole, the orbital frontal region, and the insular cortex. Moreover, Yakovlev also included in his "mesopallial" system two subcortical structures that neither Papez nor Broca had mentioned, but which today are known to be crucial to emotion and behavior—the amygdala and the dorsomedial thalamic nucleus (DMN) (Fig. 10-10 through 10-12).

Thus there arose the concept of medial limbic circuit (of Papez) strongly associated with the hypothalamus, and a basolateral limbic circuit that entertained connections with sensory cortex. In 1952,

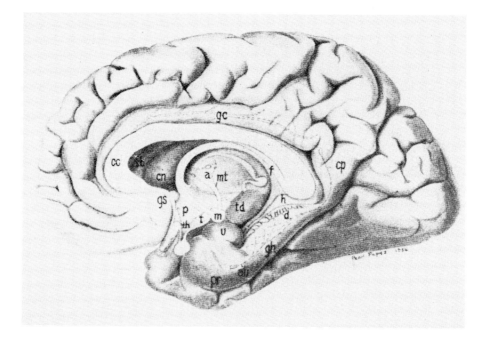

Figure 10-8. Limbic circuit of Papez. (From Papez JW, 1937: A proposed mechanism of emotion. Arch Neurol Psychiatry, 38:725–743.) Abbreviations: *a*, anterior nucleus; *ab*, angular bundle; *cn*, caudate nucleus; *cc*, corpus callosum; *cp*, cingulum posterious; *d*, gyrus dentatus; *f*, fornix; *gc*, gyrus cinguli; *gh*, gyrus hippocampi; *gs*, gyrus subcallosus; *h*, hippocampus nudus; *m*, mammillary body; *mt*, mammillothalamic tract; *p*, pars optica hypothalami; *pr*, pyriform area; *sb*, subcallosal bundle; *t*, tuber cinereum; *td*, tractus mammillotegmentalis; *th*, tractus hypophyseus; *u*, uncus.

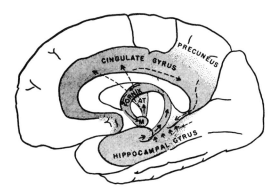

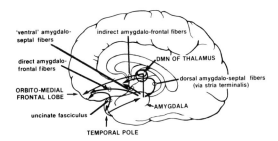

Figure 10-11. Basolateral limbic circuit. Parasagittal View of Right Hemisphere.

Figure 10-9. Papez circuit simplified by MacLean. (From MacLean PD, 1949: Psychosomatic disease and the "visceral brain." Reprinted by permission of the publisher. Psychosom Med 11:340. Vol. XI, no. 6, p. 340, copyright 1950, The American Psychosomatic Society, Inc.) M=Mammillary body; AT=Anterior thalamus.

MacLean explicitly combined these two circuits, referring to the ensemble as a "limbic system" or a "visceral brain," interposed between the ancient reptilian brain and the neocortical hemispheric convexities.

In the early 1970s Livingston and Escobar (1971) attempted to redress what they considered the disproportionate attention still being directed to the Papez circuitry at the expense of the more recently recognized basolateral circuit. They pointed out that incorporating Yakovlev's additions does not imply abandoning the notion of a limbus, but only reconceptualizing it as existing in a horizontal plane and ringing the brain stem when the brain is viewed from below (Fig. 10-13). Currently, the role of the basolateral circuit in temporal lobe epilepsy is an area of great interest to behavioral neurologists (Girgis & Kiloh, 1979). In many ways the basolateral circuit has eclipsed the Papez circuit in popularity.

Limbic connections can be summarized as follows: first, both the medial and the basolateral limbic circuits have strong *intrinsic* connections, and the Papez circuit has even been referred to as "reverberating." Second, both limbic circuits exert powerful *downward* and presumably regulating effects on the SHM continuum. Specifically, the hippocampus (medial circuit) sends precommissural forniceal fibers to the septum and postcommissural fibers both to the hypothalamus (mammillary bodies) and to the midbrain. The basolateral circuit exerts influence on the SHM continuum via dorsal (stria terminalis) and ventral amygdalofungal pathways to the septum and ventromedial hypothalamus. Other fibers of the

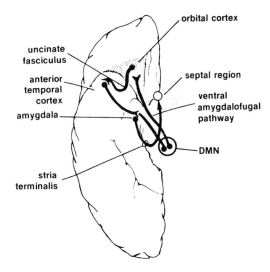

Figure 10-12. Basolateral limbic circuit viewed from under surface of brain. (Adapted from Livingston KE, & Escobar A, 1971: Anatomical bias of the limbic system concept. Arch Neurol 24:17–21. Copyright 1971, American Medical Association.)

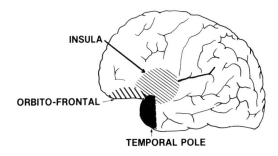

Figure 10-10. Yakovlev's cortical additions.

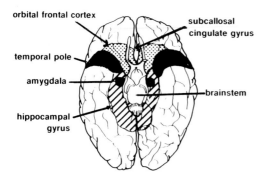

Figure 10-13. Orbital view of limbic system. (Adapted from Livingston KE, & Escobar A, 1971: Anatomical bias of the limbic system concept. Arch Neurol 24:17–21. Copyright 1971, American Medical Association.)

basolateral circuit travel from the posterior orbitofrontal cortex to the anterior SHM continuum (Nauta, 1973). Finally, the basolateral circuit enjoys strong *upward* connections to sensory and to prefrontal cortex. (For greater detail on specific limbic structures, consult Brodal, 1981; Eleftheriou 1972; Isaacson & Pribram 1975; Livingston & Hornkiewcz, 1978; Nauta & Domesick, 1981.)

SENSORILIMBIC AND FRONTOLIMBIC CONNECTIONS

The importance of the connections between sensory cortex and limbic or core-brain structures resides in the anatomic parallel these pathways provide to the process whereby experience of the external world, dependent on activity in association cortex, impacts on inner drive states conceptualized as represented in the SHM continuum. A shorthand way to speak of the influence of experience on behavior is to use the term "learning."

In macrosmatic animals olfaction has a far more extensive role in regulating behavior than it does in higher primates. In microsmatic creatures (such as man) the phylogenetic vestiges of an olfactory past remain in connections of the olfactory bulb not only to primary olfactory cortex (via lateral olfactory striae) in the mesial temporal region overlying the amygdala, but also in direct connection to the SHM continuum (via medial olfactory striae).

Even though retinohypothalamic fibers have been documented (Moore, 1973), audition, vision, and somesthesis do not appear to enjoy the intimate connections with the hypothalamus that olfaction

does. Projections from primary auditory and visual cortices do, however, travel over the inferior lateral convexity of the hemisphere and stream toward the temporal pole, a portion of the basolateral limbic circuit (Figure 10-14). Auditory fibers arise from the primary auditory cortex of Heschl's gyrus (Brodmann's areas 41 and 42), synapse in the surrounding tissue of the superior temporal gyrus, where phonemic decoding takes place (Wernicke's area, Brodmann's area 22), and project toward the temporal pole. Visual fibers from the calcarine cortex (primary visual cortex, Brodmann's area 17) synapse in peristriate cortex (Brodmann's areas 18 and 19), proceed to the posterior inferior temporal gyrus, and from there travel through the middle and inferior temporal gyri ultimately to attain the temporal pole (Powell, 1973). Sensorilimbic pathways for somesthesis are less well known: fibers arise from the entire bank of the postcentral gyrus (Brodmann's areas 3, 1, 2) and clearly travel to the superior parietal lobule (Brodmann's areas 5 and 7), but the path from there is uncertain (Keating 1971). It may be that some projections pass to the insular region (Mishkin, 1979).

Having converged on the temporal pole, unimodal association fibers from auditory and visual modalities proceed to sweep backward and medially to the lateral portions of the amygdala, a largely subcortical mass that lies deep to the uncus. Mesial portions of the amygdala are known to project strongly to the SHM continuum over dorsal and ventral amygdalofugal pathways. Some of the amygdala's numerous connections (Fig. 10-15) are (1) from sensory neocortex via temporal pole; (2) to SHM continuum through dorsal and ventral pathways; (3) to and from frontal lobe via DMN of thalamus and uncinate fasciculus; and (4) to cinguluum.

The expansion of the lateral portions of the amygdala parallels the increasing role of vision in

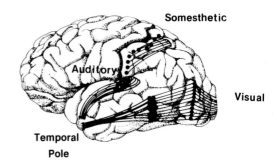

Figure 10-14. Neocortical afferents to temporal pole.

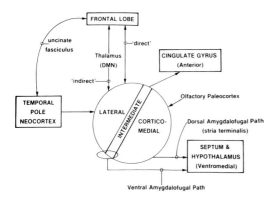

Figure 10-15. Amygdalar connections.

guiding the behavior of higher primates. Given the strong funneling of unimodal sensory fibers onto the amygdala, which itself entertains strong connections with the SHM continuum, it has been suggested that the amygdala may function as a gate or filter (Gloor, 1978) interposed between neocortical sensory representations of the external world and subcortical limbic/core-brain centers of visceral autonomic and neuroendocrine discharge. Malfunctioning of this filtering or bridging structure could have profound consequences on the regulation of emotional behavior by sensory experience, or, conversely, on the role that visceral affects play in "coloring" sensory inputs.

The amygdala possesses the lowest threshold for seizure activity in the central nervous system, making it an extremely vulnerable structure. In fact, it appears that seizure activity arising elsewhere in the brain may be capable of eventually recruiting or "kindling" the amygdala. The role that kindling of temporal pole–amygdalar connections might play in the genesis of interictal personality disorders in temporal lobe epileptics is discussed later in the section on Temporal Lobe Epilepsy. The recent demonstration of opiate receptor gradients in association cortex is of particular interest to the study of sensorilimbic connections. Lewis et al. (1981) showed that the density of μ opiate receptors (binding sites for opiates produced by the brain itself) increases "in a gradient along hierarchically organized cortical systems that sequentially process modality-specific sensory information of a progressively more complex nature"—that is, along the sensorilimbic pathway that travels toward the amygdala. They hypothesize that such gradients may play a role in emotion-induced selective attention.

The confusing term "prefrontal" refers to that portion of the frontal lobe that lies anterior to both the motor (precentral) and the premotor cortex. Freeman and Watts (1942) suggested that the prefrontal area be defined as that frontal region which entertains reciprocal connections with the thalamic DMN (Fig. 10-16). In fact, they speculated that the affective changes seen following frontal lobectomy were due to a frontothalamic disconnection, reflected ultimately in retrograde degeneration of the DMN. Although it appears that disruption of other connections (Brodal, 1981, p. 824) also plays a significant role in the behavioral changes produced by frontal lobe surgery, the DMN does appear to be a major carrefour for prefrontolimbic connections. As can be seen in the coronal section through the DMN shown in Figure 10-17, its medial (magnocellular) portion receives multiple "limbic" inputs and projects mainly to the orbital undersurface of the frontal lobe. The lateral (parvocellular) portion has less well-known afferents and projects to the dorsolateral convexity of the prefrontal region.

Recent studies (Vogt et al., 1979) have shown that, in contrast to the anterior thalamic nuclei (of Papez's circuitry), which send fibers primarily to the posterior cingulate gyrus, the DMN (along with intralaminar thalamic nuclei) is predominantly linked to the anterior cingulate gyrus, a region with major amygdalar connections. The DMN appears to be to frontolimbic connections what the amygdala is to sensorilimbic connections: a crucial bridge. In contrast, however, to the unidirectional sensorilimbic pathways traveling via the amygdala, frontolimbic connections appear to be largely reciprocal.

Frontal pathways to limbic and core-brain centers can be summarized as follows (Fig. 10-18): (1) two separate and direct pathways to the SHM continuum (see the section on the SHM continuum); (2) indirect pathways to hippocampus via cingulum and

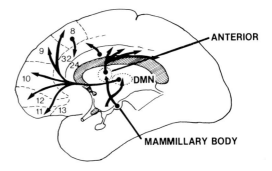

Figure 10-16. DMN–frontal lobe connections.

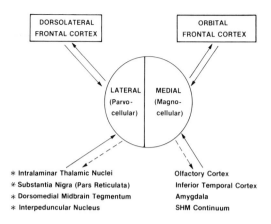

Figure 10-17. Connections of DMN. (*Data from Nauta, WJH, personal communication.)

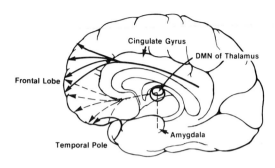

Figure 10-19. Limbicofrontal connections.

entorhinal area; and (3) indirect pathways to amygdala via DMN and uncinate fasciculus. Limbicofrontal connections travel via the following pathways (Fig. 10-19): (1) direct pathways from anterior and posterior cingulate gyrus to dorsal prefrontal region; (2) indirect pathways from subcortical amygdala and ventral tegmentum of midbrain and cortical (olfactory cortex and inferior temporal cortex) limbic areas to orbital frontal lobe via DMN; and (3) indirect pathways from amygdala to orbital and dorsal prefrontal regions via uncinate fasciculus.

There thus exist numerous pathways whereby the frontal lobes could either monitor or modify limbic activity: directly, via two distinct fronto–SHM connections; and indirectly, via either the DMN–amygdala–SHM pathway or the uncinate fasciculus–temporal pole–amygdala–SHM route. Nauta (1971) speculated that the frontal lobes exercise judgment in that they propose potential plans of action to the lower limbic regions and SHM continuum, then monitor the visceral or affective "readout." Having "tested the waters" with multiple alternative approaches, the frontal region is able to make the decision to implement a particular plan of

behavior with reference to both immediate and long-range contingencies. Nauta (1971) termed loss of this capacity "interoceptive agnosia."

FUNCTIONAL HEMISPHERIC ASYMMETRIES IN REGARD TO EMOTION

Evidence for "emotional asymmetry" in the brain comes from several sources. Among these are differing affective responses following destructive or irritative brain lesions, hemispherectomy, section of the corpus callosum, and injection of sodium amytal. The use since the early 1960s of intracarotid sodium amytal to localize cerebral dominance for language prior to neurosurgery (Wada & Rasmussen, 1960) has revealed differing affective responses following left and right-sided injections (Terzian, 1964). Because the reaction occurs as the anesthetic is wearing off (it could be a "rebound" reaction), and because investigators have not consistently reproduced the findings, caution is required in drawing inferences. Some reports, however, are compelling. Terzian (1964), for instance, reported the following.

Amytal on the left side provokes...a catastrophic reaction in the sense of Goldstein. The patient...despairs and expresses a sense of guilt, of nothingness, of indignity, and worries about his own future or that of his relatives, without referring to the language disturbances overcome and to the hemiplegia just resolved and ignored. The injection of the same dose in the contralateral carotid artery...produces on the contrary a completely opposite emotional reaction, an euphoric reaction that in some cases may reach the intensity of maniacal reaction. The patient appears without apprehension, smiles and laughs and both with mimicry and words expresses considerable liveliness and sense of well being (page 235).*

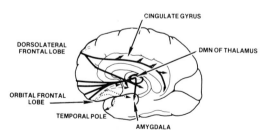

Figure 10-18. Frontolimbic connections.

*From Terzian H (1964): Behavioral and EEG affects of intracarotid sodium amytal injections. Acta Neurochir (Wien) 12:230–240. With permission.

Looking at a series of 160 brain-damaged individuals, Gainotti (1972) concluded that lesions of the left cerebral hemisphere, which is dominant for propositional language, tend to result in affective changes (predominantly depression) more frequently than do right hemispheric insults, which are associated with emotional indifference. Goldstein (1962) spoke of "catastrophic reactions" with left hemispheric pathology, and pointed to the marked anxiety and frustration accompanying cognitive and language dysfunction. Gasparrini et al. (1978) administered MMPIs to left and right hemisphere–injured patients who had been matched for severity of dysfunction. Of 16 subjects with left hemispheric dysfunction, 7 showed an elevation on depression scales. By contrast, none of the 8 patients with right hemispheric dysfunction showed elevation on depression scales.

A recent retrospective review by Sackheim et al. (1982) of emotional expression in the context of brain damage implicates left cortical irritation or disinhibition in the generation of negative emotional expression. This appears to hold for hemispherectomy, irritative temporal lobe foci, and hemispheric lesions. These authors suggested that irritative cortical lesions produce excitation of ipsilateral "centers subserving emotion," while destructive cortical lesions produce disinhibition of contralateral centers. Finklestein et al. (1982) found a significantly greater incidence of moderate to severe mood disturbance with left than with right hemispheric strokes. Interestingly, they documented that despite the absence of overt behavioral signs of depressive mood following right hemispheric vascular insult, vegetative signs (appetite or sleep changes) and neuroendocrine disturbances (abnormal dexamethasone suppression test) were nearly as frequent in this group as in those patients with left hemispheric strokes.

The behavior of split-brain subjects—patients in whom the corpus callosum has been severed surgically in an attempt to control intractable seizures—is of particular interest to those studying brain substrates of emotion. Following commissurotomy the right hemisphere has no access to the language centers in the left hemisphere. One female patient who had the image of a nude pin-up flashed tachistoscopically to her right hemisphere was observed to blush and giggle. When asked what she had seen, she responded, "Nothing, just a flash of light," and giggled again. When asked why she was laughing, her response was, "Oh, Doctor Sperry, you have some machine!" (Gazzaniga, 1970 pp. 105–106;

Galin, 1974). Thus, the experience of emotion is possible without a linguistic capacity to explain "why" one is embarrassed, happy, or angry. The possibility of such dissociations raises questions regarding the importance psychiatry has traditionally assigned to self-report and introspection (see discussions of aprosodia and alexithymia in the next section).

Dramatic displays of conflicting behavior have also been seen following commissurotomy. A patient may reach into a drawer with the right hand, only to have the drawer slammed shut by the left hand (i.e., right hemisphere). Other patients may be observed simultaneously to put on clothes with one hand and pull them off with the other (Akelaitis, 1945). This type of phenomenon has been termed the "alien hand" or *la main etrangere* (Brion & Jednyak, 1972). Gazzaniga (1970) described an individual who would attack others with one hand and try to protect the victim with the other hand. On the basis of such reports it has been suggested that repression and suppression might be mediated by selective inhibition of neuronal transmission across the corpus callosum. Galin (1974) has postulated that the right or "nonlanguage" hemisphere may be the substrate for primary process cognition—that is, for the unconscious.

Facial recognition has traditionally been associated with right brain functioning (DeRenzi et al., 1968). The specific loss of the capacity to recognize faces is termed *prosopagnosia*. While early case reports suggested the importance of right parietal pathology, recent investigators (Damasio et al., 1982; Meadows, 1974) have argued for the necessity of bilateral lesions of the temporooccipital undersurface of the brain for disruption of facial recognition. Even though intact individuals express emotion more intensely on the left side of the face (Sackheim et al., 1978), which lies in the observer's right visual field and projects to his or her left hemisphere, the right hemisphere appears to be superior to the left in the recognition both of emotions and of faces (Ley & Bryden, 1979; see also Davidson, this volume, Chapter 11, for recent work on hemispheric asymmetries in regard to ascription of affective valence).

It should be noted that voluntary and involuntary facial expressions are quite distinct. Pyramidal or voluntary motor pathways are phylogenetically more recent and are mainly crossed. Extrapyramidal pathways, on the other hand, are more primitive phylogenetically, tend to innervate axial or midline musculature, and are more likely to be ipsilateral or bilateral in their distribution. The portion of the seventh cranial (facial) nerve nucleus which innervates the lower human face receives exclusively crossed corticobulbar fibers, while that portion of the facial nucleus innervating the upper face receives both crossed and uncrossed projections (Fig. 10-20). This explains the disproportionate involvement of the lower face following an upper motor neuron lesion. The patient with an upper motor neuron lesion (contralateral hemifacial flattening of the nasolabial fold and drooping of the corner of the mouth) may be capable of spontaneous (extrapyramidal) smiling despite the paresis of voluntary musculature with attendant loss of a "social smile." On the other hand, individuals with Parkinson's disease retain some voluntary control of facial expression, yet may be incapable of smiling spontaneously. Patients with lesions in the supplementary motor area also demonstrate diminished spontaneous emotional expression, while retaining intentional facial movements (Laplane et al., 1977). As Geschwind (personal communication, 1982) has pointed out, actors who learn to smile "naturally" *appear* to have "pyramidalized" what for the rest of us tends to be an extrapyramidal (emotionally triggered) behavior. One needs to specify "appear"

since certain actors (e.g., those in the Stanislavski school) learn to voluntarily trigger extrapyramidal smiles by conjuring up emotionally charged memories or images.

In summary, it can be said that emotion is not a unitary entity. Even though the clinician needs to be aware of gross correlations between lesion site and syndromes of altered emotionality, simplistic attempts to localize emotion to a hemisphere are inappropriate and antiquated. Ross and Rush (1981) proposed that the right temporoparietal region is responsible for the "formulation of a depressive affective set." While affective coloring of speech as well as gesture is hypothesized to depend on right frontal regions, the formulation and expression of a depressive verbal/cognitive set depends in their schema on activity in subcortical regions, as well as on callosal transfer of information to left hemispheric language areas. Such a model implies that cortical and subcortical areas of both hemispheres, need to be considered in any attempt to describe anatomical correlates of emotion.

Thus, emotional behavior can be conceptualized as having afferent (sensory), efferent (motor), and central (cognitive or processing) components. Each of these may in turn depend to varying degrees on cortical and/or subcortical components from either or both hemispheres. The recent documentation of subcortical asymmetries in catecholamine (Oke et al., 1978) and indoleamine (Mandell & Knapp, 1979) neurotransmitter systems may provide a clue as to the role of right versus left subcortical regions in emotional behavior.

In the sections that follow the clinically relevant emotional concomitants of gross brain damage are described. In some syndromes the functional pathology lies in the expressive or efferent limb of emotional behavior (e.g., Parkinson's disease or progressive supranuclear palsy), whereas in others (e.g., right temporal or right parietal lesions) the problem is one of altered perception or processing of emotion. The rationale for discussion of a particular syndrome resides not in the frequency of its occurence, but rather in its potential as a window into neuroanatomic substrates of behavior.

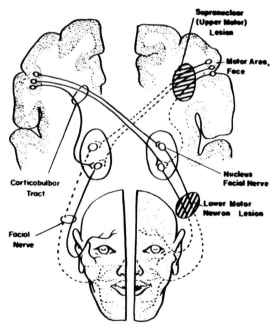

Figure 10-20.   Innervation of facial musculature. From Clark RG, 1975: *Essentials of Clinical Neuroanatomy and Neurophysiology* (ed. 5).

LANGUAGE-ASSOCIATED CHANGES IN AFFECTIVITY

Following Broca's (1861) localization of motor speech to the left frontal region and Wernicke's (1874) recognition of the role played by the left temporal lobe in receptive language, much of the late 19th century ferment concerning mind–brain issues focused on localization of language (Marx, 1966, 1967). Participants in the controversy included such figures as Jackson, Marie, Broca, Wernicke, and Freud. Thus, in addition to their clinical importance, the aphasias occupy a place of particular historical and philosophical significance.

Broca-type aphasia is produced by lesions involving the posterior portion of the inferior frontal gyrus of the dominant hemisphere (Fig. 10-21). The speech of these individuals is characteristically effortful, dysarthric, nonfluent, and "telegraphic" (consisting of short phrases in which small connecting words or "functors" are omitted). Comprehension is relatively preserved. The Russian neuropsychologist Luria (1966) spoke of "ocular palpation" to suggest the similarity between visual and manual exploration of the environment. Since speech provides a vehicle for "verbal palpation" of the human environment, patients with motor aphasia suffer from what might be considered a linguistically "locked-in" syndrome. Following recovery, individuals with a Broca or motor-type asphasia frequently report having known precisely what they wanted to say (or write) and yet having been unable to do so. Interestingly, however, the capacity to curse, sing, and pray (all presumably emotion dependent) is often preserved with Broca asphasia. The term "limbic language" (Joseph, 1982) has been used to denote these special utterances. Depression and frustration are extremely common in Broca aphasics. Sullen withdrawal and catastrophic outbursts of anger or tearfulness are seen frequently in Broca aphasics, but suicide attempts in this population are surprisingly rare (Benson, 1979). The question as to whether depression constitutes a "normal" reaction to the loss of language capacity, or whether depression might arise directly from dominant hemispheric pathology, has

been asked only recently (Robinson & Szetela, 1980; Ross & Rush, 1981).

Wernicke-type aphasias, by contrast, result from dominant hemispheric lesions of the posterior third of the superior temporal gyrus (Fig. 10-21). The speech of these individuals is characteristically fluent, contaminated with distortions of letters or of whole words ("literal" or "verbal" paraphasias), and may be mistaken for schizophrenic "word salad." Comprehension of spoken and written language is markedly impaired. A broad spectrum of emotional concomitants has been described with Wernicke-type aphasias. Patients may initially be unaware of their language problems and appear inappropriately cheerful or even euphoric (Benson, 1973). This represents a striking departure from the general rule (see previous section) that destructive lesions of the left hemisphere produce negative rather than positive emotional behavior. Altered cognition following left temporoparietal lesions may explain this anomaly. Indeed, Terzian's (1964) report of self-depreciation following left carotid amytal injection (with apparent obliviousness to both the transient impairment of language function and the resolving right hemiplegia) lends support to the argument that anosognosia (unawareness or denial of illness) occurs quite frequently in cases of posterior left hemispheric pathology (Battersby et al., 1965), but is masked by the language impairment.

On the other hand, Wernicke aphasics may develop paranoid beliefs that others are plotting against them, hiding information, or even "talking gibberish" in order to confuse them. Associated with this one may see confused wandering and frightened, impulsive behavior. Particularly in the acute stages, these patients are at high risk for self-destructive behavior arising from confusional misperceptions. If brought to an emergency room, these patients may be mistakenly diagnosed as schizophrenic or demented. Since some awareness of one's language dysfunction is a prerequisite for the initiation of speech therapy, the emergence of frustration and anger in the context of posterior aphasia is often highly appropriate and may even be a good prognostic sign. On the other hand, the risk of impulsive suicidal behavior in these individuals must not be forgotten.

Broca and Wernicke aphasias represent disorders of what Jackson (1879) termed *propositional speech*—that is, the ability to use grammar and vocabulary to formulate an idea or proposition. Monrad-Krohn (1947) coined the term *dysprosody* to refer to the absence of melody in the speech of Broca-type

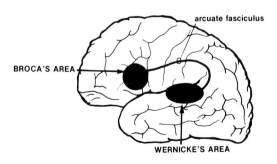

Figure 10-21. Language centers of the left hemisphere.

aphasics, parkinsonian individuals, and some demented patients. It now appears that lesions of the right or nondominant hemisphere can disrupt non-propositional language in a disastrous fashion—altering emotional gesturing, melody, rhythm, and inflexion of speech. Heilman et al. (1975) and Ross (1981) presented evidence that right hemispheric lesions homologous to those that cause aphasia in the dominant hemisphere can produce both expressive and receptive disorders of affective language.

Thus, lesions in the right frontal area may produce a *motor or expressive aprosodia* which leaves the individual unable to imbue his or her speech with affective coloring. Two fascinating cases have been reported in which patients with right frontal pathology suffered a dramatic functional impairment (Ross & Mesulam, 1979): One involved a 39-year-old school teacher who lost the ability to control her class with her voice for a period of 8 months following a right frontal infarction. In the second case a 62-year-old surgeon became unable to convey emotional warmth or sincerity in his voice, resulting in his wife's complaint that his personality had changed.

More posterior lesions, specifically those affecting the temporoparietal region of the nondominant hemisphere, may result in patients losing the ability to comprehend or appreciate the emotional or prosodic coloring of another person's speech. Analogous to the Wernicke-type aphasia (posterior dominant hemisphere lesion), the individual with a *receptive aprosodia* would be expected to produce speech that is prosodically fluent, yet disordered. Ross's work with these so-called aprosodias provides a clear example of psychiatric disturbances resulting directly from brain lesions. One can readily imagine the predicament of a therapist working with a patient who is incapable of emotional expression and gesticultion or of appreciating nuances in the inflection of the therapist's voice.

It is important to state that the term "aprosodia" implies no particular pathologic mechanism—it merely denotes the absence of emotional gesturing and/or coloration of speech. When confronting such a patient it is essential to realize that his or her subjective emotional experience may be relatively intact, despite the fact that speech and gesture betray no emotion. The possibility of such dissociations between inner emotion and outer affective display should serve as a haunting reminder that psychiatrists in particular cannot afford to be unaware of disconnection syndromes.

Several large patient populations may suffer from aprosodia. Major depressive disorders and chronic schizophrenia may both be associated with colorless, uninflected speech. Patients with idiopathic Parkinson's disease may have masked facies and "reptilian stares" accompanied by hypophonic and monotonous speech. A third and still larger group of aprosodics is made up of individuals suffering from the side effects of antipsychotic medications. Neuroleptic-induced facial immobility and achromatic speech may contribute to those factors that hinder effective reentry of schizophrenics into the community following hospitalization. Finally, as noted by Monrad-Krohn (1947), the speech of some demented individuals is amelodic. The fact that the latter group will make up an increasingly large percentage of the total population over the next few decades has led Wells (1981) to speak of an impending "deluge of dementia."

It should be remembered that unlike the aphasias, the concept of a group of aprosodias has a very short history. Few patients have been seen and reported up to this point, and pathological evidence has been limited. The presense of aprosodia has been correlated with cortical lesions, but the coexistence of subcortical pathology has not been explicitly ruled out. Depression, arising either directly from right brain lesions or as a reactive psychological process, may be associated with neurotransmitter changes that could exert major effects on relevant subcortical systems. Most importantly, the equation of affect with prosody can be misleading. Verbal communication of inner emotion may depend largely on prosody, but it is clear that stress, rhythm, and melody also play a significant role in nonemotional speech. As Weintraub et al. (1981) pointed out, patients with right hemisphere lesions have problems not only with affective prosody, but also with general (nonaffective) prosody.

Finally, the area of language disturbance secondary to right hemispheric lesions may bear some relation to the (currently popular) notion of alexithymia. *Alexithymia* (reviewed by Lesser, 1981) is an apparently constitutional inability to convert inner affective experience into propositional verbal utterances. If there are critical periods (such as those demonstrated for maturation of visual cortex; Wiesel & Hubel, 1963) for the laying down of connections between the neural substrates for central or deep emotion and the neural systems subserving propositional language, then alexithymia may represent a developmental disconnection syndrome.

SYNDROMES OF DENIAL, NEGLECT, OR INATTENTION

In 1914 Babinski coined the term *anosognosia* (*a*, without; *nosos*, illness; *gnosis*, knowledge) in describing two cases of neglect or denial of left hemiplegia following cerebral infarction. Babinski stated that his patients "either were unaware of or seemed to be unaware of their deficits. The first patient was a woman who "despite an otherwise excellent recovery (pleasant affect, normal intellect, and social comportment) never once over a period of years complained of or alluded to her hemiplegia." When asked to move her left arm, she behaved "as if someone else had been asked." His second patient, whose left arm was totally inert not only failed to respond when asked to move her arm, but would sometimes respond, *Voila, c'est fait!"* ("There, it's done"). Babinski noted that other patients, while intellectually aware of their hemiplegia, may display a striking indifference to which he gave them the name *anosodiaphoria.* Four years after his report of the two patients described above, Babinski (1918) commented that each of them had had left-sided weakness and sensory deficits in the afflicted limbs. He went on to speculate, "Could it be that anosognosia is peculiar to lesions of the right hemisphere?"

It seems unfortunate that Babinski's term has been translated "denial of illness' when in reality this constitutes only one extreme of a broad spectrum that includes inattention or relative indifference to one's illness (Critchley, 1957), outspoken hatred of a limb (Critchley, 1979), and vehement denial that a paralyzed extremity belongs to oneself (Weinstein & Kahn, 1955). Moreover, the phrase "denial of illness" imputes a psychological motivation to these individuals, implying a refusal to admit to their impairments, rather than, as Babinski suggested, a true ignorance of their deficits.

Profound inattention or neglect can be produced in animals by surgical lesions, and here one is less inclined to use the term "denial." Downer (1962) performed a study in which he produced a visuolimbic disconnection syndrome in rhesus monkeys by lesioning the amygdala unilaterally and severing all interhemispheric connections (corpus callosum, hippocampal commissure, anterior commissures, and massa intermedia). Following surgery, with both eyes open, the animal appeared to be as wild and unapproachable as prior to the operation. When the eye projecting to the side of the amygdalectomy was covered, no change in this behavior was noted.

When, however, the eye projecting to the amygdalectomized side was left open and the other eye closed, the behavioral change was dramatic. The sight of humans no longer provoked agression, and the animal would even approach humans who offered it food. This taming, however, applied only co visual stimuli since touching the animal still elicited aggression.

Working with rats, Marshall and co-workers (1971) produced a syndrome of multimodal (visual, olfactory, and tactile) neglect to contralateral stimuli following unilateral hypothalamic lesions. If a mouse appeared in the rat's visual field ipsilateral to the lesion, the rat attacked the mouse as it would do normally. On the other hand, if a mouse appeared in the contralateral visual field, there was no attack until the mouse crossed the midline into the rat's other (ipsilateral to lesion) visual field, and thus was perceived by the visual cortex of the nonlesioned hemisphere, which conveyed this information via the amygdala to the intact hemihypothalamus.

Denial of blindness (Anton's syndrome) has been known to exist since 1885 (Anton, 1899; Von Monakov, 1885). Humans who lose vision on a cortical basis may sometimes be seen walking into objects and people, complaining bitterly that the hospital does not light its corridors adequately. Infarction of both occipital cortices (secondary to bilateral posterior cerebral artery occlusions) is the most common pathologic substrate for this phenomenon, but laminar necrosis secondary to anoxia can produce a similar picture (layer 4 of the six-layered striate cortex receives geniculate projections and is particularly vulnerable to anoxia because of its high metabolic rate). Lower animals preserve considerable visual function at a subcortical level following extirpation of visual cortex, but vision in monkeys and man has become progressively "encephalized." Nevertheless, the role that extrageniculate pathways play in human vision is still being studied. Part of the impetus to such research derives from cases of cortical blindness (without denial) in which the existence of "blindsight" (i.e., perception out of conscious awareness) has been documented by patients' discriminant responses to visual stimuli (Perenin et al., 1980). Thus one can speak of "denial," or more appropriately "unawareness" of vision as well as of blindness!

Although patients with Wernicke-type aphasia may "deny" any language problems (see the section on Language-Associated Emotion), this may reflect either a comprehension deficit or an unawareness of their dysfunction. Such a patient's behavior is similar to that of the Korsakovian patient who "denies" memory problems—in order for an amnestic patient to "admit" to forgetting he would need to remember that he forgets!

Critchley (1953) chronicled the range of extraordinary phenomenology that may be found following parietal lobe lesions. Sensory, motor, and attentional hypotheses have been put forward to explain the neglect syndromes. Critchley (1953) and Schilder (1935) invoked disruption of a "body schema," while Denny-Brown et al. (1952) spoke of a failure to summate spatial impressions—"amorphosynthesis." The notion of a "hemispatial akinesia," defined as loss of the intention (despite intact sensation and strength) to perform movements in the neglected hemispace, was proposed by Heilman and Watson (1977). Attentional hypotheses were advanced early in the century and have been reformulated recently. Heilman (1979) pointed out that unilateral (especially right-sided) lesions in any of several areas (Figs. 10-22 and 10-23) may produce hemispatial neglect secondary to disruption of one or more components of a cortical–limbic–reticular activating system loop: (1) hypothalamus (medial forebrain bundle and reticular activating system fibers); (2) thalamus (intralaminar nuclei serve as an extension of the reticular activating system); (3) cingulate gyrus ("paralimbic" cortex which receives afferents from hypothalamus via anterior thalamus and from amygdala via medial thalamus); (4) dorsolateral convexity of the frontal lobe (receives inputs from auditory, visual, and somesthetic association areas, as well as from inferior parietal lobule, and exerts control over voluntary ocular pursuit); and (5) inferior parietal lobule (multi- and supramodal association cortex).

Perhaps the most dramatic example of an attentional deficit or a neglect syndrome is the phenomenon of akinetic mutism (Morariu, 1977), in which an individual whose motor and sensory path-

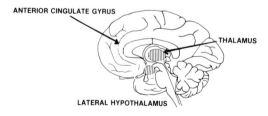

Figure 10-22. Mesial right hemispheric lesions producing neglect.

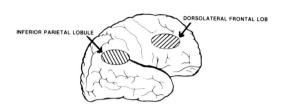

Figure 10-23. Right hemispheric convexity lesions producing neglect.

ways are intact, lies in bed awake yet unresponsive (except for visual following) to sensory stimuli. Hemorrhage in the region of the anterior cerebral arteries (usually secondary to rupture of anterior communicating artery aneurysms) with bilateral compromise of the anterior cingulate gyri is the most characteristic pathological substrate for this clinical picture, but third ventricular cysts, as well as lesions of the reticular formation, hypothalamus, and globus pallidus have all produced the syndrome (Ross & Stewart, 1981).

TEMPORAL LOBE EPILEPSY

Jackson (1881) spoke of neurologic symptoms as being "positive" or "negative." Hallucinations, involuntary utterances, and tremors are positive symptoms, whereas hemianopsia, weakness, paralysis, and mutism are negative symptoms. The ictal events of temporal lobe or complex partial seizures can be positive or negative and assume an almost infinite variety (classification of Gastaut & Broughton, 1972, is presented in Table 10-1). Motor correlates of these states may be non-existent or may consist of simple, repetitive, and stereotyped movements (automatisms) such as lip smacking, head turning, or fumbling with clothing. Alternatively, they may entail more complex behaviors such as laughing (gelastic epilepsy; Daly & Mulder, 1957), crying (dacrystic or quiritarian epilepsy; Offen et al. 1976; Sethi & Rao, 1976), running (cursive epilepsy; Sethi & Rao, 1976), or fugue states (Schenk & Bear, 1981).

When considering the phenomenology of temporal lobe epilepsy (TLE) it is important to attempt to separate ictal, postictal, and interictal periods (Lishman, 1978). Temporal lobe seizures may commence suddenly, but some patients describe an invariable "aura" lasting a few seconds to a minute that serves as a warning. Such subjective experiences have been termed "preictal" events, but they actually are part of the ictus. Blumer (1975) pro-

Table 10-1: Symptomatology of Complex Partial Seizures

1. Impaired consciousness only

2. Intellectual symptomatology
   A. Dysmnesia
   B. Ideational disturbances

3. Affective symptomatology

4. "Psychosensory" symptomatology
   A. Illusions
   B. Hallucinations

5. "Psychomotor" symptomatology
   A. Alimentary
   B. Mimetic
   C. Gestural
   E. Ambulatory
   F. Verbal

6. Compound symptomatology

From Gastaut H, & Broughton R (1972): *Epileptic Seizures.* Springfield, Ill., Courtesy of Charles C. Thomas.

posed the term *primictal* to refer to that part of the seizure which occurs before the patient becomes amnesic. Primictal events include experiences of objectless fear and sensations of jamais vu, déja vu, or their auditory equivalents. Seizures that are heralded by olfactory sensations have been termed *uncinate fits* since the primary olfactory cortex (see the section on Sensorilimbic and Frontolimbic Connections for details) lies in the uncal region overlying the amygdala.

While the range of ictal phenomena is enormous (Gastaut & Broughton, 1972), the complexity of subjective experiences may have little in the way of external behavioral correlates. Since the epileptic is usually amnesic for most of the ictus, the clinician may be barred access to much of the subjective ictal experience. Postictal periods last for varying lengths of time and may be characterized by confused behavior as the patient attempts to regain orientation. It is often impossible for an observer to determine at what point a seizure terminates and the postictal confusional period begins. Since patients in confusional states usually are incapable of laying down memories, postictal behavior is recalled vaguely, if at all.

The distinctions discussed above assume particular importance with regard to violence and aggression in temporal lobe epileptics. Without

going into the immense literature around this area, several points can be made. First, if ictal violence exists, it is extremely rare (Delgado-Escueta et al., 1981). The most frequent type of temporal lobe seizure is unemotional and characterized by disengagement, withdrawal, or psychoparesis (Penfield & Rasmussen, 1950). Second, the vast majority of violent behavior in temporal lobe epileptics occurs as an interictal event and tends to be recalled vividly. Increasing irritability over days or hours prior to a seizure has been termed the *prodrome* (Lishman, 1978) and may parallel increasing electrical disorganization in the brain of the individuals. Family members learn to recognize this period and often dread the patient's prodromal behavioral changes. Blumer (personal communication, 1982) reported that some patients intentionally discontinue their seizure medications in an attempt to terminate growing prodromal dysphoria by provoking a seizure. Finally, since postictal patients are usually confused and unable to perceive clearly events in their surroundings, attempts to touch or prod these individuals—to forcefully remove them from a given area, for example—may sometimes be met with explosive, poorly directed outbursts.

Despite the heuristic utility of categorizing the behavior of epileptic individuals, it should be stressed that ictal and postictal events may be essentially impossible to differentiate clinically. Moreover, since perhaps 20 percent of all patients with TLE have EEGs that show no abnormalities despite the use of nasopharyngeal leads and sleep deprivation (Kashnig & Celesia, 1976), even telemetric recordings may not provide an absolute correlation between electrical events and observable behavior.

The interictal personality changes that patients with TLE undergo constitute an extraordinary positive symptom complex and are of particular relevance to this chapter. Gastaut (1954) was the first to suggest that the behavior of temporal lobe epileptics might profitably be contrasted with the behavior of animals following temporal lobectomy. Blumer (1967) brought this contrast to the attention of the English-speaking world. Recently, Bear (1979) proposed that TLE be conceptualized as a syndrome of sensorilimbic *hyper*connection—that is, as the converse of the Klüver-Bucy syndrome, in which a sensorilimbic *dis*connection underlies visual agnosia. The Klüver-Bucy syndrome consists of the following remarkable features: hyperorality, hypersexuality, placidity, anterograde amnesia, and "hypermetamorphosis" (attending and reacting to all visual stimuli). The syndrome was intially described following bilateral temporal lobectomies in monkeys (Klüver & Bucy, 1937, 1938, 1939), but there have been reports of the syndrome occurring in humans following bilateral temporal ablation (Terzian & Dalle Ore, 1955) and viral encephalitis (Marlowe et al., 1975).

Within Bear's model, a functional hyperconnection between sensory information and core-brain/limbic centers is assumed to result in random pairing of motivationally neutral sensory stimuli with states of limbic arousal. When neutral experiences become imbued with a limbic aura of heightened personal relevance it becomes increasingly difficult to assign priorities to inner and outer events, to decide whether specific events are of peripheral or of central importance to one's well-being. The patient becomes unable to detach the limbic coloring or pathologic valence that a given stimulus elicits, or has been paired with, from the stimulus itself. The epileptic patient may become increasingly religious, philosophical, or moralistic (Bear & Fedio, 1977), perhaps as an expression of the effort to make sense intellectually of his or her globally deepened emotionality. In parallel with the growing sense that events have deep personal relevance, the temporal lobe epileptic may also become hypermnestic. Waxman and Geschwind (1974) suggested that temporal lobe epileptics become hypergraphic in an attempt not to lose any of their experiences. An alternative and less teleologic explanation of constant note-taking, writing a diary, or penning novels, is that this behavior is a written variant of the circumstantiality (verbal viscosity) that often characterizes the interictal speech of these patients.

The degree to which a neutral event or item can be imbued with particular significance, or, in Freud's (1895) term, "hypercathected," is illustrated by the following case report (Mitchell et al., 1954):*

For as long as he could remember, a man, aged 38, enjoyed what he described as a "thought satisfaction" when looking at a safety-pin. This was highly pleasurable and he sought the seclusion of the lavatory to indulge it, since he felt, even as a child, that this was an odd and potentially embarrassing habit. At some time between the ages of 8 and 11 years the "thought satisfaction" began to be followed by a blank period; but, since the phenomenon was kept secret, the first witness to it was his wife, who accidently observed him, aged 23, holding a safety-pin and oblivious of his environment.

*From Mitchell W, Falconer MA, & Hill D (1954): Epilepsy with fetishism relieved by temporal labotomy. Lancet 2:626–630.

During the next few years she observed more of these attacks, and the pattern became clearer. The patient would stare at the pin for a minute and then appear glassy-eyed. Next he would make a humming noise for a few seconds and for a few further seconds sucking movements with his lips. Finally he stood immobile and unresponsive for two minutes...

Every fit was produced by a safety-pin and was therefore largely voluntary. A "bright shiny" whole pin was essential, and often several of them were more effective than one.

...[The patient had] vivid memories of collecting and playing with "bright shiny safety-pins" as a very young child. These were always in his pocket in great numbers, and his favourite game was to join them in a chain and pull it along the floor...

The "thought satisfaction" was considered the greatest experience of his life—"better than sexual intercourse." ...In the last five years he had become increasingly impotent, claiming that the safety-pin had replaced his need for genital outlet (pages 626–627).*

After surgical removal of the left temporal lobe the patient lost interest in safety-pins and his wife reported that their marriage became more sexually rewarding for both of them.

Hyposexuality characterizes temporal lobe epileptics. It is as if these patients' other preoccupations (moral, religious, philisophical, etc.) grow at the expense of their sexuality. Following surgical removal of a temporal lobe focus, transient "rebound hypersexuality" may occur (Blumer, 1970).

If disruption of cortical visuo-limbic connections (see the section on Sensorilimbic and Frontolimbic Connections for details) is the substrate for visual agnosia in the Klüver-Bucy syndrome, what is the mechanism of the hyperconnected state of TLE? It has been suggested that connections between areas in the brain may be facilitated via "kindling." Repetitive subthreshold electrical stimulation has been shown to induce an altered behavioral disposition, which may manifest either as a lowered threshold for seizures or as diffuse behavioral instability reflected by irritability (Goddard, 1980).

The amygdala is known to have the lowest threshold for spiking activity in the central nervous system and it is Bear's (1979) hypothesis that facilitation of temporal pole–amygdalar connections, mediated by kindling, creates a situation wherein sensory input has inappropriately augmented access to the discharge centers for autonomic arousal. A "healthy" amygdala appears to function as a gating device or biaser (Gloor, 1978), mediating between sensory inputs and autonomic discharge mechanisms centered in the hypothalamus. TLE thus may represent a situation wherein the amygdala fails progressively in its job of mediating between internal and external worlds, becoming increasingly unable to modulate visceral autonomic discharge.

In some ways this model resembles that of Stevens (1973), who proposed that limbic forebrain structure (olfactory tubercle, nucleus of stria terminalis, and the nucleus accumbens septi) might function as a "limbic striatum" interposed between inputs from limbic cortex, amygdala, and hippocampus, on the one hand, and limbic efferents to the SHM continuum (visceral effector pathways) and frontal lobe (sensory ganglion or "comparator" for limbic inputs) on the other. Stevens suggested that the intactness of this limbic striatum or filter depends on dopaminergic input from medial forebrain bundle fibers originating in Nauta's limbic midbrain area. She hypothesized that breakdown of this filtering mechanism could be the substrate for schizophrenic disturbances of thought, affect, and behavior. Whereas Bear's model proposes a pathological facilitation of sensorilimbic connections, Steven's model suggests a facilitation of limbicofrontal and limbico-SHM connections. Both models postulate a breakdown in a filtering or gaiting function, which Stevens localizes to the anterior forebrain and Bear to the amygdala.

Despite controversy over the specificity of psychopathology seen in patients with TLE (Mungas, 1982; Stevens & Hermann, 1981), it is clear that TLE provides an exciting model for correlation of psychiatric symptomatology with altered neurophysiology and serves inexorably to remind psychiatry of its kinship with neurology.

FRONTAL LOBE PATHOLOGY AND DEMENTIA SYNDROMES

Although there are several prior anecdotal reports of individuals who survived damage to the prefrontal portions of the brain and underwent behavioral changes, the most famous case of frontal lobe damage is the "American crowbar case" which involved Phineas Gage, a 25-year-old foreman who was working on a railroad bed in Vermont at the time of the 1848 accident:

Gage...was sitting upon a shelf of rock above a drill hole. The powder and fuse had been adjusted in the hole...when Gage started tamping it with the tamping iron 3 feet 7 inches in length, 1¼ inches in diameter and weighing 13¼ pounds, the charge exploded and drove the tapered point through his head, the bar landing several rods away covered with blood and greasy to touch. The missile

entered the left side of the face, immediately anterior to the angle of the lower jaw, and, passing obliquely upward and backward, emerged in the median line near the coronal suture...The patient was thrown on his back by the explosion and gave a few convulsive motions of the extremities, but spoke in a few minutes. (Harlow, 1868).

Gage suffered from a brain infection for a few weeks, but this was treated and he appeared to do surprisingly well. On the 28th day after his injury he was described as "very clear in his mind" and able to discuss his accident. However, when seen by his physician 7 months after the injury, Harlow reported:

The equilibrium of balance, so to speak, between his intellectual faculties and his animal propensities seemed to have been destroyed. He is fitful, irreverent, indulging at times in the grossest profanity (which was not previously his custom), manifesting but little deference to his fellows, impatient of restraint or advice when it conflicts with his desires, at times pertinaciously obstinate yet capricious and vacillating, devising many plans for future operations which are no sooner arranged than they are abandoned in turn for others appearing more feasible. A child in his intellectual capacities but with the general passions of a strong man...his friends and acquaintances said that he was no longer Gage. (Harlow, 1868).

He apparently traveled across the country, spent 8 years in South America, and joined P. T. Barnum's exhibit, where he recounted his mishap and demonstrated the tamping iron which had passed through his skull. In 1861, 12 years after the accident, Gage died in California. His body and the tamping iron were later disinterred and transported from San Francisco to the Harvard Medical School, where his skull and the tamping iron may be seen in the Warren Museum (Fig. 10-24).

The planned destruction of frontal regions as an attempt to treat intractable psychoses and neuroses was initiated in the late 1930s (Moniz, 1936). After seeing a film demonstrating remarkably reduced agitation and anxiety in the behavior of two chimpanzees following frontal lobectomy, the neuropsychiatrist Moniz considered the possible application of this technique to severe mental disorders in man. He and the neurosurgeon Lima implemented prefrontal psychosurgery with the hope of disrupting "the abnormal stabilization of conditioned neural patterns" (Valenstein, 1973). In 1942 Freeman and Watts published their monograph *Psychosurgery*. During the next decade psychosurgical procedures were performed on patients who suffered from a wide range of disorders. By 1950, 1 year after

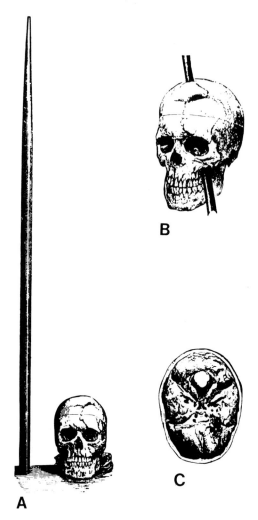

Figure 10-24. Nature of injury in "American crowbar case." (A) Comparative sizes of skull and tamping iron. (B) Front and lateral view of cranium, showing direction in which iron traversed its cavity, present appearance of line of fracture, and large anterior fragment of frontal bone, which was entirely detached, replaced, and partially reunited. (C) View of base of skull from within. Orifice caused by passage of iron had been partially closed by deposit of new bone. (From Freeman W, & Watts JW, 1942: *Psychosurgery*. Thomas, Springfield, Ill.)

Moniz received the Nobel Prize for his pioneering work, more than 10,000 psychosurgical procedures had been performed in the United States alone (Valenstein, 1980).

The earliest of these procedures destroyed, disconnected, or removed large portions of the prefrontal regions, sometimes blindly. At the zenith of enthusiasm about surgical approaches in psychiatry, a

10-minute procedure, Transorbital Leukotomy (Fig. 10-25), was in vogue (Freeman & Watts, 1950). A sharp ice-pick-like instrument was pushed through the orbital roof, inserted approximately 3 cm into brain tissue, and thrust back and forth in a coronal plane. Physiological understanding of orbital leukotomy was limited largely to the recognition that fibers passing from prefrontal and orbitomedial regions of the frontal lobe were severed en route to the dorsomedial thalamus—an area just posterior to a portion of the thalamus (anterior nucleus) which Papez (1937) had suggested might play a role in the elaboration of emotional experience.

As Brodal (1981) has pointed out, however, not only were frontal fibers to the dorsomedial thalamus destroyed, but also fibers directly passing to the SHM continuum, others traveling to the cingulate gyrus, and still others traveling to the supramodal cortex of the inferior parietal lobule (all of these pathways are probably bidirectional). Despite rather extensive ablations, many reports (e.g., Hebb, 1945) concluded that prefrontal surgery produced no significant deterioration in intellectual functioning (thus confusing "absence of proof" with "proof of absence"). What was noticed was a blunting of "higher sensitivities" as well as diminished initiative in intellectual and social spheres. In an attempt to avoid the apathy and inertia produced by the earlier procedures, more restricted targets were lesioned in later approaches (e.g., Pool, 1949, topectomy; Scoville, 1949, orbital undercutting; and anterior cingulate gyrus surgery, LeBeau, 1952).

Attempts have been made to separate cases of frontal lobe disease into two distinct clinical syndromes that reflect the degree of damage to the orbital undersurface or the dorsolateral convexity of the prefrontal region. While most patients with frontal lobe dysfunction seen by neurologists and psychiatrists will not have damage limited to one of these two areas, there appears to be heuristic value in their separation (Blumer & Benson, 1975). With damage to the convexities one tends to see apathy and indifference which can easily be mistaken for depression. On intellectual testing these patients demonstrate correct but slowed responses and require encouragement or even prodding to finish tasks. A second group of patients, those with orbitofrontal pathology, have been characterized as puerile, disinhibited, or pseudopsychopathic. The crowbar case mentioned above clearly has features from each of these syndromes.

Moria and *Witzelsucht* are terms that crop up occasionally in descriptions of altered emotionality following frontal lobe damage. Jastrowitz (1888)

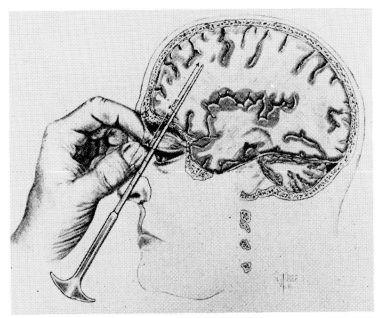

Figure 10-25. Transorbital leukotomy. (From Freeman, W., & Watts, J.W., 1950: *Psychosurgery* (ed. 2). Springfield, Ill., Thomas.)

employed the world *Moria* to describe an ongoing shallow euphoric mood. The term *Witzelsucht* was coined by Oppenheim in 1889 to denote a tendency to facetious punning. Both of these words are used most frequently in the context of the disinhibited playfulness which can follow orbitomedial frontal lobe damage. In general, however, the most characteristic quality of "frontal emotion" is its instability—a feature that parallels the instability of goal-directed behavior in patients with frontal pathology.

Hyperreflexia or spasticity of emotional expression tends to occur in the context of specific disease processes—particularly amyotrophic lateral sclerosis, multiple sclerosis, and bilateral frontal infarctions (multiinfarct dementia). All of these entities share the capacity to disconnect frontal cortex from the brain stem nuclei subserving facial expression of emotion. Autopsy studies most frequently report lesions in the genu or anterior limb of the internal capsule and also in the adjacent basal ganglia (it appears that pathological laughter may be associated with predominantly right brain destruction, while pathological crying is more likely with predominantly left brain pathology; Sackheim et al., 1982). Despite heightened emotional reactivity, most of these patients apparently do not experience altered subjective emotionality. Such patients may, on the one hand, complain that gales of laughter are trig-

gered by trivial events, and, on the other hand, admit to paroxysms of sobbing with no known precipitant. Geschwind (personal communication, 1982) related the incident of a man with pseudobulbar palsy who burst into laughter at the funeral of his son. Occasionally patients' emotional behavior may alternate between extremes (Lieberman & Benson, 1977).

Emotional changes in dementia have not as yet received real attention. There is a general sense that progressive impoverishment of emotional life accompanies most dementing processes, with alteration in the duration as well as the intensity of affective expression. In contrast, there are isolated patients who seem to become more, rather than less, emotional with the progression of dementia. Whether these patients were previously histrionic or hypomanic individuals who have lost some degree of cortical control over a tenuous emotional equilibrium, or whether they have a distinct neuropathology, remains to be determined. General paresis of the insane (tertiary syphilis) may be characterized by expansive grandiosity in 15–20 percent of cases (Merritt, 1955), and is associated with prefrontal and anterior temporal atrophy—a distribution similar to the pathology of Pick's disease.

In 1974 Albert and co-workers described progressive supranuclear palsy (PSP) as a subcortical dementia characterized by a disorder of timing and activation. It resembles Parkinson's disease but is characterized by nuchal rigidity and pseudobulbar palsy, with early impairment of extraocular movements in the vertical plane (Steele et al., 1964). Benson (1981) suggested that Parkinson's disease, Huntington's disease, normal pressure hydrocephalus, multiinfarct dementia, and Wilson's disease all might be examples of dementing processes based on a disruption of corticolimbic connections. In Parkinson's disease there is a 10-fold greater incidence of dementia than in age-matched controls (Lieberman et al., 1978), with pathology indistinguishable from that of Alzheimer's disease (Boller et al., 1980; Hakim & Mathieson, 1978). This raises the question of whether the high incidence of dementia among individuals with Parkinson's disease is simply a reflection of their greater likelihood of having Alzheimer-type degenerative changes.

Certain disease processes can produce selective distruption of limbic gray matter. The predilection of Negri bodies for the hippocampal region of rabies led Papez (1937) to associate the dramatic emotional shifts seen in this illness with damage to the medial temporal lobes. In 1968 Corsellis et al. noted the association of "limbic encephalitis" with bronchial carcinoma and commented that organic brain syndromes secondary to pulmonary malignancy may be seen in the absense of other neurological signs. Five years later, Gascon and Gilles (1973) coined the term *limbic dementia* in describing a case of necrotizing encephalitis. The patient they described had marked emotional lability (i.e., hypomania, crying, anxiety, denial of illness, and witzelsucht), impaired attention, and memory deficits. In addition to these emotional and intellectual changes, their patient also had the following features of the Klüver-Bucy syndrome: psychic blindness, oral tendencies, absence of anger or fear reactions, hypermetamorphosis (attending and responding to every visual stimulus), and somewhat sexualized language.

The Wernicke-Korsakoff syndrome (Victor et al., 1971) is usually thought of in terms of the striking memory deficits seen in the chronic stages of this illness. Often neglected, however, are the profound emotional changes that accompany the amnestic syndrome. Apathy, emotional blunting, and loss of initiative are hallmarks of the disease and can be ascribed to lesions of the SHM continuum (periventricular and periaqueductal hemorrhages), as well as destruction in the mesial (mammillary bodies) and the basolateral (dorsomedial thalamic nucleus) limbic circuits.

While the above may appear to be isolated instances, many dementias may ultimately be shown to have a limbic component (Wells, 1982). This possibility is supported by the documentation of (1) cholinergic limbicocortical projections originating in the basal forebrain (hypothalamus, nucleus basalis of Meynert, and substantia innominata) (Divac, 1975; Johnston et al., 1979; Kievit & Kuypers, 1975); (2) efferents from the subicular region of the hippocampus to widespread areas of neocortex (Rosene & VanHoesen, 1977); and (3) direct amygdaloprefrontal fibers (Jacobson & Trojanowski, 1975). A decrease in total brain choline acetyltransferase, which has been a consistently observed neurochemical defect in Alzheimer's disease (Reisine et al., 1978), could exert a selective effect on cholinergic pathways arising in core-brain or limbic regions and traveling to neocortical areas. Moreover, recent studies have demonstrated a selective and profound dropout of neurons in the nucleus basalis of Meynert of senile patients (Whitehouse et al., 1982). Thus, evidence is accumulating to suggest that multiple dementia syndromes, including those traditionally termed "cortical," have a major subcortical component and may profitably be conceptualized as arising from a disconnection between core-brain or limbic regions and the neocortex.

CONCLUSIONS

MacLean suggested that our perceptual apparatus is strongly influenced by our "paleomammalian brain" (quoted in Holden, 1979):

We try to be rational, intellectual, to be wary of our emotions. But as far as we have been able to tell to this day—and this is probably the most fundamental thing we have learned, or ever will learn about the nervous system, the only part of the brain that can tell us what we perceive to be real things is the limbic brain (page 1068).

In a similar vein, Nauta (1971) proposed that higher decision making is inseparable from "gut level" feelings generated by the SHM continuum when alternative plans of action are contemplated.

The neurosciences are starting to specify some of the pathways and mechanisms whereby "higher" mental functioning is influenced by and dependent on core-brain and limbic structures. In particular, earlier work on sensorilimbic and frontolimbic connections is increasingly complemented by specification of limbicosensory and limbicofrontal pathways. While profound disruption of these connections may produce a dementia-like picture, partial or selective disconnection of "higher" cortex from "lower" brain centers may be one mechanism whereby syndromes of neglect, inattention, denial, or decathexis arise.

On the other hand, selective hyperconnection (anatomic or transmitter-mediated) of limbicosensory or limbicofrontal connections may have a great deal to do with syndromes characterized by hypercathexis of sensation or mentation (e.g., mania, schizophrenia, or TLE), as well as with the way in which all of us assign priorities or experience meaning in our daily lives. As a bridge between visual and emotional systems, the amygdala appears to be critically involved in the investment of objects with emotional charge or significance. As a bridge between limbic and frontal regions, the dorsomedial thalamus appears to be crucial to the process whereby we structure behavior and determine our long-range goals with reference to objects whose limbic valence has been conferred by sensorilimbic connections.

Discovery of μopiate receptors (Lewis et al., 1981) in sensory association cortex may be of especial relevance to the interplay of sensory and limbic systems. If we were able to understand the mechanism whereby pathological overvaluation of ideas (delusions) arise, we might also learn how to modulate the intensity of delusional rumination. In this direction, perhaps, is the work of Watson et al. (1978), who demonstrated the reduction of auditory hallucinations in certain schizophrenic patients following administration of naloxone (an opiate antagonist).

The boundaries between anatomy and physiology, between form and function, start to break down at an ultrastructural level. Neuroleptic drugs, for instance, appear to cause supersensitivity via sprouting of postsynaptic dopaminergic receptor sites in the neostriatum (Burt et al., 1977) and may also induce similar structural changes in the mesolimbic and mesocortical systems (Stevens & Livermore, 1978). Thus, pharmacology may alter structure as well as function.

Knowledge of the brain's anatomic matrix enhances immeasurably the value of whatever physiology, chemistry, or immunology we can map onto this terrain. Freud (1912) paraphrased Napoleon when he stated, "Anatomy is destiny." It is essential for us to remember that anatomy is not static. Whether we use words (Kandel, 1979) or drugs, as psychiatrists we are in the business of facilitating or blocking neural pathways whose specificity we are actually coming to know.

REFERENCES

Akelaitis AJ (1945): Studies of the corpus callosum IV. Diagnostic dyspraxia in epileptics following partial and complete section of the corpus callosum. Am J Psychiatry 101:594–599.

Albert ML, Feldman RG, & Willis AL (1974): The subcortical dementia of progressive supranuclear palsy. J Neurol Neurosurg Psychiatry 37:121–130.

Anand BK & Brobeck JR (1951): Hypothalamic control of food intake in cats and rats. Yale J Biol Med 24:123–140.

Anton G (1899): Uber die Selbstwahrnehemung der Herderkrankungen des Gehirns durch den Kranken bei Rindenblindheit und Rindentaubheit. Arch Psychiatr Nervenkr 32:86–127.

Babinski MJ (1914): Contribution à l'etude des troubles mentaux dans l'hémiplégie organique (anosognosie). Rev Neurol 27:175–185.

Babinski MJ (1918): Anosognosie. Rev Neurol 34:365–367.

Bard P (1928): A diencephalic mechanism for the expression of rage with special reference to the sympathetic nervous system. Am J Physiol 84:490–515.

Battersby WS, Bender MB, Pollack M, & Kahn RL (1965): Unilateral spatial agnosia (inattention) in patients with cerebral lesions. Brain 79:68–93.

Bear D (1979): Temporal lobe epilepsy: A syndrome of sensory–limbic hyperconnection. Cortex 15:357–384.

Bear D & Fedio P (1977): Quantitative analysis of interictal behavior in temporal lobe epilepsy. Arch Neurol 34:454–469.

Benson DF (1973): Psychiatric aspects of aphasia. Br J Psychiatry 123:555–566.

Benson DF (1979): *Aphasia, Alexia, and Agraphia.* New York, Churchill Livingstone.

Benson DF (1981): Dementia: A clinical approach. Section 2 The Clinical Aspects of Aging - edited by JC Beck. In Roche Seminars on Aging.

Benson DF & Blumer D (1975): *Psychiatric Aspects of Neurologic Disease*, New York, Grune & Stratton.

Blumer D (1967): The temporal lobes and paroxysmal behavior disorders. Beiheft Schweiz, Z. Psychol, Anwendungen [Suppl VII] 51:273–285.

Blumer D (1970) Hypersexual episodes in temporal lobe epilepsy. Am J Psychiatry 126:1099–1106.

Blumer D (1975): Temporal lobe epilepsy and its psychiatric significance. Benson DF, & Blumer D (Eds.). In *Psychiatric Aspects of Neurologic Disease*, pp 171–198. New York, Grune & Stratton.

Blumer D & Benson DF (1975): Personality changes with frontal and temporal lobe lesions. Benson DF & Blumer D (Eds.). In *Psychiatric Aspects of Neurologic Disease*, pp 151–170. New York, Grune & Stratton.

Boller F, Mizutani T, Roessmann U, & Gambetti P (1980): Parkinson disease, dementia, and Alzheimer disease: Clinicopathological correlations. Ann Neurol 7:329–335.

Brion S & Jednyak CP (1972): Troubles du tranfert interhémisphérique (callosal disconnection) a propos de 3 observations de tumeurs du corps calleux. Le signe de la main étrangère. Rev Neurol 126:257–266.

Broca P (1861): Perte de la parole. Ramollissement chronique et destruction partielle du lobe anterieur gauche du cerveau. Paris Bull Soc Anthrop 2:219.

Broca P (1878) Anatomie comparee des circonvolutions cerebrales: Le grand lobe limbique et la scissure limbique dans la serie des mammiferes. Rev Anthropol (Ser 2) 1:385–498.

Brodal A (1981): Neurological Anatomy (Ed 3.). New York, Oxford University Press.

Burt DR, Creese, I & Snyder SH (1977): Antischizophrenic drugs: Chronic treatment elevates receptor binding in the brain. Science 196:326–328.

Cade JFJ (1949): Lithium salts in the treatment of psychotic excitement. Med J Aust 2:349–352.

Cajal S & Ramon Y (1901-2): Estudios sobre la corteza cerebral humana IV. Estructura de la corteza cerebral olfativa del hombre y mamiferos. Trabajo Laboratoria Investigativa de Madrid.

Corsellis J, Goldberg GJ, & Norton A (1968): "Limbic encephalitis" and its associations with carcinoma. Brain 91:481–496.

Critchley M (1953): The Parietal Lobes. New York, Hafner Press.

Critchley M (1957): Observations on anosodiaphoria. Encephale 46:540–546.

Critchley M (1979): Misoplegia, or hatred of hemiplegia. In The Divine Banquet of the Brain, New York, Raven Press, pp. 115–120.

Dahlstrom A, & Fuxe K (1964): A method for the demonstration of monoamine containing nerve fibers in the central nervous system. Acta Physiol Scand 60:293–295.

Daly DD, & Mulder DW (1957): Gelastic epilepsy. Neurology 7:189–192.

Damasio AR, Damasio H, & Van Hoesen GW (1982): Prosopagnosia: Anatomic basis and behavioral mechanisms. Neurology (NY) 32:331–341.

Delay J, & Deniker P (1952): Le traitement des psychoses par une methode neurolytique derivee de l' hibernothérapie. Congrès des Médecins Aliénistes et Neurologistes de France, Luxembourg 50:497–515.

Delgado-Escueta AV, Mattson RH, King L, Goldensohn ES, Spiegel H, Madsen J, Crandall P, Dreifuss E, & Porter RJ (1981): The nature of aggression during epileptic seizures. N Engl J Med 305:711–716.

Denny-Brown D, Meyer JS, & Horenstein S (1952): The significance of perceptual rivalry resulting from parietal lesions. Brain 75:434–471.

De Renzi E, Faglioni P, & Spinnler H (1968): The performance of patients with unilateral brain damage on facial recognition tasks. Cortex 4:17–34.

Dimond SJ (1980): Neuropsychology. Boston, Butterworths.

Divac I (1975): Magnocellular nuclei of the basal forebrain project to neocortex, brain stem, and olfactory bulb. Review of some functional correlates. Brain Res 93:385–398.

Downer JL (1962): Interhemispheric integration in the visual system. Mountcastle V (Ed.). In Interhemispheric Relations and Cerebral Dominance. Baltimore, Johns Hopkins Press, pp. 87–100.

Eleftheriou B (1972): The Neurobiology of the Amygdala. New York, Plenum Press.

Finklestein S, Benowitz LI, Baldessavini RJ, Arana GW, Levine D, Woo E, Bear D, Moya K, & Stoll AL (1982): Mood, vegetative disturbance and dexamethasone suppression test after stroke. Ann Neur 12:463–468.

Freud S (1912): On the universal tendency to debasement in the sphere of love (standard ed.) vol II, Hogarth, London, 1957, pp. 179–190.

Gainotti G (1972): Emotional behavior and hemispheric side of the lesion. Cortex 8:41–55.

Galin D (1974): Implications for psychiatry of left and right cerebral specialization. Arch Gen Psychiatry 31:552–583.

Gascon GG, & Gilles F (1973): Limbic dementia. J Neurol Neurosurg Psychiatry 36:421–430.

Gasparrini GS, Satz P, Heilman KM, & Coolidge FM (1978): Hemispheric asymmetries of affective processing as determined by the Minnesota Multiphasic Personality Inventory. J Neurol Neurosurg Psychiatry 41:470–473.

Gastaut H (1954): Interprétation des symptomes de l'epilepsi "psychomotrice" en fonction des données de la physiologie rhinencéphalique. Presse Méd 10:1535–1537.

Gastaut H, & Broughton R (1972): Epileptic Seizures. Springfield Ill, Thomas.

Gazzaniga MS (1970): The Bisected Brain. New York, Appleton, p. 107.

Geschwind N (1965): Disconnexion syndromes in animals and man. Brain 88:237–294, 585–644.

Gevins AS, Doyle C, Cutillo BA, Schaffer RE, Tannehill RS, Ghannam JH, Gilcrease VA, & Yeager CL (1981): Electrical potentials in human brain during cognition: New method reveals dynamic patterns of correlation. Science 213:918–922.

Girgis M, & Kiloh LG (Eds.) (1980): Limbic Epilepsy and the Dyscontrol Syndrome. New York, Elsevier/North Holland Biomedical Press.

Gloor P (1978): Inputs and outputs of the amygdala: What the amygdala is trying to tell the rest of the brain. In Limbic Mechanisms (ibid) pp. 189–209.

Glowinski J (1981): Present knowledge on the properties of the mesocorticofrontal dopaminergic neurons. Matthysse S (Ed.). In Psychiatry and the Biology of the Human Brain: A Symposium Dedicated to Seymour Kety. New York, Elsevier/North Holland, pp. 15–28.

Goddard GV (1980): The kindling model of limbic epilepsy. Girgis M, & Kiloh LG (Eds.). In Limbic Epilepsy and *the Dyscontrol Syndrome*. New York, Elsevier/North Holland, pp. 107–116.

Goldstein K (1962): The effects of brain damage on personality. Psychiatry 15:245–260.

Grossman SP (1980): The neuroanatomy of eating and drinking behavior. Krieger DT, & Hughes JC (Eds.). In *Neuroendocrinology*, Sunderland Mass, Sinauer Associates, pp. 131–140.

Hakim AM, & Mathieson G (1978): Basis of dementia in Parkinson's disease. Lancet 2:729.

Harlow JM (1868): Recovery from passage of an iron bar through the head. Publ Mass Med Soc 2:329–346.

Heath RG (1972): Pleasure and brain activity in deep and surface electroencephalograms during orgasm. J Nerv Ment Dis 154:3–18.

Hebb DO (1945): Man's frontal lobes: A critical review. Arch Neurol Psychiatry 54:10–24.

Hecaen H, & Albert ML (1978): *Human Neuropsychology*. New York, Wiley.

Heilman KM (1979): Neglect and related disorders. Heilman KM, & Valenstein E (Eds.). In *Clinical Neuropsychology*. New York, Oxford University Press.

Heilman KM, & Watson RT (1977): The neglect syndrome — A unilateral defect in the orienting response. Harnad S, Doty RW, Goldstein L, Jaynes J, & Krauthamer G (Eds.). In *Lateralization in the Nervous System*. New York, Academic Press.

Heilman KM, Scholes R, & Watson RT (1975): Auditory affective agnosia: Disturbed comprehension of affective speech. J Neurol Neurosurg Psychiatry 38:69–72.

Herrick JC (1933): The functions of the olfactory parts of the cerebral cortex. Proc Nat'l Acad Sci USA 18:7–14.

Holden C (1979): Paul MacLean and the triune brain. Science 204:1066–1068.

Isaacson RL, & Pribram KH (Eds.) (1975): *The Hippocampus*, vol I, Structure and Development, vol 2, *Neurophysiology and Behavior*. New York, Plenum Press.

Jackson JH (1881): Remarks on dissolution of the nervous sytem as exemplified by certain post-epileptic conditions. Taylor J (Ed.). In *Selected Writings of John Hughlings Jackson*, vol 2. London, Hoddert and Stoughton, 1932.

Jacobson S, & Trojanowski JQ (1975): Amygdaloid projections to prefrontal granular cortex in rhesus monkey demonstrated with horseradish peroxidase. Brain Res 100:132–139.

Jastrowitz M (1888): Beitrage zur localisation im Grosshirn und uber deren praktischen Verwerthung. Dtsch Med Wochenschr 14:81–83.

Johnston MV, McKinney MRG, & Coyle JT (1979): Evidence for a cholinergic projection to neocortex from neurons in basal forebrain. Proc Natl Acad Sci USA 76:5392–5396.

Joseph R (1982): Hemispheric laterality, limbic language, and the origin of thought. J Clin Psychol 38:4–33.

Kandel ER (1979): Psychotherapy and the single synapse. N Engl J Med 301:1028–1037.

Kashnig DM, & Celesia CG (1976): Nasopharyngeal electrodes in the diagnosis of partial seizures with complex symptoms. Arch Neurol 33:519–520.

Keating, EG (1971): Somatosensory deficit produced by parieto-temporal disconnections. Anat Rec 169:353–354.

Kiernan RJ (1981): Localization of function: The mind—body problem revisited. J Clin Neuropsychol 3:345–352.

Kievit J, & Kuypers HGJM (1975): Basal forebrain and hypothalamic connections to frontal and parietal cortex in the rhesus monkey. Science 198:315–317.

Klüver H, & Bucy P (1937): "Psychic blindness" and other symptoms following bilateral temporal lobectomy in rhesus monkeys. Am J Physiol 119:352–353.

Klüver H, & Bucy P (1938): An analysis of certain effectsof bilateral temporal lobectomy in rhesus monkeys with special reference to psychic blindness. J Psychol 5:33–54.

Klüver H, & Bucy P (1939): Preliminary analysis of functions of the temporal lobe in monkeys. Arch Neurol Psychiatry 42:979–1000.

Laplane D, Talairach J, Meininger V, Bancaud J, & Orgogozo JM (1977): Clinical consequences of corticectomies involving the supplementary motor area in man. J Neurol Sci 34:301–314.

LeBeau J (1952): The cingular and precingular areas in psychosurgery (agitated behavior, obsessive compulsive states, epilepsy). Acta Psychiatr Neurol Scand 27:305–316.

Lesser IM (1981): A review of the alexithymia concept. Psychosom Med 43:531–543.

Lewis ME, Mishkin M, Bragin E, Brown RM, Pert C, & Pert A (1981): Opiate receptor gradient in monkey cerebral cortex: Correspondence with sensory processing hierarchies. Science 211:1166–1169.

Ley RG, & Bryden MP (1979): Hemispheric differences in processing emotions and faces. Brain & Lang 7:127–138.

Lezak M (1976): *Neuropsychological Assessment* New York, Oxford University Press.

Lieberman A, Benson DF (1977): Pseudobulbar palsy. Arch Neurol 34:717–719.

Lieberman A, Dziatolowski M, Kupersmith M, Serby M, Goodgold A, Korein J, & Goldstein M (1978): Dementia in Parkinson disease. Neurology 6:355–359.

Lishman WA (1978): *Organic Psychiatry*. Oxford, Blackwell.

Livingston KE, & Escobar A (1971): Anatomical bias of the limbic system concept. Arch Neurol 24:17–21.

Livingston KE, & Hornkiewicz O (1978): *Limbic Mechanisms*. New York, Plenum Press.

Luria, AR (1966): *Higher Cortical Functions in Man*. New York, Basic Books.

MacLean PD (1967): The brain, empathy and medical education. J Nerv Ment Dis 144:374–382.

MacLean PD (1969): *A Triune Concept of Brain and Behavior*. Toronto, University of Toronto Press.

Mandell AJ, & Knapp S (1979): Asymmetry and mood, emergent properties of serotonin regulation. Arch Gen Psychiatry 36:909–916.

Marlowe WB, Mancall EL, & Thomas JJ (1975): Complete Kluver-Bucy syndrome in man. Cortex 11:53–59.

Marshall JF, Turner BH, & Teitelbaum P (1971): Sensory neglect produced by lateral hypothalamic damage. Science 174:523–525.

Marx OM (1966): Aphasia studies and language theory in the 19th century. Bull Hist Med 40:328–349.

Marx OM (1967): Freud and aphasia: An historical analysis. Am J Psychiatry 124:815–825.

Meadows JC (1974): The anatomic basis of prosopagnosia. J Neurol Neurosurg Psychiatry 37:489–501.

Merritt HH (1955): *A Textbook of Neurology.* New York, Lea & Febiger, p. 140.

Mesulam MM (1981): A cortical network for directed attention and unilateral neglect. Ann Neurol 10:309–325.

Mishkin M (1979): Analagous neural models for tactual and visual learning. Neuropsychologia 17:139–151.

Mitchell W, Falconer MA, & Hill D (1954): Epilepsy with fetishism relieved by temporal lobectomy. Lancet 2:626–630.

Moniz E (1936): *Tentatives Opératoires dans le Traitement de Certaines Psychoses.* Paris, Masson.

Monrad-Krohn GH (1947): "Dysprosody" or altered melody of language. Brain 70:405–415.

Moore RY (1973): Retinohypothalamic projections in mammals: A comparative study. Brain Res 49:403–409.

Moore RY, Bjorklund A, & Stenevi U (1971): Plastic changes in the adrenergic innervation of the rat septal nuclei in response to denervation. Brain Res 14:25–48.

Morariu MA (1977): Akinetic mutism (coma vigil). In *Major Neurological Syndromes.* Springfield, Ill., Thomas, pp. 246–255.

Moruzzi G, & Magoun HW (1949): Brainstem reticular formation and activation of the EEG. Electrophys Clin Neurophys 1:455–473.

Mungas D (1982): Interictal behavior abnormality in temporal lobe epilepsy: A specific syndrome or nonspecific psychopathology? Arch Gen Psychiatry 39:108–111.

Nauta WJH (1958) Hippocampal projections and related neural pathways to the midbrain in the cat. Brain 81:319–340.

Nauta WJH (1971): The problem of the frontal lobe: A reinterpretation. J Psychiat Res 8:167–187.

Nauta WJH (1973): Connections of the frontal lobe with the limbic system. Laitinen LV, & Livingston KE (Eds.). In *Surgical Approaches in Psychiatry.* Baltimore, University Park Press, pp. 303–314.

Nauta WJH, & Domesick VB (1981): Ramifications of the limbic system. In *Psychiatry and the Biology of the Human Brain: A Symposium Dedicated to Seymour Kety.* New York, Elsevier/North-Holland, pp. 165–188.

Offen MT, Davidoff RA, Troost BT, & Reihey ET (1976): Dacrystic epilepsy. J Neurol Neurosurg Psychiatry 39:829–834.

Oke A, Keller R, Mefford I, & Adams RN (1978): Lateralization of norepinephrine in human thalamus. Science 200:1411–1413.

Olds J (1960): Differentiation of reward systems in the brain by self-stimulation techniques. Ramey SR, & O'Doherty DS (Eds.). In *Electrical Studies on the Unanesthetized Brain.* New York, Harper & Row, p. 17.

Oppenheim H (1889): Zur Pathologie der Grosshirngeschwulste. Arch Psychiatr Nervenkr 21:560–587.

Papez JW (1937): A proposed mechanism of emotion. Arch Neurol Psychiatry 38:725–743.

Penfield W, & Rasmussen T (1950): *The Cerebral Cortex of Man: A Clinical Study of Localisation of Function.* New York, Macmillan.

Perenin PT, Ruel J, & Hecaen H (1980): Residual visual capacities in a case of cortical blindness. Cortex 16:605–612.

Pincus J, & Tucker G (1974): *Behavioral Neurology.* New York, Oxford University Press.

Pool, JL (1949): Topectomy. Proc Roy Soc Med 42: Suppl 1–3.

Powell TPS (1973): Sensory convergence in the cerebral cortex. Laitinen LV, & Livingston KE (Eds.). In *Surgical Approaches in Psychiatry.* Lancaster, England, edical Technical, pp. 266–281.

Raisman G (1969): Neuronal plasticity in the septal nuclei of the adult rat. Brain Res 14:25–48.

Reeves AG, & Plum F (1969): Hyperphagia, obesity, rage, and dementia accompanying a ventromedial hypothalamic neoplasm. Arch Neurol 20:616–624.

Reisine TD, Yamahura HI, Bird ED, Spokes E, & Enna SJ (1978): Pre- and postsynaptic neurochemical alterations in Alzheimer's disease. Brain Res 159:477–481.

Robinson RG, & Szetela B (1980): Mood change following left hemispheric brain injury. Ann Neurol 9:447–453.

Rosene DL, & VanHoesen GW (1977): Hippocampal efferents reach widespread areas of cerebral cortex and amygdala in the rhesus monkey. Science 198:315–317.

Ross ED (1981): The aprosodias: Functional-anatomic localization of the affective components of language in the right hemisphere. Arch Neurol 38:561–569.

Ross ED, & Mesulam MM (1979): Dominant language functions of the right hemisphere?: Prosody and emotional gesturing. Arch Neurol 36:144–148.

Ross ED, & Rush AJ (1981): Diagnosis and neuroanatomical correlates of depression in brain-damaged patients. Arch Gen Psychiatry 38:1344–1354.

Ross ED, & Stewart RM (1981): Akinetic mutism from hypothalamic damage: Successful treatment with dopamine agonists. Neurology (NY) 31:1435–1439.

Sackheim HA, Gur RC, & Saucy MC (1978): Emotions are expressed more intensely on the left side of the face. Science 202:434–436.

Sackheim HA, Greenberg MS, Weiman AL, Gur RC, Hungerbuhler JP, & Geschwind N (1982): Hemispheric asymmetry in the expression of positive and negative emotions. Arch Neurol 39:210–218.

Schenk L, & Bear D (1981): Multiple personalities and related dissociative phenomena in patients with temporal lobe epilepsy. J Neurol Neurosurg Psychiatry 138:1311–1316.

Schilder P (1935): *The Image and Appearance of the Human Body.* London, Kegan Paul, Trench, Trubner.

Scoville WG (1949): Selective cortical undercutting as a means to modifying and studying frontal lobe function in man. Preliminary report of 43 operative cases. J Neurosurg 6:65–73.

Sethi PK, & Rao TS (1976): Gelastic, quiritarian, and cursive epilepsy. J Neurol Neurosurg Psychiatry 39:823–828.

Snyder SH (1980): Brain peptides as neurotransmitters. Science 209:976–983.

Steele J, Richardson JC, & Olszewski J (1964): Progressive supranuclear palsy. Arch Neurol 10:333–359.

Stein M, Schleifer SJ, & Keller SE (1981): Hypothalamic influences on immune responses. Ader R (Ed.). In Psychoneuroimmunology. New York, Academic Press, pp. 429–447.

Stevens JR (1973): An anatomy of schizophrenia? Arch Gen Psychiatry 29:177–189.

Stevens JR, & Hermann BP (1981): Temporal lobe epilepsy, psychopathology, and violence: The state of the evidence. Neurology 31:1127–1132.

Stevens JR, & Livermore A (1978): Kindling of the mesolimbic dopamine system: Animal model of psychosis. Neurology 28:36–46.

Terzian H (1964): Behavioral and EEG effects of intracarotid sodium amytal injections. Acta Neurochir (Wien) 12:230–240.

Terzian H, & Dalle Ore G (1955): Syndrome of Kluver and Bucy. Neurology (Minneap) 5: 373–380.

Turner W (1890): The convolutions of the brain: A study in comparative anatomy. J Anat Physiol 25:105–153.

Valenstein ES (1973): Brain Control. New York, Wiley, p. 269.

Valenstein ES (1980): The Psychosurgery Debate. San Francisco, Freeman, p. 38.

Valzelli L (1980): An Approach to Neuroanatomical and Neurochemical Psychophysiology, Littleton, Mass, Wright.

Victor M, Adams RD, & Collins GH (1971): The Wernicke-Korsakoff Syndrome. Philadelphia, Davis.

Vogt BA, Rosene DL, & Pandya DN (1979): Thalamic and cortical afferents differentiate anterior from posterior cingulate cortex in the monkey. Science 204:1205–1207.

Von Monakov C (1885): Experimentelle und pathologisch-anatomische Untersuchungen uber die Beziehungen der sogenannten Sehsphare zu den infracorticalen Opticuscentren und zum N. opticus. Arch Psychiatr Nervenkr 16:151–199.

Wada J, & Rasmussen T (1960): Intracarotid injection of sodium amytal for the lateralization of cerebral speech dominance: Experimental and clinical observations. J Neurosurg 17:266–282.

Walsh KV (1978): Neuropsychology. New York, Churchill Livingstone.

Watson SJ, Berger PA, Akil H, Mills MJ, & Barchas JD (1978): Effects of naloxone on schizophrenia: Reduction of hallucinations in a subpopulation of patients. Science 201:73–76.

Waxman GS, & Geschwind N (1974): Hypergraphia in temporal lobe epilepsy. Neurology 24:629–636.

Weinstein EA, & Kahn RL (1955): Denial of Illness. Springfield, Thomas.

Weintraub S, Mesulam MM, & Kramer L (1981): Disturbance in prosody: A right-hemisphere contribution to language. Arch Neurol 38:742–744.

Wells CE (1981): A deluge of dementia. Psychosomatics 22:837–840.

Wells CE (1982): Chronic brain disease: an update on alcoholism, Parkinson's disease, and dementia. Hosp Community Psychiatry 33:111–126.

Wernicke C (1874): Der aphasische Symptomenkomplex. Eine psychologische Studie auf anatomischer Basis. Breslau, Kohn & Neigart. [The symptom complex of aphasia. Church (Ed.). In Modern Clinical Medicine: Disease of the Nervous System. New York, Appleton-Century-Crofts, 1908]

Whitehouse PJ, Price DL, Struble RG, Clark AW, Coyle JT, & DeLong MR (1982): Alzheimer's disease and senile dementia: Loss of neurons in the basal forebrain. Science 215:1237–1239.

Wiesel TN, & Hubel DH (1963): Single-cell responses in striate cortex of kittens deprived of vision in one eye. J Neurophysiol 26:1003–1017.

Yakovlev PI (1948): Behavior and the brain: Organization and neural coordinates of behavior. J Nerv Ment Dis 107:313–335.

SUGGESTED READINGS

Carpenter MB (1976): Human Neuroanatomy (Ed. 7). Baltimore, Williams & Wilkins, p. 479.

Chouinard G, & Jones BD (1980): Neuroleptic-induced supersensitivity psychosis: Clinical and pharmacologic characteristics. Am J Psychiatry 137:16–21.

Columbia-Greystone Associates (1949): Selective Partial Ablation of the Frontal Cortex. Metler F (Ed.). New York, Hoeber.

Freeman W, & Watts JW (1942): Psychosurgery Springfield, Ill., Thomas.

Freeman W, & Watts JW (1950). Psychosurgery (Ed. 2.). Springfield, Ill., Thomas.

Freud S (1895): Project for a Scientific Psychology (standard ed. vol 1). London, Hogarth 1966, pp. 281–397.

Himwich HE (1965): Anatomy and physiology of the emotions and their relation to psychoactive drugs. Marks J, & Pare CMB (Eds.). In The Scientific Basis of Drug Therapy in Psychiatry. Oxford, Pergamon Press, p. 7.

Iversen LI (1979): The chemistry of the brain. Sci Am 241:134–149.

Jackson JH (1878): On affections of speech from diseases of the brain. Brain 1:304–330.

Pribram K, & Gill M (1976): Freud's Project Reassessed. London, Hutchinson.

Smith JS (1980): Episodic rage. Girgis, M, & Kiloh LG (Eds.). In Limbic Epilepsy and the Dyscontrol Syndrome. New York, Elsevier/North-Holland, pp. 255–265.

Willis T (1664): Cerebri Anatome. London, Martzer and Alleftry.

11

Affect, Repression, and Cerebral Asymmetry

Richard J. Davidson

Although functional differences in the cognitive domain have been the most extensively studied of the differences between the two sides of the brain, a variety of observations from both clinical and experimental research point toward important hemispheric differences in the regulation of affective behavior. In this chapter the data on lateralization for affect in humans is reviewed and the application of this body of information to the study of individual differences in repressive defensiveness is considered. Specifically, repressive defensiveness is examined as a dissociation between verbal reports of emotion and other indices indicative of affective state. Data are presented that bear on the hypothesis that a mechanism for repression may be a functional disconnection between particular regions of the right hemisphere subserving the generation of negative affect and language centers in the left hemisphere responsible for verbal output.

ASYMMETRIES FOR AFFECTIVE PROCESSES IN HUMANS

Research on affective asymmetries in adults has received less attention than the study of cognitive asymmetries. However, during the past decade, a growing interest in the psychobiological substrates of affect has helped to stimulate more research on

Preparation of this chapter was supported in part by grants from the John D. and Catherine T. MacArthur Foundation, The Foundation for Child Development, and The Research Foundation of the State University of New York. Parts of the chapter are derived from Davidson (in press b). I thank Clifford Saron, Carrie Schaffer, and Jonathan Perl for their many contributions to the research described herein and Diana Angelini for secretarial expertise.

asymmetry and affect. Data based upon a variety of methods with both normal and clinical populations is beginning to challenge an early hypothesis suggesting right hemispheric specialization for emotion in general (e.g., Schwartz et al., 1975). The findings are more consistent with the notion of differential lateralization for at least certain positive and negative affects. More formally stated, this hypothesis holds that certain regions of the left hemisphere are specialized for the processing of certain forms of positive affect, while certain regions of the right hemisphere are specialized for the processing of certain forms of negative affect.

This hypothesis is based upon clinical data on the following: (1) the effects of unilateral cerebral lesions on emotional processes (Alford, 1933; Bear & Fedio, 1977; Benson, 1973; Denny-Brown et al., 1952; Gainotti, 1969, 1972; Goldstein, 1939; Hecaen et al., 1951; Robinson & Benson, 1981; Robinson & Szetela, 1981; Ross & Rush, 1981; Sackheim et al., 1982); (2) the effects of unilateral injections of sodium amytal on emotional processes (Hommes & Panhuysan, 1971; see also Kolb & Milner, 1981b; Milner, 1967; Perria et al., 1961; Rossi & Rosadini, 1967; Serafetinides et al., 1965; Terzian, 1964;); (3) lateralized dysfunctions in affective disorders (Abrams & Taylor, 1979; Bruder & Yozawitz, 1979; Flor-Henry, 1976; Flor-Henry & Yeudall, 1979; Flor-Henry et al., 1979; Goldstein et al., 1977; Kronfol et al., 1978; Perris & Monakhov, 1979; Sackheim & Decina, 1982; Schaffer, 1983 in press; Shagass et al., 1979; Yozawitz et al., 1979); (4) the effects of lateralized electroconvulsive therapy on depressive disorders (Cohen et al., 1974; Cronin et al., 1970; Deglin & Nikolaenko, 1975; Halliday et al., 1968; Strauss et al., 1979; Zinkin & Birthnell, 1968).

The hypothesis is also more directly supported by research on normal subjects. We have used a variety of methods to assess asymmetrical hemispheric activations in normal subjects in response to affective stimuli. These data are reviewed in the following sections.

There are two major qualifications in the statement of this hypothesis: (1) the specific hemispheric regions associated with affective asymmetries are left unstated; and (2) the precise emotions for which this asymmetry exists is not indicated. The reason for the lack of more specification on these two points is that sufficient data do not yet exist. (A number of speculations on these issues are presented at the end of this section.)

Lateral Gaze Shifts
In Response to Affective Stimuli

Lateral gaze shifts have been employed as a gross index of asymmetrical hemispheric engagement by numerous investigators (Anderson, 1977; Ehrlichman & Weinberger, 1978; Gur, 1975; Gur & Gur, 1977; Kinsbourne, 1972; Kocel et al., 1972; Schwartz et al., 1975). Considerable controversy has been generated concerning the validity of lateral gaze shifts as an index of hemispheric asymmetry. Ehrlichman and Weinberger (1978) reviewed 19 published experiments that examined the effects of reflective questions designed to activate differentially the left versus the right hemisphere on lateral eye movements (LEMs). They observed that only 9 of those experiments obtained significant effects in the predicted direction—i.e., "left hemisphere" questions eliciting a significantly greater proportion of right LEMs than "right hemisphere" questions. Numerous methodological inadequacies have plagued research using LEMs as a dependent measure (see Ehrlichman & Weinberger, 1978).

In our previous work using this measure, we reasoned that despite its methodological limitations, it may be particularly useful in the study of affective processes, as Ehrlichman and Weinberger (1978) have acknowledged. A significant component of eye movement control resides in the frontal cortex (Robinson & Fuchs, 1969); this cortical region has been implicated in the regulation of affective processes (Luria, 1966, 1973; Nauta, 1971; Pribram, 1973), and we have obtained EEG evidence suggesting that this region specifically discriminates between positive versus negative affect.

In our earlier work, we sought to examine whether greater right hemispheric involvement was associated with the processing of affective versus nonaffective questions (Schwartz et al., 1975). We

found significantly more left and fewer right eye movements in response to emotional versus non-emotional questions. (The first eye movement following the presentation of the question was scored; Ehrlichman, 1979, found this to be the most discriminating measure in a comparison of verbal versus spatial questions). These data have been successfully replicated in our laboratory with simultaneous measures of electrodermal activity (Davidson et al., 1977), which confirmed that the affective questions elicited significantly more skin resistance responses (defined as a change of at least 1,000 ohms following presentation of the question) compared with nonaffective questions. Two independent laboratories have also replicated our eye movement findings using the set of questions we developed (Hassett & Zelner, 1977; Tucker et al., 1977).

Interestingly, when we reexamined these eye movement data we found a greater number of negative compared to positive questions were employed and the negative questions elicited more left eye movements (indicative of greater right hemispheric activation) compared to the positive questions. The relative paucity of questions in these two categories did not permit a rigorous analysis of these differences.

In order to explore more systematically these preliminary observations, we designed an experiment explicitly to examine lateral gaze shifts in response to positive, negative, and neutral questions (Schwartz et al., 1979). If the asymmetrical hemispheric engagement seen in response to positive and negative affective stimuli is in part a function of the differential contribution of the left and right frontal regions, then one might expect LEMs to reflect this asymmetry. In this study 24 right-handed subjects were presented with 48 questions created such that each cell of a 2×3 matrix (verbal–spatial × positive–neutral–negative emotion) contained 8 questions. The findings revealed a significant Emotion (positive, negative, neutral) × Eye Movement Direction interaction. Negative questions elicited more left and fewer right eye movements compared to positive questions for both the verbal and spatial subsets.

Visual Field Asymmetry In
Response To Affective Stimuli

A number of studies address the issue of hemispheric activation in response to affective visual stimuli. Suberi and McKeever (1977) studied recognition memory for emotional and nonemotional faces in each visual field. They found a greater left visual field (LVF) advantage (faster reaction time) in the recognition of emotional compared with non-emotional faces. Importantly, they also observed that sad faces produced the greatest LVF (right hemispheric) advantage, while happy and angry faces were associated with the least LVF superiority.

Similarly, Ley and Bryden (1979) reported on a study in which subjects were required to recognize schematic emotional faces that were tachistoscopically exposed to each visual field. Across all emotions, subjects on the average showed an LVF advantage for this task. However, when the separate emotions were examined, it was found that subjects made more errors when extremely positive expressions were presented to the LVF compared to the presentation of extremely negative expressions to the same visual field.

Sackeim and his colleagues (1978; Sackeim & Gur, 1978) had subjects judge the intensity of emotional expression of constructed left-side and right-side composites of human faces posing six different emotions. In general, subjects judged left-side composites as expressing emotions more intensely than right-side composites. However, a posthoc analysis revealed that this effect held more strongly for the negative emotions. Overall, in 73 percent of the instances of negative emotions, mean judgements of emotional intensity were higher for left-side composites, while this held in only 45 percent of the instances of positive emotions ($p<0.05$ by chisquare). (However, see criticism by Ekman, 1980.)

Dimond and colleagues (1976; Dimond & Farrington, 1977) were explicitly concerned with examining left versus right hemispheric specialization for positive and negative affect. They developed a contact lens system whereby prolonged visual input can be projected to either the LVF or the RVF. With such a system, films were projected separately to each visual field and were subsequently rated on the nature of the affect elicited. Heart rate was recorded as a measure of autonomic reactivity. Dimond et al. (1976) found that when films were projected to the right hemisphere first (LVF) they were judged to by significantly more unpleasant than the same films initially projected to the left hemisphere (RVF). Moreover, Dimond and Farrington (1977) found that cartoons produced the greatest change in heart rate when projected to the left hemisphere, while more unpleasant or threatening films evoked the greatest heart rate changes when projected to the right hemisphere.

These findings suggest that each hemisphere may differ with respect to the valence of its affective bias. The similarities between these perceptual findings and the data on the effects of cerebral insult on the experience of emotion suggest some important similarities in the perception and the experience or expression of emotion. This hypothesis is consistent with theorizing in the cognitive area which suggests that perceptual activity calls upon certain neural mechanisms that are centrally involved in the production of that class behavior (e.g., speech perception depends critically on the structures involved in speech production; Liberman et al., 1967; Turvey, 1977; Weimer, 1977).

We recently completed an experiment (Davidson et al., 1983a) in which 19 right-handed subjects were presented with affective or neutral faces unilaterally to either the LVF or RVF for a prolonged 8-second exposure. The stimuli were exposed for this duration because pilot work had indicated that with shorter durations subjects were unable to make the complex judgments for which we asked. In order to ensure that subjects were centrally fixating throughout stimulus exposure, the electro-oculogram (EOG) was recorded and any trial associated with an eye movement of greater than $1°$ was omitted. Following presentation of the faces, subjects were asked to rate each face on the degree to which it expressed various emotions as well as on the degree to which it evoked various emotions in themselves (on 7-point scales). We believed that the asymmetry would be much stronger for ratings of subject's emotional *experience* compared with ratings of the stimulus.

Subject's ratings of the degree to which each face expressed various emotions were uninfluenced by the hemifield to which the face was presented. However, when subjects were asked to rate the degree to which the face evoked various emotions in themselves, significant visual field effects emerged. Specifically, when asked to rate how happy they felt in response to the stimuli, subjects reported experiencing significantly more happiness in response to faces presented to the RVF (i.e., initially to the left hemisphere) compared with responses to the identical faces when presented to the LVF. This effect held irrespective of the valence of the face; that is, more happiness was reported in response to RVF presentations of most faces, compared with LVF exposures.

The data on ratings of happiness and sadness in response to happy and sad faces exposed to the RVF and LVF are presented in Table 11-1. Subjects reported more happiness in response to RVF pre-

Table 11-1   Mean (±SD) Rating on 7-Point Scale of Feelings Evoked by Unilaterally Presented Faces (N=19)

	Ratings of Happiness		Ratings of Sadness	
	Happy Face	Sad Face	Happy Face	Sad Face
Hemifield				
Left	3.19±1.26	1.95±0.91	1.98±0.91	2.65±0.86
Right	3.26±1.30	2.31±0.86	1.92±0.82	2.59±1.06

Adapted from Davidson et al., 1983a.

sentations of happy and sad faces compared with LVF presentations of the identical faces. The data on sadness ratings are in the predicted direction: i.e., higher ratings of sadness in response to LVF compared with RVF presentations. However, the latter findings are nonsignificant.

In another type of study (Reuter-Lorenz & Davidson, 1981), we obtained additional evidence suggesting that the left and right hemispheres are differentially specialized for the perception of happy and sad faces. In this study 28 right-handed subjects were tachistscopically exposed to a neutral and an emotional face of the same individual presented unilaterally, one to the RVF and one to the LVF simultaneously. On each trial, subjects were required to indicate on which side the emotional face had been presented. Reaction time and accuracy were both recorded; the results are presented in Figure 11-1. Happy faces were responded to more quickly when presented to the RVF than when presented to the LVF. The opposite pattern of results was obtained in response to the sad faces.

The data reviewed in this section call into question the notion of right hemispheric involvement in all emotional behavior and support the suggestion of differential lateralization for certain positive and negative affects. The perceptual data indicate that the LVF advantage varies as a function of emotional expression, and in certain task situations actually disappears in favor of RVF advantage. Interestingly, in the Suberi and McKeever (1977) study, both happy and angry faces produced the smallest LVF advantage. The finding for angry faces calls into question the positive–negative basis for the asymmetry. A possible resolution of this apparent inconsistency may lie in classifying the emotions according to whether they are associated with approach or avoidance (considered later). If particular regions of the hemispheres are lateralized for approach versus avoidance behavior, we might expect that those negative emotions that often are

associated with approach, such as anger, would be lateralized to the left side, or at least not show strong right hemispheric specialization. While admittedly posthoc and speculative, this conceptualization would provide an explanation for the Suberi and McKeever finding.

Another important but incompletely understood issue is the differential asymmetries in the *perception* of positive and negative affective stimuli. It is commonly thought that right hemispheric posterior cortical regions (i.e., the right parietal region) are

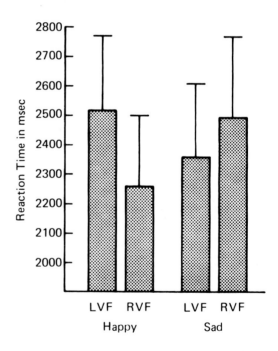

Figure 11-1. Mean reaction time (bars indicate standard errors) to happy and sad stimuli presented separately to each visual field. (Adapted from Reuter-Lorenz, P., & Davidson, R.J., 1981: Differential contributions of the two cerebral hemispheres to the perception of happy and sad faces. *Neuropsychologia* 19:609–613.)

involved in the perception of emotion, particularly in perceiving emotional faces (e.g., Luria, 1973). This specialization of right posterior areas for affective perception is thought to apply to the perception of all valences of emotion. Moreover, we have collected EEG data that indicate the right parietal region is activated in the perception of affective stimuli and that this asymmetry in parietal activation does not vary as a function of the valence of an affective stimulus (Davidson & Schwartz, 1976).

In order to account for the fact that some studies show differential lateralization effects as a function of valence and others show right hemispheric superiority for the perception of emotion in general, the following proposal is offered: Differential lateralization as a function of affective valence occurs as a function of the degree to which subjects, in the act of perception, covertly (or overtly) produce the affective expression that matches the stimulus. Contemporary models of speech perception are analagous in proposing an important role for speech production in the process of perceiving. Recent data on the perception of emotional faces (Dimberg, 1982) indicate that subjects tend to make a covert facial expression (as assessed with facial electromyography) that mimics the expression to be perceived in a task requiring facial expression identification.

Electrophysiological Studies Of Hemispheric Activation in Response To Affective Stimuli

The use of the spontaneous EEG recorded from homologous left and right scalp leads to infer asymmetrical patterns of brain activation has a number of important advantages. This procedure does not require special constraints on stimulus exposures, as do behavioral methods of inferring hemispheric involvement. This allows the investigator to present continuous stimulation that is likely to elicit emotion in the observer. For example, emotional films can be presented while the EEG is recorded from various scalp loci. Differences in patterns of EEG activation can then be examined as a function of subject self-reports of affective response to the stimulation.

This is a strategy we have used in a number of studies. We have been specifically interested in comparing frontal and parietal EEG asymmetries in response to various positive and negative affective stimuli. Based upon the literature reviewed above, we hypothesized that epochs during which subjects

report positive affect would be associated with greater relative left frontal activation compared with epochs during which subjects report negative affect. We also predicted that parietal EEG asymmetry would not differentiate between positive and negative epochs.

In one study (Davidson et al., 1979), 16 right-handed subjects were exposed to videotaped segments of popular television programs that were judged to vary in affective content. While viewing the videotapes, subjects were instructed to rate continuously the degree to which they experienced positive versus negative affect by pressing up and down on a pressure-sensitive gauge. The output of this pressure transducer was digitized to provide a quantitative measure of affective self-report.

EEG was recorded from the left and right frontal (F3 and F4) and left and right parietal (P3 and P4) regions referred to a common vertex (Cz). Activity in the alpha band was extracted from the EEG, integrated, and digitized. EOG was also recorded and epochs confounded by eye movement artifact were eliminated. In order to obtain an independent measure of the subjects' affective response to the video stimuli, two channels of facial EMG were also recorded, one from the zygomatic major region (the "smile" muscle), and one from the frontalis region (associated with tension and frowning) (Schwartz et al., 1976). EMG data were also integrated and digitized.

In order to test our major hypotheses, we compared the 30-second epoch each subject judged to be most positive with the one rated as most negative. This information was derived from the pressure transducer data. The positive and negative epochs deviated from the central neutral position by comparable amounts. It is important to emphasize that the positive and negative epochs were individually obtained for each subject on the basis of his or her self-reports. We believe that this methodological approach is superior to analyses based upon a priori classification of stimulus conditions.

We first compared the positive and negative epochs on the laterality alpha ratio score ($R-L/R+L$ alpha power). Higher numbers on this score indicate greater relative left-sided activation. We found that positive epochs elicited significantly greater relative left frontal activation compared with negative epochs ($p=0.02$). Parietal asymmetry did not distinguish between conditions (Table 11-2). Interestingly, parietal EEG indicated that subjects showed right-sided activation in both positive and negative epochs. Analysis of the separate contri-

Table 11-2   Mean (±SD) of Frontal and
Parietal Laterality Ratios* for
Self-Rated Extreme Positive and
Negative Responses

Region	Positive	Negative
Frontal	0.102 ± 0.358	−0.154 ± 0.365
Parietal	−0.046 ± 0.236	−0.119 ± 0.209

Adapted from Davidson RJ, Schwartz GE, Saron C, Bennett J,
& Goleman DJ (1979): Frontal versus parietal EEG asymmetry
during positive and negative affect. Psychophysiology 16:202–203.

*R−L/R+L alpha power.

butions of the left and right frontal sites to the ratio
score difference revealed that positive epochs were
associated with less left hemisphere and more right
hemisphere alpha compared with negative epochs.

To examine independently the impact of self-rated
positive and negative epochs on a physiological
system that previous research found discriminated
between self-generated positive and negative
imagery, we examined the integrated EMG recorded
from the zygomatic and frontalis muscle regions. As
shown in Table 11-3, positive segments elicited more
zygomatic and less frontalis activity than negative
segments ($p = 0.04$). The EMG data confirm that
subjects' self-reports were indeed associated with
expected changes in facial muscle activity.

In a second study, we presented affective (positive
and negative) and neutral words to subjects (pre-
trained on generating affective imagery) who were
then requested to generate affective imagery for a
45-second period by conjuring up personal associations to the word (Bennett et al., 1981). In response
to one set of affective words, we confirmed that subjects who rated those words more positively showed

Table 11-3   Mean (±SD) of Zygomatic Major
and Frontalis Region EMG for
Self-Rated Extreme Positive and
Negative Responses

Region	Positive	Negative
Zygomatic EMG	263.63 ± 157.71	222.19 ± 150.46
Frontalis EMG	188.88 ± 39.52	201.50 ± 44.68

Adapted from Davidson RJ, Schwartz GE, Saron C, Bennett J,
& Goleman DJ (1979): Frontal versus parietal EEG asymmetry
during positive and negative affect. Psychophysiology 16:202–203.

greater relative left frontal activation compared with
subjects who rated the words more negatively.
Parietal asymmetry again failed to discriminate
between groups. Moreover, we found that subjects'
ratings of the intensity of their affective experience
were highly correlated with frontal asymmetry and
uncorrelated with parietal asymmetry.

A number of other investigators have examined
EEG asymmetry during positive and negative affective states and obtained results consistent with ours.
Karlin et al. (1978) assessed temporal asymmetry in
respoonse to cold pressor pain bilaterally administered and found greater relative right hemispheric
activation during this condition compared with
hypnotically induced analgesia. In a second study
employing hypnotically revivified happy and sad
memories, Karlin et al. (1978) showed that sad
experiences elicited greater relative right hemispheric activation compared with happy experiences.
Tucker et al. (1981) also employed hypnotically
induced mood states as an independent variable and
reported that the induction of a depressed mood
produced significantly greater relative right
hemispheric activation compared with a euphoric
mood, but only at the frontal leads. Central,
parietal, and occipital asymmetry did not discriminate between these conditions.

Harmon and Ray (1977) found differential lateralization in the temporal region for verbally induced
positive and negative affect in a direction opposite to
our findings reported above and those by others
(Flor-Henry, 1979; Karlin et al., 1978; Tucker et al.,
1981). A number of serious methodological inadequacies in their study, however, preclude an
unambiguous interpretation of their data. They
examined broad-band activity (3–30 Hz) and
sampled for an epoch that apparently occurred prior
to the actual self-generation of affect in the subjects.
Furthermore, the experimenter was "verbally coach-
ing" the subjects during the entire epoch. Finally,
negative emotions elicited significantly more
activation across the two hemispheres.

Summary And Future
Research Directions

A variety of data derived from both clinical and
normal populations indicate that the two cerebral
hemispheres play different roles in the regulation of
affect. Aspects of the clinical and normal data suggest that asymmetries for affect are localized to
particular regions along the rostral–caudal plane
with critical involvement of the frontal lobes and

possibly the temporal lobes. The evidence indicates that the left frontal region is particularly involved in certain positive affects and the right frontal region in certain negative affects. The parietal and other cortical regions do not discriminate between affective stimuli that differ in valence.

A number of important questions remain to be resolved. The precise nature of affective asymmetry has not yet been delineated. Although the positive–negative continuum has been invoked to describe the nature of affective asymmetry, this concept is probably not quite accurate, since anger was found to be perceptually lateralized in a manner similar to happiness (Suberi & McKeever, 1977). Research is needed that uses more precise measures of an individual's affective state and examines the association between these indices and ongoing measures of brain activity. In our current research (in collaboration with Paul Ekman) subjects are exposed to films differing in emotional content. Brain and autonomic activity are being recorded, and subject's facial behavior in response to the films are being videotaped. Well-defined changes in facial expression are then used as flags to extract epochs of physiological activity. Because of the very finely differentiated nature of facial expression, specific expressions of discrete emotions can be related to patterns of central and autonomic nervous system activity. In this way, we allow for individual variability in responsiveness to the films and are able to analyze the physiological data on the basis of common subject facial responses rather than common stimulus characteristics. We hope to refine our understanding of asymmetry for affect by examining asymmetries associated with various discrete emotions.

Another important issue is the relationship between asymmetries in anterior and posterior cortical regions. We believe that this relation is central to understanding the role of hemispheric organization in affect–cognition interactions and will help to explain why depressed subjects exhibit selective deficits on tasks presumably subserved by right hemispheric posterior regions.

Finally, an issue not addressed by the data just reviewed is the ontogeny of the asymmetries for affect. What is the relation between the maturation of certain cerebral systems and the emergence of affective response systems over the first year of life? Some of these questions have been explored by our recent developmental work (with Nathan Fox). The theoretical considerations guiding this program have been reviewed elsewhere (Davidson, in press b; Fox & Davidson, in press). It was empirically established

that frontal asymmetry that discriminates between certain positive versus negative affective stimuli is present at 10 months of age (Davidson & Fox, 1982). Furthermore, frontal EEG asymmetry differences were found in newborn infants in response to sucrose versus citric acid solutions in a direction consistent with our other data (Fox & Davidson, in preparation).

REPRESSION AND CEREBRAL ASYMMETRY

The mechanisms involved in repression and repressive coping styles are undoubtedly complex and have remained elusive for quite some time. We recently initiated a program of research designed to explore some of the autonomic and central nervous system substrates of repressive coping styles. Some of these findings may further our understanding of the psychobiological substrates responsible for some of the dissociations in behavior and experience associated with repression.

This work has focused on a group of individuals, termed *repressors*, who are identified by a set of psychometric criteria. This group habitually denies or is unaware of negative affect. The core characteristics of this group of individuals were first described in detail by Freud (1959) in classic descriptions of the repressive style of defense. Individuals with this coping style often deny having elevated levels of anxiety, although they respond in a stressful manner on nonverbal behavioral and physiological indices. For example, Weinberger et al. (1979) administered a phrase association task with both affective and neutral items to repressors, truly low-anxiety subjects, and moderately high-anxiety subjects. Heart rate, spontaneous skin resistance responses, and frontalis muscle tension were recorded. On all three physiological measures, repressors showed a pattern that indicated that they were more stressed than low-anxiety subjects despite their claims of low trait anxiety.

These data led us to conceptualize repressive defensiveness as a dissociation between verbal reports of affect and other indices that reflect affective state. Repressors verbally report themselves to be in positive affective states most of the time, while other behavioral and autonomic measures suggest that their affective state is precisely the opposite. The fact that repressors exhibit this type of dissociation stimulated us to search for possible hemispheric substrates of this process. Specifically, we have been studying the possibility that repressors might show a functional disconnection between regions of the two cerebral hemispheres responsible for positive and negative affective processing. Galin (1974) was the first to propose explicitly that repression may involve a functional disconnection between certain regions of the two cerebral hemispheres. Based upon the affective lateralization data reviewed earlier, we hypothesized that negative affective information processed in the right hemisphere does not get complete access to verbal centers in the left hemisphere. Therefore, the verbal reports of repressors about how they feel are not well informed by negative affective information from the right hemisphere.

In order to test this hypothesis, we undertook a series of studies designed to explore interhemispheric transfer in repressors and nonrepressors. In the first study (Davidson et al., 1983b), repressors and non-repressors were presented with a word association task in which positive, negative, and neutral words were presented to the LVF and RVF. Reaction time of the verbal response and accuracy of word identification served as measures of interhemispheric transfer processes, based on the logic that a verbal response (controlled by the left hemisphere) to a word presented to the LVF (right hemisphere) must involve commissural transfer.

An initial pool of 319 individuals from the State University of New York at Purchase campus and surrounding communities were administered the Marlowe-Crowne Scale of Social Desirability (Crowne & Marlowe, 1964). The subjects falling in the top 10 percent were selected to constitute the repressor group. All of the repressors scored 21 or above (mean 22.6, SD 1.8) on the questionnaire. The nonrepressors were those who scored in the lower 60 percent on the questionnaire, all of whom scored 13 or below (mean 9.4, SD 3.4). The groups were selected with the constraint that they contain only right-handed individuals. A total of 12 repressors (4 men and 8 women) and 14 non-repressors (5 men and 9 women) were included.

Stimuli were one-syllable, four-letter words presented on slides. Fifteen words in each of three word categories (positive, negative, and neutral) were presented twice, once to each visual field, in random order. Words were selected on the basis of judges' rating of an initial list of 85 words. The positive words, for example, included *love*, *kiss*, *zest*, and *glee*; negative words included *doom*, *stab*, *slum*, and *wail*; neutral words included *step*, *here*, *wall*, and *foot*. The duration of stimulus presentation was 750 msec. Subjects were instructed to focus on a fixation

point and eye movements were monitored with EOG. A system was constructed to provide tone feedback to the subject whenever he or she produced an eye movement greater than 1^0 in order to facilitate central fixation. Following each stimulus presentation, subjects were instructed to say the first word that came to mind. They were also cued to say the word that was presented on that trial by a green light presented 15 seconds after their first verbal response.

We first examined accuracy of stimulus word identification. No main effect for Group, nor any interaction with Group was found. The reaction time data (Fig. 11-2) revealed a significant Group × Visual Field interaction [$F(1,24) = 4.46$, $p = .045$]. Repressors responded with a longer delay to words presented to the LVF versus RVF ($p < 0.005$), whereas nonrepressors showed no significant difference in reaction time to words presented to the two visual fields.

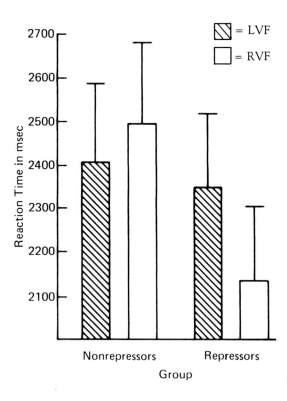

Figure 11-2. Mean verbal reaction time (bars indicate standard errors) for repressors ($N = 12$) and nonrepressors ($N = 14$) in associating to affective and neutral words presented unilaterally to each visual field. (Adapted from Davidson, Perl, & Saron, 1983.)

We performed separate analyses of variance for each group with Visual Field and Emotion as factors. Nonrepressors did not show a significant Visual Field × Emotion interaction, but repressors (Fig. 11-3) did [$F(2,21)=3.44$, $p=.05$]. Negative words elicited longer LVF compared with RVF reaction times ($p<0.0001$). Neutral words elicited a similar pattern of response ($p<0.04$). No significant visual field difference was obtained in response to the positive words.

The findings from this study lend support to our hypothesis of interhemispheric transfer differences between repressors and nonrepressors. Repressors verbally responded more slowly to words initially presented to the right hemisphere (LVF) compared to the same words initially presented to the left hemisphere (RVF) in a task designed to arouse affect. We view this finding as indicative of a deficit in interhemispheric transfer in repressors because in this task the verbal response is presumably controlled by the left hemisphere, and the input to which a response is produced is directed to the right hemisphere. Thus, in order for a response to be given, information must cross from the right to the left hemisphere. No reliable hemispheric differences were obtained among the nonrepressors. Further analysis revealed that the hemispheric differences for the repressors were mostly a function of their responses to negative affective words. Positive words elicited no reliable visual field differences.

In a second study (Davidson et al., 1983b) repressors and nonrepressors (selected on the same basis as in the previous experiment) were presented with affective faces exposed tachistoscopically to the LVF and RVF. The subjects were required to verbally name the emotion depicted on the face. We predicted that repressors would differ from nonrepressors in their accuracy of verbally identifying faces only when stimuli were presented to the LVF (right hemisphere) because verbal responses to these stimuli would require transfer of information from the right to the left hemisphere. (When stimuli are presented to the RVF no commissural transfer is required because the entire task can be performed exclusively within the left hemisphere.) As predicted, repressors and controls did not differ in their

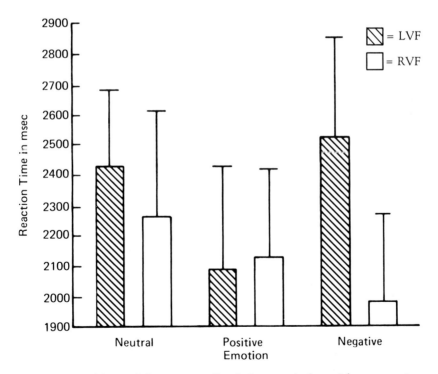

Figure 11-3. Mean verbal reaction time (bars indicate standard errors) for repressors in associating to positive, negative, and neutral words presented unilaterally to each visual field. (Adapted from Davidson, Perl, & Saron, 1983.)

accuracy of verbal identification in response to RVF information, but the repressors showed significantly worse performance ($p < .0001$) compared with controls in response to LVF presentations (Fig. 11-4).

An alternative interpretation of these data is that repressors simply show deficits in right hemisphere–mediated cognitive skills, and that is why they did worse in responding to LVF presentations. Although this interpretation does need to be explored further, other data from our study argue against it. In a second task using the identical facial stimuli as in the task described above, subjects were required to make a gender identification by saying "male" or "female" following the presentation of the face (half of the faces were male and half were female). We reasoned that in this task, affective judgments were not required; if the repressor's interhemispheric transfer deficit was functional and expressed only in response to affective challenges, then no group differences would be observed in the

gender task despite the fact that the identical stimuli were used. The results confirmed our prediction and revealed no group difference in the gender task.

CONCLUSIONS

The data on affective asymmetries in humans indicate that certain regions of the two hemispheres are specialized for the regulation of certain positive and negative emotions. Recent animal data (Denenberg, 1981) point in the same direction. Both human and animal data suggest that the frontal region is a principal area involved in this asymmetry, and specifically indicate that the left frontal region is more involved with certain positive affects and the right frontal region with certain negative affects. A more precise characteriztion of this asymmetry requires additional research, but "approach–avoidance" may provide a suitable description.

The relation between affective lateralization and repression is being investigated. Repressive defensiveness is a coping style in which verbal reports about affect are commonly dissociated from other indices indicative of affective state: the repressor frequently maintains that he or she is feeling "good," "calm," etc., while autonomic measures reveal a response pattern associated with stress. The substrates for this behavioral dissociation were considered in relation to the data on lateralization for affect. Following Galin (1974), we hypothesized that repressors exhibit a functional disconnection between right hemispheric regions involved in processing negative affect and left hemispheric verbal centers. The results of two experiments assessing interhemispheric transfer in repressors support this hypothesis and indicate that repressors have deficits in transferring affective information from the right to the left hemisphere.

An important issue remaining for future research is the association between the hypothesized neuropsychological mechanism of repression and the somatic disregulation often found in this group of individuals. For example, the recently observed relation between cardiac afferent feedback and the right hemisphere (e.g., Davidson et al., 1981) suggests that the hemispheric dissconnection may in some way be associated with cardiovascular dysfunction among repressors.

This research suggests the possibility of treatment strategies based upon neuropsychological data. Is it possible to facilitate interhemispheric interaction,

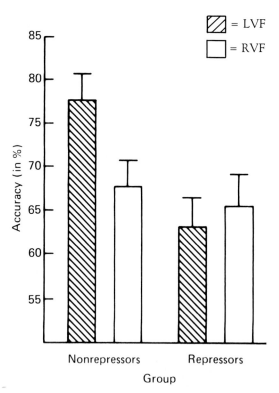

Figure 11-4. Mean accuracy (bars indicate standard errors) for nonrepressors ($N=13$) and repressors ($N=11$) in verbal identification of emotional expression of faces presented unilaterally to each visual field. (Adapted from Davidson, Perl, & Saron, 1983.)

and would such a training procedure help normalize an extremely repressive coping style? These are some of the important questions to which future research will be dedicated.

REFERENCES

Abrams R, & Taylor MA (1979): Differential EEG patterns in affective disorder and schizophrenia. Arch Gen Psychiatry 36:1355–1358.

Alford LB (1933): Localization of consciousness and emotion. Am J Psychiatry 12:789–799.

Anderson SW (1977): Language-related asymmetries of eye movement and evoked potentials. Harnad S, Doty RW, Goldstein L, Jaynes J, & Krauthamer D (Eds.). In *Lateralization in the Nervous System*. New York, Academic Press.

Bear DN, & Fedio P (1977): Quantitative analysis of interital behavior in temporal lobe epilepsy. Arch Neurol 34:454–467.

Bennett J, Davidson RJ, & Saron C (1982): Patterns of self-rating in response to verbally elicited affective imagery: Relation to frontal vs. parietal EEG asymmetry. Psychophysiology 18:158.

Benson DF (1973): Psychiatric aspects of aphasia. Br J Psychiatry 123:555–566.

Bruder GE, & Yozawitz A (1979): Central auditory processing and lateralization in psychiatric patients. Gruzelier J, & Flor-Henry P (Eds.). In *Hemisphere Asymmetries of Function in Psychopathology*. New York, Elsevier/North Holland.

Cohen BD, Penick SB, & Tarter RI (1974): Antidepressant effects of unilateral electric convulsive shock therapy. Arch Gen Psychiatry. 31:673–675.

Cronin D, Bodley P, Potts L, Mather MD, Gardner RK, & Tobin JC (1970): Unilateral and bilateral ECT· A study of memory disturbance and relief from depression. J Neurol Neurosurg Psychiatry 33:705–713.

Crowne DP, & Marlow, D (1964): *The Approval Motive: Studies in Evaluative Dependence*. New York, Wiley.

Davidson RJ (in press): Affect, cognition and hemispheric specialization. Izard CE, Kagan J, & Zajonc R (Eds.). In *Emotion, Cognition and Behavior*. New York, Cambridge University Press.

Davidson RJ, & Fox NA (1982): Asymmetrical brain activity discriminates between positive versus negative affective stimuli in ten month old human infants. Science 218:1235–1237.

Davidson RJ, Horowitz ME, Schwartz GE, & Goodman DM (1981): Lateral differences in the latency between finger tapping and the heartbeat. Psychophysiology 18: 36–41.

Davidson RJ, Moss E, Saron C, & Schaffer CE (1983a): Self-reports of emotion are influenced by the visual field to which affective information is presented. Manuscript submitted for publication.

Davidson RJ, Perl J, & Saron C (1983b): Hemispheric interaction in repressors and non-repressors during a word association task. Manuscript submitted for publication.

Davidson RJ, & Schwartz GE (1976): Patterns of cerebral lateralization during cardiac biofeedback versus the self-regulation of emotion: Sex differences. Psychophysiology 13:62–68.

Davidson RJ, Schwartz GE, Saron C, Bennet J, & Goleman DJ (1979): Frontal versus parietal EEG asymmetry during positive and negative affect. Psychophysiology 16: 202–203.

Davidson RJ, Schwartz GE, & Weinberger D (1977): Eye movement and electrodermal asymmetry during cognitive and affective tasks. Paper presented at the annual meeting of the American Psychological Association, August.

Deglin VL, & Nikolaenko NN (1975): Role of the dominant hemisphere in the regulation of emotional states. Hum Physiol 1:394–402.

Denenberg VH (1981): Hemispheric laterality in animals and the effects of early experience. Behav Brain Sci 4: 1–49.

Denny-Brown D, Meyer ST, & Horenstein S (1952): The significance of perceptual rivalry resulting from parietal lesion. Brain 75:433–471.

Dimberg U (1982): Facial reactions to facial expressions. Psychophysiology 19:643–647.

Dimond S, & Farrington L (1977): Emotional response to films shown to the right or left hemisphere of the brain measured by heart rate. Acta Psychol (Amst) 41:255–260.

Dimond S, Farrington L, & Johnson P (1976): Differing emotional response from right and left hemispheres. Nature 261:690–692.

Ehrlichman H (1979): *EOG recording of gaze direction and eye movement rate in response to verbal and spatial questions*. Paper presented to the Society for Psychophysiological Research, Cincinatti, October.

Ehrlichman H, & Weinberger A (1978): Lateral eye movements and hemispheric asymmetry: A critical review. Psychol Bull 85:1080–1101.

Ekman P (1980): Asymmetry in facial expression. Science 209:833–834.

Flor-Henry P (1976): Lateralized temporal-limbic dysfunction and psychopathology. Ann Acad Sci 280: 777–795.

Flor-Henry P (1979): On certain aspects of the localization of the cerebral systems regulating and determining emotion. Biol Psychiatry 14:677–698.

Flor-Henry P, Koles ZJ, Howarth BG, & Burton L (1979): Neurophysiological studies of schizophrenia, mania and depression. Gruzelier J, & Flor-Henry P (Eds.). In *Hemisphere Asymmetries of Function in Psychopathology*. New York, Elsevier/North Holland.

Flor-Henry P, & Yeudall LT (1979): Neuropsychological investigation of schizophrenia and manic-depressive psychoses. Gruzelier J, & Flor-Henry P (Eds.). In *Hemisphere Asymmetries of Function in Psychopathology*. New York, Elsevier/North Holland.

Fox NA, & Davidson RJ (Eds.) (in press): *The Psychobiology of Affective Development.* Hillsdale, NJ, Erlbaum.

Fox NA, & Davidson RJ (in preparation): Frontal brain electrical asymmetry distinguishes between approach and withdrawal reactions in newborn infants.

Freud S (1959): *Inhibitions, Symptoms and Anxiety.* New York, WH Norton.

Gainotti G (1969): Reactions "catotrophiques" et manifestations d'indifference au cours des atteintes cerebrais. Neuropsychologia 7:195–204.

Gainotti G (1972): Emotional behavior and hemispheric side of lesion. Cortex 8:41–55.

Galin D (1974): Implications for psychiatry of left and right cerebral specialization. Arch Gen Psychiatry 31:572–583.

Goldstein K (1939): *The Organism.* New York, Academic.

Goldstein SG, Filskov SB, Weaver LA, & Ives JO (1977): Neuropsychological effects of electroconvulsive therapy. J Clin Psychol 33:798–806.

Gur RE (1975): Conjugate lateral eye movements as an index of hemispheric activation. J Pers Soc Psychol 31:751–757.

Gur RE, & Gur RC (1977): Correlates of conjugate lateral eye movements in man. Harnad S, Doty RW, Goldstein L, Jaynes J, & Krauthamer G (Eds.). In *Lateralization in the Nervous System.* New York, Academic Press.

Halliday AM, Davison K, Browne MW, & Kreeger LC (1968): A comparison of the effects on depression and memory of bilateral ECT and unilateral ECT to the dominant and non-dominant hemispheres. Br J Psychiatry 114:997–1012.

Harmon DW, & Ray WJ (1977): Hemispheric activity during affective verbal stimuli: An EEG study. Neuropsychologia 15:457–460.

Hassett J, & Zelner B (1977): Correlations between measures of cerebral asymmetry. Psychophysiology 14:79.

Hecaen H, Ajuriaguerra JD, & Massonet J (1951): Les troubles visa, constructifs par lesions parieto-occipitales droctes: Roles des pertubbautions resticulaires. Encephale 1:122–179.

Hommes OR, & Panhuysan LHHM (1971): Depression and cerebral dominance: A study of bilateral intracarotid amytal in eleven depressed patients. Psychiatry Neurol Neurochir 74:259–274.

Karlin R, Weinapple M, Rochford J, & Goldstein L (1978): *Quantitative EEG features of negative affective states: Report of some hypnotic studies.* Paper presented to the Society of Biological Psychiatry, Atlanta.

Kinsbourne M (1972): Eye and head turning indicates cerebral lateralization. Science 76:539–541.

Kocel K, Galin D, Ornstein R, & Merrin EL (1972): Lateral eye movement and cognitive mode. Psychonom Sci 27:223–224.

Kolb B, & Milner B (1981b): Observations on spontaneous facial expression after focal cerebral exisions and after intracarotid injection of sodium amytal. Neuropsychologia 19:505–514.

Kronfol Z, Hamsher K deS, Kigre K, & Waziri R (1978): Depression and hemispheric functions: Changes associated with unilateral ECT. Br J Psychiatry 132:560–567..

Ley R, & Bryden M (1979): Hemispheric differences in processing emotions and faces. Brain Lang 7: 127–138.

Liberman AM, Cooper FS, Shankweiler D, & Studdert-Kennedy M (1967): Perception of the speech code. Psychol Rev 74:431–461.

Luria AR (1966): *Higher Cortical Functions in Man.* New York, Basic Books.

Luria AR (1973): *The Working Brain.* New York, Basic Books.

Milner B (1967): Discussion of experimental analysis of cerebral dominance in man. Millikan CH, & Darley FL (Eds.). In *Brain Mechanisms Underlying Speech and Language.* New York, Grune & Stratton.

Nauta WJH (1971): The problem of the frontal lobe: A reinterpretation. J Psychiat Res 8: 167–187.

Parcella BL, & Impastato DJ (1954): Focal stimulation therapy. Am J Psychiatry 110:576–578.

Perria L, Rosadini G, & Rossi GF (1961): Determination of side of cerebral dominance with amobarbital. Arch Neurol 4:173–181.

Perris C, & Monakhov K (1979): Depressive symptomatology and systemic structural analysis of the EEG. Gruzelier J, & Flor-Henry P (Eds.). In *Hemisphere Asymmetries of Function in Psychopathology.* New York, Elsevier/North Holland.

Pribram KH (1973): The primate frontal cortex—executive of the brain. Pribram KH, & Luria AR (Eds.). In *Psychophysiology of the Frontal Lobes.* New York, Academic.

Reuter-Lorenz P, & Davidson RJ (1981): Differential contributions of the two cerebral hemispheres to the perception of happy and sad faces. Neuropsychologia 19: 609–613.

Robinson DA, & Fuchs AF (1969): Eye movements evoked by stimulation of frontal eye fields. J Neurophysiol 32:637–648.

Robinson RG, & Benson DF (1981): Depression in aphasic patients: Frequency, severity and clinical-pathological correlations. Brain Lang 14:282–291.

Robinson RG, & Szetela B (1981): Mood change following left hemispheric brain injury. Ann Neurol 9:447–453.

Ross ED, & Rush AJ (1981): Diagnosis and neuroanatomical correlates of depression in brain-damaged patients: Implications for a neurology of depression. Arch Gen Psychiatry 38:1344–1354.

Rossi GF, & Rosadini G (1967): Experimental analysis of cerebral dominance in man. Millikan CH, & Darley FL (Eds.). In *Brain Mechanisms Underlying Speech and Language.* New York, Grune & Stratton.

Sackeim, HA, & Decina P (1982): *Lateralized neuropsychological abnormalities in bipolar adults and in children of bipolar probands.* Paper presented at the Second International Conference on Laterality on Psychopathology, Banff, Alberta, Canada, April.

Sackeim, HA, & Gur RC (1978): Lateral asymmetry in intensity of emotional expression. Neuropsychologia 16: 473–481.

Sackeim HA, Gur RC, & Saucy MC (1978): Emotions are expressed more intensely on the left side of face. Science 202:434–436.

Sackeim HA, Weinman AL, Gur RC, Greenburgh M, Hungerbuhler JP, & Geschwind N (1982): Pathological laughing and crying: Functional brain asymmetry in the experience of positive and negative emotions. Arch Neurol 39:210–218.

Schaffer CE, Davidson RJ, & Saron C (1983): Frontal and parietal EEG asymmetries in depressed and non-depressed subjects. Biol Psychiatry 18:753–762.

Schwartz GE, Davidson RJ, & Maer F (1975): Right hemisphere lateralization for emotion in the human brain: Interaction with cognition. Science 190:286–288.

Schwartz GE, Fair PL, Salt P, Mandel M, & Klerman GL (1976): Facial muscle patterning to affective imagery in depressed and non-depressed subjects. Science 192:489–491.

Schwartz GE, Ahern G, Davidson RJ, & Pusar J (1979): *Differential eye movement asymmetry in response to positive and negative affective questions.* Unpublished manuscript, Yale University.

Serafetinides EA, Hoare RD, & Driver MV (1965): Intracarotid sodium amylobarbitone and cerebral dominance for speech and consciousness. Brain 68:107–130.

Shagass C, Roemer RA, Straumanis JJ, & Amadeo M (1979): Evoked potential evidence of lateralized hemispheric dysfunction in the psychoses. Gruzelier J, Flor-Henry P (Eds.). In *Hemisphere Asymmetries of Function in Psychopathology.* New York, Elsevier/North Holland.

Strauss E, Moscovitch M, & Olds J (1979): Functional hemispheric asymmetries and depression: Preliminary findings of cognitive correlates of electroconvulsive therapy. Paper presented to the International Neuropsychological Society Convention, February.

Suberi M, & McKeever WF (1977): Differential right hemispheric memory storage of emotional and non-emotional faces. Neuropsychologia 15:757–768.

Terzian H (1964): Behavioral and EEG effects of intra-carotid sodium amytal injection. Neurochirica 12:230–239.

Tucker DM, Roth RS, Arneson BA, & Buckingham V (1977): Right hemisphere activation during stress. Neuropsychologia 15:697–700.

Tucker DM, Stenslie CE, Roth RS, & Shearer SL (1981): Right frontal lobe activation and right hemisphere performance decrement during a depressed mood. Arch Gen Psychiatry 38:169–174.

Turvey MT (1977): Preliminaries to a theory of action with reference to vision. Shaw R, & Bransford J (Eds.). In *Perceiving, Acting and Knowing.* Hillsdale, NJ, Erlbaum.

Weimer WA (1977): A conceptual framework for cognitive psychology: Motor theories of mind. Shaw R, & Bransford J (Eds.). In *Perceiving, Acting and Knowing.* Hillsdale, NJ, Erlbaum.

Weinberger DA, Schwartz GE, & Davidson RJ (1979): Low anxious, high anxious and repressive coping styles: Psychometric patterns and behavioral and physiological responses to stress. J Abnorm Psychol 88:369–380.

Yozawitz A, Bruder G, Sutton S, Sharpe L, Gurland B, Fleiss J, & Costa L (1979): Dichotic perception: Evidence for right hemisphere dysfunction in affective psychosis. Br J Psychiatry 135:224–237.

Zinkin S, & Birthnell J (1968): Unilateral electroconvulsive therapy: Its effect on memory and its therapeutic efficacy. Br J Psychiatry 114:973–988.

SUGGESTED READINGS

Davidson RJ (in press): Hemispheric specialization for cognition and affect. Gale A, Edwards J (Eds.). In *Psychological Correlates of Human Behaviour.* London, Academic Press.

d'Elia G, & Raotma H (1975): Is unilateral ECT less effective than bilateral ECT? Br J Psychiatry 126:83–89.

Kolb D, & Milner D (1981a): Performance of complex arm and facial movements after focal brain lesions. Neuropsychologia 17:491–503.

12

Behavioral Conditioning and the Immune System

Robert Ader

Psychological factors are of critical significance in the maintenance of health and the development of disease. It is only within the past 50 or so years that scientifically acceptable evidence has linked emotions or stress with physiological changes implicated in altered disease susceptibility, making the study of psychosocial factors in health and disease a respectable scientific enterprise.

Psychosomatic research has evolved from relatively superficial correlational analyses to a recognition of the indivisible nature of psychobiological processes and the potential influence of psychosocial factors in the etiology of all pathophysiological responses. The psychosomatic researcher does not seek a psychological "cause" of disease, but acknowledges that factors in addition to the biological may be important. Such factors include a genetically or experientially determined predisposition or vulnerability to a pathological process, environmental or psychosocial events that may be perceived as a threat to an individual's psychological or physiological integrity, and the personal or social resources that are available to the individual for coping with such events. Such factors play major roles in determining whether an individual becomes ill or has difficulty recovering from the superimposed or latent pathogens of which all the individuals in a given group may be equally exposed. An analysis of the

relative contribution of these interacting factors is not likely to be accomplished in a test tube.

Early studies of the physiological concomitants of emotion concentrated on the autonomic nervous system, supplemented by an emphasis on the endocrine system. It soon became evident that an understanding of adaptational processes required more integrated approaches. Modern investigators, for example, no longer speak of a central nervous system and an endocrine system, but of an organized neuroendocrine system. The immune system, however, is still commonly thought of as being independent of the central nervous system; this is no longer a tenable assumption. Research in the fields of immunology, neuroendocrinology, pharmacology, and psychology indicates that, like any other system operating in the interests of homeostasis, the immune system is integrated with other physiological processes and is therefore subject to regulation or modulation by the brain (Ader, 1981a). The immune system therefore is a potential mediator of the effects of psychosocial factors, emotions, or stress on the predisposition to and/or the precipitation or perpetuation of some disease processes.

The available data come from various biopsychosocial levels of organization. Neuroanatomical and neurochemical pathways link the central nervous system and the immune system (Bulloch & Moore, 1980; Felten et al., 1981; Giron et al., 1980; Reilly et al., 1979; Williams & Felten, 1981; Williams et al., 1981). Lymphocytes bear receptors for hormones and neurotransmitters, and hormonal interventions can influence immune function (e.g., Ahlqvist, 1981; Claman, 1972; Cohen & Crnic, 1982; Dougherty, 1952; Goldstein et al., 1978). Moreover, immune responses in vitro and in vivo are affected by serotonergic (Devoino et al., 1975), catecholaminergic

This research was supported by USPHS Research Scientist Award K05-MH-06318 from the National Institute of Mental Health, by a research grant from the W.T. Grant Foundation, Grant HD-09977 from the National Institute of Child Health and Human Development, Grant NS-15071 from the National Institute of Neurological and Communicative Disorders and Stroke, and a grant from the Kroc Foundation.

(Ernstrom & Sandberg, 1973; Hadden et al., 1970), and cholinergic (Besedovsky et al., 1979; Bourne et al., 1974; Hadden et al., 1970; Lane, 1978; Strom et al., 1974) stimulation. Drug-mediated interferences with these neuroendocrine changes can also alter immune responses (Maestroni & Pierpaoli, 1981). Not only does antigenic stimulation elicit neuroendocrine changes, but it has been reported that there are also changes in the firing rate of neurons within the ventromedial hypothalamus of the rat corresponding to the time of peak antibody production (Besedovsky et al., 1977). Much of this material has recently been reviewed by Besedovsky and Sorkin (1981) and Hall and Goldstein (1981).

Other direct evidence of central nervous system involvement in the regulation of immunogenesis is provided by studies in which immune responses have been altered by direct electrical stimulation or ablation of specific hypothalamic areas (e.g., Korneva & Khai, 1963, 1967; Spector & Korneva, 1981). Midbrain lesions have been shown to offer protection against anaphylaxis (Freedman & Fenichel, 1958; Luparello et al., 1964; Szentivanyi & Filipp, 1958). With minor exceptions, (Thrasher et al., 1971), there is general agreement that anterior hypothalamic lesions protect against anaphylaxis, lower circulating antibody titers, and depress delayed hypersensitivity reactions (Jankovic & Isakovic, 1973; Stein et al., 1976; Stein et al., 1981).

Evidence that behavioral factors can influence immune function is presented in this chapter. Several studies have demonstrated that stress can influence susceptibility to a variety of disease processes that are thought to involve immune mechanisms, and an even newer literature is beginning to delineate the effects of stress on different parameters of immunological reactivity in vitro and in vivo. This material has been reviewed in the past (Amkraut & Solomon, 1974; Bahnson, 1969; Friedman & Glasgow, 1966; LaBarba, 1970; Rogers et al., 1979) and recently (Monjan, 1981; Palmblad, 1981; Plaut & Friedman, 1981; Riley et al., 1981; Solomon & Amkraut, 1981). Some of this information is discussed by Solomon and Amkraut (this volume, Chapter 14); therefore, this material is only briefly reviewed here; the major focus is on the impact of behavioral conditioning in modifying immune responses.

BEHAVIORAL FACTORS AND SUSCEPTIBILITY TO DISEASE

Retrospective clinical studies have provided most of the evidence for a relationship between "life change" or "stress" in humans and a variety of diseases, including those that are thought to involve immunological competence (e.g., Gunderson & Rahe, 1974; Plaut & Friedman, 1981). Both susceptibility to (Jacobs et al., 1970; Kasl et al., 1979; Meyer & Haggerty, 1962) and recovery from (Greenfield et al., 1959; Imboden et al., 1961) infectious disease have been related to stressful life experiences. Similar data have been reported for allergic conditions (Engels & Wittkower, 1975) and autoimmune disorders (Solomon, 1981). Most of the experimental data has been obtained from experiments in animals.

In general, stress appears to increase susceptibility to a variety of infectious agents. It should be noted, however, that the results are neither uniform nor simple, and the observed effects are frequently small and sometimes equivocal. Furthermore, it is not entirely clear that all the behavioral manipulations that have been imposed can be subsumed under the single rubric of stress. In any case, stimulation that is usually referred to as stressful (such as avoidance conditioning) has been shown to increase susceptibility to herpes simplex (Rasmussen et al., 1957), Coxsackie B (Johnson et al., 1959), polyoma (Chang & Rasmussen, 1965), and vesicular stomatitis (Jensen & Rasmussen, 1963; Yamada et al., 1964) viruses in mice. Paralleling a clinical paradigm (Holmes et al., 1951), Friedman et al. (1965) found that neither stress nor an inoculation of Coxsackie B virus administered alone was sufficient to elicit symptoms of disease in adult mice. The combination of stress and virus, however, could induce manifest disease.

The response to parasitic infection is also influenced by stressful environmental conditions. Weinmann and Rothman (1967) showed that resistance to Hymenolepsis nana, a tapeworm, was decreased when intense fighting occurred among male mice. Hamilton (1974) found decreased resistance to H. nana in direct proportion to the frequency with which immunized mice were exposed to a predator. In contrast, resistance to Plasmodium berghei, a rodent malaria, is increased when rats are subjected to stressful environmental conditions (Friedman et al., 1973).

Other data also point out the bidirectionality of the effects of stress. An increased resistance to poliomyelitis has been shown to follow avoidance conditioning in monkeys (Marsh et al., 1963), and physical restraint (but not the stimulation of a cold bath) suppresses development of experimental allergic encephalomyelitis in rats (Levine et al., 1962). Group housing or other manipulations that alter social interactions have been found to increase resistance to encephalomyocarditis virus (Friedman et al., 1969) and *Escherichia coli* (Gross & Siegel, 1965), while increasing susceptibility to trichinosis (Davis & Read, 1958), malaria (Plaut et al., 1969), and a *Salmonella* infection (Edwards & Dean, 1977). Amkraut et al. (1971) reported that crowding increases susceptibility to an adjuvant-induced arthritis in the rat. Rogers et al. (1980) observed an increased resistance to collagen-induced arthritis among rats exposed to a cat, but also found that auditory stress exacerbates the incidence of this autoimmune disorder (Rogers et al., 1981).

These are some of the findings that document the effects of environmental factors on immune processes. There are data suggesting that psychosocial factors have an effect on susceptibility and response to neoplastic diseases (Bammer & Newberry, 1981); however, at this point, the extent to which immune mechanisms may be involved is conjectural. The development of and/or response to spontaneously developing or experimentally induced neoplastic diseases in animals can be influenced by a variety of psychosocial manipulations, including early life experiences, differential housing, noxious stimulation, the opportunity for effective coping behavior, etc. (For recent reviews of this literature see Riley et al., 1981, and Sklar & Anisman, 1981). These are experimental manipulations that do have the capacity to modify immunological reactivity. Thus, research into the immunological mediation of the effects of psychosocial factors on tumorigenesis is of interest.

BEHAVIORAL FACTORS AND IMMUNOLOGICAL REACTIVITY

The effects of stress or psychosocial events have been detected within some components of the immune system. Long ago it was noted that emotional states in man could result in a change in the number of lymphocytes (Farris, 1938; Mora et al., 1926). Only recently, however, has real interest in this area been generated. Bartrop et al. (1977) reported that the grief response to the death of a spouse is accompanied by a depression in lymphocyte function that is independent of the hormonal responses that are concomitantly measured. Preliminary observations by Schleifer et al. (1980) confirmed these findings. Several other programs have now been initiated to explore the relationship between stressful life events, coping behavior, and immunological competence, e.g., lymphocyte cytotoxicity and natural killer cell activity (Dorian et al., 1981; Greene et al., 1978; Locke et al., 1978; Roessler et al., 1979). Preliminary results suggest that the combination of high stress scale scores and

inadequate coping skills correlate with depressed immunological defenses.

Most of the available data come from animal research (Monjan, 1981). Increases as well as decreases in immunological reactivity follow stressful experiences. Repeated sampling procedures, for example, have revealed a biphasic response: a depression followed by an increase in the lymphocyte response to mitogenic stimulation (Folch & Waksman, 1974; Monjan & Collector, 1976). Gisler et al. (1971) found suppressed activity in splenic lymphocytes obtained from mice subjected to acceleration or anesthetization. These in vitro effects could be mimicked by ACTH (Gisler & Schenkel-Hulliger, 1971), but neither Gisler nor Solomon (Solomon et al., 1979) were able to reproduce in vivo effects by ACTH treatment.

Electric shock has been reported to increase the immune response to a topically applied irritant in guinea pigs (Guy, 1952; Mettrop & Visser, 1969), and auditory stimulation has been observed to reduce the inflammatory response in mice (Christian & Williamson, 1958; Funk & Jensen, 1967; Smith et al., 1960). A reduced hypersensitivity response in mice exposed to high temperature was reported by Pitkin (1965), and Wistar and Hildemann (1960) observed prolonged survival of a skin allograft in mice subjected to an avoidance conditioning regimen. A depressed graft-versus-host response was also observed among animals subjected to a limited feeding schedule (Amkraut et al., 1973).

Increases and decreases in primary and secondary humoral responses to different antigens have been observed in several species subjected to a variety of noxious stimuli or to some manipulation of social interactions (Edwards et al., 1980; Glenn & Becker, 1969; Hill et al., 1967; Joasoo & McKenzie, 1976; Solomon, 1969; Vessey, 1964). Furthermore, macrophages from mice subjected to physical immobilization show a decreased nonspecific tumoricidal activity (Pavlidas & Chirigos, 1980). In another recent study (Keller et al., 1981), suppression of lymphocyte function was directly related to the degree of stress experienced by rats. Early life experiences, which can chronically alter behavioral and physiological reactivity, have also been found to alter subsequent aspects of immunological reactivity (Michaut et al., 1981; Monjan & Mandell, 1980; Solomon et al., 1968).

There are abundant data, then, indicating that psychosocial or stressful environmental circumstances are capable of modifying humoral and cell-mediated immune responses. Like the data on disease susceptibility, however, the results are neither uniform nor simple. It is quite evident that the impact of stress or psychosocial variables on immune function is determined by several major factors: the quality and quantity of stressful stimulation; the quality and quantity of immunogenic stimulation; the myriad host factors (such as species, strain, sex, age, diet, circadian rhythmicity, etc.) upon which stress and immunogenic stimulation are superimposed; the chronicity of stress and immunogenic stimulation; the temporal relationship between stress and immunogenic stimulation; procedural variables such as the nature of the dependent variable and sampling parameters; and the interaction among these factors.

CONDITIONING STUDIES: BACKGROUND AND DESIGN

Classical conditioning is probably the oldest experimental approach to the study of the relationship between the central nervous system and the immune system. The first studies were initiated in the Soviet Union more than 50 years ago. Peritoneal exudate normally consists primarily of mononuclear leukocytes. When antigen is introduced, however, there is a rapid increase in the number of polynuclear cells. Metal'nikov and Chorine (1926) attempted to condition this reaction. Guinea pigs were subjected to the repeated pairing of intraperitoneal injections of foreign material and certain specific external (conditioned) stimuli. After a rest period to allow the peritoneal exudate to return to normal, the conditioned stimulus (CS), was presented without the injection of antigen. Within 5 hours of antigenic stimulation (the unconditioned stimulus, US), approximately 90 percent of the peritoneal exudate consisted of polynuclear cells. In response to the CS, polynuclear cells increased from approximately 0.6 to 62 percent within 5 hours.

These original observations on conditioned leukocyte reactions were verified in several other experiments (Benetato, 1955; Diacono, 1933; Nicolau & Antinescu-Dimitriu, 1929; Ostravskaya, 1930; Podkopaeff & Saatchian, 1929; Riha, 1955; Ul'yanov, 1953; Vygodchikov & Barykini, 1927). Other nonspecific defense mechanisms—such as phagocytosis (Golovkova, 1947; Hadnagy & Kovats, 1954; Pel'ts, 1955; Strutsovskaya, 1953), complement (Berezhnaya, 1956; Dolin et al., 1960), and lysozyme activity (Gasanov, 1953)—were found to be influenced by conditioning.

Metal'nikov and Chorine (1928) were also the first to report that the repeated association of a neutral CS with antigenic stimulation resulted in an increase in specific antibody titer when experimental animals were subsequently reexposed to the CS alone. These observations, too, were confirmed under a variety of experimental conditions, with a variety of antigens (bacterial, cellular, viral, anatoxic), and in different species (Luk'ianenko, 1961). A detailed review of this early Soviet research has been provided elsewhere (Ader, 1981b).

Unaware of the literature from the Soviet Union, we derived our own studies from the serendipitous observation of mortality among animals that were being tested in a taste-aversion learning situation (Ader, 1974). In this passive avoidance conditioning paradigm, consumption of a novel, distinctively flavored drinking solution may be followed by the injection of a drug that induces a transient gastrointestinal upset. For example, water-deprived animals might be provided with a saccharin-flavored drinking solution, the CS, and then injected with any of several drugs with noxious internal effects, the US. After a single CS–US pairing, animals will avoid further consumption of the flavored solution when they are given a choice of solutions or when the CS solution is presented alone. Another relevant feature of this experimental paradigm is that acquired preferences for distinctively flavored drinking solutions can be established if such solutions are paired with recovery from illness or with substances that correct experimentally induced deficiency states (Garcia et al., 1967; Soughers & Etscorn, 1980; Sparenborg et al., 1981; Zahorik et al., 1974).

In one study we varied the volume of a saccharin drinking solution that was paired with a constant dose of cyclophosphamide (CY). As expected, the magnitude of the initial aversion to saccharin and resistance to extinction was directly related to the volume of saccharin consumed on the single conditioning trial. During the course of extinction trials, however, some rats died and the mortality rate tended to vary directly with the amount of saccharin consumed on the single conditioning trial. As it happens, CY, the US in this study, is a potent cytotoxic drug that suppresses immunological responses. Therefore, in order to account for these observations, it was hypothesized that pairing a neutral stimulus with an immunosuppressive drug could result in the conditioning of an immunosuppressive response. If conditioned rats were repeatedly reexposed to such a CS and, as a result, immunologically impaired, they might have become susceptible to the superimposition of latent pathogens that existed in the environment. These speculations were translated into a series of studies specifically designed to examine conditioned immunosuppression.

The essential features of the experimental protocol are outlined in Table 12-1. Individually caged rats or mice were first adapted to drinking their total daily allotment of water during a single 15- or 30- minute period occurring at the same time each day. On the training (conditioning) day, animals were randomly assigned to conditioned, nonconditioned, and placebo groups. Conditioned animals were provided with a 0.1–0.15 percent solution of sodium saccharin in tap water (the CS) instead of plain water; immediately thereafter they were injected intraperitoneally with CY (generously supplied by the Mead Johnson Research Center, Evansville, Indiana). Nonconditioned animals also received a saccharin drinking solution and an injection of CY, but these stimuli were not paired; they were introduced on different days. Placebo animals received plain water (or saccharin) and were injected with saline. Some time after conditioning (from 3 days to 7 weeks in different experiments), all animals were exposed to antigenic stimulation.

At the time that animals were injected with antigen (e.g., sheep red blood cells, SRBC), previously conditioned animals were randomly divided into three subgroups. Group US was provided with plain water and injected with CY in order to define the unconditioned immunosuppressive effects of the drug. Group CSo was also supplied with plain water and served to control for the effects of prior conditioning. Group CS, the critical experimental group, was reexposed to the CS on one or more occasions on or following the day of antigen treatment; i.e., this group was provided with the saccharin-flavored drinking solution and injected intraperitoneally with saline (the complex of stimuli that defines the CS). Nonconditioned (NC) animals were provided with the saccharin drinking solution on the same schedule as animals in Group CS. Placebo-treated animals received either plain water or saccharin during the regularly scheduled drinking periods.

Immunological reactivity was assessed one or more times following antigenic stimulation. Assays were performed according to standard procedures and without knowledge of the group to which an animal belongs.

CONDITIONED IMMUNOPHARMACOLOGICAL EFFECTS

Conditioned Suppression Of Humoral Responses

Based on the hypothesis that immunosuppression could be conditioned, the following pattern of antibody responses was predicted: Placebo-treated animals who had not been treated with CY would show high hemagglutinating antibody titers in response to the injection of SRBC. Nonconditioned animals and conditioned animals that were *not* reexposed to the saccharin drinking solution (Groups NC and CS0) were expected to have relatively high antibody

Table 12-1:   Experimental Protocol

Group	Adaptation	Treatment* on Conditioning Day	Treatment on Day of Antigenic Stimulation†	
			Sub-group	Treatment
Conditioned	H_2O (15–30 min)	SAC + CY	US	H_2O + CY
			CS0	H_2O
			CS	SAC + Sal
Nonconditioned	H_2O (15–30 min)	H_2O + CY‡	NC	SAC
Placebo	H_2O (15–30 min)	H_2O or SAC + saline	P	H_2O or SAC

*CY, intraperitoneal injection of cyclophosphophamide; SAC, 0.1–0.15 percent solution of sodium saccharine in tap water.
† Antigen administered 3–48 days after conditioning.
‡ SAC administered on different day.

titers. However, because these animals had been treated with CY on the conditioning day, they were expected to show lower antibody titers than the placebo group. Animals that were treated with CY at the same time that antigen was injected (Group US) were expected to show a minimal antibody response. The critical experimental group, conditioned animals that were reexposed to saccharin at the time of antigenic stimulation (Group CS), were expected to show an attenuated antibody response relative to NC and CS0 animals, the most relevant control groups.

The initial results (Ader & Cohen, 1975), based on hemagglutinating antibody titers sampled 6 days after treatment with SRBC, conformed precisely to the predicted relationship among the groups (Fig. 12-1). Placebo-treated rats had the highest antibody titers, and CY administered at the time of antigenic stimulation suppressed antibody production. There was no difference between NC and CS0 animals; both groups had lower antibody titers than placebo-treated animals (a difference that presumably reflects the residual effects of CY). Conditioned animals that were reexposed to the CS on the day that antigen was injected or 3 days later (Group CS1), or reexposed to the CS on both of these days (Group CS2), had antibody titers that were significantly lower than the titers in Groups NC and CS0. These

findings were taken as evidence of conditioned immunosuppression. Studies by Rogers et al. (1976) and Wayner et al. (1978) have provided independent confirmation of the phenomenon (Fig. 12-1).

The phenomenon of conditioned immunosuppression has been observed repeatedly under a variety of experimental circumstances. We have defined the dose-related residual effects of CY (Ader et al., 1979) and, accordingly, lengthened the interval between conditioning and the introduction of antigen. We have used a different CS solution and a different immunosuppressive drug, and we have varied the concentration of CY and the concentration of SRBC. Moreover, we have eliminated intraperitoneal injections of saline administered to the control groups in our first experiments on the grounds that the injection associated with CY treatment could function as a CS; we have physically separated experimental and control groups in order to decrease olfactory cues associated with the reexposure of some animals (Group CS) to the conditioned stimulus; and we have introduced a preference testing procedure instead of the forced exposure to the CS solution used in our initial experiments in order to equate total fluid consumption among experimental and control groups. In all of these experiments (Ader & Cohen, 1981) we have observed a conditioned suppression of the antibody

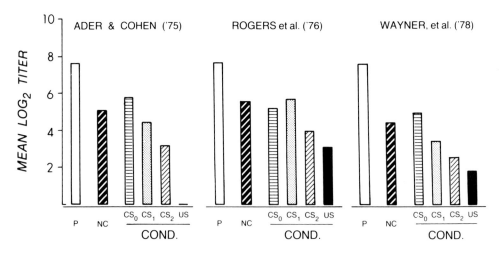

Figure 12-1. Mean Hemagglutinating antibody titers measured 6 days after injection of SRBC. P, placebo-treated animals; NC, nonconditioned animals; CS_0, conditioned animals not reexposed to CS after antigen treatment; CS_1, conditioned animals reexposed to CS on one occasion; CS_2, conditioned animals reexposed to CS on two occasions; US, conditioned animals treated with CY at the time of antigenic stimulation. From Ader (1981c): The central nervous system and immune response: Conditioned immunopharmacologic effects. In *Advances in Immunopharmacology*, Hadden J., Chedid L., & Spreafico F. (Eds.)., pp 427–434. Pergamon Press.

response to SRBC. The magnitude of the conditioning effect has not been large; it has, however, been quite consistent. Using mice, we have also found (Cohen et al., 1979) that conditioned immunosuppression occurs in response to the hapten 2, 4, 6-trinitrophenyl coupled to lipopolysaccharide (TNP–LPS) a T cell–independent antigen, providing evidence for the generality of the phenomenon.

As a reflection of immunological reactivity, antibody titer is the result of a complex chain of events which, at any of several levels, might be influenced by the neuroendocrine changes that accompnay a conditioned response or that are the direct effect of conditioning (Ader, 1976). Adrenocortical steriods can, under certain circumstances, be immunosuppressive. Therefore, it was hypothesized that the attenuated antibody response of conditioned animals resulted from a conditioned elevation in corticosterone level. Experiments designed to evaluate this possibility (Ader & Cohen, 1975; Ader et al., 1979), however, failed to confirm the hypothesis.

Lithium chloride, like CY, is an effective stimulus for taste-aversion learning and unconditionally elicits an adrenocortical response. Lithium chloride, however, is not immunosuppressive and rats conditioned with this drug instead of CY did not show an attenuated antibody response to SRBC. Additional experiments were conducted to determine if an elevation in steroid level superimposed upon the residual immunosuppressive effects of CY might be responsible for the conditioning effect. Extra groups of rats conditioned with CY were subsequently injected with lithium chloride or corticosterone instead of simply being reexposed to the CS previously paired with CY. Neither of these circumstances reduced antibody titer relative to Groups NC or CS0, whereas conditioned animals that were reexposed to the CS again showed an attenuated antibody response. These results provided no support for the hypothesis that conditioned immunosuppression is mediated by an experimentally induced differential elevation of adrenocortical steroids.

Conditioned Suppression of a Graft-Versus-Host Response

Further evidence of the generality of conditioned immunosuppression was provided by our observation that the phenomenon applies to a cell-mediated as well as a humoral response (Bovbjerg et al., 1982). It was reported by Whitehouse et al. (1973) that multiple low doses of CY could suppress a popliteal graft-versus-host response if CY was injected on the day of and the 2 days following the injection of splenic lymphocytes. We were able to repeat these results and, in addition, found that a *single* low-dose injection of CY was only moderately immunosuppressive. Taking advantage of the difference between one and three low-dose injections of CY, we based a study of conditioning effects on the possibility that a single low-dose injection of CY in conjunction with repeated reexposure to a CS previously paired with CY would suppress a graft-versus-host response to a greater extent than a single injection of CY alone, and that the effects of a single low-dose injection of CY plus reexposure to the CS might approximate the effects of three low-dose injections of CY.

The rats in this study were conditioned by pairing saccharin consumption with CY 48 days before grafting. Recipient Lewis X Brown Norwegian hybrid females were initially divided into conditioned, nonconditioned, and placebo groups. On the day of grafting (Day 0), all animals were injected subdurally into a hind footpad with a suspension of splenic leukocytes obtained from female Lewis donors. At this point, conditioned animals were subdivided as in previous studies. The critical group of conditioned rats (Group CS_r) was treated as follows: On Day 0 they were reexposed to the CS (in a preference-testing procedure) and injected intraperitoneally with saline. On Day 1 they were reexposed to the CS and injected intraperitoneally with 10 mg/kg CY. On Day 2 they were again reexposed to the CS and injected with saline. Another conditioned group (Group CS_0) was not reexposed to the CS, but did receive the single injection of 10 mg/kg CY on Day 1 (as did Group CS). A US group was injected with CY on Days 0, 1, and 2 to define the unconditioned immunosuppressive response to three low-dose CY treatments. As in previous studies, nonconditioned animals (Group NC) were exposed to saccharin and CY on the same days as the experimental group.

As shown in Figure 12-2, three low-dose injections of CY suppressed the graft-versus-host response relative to placebo-treated animals. A single low-dose injection of CY, however, only resulted in a slight attenuation of the response; that is, Group NC did not differ from placebo-treated animals, but Group CS_0 did show a lower node weight response than Group P. The control groups that received a single low-dose injection of CY (Groups NC and CS_0) did not differ from each other and showed a greater graft-versus-host response than animals that received three injections of CY (Group US). In con-

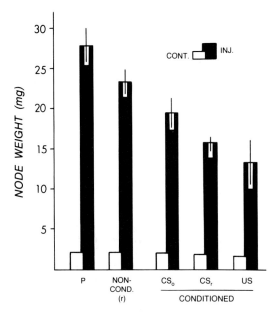

Figure 12-2. Popliteal lymph node weights determined 5 days after inoculation with splenic leukocytes: values for injected and contralateral footpads. P, placebo-treated animals; Non-cond (r), nonconditioned animals exposed to a single low dose of CY administered 1 day after cellular graft; CS_0, conditioned animals given a single low dose of CY and provided with plain water; CS_r, conditioned animals given a single low dose of CY and reexposed to CS on Days 0, 1, and 2 after cellular graft; US, conditioned animals given three low-dose injections of CY (on Days 0, 1, and 2) and provided with plain water. (From Ader R., & Cohen N., 1981: Conditioned immunopharmacologic responses. In Ader R. (Ed.). *Psychoneuroimmunology*, pp 281–320. Academic Press, New York.

trast, animals that received a single low-dose injection of CY *and* reexposure to the saccharin drinking solution previously paired with CY showed a suppressed graft-versus-host response. Stimulated lymph nodes obtained from Group CS_r rats weighed significantly less than those from NC and CS_0 animals, and there was no significant difference in lymph node weights between Group CS_r and animals that received three injections of CY.

Although there is no evidence to implicate elevated adrenocortical steroid levels in the conditioned suppression of humoral responses, that possibility can not be completely excluded in the case of a graft-versus-host response. Conditioning could involve effects on host cells, donor cells, or both, and although initiating donor cells are resistant to changes in circulating corticosterone level,

treatment of recipients with hydrocortisone does reduce splenomegally (Cohen & Claman, 1971). We did not measure steroid levels in this study, but we did use a preference-testing procedure that does not differentially influence corticosterone level (Smotherman et al., 1976). Furthermore, it is not likely that there was a differential adrenocortical response attributable to nonspecific treatment procedures. All animals were handled in the same manner, although experimental animals did receive, in addition, three intraperitoneal injections (compared to one intraperitoneal injection in Groups NC and CS_0). Since our own pilot studies as well as the results reported by Whitehouse et al. (1973) showed that even three injections of CY (in doses up to 5 mg/kg) did not reduce the graft-versus-host response any more than a single injection of 10 mg/kg CY (the dose used in the present experiment), it is unlikely that in the absence of conditioning the injection of saline alone would significantly reduce the graft-versus-host response.

Conditioned Immunosuppression in Murine Systemic Lupus Erythematosus

We have made a point of noting that the magnitude of the effects of conditioning in suppressing immune responses has been small. The phenomenon has, however, been quite reproducible and extends to cell-mediated as well as humoral responses. In an effort to assess the biological significance of conditioned changes in immunological reactivity, we have initiated studies to determine the effect of conditioned immunosuppressive responses in New Zealand mice (Ader & Cohen, 1982). The NZB×NZW F_1 female has become a standard model for experimental studies of systemic lupus erythematosus (Steinberg et al., 1981; Talal, 1976; Theofilopoulos & Dixon, 1981). These hybrids develop a lethal glomerulonephritis between approximately 8 and 14 months of age. The onset of proteinuria and mortality can be delayed, however, if mice are placed on a weekly regimen of immunosuppressive therapy (Casey, 1968; Hahn et al., 1975; Lehman et al., 1976; Morris et al., 1976; Russell & Hicks, 1968; Steinbert et al., 1975). Having demonstrated conditioned immunosuppression, we hypothesized that substituting conditioned stimuli for an active immunosuppressive drug might delay the development of autoimmune disease in conditioned mice relative to nonconditioned animals treated with the same amount of drug; that is, an attempt was made to determine the applicability of conditioning procedures in the regulation and control of an immunological disorder.

Female NZB×NZW F$_1$ mice were placed on an 8-week chemotherapeutic regimen when they were 4 months of age. All animals were given a 0.15 percent sodium saccharin solution by pipette (up to a maximum of 1.0 ml) on 1 day of each week. CY (30 mg/kg) was injected according to the following schedule: Group C100 was administered the drug on a "traditional" chemotherapeutic regimen; that is, CY was injected once each week immediately after mice drank the saccharin solution. This occurred at the same time and on the same day of each week. As expected, this dosage of CY and this duration of treatment effectively prolonged survival but was not sufficient to prevent the ultimate development of autoimmune disease.

Group C50 also received saccharin at the same time and on the same day of each week, but for these conditioned animals injections of CY followed exposure to saccharin on only one-half of the weekly trials; on 2 of every 4 weeks, these mice received an intraperitoneal injection of saline instead of CY. In effect, these conditioned animals were treated under a partial reinforcement schedule; saccharin consumption was pharmacologically reinforced on only 50 percent of the occasions when saccharin was administered.

Group NC50 was a nonconditioned group that received the same weekly exposures to saccharin and the same number of CY and saline injections as Group C50. For this group, however, CY (or saline) injections were not paired with consumption of saccharin; the taste stimulus and pharmacological stimulus were introduced on different days of the same week.

A control group received no CY. These mice did, however, receive weekly exposures to saccharin and saline injections on a noncontingent basis.

Nonconditioned mice that received only one-half the total amount of CY administered under the customary kind of therapeutic schedule were expected to show symptoms of autoimmune disease and die sooner than animals treated weekly, and somewhat later than animals that were not treated with CY at all. Animals in Group C50 were also treated with one-half the amount of drug given to animals in Group C100. Assuming that the pairing of saccharin and CY results in a conditioned immunosuppressive response, however, we predicted that Group C50 would develop systemic lupus erythe-

matosus at a slower rate than nonconditioned animals treated with exactly the same number and distribution of CY injections. This is precisely what happened.

Weekly treatment with CY (the "traditional" chemotherapy protocol) delayed the onset of proteinuria and prolonged survival in NZB×NZW mice. Considering the entire population of animals that developed autoimmune disease (Fig. 12-3), there was a significant difference in the rate of development of unremitting proteinuria. In any such situation wherein all animals are expected to develop disease symptoms and die, the longer one monitors the progression of disease the less likely it is to discriminate statistically among groups that are subjected to different treatment conditions. As is evident in Figure 12-3, differences among the differentially treated groups are particularly dramatic when systemic lupus erythematosus is measured by the rate of development of proteinuria for the initial 50 percent of the population to develop disease. Group C100 developed proteinuria later than the groups treated with one-half the amount of drug or untreated controls. Group NC50 did not differ significantly from untreated controls. Group C50, however, developed proteinuria significantly later than untreated controls and nonconditioned animals treated with the same amount of CY.

The same results were observed with respect to mortality (Fig. 12-4): there was an overall difference among the total population of animals and the differences were especially apparent in the rate at which the first half of each group died. Mice treated weekly with CY died at a significantly slower rate than untreated controls and Group NC50. Group NC50 did not differ significantly from untreated animals, but conditioned animals that received the same amount of drug survived significantly longer than untreated controls and nonconditioned animals. The difference between Groups C50 and C100 was not statistically significant.

The results of this study conformed precisely to predictions based on the hypothesis that pairing saccharin consumption with immunosuppressive treatment would enable saccharin, acting as a CS, to suppress immunological reactivity and thereby delay the onset of systemic lupus erythematosus under a regimen of chemotherapy that was not, in itself, sufficient to influence the development of autoimmune disease. These observations, then, constitute a further elaboration of conditioned immunopharmacological effects and document the biological impact of conditioned immunosuppressive responses.

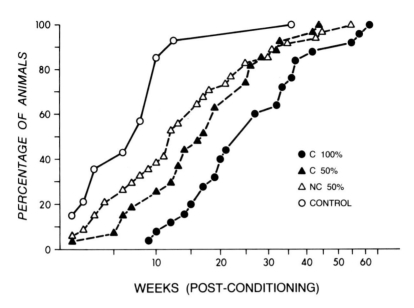

WEEKS (POST-CONDITIONING)

Figure 12-3. Rate of development of an unremitting proteinuria in NZB×NZW F_1 female mice under different chemotherapeutic regimens. Group C100 (N = 25) received weekly presentations of saccharin followed by intraperitoneal injection of 30 mg/kg CY; Group C50 (N = 27) received weekly presentations of saccharin with injection of CY following saccharin on 2 of every 4 weeks; Group NC50 (N = 34) received weekly presentations of saccharin and unpaired injections of CY on 2 of every 4 weeks; control mice (N = 14) received weekly presentations of saccharin but no CY. (From Ader R., & Cohen N., 1982: Behaviorally conditioned immunosuppression and murine systemic lupus erythematosus. *Science* 25:1534–1536. Copyright 1982 by the American Association for the Advancement of Science.

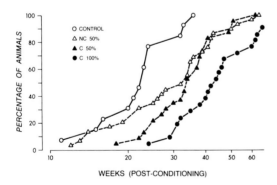

WEEKS (POST-CONDITIONING)

Figure 12-4. Cumulative mortality rate in NZB×NZW F_1 female mice following different chemotherapeutic regimens. Group C100 (N = 21), C50 (N = 23), NC50 (N = 29), and control (N = 13) are defined as in Figure 12-3. (From Ader R., & Cohen N., 1982: Behaviorally conditioned immunosuppression and murine systemic lupus erythematosus. *Science* 25:1534–1536. Copyright 1982 by the American Association for the Advancement of Science.

DISCUSSION

It was hypothesized that pairing a neutral, gustatory stimulus with the immunosuppressive effects of a pharmacological agent would enable the neutral or conditioned stimulus to suppress immunological reactivity, i.e., immunopharmacological responses would be conditioned. In a one-trial passive avoidance conditioning paradigm, consumption of saccharin—a novel, distinctively flavored drinking solution—was followed by an injection of CY, an immunosuppressive drug. When subsequently treated with SRBC, a T cell–dependent antigen, or TNP-LPS, a T cell–independent antigen, conditioned animals that were reexposed to the saccharin drinking solution displayed attenuated antibody responses relative to a group of conditioned animals that were *not* reexposed to the CS and a group of nonconditioned animals that were exposed to saccharin. Observations of conditioned immunosuppression have been repeated in our laboratory under a variety of experimental circumstances (Ader 1981c) and verified by other studies (Rogers et al., 1976; Wayner et al., 1978). We have also demonstrated conditioned suppression of a cell-mediated immune response, which attests to the generality of the phenomenon. Forty-eight days after saccharin consumption was paired with an injection of CY, the reexposure of conditioned animals to saccharin significantly reduced a graft-versus-host response.

Conditioned immunosuppression appears to be a highly reproducible phenomenon and, although the effects of conditioning are relatively small, the biological consequences are clearly demonstrable. Introduction of conditioning techniques (and, presumably, conditioned immunosuppressive responses) within a chemotherapeutic protocol for the treatment of systemic lupus erythematosus in New Zealand mice resulted in a delay in the onset of proteinura and mortality with the administration of an amount of drug that, by itself, was only minimally effective in influencing the development of the disease.

Hemagglutinating antibody titers several days after antigenic stimulation may not be the most sensitive index of the effects of conditioning. Conditioning and reexposure to the CS may, for example, exert effects early in the complex chain of events that determine the ultimate level of circulating antibody. Since CY has different effects upon different populations of lymphocytes, a CS associated with CY may also have such differential effects. The temporal relationship between reexposure(s) to a CS and antigenic stimulation thus becomes an important variable in assessing the effects of conditioning.

There are, in addition, behavioral issues that lead one to suspect that we may not yet have devised an optimal experimental paradigm or model for examining the effects of conditioning in modifying immune response. In conditioning terms, an antigen is a US. Operationally, then, we eventually pair a CS for suppression of an immune response with a US for initiation of that very same response. This description of our current procedures is consistent with the data we have obtained thus far and is discussed in greater detail elsewhere (Ader & Cohen, 1981). It should be noted here, however, that this analysis implies that enhancement of immunological reactivity could be a sensitive model for exploring conditioned immunopharmacological effects.

Although the mechanisms mediating conditioned humoral or cell-mediated responses remain to be determined, direct and indirect evidence for anatomical and neurochemical innervation of lymphoid organs, the presence of receptors for hormones and neurotransmitters on lymphocytes, the endocrine involvement in immune responses and autoimmune disorders (and vice versa), and the myriad host factors (age, sex, nutritional state, circadian rhythmicity, etc.) that influence immunological reactivity already provide compelling evidence for a dynamic flow of information among the central nervous system, the endocrine system, and the immune system. There are therefore many neuroendocrine pathways that might be explored in analyzing the effects of behavioral factors on immune responses.

REFERENCES

Ader R (1974): Letter to the editor. Psychosom Med 36:183–184.

Ader R (1976): Conditioned adrenocortical steroid elevations in the rat. J Comp Physiol Psychol 90:1156–1163.

Ader R, (Ed.) (1981a): *Psychoneuroimmunology*. New York, Academic Press.

Ader R (1981b): An historical account of conditioned immunobiologic responses. Ader R (Ed.). In *Psychoneuroimmunology*. New York, Academic Press, pp. 321–354.

Ader R (1981c): The central nervous sytem and immune responses: Conditioned immunopharmacologic effects. Hadden J, Chedid L, & Spreafico F (Eds.). In *Advances in Immunopharmacology*. Oxford, Pergamon Press, pp. 427–434.

Ader R, & Cohen N (1975): Behaviorally conditioned immunosuppression. Psychosom Med 37:333–340.

Ader R, & Cohen N (1981): Conditioned immunopharmacologic responses. Ader R (Ed.). In *Psychoneuroimmunology*. New York, Academic Press, pp. 231–320.

Ader R, & Cohen N (1982): Behaviorally conditioned immunosuppression and murine systemic lupus erythematosus. Science 25:1534–1536.

Ader R, Cohen N, & Grota LJ (1979): Adrenal involvement in conditioned immunosuppression. Int J Immunopharmacol 1:141–145.

Ahlqvist J (1981): Hormonal influences on immunologic and related phenomena. Ader R (Ed.). In *Psychoneuroimmunology*. New York, Academic Press, pp. 355–404.

Amkraut AA, & Solomon GF (1974): From the symbolic stimulus to the pathophysiologic response: Immune mechanisms. Int J Psychiat Med 5:541–563.

Amkraut AN, Solomon GF, Kasper P, & Purdue P (1973): Stress and hormonal intervention in the graft-versus-host response. Jankovic BD, & Isakovic K (Eds.). In *Microenvironmental Aspects of Immunity*. New York, Plenum Press, pp. 667–674.

Amkraut AA, Solomon GF, & Kraemer HC (1971): Stress, early experience and adjuvant-induced arthritis in the rat. Psychosom Med 33:203–214.

Bahnson CB (Ed.) (1969): Second conference on psychophysiological aspects of cancer. Ann NY Acad Sci 164:307–634.

Bammer K, & Newberry BH (Eds.) (1981): *Stress and Cancer.* Toronto, Hogrefe.

Bartrop RW, Lazarus L, Luckhurst E, Kiloh LG, & Penny R (1977): Depressed lymphocyte function after bereavement. Lancet 1:834–836.

Benetato GR (1955): Le mechanisme nerveux central de la reaction leucocytaire et phagocytaire. J Physiol 47:391–403.

Berezhnaya NM (1956): In *Principles of Immunity.* (Proceedings of a Scientific Conference) vol 3: 185.

Besedovsky HO, del Ray A, Sorkin E, DePrada M, & Keller HH (1979): Immunoregulation mediated by the sympathetic nervous system. Cell Immunol 48:346–355.

Besedovsky HO, & Sorkin E (1981): Immunologic-neuroendocrine circuits: Physiological approaches. Ader R (Ed.). In *Psychoneuroimmunology.* New York, Academic Press, pp. 545–574.

Besedovsky HO, Sorkin E, Felix D, & Haas H (1977): Hypothalamic changes during the immune response. Eur J Immunol 7: 323–325.

Bourne HR, Lichtenstein LM, Melmon KL, Henny CS, Weinstein Y, & Shearer GM (1974): Modulation of inflammation and immunity by cyclic AMP. Science 184: 19–28.

Bovbjerg D, Ader R, & Cohen N (1982): Behaviorally conditioned immunosupression of a graft-vs-host response. Proc Nat Acad Sci USA 79: 583–585.

Bulloch K, & Moore RY (1980): Nucleus ambiguus projections to the thymus gland: Possible pathways for regulation of the immune response and the neuroendocrine network. Anat Rec 196: 25A.

Casey TP (1968): Immunosuppression by cyclophosphamide in NZB/NZW mice with lupus nephritis. Blood 32: 436–444.

Chang S, & Rasmussen AF Jr (1965): Stress-induced suppression in interferon production in virus-infected mice. Nature 205: 623–624.

Christian JJ, & Williamson HO (1958): Effect of crowding on experimental granuloma formation in mice. Proc Soc Exp Biol Med 99: 385–387.

Claman HN (1972): Corticosteroid and lymphoid cells. N Engl J Med 287: 388–397.

Cohen N, Ader R, Green N, & Bovbjerg D (1979): Conditioned suppression of a thymus-independent antibody response. Psychosom Med 41: 487–491.

Cohen JJ, & Claman HN (1971): Hydrocortisone resistance of activated initiator cells on graft-versus-host reactions. Nature 229: 274–275.

Cohen JJ, & Crnic LS (1982): Glucocorticoids, stress and the immune response. Webb, DR Jr (Ed.). In *Immunopharmacology and the Regulation of Lymphocyte Function.* New York, Dekker, pp. 61–91.

Davis DE, & Read CP (1958): Effect of behavior on development of resistance in trichinosis. Proc Soc Exp Biol Med 99: 269–272.

Devoino L, Elsicera L, Eremina O, Idova G, & Cheido M (1975): 5-hydroxytryptophan effect on the development

of the immune response: IgM and IgG antibodies and rosette formation in primary and secondary responses. Eur J Immunol 5: 394–399.

Diacono H (1933): Le phénomène hemolytique: Contribution a l'étude de l'hemolyse: XI. Réflexes conditionnels et hemolyse. Arch Inst Pasteur Tunis 22: 376–385.

Dolin AO, Krylov VN, Luk'ianenko VI, & Flerov BA (1960): New experimental data on the conditioned reflex reproduction and suppression of immune and allergic reactions. Zh Vyssh Nerv Deiat 10: 832–841.

Dorian BJ, Keystone E, Garfinkel PE, & Brown GM (1981): Immune mechanisms in acute psychological stress. Psychosom Med 43: 84.

Dougherty TF (1952): Effect of hormones on lymphatic tissue. Physiol Rev 32: 379–401.

Edwards EA, & Dean LM (1977): Effects of crowding of mice on humoral antibody formation and protection to lethal antigenic challenge. Psychosom Med 39: 19–24.

Edwards EA, Rahe RH, Stephens PM, & Henry JP (1980): Antibody response to bovine serum albumin in mice: The effects of psychosocial environmental change. Proc Soc Exp Biol Med 164:478–481.

Engels WD, & Wittkower ED (1975): Psychophysiological allergic and skin disorders. Freedman AM, Kaplan HJ, & Sadock BJ, (Eds.). In *Comprehensive Textbook of Psychiatry,* vol II. Baltimore, Williams & Wilkins, 1685–1694.

Ernstrom U, & Sandberg G (1973): Effects of adrenergic alpha- and beta-receptor stimulation on the release of lymphocytes and granulocytes from the spleen. Scand J Haematol 11:275–286.

Farris EJ (1938): Increase in lymphocytes in healthy persons under certain emotional states. Am J Anat 63:297–323.

Felten DL, Overhage JM, Felten SY, & Schmedtje JF (1981): Noradrenergic sympathetic innervation of lymphoid tissue in the rabbit appendix: Further evidence for a link between the nervous and immune systems. Brain Res Bull 7:594–612.

Folch H, & Waksman BH (1974): The splenic suppressor cell: Activity of thymus dependent adherent cells: Changes with age and stress. J Immunol 113:127–139.

Freedman DX, & Fenichel D (1958): Effect of midbrain lesion in experimental allergy. Arch Neurol Psychiatry 79:164–169.

Friedman SB, Ader R, & Glasgow LA (1965): Effects of psychological stress in adult mice inoculated with Coxsackie B viruses. Psychosom Med 27:361–368.

Friedman SB, Ader R, & Grota LJ (1973): Protective effect of noxious stimulation in mice infected with rodent malaria. Psychosom Med 35:535–537.

Friedman SB, & Glasgow LA (1966): Psychologic factors and resistance to infectious disease. Pediatr Clin North Am 13:315–335.

Friedman SB, Glasgow LA, & Ader R (1969): Psychosocial factors modifying host resistance to experimental infections. Ann NY Acad Sci 164:381–393.

Funk GA, & Jensen MM (1967): Influence of stress on granuloma formation. Proc Soc Exp Biol Med 124:653–655.

Garcia J, Ervin FR, Yorke CH, & Koelling RA (1967): Conditioning with delayed vitamin injections. Science 155:716–718.

Gasanov GT (1953): Experimental data on the study of the effect and excretion of lysozyme. Unpublished dissertation.

Giron LT Jr, Crutcher KA, & Davis JN (1980): Lymph nodes—A possible site for sympathetic neuronal regulation of immune responses. Ann Neurol 8:520–525.

Gisler RH, Bussard AE, Mazie JC, & Hess R (1971): Hormonal regulation of the immune response: I. Induction of an immune response in vitro with lymphoid cells from mice exposed to acute systemic stress. Cell Immunol 2:634–645.

Gisler RH, & Schenkel-Hulliger L (1971): Hormonal regulation of the immune response: II. Influence of pituitary and adrenal activity on immune responsiveness in vitro. Cell Immunol 2:646–657.

Glenn WG, & Becker RE (1969): Individual versus group housing in mice: Immunological response to time-phased injections. Physiol Zool 42:411–416.

Goldstein AL, Thurman GB, Low TLK, Rossio JL, & Trivers GE (1978): Hormonal influences on the reticuloendothelial system: Current status of the role of thymosin in the regulation and modulation of immunity. J Reticuloendothel Soc 23:253–266.

Golovkova IN (1947): The influence of nociceptive and conditioned reflex stimulation on phagocytic capability or leukocytes in the organism. Bull Exp Biol Med 24:268–270.

Greene WA, Betts RF, Ochitill HN, Iker HP, & Douglas RG (1978): Psychosocial factors and immunity: Preliminary report. Psychosom Med 40:87.

Greenfield NS, Roessler R, & Crosley AP (1959): Ego strength and length of recovery from infectious mononucleosis. J Nerv Ment Dis 128:125–128.

Gross WB, & Siegel HS (1965): The effect of social stress on resistance to infection with Escherichia coli or Mycoplasma gallisepticum. Poult Sci 44:98–100.

Gunderson E, & Rahe RH, (Eds.) (1974): *Life Stress and Illness*. Springfield, Ill., Thomas.

Guy WB (1952): Neurogenic factors in contact dermatitis. Arch Dermatol Syphil 66:1–8.

Hadden JW, Hadden EM, & Middleton E Jr (1970): Lymphocyte blast transformation: 1. Demonstration of adrenergic receptors in human peripheral lymphocytes. Cell Immunol 1:583–595.

Hadnagy CS, & Kovats I (1954): Die rolle der hirnrinde bei den veranderungen der fahigkeit des serums zur stimulation der phagozytose. Acta Physiol Acad Hung 5:325–330.

Hahn BH, Knotts L, Ng M, & Hamilton TR (1975): Influence of cyclophosphamide and other immunosuppressive drugs on immune disorders and neoplasia in NZB/NZW mice. Arthritis Rheum 18:145–152.

Hall NR, & Goldstein AL (1981): Neurotransmitters and the immune system. Ader R (Ed.). In *Psychoneuroimmunology*. New York, Academic Press, pp. 521–543.

Hamilton DR (1974): Immunosuppressive effects of predator induced stress in mice with acquired immunity to Hymenolepsis nana. J Psychosom Res 18:143–153.

Hill CW, Greer WE, & Felsenfeld O (1967): Psychological stress, early response to foreign protein, and blood cortisol in vervets. Psychosom Med 29:279–283.

Holmes TH, Treuting T, & Wolff HG (1951): Life situations, emotions and nasal disease: Evidence on summative effects exhibited in patients with "hay fever." Psychosom Med 13:71–82.

Imboden JB, Canter A, & Cluff LE (1961): Convalescence from influenza: A study of the psychological and clinical determinants. Arch Intern Med 108:393–399.

Jacobs MA, Spilken AZ, Norman MM, & Anderson LS (1970): Life stress and respiratory illness. Psychosom Med 32:233–242.

Jankovic BD, & Isakovic K (1973): Neuroendocrine correlates of immune response: I. effects of brain lesions on antibody production, Arthus reactivity and delayed hypersensitivity in the rat. Int Arch Allergy Appl Immunol 45:360–372.

Jensen MM, & Rasmussen AF Jr (1963): Stress and susceptibility to viral infections: II. Sound stress and susceptibility to vesicular stomatitis virus. J Immunol 90:21–23.

Joasoo A, & McKenzie JM (1976): Stress and the immune response in rats. Int Arch Allergy Appl Immunol 50:659–663.

Johnson T, Lavender JF, & Marsh JT (1959): The influence of avoidance learning stress on resistance to Coxsackie virus in mice. Fed Proc 18:575.

Kasl SV, Evans AS, & Neiderman JC (1979): Psychosocial risk factors in the development of infectious mononucleosis. Psychosom Med 41:445–466.

Keller SE, Weiss J, Schleifer SJ, Miller NE, & Stein M (1981): Suppression of immunity by stress: Effect of a graded series of stressors on lymphocyte stimulation in the rat. Psychosom Med 43:91.

Korneva EA, & Khai LM (1963): Effect of destruction on hypothalamic areas on immunogenesis. Fizio Zh SSSR 49:42–48.

Korneva EA, & Khai LM (1967): The effect of stimulating different mesencephalic structures on protective immune response patterns. Fizio Zh SSR 53:42–47.

LaBarba RC (1970): Experiential and environmental factors in cancer. Psychosom Med 32:259–276.

Lane MA (1978): Muscarinic cholinergic activation of mouse spleen cells cytotoxic to tumor cells in vitro. J Natl Cancer Inst 61:923–926.

Lehman DH, Wilson CB, & Dixon FJ (1976): Increased survival times of New Zealand hybrid mice immunosuppressed by graft-versus-host reactions. Clin Exp Immunol 25:297–302.

Levine S, Strebel R, Wenk EJ, & Harman PJ (1962): Suppression of experimental allergic encephalomyelitis by stress. Proc Soc Exp Biol Med 109:294–298.

Locke SE, Hurst MW, Heisel J, & Williams RM (1978): The influence of stress on the immune response. Paper presented at the meetings of the American Psychosomatic Society. March, Washington, DC.

Luk'ianenko VI (1961): The problem of conditioned reflex regulation of immunobiologic reactions. Usp Sovrem Biol 51:170–187.

Luparello TJ, Stein M, & Park CD (1964): Effect of hypothalamic lesions on rat anaphylaxis. Am J Physiol 207:911–914.

Maestroni GJM, & Pierpaoli W (1981): Pharmacologic control of the hormonally mediated immune response. Ader R (Ed.). In *Psychoneuroimmunology.* New York, Academic Press, pp. 405-428.

Marsh JT, Lavender JF, Chang S, & Rasmussen AF Jr (1963): Poliomyelitis in monkeys: Decreased susceptibility after avoidance stress. Science 140:1415–1416.

Metal'nikov S, & Chorine V (1926): Rôle des réflexes conditionnels dans l'immunité. Ann Inst Pasteur 40:893–900.

Metal'nikov S, & Chorine V (1928): Rôle des réflexes conditionnels dans la formation des anticorps. C R Soc Biol (Paris) 99:142–145.

Mettrop PJG, & Visser P (1969): Exteroceptive stimulation as a contingent factor in the induction and elicitation of delayed-type hypersensitivity reactions to 1-chloro-2, 4-dinitrobenzene in guinea pigs. Psychophysiology 5:385–388.

Meyer RJ, & Haggerty RJ (1962): Streptococcal infections in families: Factors altering individual susceptibility. J Pediatr 29:339–349.

Michaut RJ, DeChambre RP, Doumerc S, Lesourd B, Devillechabrolle A, & Moulias R (1981): Influence of early maternal deprivation on adult humoral immune response in mice. Physiol Behav 26:189–191.

Monjan AA (1981): Stress and immunologic competence: Studies in animals. Ader R, (Ed.). In *Psychoneuroimmunology.* New York, Academic Press, pp. 185–229.

Monjan AA, & Collector MI (1976): Stress-induced modulation of the immune response. Science 196:307–308.

Monjan AA, & Mandell W (1980): Fetal alcohol and immunity: Depression of mitogen-induced lymphocyte blastogenesis. Neurobehav Toxicol 2:213–215.

Mora JM, Amtman LE, & Hoffman SJ (1926): Effect of mental emotional states on the leukocyte count. Jama 86:945–946.

Morris AD, Esterly J, Chase G, & Sharp GC (1976). Cyclophosphamide protection in NZB/NZW disease. Arthritis Rheum 19:49–55.

Nicolau I, & Antinescu-Dimitriu O (1929): L'influence des réflexes conditionnels sur l'exsudat peritoneal. C R Soc Biol (Paris) 102:144–145.

Ostravskaya OA (1930): Le reflex conditionnel et les reactions de l'immunite. Ann Inst Pasteur 44:340–345.

Palmblad J (1981): Stress and immunologic competence: Studies in man. Ader R (Ed.). In *Psychoneuroimmunology.* New York, Academic Press, pp. 229–258.

Pavlidas N, & Chirigos M (1980): Stress-induced impairment of macrophage tumoricidal function. Psychosom Med 42:47–54.

Pel'ts DG (1955): The role of the cerebral cortex in the modification of phagocytic activity of blood leukocytes of animals from the application of electrocutaneous stimuli. Bull Exp Biol Med 40:55–58.

Pitkin DH (1965): Effect of physiological stress on the delayed hypersensitivity reaction. Proc Soc Exp Biol Med 120:350–351.

Plaut SM, & Friedman SB (1981): Psychosocial factors in infectious disease. Ader R (Ed.). In *Psychoneuroimmunology.* New York, Academic Press, pp. 3–30.

Plaut SM, Ader R, Friedman SB, & Ritterson AL (1969): Social factors and resistance to malaria in the mouse: Effects of group vs individual housing on resistance to Plasmodium berghei infection. Psychosom Med 31:536–552.

Podkopaeff NA, & Saatchian RL (1929): Conditioned reflexes for immunity: I. Conditioned reflexes in rabbits for cellular reaction of peritoneal fluid. Bull Battle Creek Sanit Hosp Clin 24:375–378.

Rasmussen AF Jr, Marsh JT, & Brill NC (1957): Increased susceptibility to herpes simplex in mice subjected to avoidance-learning stress or restraint. Proc Soc Exp Biol Med 96:183–189.

Reilly FD, McCuskey PA, Miller ML, McCuskey RS, & Meineke HA (1979): Innervation of the periarticular lymphatic sheath of the spleen. Tissue Cell 11: 121–126.

Riha I (1955): A contribution to the question of conditioned reflex formation of antibodies. Folia Biol (Praha) 1: 139–143.

Riley V, Fitzmaurice MA, & Spackman DH (1981): Psychoneuroimmunologic factors in neoplasia: Studies in animals. Ader R (Ed.). In *Psychoneuroimmunology.* New York, Academic Press, pp. 31–102.

Roessler R, Cate TR, Lester JW, & Couch RB (1979): Ego strength, life events, and antibody titers. Paper presented at the annual meetings of the American Psychosomatic Society. March, Dallas, Texas.

Rogers MP, Dubey D, & Reich P (1979): The influence of the psyche and the brain on immunity and disease susceptibility. Psychosom Med 41:147–164.

Rogers MP, Reich P, Strom TB, & Carpenter CB (1976): Behaviorally conditioned immunosuppression: Replication of a recent study. Psychosom Med 38:447–452.

Rogers MP, Trentham DE, McCune WJ, Ginsberg BI, Rennke HG, Reich P, & David JR (1980): Effect of psychological stress on the induction of arthritis in rats. Arthritis Rheum 23:1337–1342.

Rogers MP, Trentham DE, & Reich P (1981): Modulation of collagen-induced arthritis by different stress protocols. Psychosom Med 42:72.

Russell PJ, & Hicks JD (1968): Cyclophosphamide treatment of renal disease in (NZBxNZW) F1 hybrid mice. Lancet 1:440–446.

Schleifer SJ, Keller SE, McKegney FP., & Stein M (1980): Bereavement and lymphocyte function. Paper presented at the meetings of the American Psychiatric Association. March, San Francisco, California.

Sklar LS, & Anisman H (1981): Stress and cancer. Psychol Bull 89:369–406.

Smith LW, Molomut N, & Gottfried B (1960): Effect of subconvulsive audiogenic stress in mice on turpentine induced inflammation. Proc Soc Exp Biol Med 103: 370–372.

Smotherman WP, Hennessy JW, & Levine S (1976): Plasma corticosterone levels during recovery from LiCl produced taste aversions. Behav Biol 16:401–412.

Solomon GF (1969): Stress and antibody response in rats. Int Arch Allergy Appl Immunol 35:97–104.

Solomon GF (1981): Emotional and personality factors in the onset and course of autoimmune disease, particularly rheumatoid arthritis. Ader R (Ed.). In *Psychoneuroimmunology.* New York, Academic Press, pp. 159–184.

Solomon GF, & Amkraut AA (1981): Psychoneuroendocrinological effects on the immune response. Ann Rev Microbiol 35:155–184.

Solomon GF, Amkraut AA, & Rubin RT (1979): Stress and psychoimmunological response. Stoll BA (Ed.). In *Mind and Cancer Prognosis.* New York, Wiley, pp. 73–84.

Solomon GF, Levine S, & Kraft JK (1968): Early experience and immunity. Nature 220:821–822.

Soughers TK, & Etscorn F (1980): A learned preference in the mouse using potassium deficiency as the induced need state. Bull Psychonomic Soc 16:62–64.

Sparenborg SP, Buskist WF, Miller HL Jr, Fleming DE, & Duncan PC (1981): Attenuation of taste-aversion conditioning in rats recovered from thiamine deficiency: Atropine vs lithium toxicosis. Bull Psychonomic Soc 17:237–239.

Spector NH, & Korneva EA (1981): Neurophysiology, immunophysiology, and neuroimmunomodulation. Ader R (Ed.). In *Psychoneuroimmunology.* New York, Academic Press, pp. 449–474.

Stein M, Schiavi RC, & Camerino M (1976): Influence of brain and behavior on the immune system. Science 191: 435–440.

Stein M, Schleifer SJ, & Keller SE (1981): Hypothalamic influences on immune responses. Ader R (Ed.). In *Psychoneuroimmunology.* New York, Academic Press, pp. 429–448.

Steinberg AD, Gelfand MC, Hardin JA, & Lowenthal DT (1975): Therapeutic studies in NZB/W mice: III. Relationship between renal status and efficacy of immunosuppressive drug therapy. Arthritis Rheum 18:9–14.

Steinberg AD, Huston DP, Taurog JD, Cowdery JS, & Raveche ES (1981): The cellular and genetic basis of murine lupus. Immunol Rev 55:121–154.

Strom TB, Bear RA, Carpenter CB, & Merril JP (1974): Modulation of GvH proliferation by cyclic nucleotides. J Clin Invest 53:79–84.

Strutsovkaya AL (1953): An experiment on the formation of conditioned phagocytic reactions in children. Zh Vyssh Nerv Deiat 3:238–246.

Szentivanyi A, & Filipp G (1958): Anaphylaxis and the nervous sytem: II. Ann Allergy 16:143–151.

Talal N (1976): Disordered immunologic regulation and autoimmunity. Transplant Rev 31:240–263.

Theofilopoulos AN, & Dixon FJ (1981): Etiopathogenesis of murine SLE. Immunol Rev 55:179–216.

Thrasher SG, Bernardis LL, & Cohen S (1971): The immune response in hypothalamic-lesioned and hypophysectomized rats. Arch Allergy 41:813–820.

Ul'yanov MI (1953): On the question of cortical regulation of the leukocyte composition of peripheral blood. Klin Med 31:52–56.

Vessey SH (1964): Effects of groupings on levels of circulating antibodies in mice. Proc Soc Exp Biol Med 115: 252–255.

Vygodchikov GV, & Barykini O (1927): The conditioned reflex and protective cell reactions. J Biol Med Exp (Moscow) 6:538–541.

Wayner EA, Flannery GR, & Singer G (1978): Effects of taste aversion conditioning on the primary antibody response to sheep red blood cells and Brucella abortus in the albino rat. J Comp Physiol Behav 21:995–1000.

Weinmann CJ, & Rothman AH (1967): Effects of stress upon acquired immunity to the dwarf tapeworm Hymenolepsis nana. Exp Parasitol 21:61–67.

Whitehouse MW, Levy L, & Beck FJ (1973): Effect of cyclophosphamide on a local graft-versus-host reaction in the rat. Influence of sex, disease and different dosage regimens. Agents Actions 3:53–60.

Williams JM, & Felton DL (1981): Sympathetic innervation of murine thymus and spleen: A comparative histofluorescence study. Anat Rec 199:531–542.

Williams JM, Peterson RG, Shea PA, Schmedtje JF, Bauer DC, & Felten DL (1981): Sympathetic innervation of murine thymus and spleen: Evidence for a functional link between the nervous and immune systems. Brain Res Bull 6:83–94.

Wistar R Jr, & Hildemann WH (1960): Effect of stress on skin transplantation immunity in mice. Science 131: 159–160.

Yamada A, Jensen MM, & Rasmussen AF Jr (1964): Stress and susceptibility to viral infections: III. Antibody response and viral retention during avoidance learning stress. Proc Soc Exp Biol Med 116:677–680.

Zahorik DM, Maier SF, & Pies RW (1974): Preferences for tastes paired with recovery from thiamine deficiency in rats: Appetitive conditioning or learned satiety? J Comp Physiol Psychol 87:1083–1091.

13

Endorphins in Emotions, Behavior, and Mental Illness

Philip A. Berger

The discovery of peptide molecules in the human brain with pharmacological activity similar to that of morphine, heroin, and other opiates is an exciting advance in neurobiology. The discovery was not an accident. Endogenous opiate peptides were found as a result of a systematic search that began with a pharmacological observation and a physiological finding. In 1972, Akil et al. reported that analgesia produced by electrical stimulation of certain brain areas in the rat could be partially reversed by the potent opiate antagonist naloxone. This observation suggested that electrically stimulated analgesia was mediated, in part, by a natural substance with actions like those of morphine. In 1973 three groups of investigators, using a model proposed by Goldstein et al. (1971), found highly specific opiate receptors in mammalian brain (Pert & Snyder, 1973; Simon et al., 1973; Terenius, 1973). Numerous investigators then suggested that the brain opiate receptors must be the target of a naturally occurring or endogenous opiate.

The first endogenous opiates found were two small peptides of five amino acids each called *methionine-enkephalin* (met-ENK) and *leucine-enkephalin* (leu-ENK) by their discoverers, Hughes et al. (1975). These investigators also reported that the amino acid sequence of met-ENK was found within the pituitary peptide β-lipotropin (β-LPH), which had been discovered by Li in 1964. Met-ENK is β-LPH amino acid 61–65; leu-ENK has the same amino acid sequence but its terminal amino acid is leucine instead of methionine. Soon after the discovery of met- and leu-ENK, other endogenous opiates were discovered. These endogenous opiates are now called *endorphins*, a contraction of "endogenous morphinelike" substances. Other endorphins are also found in the sequence of β-LPH, including β-endorphin (β-END; β-LPH 61–69), a-END (β-LPH 61–76), and γ-END (β-LPH 61–77) (Bradbury et al., 1976; Guillemin et al., 1976; Li & Chung, 1976; Teschemacher et al., 1975). Endorphins have now been found in human pituitary gland, human brain, gastrointestinal tract, placenta, and adrenal medulla (Berger, 1978; Herz et al., 1980; Pert et al., 1976; Schulz et al., 1980; Wahlström & Terenius, 1976). Endorphins have also been reported to be in blood, urine, and spinal fluid (Berger, 1978; Herz et al., 1978; Lewis et al., 1980; Pert et al., 1976; Schulz et al., 1980; Wahlström & Terenius, 1976). Udenfriend and colleagues (Lewis et al., 1980) reported that perhaps as many as 12 endorphin peptides of various sizes are contained in the cells of the adrenal medulla that secrete epinephrine. Some of these peptides contain two or more copies of the five amino acid sequences of either met- and/or leu-ENK.

β-END was first thought to be the precursor of met-ENK since the amino acid sequence of met-ENK is contained in β-END. However, it is now known that β-END and met-ENK occur in separate areas of the brain. The enkephalins are widely distributed throughout the brain in numerous cell groups with very short tracts (Watson et al., 1979). The short biological half-life of the enkephalins suggests that they may act as neurotransmitters in numerous

The investigations reported in this chapter were accomplished with Huda Akil, Jack D. Barchas, Kenneth L. Davis, Glen R. Elliott, Avram Goldstein, James Kilkowski, Helena Kraemer, Choh Hao Li, Adolf Pfefferbaum, Maureen Ross, and Robert T. Rubin. This research was supported by the Medical Research Service of the Veterans Administration, by NIMH Specialized Research Center Grant MH 30854, NIMH Grants MH 23861, MH 29491, MH 30245, and NIDA Grant DA 02265.

pathways. β-END is present both in the pituitary and in at least one area of the brain. The brain β-END system seems to be located in a single set of hypothalamic neurons, with axons innervating midbrain and limbic structures (Watson et al., 1979). β-END has a longer half-life than the enkephalins; it may act as a hormone or neuromodulator.

The biochemical steps involved in the synthesis of endorphins remains unknown. However, Mains et al. (1977) demonstrated that a single molecule with a molecular weight of about 31,000 daltons is a common precursor for both β-LPH and ACTH, suggesting possible links between endorphins and other important hormonal systems. The common precursor protein is called pro-opiomelanocortin (POMC) or the 31K precursor because of its molecular weight. Watson and co-workers (1979) showed that hypothalamic cells that react to immunohistochemical staining for ACTH also stain for β-LPH. Since ACTH is released in times of stress, β-END would presumably be released at the same time. It is easy to speculate on why it would be useful for the body to react to stress with both steroids and a morphinelike agent such as β-END.

Recent research has shed more light on the structure and location of the presumed precursor of ACTH and β-END. There are two pituitary cell groups that contain this peptide and probably several of its smaller components. The anterior lobe of the pituitary gland contains POMC in the corticotrophs (the pituitary cells which produce ACTH), previously thought to produce only ACTH. The intermediate lobe of the pituitary, which is found in animals and probably occurs as a distinct structure in humans only during pregnancy, also contains POMC. Surprisingly, in animal and human brains there are neurons or nerve cells that also contain this precursor protein. These neurons are located in the arcuate nucleus of the hypothalamus with fiber projections to many limbic system and brain stem structures.

Mains and colleagues (1977) and Roberts and Herbert (1977) used different methods to further define the structure of POMC. Preliminary evidence suggests that this protein contains β-LPH, β-END, ACTH, a-melanocyte-stimulating hormone (a-MSH), corticotropinlike intermediate lobe peptide (CLIP), β-MSH, and γ-MSH. POMC is probably the precursor for many of these compounds and presumably for numerous other compounds yet to be discovered. Recent evidence suggests that the anterior lobe of the pituitary probably processes the precursor mainly to ACTH and β-LPH with a small amount of β-END. However, the intermediate lobe of the pituitary and the brain process POMC differently, producing a-MSH, CLIP β-END, and γ-MSH (Berger et al., 1982). The role of the peptides that derive from POMC in normal physiology and in pathological states has not been determined.

Two new opiate peptides were recently discovered. Goldstein and co-workers (1979) at Stanford isolated an endorphin and named this new compound *dynorphin* (from *dynis*, meaning "powerful"). Dynorphin includes the full structure of leu-ENK as its first five amino acids, followed by 12 amino acids in a sequence distinct both from enkephalins and β-END. Dynorphin is extremely potent in one biological assay for endorphins but its pharmacological actions have not been thoroughly studied. Anatomical studies suggest it occurs in the posterior pituitary gland, in the hypothalamus, and in the brain with a distribution distinct from β-END. The second new endorphin, *a-neoendorphin* (a-neoEND) was discovered by Matsuo and colleagus in Japan (Kangawa et al., 1981). Like dynorphin, a-neoEND and the numerous endorphins from the adrenal medulla contain the structure of either leu-ENK or met-ENK. An important area of current investigation is the attempt to determine how dynorphin, a-neoEND, the adrenal endorphins, and met- and leu-ENK are related. One or all of these substances may come from a common precursor protein yet to be discovered.

Thus, there is evidence that at least five endorphins occur in mammalian brain: β-END, met- and leu-ENK, dynorphin, and a-neoEND. A massive research effort is investigating the role of these endorphins in normal and abnormal physiology. Part of this research focuses on the possible role of endorphins in psychopathology. Curiously, there is controversial evidence for both an excess and a deficiency of endorphin activity in mental illnesses.

REVIEW OF STUDIES ON ENDORPHINS IN PSYCHOPATHOLOGY

Schizophrenia

Several types of evidence support the hypothesis that schizophrenia reflects a deficiency of endorphins. Enthusiastic reports of the effects of exogenous opiates on schizophrenic symptoms have appeared in the medical literature of the past 130 years; however, none of these reports is based on double-blind study designs (Berger, 1978). A synthetic analogue of enkephalin, FK 33-824, has been reported to decrease psychotic symptoms in some schizophrenic patients. In an uncontrolled pilot study, nine patients received 0.5 and 1 mg FK 33-824 for 2 days (Nedopil & Ruther, 1979). A significant improvement in symptoms, lasting 1–7 days was reported. In a single-blind study, researchers reported that FK 33-824 had a strikingly positive effect on hallucinations in nine chronic psychotic patients (Jorgenson et al., 1979).

Des-tyrosine1-γ-endorphin (DTγE; β-LPH 62–77) is structurally related to endorphins, but has no opiate activity. Burbach and de Wied (1980) found evidence of DTγE in rat pituitary, rat brain, and human spinal fluid. Incubation of β-END with homogenates of rat forebrain yield DTγE, suggesting that DTγE is an endogenously formed compound (Burbach & de Wied, 1980). A decrease in schizophrenic symptoms following the administration of DTγE was reported in a single-blind study of six patients and in a double-blind study of eight patients (Verhoeven et al., 1979). However, a study by Emrich and colleagues (1980) revealed only slight differences between placebo and DTγE, and these differences occurred in only a few patients.

Recently, the group from the Netherlands, (Verhoeven et al., 1979) reported that a new compound, des-enkephalin-γ-endorphin (DEγE; β-LPH 66–77), has behavioral effects on rodents similar to those of DTγE, suggesting that this compound might also have antischizophrenic activity. DEγE might be formed from DTγE in mammalian brain. Preliminary clinical studies suggest that DEγE may also decrease schizophrenic symptoms in some patients. In this preliminary report, the antischizophrenic actions of DEγE were similar to those of DTγE (van Praag et al., in press).

Jacquet and Marks (1976) compared the stiffness from intraventricular β-END injections in rats to the catalepsy caused by the administration of antischizophrenic neuroleptics to these animals. Although not all investigators agree (Segal et al., 1978), this finding suggests that β-END is an endogenous neuroleptic and that schizophrenic symptoms might reflect an endorphin deficiency (Jacquet & Marks, 1976). Furthermore, in the single-blind study of Kline and Lehmann (1979), three of four schizophrenic patients were reported to benefit from intravenous administration of 1.5 – 9 mg β-END.

In contrast to the studies suggesting an endorphin deficiency in schizophrenia, there are several studies that indicate an increase in endorphin activity in schizophrenia. In the double-blind crossover study by Gerner et al. (1980), the condition of six of eight schizophrenic patients worsened after β-END treatment when compared with placebo trials. In another double-blind study by Pickar et al. (1981), six schizophrenic subjects received β-END, 4 – 15 mg intravenously. While there were no statistically significant changes in these six patients, there was a trend for the schizphrenic patients to worsen after β-END administration (Pickar et al., 1981).

According to Terenius et al., (1976) and Wahlström and Terenius (1976), endorphin fractions different from β-END and enkephalin are increased in the cerebrospinal fluid (CSF) of unmedicated schizophrenic patients. When these patients are medicated, the increased levels return toward normal. The exact structure of this endorphin fraction is not yet known. There are also reports of elevated CSF concentrations of β-END in some schizophrenic subjects. Domschke et al. (1979) reported that normal subjects have values of 72 femtomoles (fmole; 10^{-15} moles) β-END per milliliter and neurological controls have 92 fmole/ml, whereas chronic schizophrenic patients have 35 fmole/ml, and acute schizophrenics have 760 fmole/ml.

The reported improvement in schizophrenic symptoms following hemodialysis also suggests an endorphin excess in schizophrenia. Palmour et al. (1979) and Wagemaker and Cade (1977) proposed that the improvement results from the removal of leucine^5-β-endorphin (leu^5-β-END), a previously unknown endorphin. Unfortunately, the hemodialysis trial was not double blind, and the finding of elevated leu^5-β-END concentrations in either the dialysate or the plasma of schizophrenic patients was not confirmed (Lewis et al., 1979; Ross et al., 1979).

Bloom et al. (1976) reported that rats exhibited catatoniclike behavior when given β-END, which is further evidence for a possible increase in endorphin activity in schizophrenia. However, this "catatonia" is the same stiffness that Jacquet and Marks thought was like the catalepsy produced by neuroleptics; thus, two groups of investigators observing similar phenomena came to opposite conclusions on the role of β-END in schizophrenia.

Finally, an improvement in schizophrenic symptoms has been found in five controlled double-blind studies following intravenous administration of the opiate antagonist naloxone. One study reported a decrease in unusual thought content of schizophrenic patients (Davis et al., 1979); two of the studies reported a decrease in schizophrenic hallucinations (Emrich et al., 1977; Watson et al., 1978); and a fourth study reported an overall amelioration of psychotic symptoms (Lehmann et al., 1979).

While some investigators have not been able to duplicate these findings, a recent World Health Organization (WHO) collaborative study involving 32 schizophrenic patients reported that naloxone produced a significant reduction in hallucinations (Pickar & Bunney, 1981).

Affective Disorders

Several studies have suggested that endorphins are deficient in patients with depression. Angst and colleagues (1979) reported that three of six depressed patients became hypomanic after a 10-mg intravenous injection of β-END. This mood change could be due to low endorphin levels in depressed patients, although other factors such as the stress of the experimental situation or patient expectation might be involved. Kline et al. (1977) reported positive changes in several psychotic symptoms in depressed patients following intravenous administration of 1–9 mg β-END. However, these trials were not double blind, and a relatively low dose of β-END was used. β-END also seemed to briefly improve depression in two double-blind investigations (Catlin et al., 1980; Pickar et al., 1981). In the double-blind, placebo-controlled, crossover study by Gerner and colleagues (1980), nine depressed patients showed significant improvement 2–4 hours after β-END administration when compared with placebo trials. This report supports the hypothesis that depressed patients may have a deficit of endorphin activity.

As described above, Terenius and colleagues (1976) isolated two CSF endorphin fractions (labeled Fractions I and II) that are neither β-END nor enkephalins. Fraction I was reported to be increased in three of four manic subjects. Interestingly, these patients also had increased levels of Fraction II during normal mood states. Judd et al. (1978) reported a reduction in the symptoms of mania in four of eight manic patients after the administration of 20 mg naloxone. Using generally lower doses of naloxone, other investigators found no change in the symptoms of patients with affective disorders (G. C. Davis et al., 1978b). Finally, in the recent collaborative study organized by WHO, a larger number of manic patients had no change in symptoms following administration of high doses of naloxone (Pickar & Bunney, 1981).

Janowsky and co-workers (1974) reported a recrudescence of depressive symptoms in patients with a history of depression following the infusion of the cholinesterase inhibitor, physostigmine (which increases brain acetylcholine). Antimanic properties of physostigmine have also been described (K. Davis et al., 1978; Janowsky et al., 1973). In an investigation with normal volunteer subjects, Risch et al. (1980) reported that physostigmine-induced mood changes, particularly the depressive components, were significantly correlated with increases in plasma β-END levels. Changes reported included an increase in depression, hostility, and confusion, and a decrease in arousal and mania. This study suggests that acetylcholine and β-END interact, which supports the hypothesis that increased endorphin activity causes depressive symptoms.

HUMAN STUDIES ON ENDORPHINS AND MENTAL ILLNESS AT STANFORD UNIVERSITY

Our studies of the possible role of endorphins in mental illness have employed three strategies. First, we measured endorphin concentrations in various biological fluids in schizophrenic patients and normal volunteers. Our second strategy was to administer the opiate and endorphin antagonist naloxone in an attempt to improve schizophrenic symptoms. Finally, we gave β-END as an experimental treatment for schizophrenic patient volunteers.

β-Endorphin in Biological Fluids

What is the relationship between leu^5-β-END and the hemodialysis "treatment" of schizophrenia? If schizophrenic patients have extremely high levels of endorphins in their dialysate, than these high concentrations should be evident in their blood. In 98 schizophrenic patients and 42 normal subjects, we found strikingly similar plasma concentrations of endorphinlike immunoreactivity using an antibody sensitive to both leu^5-β-END and met^5-β-END (2.8 fmole/ml average for the schizophrenic patients, and 2.4 fmole/ml for the normals) (Ross et al., 1979). The antibodies were developed and the assays were performed by Maureen Ross, Ph.D., and Avram Goldstein, M.D., of Stanford University. We were also unable to find increased concentrations of β-END or leu^5-β-END in the dialysate of 10 schizophrenic patients (Ross et al., 1979). Although hemodialysis might eventually be demonstrated to improve schizophrenic symptoms, our results suggest that if such an improvement occurs, it is not likely to be due to the removal of leu^5-β-END, as proposed by Palmour et al. (1979).

In a second study, we examined over 60 CSF samples from chronic schizophrenic patients and normal controls. We found β-END-like immunoreactivity measured by radioimmunoassay to be between 3 and 12 fmole/ml. No differences were found between normal and schizophrenic CSF β-END-like immunoreactivity (Akil et al., in preparation). β-END-like immunoreactivity probably accurately reflects β-END concentrations in CSF. In a study by Emrich et al. (1977), normals and groups of patients with schizophrenia, meningitis, disk herniation, and lumbago all showed approximately the same concentration of CSF endorphins (10–15 fmole/ml). These studies revealing lower concentrations of β-END used more sophisticated calibration methods for antisera, more accurate extraction procedures, and more elaborate controls than the studies that reported normal β-END CSF concentrations of 72 fmole/ml (Domschke et al., 1979). The results of the studies on CSF concentrations of endorphins described above show great disparity in the CSF endorphin level of schizophrenic patients and in the levels in normal controls. Thus, the question of CSF β-END levels remains unanswered.

We are now studying concentrations of dynorphin, enkephalins, and other endorphins in schizophrenic patients and normal controls. However, we have found no major differences between these groups in our preliminary data analysis. Our failure to find differences in CSF endorphin concentrations between schizophrenic patients and control subjects using radioimmunoassay should be contrasted with the success of two groups of investigators who found that schizophrenics have altered CSF endorphin concentrations using radioreceptor assay methods. As described above, Terenius et al. (1976) and Wahlström and Terenius (1976) reported that one endorphin fraction, isolated in part by radioreceptor assay, is elevated in the CSF of unmedicated schizophrenic subjects. However, Naber and colleagues (Naber et al., 1981), using a different radioreceptor assay, found decreased endorphin concentrations in schizophrenic patients. These discrepant results suggest the need for further investigations using common assay methods.

Naloxone in Schizophrenia

We used naloxone, the potent endorphin and opiate antagonist, to study the possible role of endorphins in schizophrenia (Watson et al., 1978). Our naloxone study involved 14 male veteran volunteer subjects who reported frequent hallucinations and had relatively stable psychotic symptoms, either on or off antischizophrenic medications. The

subjects who gave informed consent to participate in this double-blind, randomized, crossover study received naloxone (10 mg) and placebo infusions given at least 48 hours apart. Seven of the schizophrenic subjects had not received neuroleptics for at least 2 weeks prior to the study, and the rest were maintained on their routine doses of neuroleptics. The patients were interviewed and rated on the National Institute of Mental Health rating scale by trained raters at baseline, 15 minutes, and 1, 2, and 4 hours after the infusion of naloxone (naloxone was supplied by Endo Laboratories, Delaware).

During 15 trials with the 14 chronic schizophrenic patients, naloxone produced a statistically significant decrease in auditory and (in one subject) visual hallucinations ($p < 0.05$) (Berger et al., 1980). In 10 of the 15 trials, a reduction in hallucinations was reported; in the shortest responses, hallucinations returned in 3 hours. Since naloxone usually reverses the action of morphine for about 1 hour, we expected the hallucinations to be changed, if at all, during the first hour after infusion; however, all schizophrenic subjects who had a loss or a decrease in hallucinations reported that it began 2–3 hours after the naloxone infusion.

Comparative reading of earlier studies with naloxone in schizophrenia reveals conflicting results. Some studies claimed naloxone is ineffective in decreasing hallucinations. However, these studies generally used lower doses of naloxone, were not doubleblind, or examined only a relatively short time period after the infusion (Janowsky et al., 1977; Kurland et al., 1977; Volavka et al., 1977). Finally, the recent WHO collaborative study found a significant reduction in schizophrenic hallucinations in 32 schizophrenic patients given naloxone, 0.3 mg/kg subcutaneously (Pickar & Bunney, 1981).

β-Endorphin and Schizophrenia

Our β-END study was designed to test the reported antipsychotic actions of intravenously administered β-END (Berger et al., 1980). We chose a placebo-controlled, double-blind, crossover design. As β-END is thought to have opiate agonist activity, and opiate agonists such as morphine stimulate prolactin (PRL) secretion from the pituitary gland, we also measured serum PRL concentrations. In addition, we sought preliminary data on the pharmacokinetics of β-END and its effects on the EEG.

Ten male veterans with schizophrenia from the Palo Alto Veterans Administration Medical Center at Stanford University gave informed consent to participate in the study. The ages of the subjects ranged from 27 to 47 years, with a mean age of 37. Each patient was interviewed and diagnosed by a research psychiatrist, using the Research Diagnostic Criteria (Spitzer et al., 1978a; 1978b), as having either chronic schizophrenic or chronic schizoaffective disorder, depressed type. All schizophrenic subjects were free of psychotropic medications for at least 2 weeks prior to the study. Subjects received a single weekly injection on Monday for 3 weeks. The first week's injection was always saline and the first week was considered to be an acclimatization period for data analysis. The next two randomized infusions were either saline control or 20 mg β-END. Both the schizophrenic patients and the staff who rated the patients were blind to the content of the injections.

β-END was supplied by Choh Hao Li of the University of California, San Francisco, and was given as a liquid solution (4 mg/ml) in sterile saline for the first five patients. The next five patients received β-END supplied as a white powder. Immediately prior to the infusion, the β-END was dissolved in 10 ml normal saline, forced through a filter to remove particulates, and taken up in a human albumin-coated glass syringe. To minimize the changes of possible biases, the 5- or 10-ml saline control solution was also administered in an albumin-coated glass syringe. Nine of the subjects had all three intravenous injections administered as a bolus; one subject was given three slow intravenous injections from non–albumin-coated syringes.

The patients' symptoms were rated by two investigators using the Brief Psychiatric Rating Scale (BPRS; Overall & Gorham, 1962) and the Clinical Global Inventory (CGI; Psychopharmacology Research Branch, 1967). Baseline BPRS and CGI ratings were taken just prior to each injection. The ratings were repeated 3 and 5 hours later, and on the third and fifth days after each infusion. CGI ratings alone were also performed on the second and fourth days. Our interrater reliability for the BPRS was 0.94 (Pearson product moment correlation coefficient).

Venous blood was taken each week for serum PRL determinations at 60, 40, and 20 minutes and immediately prior to the infusion, and at 10, 30, 60, 120, and 180 minutes after the infusion. Serum PRL was measured using an established and reliable double antibody and radioimmunoassay technique (Sinha et al., 1973), with an intraassay variability of 8.9 percent, interassay variability of 13.8 percent, and sensitivity of 0.1 ng/tube. Human PRL (hPRL AFP

1562-C) for iodination and standard was provided by Albert F. Parlow, Ph.D. (Harbor UCLA Medical Center, Torrance, California). Iodination was performed according to the glucose oxidase–lactoperoxidase technique (Tower et al., 1977), and the suitability of the ^{125}I-labeled PRL was verified by the talc–resin–trichloroacetic acid method (Tower et al., 1978). Anti-hPRL (AFP-1) was supplied by the National Pituitary Agency. For these assays, the values were reported in nanograms hPRL AFP 1562-C per milliliter serum. The PRL assays were performed by Robert T. Rubin, M.D., of the University of California, Los Angeles.

Venous blood was also drawn each week for β-END measurement immediately prior to infusion, and 2, 5, 10, 30, 60, 120, and 180 minutes after the infusion. The β-END concentrations were determined using a specific and sensitive radioimmunoassay developed by Huda Akil, Ph.D. at the University of Michigan at Ann Arbor (Akil et al., 1979). The detection range of this assay is from 15 fmole/ml to 600 picomoles (pmole; 10^{-12} moles) per milliliter plasma.

For one patient, an EEG was recorded from central and parietal electrode sites with disc electrodes referenced to linked ear electrodes for all infusions. The EEG underwent fast Fourier analysis, which resulted in a power spectrum with 0.5 Hz resolution for the 0–32 Hz components. This schizophrenic patient also received a single 10-mg infusion of morphine sulfate under double-blind conditions. The patient was studied by Adolf Pfefferbaum, M.D., of Stanford University.

The slow intravenous infusion from the non–albumin-coated syringe produced a plasma β-END concentration of 1.3 pmole/ml at 5 minutes and 0.45 pmole/ml at 30 minutes after infusion. However, in six patients bolus injections from albumin-coated syringes produced the following mean plasma β-END concentrations: 197.6 ± 37 (SE) pmole/ml at 2 minutes, 80 ± 37 pmole/ml at 30 minutes, and 1.8 ± 0.4 pmole/ml at 3 hours. The β-END two-component half-life in human plasma was 15 and 39 minutes. Thus, the patient who received the slow infusion had a plasma β-END concentration only 0.01 of the mean of six other patients. For this reason, his PRL and clinical results were not included in the data analysis.

For each patient, serum PRL concentrations from the saline control day were subtracted from PRL concentrations from the same time points on the β-END infusion day; the difference was statistically significant ($p<0.001$) (Siegel, 1956). β-END infusion was associated with a maximum plasma PRL concentration of 27 ± 7 (SE) ng/ml at 30 minutes; PRL levels returned to normal levels of 5 ± 1 ng/ml by 3 hours.

For one patient described above, the EEG changes were monitored during each infusion and during one 10-mg infusion of morphine. Following the injection of either morphine or β-END, spectral analysis revealed changes in the alpha frequency range (8 – 12 Hz). The alpha activity increased rapidly and remained high for about 50 minutes after the morphine injection. After β-END, there was a rise in alpha activity that was similar to but faster than that produced by morphine. The increase following β-END lasted less than 30 minutes. No changes in alpha EEG activity were observed after the saline injections (Pfefferbaum et al., 1979).

Patients were rated on the BPRS five times each week and on the CGI seven times each week. The degree of change in each patient was quantified by selecting the lowest postinjection BPRS score and subtracting it from the baseline score. A positive score reflected improvement in symptoms, as the postinjection BPRS was lower than the baseline score; a negative score reflected a relative worsening in symptoms. One of the 10 patients withdrew from the study after two injections. Nine of the medication-free schizophrenic patients completed the study. As previously mentioned, one patient was not included in the data analysis because of extremely low plasma β-END concentration after infusion. Since eight patients exhibited an average improvement of 10 points on the BPRS after the first saline injection, the first week acclimatization period was obviously very important. This compares with an average improvement of 4 points on the PBRS after the saline control injection and 6 points after the β-END injection. No changes were recorded on the CGI during the entire 3-week period for any patient. These CGI scores were consistent with the impressions of both patients and staff that neither could distinguish the response to β-END from the response to saline.

Of the eight patients with higher plasma concentrations of β-END, six patients were found to have improved. This improvement was statistically significant when the total BPRS scores following β-END injecton were compared to scores following the saline injection in all eight patients ($p < 0.05$) (Siegel, 1956).

In an earlier study, a single intravenous infusion of 9 mg β-END produced a plasma concentration of 80 – 90 ng/ml (27.3 pmole/ml) (Kline et al., 1977; Lehmann et al., 1979). These values easily fit a single-component elimination time with a half-life of about 20 minutes (Kline et al., 1977). In our β-END study, we were about three times more efficient in achieving an initial plasma concentration per milligram of the β-END. The average of our 15- and 39-minute half-lives is similar to the 20-minute half-life reported by Kline and Lehmann, (1979) even though our two-component elimination curve differed significantly from the single component curve they reported (Kline et al., 1977; Lehmann et al., 1979; Siegel, 1956).

The significant increase in serum PRL levels observed in our patients following β-END administration suggested that β-END has opiate agonist activity in humans. Elevated PRL levels have been reported in rats following morphine, met-enkephalin, and β-END infusions (Cusan et al., 1977; Guidotti & Grandison, 1979; Labrie et al., 1979; Rivier et al., 1977). Morphine and methadone are also reported to increase human serum PRL concentrations (Gold et al., 1977; Tolis et al., 1975). The mechanism of PRL stimulation by opiate agonists has not yet been determined, but it might be mediated by dopamine neurons. Dopamine exerts tonic inhibitory control of PRL secretion (Ojeda et al., 1974). The acute response of plasma PRL to a maximal dose of morphine in the rat could not be further increased by haloperidol in a study by Ferland et al. (1978). These investigators claimed that this suggests that the effect of morphine on PRL is secondary to inhibition of dopaminergic activity, perhaps through presynaptic inhibitory opiate receptors on dopamine neurons (Ferland et al., 1978).

The effect of morphine on EEG activity that we observed in one patient is consistent with previous reports (Fink et al., 1971; Wikler, 1954). The acute increase in alpha EEG activity produced by both morphine and β-END could be secondary to the peripheral actions of morphine and β-END; however, a direct effect of both compounds on central opiate systems is a more likely explanation (Pfefferbaum et al., 1979). The fact that the met-ENK analogue FK 33-824 also increases the alpha power of the EEG is further evidence that this effect is mediated by brain opiate receptors (Krebs & Roubicek, 1979). Furthermore, there is evidence that in the rabbit, CSF levels of β-END are significantly elevated following intravenous injection, and that four modified opiate peptides enter the central nervous system after peripheral administration in the rat (Pezalla et al., 1978; Rapoport et al., 1980). These observations support the suggestion that β-END administered peripherally enters the mammalian brain (Pezalla et al., 1978).

Kline and Lehmann (1979; Kline et al., 1977), in their single-blind study, found a dramatic improvement in three of four patients following β-END administration. They reported that a patient with schizoaffective schizophrenia showed improvement after doses of 1.5, 3, 6, and 9 mg β-END; the greatest improvement was after 9 mg. One patient with chronic undifferentiated schizophrenia showed no improvement after 1.5 mg β-END, had diminished hallucinations and more "appropriate behavior" after 3 mg, and showed "marked improvement" after 6 mg. Interestingly, this patient later failed to respond to a dose of 6 mg β-END. The third patient, with a diagnosis of paranoid schizophrenia, was "more active" and "less withdrawn" after 6 mg β-END, but did not respond to lower levels of the compound. Two intravenous injections of 9 mg β-END had no apparent effect on a patient with catatonic schizophrenia (Kline et al., 1977; Kline & Lehmann, 1979).

In our study, neither the schizophrenic patients nor the staff could distinguish between the effects of β-END and saline on the basis of clinical changes. This observation is in agreement with the constant level of pathology recorded on the CGI rating scale. Although a statistically significant improvement was observed in BPRS scores following β-END compared to the change in scores following saline, the improvement just reached statistical significance with a one-tailed test, was not clinically obvious, and was less than the improvement on the BPRS noted during the acclimatization period. Use of a one-tailed statistical test might be questioned, as there is controversial evidence for both a deficiency and an excess of endorphin activity in schizophrenia; however, since the reports of Kline et al. led us to predict that patients would show improvement following β-END administration, we used a one-tailed statistical test.

Our study design was not the best for testing the antischizophrenic activity of an experimental treatment. We used a double-blind comparison of a single injection of β-END with a single injection of saline because of the limited availability of β-END and the report of Kline et al., (1977; Kline & Lehmann, 1979), of improvement in schizophrenic symptoms following a single injecton of β-END. However, the comparison of saline with an antischizophrenic drug already known to be effective

such as chlorpromazine given to eight patients with our β-END study design might yield only slightly positive results or might fail to demonstrate any antischizophrenic activity of the chlorpromazine. Thus, a single 20-mg infusion of β-END reproduced a statistically significant yet not clinically obvious improvement in schizophrenic symptoms. Further studies with repeated doses of β-END in the same patient are needed to determine if these statistical improvements can become clinically obvious.

Our β-END findings can be summarized as follows: 20 mg of intravenously infused β-END in humans has pharmacological activity on both PRL and the EEG. β-END shares this PRL-stimulating ability with other opiate agonists in rats and humans. The increase in alpha EEG power following intravenous β-END administration was similar to that seen following intravenous morphine administration. The method of intravenous injection has a profound effect on the plasma concentration of β-END. Slow intravenous infusion from non–albumin-coated syringes yielded markedly lower plasma levels than a bolus injection from an albumin-coated syringe. Finally, in our double-blind crossover study, a statistically significant, but not clinically obvious improvement in schizophrenic symptoms was observed after a 20-mg intravenous injection of β-END when compared with a saline injection. (Berger et al., 1980).

DISCUSSION

Endorphin research has led to exciting, although conflicting findings in the field of mental illness. Evidence exists for both an excess and deficiency of endorphin activity in depression and schizophrenia. The report of a decrease in schizophrenic hallucinations in an open study by Gunne et al. (1977) led to our successful double-blind trial of naloxone in schizophrenic hallucinations (Berger et al., 1981). Positive reports of β-END infusion in psychiatric patients by Kline and Lehmann, Angst, and others prompted us to perform our double-blind, placebo-controlled, crossover study with intravenously administered β-END. The lack of a clinically obvious patient response in our study may have been due to the method of injection. More recent Japanese studies with intrathecally administered β-END for analgesia are promising (Dyama et al., 1980), and studies using this method would enable researchers to study the effectiveness of β-END at lower doses. Other study designs, such as the use of multiple doses, are needed to investigate further the activity of β-END in psychiatric patients. Such studies might may yield a new treatment for depression or schizophrenia and should improve our understanding of the role of endorphins in normal and abnormal physiology.

USE OF NALOXONE IN THE STUDIES OF ENDORPHINS

Naloxone (N-allylnoroxymorphone) has been thought to be a potent and pure opiate antagonist with no opiate agonist activity (Blumberg et al., 1961; Blumberg et al., 1965; Fink, 1968; Jasinski et al., 1967; Pearl & Harris, 1966) and no other pharmacological activity apart from competitive opiate receptor binding (Aronski & Kubler, 1977; Martin, 1976). Naloxone should theoretically reverse both the effects of exogenously administered opiates and the effects of the endorphins. For these reasons, a major strategy for investigating the endorphins has been to administer naloxone to humans and animals to observe its effects on physiology and behavior. This strategy is limited by the fact that naloxone may have pharmacological activities other than competitive opiate receptor binding (Sawynok et al., 1979). Thus, naloxone antagonism suggests but does not prove that a behavior or a physiological response is mediated or influenced by the endorphins.

In studies of pain and analgesia, naloxone has been reported to have some remarkable effects. In rats, naloxone reversed the diurnal fluctuation in pain sensitivity, reversed the normal increase in pain threshold during pregnancy and decreased food deprivation–induced analgesia (G. C. Davis et al., 1978a; McGivern & Bernston, 1980; McGivern et al., 1979). In addition, several groups of investigators have reported that environmental stresses of various types can cause analgesia in rodents which can be reversed by naloxone. The stresses include electroshock, heat, acetic acid, cold swim, and immobilization (Bodnar et al., 1978; Buckett, 1979; Fanselow & Bolles, 1979; Kokka & Fairhurst, 1977; Kulkarni, 1980). Stress-induced analgesia that is reversible by naloxone has also recently been reported in human subjects (Willer et al., 1981).

In rodents, naloxone has been shown to inhibit or reverse the analgesia produced by the anesthetics nitrous oxide, cycloproprane, halothane, and enflurane (Berkowitz et al., 1977; Finck et al., 1977). Several studies have shown that naloxone antagonizes acupuncture analgesia in both humans and animals (Mayer et al., 1977; Pomeranz & Chiu, 1976; Tsunoda et al., 1980). Naloxone has also been reported to reverse the increase in tooth pain threshold produced by placebo injection; that is, in at least one paradigm naloxone seems to antagonize placebo analgesia (Levine et al., 1979). Naloxone has produced mixed results when given in attempts to antagonize the analgesia produced by alcohol intoxication, hypnosis or acetylsalicylic acid (Goldstein & Hilgard, 1975; Jeffcoate et al., 1979; Mackenzie, 1979).

Naloxone has been used to investigate the possible role of endorphins in shock, sleep, and in sexual, separation, and feeding behavior. It has also been used in attempts to reverse certain drug intoxication states. Experimentally induced hypovolemic and endotoxic shock in animals is antagonized by naloxone, which increases mean arterial pressure, pulse pressure, and survival compared to control animals (Faden & Holaday, 1979; 1980a; 1980b). In addition, naloxone is effective in antagonizing hypotension, hypothermia, and respiratory depression in animals following spinal cord transection or experimental injury (Faden et al., 1981; Holaday & Faden, 1980). Naloxone seems to improve neurological recovery in cats after spinal cord injury (Faden et al., 1981; Holaday & Faden, 1980). These important and exciting findings in animal studies have led to numerous case reports of trials of naloxone as an experimental treatment for human hypovolemic and endotoxic shock (Dirksen et al., 1980; Wright, 1980). Several of these preliminary reports suggest that naloxone may have a therapeutic role in treating shock of several types in human patients (Peters et al., 1981).

Naloxone does not appear to alter normal human sleep, although further studies are needed. However, naloxone has been reported to awaken hibernating hamsters. In addition, naloxone injected into sexually inactive male rats induced successful copulatory behavior (Gess et al., 1979). Naloxone has also been reported to alter behavioral expressions of distress. Separation distress vocalizations in juvenile and adult guinea pigs are reliably increased by naloxone and decreased by opiates (Herman & Panksepp, 1978). In addition, injection of naloxone both centrally and peripherally reduces feeding and drinking behavior in rats (Fanselow & Bolles, 1979; Holtzman, 1974; Reid et al., 1980; Schulz et al., 1980).

Several studies have suggested that naloxone may reverse some of the effects of ethanol. For example, naloxone may antagonize ethanol withdrawal convulsions in mice (Blum et al., 1977), alcohol-induced epileptiform activity in monkeys (Bell et al., 1980), and alcohol-induced psychomotor impairment in humans (Jeffcoate et al., 1979). One group of investigators studied 100 patients admitted to a hospital with coma due to suspected overdose of ethanol. Naloxone reversed the coma in 20 percent of these patients, even though they had no evidence of concomitant opiate intoxication (Jefferys et al., 1980). However, other investigators have not found effects of naloxone on alcohol intoxication, tolerance, or withdrawal in rats (Hemmingsen & Sorensen, 1980; Miceli et al., 1980).

Naloxone may also inhibit some of the effects of benzodiazepines such as diazepam (Valium). Naloxone reduces the duration of diazepam-induced loss of the righting reflex in mice and rats (Walz & Davis, 1979). Naloxone has also been reported to antagonize diazepam-induced feeding in rats (Stapleton et al., 1979) and to inhibit diazepam-induced release of behavior in aversive situations (Soubrie et al., 1980). Naloxone may also inhibit certain behavioral and respiratory effects of chlordiazepoxide (Librium) in rats and cats (Billingsley & Kubena, 1978; Grevert et al., 1978). Finally, there is a single case report of naloxone reversal of coma in a 27-month-old infant, where toxicological studies suggest that diazepam caused the coma (Bell, 1975).

We conclude that studies using naloxone suggest that endorphins may be involved in numerous physiological states, pharmacological reactions, and behaviors. However, since naloxone itself may have pharmacological actions that are independent of opiate systems, these studies should be viewed as generating hypotheses for the roles of endorphins rather than establishing that a given phenomenon is mediated by endorphins. Thus, further research is necessary to define more precisely and understand more fully the function of the endorphins in normal and abnormal physiology and behavior.

REFERENCES

Akil H, Berger PA, Watson SJ, & Barchas JD (in preparation).

Akil H, Mayer DJ, & Liebeskind JC (1972): Comparison chez le rat entre l'analgesie induite par stimulation de la substance grise periaqueducale et l'analgesie morphinique. CR Acad Sci (Paris) 274:3603.

Akil H, Watson SJ, Brachas JD, & Li CH (1979): Beta-endorphin immunoreactivity in rat and human blood: Radioimmunoassay, comparative levels and physiological alterations. Life Sci 24:1659–1666.

Angst J, Autenrieth V, Brem F, Koukkou M, Meyer H, Stassen H, & Storek U (1979): Preliminary results of treatment with β-endorphin in depression. Usdin E, Bunney WE Jr, & Kline NS (Eds.). In *Endorphins in Mental Health Research*. New York, Macmillan, pp. 581–528.

Aronski A, & Kubler A (1977): Examination of the effects of naloxone. Anaesthesist 26:354–356.

Bell EF (1975): The use of naloxone in the treatment of diazepam poisoning. J Pediatr 87:803–804.

Bell EF, Triana E, Francis RJ, Stokes PE (1980): The relationship between endorphins and alcohol-induced subcorticol activity. Am J Psychiatry 137:491–493.

Berger PA (1978): Investigating the role of endogenous opioid peptides in psychiatric disorders. Neurosci Res Progr Bull 16:585–599.

Berger PA, Akil H, Watson SJ, & Barchas JD (1982): Behavioral pharmacology of the endorphins. Ann Rev Med 33:397–415.

Berger PA, Watson SJ, Akil H, Barchas JD, & Li CH (1980): Clinical studies with naloxone and beta-endorphin in chronic schizophrenia. Usdin E, Sourkes TS, & Youdim MBH (Eds.). In *Enzymes and Neurotransmitters in Mental Disease*. New York, Wiley, pp. 45–64.

Berger PA, Watson SJ, Akil H, & Barchas JD (1981): Effects of naloxone in chronic schizophrenia. Am J Psychiatry 138:913–918.

Berkowitz BA, Finck AD, & Ngai SH (1977): Nitrous oxide analgesia: Reversal by naloxone and development of tolerance. J Pharmacol Exp Ther 203:539–547.

Billingsley ML, & Kubena RK (1978): The effects of naloxone and picrotoxin on the sedative and anticonflict effects of benzodiazepines. Life Sci 22:897–906.

Bloom F, Segal D, Ling N, & Guillemin R (1976): Endorphins: Profound behavioral effects in rats suggest new etiological factors in mental illness. Science 194:630–632.

Blum K, Futterman S, Wallace JE, & Schwertner HA (1977): Naloxone-induced inhibition of ethanol dependence in mice. Nature 265:49–51.

Blumberg H, Dayton HB, George M, & Rappaport DN (1961): N-Allylnoroxymorphone: A potent narcotic antagonist. Fed Proc 20:311.

Blumberg H, Wolf PS, Dayton HB (1965): Use of writing test for evaluating analgesic activity of narcotic antagonists. Proc Soc Exp Biol Med 118:763–766.

Bodnar RJ, Kelly DD, Spiaggia A, Ehrenberg C, & Glusman M (1978): Dose-dependent reductions by naloxone of analgesia induced by cold-water stress. Pharmacol Biochem Behav 8:667–672.

Bradbury AF, Feldberg WF, Smyth DG, & Snell CR (1976): Lipotropin c-fragment: an endogenous peptide with potent analgesic activity. Kosterlitz HW (Ed.). In *Opiates and Endogenous Opioid Peptides*. Amsterdam, Elsevier/North Holland, pp. 9–17.

Buckett WR (1979): Peripheral stimulation in mice induces short-duration analgesia preventable by naloxone. Eur J Pharmacol 58:169–178.

Burbach P, & de Wied D (1980): Usdin E, Sourkes TS, & Youdim MBH (Eds.). In *Enzymes and Neurotransmitters in Mental Disease*. New York, Wiley, pp. 103–114.

Catlin DH, Gorelick D, Gerner RH, Hui KK, & Li CH (1980): Costa E, & Trabucchi EM (Eds.). Clinical effects of β-endorphin infusions. In *Neural Peptides and Neuronal Communication*, Vol 22. New York, Raven Press, pp. 465–472.

Cusan L, Dupont A, & Kledzik GS (1977): Potent prolactin and growth hormone releasing activity of more analogues of met-enkephalin. Nature 268:554–557.

Davis K, Berger PA, Hollister LE, & de Fraites EG (1978): Physostigmine in mania. Arch Gen Psychiatry 35:119–222.

Davis GC, Buchsbaum MS, & Bunney WE Jr (1978a): Naloxone decreases diurinal variation in pain sensitivity and somatosensory evoked potentials. Life Sci 23:1449–1459.

Davis GC, Bunney WE Jr, de Fraites EG, Extein I, Goodwin FK, Hamilton W, Kleinman J, Mendelson W, Post R, Reus V, Shiling D, van Kammen D, Weinberger D, Wyatt RJ, & Li CH (1978b): Endogenous opioids: Basic and clinical aspects. Presented at the Seventeenth Annual Meeting of the American College of Neuropsychopharmacology, Hawaii.

Davis GC, Bunney WE Jr, Buchsbaum MS, de Fraites EG, Duncan W, Gillin JC, van Kammen DP, Kleinman J, Murphy DL, Post RM, Reus V, & Wyatt RJ (1979): Use of narcotic antagonists to study the role of endorphins in normal and psychiatric patients. Usdin E, Bunney WE Jr, & Kline NS (Eds.). In *Endorphins in Mental Health Research*. New York, Macmillan, pp. 393–406.

Dirksen R, Otten MH, Wood GJ, Verbaan CJ, Haalebos MP, Verdouw PV, & Nighuis GMM (1980): Naloxone in shock. Lancet 2:1360–1361.

Domschke W, Dickschas A, & Mitznegg PCSF (1979): Beta-endorphin in schizophrenia. Lancet 1:1024.

Emrich HM, Cording C, & Piree S (1977): Indication of an antipsychotic association of the opiate antagonist naloxone. Pharmakopyschiatr Neuropsychopharmakol 10:265–270.

Emrich HM, Zaudig M, Kissling W, Dirlich G, Zerssen DV, & Herz A (1980): EEG and clinical profile of a synthetic analogue of methionine-enkephalin-FK 33-824. Pharmakopyschiatr Neuropsychopharmakol 12:86–93.

Faden AI, & Holaday JW, (1979): Opiate antagonists: A role in the treatment of hypovolemic shock. Science 13:290–298.

Faden AI, & Holaday JW (1980a): Experimental endotoxin shock. The pathophysiologic function of endorphins and treatment with opiate antagonists. J Infec Dis 142:229–238.

Faden AI, & Holaday JW, Naloxone treatment of endotoxin shock: Stereospecificity of physiologic and pharmacologic effects in the rat. J Pharmacol Exp Ther 213:441–447.

Faden AI, Jacobs TP, & Holaday JW (1981): Opiate antagonist improves neurologic recovery after spinal injury. Science 211:493–494.

Fanselow MS, & Bolles RC (1979): Naloxone and shock-elicited freezing in the rat. J Comp Physiol Psychol 93:736–744.

Ferland L, Kelly P, Denizeau F, & LaBrie F (1978): Role of dopamine and serotonin in the stimulatory effect of opiates on prolactin secretion. van Ree JM, & Terenius L (Eds.). In *Characteristics and Function of Opiods*. Amsterdam, Elsevier/North Holland, pp. 353–354.

Finck AD, Ngai SH, & Berkowitz BA (1977): Antagonism of general anesthesia by naloxone in the rat. Anesthesiology 46:241–245.

Fink M (1968): Naloxone in heroin dependence. Clin Pharmacol Ther 9:568–577.

Fink M, Zaks A, Volavka J, & Roubicek J (1971): Clouet DH (Ed.). In *Narcotic Drugs: Biochemical Pharmacology*. New York, Plenum Press, pp. 452–467.

Gerner RH, Catlin DH, Gorelick DA, Hui KK, & Li CH (1980): Beta-endorphin: Intravenus infusion causes behavioral change in psychiatric patients. Arch Gen Psychiatry 37:642–647.

Gess GL, Pagliet E, & Quarantot BP (1979): Induction of copulatory behavior in sexually inactive rats by naloxone. Science 204:203–204.

Gold MS, Donabedian RK, Dillard M Jr, Slobetz FW, Riordan CE, & Kleber HD (1977): Antipsychotic effect of opiate antagonists. Lancet 2:398–399.

Goldstein A, & Hilgard ER (1975): Failure of the opiate antagonist naloxone to modify hypnotic analgesia. Proc Natl Acad Sci USA 72:2041–2043.

Goldstein A, Lowney LI, & Pal BK (1971): Stereospecific and nonspecific interactions of the morphine cogener levorphanol in subcellular fractions of mouse brain. Proc Natl Acad Sci USA 68:1742–1747.

Goldstein A, Tachibana S, Lowney L, Hunkapiller M, & Hood L (1979): Dynorphin-(1-13), an extraordinarily potent opioid peptide. Proc Natl Acad Sci USA 76:6666–6670.

Grevert P, Baizman ER, & Goldstein A (1978): Naloxone effects on a nociceptine response of hypophysectomized and adrenalectomized mice. Life Sci 23:723–728.

Guidotti A, & Grandison L (1979): Participation of endorphins in the regulation of pituitary function. Usdin E, Bunney WE Jr, & Kline NS (Eds.). In *Endorphins in Mental Health Research*. New York, Macmillan, pp. 416–422.

Guillemin R, Ling N, & Burgus R (1976): Endorphines, peptides, d'origine hypothalamique et neurohypophysaire a activite morphinominetique. Isolement et structure moleculaire de l'alpha-endorphine. CR Acad Sci (Paris) 282:783–785.

Gunne LM, Lindstrom L, & Terenius L (1977): Naloxone-induced reversal of schizophrenic hallucinations. J Neural Transm 40:13–19.

Hemmingsen R, & Sorensen S (1980): Absence of an effect of naloxone on ethanol intoxication and withdrawal reactions. Acta Pharmacol Toxicol 46:62–65.

Herman BH, & Panksepp J (1978): Effects of morphine and naloxone on separation distress and approach attachment: Evidence of opiate mediation for social affect. Pharmacol Biochem Behav 9:213–220.

Herz A, Duka T, Gramsch C, Hollt V, Osborne H, Przewlocki R, Schulz R, & Wuster M (1980): Pharmacologic manipulation of brain and pituitary endorphin content and release. Costa E, & Trabucchi M (Eds.). In *Neural Peptides and Neuronal Communication,* vol 22. New York, Raven Press, pp. 323–333.

Holaday JW, & Faden AI (1980): Naloxone acts at central opiate receptors to reverse hypotension, hypothermia and hypoventilation in spinal shock. Brain Res 189:295–299.

Holtzman SF (1974): Behavioral effects of separate and combined administration of naloxone and d-amphetamine. J Pharmacol Exp Ther 189:51–60.

Hughes J, Smith TW, Kosterlitz HW, Fothergill L, Morgan B, & Morris H (1975): Identification of two related pentapeptides from the brain with potent opiate agonist activity. Nature 258:577–579.

Jacquet YR, & Marks N (1976): The C-fragment of beta-lipotrophin: An endogenous neuroleptic or antipsychotogen? Science 194:632–636.

Janowsky DS, El-Yousek, Davis JM, & Sekerke HI (1973): Parasympathetic suppression of manic symptoms by physostigmine. Arch Gen Psychiatry 28:542–547.

Janowsky DS, Khaled MK, & Davis JM (1974): Acetylcholine and depression. Psychosom Med 36:248–257.

Janowsky DS, Segal DS, & Bloom F (1977): Lack of effect of naloxone on schizophrenia symptoms. Am J Psychiatry 134:926–927.

Jasinski DR, Martin WR, & Haertzen CA (1967): The human pharmacology and abuse potential of N-allylnoroxymorphone (naloxone). J Pharmacol Exp Ther 157:420–426.

Jeffcoate WJ, Cullen MH, Herbert M, Hastings AG, & Walder CP (1979): Prevention of effects of alcohol intoxication by naloxone. Lancet ii:1157–1159.

Jefferys DB, Flanaga RJ, & Volans GN (1980): Reversal of ethanol-induced coma with naloxone. Lancet 1:308–309.

Jorgenson A, Fog R, & Veilis B: Synthetic enkephalin analogue in treatment of schizophrenia. Lancet 1:935.

Judd LL, Janowsky DS, Segal DS, & Huey LY (1978): Naloxone related attenuation of manic symptoms in certain bipolar depressives. van Ree J, & Terenius L (Eds.). In *Characteristics and Function of Opiods.* Amsterdam, Elsevier/North Holland, pp. 173–174.

Kangawa K, Minamino N, Chino N, Shabakibara S, Matsuo H (1981): The complete amino acid sequence of alpha-neo-endorphin. Biochem Biophys Res Commun 99:871–878.

Kline NW, & Lehmann HE (1979): -Endorphin therapy in psychiatric patients. Usdin E, Bunney WE Jr, & Kline NS (Eds.). In *Endorphins in Mental Health Research.* New York, Macmillan, pp. 500–517.

Kline NS, Li ChH, Lehmann HE, Lajtna A, Laski E, & Cooper T (1977): Beta-endorphin-induced changes in schizophrenia and depressed patients. Arch Gen Psychiatry 34:1111–1113.

Kokka N, & Fairhurst AS (1977): Naloxone enhancement of acetic acid-induced writhing in rats. Life Sci 21:975–980.

Krebs E, & Roubicek (1979): J Pharmakopsychiatr Neuropsychopharmakol (1979), 12:86–93.

Kulkarni SK (1980): Heat and other physiological stress-induced analgesia: Catecholamine medicated and naloxone reversible response. Life Sci 27:185–188.

Kurland AA, McCabe O, Hanlon TE, & Sullivan D (1977): The treatment of perceptual disturbances in schizophrenia with naloxone hydrochloride. Am J Psychiatry 134:1408–1410.

Labrie F, Dupont A, & Cusan L, Lissitzky JC, Lepine J, Raymond V, & Coy DH (1979): Effects of endorphins and their analogues on prolactin and growth hormone secretion. Usdin E, & Bunney WE Jr, & Kline NS (Eds.). In *Endorphins in Mental Health Research.* New York, Macmillan, pp. 335–343.

Lehman H, Vasavan Nair NP, & Kline NS (1979): Beta-endorphin and naloxone in psychiatric patients: Clinical and biological effects. Am J Psychiatry 136:762–766.

Levine JD, Gordon NC, & Fields HL (1979): Naloxone dose dependently produces analgesia and hyperanalgesia in postoperative pain. Nature 278:740–741.

Lewis RV, Gerber LD, Stein S, Stephen RL, Grosser BI, Velick SF, Udenfriend S (1979): On beta$_H$leu^5-endorphin and schizophrenia. Arch Gen Psychiatry 36:237.

Lewis RV, Stern AS, Kimura S, Rossier J, Stein S, & Udenfriend S (1980): An about 50,000 dalton protein in the adrenal medulla: A common precursor of [met]-and [leu]-enkephalin. Science 208:1459–1461.

Li CH, & Chung D (1976): Isolation and structure of an untriakontapeptide with opiate activity from camel pituitary glands. Proc Natl Acad Sci USA 73:1145–1148.

Mackenzie AI (1979): Naloxone in alcohol intoxication. Lancet 1:733–734.

Mains RE, Eipper BA, & Ling N (1977): Common precursor to corticotrophins and endorphins. Proc Natl Acad Sci USA 74:3014–3018.

Martin WR (1976): Naloxone-diagnosis and treatment, drugs five years later. Ann Intern Med 85:765–768.

Mayer DJ, Price DD, & Rafii A: Antagonism of acupuncture analgesia in man by the narcotic antagonis+naloxone. Brain Res 121:368–372.

McGivern RF, Berka C, Bernston CG, Walker JM, & Sandman CA (1979): Effects of naloxone on analgesia induced by food deprivation. Life Sci 25:885–888.

McGivern RF, & Bernston GG: Mediation of diurinal fluctuations in pain sensitivity in the rat by food intake patterns: Reversal by naloxone. Science 210:210–211.

Miceli D, Marfaing-Jallat P, Le Magnen J (1980): Failure of naloxone to affect initial and acquired tolerance to ethanol in rats. Eur J Pharmacol 63:327–333.

Naber D, Pickar D, Post RM, van Kammen DP, et al. (1981): Perris C, Struwe G, Jansson B (Eds.). In *Proceedings of IIIrd World Conference of Biological Psychiatry, Stockholm.* Amsterdam, Elsevier/North Holland.

Nedopil W, & Ruther E (1979): Effects of the synthetic analogue of methionine-enkephalin FK33-824 on psychotic symptoms. Pharmakopsychiatr Neuropsychopharmakol 12:277–280.

Ojeda SR, Harms PG, & McCann SM (1974): Possible role of cyclic AMP and prostaglandin E in the dopaminergic control of prolactin release. Endocrinology 95:1694–1703.

Oyama T, Matsuki A, Taneichi T, Ling N, Guillemin R (1980): -Endorphin in obstetric analgesia. Am J Obstet Gynecol 137:613–616.

Overall JE, & Gorham DR (1962): The brief psychiatric rating scale. Psychol Rep 10:799–812.

Palmour R, Ervin R, Wagemaker H, & Cade R (1979): Characterization of a peptide from the serum of psychotic patients. Usdin E, Bunney WE Jr, Kline NS (Eds.). In *Endorphins in Mental Health Research*. New York, Macmillan, pp. 581–593.

Pearl J, & Harris LS (1966): Inhibition of writing by narcotic antagonists. J Pharmacol Exp Ther 154:319–323.

Pert CB, Pert A, & Tallman JF (1976): Isolation of a novel endogenous opiate analgesic from human blood. Proc Natl Acad Sci USA 73:2226–2230.

Pert CB, & Snyder SH (1973): Opiate receptor: Demonstration in nervous tissue. Science 179:1011–1014.

Peters WP, Johnson MW, Friedman PA, & Nitch WE (1981): Pressor effect of naloxone in septic shock. Lancet 1:529–532.

Pezalla PD, Lis M, Seidah NG, Chretian M (1978): Lipotropin, melanotropin and endorphin: In vivo catabolism and entry into cerebrospinal fluid. Can J Neural Sci 5:183–188.

Pfefferbaum A, Berger PA, Elliot GR, Tinklenberg JR, Kopell BS, Barchas JD, & Li CH (1979): Human EEG response to beta-endorphin. Psychiatry Res 1:83–88.

Pickar D, & Bunney WE Jr (1981): Acute naloxone administration in schizophrenic patients: A World Health Organization study. Perris C, Struwe G, Jansson B (Eds.). In *Proceedings of IIIrd World Conference of Biological Psychiatry, Stockholm*. Amsterdam, Elsevier/North Holland.

Pickar D, Davis GC, Schulz SC, Extein I, Wagner R, Naber D, Gold PW, van Kammen DP, Goodwin FK, Wyatt RJ, Li CH, & Bunney WE: Behavioral and biological effects of acute beta-endorphin injection in schizophrenic and depressed patients. Am J Psychiatry 138:160–166.

Pomeranz B, Chiu D (1976): Naloxone blockade of acupuncture analgesia: Endorphin implicated. Life Sci 19:1757–1762.

Psychopharmacology Research Branch and National Institute of Mental Health (1967): Clinical Global Inventory (CGI): The Clinical Global Impressions Scale. Bethesda, Md.

Rapaport SI, Klee WA, Pettigrew KD, Ohno K (1980): Entry of opioid peptides into the central nervous system. Science 207:84–86.

Reid LD, Stapelton JM, Ostrowski NL, Noble RG (1980): Way EL (Ed.). In *Endogenous and Exogenous Opiate Agonists and Antagonists*. New York, Pergammon Press, pp. 427–430.

Risch SC, Cohen RM, Janowsky DS, Kalin NH, & Murphy DL (1980): Mood and behavioral effects of physostigmine in humans are accompanied by elevations in plasma beta-endorphins and cortisol. Science 209:1545–1546.

Rivier C, Vale W, Ling N, Brown M, & Guilleman R (1977): Stimulation in vivo of the secretion of prolactin and growth hormone by beta-endorphin. Endocrinology 100:238–241.

Roberts JL, & Herbert E (1977): Characterization of a common precursor to corticotropin and beta-lipotropin: Identification of beta-lipotropin peptides and their arrangement relative to corticotrophin in the precursor synthesized in a cell-free system. Proc Natl Acad Sci USA 74:5300–5304.

Ross M, Berger PA, Goldstein A (1979): Plasma beta-endorphin immuno-reactivity in schizophrenia. Science 205:1163–1164.

Sawynok J, Pinsky C, & LaBella FS (1979): Microview on the specificity of naloxone as an opiate antagonist. Life Sci 25:1621–1632.

Schulz R, Wuster M, & Herz A: Interaction of amphetamine and naloxone in feeding behavior in guinea pigs. Eur J Pharmacol 63:313–319.

Segal DS, Brown RG (1978): -endorphin- and opiate-induced immobility: behavioral characterization and tolerance development. van Ree JM, & Terenius L (Eds.). In *Characteristics and Function of Opioids*. Amsterdam, Elsevier/North Holland. pp. 413–414.

Siegal S (1956): *Nonparametric Statistics: For the Behavioral Sciences*. New York, McGraw-Hill.

Simon EJ, Hiller JM, & Edelman I (1973): Stereospecific binding of the potent narcotic analgesic [^{3}H] etrophine to rat-brain homogenate. Proc Nat Acad Sci USA 70:1947–1949.

Sinha YN, Selby FW, Lewis UJ, & Vanderlaan WP (1973): A homologous radioimmunoassay for human prolactin. J Clin Endocrinol Metab 36:509–516.

Soubrie P, Jobert A, & Thiebot MH (1980): Differential effects of naloxone against diazepam-induced release of behavior in rats in three aversive situations. Psychopharmacologia 69:101–105.

Spitzer RL, Endicott J, & Robins E (1978a): *Research Diagnostic Criteria (RDC) for a Selected Group of Functional Disorders* (Ed. 3). New York, Biometrics Research, New York State Psychiatric Institute.

Spitzer RL, Endicott J, & Robins E (1978b): Research diagnostic criteria: Rationale and reliability. Arch Gen Psychiatry 35:773–782.

Stapleton JM, Lind MD, Merriman VJ, & Reid LD (1979): Naloxone inhibits diazepam-induced feeding in rats. Life Sci 24:2421–2426.

Terenius L (1973): Characteristics of the "receptor" for narcotic analgesics in synaptic plasma membrane fraction from rat brain. Acta Pharmacol Toxicol 33:377–384.

Terenius L, Wahlstrom A, Lindstrom L, & Widerlov E (1976): Increased CSF levels of endorphins in chronic psychosis. Neurosci Lett 3:157–162.

Teschemacher H, Opheim KE, Cox BM, & Goldstein A (1975): A peptide-like substance from pituitary that acts like morphine. Life Sci 16:1771–1776.

Tolis G, Hickey J, & Guyda H (1975): Effects of morphine on serum grown hormone, cortisol, prolactin and thyroid stimulating hormone in man. J Clin Endocrinol Metab 41:797–800.

Tower BB, Clark BR, Rubin RT (1977): Preparation of ^{125}I polypeptide hormones for radioimmunoassay using glucose oxidase with lactoperoxidase. Life Sci 21:959–966.

Tower BB, Sigel MB, Rubin RT, Poland RE, & Vanderlaan WP (1978): The talc-resin-TCA test: Rapid screening of radioiodinated polypeptide hormones for radioimmunoassay. Life Sci 23:2183–2192.

Tsunoda Y, Sakahira K, Nakano S, Matsumoto I, Yoshida T, Nagayama K, & Ikezono E (1980): Antagonism of acupuncture analgesia by naloxone in unconscious man. Bull Tokyo Med Dent Univ 27:89–94.

van Praag HM, Verhoeven WMA, van Ree JM, de Wied D (1983): Treatment of schizophrenia with gamma endorphin fragments. Perris C, Struwe G, Jansson B (Eds.). Abstracted in *Proceedings of IIIrd World Conference of Biological Psychiatry, Stockholm*. Amsterdam, Elsevier/North Holland.

Verhoeven WM, van Praag HM, van Ree JM, & de Wied D (1979): Improvement of schizophrenic patients treated with [Des-Tyr^1]- -endorphin (DT E). Arch Gen Psychiatry 36:294–298.

Wolavka J, Mallya A, Baig S, & Perez-Cruet J (1977): Naloxone in chronic schizophrenia. Science 196:1227–1228.

Wagemaker H, & Cade R (1977): The use of hemodialysis in chronic schizophrenia. Am J Psychiatry 134:684–685.

Wahlstrom A, Johansson L, & Terenius L (1976): Characterization of endorphins (endogenous morphine-like factors) in human CSF and brain extracts. Kosterlitz HW (Ed.). In *Opiates and Endogenous Opioid Peptides*. Amsterdam, Elsevier/North-Holland, pp. 49–56.

Walz MA, & Davis WM (1979): Experimental diazepam intoxication in rodents: Physostigmine and naloxone as potential antagonists. Drug Chem Toxicol 2:256–267.

Watson SJ, Berger PA, Akil H, Mills MJ, & Barchas JD (1978): Effects of naloxone on schizophrenia: Reduction of hallucinations in a subpopulation of subjects. Science 201:73–75.

Watson SJ, Akil H, & Barchas JD (1979): Immunohistochemical and biochemical studies of the enkaphalins, -endorphin and related peptides. Usdin E, Bunney WE, & Kline NS (Eds.). In *Endorphins in Mental Health Research*. London, Macmillan, pp. 30–44.

Wikler A (1954): Clinical and electroencephalographic studies on effect of mescaline, etc. J Nerv Ment Dis 120:157–175.

Willer JC, Dehen H, & Cambier J (1981): Stress-induced analgesia in humans: Endogenous opioids and naloxone-reversible depression of pain reflexes. Science 212:689–691.

Wright DJM, Phillips M, & Weller MPI (1980): Naloxone in shock. Lancet 2:1360.

14

Emotions, Immunity, and Disease

George F. Solomon   *Alfred A. Amkraut*

In 1964 Solomon and Moos suggested that "emotions play an important role in the pathogenesis of physical diseases associated with immunological dysfunction," especially the autoimmune diseases and certain cancers; we now believe infectious and allergic diseases can be added to that list. Salk (1962) had speculated that disease might involve genetic, behavioral, nervous, and immune interrelationships; Solomon and Moos (1964) thought the presence of autoimmune phenomena and dysproteinemias in conjunction with mental illness, particularly schizophrenia, was added evidence for a relationship between mental stress and immune dysfunction and the influence of the central nervous system on immunity. It seemed logical to link the central nervous and immune systems, as both relate the organism to the outside world, serve functions of defense and adaptation, illness ensues from inappropriate defenses in either system (neurosis on the one hand, and allergy on the other), and either can turn against the self (depression and autoimmunity). Finally, both systems have the property of memory and "learn" by experience.

Psychoneuroimmunology (a term aptly coined by Ader in 1981) is now based on reliability replicable experimental and clinical data in animals and humans. If the central nervous system influences immunological function, it should be possible to gather evidence supporting the following hypotheses:

1. Emotional upset and distress should alter the incidence or severity of those diseases to which there is immunologic resistance (infectious and neoplastic) and those associated with aberrant immunologic function (allergic and autoimmune).
2. Severe emotional disturbance and mental dysfunction should be accompanied by immunologic abnormalities.

3. Diseases of immunologic aberration should, at times, be accompanied by psychological or neurological symptoms.
4. Hormones regulated by the central nervous system (neuroendocrines) should influence immune mechanisims.
5. Experimental manipulation of appropriate portions of the central nervous system should have immunologic consequences.
6. Experimental behavioral manipulation (e.g., stress, conditioning, differential early experience) should have immunologic consequences.
7. Immunologically competent cells should have receptor sites for neuroendocrines, neurotransmitters, or for substances regulated by them.
8. Activation of the immune system (e.g., immunization) should be accompanied by central nervous system phenomena.
9. Factors elaborated by the immune system should affect the central nervous system and substances regulated by it.
10. Feedback mechanisms in immune regulation should act, at least in part, via central nervous system mediation.

Before the data in support of these hypotheses are discussed, a brief description of the immune system is presented.

IMMUNE SYSTEM

The immune system defends the organism against foreign invaders—bacteria, viruses, and chemical toxins—and appears to operate as a surveillance mechanism against mutant neoplastic cells that are antigenically different from normal cells. These mutant cells may be induced by chemical carcinogens, radiation, viruses, or chance somatic mutation. The immune system operates via specific antibodies (humoral immunity) and sensitized immunologically competent cells (cellular immunity). The elements of the immune response are B cells (producers of antibodies), T cells and macrophages. The immune response can be divided into three elements: an afferent limb concerned with induction of immunity; a central limb concerned with elaboration of immunity or of tolerance; and an efferent limb concerned with activation of complement components, which in turn, act either directly on the toxic agent or activate phagocytes that remove such agents.

Five classess of immunoglobulins (Ig) are known. One of these, IgE is responsible for allergic reactions. Substances known as *lymphokines* are released by T cells on encounter with antigen and can cause the activation, aggregation, and attraction of macrophages. They also have a direct cytolytic effect on target cells and can stimulate or depress lymphocyte proliferation, for purposes of regulation of the immune response. *Transfer factor* can confer specificity on sensitized cells and may therefore "broadcast" the immune response. Cascades of *kinins* and the release of *lytic enzymes* contribute to the inflammatory process. Tumor cells can be attacked directly by special T cells known as *killer cells* or by *macrophages* after being coated with antibody (opsonin). *Natural killer (NK) cells* do not require prior sensitization and may be the first line of defense against tumor cells. Other T cells called *helpers* and *suppressors* serve as modulators of the immune response; the latter control the proliferation of both B and other T cells. Failure of suppressor cell function is now felt to be critical to the development of sensitivity to a self-component (i.e., autoimmunity). Macrophages are important in both the afferent and efferent limbs of the immune response: they present antigent to T cells and attack invaders. Contact with B cells may stimulate suppressor cells to multiply. The site in which the immune reaction develops may be critical. A variety of feedback and self-regulatory systems appear to be involved, including *interferon*, which our work has shown to be enhanced by stress (Solomon et al., 1967).

EMOTIONAL FACTORS IN IMMUNOLOGICALLY RELATED DISEASES

Infectious Diseases

Many studies have linked the onset or course of infectious diseases to emotional factors. Psychologi-

cal health ("ego strength") is correlated with speed of recovery from infectious mononucleosis (Greenfield et al., 1959). High "stress" scores in families studied longitudinally are related to rate of acquisition of streptoccocal infections and to antistreptolysin 0 responses (Meyer & Haggerty, 1962). Prolonged convalescence frum brucellosis (Imboden et al., 1959) and from influenza (Imboden et al., 1961) is correlated with depression. Of particular interest is the fact that the oral disease, acute necrotizing ulcerative gingivitis (or trenchmouth), in which the normal bacterial flora of the mouth become invasive, is well known by dentists to be associated with acute stress (Engel, 1953). It was recently demonstrated that this disease is associated with both emotional factors and decreased immunological responsiveness (i.e., lowered lymphocyte stimulation by concanavalin A; Cohen-Cole et al., 1981). Similarly, herpes simplex is a condition in which a resident virus, usually kept in check by T lymphocytes "monitoring" infected cells, is "released" by stresses such as fever, ultraviolet radiation, or emotional upset. Avoidance learning and restraint lead to increased susceptibility to herpes simplex virus in mice (Rasmussen et al., 1957) among a variety of experimental conditions altering infectious disease in animals.

Allergic Disease

Personality and stress factors are related to contact dermatitis (Brown & Young, 1965). In guinea pigs, the probability of delayed-type skin hypersensitivity to dinitrochlorobenzene in a subthreshold concentration is increased in a stressed group (Metrop & Vesser, 1969). In humans the psychological state of "suppressed weeping" is tied to attacks of urticaria (Saul & Bernstein, 1941). In a review of the very extensive literature on psychosocial and psychophysiological aspects of bronchial asthma, Weiner (1977) noted that in genetically predisposed individuals, exposure to allergens, infections, and psychological factors can provoke attacks of asthma. Psychological studies make four major points: (1) there is no "asthmatic personality," (2) asthmatic patients have unconscious dependency wishes, (3) dependency conflicts are the result of specific parental attitudes and behaviors, and (4) the asthmatic attack occurs when the dependency wish is frustrated or conflict is activated. Asthmatic patients generally have elevated levels of IgE. (We have shown that stress may increase IgE levels in animals, Solomon & Amkraut, unpublished data.)

Autoimmune Disease

Solomon (1981) reviewed the literature on emotional and personality factors in the onset and course of autoimmune diseases, particularly rheumatoid arthritis. The critical factor in the immunological deficiency state of autoimmunity appears to be compromised suppressor T cell function (Horowitz et al., 1977; Reinberg et al., 1979). Arthritics are described as quiet, introverted, reliable, conscientious, restricted in the expression of emotion (especially anger), conforming, self-sacrificing, tending to allow themselves to be imposed upon, sensitive to criticism, distant, overactive and busy, pseudoindependent in order to deny dependency, stubborn, rigid, and controlling. Onset of disease often follows either a period of psychological stress or loss of the ability to maintain previous patterns of defense and adaptation.

Similar psychological findings have been reported in patients with other probable autoimmune diseases such as multiple sclerosis (Grinker & Robbins, 1954), systemic lupus erythematosus (Otto & Mackay, 1967), ulcerative colitis (Engel, 1953), and autoerythrocyte sensitization (Boehme & Kurnick, 1981). Rapid progress of disease (Moos & Solomon, 1969), degree of incapacitation (Moos & Solomon, 1965), and lack of response to treatment (Moos & Solomon, 1965a) are correlated with failure of psychological defenses and concomitant anxiety, depression, and alienation. Of special interest is a psychological comparison by Solomon and Moos (1965b) of relatives of arthritic patients who were physically healthy and either had or did not have rheumatoid factor, an IgM anti-IgG autoantibody. The rheumatoid factor–negative relatives were a cross section of the general population, ranging from psychologically healthy to near psychotic; whereas the rheumatoid factor–positive group was uniformly emotionally healthy, with high ego strength (i.e., capacity for successful psychological defense, coping, mastery, and integration) and good impulse control. Based on these findings, a reasonable hypothesis is that, given a genetic predisposition to autoimmune disease (e.g., individuals of HLA-B type 27 are more likely to develop rheumatoid arthritis and individuals of HLA-D type 7 are more likely to develop multiple sclerosis; Gowdy, 1980) only individuals with significant emotional conflict, psychological distress, and failure of psychological defenses develop overt disease.

Neoplastic Disease

A large number of studies have tied personality factors to the presence and rate of dissemination of cancer. Rapid progress of cancer is associated with unsuccessful psychological defenses and psychic distress. Four consistent factors recur in reports of personality studies on patients with cancer: (1) loss of an important relationship prior to the development of a tumor; (2) inability to express hostile feelings and emotion; (3) unresolved tension concerning a parent figure; and (4) sexual disturbance (LeShan & Worthington, 1956). In a predictive study, Klopfer (1957) related prolonged survival in patients with metastastic cancer to either a successful denial of reality or, more rarely, a mature, calm acceptance of reality. In contrast, death was associated with ego defensiveness and a high degree of subjective distress. (Note that the emotional and personality factors cited in relation to the onset and course of cancer are similar to those that have been related to autoimmune disease.)

LaBarba (1970) reviewed the effects of stress on induction and growth of a variety of experimental tumors in animals without reference to immunological factors. Increases as well as decreases in tumor induction and growth were found to be associated with stress; however, a number of experiments failed to show any effect of stress on the particular system under study. The wide variation in results may reflect the multiplicity of tumor systems, the different species and stress procedures used in the experiments, or the different effects of stress on specific aspects of immunological resistance. LaBarba concluded that scientific evidence strongly supports the notion that cancer in animals can be influenced by experiential manipulation.

In summary, stress, failure of psychological defenses, and concomitant psychological distress are associated with hypofunction and dysfunction of the immune system in a variety of clinical diseases, suggesting that noxious affect can be immunosuppressive.

IMMUNOLOGICAL ABNORMALITIES IN MENTAL ILLNESS

Evidence for links between the central nervous system and immunological function are inferred from the immunological abnormalities observed in mental illness, particularly in schizophrenia.

Immunoglobulins

Numerous studies have produced rather confusing and somewhat contradictory results regarding immunoglobulin abnormalities in psychiatric patients. Quantitative and qualitative changes in serum globulins have been reported in schizophrenic patients (Fessel & Grunbaum, 1961; Grunbaum et al., 1964). We found correlations between severity of psychotic symptomatology and 19S ultracentrifugal class immunoglobulin (primarily IgM) levels (Solomon et al., 1966), elevation of IgA and IgM in psychotic inpatients (Solomon et al., 1969), and poorer prognosis, with or without pharmacotherapy, in those patients with high immunoglobulin levels (Amkraut et al., 1973). Others found elevation of only IgA or IgM in psychiatric patients; however, these were not specific to the diagnosis of schizophrenia (Hendrie et al., 1972). In contrast, Bock (1978) found a decrease of IgA and IgM. In a sophisticated study the highest IgM levels were found in withdrawn schizophrenics and the lowest in paranoid patients; in contrast to our findings, higher IgA and IgM levels were associated with a shorter hospital stay (Pulkkinen, 1977). Gowdy (1980) reported significantly elevated IgG levels in acute schizophrenic patients; levels peaked after 12 years of disease, and dropped with increased phenothiazine dosage.

Autoantibodies

An increased incidence of autoantibodies has been reported in schizophrenia; these include rheumatoid factor (in spite of the reportedly low coincidence of rheumatoid arthritis and schizophrenia), antinuclear factor (of particular note in view of the fact there is a 22 percent incidence of schizophreniform psychosis in patients with systemic lupus erythematosus), and antithymic antibodies (Burian et al., 1964; Domashneva & Maznina, 1976; Fessel, 1961; Fessel & Solomon, 1960; Goldstein & Rossio, 1980; Rothermich & Philips, 1963). However, some workers claim that autoantibodies are induced by antipsychotic medication (Alarcon-Segovia et al., 1973).

The original idea by Solomon—that schizophrenia might be a "psychosomatic disease" in which genetic, personality, and stress factors lead to a physiological abnormality, which in turn affects brain function—was supported by the controversial and essentially unconfirmed work of Heath and co-workers (1957) claiming the presense of a specific antibrain antibody ("taraxein") in schizophrenia. Earlier work

with heterologous brain antigens was also suggestive of this (Fessel, 1963). Heath claimed that taraxein, eventually identified as an IgG, could produce psychotic symptoms in human volunteers or in monkeys, with the latter demonstrating focal EEG changes in the septal area. Sheep antibodies administered to septal and caudate areas of monkey and human brains produced similar results (Heath, 1969; Heath & Krupp, 1967; Heath et al., 1957; Heath et al., 1967a, b). When administered intravenously these antibodies attached to nuclei of septal and caudate neurons in recipient monkeys, whose EEGs and behavior were altered by the injections (Heath, 1969). Health's work is subject to much theoretical and methodological criticism and has been supported mainly by Soviet work (Glebov & Zil'bersheteyn, 1975; Gosheva et al., 1969; Kolyaskina & Kushnir, 1969). Although evidence that autoimmunity, particularly antibrain reactivity, plays a pathogenic role in schizophrenia is unconvincing, it seems clear that an increased incidence of nonspecific autoimmune reactions occurs in schizophrenia illness.

Immune Responsivity

If autoimmunity is relevant to schizophrenia, relative immunological incompetence might be expected. Some studies demonstrated diminished immunological responsivity in schizophrenic patients to several agents, including guinea pig serum (Molholm, 1942), pertussis vaccine (Vaughn et al., 1949), tularemia vaccine (Matvetts et al., 1957), and a variety of other antigens (Certcov, 1969). However, others showed no decrease in response to diptheria toxoid (Hussar et al., 1971) or tetanus toxoid (Solomon et al., 1968). In one study antibody titers to cholera vaccine were higher in schizophrenics than in normal or depressed patients (Friedman et al., 1967). Soviet researchers claim that immune reactivity is decreased only in certain forms of schizophrenia (Kerbikov, 1961). Thus, there is no convincing body of evidence for altered immunological responsivity (i.e., antibody response) in schizophrenia.

Lymphocyte Abnormalities

The hypothesis that abnormal immunological reactivity would be reflected in morphological abnormalities of lymphocytes was examined in several studies in the 1960s (Erban 1965; Kamp, 1962; Pennington, 1963; Vanderkamp, 1962;

Hollister & Kosek, personal communication, 1962). Fessel and Hirata-Hibi (1963) found three types of abnormal lymphocytes in the peripheral blood of most schizophrenic patients; only one type corresponded to the so-called stress lymphocyte of Frank and Dougherty (1953). In their impressive blind study of coded pairs of slides from 50 schizophrenic patients and 50 controls, Fessel and Hirata-Hibi correctly diagnosed 49 pairs. Extending their work to the bone marrow, these authors described the lymphocyte abnormalities as consisting of the following: strong basophilic cytoplasm with a prominent perinuclear clear zone, which contained small vacuoles, a faintly lamellar structure, or both; an indented lobulated nucleus; and variably fine or coarse chromatin structure, often heterogeneously within the same nucleus (Hirata-Hibi & Fessel, 1964). The families of *process* schizophrenics (i.e., insidious onset of disease, poor premorbid history, and little or no apparent precipitating stress), but not of *reactive* schizophrenics (i.e., rapid onset, good premorbid history, and precipitating event) had 30 times as many "schizophrenic lymphocytes" as did normal families (Fessel et al., 1965). These findings have been confirmed in chronic schizophrenics and their family members (Sethi et al., 1973) and in schizophrenic children (Fowle, 1968). This work suggests that similar genetic factors affect both the immune system and susceptibility to schizophrenia. Chromatin structure of neutrophils as well as lymphocytes may be altered in schizophrenia, with the former reflecting alteration of nucleohistones (Issidorides et al., 1975).

On a functional level, Soviet workers reported a deficient response to T cell mitogens by lymphocytes from schizophrenic patients cultured in vitro (Liedermann & Prilipko, 1978). They also reported that serum of schizophrenic patients inhibits phytohemagglutinin (PHA) stimulation of lymphocytes of normal individuals (Vartanian et al., 1978). On the other hand, recent work suggests lymphocytes from schizophrenic individuals have elevated responses to both concanavalin A and PHA (Goldstein & Rossio, 1980).

It seems likely that abnormalities of lymphocytes are present in schizophrenia; however, their significance is unclear. Obviously, comparison of T and B cell numbers and examination of lymphocytes by schizophrenic patients by transmission and scanning electron microscopy would be of value. Of even more interest would be the utilization of new techniques to differentiate subpopulations of T cells that contain suppressor cells or helper cells (Reinberg et

al., 1979). Work in progress suggests a deficiency of suppressor T cells in schizophrenia, which might account for the autoimmune phenomena reported in conjunction with schizophrenia already discussed (JD Berman, personal communication, 1981).

To conclude, evidence overwhelmingly supports the presence of a variety of immunological abnormalities in schizophrenia, and possibly in other major mental illnesses. This evidence lends credence to a relationship between immunity and central nervous system functioning; but its significance for the etiology and pathogenesis of mental illness is unclear. Some authors claim that the various immunological abnormalities in schizophrenia, particularly the dysglobulinemias, support a viral hypothesis (especially a slow virus) for the etiology of schizophrenia (Torrey & Peterson, 1976).

HYPOTHALAMIC INFLUENCES ON IMMUNE RESPONSE

The hypothalamus, a small area of the diencephalon is rich in neural connections to the limbic system of the brain and has receptors for humoral influences from blood and CSF. The hypothalamus influences the pituitary through a variety of polypeptide releasing or inhibiting factors (thyrotropin releasing hormone, luteinizing hormone releasing hormone, corticotropin releasing factor and somatostatin) and is at the interface between the brain and a range of critical peripheral regulatory functions. It is rich in neurohormones and neurotransmitters that may affect immune function and it has been implicated in immune function by direct research. a^1-thymosin is found in the hypothalamus (N. Hall, personal communication, 1981). Lesions or electrical stimulation of the hypothalamus can, respectively, suppress or enhance the Arthus reaction in the rat (Jankovic & Isakovic, 1973a, 1973b; Luparello et al., 1964). Electrolytic lesions in the anterior basal hypothalamus in the rat protect against lethal anaphylaxis (Luparello et al., 1964), as do anterior hypothalamic lesions in the guinea pig (Schiavi et al., 1966). Changes in antibody levels are not required for this protective effect (Stein et al., 1976), and the effect also occurs in the case of passive anaphylaxis (Macris et al., 1972). The mechanism remains unclear, but bilateral anterior medial lesions protect against lethal histamine shock (Schiavi et al., 1966).

In regard to antibody production, early work demonstrated alteration in γ globulin levels as a result of the electrical stimulation of the lateral hypothalamus of rats (Fessel & Forsythe, 1963). Significant Soviet work revealed that a destructive lesion in a specific portion of the dorsal hypothalamus of rabbits led to complete suppression of primary antibody response, prolonged retention of antigen in the blood, inability to induce streptoccocal antigen myocarditis, and prolonged graft retention (Korneva & Khai, 1963). Electrical stimulation of the same region enhanced antibody response (Korneva, 1967). Destruction of the posterior hypothalamus aggravated experimental allergic polyneuritis, which was related to the absence of antibodies to myelin (Konovalov et al., 1971). However, some workers found no effect on antibody levels following lesions in a variety of hypothalamic sites (Ado & Goldstein, 1973; Thrasher et al., 1971).

Hypothalamic lesions also affect cell-mediated immunity. Anterior lesions in the guinea pig suppressed delayed cutaneous hypersensitivity to picryl chloride and turberculin (Macris et al., 1972). Lesions produced decreased delayed cutaneous hypersensitivity, while stimulation enhanced the response (Jankovic & Isakovic, 1973a, 1973b). Electrolytic lesions of the ventromedial and posterior nuclei of the hypothalamus of hybrid rats impaired the graft-versus-host reaction in the recipient (Solomon, Amkraut, Kaspar, & Pudue, unpublished data). We did not find an effect on antibody formation. Guinea pigs with anterior hypothalamic lesions had significantly smaller cutaneous tuberculin reactions than nonoperated or sham-operated controls (Keller et al., 1980). While the absolute number or percentage of T and B cells was not changed, there was decreased stimulation in vitro of lymphocytes from animals with hypothalamic lesions by both PHA and purified protein derivative in whole blood (but not in isolated lymphocyte cultures). This implies that humoral factors were responsible for the decreased stimulation. Besedovsky and Sorkin (1977) and Korneva (1967) suggested that the hypothalamus is directly involved in regulation of immune response following exposure to antigen. The neuronal firing rate of specific hypothalamus nuclei was increased following immunization, implicating a feedback loop between the immune response and the hypothalamus.

Evidence that the hypothalamus can influence immune function is strong, although there is disagreement regarding specific critical hypothalamic loci. The variability in findings regarding the effect of hypothalamic lesions on antibody levels may result from the heterogeneity of study designs.

Most likely, hypothalamic influences are hormonally mediated (discussed later). The suggestive evidence for a direct role of the hypothalamus in modulation of immune response is intriguing and deserves further investigation.

STRESS AND IMMUNOLOGICAL RESPONSE

Stress

One of the major pitfalls in approaching the problem of stress and immunological response is in the definition of *stress*. In the context of this discussion, we assume that *stress* represents an extraordinary demand on physiological or psychological defenses, with concomitant responses of neuroendocrine systems to the external elicitor. One should note that in animal experiments it is not always clear whether what is considered to be a "control" group may not in fact be exposed to stresses unknown to the experimenter. It was once commonly believed that the neuroendocrine stress-response status of the animal could be determined by the measurement of relatively few hormones. With increased sophistication in understanding hormonal responses, it has become clear that no simple or limited set of measurements can be considered adequate. In addition, many investigators have pointed out the difficulty in achieving the desired degree of reproducibility in stress experiments. These observations, coupled with the complex interactions of the immune and neuroendocrine systems, indicate the need for as many measurements as possible in both systems. It is incumbent on the researcher to determine whether the psychological stresses experimentally applied have resulted in changes in physiological parameters such as food intake, sleep, body temperature, or blood pressure—all of which could directly affect immune responses. Similarly, in assessing the effects of physiological stress (e.g., food deprivation), it is important to determine whether psychological distress has resulted in a hormonal shift.

Stress and Immune Response in Man

Striking correlations between stress and disease, particularly respiratory disease, have been observed in a number of clinical studies (Holmes et al., 1957; Horowitz et al., 1977; Jacobs et al., 1969; Jacobs et al., 1970; Meyer & Haggerty, 1962; Rahe et al., 1974). Some of these observations may reflect physiological alterations in the respiratory system. In light of these reports and the findings of reduced alveolar macrophage activity following experimental stress in rabbits (Lockard et al., 1973), the role of these cells in respiratory disease appears to be important.

Palmblad and associates carried out a number of experiments on the effects of food deprivation and sleep deprivation on immune mechanisms in man (Palmblad, 1979; Palmblad et al., 1977a; Palmblad et al., 1977b; Palmblad et al., 1979a; Palmblad et al., 1979b). Both stresses led to similar findings. Acute phase elements were depressed, as were neutrophil function and lymphocyte response to PHA. The levels of all immunoglobulins and specific antibody levels were unaffected, but antibody levels increased following discontinuation of the stress. Delayed hypersensitivity reactions in the subjects were not altered by the stress. Changes in levels of adrenal medullary and cortical hormones, growth hormone, and thyroid hormones were present, but they did not correlate with decreased function.

Quantification of stress by measuring recent life change further confirmed its contribution to illness (Gunderson & Rahe, 1974; Rahe, 1978). Cobb (1974, 1976) found that low levels of social support in combination with loss of work led to a markedly increased incidence of disease.

A few studies have been concerned with direct measurement of elements of the immune system in the presence of stress. Changes in immunoglobulin levels with emotional state were reported in breast cancer (Pettingale et al., 1977) and rheumatoid arthritis (Hendrie et al., 1971). Bereavement was found to be associated with depressed T cell response to the mitogens concanavalin A and PHA (Bartrop et al., 1977). While there was no difference in this response 2 weeks after the death of a spouse, a 10-fold difference between controls and bereaved subjects was found at 5 weeks. There was no difference in the number of T and B cells, antibody titers, and presence of antibodies; nor was there an alteration in the measured serum levels of thyroid, adrenocortical, and pituitary hormones. The importance of successful coping for return of full immunological responsivity was pointed out. Suppression of T cell function was confirmed in recent widowers, followed longitudinally before and after the death of their wives. Their B cell function was also found to be suppressed as measured by pokeweed mitogen. Immunosuppression generally lasted at least 6 months (M. Stein, unpublished data, 1981). In another study (Green et al., 1978), in vitro lymphocyte cytotoxicity was reduced in the presence of inadequate coping with a life change situation.

The stress of an oral examination for psychiatry residents caused significantly reduced lymphocyte response to PHA and pokeweed mitogen followed by elevation after the examination (Dorian et al., 1981). In a well-controlled study with college students, a significant correlation was found between high stress combined with poor coping and a decline in NK cells (Locke et al., 1978). It is possible that the decrease in reactive T cells in older people (Weksler & Hutteroth, 1974) and the increased incidence of autoimmune phenomena and cancer in the elderly could be the cumulative result of stress or could be influenced by the relative frequency of depressive affect in the older age group.

Stress and Immune Response in Animals

Animal experiments in this area are numerous, and at first glance the results appear to be confusing and contradictory. They cover different age and sex groups as well as a large array of immune stimuli. The studies examine phenomena that are intrinsically immunological in nature, but also extend to the areas of infectious diseases and tumors, in which the contribution of immunity and, in particular, acquired immunity is not always clear. The review that follows is intended to illustrate the variety of studies, and particularly, to point out unifying principles that may allow conclusions concerning mechanisms of stress effects.

Studies on infectious diseases are the most difficult to interpret. The outcome depends not only on the contributions of the immune system, but also on the distribution and reproduction of the infective agent. The first barriers to infection are those of natural immunity; Immunity acquired on the first exposure to the infectious agent enters the picture rather late. The stresses used in these experiments are mainly shock avoidance, confinement, sound stress, and electric shock. The outcome does not appear to differ significantly among these stresses. In mice, severity of infection by Coxsackie B virus (Friedman et al., 1971; Johnsson et al., 1963), polio virus (Johnsson & Rasmussen, 1965), herpes virus, and vesicular stomatitis virus (Jensen & Rasmussen, 1963; Rasmussen et al., 1957) was increased by stress, although with vesicular stomatitis virus the disease was decreased when stress was applied before infection. Stresses that increased Coxsackie virus infection (in the hands of the same investigators) decreased malarial infection with *Plasmodium berghei* (Friedman et al., 1973). On the other hand, *Plasmodium* infection was increased in animals stressed by group housing (Friedman & Glasgow, 1973; Plaut et al., 1971).

Since documentation of emotional and stress factors in the onset and course of cancer has received much attention, tumorigenesis (i.e., spontaneous, chemical carcinogen, tumor implantation, or tumor viruses), has been extensively studied. The subject was reviewed by Riley in 1979. The incidence of mammary tumors can be affected by stresses as mild as those found in a "normal" animal-house environment (Riley, 1979). It should be pointed out that these tumors are not only steroid sensitive, but also prolactin sensitive, and the role of the immune system is not clear. Experimental stresses increased the incidence of polyoma (Chang & Rasmussen, 1964) but decreased that of Rauscher virus–induced leukemia (Jensen, 1969). Introducing chickens into a new "pecking order" increased the incidence of Marek's disease (Gross, 1972). The incidence and size of murine sarcoma virus-induced tumors significantly increased when stressful housing conditions, electric shock, or restraint were applied following injection of the virus (Amkraut & Solomon, 1972; Seifter et al., 1973); stress of crowding and electric shock prior to administration of the virus decreased these parameters. There were no differences in neutralizing antibodies in these animals (Amkraut & Solomon, 1974). Inbred female mice that spontaneously developed fighting behavior were more resistant to murine sarcoma virus tumors than nonfighting females (Amkraut & Solomon, 1972).

Effects of stress on efferent mechanisms of the immune system have also been studied. Effects on asthma and allergy were reviewed by Stein et al. (1981). Since a limited number of elements participate in passive anaphylaxis, which is stress susceptible (Rasmussen et al., 1959), it should be possible to use this paradigm for the determination of stress effects on different mechanisms. A more complex model is adjuvant-induced arthritis in the rat, felt by some to analogous to rheumatoid arthritis in humans. Crowding in these animals led to significantly increased inflammation in males. The rate of decrease of the swelling, however, was accelerated in stressed animals (Amkraut et al., 1971). Different stress procedures either increased or decreased the incidence of collagen-induced arthritis in the rat (M. Rogers, personal communication, 1981).

Experiments involving antibody production and expression of cell-mediated hypersensitivity offer a more direct measure of the effect of stress on immune mechanisms. A variety of stresses, in particular that of overcrowding, reduced the primary and secondary response of rats to flagellin, a potent bacterial antigen to which animals have no natural exposure (Solomon, 1969). Overcrowding of rats caused steroid elevation in the first 2 weeks, and the stress had to be applied prior to, or concurrently with administration of antigen. Electric shock stress was ineffective in this model. Large amounts of antigen could overcome these stress effects. This phenomenon could be mediated by reduction in macrophage or helper T cell activity, which may be required for immunization with small (1- μg) but not large amounts of antigen. (It is interesting to speculate that overcrowding-induced immunosuppression might be a mechanism by which nature regulates populations).

Similar effects were shown when environmental stresses, such as noise and light flashes, were used on monkeys accompanied or followed by administration of either bovine serum albumin (Hill et al., 1967) or a bacterial lipopolysaccharid (Felsenfield et al., 1966). Adult rats that were handled in infancy had higher antibody titers than unhandled controls in response to both primary and secondary immunization with flagellin (Solomon et al., 1968). It should be remembered that even a low level of "stress," such as that induced by handling (better termed "stimulation"), can affect immune-related phenomena, as has been shown with spontaneous tumor appearance. The early handling increased the production of IgM, which may reflect more efficient processing by macrophages.

Restricting the feeding of rats to 2 hours in the early morning caused a three- to fivefold rise of late night and early morning corticosteroid levels. This stress reduced IgG production somewhat, but only after 3 weeks' duration. IgE production, on the other hand, was significantly increased by this restricted feeding treatment, but the difference in IgE production vanished in 5–6 weeks (Solomon & Amkraut, unpublished data). This pattern may reult from decreased T cell activity early in the response, which is self-repairing. In contrast to these findings, Kamoshita et al. (1979) reported that restraint stress prior to immunization suppressed IgE production.

Cell-mediated responses are also susceptible to stress. Suppression of granuloma formation with crowding and sound was reported (Christian & Williamson, 1958; Funk & Jensen, 1967). Restricted feeding schedules greatly reduced the graft-versus-host response in rats (Amkraut et al., 1972). The stress had to be applied in the first 3 days of the reaction, whose magnitude was then measured on day 7. Stress during the last 4 days had no effect. Administration of ACTH (5 mg twice daily) caused a reduction in the response, which was less severe than that induced by stress and showed a different time course. This difference indicates that the rise in corticosteroids was not the sole mediator of the effect. Furthermore, the animals could not be restored to normal activity by administration of bone marrow, thymus, and spleen cells. Trapping of tagged donor cells in popliteal lymph nodes following foot pad injection was significantly decreased in stressed animals but could not account for the quantitative decrease in reactivity. The cells from stressed animals used as donors elicited normal reactions in recipients, indicating that the effect was probably not one of shift in cell populations but rather was determined by environmental conditions.

It has long been known that the antibody response shows an impressive self-stabilizing capability. This capability is, in part, the result of feedback loops, such as the effect on the immune system of (1) specific and nonspecific suppressor cell populations, (2) the production of inhibitor factors by eosinophils (Goetzl & Austin, 1977), and (3) neuroendocrines. Since it is to be expected that in vivo measurements will show very small effects, a number of investigators have attempted to use in vitro systems to isolate the targets of stress within the immune system.

Studies with in vitro lymphocyte stimulation in man were described above. In animal systems, studies following application of standard stresses have led to reports of both increases and decreases of in vitro responses. When adherent suppressor cells were removed from populations of whole spleen cells, the nonadhering population, although it showed PHA excess suppression, demonstrated a greatly reduced response. This reduced response could be restored to that of the whole population by the addition of 2 percent macrophages. The restored population did, however, show excess mitogen suppression. The phenomenon could be reproduced either by cortisone acetate or by water-deprivation stress. A very large excess of suppressor cells was produced 15 days after the administration of hydrocortisone acetate, i.e., an overshoot took place as a consequence of the suppressive maneuver. These results point to the macrophage as a critical cell in

stress-induced immunosuppression (Folch & Wakeman, 1974). In other work, a significantly graduated suppression of lymphocyte stimulation to PHA was found in response to graded increases in the intensity of stressors (Keller et al., 1981).

Antigen-induced thymidine uptake in vitro was increased in rats after 5 weeks of crowding (Joassod & McKenzie, 1976). In another series of experiments (Monjan, 1981; Monjan & Collector, 1977), the time course of stress effects on in vitro lymphocyte stimulation was studied. It was shown that 2 weeks of sound stress decreased the in vitro thymidine uptake due to concanavalin A or PHA. In contrast, 2 months of the same stress increased this uptake significantly. These observations may explain some of the contradictory findings referred to previously. They also suggest an explanation for the failure of certain stress experiments, since the time element varies from animal to animal, antigen to antigen, and reaction to reaction.

The most thorough study of mechanisms of stress-induced reduction of in vitro response was reported by Gisler and co-workers (Gisler, 1974; Gisler & Schenkel-Hullinger, 1971; Gisler et al., 1971). They showed a 10-fold reduction in plaque-forming cell response in tissue culture to sheep red blood cells following a variety of stresses; these included acceleration, ether anesthesia, restraint, and overcrowding. The response was greatest in spleens explanted 6 hours following the application of stress, but returned to normal in 72 hours. Although the stresses raised corticosteroid levels, the reduction in plague-forming cells was not a direct function of this rise.

The effect of stress on ^{51}Cr-labeled lymphocyte distribution was studied. B cells were significantly decreased in the spleen and increased in the liver. The effect on T cells was the reverse, except that T cells were also increased in the bone marrow. Addition of B cells, T cells, or macrophages alone did not restore the in vitro response, but the addition of both cells and macrophages was effective. Administration of diazepam (Valium), an "antianxiety" drug that has muscle relaxant and sedative effects, interfered with the suppressive action of immobilization stress, but not with that of ether stress. This experiment, too, focused attention on the macrophages. Unfortunately, it is not clear whether stress reduced the macrophage population in the spleen or reduced macrophage activity.

Direct effects on macrophage activity by hormones were reported by Pavlidis and Chirigos (1980). The stress was that of acute immobilization, and macrophage activity was induced by either interferon or bacterial lipopolysaccharide. The presence or contribution of NK cells in these reactions cannot be judged from the data presented. The results show an interesting parallel to those stress responses in man described previously. It is interesting to note that interferon, which activates NK cells, is increased by stress (Solomon et al., 1969).

EFFECT OF CONDITIONING AND HYPNOSIS ON IMMUNE RESPONSE

The enormous influence exercised by Pavlovian thinking and experimentation on early Russian biology led to extensive experiments on conditioning of the immune response. Several reviews of the field are available (Ader, 1981; Dolin et al., 1960; Il'enko & Kovaleva, 1960; Luk'ianenko, 1961; Talwar et al., 1975). Many reports of successful conditioning of immune responses can be found in the Russian literature. Virtually all of the experiments were carried out with bacterial or viral antigens. A number of the reports refer to nonspecific effects, such as an increase in phagocytic activity and an increase in polymorphonuclear cells in peritoneal fluid. Specific responses were usually on the order of only a two- to fourfold increase in titer; but in one experiment involving four monkeys undergoing chair confinement stress and administered paratyphoid vaccine, quite large rises in titers were observed when a conditioned stimulus was administered along with saline (Luk'ianenko, 1959).

More recently, a series of experiments on conditioning of immunosuppression were reported by Ader and Cohen (1975, 1981; described in detail in Chapter 12). Cyclophosphamide, an immunosuppressive drug, is one of many agents that cause gastric upset in animals. If a rodent is given flavored water prior to administration of the aversive stimulus, the animal subsequently avoids the flavor. In these experiments saccharin-flavored drinking water was used as the conditioned stimulus. Animals administered this stimulus along with an antigen, following conditioning with injection of cyclophosphamide, showed significantly decreased responses to the antigen (Ader & Cohen, 1975). Thus, the "placebo" produced immunosuppression (significant but somewhat less than with the immunosuppressant drug in these classically conditioned animals). Two other groups replicated this

experiment with no deviation from the original protocol (Rogers et al., 1976; Wayner et al., 1978). The antigen used in this work was sheep red blood cells, a T cell–dependent antigen in the rat. *Brucella*, a T cell–independent antigen, did not show this phenomenon of conditioned suppression (Wayner et al., 1978). Based on the finding that B cells, which are refractory to corticosteroids but suppressed by cyclophosphamide, do not seem to respond to conditioning, Wayner and co-workers (1978) attributed the conditioning effect to a rise in corticosteroids as a result of the aversive behavior rather than to a recall of the immunosuppressive action of cyclophosphamide. However, lithium chloride, which causes similar aversive behavior, did not lead to immunosuppression when conditioned aversion to it was evoked, suggesting recall of immunosuppression by the conditioned stimulus after its initial pairing with the immunosuppressive drug (the unconditioned stimulus) (Ader et al., 1979). Furthermore, trinitrophenyl-coupled lipopolysaccharide, assumed to be a T cell–independent antigen, also showed conditioned immunosuppression when cyclophosphamide was used for conditioning (Cohen et al., 1979). Apparently, suppression of cellular as well as humoral immunity can be conditioned, as evidenced by the reduction of the graft-versus-host response. Conditioned immunosuppression can also help prolong life in NZB mice that develop spontaneous autoimmune disease. Preliminary work of Ader (like old Soviet research) suggests an ability to condition immunoenhancement (personal communication, 1982).

It is difficult to accept the notion of specific responses being controlled by the central nervous system, as claimed by Soviet authors. This specificity would indicate that the central nervous system has recognition capability identical to that of the immune system. The Soviet claims for specific conditioning are controversial because of their choice of antigens and assays. In no instance was this phenomenon controlled for specificity by using two different antigens. Should such phenomena be reproducible with stringent controls, one would have to look for release of stored antigen by the conditioned stimulus. Nonspecific responses, in particular immunosuppression, are much more acceptable and appear to be well proven.

The successful experimental model of immunosuppression described above should serve as a basis for studying the mechanisms of this particular central nervous system intervention and immune response. It is interesting that a bacterial antigen could overcome the effects of suppressive conditioning. Bacterial components may exert an adjuvant activity on the mechanisms that respond to conditioning.

Hypnosis has been used to suppress immune responses but, understandably, only efferent responses. Allergic dermatitis, food allergy (Ikemi & Makagawa, 1963), and urticaria (Kaneko & Talaishi, 1963) were tested. Response to tuberculin was also suppressed by hypnosis in previously sensitized subjects (Black et al., 1963). In the absense of the acute skin reaction, biopsies showed the presence of cellular infiltration, indicating that either lymphokine release was affected or, more probably, there was a lack of response by the target organ (i.e., the capillary system). Recently, it was claimed that hypnosis with imaging (i.e., feeling white blood cells increasing in number and swimming around like strong, powerful sharks attacking weak, confused germs) enhanced pokeweed mitogen stimulation of lymphocytes in young, but not old, subjects (Hall et al., 1981). Only highly hypnotizable subjects were able to increase lymphocyte response.

EFFECT OF NEUROENDOCRINES AND NEUROTRANSMITTERS ON THE IMMUNE RESPONSE

The effect of hormones on immune responses has been the subject of many reviews (Ahlqvist, 1976; Claman, 1975; Dougherty, 1952; Parrillo & Fauci, 1979; Reichlin & MacLean, 1981; Talwar et al., 1975; Wolstenholme & Knight, 1970). The discussion here is restricted to those hormones that are clearly under central nervous system control and have important effects on immune function. Some interaction with immune function has been postulated for virtually all hormones. It is to be hoped that further research in this area will serve to define the important neurohumoral pathways by which the psyche influences the immune response.

Determining which endogenous hormonal functions are important in causing particular physiological effects is not a simple task. Studies that have been carried out in vitro using pharmacological levels of hormones or in vivo by removal of endocrine glands may bypass or significantly alter the very close interrelationship among the various elements of the endocrine system. Profound effects of glucocorticosteroids on the lymphatic system, as well as their extensive and effective use in the

therapy of allergy and inflammation, have conferred a unique position on these hormones in the study of immunology. One is tempted to explain all immunological stress effects by their fate and action; however, in the previous section a number of situations were pointed out in which stress effects do not totally correspond to the levels and kinetics of corticosteroids. Nevertheless, they are probably the most important and certainly the best studied.

Stimulating effects of corticosteroids on lymphocyte proliferation at low concentrations and an inhibitory effect at high concentrations was demonstrated in vitro for animal species (Ambrose, 1964, 1970). An interesting report showed suppression by physiological concentrations of hydrocortisone on in vivo mixed lymphocyte reactions between autologous T and B cells, but not between allogeneic (from different individuals) T and B cells (Ilfeld et al., 1977). This finding suggests that corticosteroids may have a role in suppressing T cell reactions to autoantigens and might explain postulated effects of stress and emotional distress in autoimmune diseases. Corticosteroids were shown to depress lymphoid cytotoxicity in vitro (Rosenau & Moon, 1962). Profound effects of corticosteroids in vitro on NK cell activity were also reported by Parrillo and Fauci (1978).

The hypothesized existence of a feedback loop between the immune system and the hypothalamic-endocrine system has already been mentioned (Besedovsky & Sorkin, 1977). In support of this theory, a series of experiments demonstrated that cortisol levels in the circulation were elevated in response to antigenic stimulation. Levels were highest on day 5 after injection of the primary antigen. Such an endocrine response was postulated as an explanation of the phenomenon of antigenic competition, in which response to one antibody inhibits that to another (Besedovsky et al., 1979). This hypothesis stems from the known fact that corticosteroids suppress precursor cells but not antibody-producing cells; that is, corticosteroids will suppress initiation of responses more profoundly than their persistence. One may speculate broadly as to the usefulness of this hormonal response in restricting the immune response. Such restriction may be useful in preventing the reaction to altered self in the presence of an invading organism that causes tissue destruction. Recently, another effect of the immune response on a neurotransmitter-neurohormone was found, namely, an inverse relationship between the intensity of the immune response and the lowering of splenic epinephrine (Besedovsky et al., 1979).

Receptors for a number of central nervous system–controlled hormones, as well as for neurotransmitters, have been found on lymphocytes or thymocytes. They include receptors for corticosteroids (Cake & Litwack, 1975), insulin (Helderman & Strom, 1978; Krug et al., 1974), testosterone (Abraham & Bug, 1976; Gillette & Gillette, 1979; Grossman et al., 1978), β-endrenergic agents (Hadden et al., 1970; Singh et al., 1979), estrogens (Grossman et al., in press), histamine (Roszkowski et al., 1977), and acetylcholine (Richman & Arnason, 1979). Receptors for growth hormone (Gavin, 1977), but not for prolactin (Arrenbrecht, 1974), have also been reported. A number of these receptors have been identified as playing a role in differentiation of lymphocytes (Cantor & Gershon, 1979; Fabris et al., 1971; Hollenberg & Cuatrecasas, 1974) and in controlling their activity (Helderman & Strom, 1978; Strom et al., 1977).

The pituitary–thymic interaction has long been known (Pierpaoli et al., 1971), and the control of pituitary hormones by the thymus has been proposed (Pierpaoli & Sorkin, 1973). Infused radioactive a^1-thymosin can be found in circumventricular areas that regulate neurohormones (N. Hall, personal communication, 1981). The pituitary hormone that influences immune responses most extensively is growth hormone. It increases the weight of the thymus (Ahlqvist, 1976) and appears to be required in the maturation of antigen percursor cells. It was shown that the production of spleen plague-forming cells from hypophysectomized mice is depressed significantly unless both ACTH and growth hormone are administered (Gisler, 1974; Gisler & Schenkel-Hullinger, 1971). Prolactin appears to increase later antigen expression in vitro (Singh & Owen, 1976). Prolactin may play a significant role in differentiation of T cells during thymic residence. It has been postulated that androgens promote the function of suppressor cells, whereas estrogens favor the development of helper T cells (Graff et al., 1969; Roubinian et al., 1978). Thyroid hormones and thyrotropin are generally thought to be stimulators of immune actions (Ahlqvist, 1976; Aoki et al., 1976). Insulin may have a function in modulating effector activities of lymphocytes. It has been shown that the number of insulin receptors increases in antigen-stimulated lymphocyte membranes and that the cytotoxic effect is augmented by this hormone (Strom et al., 1977). Ahlqvist (1976) proposed a role for such effects in the susceptibility of diabetics to infection.

Not only may immunologically relevant neuroendocrines and neurotransmitters be altered by stress, but immunoactive polypeptides may also be affected by stress. The immunosuppression followed by immunoenhancement of chronic sound stress previously noted can be shown to take place in lymphocytes from normal animals incubated with sera from stressed animals. Separation of these sera by molecular weight suggests a role of polypeptides and cannot be accounted for solely by adrenal cortical steroid hormones (Monjan et al., 1981).

The impact of endorphins on the immune system is under intensive investigation. For example, endorphins have been shown to enhance lymphocyte proliferation (Gilman et al., 1981). Although the issue is still controversial, it seems likely that endorphins are increased in depression, in view of reports of increased analgesia to painful stimuli in affective illness (Davis et al., 1979). This would not be supportive of a role for endorphins in depression-induced immunosuppression. However, endorphin levels appear to be lower in patients with rheumatoid arthritis (Denko, 1981). These patients tend to show decreased immune response, as do patients with other autoimmune diseases; depression and other negative emotions are often prominent in patients with autoimmune diseases.

The catecholamines and histamines are closely involved with the effector activities of the immune system (reviewed by Bourne et al., 1974; Kaliner & Austen, 1974). Briefly, it was shown that β-adrenergic agonists and histamine regulate the release of mast cell granule contents, which have a toxic effect. The effect was closely tied to that of the prostaglandin system. Interaction of these agents with the receptors on the cell membrane caused an increase in intracellular cyclic adenosine 3^1, 5^1-mono phosphate (cAMP) concentration. Similarly, by affecting cAMP/cyclic guanosine 3^1, 5^1-monophosphate (cGMP) ratios, these receptors modulated effects of mitogens on lymphoid cells, strength of mixed lymphocyte reactions, B cell activation and antibody formation, T cell helper functions, antibody-mediated killer cell cytotoxicity, and the release of lysosomal enzyme from neutrophils and macrophages (Coffey et al., 1977; Lee & Reed, 1977; Lee et al., 1977). It has now been found that infusions of norepinephrine significantly increase NK cell activity (S. Locke, personal communication, 1981) and norepinephrine has been tied to behaviors that include outward aggression rather than inward aggression or depression (Antelman & Cagguilo, 1977). On the other hand, it was shown that β-adrenergic agonists can depress the immune response in vivo (Ahlqvist, 1976). Serotonin or a precursor produced marked depression of T cell–dependent, humoral, hemolytic primary immune response in mice and reduction in thymus weight (Bliznakov, 1980).

It is likely that many of the effects of psychological events on the immune system are the result of neuroendocrine and neurotransmitter influences on cyclic nucleotides, the "second messengers," that may have parallel mechanisms in both the central nervous and immune systems (Amkraut & Solomon, 1974; Horowitz et al., 1972).

POSSIBLE MECHANISMS OF STRESS EFFECTS ON IMMUNITY: STRESS-ENDOCRINE RELATIONS

The term "stress" is used primarily to denote pressing *external* demands on the organism, rather than the organism's response to the external stimulus (Mason, 1975a, 1975b). However, in humans the subjective response to the stimulus ("distress," "strain"), not the event itself, seems critical (Jumping out of an airplane presumably is not as stressful to the inveterate sky-diver as to the uninitiated parachutist.) Perhaps the most accepted definition is that of David Glass, who calls stress, "the perception of threat to physical or psychological well-being and the perception that the individual's responses are inadequate to cope with it" (quoted in Holden, 1978).

We assume that an animal is stressed in the presence of an adrenal cortical response, but we should be very cautious about the analogy to human noxious affect. Animals presumably cannot ward off such affects through psychological defenses. Early life experiences in animals, such as holding, or rearing in isolation, can affect adult physiological responses to stress (and immunity as well) (Henry, 1967; Newton & Levine, 1968; Solomon et al., 1966). In monkeys, adrenal cortical activation occurs especially in stresses with a psychological component (e.g., capture, chair restraint, shock avoidance) (Mason et al., 1976). In humans, adrenal cortical activation precedes an unfamiliar anticipated experience, undergoes rapid adaptation as mastery of the situation is gained, and is higher when some kind of task performance (coping) is required (Rahe et al., 1974).

Growth hormone secretion is provoked by a variety of stimuli (Brown & Reichlin, 1972). Such responsiveness is diminished in patients with depressive illness, in whom (in contrast to animals) growth hormone can be stimulated by thyrotropin-releasing hormone (DeLaFuente & Wells, 1981). Usually ACTH and growth hormone responses to stress are dissimilar (Yalow et al., 1969). The responsivity of growth hormone to stress may be related to such personality characteristics as "neuroticism" (Miyabo et al., 1976) and "coronary-proneness" (Friedman et al., 1971). Prolactin is responsive to stress in man, with a secretion pattern different from that of growth hormone (Mirsky, 1957). Direct measurement of thyrotropin-releasing hormone indicates small, if any, increase following psychological stress (Mason et al., 1975). However, it is well documented that clinical hyperthyroidism can be precipitated by an acute emotional stress (Mandelbrote & Wittkower, 1955). Hyperthyroidism may result from failure of specific suppressor T cells in genetically predisposed individuals (Volpe, 1978), or from the direct action of a (stress-precipated?) autoantibody, long-acting thyroid stimulator (Kriss, 1968). Most studies show a clear decrease in testosterone levels during stress, with a poststress recovery to normal levels (Kruez et al., 1972; Nakashima et al., 1975).

Important issues are how these multiple hormone responses may be interrelated and what their ultimate metabolic effect may be at the target tissue level, in this case the immunologically competent cell (Mason, 1968). The ultimate metabolic consequences of a given hormone are influenced strongly by the existing overall "hormonal milieu." Mason (1975a, 1975b), on the basis of considerable experimental evidence, suggested that the multiple endocrine responses to an acute stress are organized in a catabolic–anabolic sequence. The result is enhanced availability of energy substrate (glucose) during the stress as a preparation for "fight or flight," and then poststress restoration of protein and other tissue stores (e.g., glycogen). He postulated a central nervous system "organizer" of these multiple hormonal responses via the autonomic nervous system and the hypothalamic–pituitary–endocrine axis.

Most hormones are secreted in a pulsatile, episodic fashion. Many hormones have 24-hour secretory rhythms; components of the immune system also show a 24-hour periodicity. For example, stimulation of lymphocytes in vitro by mitogens varies directly with the cortisol rhythm (Tavadia et al.,

1975). Thus, timing of stress in relation to naturally occurring rhythms may influence its immunological consequences.

CONCLUSION

There is abundant evidence that emotional factors, particularly failure of psychological defenses, play a role in the onset and course of infectious and neoplastic diseases, resistance to which is immunological, and in the onset and course of allergic and autoimmune diseases, which are associated with immunological abnormalities. Documentation of immunological abnormalities during profound disturbance of CNS function, (namely, mental illness), evidence of stress effects on immunity in animals and humans, neurophysiological data on hypothalamic influences on immunity, and psychological data for behavioral conditioning of immunosuppression all point to a critical role of hormones under CNS control on various aspects of the immune response.

There are a number of mechanisms by which hormones can influence the immunologically competent cell. Stresses that affect these hormones must therefore be considered to be immunomodulators. The stresses may have different effects depending on such factors as sex, metabolic state, age, and the immunogenetic make-up of the subject. General effects may depend on the thymus development of the subject and states of immunological suppression or stimulation, which may be a consequence of the presence of infective agents or their products. Effects on a specific immune response may depend on the state of development of the response at the time at which the stimulus occurs (i.e., the developmental stage of the specific T or B cells). Selective effects on a stage of cell development may also have general consequences. For example, altered immunoglobulin levels in schizophrenics may be due to arrested or accelerated B cell development during transition from the production of one immunoglobulin to the next. Specific effects on different stages of cell development are also implied by the different consequences of stress when applied at different time intervals following the initiation of an immune response.

The effects of numerous hormones on the immune response put in doubt the validity of experiments in which the consequences of administering a single hormone are studied. Clearly, such effects are not akin to the sequence of hormonal changes that occur following an endogenous event. It obviously would be useful to determine the pathways by which the central nervous system is most likely to affect the immune response and the hormones that are involved in this pathway.

The parallel activities of the immune and central nervous systems have been pointed out frequently. The two-way interaction, which as been demonstrated recently by Besedovsky, and co-workers (Besedovsky & Sorkin, 1977; Besedovsky, 1979) makes it appealing to postulate that a cooperative evolutionary development between these two systems has occurred. It is possible that the central nervous system has used the immune system to elicit modification of behavior, e.g., by emitting alarm signals in emergency situations. This function might explain the role of such apparently useless responses as the allergic reaction mediated by IgE. Responses such as itching may constitute a warning against otherwise toxic materials or otherwise unnoticed parasites and may cause useful conscious action to eliminate the intruder. Prior experience certainly modifies the response to current stimuli in both systems.

It is apparent that in the future significant contributions to the behavioral sciences will come from immunologists, as well as from neuropsychologists and endocrinologists. Important developments in prophylaxis and treatment of disease should be expected from the emerging new field of psychoneuroimmunology. The possible role of psychological interventions in prevention and amelioration of distress-induced immunosuppression and in immune enhancement should be studied. Is the "relaxation response," with its vagotonia (as observed during grooming in animals or meditation, biofeedback, and progressive relaxation in man) and euphoria or a sense of well-being, accompanied by immune enhancement (Henry & Meehan, 1981)?

If the immune and central nervous systems are closely linked, not only may understanding of psychophysiology enhance understanding of immune mechanisms, but, as Salk suggested (personal communication, 1981), understanding of cellular and molecular immunology may enhance understanding of mechanisms within the nervous system.

REFERENCES

Abraham AD, & Bug G (1976): Mol Cell Biochem 13:157–163.

Ader R (1981): A historical account of conditioned immunobiologic responses. Ader R (Ed.). In *Psychoneuroimmunology*. New York, Academic Press, pp. 321–354.

Ader R (1982): Behaviorally conditioned immunosuppression and murine systemic lupus erythematosus. Science 215:1534–1536.

Ader R, & Cohen N (1975): Behaviorally conditioned immunosuppression. Psychosom Med 37:333–340.

Ader R, Cohen N, & Grota LJ (1979): Adrenal involvement in conditioned immunosupression. Int J Immunopharmacol 1:141–145.

Ado A, & Goldstein MM (1973): The primary immune response in rabbits after lesion of the different zones in the medial hypothalamus. Ann Alergy 31:585–589.

Ahlqvist J (1976): Endocrine influences on lymphatic organs, immune responses, inflammation and autoimmunity. Acta Endocrinol [Suppl.] (Kbh) 206.

Alarcon-Segovia D, Fishbein E, Centina JA, Rais RJ, & Barrera E (1973): Antigenic specificity of chlorpromazine-induced antinuclear antibodies. Clin Exp Immunol 15:543–548.

Ambrose CT (1964): The requirement for hydrocortisone in antibody forming tissue cultivated serum-free medium. J Exp Med 119:1027–1049.

Ambrose CT (1970): Wolstenholme GEW, Knight J (Eds.). In *Hormones and the Immune Response*. London, Churchill.

Amkraut A, & Solomon GF (1972): Stress and murine sarcoma virus (Maloney)-induced tumors. Cancer Res 32:1428–1433.

Amkraut A, & Solomon GF (1974): From the symbolic stimulus to the pathophysiological response: Immune mechanisms. Int J Psychiatr Med 5:541–563.

Amkraut A, Solomon GF, Allansmith M, McClellan B, & Rappaport M (1973): Immunoglobulins and improvement in acute schizophrenic reactions. Arch Gen Psychiatry 28:673–677.

Amkraut A, Solomon GF, Kasper P, & Purdue A (1972): Adv Exp Med Biol 29:667–674.

Amkraut A, Solomon GF, & Kraemer HC (1971): Stress, early experience and adjuvant-induced arthritis in the rat. Psychosom Med 33:203–214.

Antelman JM, & Cagguilo AR (1977): Norepinephrine-dopamine interactions and behavior. Science 195:646–653.

Aoki N, Wakisaka G, & Nagata I (1976): Effects of thyroxine on T-cell counts and tumour cell rejection in mice. Acta Endocrinol (Kbh) 81:104–109.

Arrenbrecht S (1974): Specific binding of growth hormone to thymocytes. Nature 252:255–257.

Bartrop RW, Lazarus I, Luckhurst E, et al. (1977): Depressed lymphocyte function after bereavement. Lancet 1:834–836.

Besedovsky HO, del Rey A, Sorkin E, DaPrada M, & Keller HH (1979): Immunoregulation mediated by the sympathetic nervous system. Cell Immunol 48:346–355.

Besedovsky HO, & Sorkin E (1977): Network of immune–neuroendocrine interactions. Clin Exp Immunol 27:1–12.

Black S, Humphrey JH, & Niven JS (1963): Inhibition of mantou reaction by direct suggestion under hypnosis. Br Med J 1649–1653.

Bliznakov EG (1980): Serotonin and its precursors as modulators of the immunological responsiveness in mice. J Med (Basel) 11:81–105.

Bock E (1978): Protein in blood and cerebrospinal fluid. Bergsma D, Goldstein AL (Eds.). In *Neurochemical and Immunologic Components in Schizophrenia*. New York, Liss, pp. 283–295.

Boehme NM, & Kurnick JE (1981): Autoerythrocyte sensitization. West J Med 134:441–442.

Bourne HR, Lichtenstein LM, Melmon KL, Henney CS, Weinstein Y, & Shearer GM (1974): Modulation of inflammation and immunity by cyclic AMP. Science 184:19–28.

Brown DG, & Young AJ (1965): The effect of extraversion on susceptibility to disease: A validatory study on contact dermatitis. J Psychosom Res 8:421–429.

Brown GM, & Reichlin S (1972): Psychologic and neural regulation of growth hormone secretion. Psychosom Med 34:45–61.

Burian L, Kubikova A, & Krejeova O (1964): Human antiglobulins in the serum of schizophrenic patients. Cesk Psychiatr 60:26–29.

Cake MH, & Litwack G (1975): Litwack G (Ed.). In *Biochemical Actions of Hormones*. New York, Academic Press, pp. 317–390.

Cantor H, & Gershon RK (1979): Immunological circuits: Cellular composition. Fed Proc 38:2058–2064.

Certcov D (1969): Immunity and mental illness. Ann Med Psychol (Paris) 127:733–742.

Chang SS, & Rasmussen AF Jr (1964): Bacteriol Proc 64:134.

Christian JJ, & Williamson HO (1958): Effects of crowding on experimental granuloma formation in mice. Proc Soc Exp Biol Med 99:385–387.

Claman HM (1975): How corticosteroids work. J Allergy Clin Immunol 55:145–151.

Cobb S (1974): Physiologic changes in men whose jobs were abolished. J Psychosom Res 18:245–258.

Cobb S (1976): Social support as a moderator of life stress. Psychosom Med 38:300–314.

Coffey RG, Hadden EM, & Hadden JW (1977): Evidence for cyclic GMP and calcium mediation of lymphocyte activation by mitogens. J Immunol 119:1387–1394.

Cohen N, Ader R, Green N, & Bovbjerg D (1979): Conditioned suppression of a thymus-independent antibody response. Psychosom Med 41:487–491.

Cohen-Cole S, Cogen R, Stevens A, Kirk K, Gaitan E, Hein J, & Freeman A (1981): Psychosocial, endocrine, and immune factors in acute necrotizing ulcerative gingivitis (trenchmouth). Psychosom Med 43:91 (Abstract).

Davis GC, Buchsbaum MS, & Bunney WE Jr (1979): Analgesia to painful stimuli in affective illness. Am J Psychiatry 136:1148–1151.

DeLaFuente JR, & Wells LA (1981): Human growth hormone in psychiatric disorders. J Clin Psychiatry 42:270–274.

Denko CW (1981): B-Endorphin levels lower in arthritis patients. JAMA 246:203.

Dolin AO, Krylov VN, Luk'ianenko VI, & Flerov BA (1960): Zh Vyssh Nerv Deiat 10:832–841.

Domashneva IV, & Maznina TP (1976): Clinical–immunological correlations in the study of antithymic antibodies in schizophrenia. Zh Nevropatol Psikhiatr 76:78–81.

Dorian BJ, Keystone E, Garfinkel PE, & Brown GM (1981): Corticosteroids and lymphoid cells in vitro. I. Hydrocortisone lysis of human guinea pig, and mouse thymus cells. Science 213:1397–1400.

Dougherty TF (1952): Effect of hormones on lymphatic tissue. Physiol Rev 32:379–401.

Engel G (1953): Studies of ulcerative colitis III. Am J Med 19:231–256.

Erban L (1965): Viability changes of white blood cells in patients with schizophrenic reaction. J Psychiatr Res 3:73–77.

Fabris N, Pierpaoli W, & Sorkin E (1971): Hormones and the immunological capacity. IV. Restorative effects of developmental hormones or of lymphocytes on the immunodeficiency syndrome of the dwarf mouse. Clin Exp Immunol 9:227–240.

Felsenfeld O, Hill CW, & Green WE (1966): Trans R Soc Trop Med Hyg 60: 514–518.

Fessel WJ (1961): Disturbed serum proteins in chronic psychosis. Arch Gen Psychiatry 4:154–159.

Fessel WJ (1963): The antibrain factors in psychiatric patients' sera. Arch Gen Psychiatry 8:614–621.

Fessel WJ, & Forsythe RP (1963): Hypothalamic role in control of gamma globulin levels. Arthritis Rheum 6:770 (Abstract).

Fessel WJ, & Grunbaum BW (1961): Electrophoretic and analytical ultracentrifuge studies in sera of psychotic patients: Elevation of gamma globulins and macroglobulins and splitting of alpha globulins. Ann Intern Med 54:1134–1145.

Fessell WJ, & Hirata-Hibi M (1963): Abnormal leukocyte in schizophrenia. Arch Gen Psychiatry 9:91–103.

Fessel WJ, Hirata-Hibi M, & Shapiro IM (1965): Genetic and stress factors affecting the abnormal lymphocyte in schizophrenia. J Psychiatr Res 3:275–283.

Fessel WJ, & Solomon GP (1960): Psychosis and systematic lupus erythematosus. A review of the literature and case reports. Calif Med 92:265–270.

Folch H, & Wakeman BH (1974): The splenic suppressor cell. (1) Activity of thymus-dependent adherent cells: Change with age and stress. J Immunol 113:127–139.

Fowle AM (1968): Atypical leukocyte pattern of schizophrenic children. Arch Gen Psychiatry 18:666–680.

Frank JA, & Dougherty TF (1953): Evaluation of susceptibility to stress stimuli determined by "stress" lymphocytes. Fed Proc 12:45–46.

Friedman M, Byers SO, Rosenman RH, & Neuman R (1971): Cornary-prone individuals (Type A behavior patterns) growth hormone responses. JAMA 217:929.

Friedman SB, Ader R, & Glasgow LA (1965): Effects of psychological stress in adult mice inoculated with Coxsackie B viruses. Psychosom Med 27:361–368.

Friedman SB, Cohen J, & Iker H (1967): Antibody response to cholera vaccine. Arch Gen Psychiatry 16:312–315.

Friedman SB, Ader R, & Grota LJ (1973): Protective effect of noxious stimulation in mice infected with rodent malaria. Psychosom Med 35:535–537.

Friedman SB, & Glasgow LA (1973): Interaction of mouse strain and differential housing upon resistance to plasmodium berghei. J Parasitol 59:851–854.

Funk GA, & Jensen MM (1967): Influence of stress on granuloma formation. Proc Soc Exp Biol Med 124:653–655.

Gavin JR III (1977): Comprehensive immunology. Hadden JW, & Coffey RG (Eds.). In *Immunopharmacology.* New York, Plenum Press, pp. 357–388.

Gilman LC, Schwartz JM, Milner J, Bloom LE, & Feldman JD (1981): *Enhancement of lymphocyte proliferative responses by beta-endorphins. Paper presented to Society for Microscience.*

Gillette S, Gillette RW (1979): Changes in thymic estrogen receptor expression following orchidectomy. Cell Immunol 2:194–196.

Gisler RH (1974): Psychother Psychosom 23:197–208.

Gisler RH, Bussard AE, Mazie JC, & Hess R (1971): Hormonal regulation of the immune response: Induction of an immune response in vitro with lymphoid cells from mice exposed to acute system stress. Cell Immunol 2:634–645.

Gisler RH, & Schenkel-Hullinger L (1971): Hormonal regulation of the immune system. II. Influence of pituitary and adrenal activity on immune responsiveness in vitro. Cell Immunol 2:646–657.

Glebov VS, & Zil'bersheteyn AA (1975): Zh Nevropatol Psikhiatr 75:82–87.

Goetzl EJ, Austin KF (1977): Comprehensive immunology. Hadden JW, & Coffey RG (Eds.). In *Immunopharmacology.* New York, Plenum, pp. 113–124.

Goldstein AL, & Rossio J (1980): Immunological components in schizophrenia. Baxter C, & Melnechak T (Eds.). In *Perspectives in Schizophrenia Research.* New York, Raven Press, pp. 249–267.

Gosheva AE, Domashneva IV, Kobrinsky GD, Kushner SG, & Podozerova NP (1969): A study into immunological reaction of delayed type in schizophrenic patients. News Sci Acad Med USSR 4:70–75.

Gowdy JM (1980): Immunoglobulin levels in psychotic patients. Psychosomatics 21:751–756.

Graff RJ, Lappe MA, & Snell GD (1969): The influence of the gonads and adrenal glands on the immune response to skin grafts. Transplantation 7:105–111.

Greene WA, Betts RF, Ochitill HN, Iker HP, & Douglas RG (1978): Paper presented at annual meeting of the American Psychosomatic Society, Washington, DC, March.

Greenfield ML, Roessles R, & Crosby AP (1959): Ego strength and length of recovery from infectious mononucleosis. J Nerv Ment Dis 128:125–128.

Grinker RR Jr, & Robbins FP (1954): Some factors concerned in a case of multiple sclerosis. In *Psychosomatic Case Book*. New York, Blakeston.

Gross WB (1972): Effect of social stress on occurrence of marek's disease in chickens. Am J Vet Res 33:2275–2279.

Grossmon CJ, Nathan P, & Sholiton LJ (1978): Biol Rep 18: [Suppl 1] 48A.

Grossman CJ, Sholiton LJ, & Blaha GC (in press): J Steroid Biochem.

Grunbaum BW, Forrest FM, & Kirk PL (1964): The serum proteins in the alcoholic and mentally ill treated with chlorpromazine. Proc Soc Exp Biol Med 117:195–198.

Gunderson EK, & Rahe RH (Eds.). (1974): *Life Stress and Illness*. Springfield, Ill, Thomas.

Hadden JW, Hadden EM, & Middleton E Jr (1970): Lymphocyte blast transformation. I. Demonstration of adrenergic receptors in human peripheral lymphocytes. J Cell Immunol 1:583–595.

Hall H, Lango S, & Dixon R (1981): Endocrine influences on lymphatic organs, immune responses, inflammation and autoimmunity. Unpublished manuscript.

Heath RG (1969): Schizophrenia: Evidence of a pathologic immune mechanism. Proc Am Psychopathol Assoc 58: 234–236.

Heath RG, & Krupp IM (1967): Schizophrenia as an immunologic disorder. I. Demonstration of antibrain globulins by fluorescent antibody techniques. Arch Gen Psychiatry 16:1–9.

Heath RG, Martens S, Leach BE, Cohen N, & Angel C (1957): Effect on behavior in humans with the administration of taraxein. Am J Psychiatry 114:14–24.

Heath RG, Krupp IM, & Byers LW (1967a): Schizophrenia as an immunologic disorder. II. Effects of serum protein fractions on brain function. Arch Gen Psychiatry 16:10–23.

Heath RG, Krupp IM, Byers LW, & Liljekvist JI (1967b): Schizophrenia as an immunologic disorder. III. Effects of antimonkey and antihuman brain antibody on brain function. Arch Gen Psychiatry 16:24–33.

Helderman JH, & Strom TB (1978): Specific insulin binding site on T and B lymphocytes as a marker of cell activation. Nature 274:62–63.

Hendrie HC, Paraskevas F, Batagar FD, & Adamson JD (1971): Stress immunoglobulin levels and early polyarthritis. J Pschosom Res 15:337–342.

Hendrie HC, Paraskevas F, & Varsamis J (1972): Gamma globulin levels in psychiatric patients. Can Psychiatr Assoc J 17:93–97.

Henry JP (1967): The use of psychosocial stimuli to induce prolonged systolic hypertension in mice. Psychosom Med 29:408–432.

Henry JP, & Meehan JP (1981): Psychosomatic medicine, its principles and application. Weiner H, Hofer MA,

Stunkard AJ, (Eds.). In *Brain Behavior and Bodily Disease*. New York, Raven Press, pp. 305–333.

Hill CW, Greer WE, & Felsenfeld O (1967): Psychological stress, early response to foreign protein and blood cortisol in vervets. Psychosom Med 29:279–283.

Hirata-Hibi M, & Fessel WJ (1964): The bone marrow in schizophrenia. Arch Gen Psychiatry 10:414–419.

Holden C (1978): Cancer and the mind: How are they connected? Science 200:1363–1369.

Hollenberg MD, & Cuatrecasas P (1974): Clarkson B, Basegas R (Eds.). In *Control of Proliferation of Animals Cells*. Cold Spring Harbor, NY, Cold Spring Harbor Laboratories, pp. 423–434.

Holmes TH, Hawkins NG, Bowerman CE, Clarke ER, & Joffe JP (1957): Psychosocial and psychophysiologic studies of tuberculosis. Psychosom Med 19:134–143.

Horowitz S, Borcherding W, Moorthy AV, Chesney R, Schulte-Wisserman H, & Hong R (1977): Induction of suppressor T cells in systemic lupus erythematosus by thymosin and cultured thymic epithelium. Science 197: 999–1001.

Horowitz ZP, Beer B, Clody DE, Vogel JR, & Chasin M (1972): Cyclic AMP and anxiety. Psychosomatics 13:85–92.

Hussar AE, Cradle JL, & Beiser SM (1971): A study of the immunologic and allergic responsiveness of chronic schizophrenics. Br J Psychiatry 118:91–92.

Ikemi Y, & Makagawa S (1963): Psychological factors affecting the occurence of bronchial asthma. J Med Psychol 50:454–474.

Il'enko VI, & Kovaleva GA (1960): Zh Mikrobiol Epidemiol Immunobiol 31:108–113.

Ilfeld DN, Krakauer RS, & Blaese RM (1977): Suppression of the human autologus mixed lymphocyte reaction by physiologic concentrations of hydrocortisone. J Immunol 119:428–434.

Imboden JB, Carter A, & Leighton EC (1961): Convalescence from influenza. Arch Intern Med 108:393–399.

Imboden JB, Carter A, Leighton EC, & Treva AU (1959): Brucellosis. Arch Intern Med 103:406–414.

Issidorides MR, Stefanis CN, Varsou E, & Katsorchis T (1975): Altered chromatin ultrastructure in neutrophils of schizophrenics. Nature 258:612–614.

Jacobs MA, Spilken A, & Norman M (1969): Relationship of life change, maladaptive aggression and upperrespiratory infection in male college students. Psychosom Med 31:33–42.

Jacobs MA, Spilken A, Norman M, & Anderson LS (1970): Life Stress and respiratory illness. Psychosom Med 32:233–242.

Jankovic BD, & Isakovic K (Eds.). (1973a): *Microenvironmental Aspects of Immunity*. New York, Plenum Press, pp. 667–674.

Jankovic BD, & Isakovic K (1973b): Neuro-endocrine correlates of immune response: I. Effects of brain lesions on antibody production, arthus reactivity and delayed hypersensitivity in the rat. Int Arch Allergy 45:360–372.

Jankovic BD, Jovanova K, & Markovic BM (1979): Periodocum Biol 81:211–212.

Jensen MM (1969): Influence of stress on murine leukemia virus infection. Proc Soc Exp Biol Med 127:610–614.

Jensen MM, & Rasmussen AJ (1963): Stress and susceptibility to viral infection. J Immunol 90:17–20.

Joassod A, & McKenzie JM (1976): Int Arch Allergy Appl Immunol 50:659–663.

Johnsson T, Lavender JF, Hultin F, & Rasmussen AF Jr (1963): The influence of avoidance-learning stress on resistance to Coxsackie B virus in mice. J Immunol 91:569–575.

Johnsson T, & Rasmussen AF Jr (1965): Arch Gesamte Virusforsch 18: 393–396.

Kaliner M, & Austen KF (1974): Cyclic nucleotides and modulation of effector systems of inflammation. Biochem Pharmacol 23:763–771.

Kamoshita J, Yamaguchi M, Katsura J, Amaki I, & Makjima A (1979): Acta Med Kinki Univ 4:447–458.

Kamp HV (1962): Nuclear changes in the white blood cells of patients with schizophrenic reaction. A preliminary report. J Neuropsychiatry 4:1–3.

Kaneko A, & Takaishi N (1963): Psychosomatic studies on chronic urticaria. Folia Psychiatr Neurol Jpn 17:16–24.

Keller SE, Stein M, Camerino MS, Schleifer SJ, & Sherman J (1980): Cellular Immunology.

Keller SE, Weiss J, Schliefer SJ, Miller MD, & Stein M (1981): Suppression of immunity by stress: Effect of a graded series of stressors on lymphocyte stimulation in the rat. Science 213:1397–1400.

Kerbikov OV (1961): Immunological reactivity in schizophrenia as influenced by some modern drugs. Ann NY Acad Sci 92:1098–1104.

Klopfer B (1957): Psychological variables in human cancer. J Prof Tech 21:331–340.

Kolyaskina GT, & Kushnir SG (1969): Concerning some regularities in the appearance of antibrain antibodies in the blood serum of schizophrenic patients. J Neuropathol Psychol USSR 69:1679–1682.

Konovalov GV, Korneva EA, & Khai LM (1971): Effect of destruction of the posterior hypothalamic area on the experimental allergic polyneuritis. Brain Res 29:283–386.

Korneva EA (1967): The effects of stimulating different mesencephalic structures on protective immune response pattern. Fiziol Zh SSSR 53:42–45.

Korneva EA, & Khari LM (1963): Effects of destruction of hypothalamic areas on immogenesis. Fiziol Zh SSSR 49:42–46.

Kreuz LE, Rose RM, & Jennings JR (1972): Suppression of plasma testosterone levels and psychological stress. Arch Gen Psychiatry 26:479.

Kriss JP (1968): The long-acting thyroid stimulator. Calif Med 109:202–213.

Krug U, Krug F, & Cuatrecasas P (1974): Emergence of insulin receptors on human lymphocytes during in vitro transformation. Proc Natl Acad Sci USA 69:2604–2608.

LaBarba RC (1970): Experimental and environmental factors in cancer. A review of research with animals. Psychosom Med 32:259–276.

Lee TP, Bussee WW, & Reed CE (1977): Effects of beta adrenergic agonists, prostaglandins and cortisol on lymphocyte levels, cyclic adenosine monophosphate and glycogen J Allergy Clin Immunol 59:408–413.

Lee TP, & Reed CE (1977): Effects of steroids on the regulation of the levels of cyclic AMP in human lymphocytes. Biochem Biophys Res Commun 78: 998–1004.

LeShan LL, & Worthington RE (1956): Personality as factor in pathogenesis of cancer: Review of literature. Br J Med Psychol 29:49–56.

Liedermann RR, & Prilipko LL (1978): The behavior of T lymphocytes in schizophrenia. Bergsma D, Goldstein AL, (Eds.). In *Neurochemical and Immunologic Components in Schizophrenia*. New York, Liss, pp. 365–377.

Lockard VG, Grogan JB, & Brunson JG (1973): Alterations in the bactericidal ability of rabbit alveolar macrophages as a result of tumbling stress. Am J Pathol 70:57–62.

Locke SE, Hurst MW, Heisel JS (1978): Paper presented at annual meeting of the American Psychosomatic Society, Washington, DC, April.

Luk'ianenko VI (1959): On the role of the conditioned reflex in the regulation of the immune reaction. Zh Mikrobiol Epidemiol Immunobiol 30:53–59.

Luk'ianenko VI (1961): The problem of conditioned reflex regulation of immuno-biological reactions. Usp Sovrem Biol 51:170–187.

Luparello TJ, Stein M, & Park CD (1964): Effect of hypothalamic lesions on rat anaphylaxis. Am J Physiol 209:911–914.

Macris NT, Schiavi RC, Camerino MS, & Stein M (1972): Effect of hypothalamic lesions on immune processes in the guinea pig. Am J Physiol 219:1205–1209.

Mandelbrote BM, & Wittkower E (1955): Emotional factors in Grave's disease. Psychosom Med 17:109–117.

Mason JW (1968): "Over-all" hormonal balance as a key to endocrine organization. Psychosom Med 30:791–808.

Mason JW (1975a): A historical view of the stress field. J Hum Stress 1(1):6,1(2):22.

Mason JW (1975b): Levi L (Ed.). In *Emotions—Their Parameters and Measurement*. New York, Raven, pp. 143–181.

Mason JW, Hartley LH, Kotchen TA, Wherry FE, Pennington LL, & Jones JG (1975): Plasma thyroid-stimulating hormone response in anticipation of muscular exercise in humans. J Clin Endocrinol Metab 37:403.

Mason JW, Maher JT, Hartley LH, Mougey EH, Perlow MJ, & Jones LG (1976): Serban G (Ed.). In *Psychopathology of Human Adaptation*. New York, Plenum Press, pp. 147–171.

Matvetts LS, Olsuf'ev NG, Il'inshii Yua A, & Zharikov NM (1957): Immunological reactivity in persons suffering from derangement of the central nervous system to tularaemia vaccination. Zh Mikrobiol Epidemiol Immunobiol. 9:1263-1268.

Metrop PJG, & Vesser P (1969): Influence on the induction and elicitation of contact-dermatitis in guinea pigs. Phychophysiology 8:45-53.

Meyer RJ, & Haggerty RJ (1962): Streptococcal infections in families: Factors altering individual susceptibilities. J Pediatr 29:539-549.

Mirsky A (1957): The psychosomatic approach to the etiology of clinical disorders. Psychosom Med 19:424-430.

Miyabo S, Hisada T, Asata T, Mizushima N, & Ueno K (1976): Growth hormone and cortisol responses to psychological stress: Comparison of normal and neurotic subjects. J Clin Endocrinol Metab 42:1158.

Molholm HB (1942): Hyposensitivity to foreign protein in schizophrenic patients. Psychiatr Q 16:570-571.

Monjan AA (1981): Stress and immunologic competence studies in animals. Ader R (Ed.). In *Psychoneuroimmunology*. New York, Academic Press, pp. 185-217.

Monjan AA, & Collector MI (1977): Stress-induced modulation of the immune response. Science 196:307-308.

Monjan AA, Collector MI, & Guchait RB (1981): Stress-induced modulation of lymphocyte reactivity: Role of humoral factors. Unpublished manuscript, Johns Hopkins University.

Moos RH, & Solomon GF (1965): Personality correlates of the degree of functional incapacity of patients with physical disease. J Chronic Dis 18:1019-1038.

Moos RH, & Solomon GF (1969): Personality correlates of the rapidity of progression of rheumatoid arthritis. Ann Rheum Dis 23:145-151.

Nakashima A, Koshiyama K, Uozumi T, Monden Y, Hamanaka Y, Kurachi K, Aono T, Mizutani S, & Matsumoto K (1975): Effects of general anesthesia and severity of surgical stress on serum LH and testosterone in males. Acta Endocrinol 78:258.

Newton G, & Levine S (Eds.) (1968): *Early Experience and Behavior. The Psychobiology of Development.* Springfield, Ill, Thomas.

Otto R, & Mackay I (1967): Psychosocial and emotional disturbance in systemic lupus erythematosus. Med J Aust 2:488-493.

Palmblad J (1979): Activation of the bacteriocidal capacity of polymorphonuclear granulocytes after surgery, measured with a new in vitro assay. Scand J Haematol 23:10-16.

Palmblad J, Cantell K, Holm G, Norberg R, Strander H, & Sundblad L (1977a): Acute energy deprivation in man: Effect on serum immunoglobulins antibody response, complement. Clin Exp Immunol 30:50-55.

Palmblad J, Levi L, Burger A, Melander A, Westgren U, von Schenk H, & Skude G (1977b): Effects of total energy withdrawal (fasting) on the levels of growth hormone, thyrotropin, cortisol, adrenaline, noradrenaline, T4, T3, and rT3 in healthy males. Acta Med Scand 201:15-22.

Palmblad J, Karlson CG, Levi L, & Liberg T (1979a): The erythrocyte sedimentation rate and stress. Acta Med Scand 205:517-520.

Palmblad J, Petrini B, Wasserman J, & Akerstedt T (1979b): Lymphocyte and granulocyte reactions during sleep deprivation. Psychosom Med 41: 273-278.

Parrillo JE, & Fauci AS (1978): Comparison of the effector cells in human spontaneous cellular cytotoxicity and antibody-dependent cellular cytotoxicity: Differential sensitivity of effector cells to in vivo and in vitro corticosteroids. Scand J Immunol 8:99-107.

Parrillo JE, & Fauci AS (1979): Mechanisms of glucocorticoid action on immune processes. Ann Rev Pharmacol Toxicol 19:179-201.

Pavlidis N, & Chirigos M (1980): Stress-induced impairment of macrophage tumoricidal function. Psychosom Med 42:47-54.

Pennington VM (1963): A study to determine possible difference in the formed blood elements of normal and schizophrenic subjects. J Neuropsychiatry 5:21-28.

Pettingale KW, Greer S, & Tee DE (1977): Serum IgA and emotional expression in breast cancer patients. J Psychosom Res 21:395-399.

Pierpaoli W, & Sorkin E (1973): Adv Exp Med Biol 29:651-654.

Pierpaoli W, Fabris N, & Sorkin E (1971): Cohen S, Cuckowicz G, & McCluskey RT (Eds.). In *Cellular Interaction in the Immune Response.* Basel, Karger, pp. 25-30.

Plaut SM, Friedman SB, & Grota JL (1971): Plasmodium berghei: Resistance to infection in group and individually housed mice. Exp Parasitol 29:47-52.

Pulkkinen E (1977): Immunoglobulins, psychopathology and prognosis in schizophrenia. Acta Psychiatr Scand 56:173-182.

Rahe RH (1978): Life changes and illness studies: Past history and future direction. J Hum Stress 4:3-15.

Rahe RH, Rubin RT, & Arthur RJ (1974): The three investigators study. Serum uric acid, cholesterol and cortisol variability during stresses of everyday life. Psychosom Med 36:258-268.

Rasmussen AF, Marsh JT, & Brill NQ (1957): Increased susceptibility to herpes simplex in mice subjected to avoidance learning stress or restraint. Proc Soc Exp Biol Med 96:183-189.

Rasmussen AF Jr, Spencer ES, & Marsh JT (1959): Decrease in susceptibility of mice to passive anaphylaxis following avoidance-learning stress. Proc Soc Exp Biol Med 100:878-879.

Reichlin S, & MacLean DB (1981): Neuroendocrinology and the immune process. Ader R (Eds.). In *Psychoneuroimmunology*. New York, Academic Press, pp. 475-520.

Reinberg EL, Rubenstin A, Geha RS, Strelkouskas AJ, Rosen FS, & Schlossman SF (1979): Abnormalities of immunoregulatory T cells in disorders of immune function. New Engl J Med 301:1018-1022.

Richman DP, & Arnason BG (1979): Nicotinic acetyl-choline receptor: Evidence for a functionally distinct receptor on human lymphocytes. Proc Natl Acad Sci USA 76:4632–4635.

Riley V (1979): Cancer and stress: Overview and critique. Cancer Detect Prev 2:163–195.

Rogers MP, Reich P, Strom TB, & Carpenter CB (1976): Behaviorally conditioned immunosuppression: Replication of a recent study. Psychosom Med 38:447–452.

Rosenau W, & Moon HD (1962): The inhibitory effect of hydrocortisone on lysis of homologous cells by lymphocytes in vitro. J Immunol 89:422–426.

Roszkowski W, Plaut M, & Lichtenstein LM (1977): Selective display of histamine receptors on lymphocytes. Science 195:683–685.

Rothermich NO, & Philips VL (1963): Rheumatoid arthritis in criminal and mentally ill populations. Arthritis Rheum 6:639–640.

Roubinian JR, Talal N, Greenspan JS, Goodman JR, & Siiteri PK (1978): Effect of castration and sex hormone treatment on survival, anti-nucleic acid antibodies and glomerulonephritis in NZB/NZW F1 Mice. J Exp Med 147:1568–1581.

Salk J (1962): Biological basis of disease and behavior. Perspect Biol Med 5:198–206.

Saul LJ, & Bernstein C (1941): Emotional settings of some attacks of urticaria. Psychosom Med 3:349–369.

Schiavi RC, Adams J, & Stein M (1966): Effect of hypothalamic lesions on histamine toxicity in the guinea pig. Am J Physiol 211:1269–1273.

Seifter E, Rettura G, Zisblatt M, Levenson SM, Levine N, Davidson A, & Seifter J (1973): Enhancement of tumor development in physically-stressed mice inoculated with an oncogenic virus. Experientia 29:1379–1382.

Sethi N, Sethi BB, & Kumar RAJ (1973): A family study of atypical lymphocytes in schizophrenia. Indian J Psychiatry 15:267–271.

Singh U, Millson DS, Smith P, & Owen JJT (1979): Identification of beta adrenoreceptors during thymocyte otogeny in mice. Eur J Immunol 9:31–35.

Singh U, & Owen JJT (1976): Studies on the maturation of thymus stem cells—The effects of catecholamines, histamine and peptide hormones on expression of T-cell alloantigens. Eur J Immunol 6:59–62.

Solomon GF (1969): Stress and antibody response in rats. Int Arch Allergy 35:97–104.

Solomon GF (1981): Emotional and personality factors in the onset and cause of auto-immune disease, particularly rheumatoid arthritis. Ader R (Ed.). In Psychoneuroimmunology. New York, Academic Press, pp. 159–184.

Solomon GF, Allansmith M, McClellan B, & Amkraut AA, (1969): Immunoglobulins in psychiatric patients. Arch Gen Psychiatry 20:272–277.

Solomon GF, & Amkraut AA, Psychoneuroendocrine effects on the immune response. Ann Rev Microbiol 35:155–184.

Solomon GF, Merigan TC, & Levine S (1967): Variations in adrenal cortical hormones within physiologic ranges, stress and interferon production in mice. Proc Soc Exp Biol Med 126:74–79.

Solomon GF, Moos RH, Fessel WJ, & Morgan EE (1966): Globulins and behavior in schizophrenia. Int J Neuropsychiatry 2:20–26.

Solomon GF, & Moos RH (1964): Emotions, immunity and disease. Arch Gen Psychiatry 11:657–674.

Solomon GF, & Moos RH (1965a): Psychological aspects of response to treatment in rheumatoid arthritis. GP 32:113–119.

Solomon GF, & Moos RH (1965b): The relationship of personality to the presence of rheumatoid factor in asymptomatic relatives of patients with rheumatoid arthritis. Psychosom Med 27:350–360.

Stein M, Schiavi RC, & Camerino MS (1976): Influence of brain and behavior on the immune system. Science 191:435–440.

Stein M, Schleifer SJ, & Keller JE (1981): Hypothalamic influences on immune responses. Ader R (Ed.). In Psychoneuroimmunology. New York, Academic Press, pp. 429–448.

Strom TB, Lundin AP, & Carpenter CB (1977): The role of cyclic nucleotides in lymphocyte activation and function. Prog Clin Immunol 3:115–153.

Talwar GP, Hanjan SNS, Saxena RK, Pandian MR, Gupta PD, & Bhattarai QB (1975): Talwar GP (Ed.). In Regulation of Growth and Differentiated Function in Eukaryote Cells. New York, Raven Press, pp. 271–281.

Tavadia HB, Fleming KA, Hume PD, & Simpson HW (1975): Circadian rhythmicity of human plasma cortisol and PHA-induced lymphocyte transformation. Clin Exp Immunol 22:190.

Thrasher SG, Bernardis LL, & Cohen S (1971): The immune response in hypothalamic-lesioned and hypophysectomized rats. Int Arch Allergy 41:813–820.

Torrey EF (1977): CSF better than serum in study of immunology in mental patients. Clin Psychiatry News 5:5.

Torrey EF, & Peterson MR (1976): The viral hypothesis of schizophrenia. Schizo Bull 2:136–146.

Vanderkamp H (1968): The abnormal lymphocytes in schizophrenia. Int J Neuropsychiat 4:4–5.

Vartanian ME, Kolyaskina GI, Lozovsky DV, Burbaeva G Sh, & Ignatov SA (1978): Aspects of humoral and cellular immunity in schizophrenia. Bergsman D, & Goldstein AL (Eds.). In Neurochemical and Immunologic Components in Schizophrenia. New York, Liss, pp. 339–364.

Vaughn WT Jr, Sullivan JD, & Elmadjian F (1949): A survey of the ability of schizophrenic patients to develop an active immunity following the injection of pertussis vaccine. Psychosom Med 2:327–333.

Volpe R (1978): The pathogenesis of Grave's disease—An overview. Clin Endocrinol Metab 7:3.

Wayner ER, Flannery GR, & Singer G (1978): Physiol Behav 21:995–1000.

Weiner H (1977): Bronchial asthma. In Psychobiology and Human Disease. New York, Elsevier, pp. 223–317.

Weksler ME, & Hutteroth TH (1974): Impaired lymphocyte function in aged humans. J Clin Invest 53:99–104.

Wolstenholme GEW, & Knight J (1970): Hormones and the Immune Response. London, Churchill.

Yalow RS, Versano-Sharon N, Echemendia E, & Berson SA (1969): HGH and ACTH secretory responses to stress. Horm Metab Res 1:3.

PART IV

Theoretical Perspectives

15

Emotion: Toward A Biopsychosocial Paradigm

Bruce W. Heller

The search for an adequate understanding of emotion began with the earliest myths, art, and folk beliefs of our species. It was initiated in a more formal way by the Pre-Socratics (Cleve, 1969), and carried on during the ensuing two millennia by many great minds, including such philosophers as Plato, Aristotle, Aguinas, Descartes, Hobbes, Spinoza, Nietzsche, and Sartre (Gardiner et al., 1937), psychologists such as Wundt, James, McDougall, and Freud, and biologists such as Darwin and Cannon.

Unfortunately, neither philosophical nor scientific methods have prevailed: an adequate theory—or even a commonly agreed-upon definition of the phenomenon—remains elusive. Summing up previous work in the field, Claparede (1928), for example, declared that emotion was "the most confused chapter in all psychology." Subsequent evaluations of the state of the art have continued to reaffirm this view (Hebb, 1949; Lazarus et al., 1970; Plutchik, 1962). Within the past 10 years, however, the investigation of this phenomenon has become more systematic. Instruments and methods have been developed that point toward a growing commonality of approach, and, ultimately, of findings.

Questions proliferate in the field of emotion; answers are scarce. At the most basic level, one might ask if the term "emotion" has any meaning at all. For some investigators the term is too vague to be useful (Kagan, 1978). For some, emotions do not all fit into a single class (Rorty, 1980). For others, emotional terms are confusing and unnecessary; they exclude them from their lexicon, substituting terms such as "activation" or "arousal" (Duffy, 1962; Lindsley, 1951). Still others consider "arousal" itself an imprecise and useless label for a group of processes that do not themselves fit into a single class (Lacey, 1967).

If one grants that the terms "emotion" and "arousal" *do* have meaning, many other questions arise. Is arousal a necessary condition for emotional experience (Schachter & Singer, 1962), or is it inessential (Leventhal, 1979)? Are emotions passive, representing unlearned reaction patterns (Watson, 1929), learned responses (Hebb, 1949), or autonomic system arousal (Wenger et al., 1956); or are they active, representing constructions of cognitions and arousal (Mandler, 1975), adaptive coping mechanisms (Lazarus, 1968) and judgments (Jung 1923; Solomon, 1980)? Are emotions irrational or rational (De Sousa, 1980)? Are emotions universal (Darwin, 1872; Eibl-Eibesfeldt, 1971; Ekman et al., 1969; Izard, 1971) or culturally relative (Birdwhistell, 1970; Klineberg, 1938; La Barre, 1947; Mead, 1975)?

There is disagreement as to whether cognitions must precede emotions (Lazarus, 1982) or emotions may precede cognitions (Zajonc, 1980). Emotions may be the primary motivational system of the organism (Tomkins, 1970); or this function may reside in cognitions (Schachter, 1966), external stimuli (Millenson, 1967), physiological responses (James, 1884), drives (Freud, 1915), or central neural processing (Cannon, 1928). Some authors maintain that emotions disrupt, interrupt, and disorganize ongoing behavior (Arnold, 1960; Lazarus, 1968; Mandler, 1964; Young, 1949), whereas others believe they sustain, potentiate, and organize behavior (Leeper, 1948; Mowrer, 1960; Schachtel, 1959; Tomkins, 1980). It is also arguable whether a finite number of primary emotions exist or an infinite number of emotions are arrayed along a continuum, and whether the emotional system is separate from or inextricably linked to cognitive processing.

This series of questions and issues could easily be multiplied. Suffice it to say that the area remains ill defined, poorly understood, and characterized by a plethora of conflicting views and findings. Theory and research in emotion are at the stage of development that Kuhn (1970) describes as "preparadigmatic." This situation is marked by a multiplicity of competing models, fragmenting research endeavors. Each model may offer a different definition of the phenomenon, central issues in the field, methods of investigation, and rules of evidence by which knowledge may be derived. Nevertheless, given the advances of science in so many other areas, it seems fair to ask why an understanding of emotion has remained so obscure.

Emotions are brief and evanescent. They are emergent phenomena of great complexity, subtlety, and variety, arising from transactions among many organs and organ systems, and influenced by external and internal stimuli. Emotions do not lend themselves to study in the laboratory. Aspects of the experimental situation may inhibit, distort, or mask expressive behaviors. Spontaneity—an essential element—is often lost. In the field, however, crucial experimental parameters may be difficult to control and many response characteristics difficult to measure.

Researchers in this area often encounter the Heisenbergian dilemma that study of a phenomenon may change it, thereby invalidating findings. Furthermore, investigation of emotion involves a self-reflexive paradox: the object under scrutiny also does the scrutinizing. This problem is most cogent for the investigation of the phenomenology of emotion, although it pervades other areas as well.

Emotions have often been denigrated by scientists, philosophers, and the general public as primitive, childish, bestial, and uncontrollable in comparison to "rational thought." Descartes, after all, did not say "I *feel*, therefore I am," and Kant pointedly declared emotions inimical to reason. There have been countertrends, but the general view has been overwhelmingly pejorative. The prejudice that emotions are a lower form of life has profoundly distorted Western approaches to emotion, influencing culture, thought, and research in this area, as well as our very experience of affect.

Rational thought is often said to be the result of the exclusion of the unsuitable (e.g., emotion). Civilization has often been considered possible only with repression and sublimation of drives and emotions. Human beings, however, have the richest, most complex, and expressive affective repertoire of any animal. Logically, if emotions were inferior, disorganizing, and maladaptive, they would have

dropped out as encephalization, cognitive development, and natural selection proceeded. In fact, just the opposite has been the case.

FIVE TRADITIONS IN EMOTION THEORY

The neglect or denigration of emotion has reversed itself during the past decade. More and more, emotion is conceived of as a topic within the mainstream of behavioral science research and theory. The chapters in Part IV illustrate this trend. The work of the present, however, is based upon the work of the past. Therefore, in order to provide a context within which to understand the ideas presented in Part IV, I will briefly sketch five major antecedent traditions that originated in the Dark Ages of emotion theory.

Expressive or Differential Emotion Theory

In 1872 Darwin introduced or first systematically employed many of the major sources of information, research methods, and conceptual perspectives that continue to dominate the field. He approached the subject from several complementary, overlapping perspectives, each of which has been elaborated by later investigators (reviewed by Davis, 1979; Ekman, 1973). Certain assumptions are shared by subscribers to this tradition (e.g., Eibl-Eibesfeldt, 1971; Ekman, 1977; Izard, 1977; Plutchik, 1980; Tomkins, 1962; 1963; 1980): (1) Emotions arise from an adaptive, biological base, modifiable by social learning. (2) A stimulus or eliciting situation is perceived (appraised), producing activity in neural and other structures. (3) Activity in underlying neural structures results in a felt experience of emotion and expressive motor behavior as well as physiological correlates. (4) The pattern of central and autonomic neural activity, behavior, physiology, and subjective experience is specific to each emotion, of which there are a discrete number. (5) There is a feedback loop between expressive motor action and subjective experience of emotion.

Visceral or Autonomic Reaction Theory

The next tradition began with the two separately derived but similar theories of James (1884) and Lange (1887). Each reversed the common sense notion that behavioral, autonomic, and other activity is the result of perception and emotion. Instead, James and Lange argued, external stimuli elicit motor, physiological, and other activity, the experiential transform of which (especially visceral reactions) is felt emotion. Therefore, we are afraid because we run, we are sad because we cry, and the like. Emotion is the perception of physiological arousal. This theory has been elaborated by later investigators (e.g., Leeper 1948, Schlosberg, 1954; Wenger et al., 1956; Young, 1961), as well as the cognitive-arousal theorists discussed below.

Central Neural Theory

Cannon (1928, 1939) strongly opposed the James-Lange view. An early proponent of a systems view, he argued that the viscera were a part of the organism's homeostatic system, and changed their levels of activity to deal with fluctuations in the internal and external environment. Emotion, thought Cannon, was generated by thalamic-cortical interactions. He noted that the viscera are an unlikely source for emotion because they are insufficiently differentiated in activity level, slow in response time, relatively insensitive to external stimuli, and without demonstrable impact on emotional processes when sectioned or when stimulated artifically (with an epinephrine injection, for example). Later researchers deriving impetus from Cannon's work include Papez (1937), MacLean (1963), and Pribam (1971).

Psychoanalytic Theory

The psychoanalytic tradition (Freud, 1915, 1926; Rapaport, 1950) dispenses with the problem of causal relations among emotional expression, experience, and physiological change by positing that all three are discharge products of conflicting drive energies. Psychoanalytic theory proposes the following: (1) Sense data impinging on the organism are unconsciously evaluated and mobilize relevant drive energies. (2) The drives—which are considered peremptory, cyclic, selective, and displacable, and classified as pleasure oriented (sexual) and reality oriented (ego)—often conflict. (3) If no free (unconflicted) pathway is available for discharge of these energies—and Rapaport (1953) reminds us that in our culture open pathways for drive energy discharge are rare—emotional expressivity, emotional experience, and neurophysiological changes occur in place of voluntary goal-oriented motility. Classical drive theory has been modified and updated to incorporate concepts compatible with ego psychology and object relations theory, as well as information and general systems theory (Holt, 1967; Peterfreund, 1971; Rosenblatt & Thickstun, 1977).

Cognitive-Arousal Theory

Cognitive-arousal theory has a fairly lengthy history (Ruckmick, 1936; Russell, 1927; Sully, 1903), although it really became a force in psychology only with Schachter's widely discussed experiments (Schachter, 1966; Schachter & Singer, 1962; Schachter & Wheeler, 1962). This theory holds the experience of emotion to be a construction of the interaction between physiological arousal and cognitive set. Cognitive set includes object and self representations, schemata, plans, expectations, learning, memory, and the like. Cognitive-arousal theories borrow from the James and Lange focus on the viscera and autonomic activity as well as cognitive theory's focus on representations, "processes" (Mandler, 1975), and coping strategies (Lazarus, 1968). Assumptions of members of this group include the following: (1) Arousal, a necessary but not sufficient condition for emotion, occurs when there is a mismatch between experience and cognitive set. (2) When aroused, individuals search for the cause of their arousal. (3) This attribution is the resultant of the situation and the cognitive set of the individual. (4) The cognitive set provides the sufficient condition and determines the specific quality of the emotion felt. (5) Emotions arise from the meaning of the eliciting situation, rather than the eliciting situation per se.

Overview

Each of these five theories has had a major influence on both research and theory in the field. In terms of a research example, Davidson's work, presented in Chapter 11 of the previous section, incorporates elements from all five traditions, as well as general systems and information theories. His well-designed studies utilize self-report, behavioral, central neural, autonomic, and physiological sources of information. Especially noteworthy is his use of the Facial Affect Coding System, developed by Ekman and Friesen (1977), lateral eye movements, electromyography, electroencephalography, and the Marlowe-Crowne scale (Crowne & Marlowe, 1964) to better understand the cognitive psychobiology of emotion. These are some of the new methods which, enhanced by sophisticated concepts and elegant designs, as well as multichannel online computer capability, have resulted in an increased understanding of emotion in the past 10 years.

In terms of theoretical explanations, none of the five theories has been able to account for all the phenomena associated with emotion. Taken together, however, they provide a grid of some power, suggesting parameters of the phenomena of emotion. What might these parameters be? Clearly, emotion is emergent from biological, psychological, and sociocultural phenomena. Any model of emotion must be able to integrate and explain findings across all three domains. It must integrate data from central neural, autonomic, and physiological functioning, from observed behavior, and from reports of subjective experience. The model must provide sensitivity to genetic predisposition as well as cultural press, and to the influence of innate response patterns as well as social learning, expectations, and unconscious wishes. The two current theories discussed below incorporate many of these desiderata.

TWO CURRENT THEORIES OF EMOTION

Mandler's Theory

For Mandler (Chapter 16), the experience of emotion is constructed from the interaction of autonomic, particularly sympathetic, nervous system arousal and evaluative cognitions. Autonomic nervous system arousal is triggered when an ongoing, organized activity or thought process is interrupted by input that is unexpected or mismatched to cognitive set. Evaluative cognitions are products of social learning, memory, and cultural press; they are organized as representations, and operated on by cognitive processes (programs).

Mandler draws upon psychoanalytic, general systems, information, cognitive, social, and bodily arousal traditions to construct an intentionally psychological theory. His argument rests on three propositions: that arousal is necessary for emotion to arise at all; that arousal is a generalized phenomenon (rather than specific to each emotion); and that cognitions, mediating between arousal and the experience of emotion, give this generalized arousal its specific emotional caste. Mandler impressively argues these propositions on both logical and empirical grounds, although they have been disputed by others.

Certainly, Schachter's experiments provide support for these ideas, although their methodology (Plutchik & Ax, 1967) and their replicability (Maslach, 1979) have been questioned. Furthermore, data from a recently completed experiment by Ekman and Levenson (in press) indicate patterning of autonomic functioning for different emotions. Cognitive-arousal theory would not predict such differentiation. Finally, data from false feedback studies, animal studies, and studies of the emotional experience of paraplegics have also been offered to dispute this view (Leventhal, 1979).

Mandler's theory—as has been the case with cognitive-arousal theory in general—has stimulated much speculation, discussion, research, and important findings. His erudite, well-articulated, and wide-ranging theory has made major contributions to the field's acceptance of emotion as a legitimate area of investigation, as well as materially advancing our understanding of this complex phenomenon.

Temoshok's Theory

Temoshok's intriguing and synthetic theory of emotion, adaption, and consciousness (Chapter 17) draws upon all five major traditions as well as a host of other sources. She develops a hierarchically-structured, information processing model incorporating systems and subsystems which, through transaction and transformation, give rise to the emergent properties of consciousness, including emotion.

The central organizing principle in her theory is that of *information and meaning transformation*. Information is both transmitted and transformed at system and subsystem boundaries. Transformation of information and meaning across boundaries or levels of consciousness may occur, according to Temoshok, in forward (adaptive) or reverse (potentially maladaptive) directions. The symptomatic form that psychological or somatic emotion concomitants may take arises in large part because of information processing predispositions of the organism. These are internalization (a proclivity toward environment-to-organism exchange and externalization (a proclivity toward organism-to-environment exchange). Individuals whose major mode is internalization are prone, according to this theory, to physical ills; those who employ externalization are prone to psychological distress.

The theory draws from multiple perspectives and addresses the salient dimensions of emotion. It is impressive, rich in implications and potential applications, and promises a great deal. It could go further, however, in specifying how the propositions might be operationalized, measured, or evaluated. If this theory is to be adequately validated, more empirical investigation must address its testable hypotheses. For example, if internalization and externalization are in fact, mutually exclusive as postulated, then we would not expect to see many individuals suffering from both cancer and premorbid psychoticism. Epidemiological studies could resolve this point.

Nevertheless, Temoshok's theory stands as a challenging, innovative, and welcome addition to the literature on emotion. It integrates the biological, psychological, behavioral, and sociocultural data available. It is truly a biopsychosocial theory. As such, and on its own intrinsic merits, it points the way toward an understanding, and ultimately, the utilization of such understanding to better address one of *Homo sapiens'* most pressing concerns: how to deal with feelings.

SUMMARY

Emotions are complex, emergent, often quite brief phenomena, arising from numerous organs and organ systems, influenced by multiple sources of input, and expressed by multiple means of output. Their study demands an integration of multiple perspectives, conceptual expertise, technological sophistication, and methodological ingenuity, as well as a lack of prejudice. It is apparent that past investigators, each from his or her own perspective, have been studying different aspects of this most crucial problem. Integrative, multidisciplinary, multidimensional study of emotion as a multidetermined, biopsychosocial entity will be most fruitful in the future. The chapters that follow indicate the power of such an integrated view. It is unfortunate that it has only been quite recently that the conceptual, methodological, and instrumental bases have been available to facilitate the study of this organized system of phenomena that stand between fantasy and reality, between stimulus and response, between mind and body, and between behavioral science and medicine.

REFERENCES

Arnold MB (1960): *Emotion and Personality* (2 vols.). New York, Columbia University Press.

Birdwhistell R (1970): *Kinesics and Context.* Philadelphia, University of Pennsylvania Press.

Cannon WB (1928): Neural organization for emotional expression. Reymert ML (Ed.). In *Feelings and Emotions:* *The Wittenberg Symposium.* Worchester, Mass., Clark University Press.

Cannon WB (1939): *The Wisdom of the Body.* New York, Norton.

Claparede E (1928): Feelings and emotions. Reymert ML (Ed.).: In *Feelings and Emotions: The Wittenberg Symposium.* Worchester, Mass., Clark University Press.

Cleve FM (1969): *The Giants of Pre-Socratic Philosophy: An Attempt to Reconstruct Their Thoughts* (Vol. 2). The Hague, Martinus Nijhoff.

Crowne DP, & Marlow D (1964): *The Approval Motive: Studies in Evaluative Dependence.* New York, Wiley.

Darwin CR (1872): *The Expression of the Emotions in Man and Animals.* Chicago, University of Chicago Press.

Davis M (1979): The state of the art: Past and present trends in body movement. Wolgang A (Ed.). In *Nonverbal Behavior: Applications and Cultural Implications.* New York, Academic Press.

de Sousa R (1980): The rationality of emotions. Rorty AC (Ed.). In *Explaining Emotions.* Berkeley, University of California Press.

Duffy E (1962): *Activation and Behavior.* New York, Wiley.

Eibl-Eibesfeldt I (1971): *Love and Hate: The Natural History of Behavior Patterns.* New York, Holt, Rinehart, & Winston.

Ekman P (Ed.) (1973): *Darwin and Facial Expression: A Century of Research in Review.* New York, Pergamon Press.

Ekman P (1977): Biological and cultural contributions to body and facial measurement. Blacking J (Ed.). In *The Anthropology of the Body.* London, Academic Press.

Ekman P, & Friesen WV (1977): *The Facial Action Coding System: A Manual for the Measurement of Facial Movement.* Palo Alto, CA, Consulting Psychologists Press.

Ekman P, & Levenson R (in press): *Emotions differ in ANS activity.* Accepted for publication. Science, 1983.

Ekman P, Sorenson ER, & Friesen WV (1969): Pancultural elements of facial displays of emotion. Science 164:86–88.

Freud S (1915): The unconscious. Freud S. In *Collected Papers,* (vol. 4). London, Hogarth Press, 1949.

Freud S (1926): *Inhibitions, Symptoms, and Anxiety.* London, Hogarth Press.

Gardiner HM, Metcalf RC, & Beebe-Center JC (1937): *Feeling and Emotion: A History of Theories.* Westport, Greenwood Press.

Hebb DO (1949): *The Organization of Behavior.* New York, Wiley.

Holt RR (1967): Beyond vitalism and mechanism: Freud's concept of psychic energy. Masserman JH (Ed.). In *Science and Psychoanalysis.* New York, Grune & Stratton.

Izard CE (1971): *The Face of Emotion.* New York, Appleton-Century-Crofts.

Izard CE (1977): *Human Emotions.* New York, Plenum Press.

James W (1884): What is emotion? Mind 19:188–205.

Jung CG (1923): *Psychological Types.* Princeton, University Press, NJ, 1971.

Kagan J (1978): On emotion and its development: A working paper. Lewis M, & Rosenblum IA (Eds.). In *The Development of Affect.* New York, Plenum Press.

Klineberg O (1938): Emotional expressions in Chinese literature. J Abnorm Soc Psychol 33:517–520.

Kuhn T (1970): *The Structure of Scientific Revolutions* (Rev. ed.). Chicago, University of Chicago Press.

La Barre W (1947): The cultural basis of emotions and gestures. J Pers 16:49–68.

Lacey JI (1967): Somatic response patterning and stress: Some revisions of the activation theory. Appley MH, & Trumbull R (Eds.). In *Psychological Stress.* New York, Appleton-Century-Crofts.

Lange C (1887): *Uber Gemuthsbewegungen.* Leipzig, Theodore Thomas.

Lazarus RS (1968): Emotions and adaption: Conceptual and empirical relations. Arnold MB (Ed.). In *Nebraska Symposium on Motivation.* Lincoln, University of Nebraska Press.

Lazarus RS (1982): Thoughts on the relations between emotion and cognition. Am Psychol 37:1019–1024.

Lazarus RS, Averill J, & Opton EM Jr. (1970): Towards a cognitive theory of emotion. Arnold MB (Ed.). In *Feelings and Emotions.* New York, Academic Press.

Leeper RW (1948): A motivational theory of emotion to replace "emotion as a disorganized response." Psychol Rev 55:5–21.

Leventhal H (1979): A perceptual-motor processing model of emotion. Blankstein KR, Pliner P, & Spigel IM (Eds.). In *Perception of Emotion in Self and Others.* New York, Plenum Press.

Lindsley DB (1951): Emotion. Stevens SS (Ed.). In *Handbook of Experimental Psychology.* New York, Wiley.

MacLean PD (1963): Phylogenesis. Knapp P (Ed.). In *Expression of the Emotions in Man.* New York, International Universities Press.

Mandler G (1964): The interruption of behavior. Levine D (Ed.). In *Nebraska Symposium on Motivation.* Lincoln, University of Nebraska Press.

Mandler G (1975): *Mind and Emotion.* New York, Wiley.

Maslach C (1979): Negative emotional biasing of unexplained arousal. Izard C (Ed.). In *Emotion, Personality, and Psychopathology.* New York, Plenum Press.

Mead M (1975): Review of *Darwin and Facial Expression.* Ekman P (Ed.). J Commun 25:209–213.

Millenson JR (1967): *Principles of Behavioral Analysis.* New York, Macmillan.

Mowrer OH (1960): *Learning Theory and Behavior.* New York, Wiley.

Papez JW (1937): A proposed mechanism of emotion. Arch Neurol Psychiatry 38:725–743.

Peterfreund E (1971): Information, systems, and psychoanalysis: An evolutionary biological approach to psychoanalytic theory (with Schwartz JT). Psychol Issues 7:1–399.

Plutchik R (1962): *The Emotions: Facts, Theories, and a New Model.* New York, Random House.

Plutchik R (1980): *Emotion: A Psychoevolutionary Synthesis.* New York, Harper & Row.

Plutchik R, & Ax AF (1967): A critique of determinants of emotional state by Schachter and Singer (1962). Psychophysiology 4(1):79–82.

Pribram KH (1971): *Languages of the Brain.* Englewood Cliffs, Prentice-Hall.

Rapaport D (1950): *Emotion and Memory.* New York, International Universities Press.

Rapaport D (1953): On the psychoanalytic theory of affects. Int J Psychoanal 34:177–198.

Rorty AO (1980): Explaining emotions. Rorty AO (Ed.). In *Explaining Emotions.* Berkeley, University of California Press.

Rosenblatt AD, & Thickstun JT (1977): Modern psychoanalytic concepts in a general psychology. Psychol Issues 11:1–338.

Ruckmick C (1946): *The Psychology of Feeling and Emotion.* New York, McGraw-Hill.

Russell B (1927): *An Outline of Philosophy.* New York, Meridian, 1960.

Schachtel EG (1959): *Metamorphosis.* New York, Basic Books.

Schachter S (1966): The interaction and physiological determinants and emotional state. Spielberger CD (Ed.). In *Anxiety and Behavior.* New York, Academic Press.

Schachter S, & Singer JE (1962): Cognitive, social, and physiological determinants of emotional state. Psychol Rev 69:379–399.

Schachter S, & Wheeler L (1962): Epinephrine, chlorpromazine, and amusement. J Abnorm Soc Psychol 65:121–128.

Schlosberg H (1954): Three dimensions of emotion. Psychol Rev 61:81–88.

Solomon RC (1980): Emotions and choice. Rorty AO (Ed.). In *Explaining Emotions.* Berkeley, University of California Press.

Sully J (1903): *Essay on Laughter.* London, Longmans, Green.

Tomkins SS (1962): *Affect, Imagery, and Consciousness,* vol. 1: *The Positive Effects.* New York, Springer.

Tomkins SS (1963): *Affect, Imagery, and Consciousness,* vol. 2: *The Negative Affects.* New York, Springer.

Tomkins SS (1970): Affect as the primary motivational system. Arnold MB (Ed.). In *Feelings and Emotions.* New York, Academic Press.

Tomkins SS (1980): Script theory: Differential magnification of affects. Howe HE Jr, & Dienstbier RA (Eds.). In *Nebraska Symposium on Motivation,* vol 26. Lincoln, University of Nebraska Press.

Watson JB (1929): *Psychology from the Standpoint of a Behaviorist* (ed. 3). Philadelphia, Lippincott.

Wenger MA, Jones FN, & Jones MH (1956): *Physiological Psychology.* New York, Holt, Rinehart, & Winston.

Young PT (1949): Emotion as disorganized response—A reply to Professor Leeper. Psychol Rev 56: 184–191.

Young PT (1961): *Motivation and Emotion.* New York, Wiley.

Zajonc RB (1980): Feeling and thinking: Preferences need no inferences. Am Psychol 35:151–175.

16

Emotion and Stress: A View from Cognitive Psychology

George Mandler

The major concern of this chapter is to present a perspective on emotion and stress that is representative of recent theoretical developments in cognitive psychology. The trends that characterize contemporary cognitive psychology are introduced, and then a general approach to the construction of emotional experience is outlined, followed by a specific discussion of problems of emotion and stress.

CENTRAL ISSUES IN CONTEMPORARY COGNITIVE PSYCHOLOGY

During the past two decades, the field of psychology, experimental psychology in particular, has turned from the rather impoverished theoretical notions that it inherited from the behaviorists and their successors to its earlier theoretical traditions. Psychological theory has become cognitive in the sense of being both structuralist and constructivist: structuralist because of its concerns with the processes that underlie the observable world of action and behavior; and constructivist in its concern with specifying how those observables could be and are derived from the processes hidden in underlying mechanisms and deep structures. Modern cognitive psychology claims that representations and processes can be developed to fit the full range of human thought and action; it differs from the more traditional study of cognition, which was concerned with conscious knowledge and conscious thought.

An acceptable theory of human thought and action must represent the full range of the organisms's knowledge. Representational systems are postulated as underlying (and generating) the thoughts and actions of the organism. There is no one-to-one correspondence between an act and its representation; representation is not a symbol that "stands for" some other event. The representation of knowledge is the theoretical system that is used to explain, understand, and predict the behavior of organisms.

Representation by itself would only provide more or less static sources of cognition; it is useless without processes that shape representations, transform them, and finally construct experience and action. Thus, the second central concern of cognitive psychology is the production of thoughts and acts, as well as the specification of the processes that operate on representations, which include operators, search and storage mechanisms, inferential processes, and many others. The postulation of representation and process is only a convenient way of dividing up overlapping concepts and inextricable components of mental functioning. In fact, we talk about the representation of processes and about the possible distinction (within representational systems) between declarative and procedural knowledge.

The theoretical concepts of modern cognitive psychology do not, in principle, seek to have physiological content. Psychology is not constrained by current physiological theory and has built a data base and a theoretical structure that can now be related

Parts of this chapter have been adapted from two previous publications, both copyrighted by the author. (1) Mandler, G. (1979): Thought processes, consciousness, and stress. In Hamilton, V., & Warburton, D.A. (Eds.), *Human Stress and Cognition: An Information Processing Approach.* Wiley, London. (2) Mandler, G. (1981): *What is cognitive psychology? What isn't?* Invited address before the American Psychological Association, Los Angeles, August.

to some of the more sophisticated models and data bases in physiology. The growth of cognitive neuropsychology in the past ten or twenty years attests to this development.

EMOTION AND COGNITIVE THEORY

Classical theories of emotion were unsatisfactory for a contemporary cognitive psychology, and cognitive theories of emotion started to become popular about 20 years ago. Theories that postulated unanalyzable fundamental emotions as building blocks of other, more complex emotions were opaque to a constructivist approach. Cognitive psychologists ask questions about the representations and processes that construct the emotional experience; my work is about the representation of arousal and the evaluative processes that combine into a single emotional experience. Cognitive psychology goes beyond phenomenalism by specifying the processes that produce the experiences themselves. Similarly, speculations about the neurophysiological structures that produce emotions are also unsatisfactory because they bypass the entire process of discovering underlying psychological mechanisms and their relation to other cognitive processes.

The work that culminated in the first extensive statement of my constructivist position (Mandler, 1975) began with a focus on the role of autonomic feedback in the experience of emotion. Schachter's work on the cognitive and physiological determinants of emotion (e.g., Schachter & Singer, 1962) was one of the catalysts that spurred the development of a constructivist theory of emotional experience. That approach focused on the theoretical analysis of the processes that underlie the experience of the various emotions, rather than the labelling or attributional aspects of emotional experience. The constructivist approach has been extended into the cognate areas of thought and stress (Mandler, 1979, 1982b), the development of emotion (Mandler, 1982a), affective judgments (Mandler, 1982c), and life stress and coping.

The general character of this approach embodies the notion that the experience of emotion is derived from two sets of events: the arousal factor, which depends on gross perceivable activations of the autonomic nervous system, particularly of the sympathetic nervous system; and evaluative cognitions, which determine the quality of an emotion. A constructivist approach to consciousness postulates that the holistic experience of an emotion is derived from the

combination of two or more activated structures, in this case arousal and evaluation. The conditions that lead to arousal and the processes of evaluative cognitions are discussed in the next sections.

Functions of Autonomic Nervous System Arousal

How does peripheral autonomic activity interact with the information processing apparatus? The autonomic nervous system has adaptive functions that go well beyond its role in homeostasis. It can be viewed as a system that responds to certain events that require extensive cognitive interpretation. Central to this argument is the realization that autonomic arousal is triggered by the interruption of and discrepancies among thoughts and actions. When an individual is focused on a particular set of events, another occurrence in the environment might signal an unexpected and unprepared-for set of circumstances. In addition to some direct reaction to the discrepant event, the interruption automatically triggers the autonomic nervous system. The autonomic response reacts more slowly to the discrepant event and functions as a secondary alerting mechanism that draws the organism's attention to the new state of affairs. If no coping mechanism is available to deal with that occurrence directly, the feedback from the autonomic reaction draws attention to the new situation.

The evidence for an attentional effect of autonomic arousal is threefold. First, Lacey and Lacey, (1974) have shown that attentional activity is accompanied by cardiac deceleration. Such deceleration would attenuate the internal attention-demanding "noisy" apsect of cardiac activity (acceleration). Note that, in general, the primitive response of the organism is a parasympathetic one (Pick, 1970), one that conserves energy and prepares the organism for more adequate coping with the environment. Second, there is an independent response of cardiac deceleration in response to acceleration. Here again, although with a longer latency (1–1.5 seconds), a noise-reducing response occurs automatically in response to sympathetic activation. Thus, attention first reduces internal "noise," and then internal "noise" produces its own negative feedback. The third line of evidence comes primarily from Frankenhaeuser (1975, 1976), who has suggested that autonomic activity and the accompanying catecholamine release are not obsolete "primitive" responses; rather, such activity facilitates adjustment to cognitive and emotional pressure. In brief, there is evidence that the autonomic nervous system may be involved in the instigation of environmental scanning and attention to important events.

The function of the autonomic nervous system can be viewed as an important adaptive process, going well beyond the homeostatic functions that have been assigned to it. Central to this argument is the dependence of autonomic arousal on the interruption of ongoing thought and actions.

Interruption and Arousal

The problem of autonomic arousal can be approached from the point of view of interruption theory (Mandler, 1964, 1975). The basic premise is that autonomic activity results whenever an organized action or thought process is interrupted. Interruptions occur when thought or behavior is stopped in its flow due to active or passive blocking by environmental events, when an internal thought process prevents the completion of some other internal process, or when a plan or processing strategy cannot be brought to completion because it is inconsistent or discrepant with another currently active processing activity. Such inconsistencies also occur when environmental demands cannot be met, when no appropriate cognitive activity (schema) is available. Interruptions can occur in the perceptual, cognitive, or behavioral domains, but the consequence will always be the same—autonomic activity. It is important to note that interruption should not be imbued with negative characteristics; it is simply the disconfirmation of an expectancy or the noncompletion of some initiated action. Interruption may be interpreted emotionally in any number of ways, ranging from the joyful to the noxious. Thus, the unexpected occurrence of a positive event is just as arousing as the unexpected negative event.

The amount of autonomic activity depends primarily on two factors: the degree of organization of the interrupted process, and the severity of the interruption. Degree of organization reflects the stereotype and habitual character of the act or thought process. An action or thought sequence that is in the process of organization is highly variable, and much irrelevant thought and behavior occurs within the sequence; there is no well-organized structure to be interrupted. However, when the sequence has become invariant and its stages occur with a high degree of expectancy and even certainty, then interruptions will have their maximal effect.

Autonomic arousal potentiates, colors, and distinguishes the experiences usually called "emotional." It is the presence of arousal that turns "cold" evaluative actions and thoughts into "hot" emotions. Arousal also significantly influences the memory system; events are stored and retrieved with reference to the emotional state within which they are experienced. It would be a rather drab life if autonomic arousal did not lend passion and color to our experiences.

STRUCTURE OF EVALUATIONS

Cognitive Evaluations

Cognitive evaluation of the world is an important determiner not only of the kinds of complex emotions that the individual will experience, but also of the specific emotions that any particular event is likely to elicit. However, there are many emotions that seem to occur cross-culturally and transsocially. All human beings apparently experience fear, grief, and joy. There appear to exist general cognitive conditions that we label with these emotions. For example, joy is often related to the occurrence of an unanticipated positively valued event, grief to the absence of an important object (usually, but not always, human), and anxiety to helplessness (the unavailability of appropriate coping mechanisms). It is well known, however, that there are important individual and cultural differences in the experience of and the occasions for these emotions. Emotional labels are convenient categories that facilitate communication, but they do not reflect the nuances of emotional experience. Cultural influences on the pervasive and the individual emotions are reflected in the frequency with which certain emotions are encountered in a culture or society, as well as the distribution of their intensities. The values, categories, and schemas that encode a particular societal structure (culture) determine in part how and when anxiety, grief, depression, and fear are experienced.

The cognitive evaluations that are at the basis of the qualitative nature of emotions have three general sources (Mandler, 1982a). *Innate evaluations* include such things as the preference for sweet over bitter substances, and shrinking from looming objects. *Culturally learned evaluations* do not necessarily involve first hand acquaintance with the valued object. Cultural predications are typically learned early in life and tell us with whom we might associate, what foods are acceptable, what clothes should be worn, what beliefs held. *Structurally based evaluations* are at the basis of the observations that we like what we know, but also that we know what we like. This structural value is based on an appreciation of the internal structure of an event, of the relations among its features, not just on the presence of such features. Thus, I might recognize a picture to represent a dancer, but I like it because of certain relational characteristics represented in the dancer or in the painter's style.

Representation and Consciousness

How are expectations and valuations represented in the human mind? The concept of the schema is the general vehicle for the representation of current and potential thoughts and action. Schemas are organized mental representations that are built up in the course of interaction with the environment. They are available at various levels of generality and abstraction, and may represent organized experience ranging from discrete features to general categories. Schemas are mental structures that organize past experience; they structure our experience and are being structured by it. They are activated by external events or by intrapsychic occurrences, by input from sensory data and from other schemas. Most, if not all, of the activation processes occur automatically and without awareness on the part of the perceiver/comprehender. We identify our surroundings in terms of the congruity between the environmental evidence and our stored schemas (Rumelhart & Ortony, 1978). Generic schemas have modal values of variables; and there exist schematic prototypes (Rosch, 1978) that affect the congruity of specific instances of objects and events.

My account of consciousness is derived in part from Marcel (in press a and b), who addresses the problem of consciousness for perceptual processes in general. In contrast to the view that consciousness is simply a different state of a structure, consciousness is seen as a constructive process in which the phenomenal experience is a novel construction to which two or more activated schemas have contributed. We can be conscious only of experiences that are constructed out of activated schemas. When a schema is activated, either by evidence from the environment or by intrapsychic processes, it can potentially become part of a conscious content. However, neither the process whereby the schema is activated nor the components of the schema are available in consciousness. Two or more schemas may combine to form a single conscious experience, and the fac-

tors that determine which schemas are combined are found in the demands of the task and situation and regulated by attentional processes. Phenomenal experience is "an attempt to make sense of as much data as possible at the highest or most functionally useful level possible. . . ." (Marcel, in press b).

When a conscious evaluative judgment is sought, by an actor's intentions or by an experimenter's instructions, the "most functionally useful" level of abstraction is the relational aspect of the relevant schemas. The difference between an identifying and an evaluating construction is that the former accesses the congruity between the event to be judged and the features of the schemas, while the latter accesses the relationship among those features. What is represented in consciousness is a direct phenomenal experience of "value," and not the relations among features that have constructed that value. We are aware of beauty and horror, not of the characteristics that determine that judgment.

Value is abstracted from the structural representation of an object or event (Mandler, 1982c). In brief, the relations among the features of an event, the relations among the components of a schema determine value. As indicated above, the identification of an object depends on the similarities between the evidence in the world and the features in the stored schema. The judgment of value, however, depends on the congruity between the evidence in the world and the relations among the constituent elements of a schema. From a structural point of view, we like things not because they are what they are but because of the particular structure of these objects and events. The judgment of liking the familiar is likewise dependent on the availability of well-established structural aspects of the event. Conversely, of course, the new and strange needs examination and adaptation before it can enter the realm of the known and the liked.

The discussion of value has centered on relatively simple objects and events. The same kind of argument, with respect to both schematic representation and evaluative cognitions, applies to more complex life events, especially those that enter into the development of stress. In principle, we represent our homes, families, jobs in the same way that we represent simple objects such as tables, apples, and paintings. The more complex life events also engender predictions and expectations, discrepancies and interruptions. Furthermore, our evaluations of our life situations are driven by the same considerations as our evaluations of paintings and melodies. The structure of our life and of our expectations about it can be analyzed within schema theory and value theory to yield important insights into the causes and consequences of stress.

CAUSES AND CONSEQUENCES OF STRESS

A Definition of Stress

Questions about the conditions that produce psychological stress have bedeviled most theories of stress and emotion. Stressors have usually been defined as the class of events that produce stress in the individual. This circular approach produces enumerations of what circumstances might be evaluated as potentially stressful, but does not provide any principle that links these circumstances.

Let us start with a psychological, rather than a physiological, definition of stress. External "stressors" are effective to the extent that they have organismic consequences. In order for some external event to acquire these consequences, it must be processed by the cognitive mechanisms. In a critique of Selye's stress concept, Mason (1975) notes that "emotional arousal" is one of the most ubiquitous reactions common to a great many situations that are considered stressful. These emotional responses depend on psychological interpretive mechanisms. What determines the emotional quality of an event is a combination of autonomic arousal and cognitive evaluation. The consequences of the processing of an external event must be perceptible before it becomes an actual stressor. It is the perception of autonomic activity in particular that represents the perceptible, stressful part of the stress reaction. Continued excessive or strong autonomic reactions have, in the long run, deleterious effects on the health of the individual.

It can be assumed that the primary condition that leads to autonomic arousal is interruption. Rather extensive consequences will result if repeated interruptions are inevitable. If the execution of some particular action or cognitive process is interrupted, the organism attempts to take up the sequence again, repeated interruptions, will potentiate the arousal. Interruption, and the subsequent arousal, will be most severe when the action sequence is continuously reinitiated and interrupted, and when the action is most salient to current plans and goals of the individual.

There are two clearly distinguishable consequences of stress. The first one is short-term and primarily subsumed under the rubric of the effect of stress on immediate coping, on thought processes, and on intellectual and performance efficiency (Mandler, 1979, 1982b). The second consequence of stress, and the one to be addressed here, is generally labeled as the problem of life stress: the effect of stresses on the ongoing life of the individual, on longterm functioning, health, and psychological processes in general.

Life Stress and Interruption Theory

The interpretation of life stresses within the framework of interruption theory suggests that any event that involves a normal and expected outcome is capable of generating autonomic nervous system arousal if and when the world changes in such a way that that outcome no longer occurs or is no longer possible. More generally, any change in the life of the individual in which the expected no longer happens is potentially stressful. The definition of what can be or is expected must be seen as very broad. It ranges from the place where one expects to find one's toothpaste in the morning, to the items that are usually on the menu of the restaurant where one eats lunch, to the people one encounters in the workplace, or to the friends with whom one goes bowling.

It is important to note that the relevance of a life event is not defined by how much one likes or dislikes it, or whether one classes a particular event as important or not. The crucial aspect of a life event and its changes is the degree to which the changes are discrepant with one's expectations, the degree to which the new state of world is subjectively perceived as different from the "normal" modal one.

Berscheid (1982) has used interruption theory to provide an extensive, insightful, and original analysis of close relationships. She notes that the closeness of a relationship stems from the frequency, strength, and diversity of the interconnections between two individuals' sequences of life events. The sequences may be casually interconnected, such that the occurrence of an action by one is a necessary and sufficient condition for some action on the part of the other. The organized actions of the two people are then said to be "meshed," that is, each person facilitates and augments the other person's actions. Whenever such meshing fails, the action sequences of one or both people will be interrupted, arousal will result, and stress and emotional experiences will follow. If a relationship is characterized by a large number of well-meshed causal interconnections, little emotion (or stress) will be observable in the normal course of events. However, such well-meshed relationships contain what Berscheid calls "hidden ticking emotional bombs." Any significant change of these relationships will result in many extensive interruptions. Conversely a relationship that is not closely interconnected (a "parallel" relationship) is much less likely to produce severe emotional consequences if, for example, one of the partners leaves or dies.

Berscheid notes that these analyses suggest important consequences: The closeness of a relationship cannot be defined in terms of the attitudes toward each other or by the frequency or intensity of emotions that the involved people typically experience. Frequently intense emotional reactions can be experienced following the loss of a partner even though the relationship itself may not have been characterized by much ongoing emotional coloring. Furthermore, global feelings of liking or disliking a situation may not represent the degree of interconnections, and thus may not predict emotional reactions (e.g., to desertion or death). Finally, the general appraisal of a person or situation may not predict one's emotional reactions to that person. One may like or dislike a person, but how one reacts to his or her actions, will depend on the interconnectedness of the two lives and the conditions under which actions by the other are discrepant. Events, relationships, and life situations must be studied in the context of the manner in which individual needs, aspirations, and goals are acted out.

Berscheid's analysis clearly extends far beyond the realm of close relationships. It can be applied to the work situation, to the family situation in general, and to practically all aspects of an individual's life. It is with this additional analysis in mind that some of the current studies of life stress in the next section can be considered.

LIFE STRESS AND PHYSICAL AND PSYCHOLOGICAL WELL BEING

How could life stress affect the long-range welfare of the individual? An initial analysis will require us to know something about the individual's important life situations, to know the expectations that are elicited by the world and the interactions with it. Potentially stressful situations must be analyzed in terms of the interconnectedness of the life of the individual with situational demands and with other people. If we assume that interruptions are a sufficient (and possibly necessary) condition for the activation of autonomic, and particularly sympathetic, nervous system activity, then repeated life stresses will increase the general level of arousal of the individual. Such arousal is likely to have three consequences: First, in the short-run, continuing autonomic arousal will interfere with the effectiveness of the individual's intellective functioning. One consequence of extensive and continuing autonomic arousal is conscious preoccupation with such arousal and with the causes of the interruption. Furthermore, the limited capacity of human consciousness will force constriction of thought, stereotyping of plans, limitation of creative problem solving, and general interference with efficient cognitive functioning (Mandler, 1979). Second, the continuous arousal of autonomic nervous system activity is likely to overload the system, require sustained extraordinary cardiac activity, and may be responsible for general deleterious effects on cardiac and visceral functions. Finally, recent evidence has suggested that continuing elevated epinephrine levels in the blood stream may interfere with the immune system (cf. Bourne et al., 1974; Rogers et al., 1979). If in fact there are immunosuppressive effects of continuing high levels of catecholamine, then continuing life stress will make the individual more vulnerable to illness.

The current concern with life stress and the intensive empirical attack on the attendant phenomena can be dated to the appearance of the Social Readjustment Rating Scale developed by Holmes and Rahe (1967). That scale has been the basis for variant versions and has undergone changes in content and wording and scoring procedures (for a review see Rahe, 1978); other scales have been developed with similar intent and content (e.g., Dohrenwend et al., 1978). The general conclusion is that retrospective studies show a reasonably high correlation between current illness and prior life stresses, but that prospective studies are much less promising; many people who have been exposed to the life stresses listed in the various scales do not display any illness or disturbance. It is also the case that individuals with a history of depression, for example, are more sensitive than average people to the deleterious effects of life stress. Finally, social support seems to have some, but often not very effective, role in ameliorating the effect of life stresses. (For a review and summaries of the relevant data see Rahe, 1978; Rahe & Arthur, 1978; Silver & Wortman, 1980; Wallston et al., 1981.)

Even a cursory examination of the life stresses listed in these various questionnaires and inventories shows that they are all consistent with the basic tenets of interruption theory. The events listed represent life events in which a usual situation is changed, in which novel events are encountered, and in which the new life situation is discrepant from the old. In fact, the questions are posed frequently in terms of "changes" in the life situation. Equally consistent with interruption theory is the fact that positive as well as negative changes are listed and often the positive events are given greater weight than the negative ones. It must be remembered, however, that weights for the items on the scales are typically determined by having people rate the degree of adjustment and coping necessary to deal with the target events. As various commentators have noted, this does not tell how the individual who is being rated by such a scale can or does cope with the actual event. It is therefore misleading to consider the scales to be objectively reliable measures of life stress. Even though the population at large may consider some event difficult to deal with, it may not be difficult for the individual involved. Beyond such considerations, it is important to be wary of the introspective or retrospective reports of individuals concerning either their current state or prior experiences. Reports of such experiences or of current sensitivities are frequently shaped more by beliefs and hypotheses than by veridical perceptions (Nisbett & Wilson, 1977).

In discussing the low prospective utility of these scales, it does not seem appropriate to ask how "the majority of individuals tolerate their recent life change experiences and remain healthy?" or to state that "(n)ew research needs to be done in the area of systematic quantification of subjects' stress tolerance characteristics." (Rahe, 1978, p. 9). Rather than talking about the tolerance for events that are assumed to be equally stressful for all people, we must ask which events are actually effective stresses for the individual. If the event is not stressful, no tolerance is required. Remember Berscheid's argument that similar appearing relationships may in fact hide quite different degrees of potential for interruption. Rather than looking for complex new models that integrate social, psychological, and physiological aspects, we should look at particular events and determine their potential stressfulness in terms of their interruptive potential.

Coping and Mastery

When a situation is in fact subjectively stressful, then strategies and mechanisms of coping enter into the picture. Extensive evidence exists that stress situations will tend to draw attention to centrally important aspects of the environment (for a review see Mandler, 1979). This effect is relevant to the mastery of stress, i.e., to our ability to control a particular situation. Mastery refers to our perception that the events in our personal world may be brought under our control. This sense of mastery may be important not so much because of the direct effects it has on our actions, but because a sense of control or mastery colors the cognitive interpretation of our world. It is generally seen as "good" to be in control, and as the world is appraised as "good" the emotional tone will be positive. What frightens us may become affectively neutral when we have a sense of mastery, even though our actual control of the situation has not changed. What has changed is the relevance of the events to our ongoing plans—if the events are seen as relevant and as impeding (interrupting) ongoing action, they may become frightening. If they are seen as irrelevant, or impeding only in the short term, they may become tolerable or even amusing.

The objective absense of control is not necessarily seen as negative; it is the subjective sense of control that is important, rather than the objective control of the environment. In general, the phenomenal sense of control is a function of the predictability of the world. If we can predict with some degree of certainty what will happen in our environs and in response to our actions, we experience a sense of control. There is no doubt that the sense of mastery in many cases does reduce the deleterious effects of stress and does alleviate the subjective sense of emotional disturbance. This effect may occur under two conditions: First, any action directly related to the threatening, interrupting situation or event may change that event and reduce its threatening (interrupting) effect. In that case, an action by the individual has changed the situation from one that is arousing (and interpreted as threatening) to a nonarousing one, thereby removing its threatening aspects. Second, without changing any of its objective aspects, a situation may be reinterpreted in such a way that the events are no longer perceived as interrupting. The overall structure or plan under which the situation or event is perceived is changed significantly to remove its interrupting aspect or to view the interruption as beneficial. In the latter case, the autonomic arousal will persist but will be positively interpreted. The roller coaster ride is seen as a joyful situation that will terminate when planned (at the end of its run) and will thus not be frightening. The other kind of event, the cognitive removal of interruptive aspects, occurs less frequently. Consider the case of the student who has received his graded examination paper with a grade of 66 percent. He had hoped (planned) for at least a 75 in order to pass the course. These plans have been disrupted; he is in a state of autonomic arousal and his emotional state is negative. Then he notices a slip of paper appended to the examination which says that the examination was unusually difficult and that 66 percent will be recorded as a passing grade. The same event has now been reinterpreted, its interruptive, as well as negative, aspect are removed.

Both action structures and intrapsychic cognitive structures may be interrupted for one of two reasons. One involves the situation where an expected event or sequence fails to occur, the other when something unexpected happens. Both of these involve interruption, both involve autonomic arousal and both usually (in the kind of situation considered in this chapter) are interpreted as negative and unpleasant. In either case, the interruption of a current cognitive structure automatically focuses consciousness on that structure and the interruptive event or thought. One of the functions of consciousness is that it becomes the arena for trouble shooting when conscious or unconscious structures fail. This phenomenon has been labelled the law of awareness by Claparède (1934); people become aware of automatic actions when they are disrupted or when they fail.

It is reasonable to assume that one of the adaptive functions of interruption is to bring some problem into consciousness, where repair and coping activities can take place. If such "snapping into consciousness" takes place we expect the field of focal attention to be narrowed, and, under many circumstances, other ongoing activity to be impaired because of the restricted amount of focal capacity that remains available. However, it should be noted that much trouble-shooting occurs without any stressing sequelae. When working on a complex problem, we often expect to find one or more structures to be inadequate for the solution of the problem at hand. In that case, the operative executive plan "expects" interruptions and the expectation does not lead to autonomic arousal. Expected interruptions of this kind will only be innocuous if they are not perceived as destructive of the executive plan. In contrast, the anxious individual, who "expects" to fail will perceive these interruptions as fatal or at least deleterious to the goal at hand. Well-trained individuals (e.g., the astronauts) have exactly the useful kinds of expectations in which trouble shooting is expected, and interruptions may not produce a stress response.

This discussion leads into the general topic of coping, appraisal, and reappraisal. A most important contribution to this problem has been made by Lazarus and his colleagues (Folkman et al., 1979; Lazarus, 1975). In that context, Gal and Lazarus (1975) have addressed the issue of mastery and stress. They asked why activity as such apparently has the capacity to lower stress reactions. Gal and Lazarus distinguish between threat-related and non–threat-related activities. The former lower stress reactions because they provide a feeling of control or mastery. In the case of non–threat-related activities, however, the effect derives from the fact that they distract or divert attention from threat. It is the latter explanation that should be added to the account given here. It is certainly likely that in certain cases of threat some restriction of attention may reduce the perception of both the threatening event and the internal autonomic activity. In general, the issue of mastery and control, as well as of the effects of activity as such, requires detailed analyses of the task, the perceived situation, and the structures that guide thought and action at each point in time.

Another characteristic of human cognition that may produce fearful (arousing and negatively interpreted) reactions involves the presence of events and perceptions that are new, i.e., for which no current schemas or structures are appropriate. Human beings will always search for an appropriate way to interpret the surroundings ("meaning analysis"), a process that is automatic. Given a genuinely novel situation, an appropriate structure may not be found, but in the process each attempted structure fails in environmental support and is thus interrupted. This unavailability of appropriate response or action alternatives, this helplessness in the face of the environment, I consider to be the essential psychological basis of the set of subjective reactions subsumed under "anxiety."

If we consider the hierarchical structure of plans and cognitive structures (Miller et al., 1960), the stress produced by the interruption of a particular plan will vary with the number of other plans (subordinate and superordinate to the interrupted one) that are disrupted at the same time. For example, the interruption of a low-level plan ("I want to have eggs for breakfast but there aren't any in the house") may not be too arousing and stressful because a higher one is not affected ("I want to have breakfast and might as well eat some cereal"). The important point to be noted is that any interruptive event must be analyzed in terms of the level of plans and relevant hierarchies involved. Thus when all levels of plans are threatened by some event, the degree of autonomic arousal will be intense and the stress most severe. An unresolved question about the severity of stress is whether the severity is determined by the level of the stress within a hierarchy or by the number of different alternatives that are blocked. The higher the level within the hierarchy that is blocked, the more subordinate goals are interrupted, but the specific relationship between level and severity of stress requires further investigation.

Stress, Mastery, and Arousal

One of the most impressive programs of research on the relationship between stress and autonomic (endocrine) functions has been carried out over many years by Frankenhaeuser at the University of Stockholm. In a review (Frankenhaeuser, 1979), she stressed that neuroendocrine responses reflect the emotional impact of the individual's psychosocial environment, which "is determined by his or her cognitive appraisal of stimuli and events" (p. 125). Her data show that "stimulus conditions that are perceived as deviating from those to which the person is accustomed will induce a change in adrenalin output, whereas stimuli and events that are perceived as part of the familiar environment will not affect secretion. Novelty, change, challenge, and anticipation may be considered key components in the psychosocial conditions triggering the adrenal-medullary response" (p. 128).

Several studies have shown that deviations from the level of stimulation that the individual expects lead to increased adrenalin output. For example, both a monotonous vigilance task and a complex choice-reaction time task produced adrenalin levels higher than that produced by a situation that matched the average complexity of a normal environment. However, when the situation is subjectively restructured so that the individual perceives that he or she is able to exercise control over the environment, then the adrenalin output is determined by degree of perceived control (Frankenhaeuser & Rissler, 1970). In terms of my formulation, interruption is determined by subjective expectancies, and when control is perceived as being exercised over the situation it becomes more predictable and less interrupting, and therefore less effective in terms of autonomic arousal. Similarly, commuters who entered a crowded train (where seat selection was difficult) showed higher adrenalin levels that those entering the train when it was less crowded and seat selection was more under their

control; that is, length and duration of the trip were not the determiners of adrenalin, but perceived control was (Singer et al., 1978). Frankenhaeuser (1979) also reported on a series of studies in the workplace indicating that highly constricted, machine-paced work and repetitive, physically constrained work in which the pace is outside the worker's control contribute to high and continuing levels of adrenalin output.

On the question of the relationship between health and stress, Frankenhaeuser (1979) noted that the cardiovascular system may be adversely affected if "periods of high secretion [of catecholamines] are prolonged or repeated frequently" (p. 142). Data from her laboratory show that individuals whose adrenaline response returns quickly to baseline after stress are psychologically better balanced and more efficient than are "slow decreasers." She also suggests that the coronary prone behavior pattern (type A) may be related to "low flexibility in physiological arousal relative to situational demands" (p. 143).

McClelland and his associates (Jemmott et al., 1981; McClelland et al., 1980; McClelland & Jemmott, 1980) have reported some interesting results on the study of individuals with a great need for power. Individuals high in need for power are defined by the fact that they write imaginative stories about having impact on others by aggression; they also play more competitive sports and generally try to increase their impact on others. Subjects were selected in whom such characteristics were also associated with high scores on inhibition, as well as on items from the Holmes and Rahe scale which indicate stress in the power/achievement areas. These individuals showed higher adrenalin excretion rates and lower concentrations of immunoglobulin A, as well as more frequent reports of illnesses than did subjects not characterized by this triple identification. The authors conclude that a "strong need for power, if it is inhibited and stressed, leads to chronic sympathetic overactivity which has an immunosuppressive effect," which in turn leads to a greater susceptibility to illness (McClelland et al., 1980, p. 11).

In terms of my formulation, the need for power is indicated by a set of habitual actions in and reactions to a variety of situations. Individuals have, in a sense, a script or schema that determines how they are to deal with situations that require aggressive and power-defined social interactions. When these actions are blocked by the environment (as indicated by the power stress measures) or when they are inhibited intrapsychically from being executed, then interruptive events occur that lead to autonomic nervous system arousal.

CONCLUSIONS

A brief overview of the most important aspects of contemporary cognitive theory has been presented, and the application of some of the tools of the cognitive theorist to problems of human emotional experience has been illustrated. The utility of a cognitive analysis has been shown for problems of stress and stress management, the analysis of life stress in terms of the interconnectedness of people's lives and actions, the relationships between interruption and arousal, and the construction of subjective emotions and stress from a conjunction of arousal and value. I hope that in pointing out how current cognitive theory can be put to use in such efforts, better understanding and communication among the various practitioners of the life sciences can be fostered.

REFERENCES

Berscheid E (1982): Attraction and emotion in interpersonal relationships. Clark MS, & Fiske ST (Eds.). In *Affect and Cognition: The Seventeenth Annual Carnegie Symposium on Cognition.* Hillsdale, NJ, Erlbaum.

Bourne HR, Lichtenstein LM, Melmon RL, Henny CS, Weinstein Y, & Shearer GM (1974): Modulation of inflammation and immunity by cyclic AMP. Science 184:19–28.

Claparede E (1934): *La genese de l'hypothese.* Geneva, Kundig.

Dohrenwend BS, Krasnoff L, Askenasy AR, & Dohrenwend BP (1978): Exemplification of a method for scaling life events: The PERI life events scale. Health Soc Behav 19:205–229.

Folkman S, Schaefer C, & Lazarus RS (1979): Cognitive processes as mediators of stress and coping. Hamilton V, & Warburton DM (Eds.). In *Human Stress and Cognition: An Information Processing Approach.* London, Wiley.

Frankenhaeuser M (1975): Experimental approaches to the study of catecholamines and emotion. Levi L (Ed.). In *Emotions: Their Parameters and Measurement.* New York, Raven Press.

Frankenhaeuser M (1976): The role of peripheral catecholamines in adaptation to understimulation and overstimulation. Serban G (Ed.). In *Psychopathology of Human Adaptation.* New York, Plenum Press.

Frankenhaeuser M (1979): Psychoneuroendocrine approaches to the study of emotion as related to stress and coping. Howe HE, & Dienstbier RA (Eds.). In *Nebraska Symposium on Motivation 1978.* Lincoln, University of Nebraska Press.

Frankenhaeuser M, & Rissler A (1970): Effects of punishment on catecholamine release and efficiency of performance. Psychopharmacologia 17:378–390.

Gal R, & Lazarus RS (1975): The role of activity in anticipating and confronting stressful situations. J Hum Stress 1:4–20.

Holmes TH, & Rahe RH (1967): The social readjustment rating scale. J Psychosom Res 11:213–219.

Jemmott JB, Borysenko M, Borysenko J, McClelland DC, Chapman R, Meyer D, & Benson H (1981): *Stress, power motivation, and immunity.* Unpublished manuscript, Harvard University.

Lacey BC, & Lacey JI (1974): Studies of heart rate and other bodily processes in sensorimotor behavior. Black A, Brener J, Dicara L, & Obrist PA (Eds.). In *Cardiovascular Psychophysiology: Current Mechanisms, Biofeedback and Methodology.* Chicago, Aldine-Atherton.

Lazarus RS (1975): The self-regulation of emotion. Levi L (Ed.). In *Emotions: Their Parameters and Measurement.* New York, Raven Press.

Mandler G (1964): The interruption of behavior. Levine D (Ed.). In *Nebraska Symposium on Motivation: 1964.* Lincoln, University of Nebraska Press.

Mandler G (1975): *Mind and Emotion.* New York, Wiley.

Mandler G (1979): Thought processes, consciousness, and stress. Hamilton V, Warburton DM (Eds.). In *Human Stress and Cognition: An Information Processing Approach.* London, Wiley.

Mandler G (1982a): The construction of emotion in the child. Izard CE (Ed.). In *Emotions in Infants and Measuring Children.* New York, Cambridge University Press.

Mandler G (1982b): Stress and thought processes. Breznitz S, Goldberger L (Eds.). In *Handbook of Stress.* New York, Free Press/Macmillan.

Mandler G (1982c): The structure of value: Accounting for taste. Clark MS, & Fiske ST (Eds.). In *Affect and Cognition: The Seventeenth Annual Carnegie Symposium on Cognition.* Hillsdale, NJ, Erlbaum.

Marcel AJ (In press a): Conscious and unconscious perception: I. Experiments on visual masking and word perception. Cognitive Psychol.

Marcel AJ (In press b): Conscious and unconscious perception: II. An approach to consciousness. Cognitive Psychol.

Mason JW (1975): A historical view of the stress field. Hum Stress 1:6–12, 22–36.

McClelland DC, Floor E, Davidson RJ, & Saron C (1980): Stressed power motivation, sympathetic activation, immune function, and illness. J Hum Stress 6(2):11–19.

McClelland DC, & Jemmott JB III (1980): Power motivation, stress and physical illness. J Hum Stress 6(4):6–15.

Miller GA, Galanter EH, & Pribram K (1960): *Plans and the Structure of Behavior.* New York, Holt.

Nisbett RE, & Wilson TD (1977): Telling more than we can know: Verbal reports on mental processes. Psychol Rev 84:231–259.

Pick J (1970): *The Autonomic Nervous System.* Philadelphia, Lippincott.

Rahe RH (1978): Life change events and mental illness: An overview. J Hum Stress 5:2–9.

Rahe RH, & Arthur RJ (1978): Life change and illness studies: Past history and future directions. Stress 4:3–15.

Rogers MP, Dubey D, & Reich P (1979): The influence of the psyche and the brain on immunity and susceptibility to disease: A critical review. Psychosom Med 41:147–167.

Schachter S, & Singer JE (1962): Cognitive, social and physiological determinants of emotional state. Psychol Rev 69:379–399.

Silver RL, & Wortman CB (1980): Coping with undesirable life events. Gaber J, & Seligman MEP (Eds.). In *Human Helplessness: Theory and Applications.* New York, Academic Press, pp. 279–375.

Singer JE, Lundberg U, & Frankenhaeuser M (1978): Stress on the train: A study of urban commuting. Baum A, Singer JE, & Valins S (Eds.). In *Advances in Environmental Psychology,* vol 1. Hillsdale, NJ, Erlbaum.

Wallston BS, Alagna SW, DeVellis BM, & DeVellis RF (1981): *Social Support and Physical Health.* Unpublished manuscript.

17

Emotion, Adaptation, and Disease:
A Multidimensional Theory

Lydia Temoshok

AN INFORMATION PROCESSING THEORY OF ADAPTATION

Hierarchical Organization of Information Transforming Mental Subsystems

The mind, like a living cell, is an *open system* according to Bertalanffy's (1968) definition: "a system in exchange of matter with its environment, presenting import and export, building up and breaking down of its material components" (p. 141). Open systems tend toward increased order or "negative entropy." The elaboration of order or structure through the import of matter depends upon the existence of ways to process that matter (Buckley, 1967).

The difference between the mind and other open systems, however, is that the mind imports, exports, and orders information rather than matter. Matter, energy, and information always flow together, in that information is carried via electrochemical impulses in a substrate of physical matter (brain, body). It is the *relations* of these impulses, rather than the impulses themselves, that create information and potential meaning as mental phenomena. Information is an abstract formal patterning that describes relations between entities, acts, emotions, abstractions, and the like. Bateson (1972) called it "the difference that makes a difference." The difference that information makes may be seen as a change in state that can be represented by a means of a change in a symbolic model.

Information from the external environment or from endogenous systems can be utilized by the mind system only if it is transformed into "matter for mind," literally "food for thought." This process of information transformation involves certain rules, just as there are rules for the transformation of matter and energy. Kuhn (1977) suggested that there are different sets of transformation rules, such that information or pattern remains *qualitatively* equivalent when transformed, whereas matter and energy remain *quantitatively* the same.

In the theory presented in this chapter, the mind and environment systems, as well as mental subsystems, are separated from each other by *information boundaries*. Because "goings-on" on one side of an information boundary are qualitatively different from those on the other side, it is hypothesized that a reorganization or a transformation of pattern is required before information can be represented in another subsystem. Qualitative differences between representations in different subsystems involve the concept of *meaning* as both distinct from and more than information. Meaning is the significance of information to a system that processes it (Miller, 1959). Meaning both arises out of and creates organization. Organization can be both biologically "hard-wired" or mentally acquired.

The basic idea of a hierarchically organized series of mental subsystems has been elaborated in two nearly parallel theories by Battista (1978) and John (1976), which are themselves related to Tart's (1975)

I am extremely grateful to Bruce W. Heller, Kent Bach, Jesse D. Geller, Jeffrey Wagner, and Lynn Pierson for their comments on previous versions of this chapter, and to David M. Sweet for his critical assistance in the preparation of the manuscript. Special appreciation is due to Paul Ekman, Silvan S. Tomkins, and Claus B. Bahnson, whose thoughtful suggestions regarding certain problematic points and concepts in the manuscript were invaluable, and whose work has been a continual source of scholarship and inspiration.

nonhierarchical, but similarly organized theory of emotional subsystems. The theory presented here retains the notion of hierarchical organization and posits an analogous series, but defines the mental subsystems somewhat differently. More importantly, the organizing principle in this theory is that of *information and meaning transformation* (Temoshok, 1983).

In Table 17-1 components of Tart's, Battista's, and John's theories are compared (this comparison is adapted from Heller, 1978). Brief definitions, which are consistent with Wolman (1973), for the elements in my system follow.

Sensation refers to stimulus-related sense organ (e.g., eye, ear) and associated nervous system activity leading to a particular sensory area in the brain.

Perception is more complex than sensation and more dependent upon mental processes (e.g., learning, motivation, social, and personality factors). In gestalt psychology, perception results from an innate organizing process between perceived configurations and chemical-electrical events in the brain.

The term *appraisal* corresponds largely to Lazarus' definition (e.g., Lazarus & Launier, 1978) of it as a first evaluation of an organism–environment transaction in terms of the significance for that orga-

nism's well-being. (The difference in my use of the term is that it has a less conscious and less cognitive tone). Two subprocesses are subsumed under the rubric of appraisal: *arousal* is an increase in the complexity (amount of information) of neural organization, manifested by brain activation (desynchronized EEG); *attention* is the selective perception of a certain stimulus from a complex situation.

Motivation is the regulation of need-satisfying and goal-directed behaviors. It may be used more simply to designate direction toward a goal or goals that controls attention at any given time (Simon, 1967). It is used in a very broad sense here to include both the traditional implication of primary and acquired drives, as well as the concept of the feedback loop in the test–operate–test–exit (TOTE) unit proposed by Miller et al. (1960). The TOTE model holds that performed operations are constantly guided by the outcome of various tests. Aspects of this pattern may be combined to represent both complex behaviors and the continuous feedback relations between plans, behaviors, and changes in the environment. Miller et al. emphasized the role of plans in initiating and guiding behavior. A plan does not have to be conscious; it is defined as "any hierarchical process in the organism that can control the order in which

Table 17-1:   Comparison of Subsystems in Four Theories of Consciousness

Author	Subconscious		Preconscious		Conscious	
Tart (1975)*	Exteroception (sensing environmental stimuli)	Input processing (selection and abstraction of sensory information)	Emotions	Space–time sense	Sense of identity Evaluation Cognitive processing; Decision making	Pure awareness
	Interoception (sensing bodily stimuli)	◄ — — — — — —	Memory	— — — — — — ►		
				Consciousness		
John (1976)*	Sensation	Perception		Subjective experience; the self	Self-awareness	Unition (awareness of being aware)
Battista (1978)*	Sensation	Perception	Emotion	Awareness	Self-awareness (awareness of being aware)	
Temoshok (1983)	Sensation Perception	Appraisal Arousal Attention	Motivation	Appositional consciousness	Propositional consciousness	

*Comparison of these three systems is adapted from Heller (1978).

a sequence of operations is to be performed" (Miller et al., 1960, p. 16).

Motivation is manifested by increased activity in the autonomic nervous system. Leeper (1948) argued that emotions serve the functions of arousing, sustaining, and directing activity. Consistent with this view is that of Tomkins (1962, 1963, 1979), which emphasized that affects are the primary biological motivating mechanism, stronger than drives, and necessary for a signal of bodily need to be transformed into action.

The terms *appositional* and *propositional consciousness* were proposed by Bogen (1973) to avoid the semantic problem with "nonverbal" versus "verbal," "unconscious" versus "conscious," or some other potentially problematic pair of terms. These approximate distinctions emphasize the different organizational modes of the two cerebral hemispheres (cf. Bakan, 1978; Galin, 1974). *Appositional* implies a capacity for apposing or comparing perceptions, but in proximity or juxtaposition, rather than in sequence or syntax. A translation into Freudian terms would be "primary process" thinking (Freud, 1946), which is characterized by the following: an absence of any negatives, conditionals, or other qualifying conjunctions; the lack of any sense of time; and the use of allusion, analogy, and symbolic representation (Hinsie & Campbell, 1970). The rules of *propositional* thought may be analyzed by syntax, semantics, and mathematical logic. A proposition is a statement in which something is affirmed or denied so that it can be significantly characterized as either true or false. Thus, it has pretensions to objective reality. Propositional thought is equivalent to Freud's (1946) term "secondary process," the mode of operation of the ego, regulating the discharge of excitations arising from either external stimuli or instinctual demands through reality testing, logic, and judgment.

By presenting this theory in terms of a hierarchically organized series, I do not mean to say that information processing is limited to a forward (left to right) direction. A more accurate depiction would include all possible influences of thoughts and emotions upon attention, and all interactions of positive and negative feedback across levels and systems, including feedback from facial muscles that influences emotion, the effects of efferent modulation of afferent input (e.g., Spinelli & Pribram, 1967), and so forth. In other words, there should be bidirectional arrows from every element in the theory to every other element in Table 17-1. The hierarchical organization presented here is intended

to illustrate the proposed increasingly more complex types of information transformations that are made possible by the evolution of more complex brain structures.

Neural Substrates and Forms of Encoding

The organizing biological structure for these mental subsystems is the neural substrate. It may be said that the mind as a system emerges from neurophysiology and brain structure (John, 1976; Schwartz, 1975; Sperry, 1969, 1976). I further propose that this emergence is not an all-or-nothing state, but that mental subsystems early in the hierarchical series are more embedded in biology and neurobiology, while mental subsystems later in the series are increasingly less dependent upon biological structure.

The proposed neural substrates for a hierarchical series of information processing subsystems are depicted in Figure 17-1. Since Mueller describes the neuroanatomical correlates of emotion in authoritative detail in Chapter 10, and the proposed neural substrates in Figure 17-1 are consistent with his review, they are not elaborated in this chapter.

In my theory, each mental subsystem has its own mode of representation, which is based on the respective neural substrate. These representative modes are also conceived of as hierarchically organized such that the more basic modes are concretely bound to the underlying neural substrates, while the more complex modes are more emergent, in the systems sense.

In Table 17-2 forms of stimulus encoding are hypothetically assigned to levels of information transformation (according to my interpretation of the extensive literature in this area). The interested reader is referred to reviews on psychophysiology (Grings & Dawson, 1978), psychoneuroendocrinology (Frankenhaeuser, 1979), neurotransmitters (McGreer & McGreer, 1980), and pituitary hormones in the brain (Krieger & Liotta, 1979).

Mental structures are considered phylogenetically continuous with biologically hard-wired structures. *Structure* refers to a system of generalized representations of past organism–environment transactions that determine an organism's habitual and potential action tendencies. In Davidson's (1980) discussion of consciousness and information processing, there is an unconscious system of information processing comprising certain neural structures whose function is to transform input according to certain rules or algorithms. My elaboration of Davidson's use of the

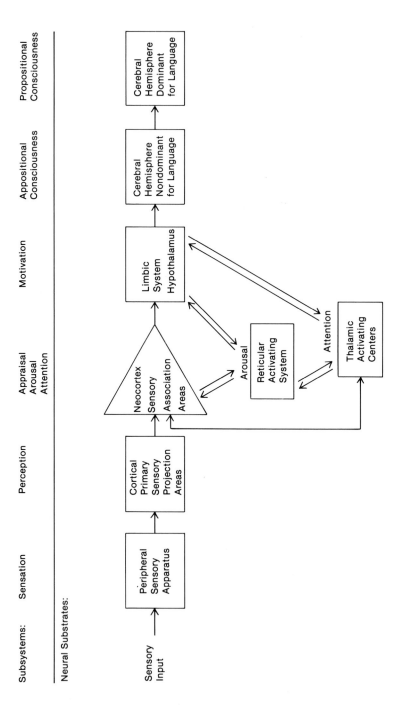

Figure 17-1. Proposed neural substrates for information processing systems.

Table 17-2:   Stimulus and Memory Encoding

Sensation	Perception	Appraisal	Motivation	Appositional Consciousness	Propositional Consciousness
		Form of Stimulus Encoding			
Transduction		Electrochemical	Neuroendocrine	Neurotransmitters	
Transformation of external energy into nerve impulses	Sensory signals received by feature	Cortical evoked potential EEG desynchronization	Autonomic nervous system	Acetylcholine, dopamine, noradrenaline, serotonin, etc.	
			Endocrine system	Symbolic Representation	
			Enkephalins, β–endorphin	Spatiotemporal patterns and regulations	Linguistic, sequential relations
		Form of Memory Encoding			
"Hard-Wired" Structures		Biocognitive Structures		Affective–Cognitive Structures	
Peripheral sensory apparatus	Short-term ionic and echoic storage	Recognition memory	Hippocampal consolidation of memory from short to long-term storage with hemispheric diffentiation		
				Episodic Memory	Semantic Memory
	Pattern recognition	"Affective attitudes" (Arnold, 1960)	Physiological state-labeled memory	Affective state-labeled memory	Verbally labeled memory
				Nonverbal imagery process	Verbal symbolic process

Immune System Recognition and Memory

concept of "biocognitive structures" is that these represent the intermediate level of memorial encoding in the emergence of more "purely mental" affective-cognitive structures from the hard-wired neural substrate.

Adaptiveness of Hierarchical Levels of Mental Organization

Adaptation

Hierarchically organized mental subsystems emerge from increasingly complex brain structures that are phylogenetically ordered. It is proposed that the mind's capacity to transform information and meaning developed, as did other functions, gradually over the course of evolution. The mind is a unique adaptive tool not only because it utilizes information instead of matter, but because it can ela-

borate and create meaning. The latter capability is maximally adaptive in the sense that it facilitates a potentially infinite number of information–meaning transformations. The term "adaptive" is used in Piaget's (1952) sense, in which the organism is transformed by the environment (and also transforms the environment in the process) so as to increase the probability of favorable interchanges between the environment and itself.

The proposed functions served by different organizations of information and meaning across different mental subsystems are presented in Table 17-3. At the more basic levels, information is dealt with much as matter is processed: it is either taken in (incorporated) or not, based on biological programs and needs. In general, it may be said that with ascension of the phylogenetic scale, there is decreased reliance on "wired-in" stimulus–response linkages, and concomitantly more emphasis on learning and

Table 17-3:   Proposed Functions Served by Information Processing Subsystems

Sensation	Perception	Appraisal	Motivation	Appositional Consciousness	Propositional Consciousness
			Function		
Internal and external regulation		Danger avoidance: survival–related approach	Preparation for action, drive-satisfying behavior, basic social signalling, learning and memory	Exploration and sustained activity, social bondings, more complex communication; maintenance of social order	Purposeful action, social cooperation in goal-directed activity, identity and cultural growth
			Means		
"Hard-wired" reflexes and responses; incorporation and elimination-rejection; perception of pain and satisfaction		Good–bad discriminations; experiences of pleasure–displeasure	Biological response patterns, drives, emotional behavior display, autonomic nervous system arousal	Experience of interest, facial expressions	Digital codification, verbal representation, self-system

symbolic thought. Thus, what increases is the potential for variability of response. The basic emotion language may be considered a primary means of "knowing" beyond sensation and perception. It involves an encoding of a gestalt, a patterning of stimuli that includes a distinctive perceptual quality of a particular emotion associated with that pattern. The animals that best "knew" when to be attracted or repulsed from objects, when to withdraw, and when to attend to their own internal evaluative messages would have had survival advantages over animals whose brains could not pattern stimuli in this way.

The proposed expressive concomitants of information processing subsystems are presented in Table 17-4. The components of Table 17-2 and -4 are elaborated in the following sections.

Preemotional Phenomena

Some researchers and emotion theorists have made explicit distinctions between emotional and behavioral phenomena. For example, Ekman and his colleagues (1982) pointed out the characteristics of startle that distinguish it from emotion: the invariability of its occurrence given a certain elicitor; the limited number of elicitors; the stereotypy of the facial and bodily reactions consequent to the elicitor; and the rapid onset of these reactions. In Table 17-4 startle as a phenomenon is located at the boundary of emotional and behavioral expressions because I believe it represents a form of adaptation

to environmental stimuli that is more mutable and responsive to environmental changes than are other reflexes (e.g., the Babinski reflex).

Other behavioral concomitants of preemotional phenomena in Table 17-4 are attention, orienting and defensive reactions, sensitization, and habituation. In Sokolov's (1960) theory, *orienting reactions* to intense and/or novel stimuli include increased skin conductance, peripheral vasoconstriction, and cephalic vasodilation. Graham and Clifton (1966) also found a decrease in heart rate. *Defensive reactions*, which occur in response to very intense or aversive stimuli, include heart rate acceleration, cephalic vasoconstriction, and high amplitude sympathetic nervous system activity. *Habituation* and *sensitization* are two opposing processes that occur as a function of repeated or constant stimuli. While sensitization is an increase in a response, habituation is the decrease in the size of an orienting response during constant or repetitive simulation (Graham, 1973; Groves and Thompson, 1970).

Good–Bad Discrimination

All of the aforementioned terms have in common a reaction to stimuli that is based on sheer newness. At the next level of complexity, *appraisal*, valence is added. Valence is the most basic ingredient of an emotional response. At this level, "newness" is given a *soupçon* of valence such that a perceived old–new distinction becomes familiar–unfamiliar. Zajonc (1968) conducted many experiments in this arena

Table 17-4:   Proposed Expressive Concomitants of Information Processing Subsystems

Subsystems:	Sensation	Perception	Appraisal	Motivation	Appositional Consciousness	Propositional Consciousness
					Stimulus Source	
Emotional concomitants			Subjective orientation: displeasure, pleasure	Physiological system: drive and need states	Endogenous systems: awareness of need status, repressed emotional states	Endogenous systems: subjective feelings
	Perturbation stability (regularity)	Pain (new) satisfaction (comfort, old)	Objective orientation: dislike, like	Exogenous systems: unmodulated emotions	Exogenous systems: modulated emotions	Exogenous systems, reappraisal, affective judgments, propositional attitudes
				Mental system: anxiety depression		
(Transformation)						
— — — — — — — —	— — —	Startle — — —	Alertness — — —	— — — — — —	— — — — — —	— — — — — —
Behavioral concomitants	Incorporation Elimination-rejection	Attention orienting and defensive reactions	Focused attention	Emotional display	Spontaneous facial expressions	Non-spontaneous facial expressions
	Sensory adaption	Habituation Sensitization		Appetitive and consummatory behaviors	Automatic behaviors	Goal-directed behaviors
		Unconditioned approach and avoidance		Biological response patterns	Impulsive actions	Voluntary and intended actions
		Distress, crying				
		Conditioned learning		Instrumental learning	Habits	Modification of habitual actions

that suggest that familiarity ("mere exposure") in almost every instance breeds liking. Furthermore, he demonstrated that the subject need not be able to identify an object to like it; the individual merely needs to feel it to be familiar (Moreland & Zajonc, 1977, 1979).

We can only speculate as to why this emotionlike phenomenon would be adaptive. There is high survival value in making judgments about stimuli quickly, before conscious recognition, followed immediately by a ready response appropriate to that evaluation. Basically, animals need to know whether something is familiar and thus "okay," if not good and worthy of approach, or unfamiliar and thus probably dangerous and to be avoided. These evaluations are truly matters of life and death that should not be left to the slower working cognitive processing system.

In this theory, the basic affective experiences of pleasure and displeasure—as more affective transformations of perceived satisfaction or pain—originate at the level of appraisal. What is experienced as pleasant (rewarding) or unpleasant (punishing) by an animal is probably not determined by chance associations between internal need states and environmental events. First, except for the early, relatively undifferentiated experience of the infant, there are many specific sensory qualities (e.g., tastes, smells, visual images) that are associated with such experiences.

Second, the connection of these more specific sensations with need reduction is probably genetically based, in that there may be natural selection of only those animals that have found certain sensations rewarding. Along similar lines, the sociobiologists (e.g., Barash, 1977) have argued that we are preprogramed to react to certain stimuli that have biological meaning for us. Pleasure is nature's way of reinforcing reactions to certain stimuli that satisfy biological needs. Sugar tastes sweet to us, or rather, we perceive its chemical configuration as "good sweetness" because those primordial primates who could detect sweetness, which was associated with ripe fruit, derived more nutrition from eating these ripe fruit, and so were better fortified to survive and multiply than their associates who ate unripe fruit. "Sweetness" as a sensory quality is connected with the mouth and with eating, and is accompanied by an affect of pleasure. It would be difficult if things were wired otherwise. In Tomkins' (1979) vivid example: "If instead of pain, we always had an orgasm to injury, we would be biologically destined to bleed to death."

Emotional Response Patterns

At the level of *motivation*, drive and need states (hunger, thirst, sex) lend urgency to approach, appetitive, consummatory, or avoidance behaviors (Tomkins, 1979). The strength of these states makes *instrumental learning* possible. In this sense, emotions replace biologically hard-wired response proclivities (which include the reflexes) that may underlie unconditioned responses and classical conditioning.

Memory encoding at the level of motivation relies on sequentially or temporally tagged scenes. Retrieval in such "episodic memory" (Tulving, 1972) is accomplished by contextual coding, that is, what happens inside and outside the organism at the time of the occurrence on which the memory is based. Physiological states may serve as cues to retrieve the memory because they were part of the original context. These features nominate episodic memory as a good candidate for the mediation of state-dependent learning (Reus et al., 1979). State-dependent learning was first demonstrated in animal studies that focused on whether an animal could discriminate one state defined by a drug or a certain dosage of

that drug from another dosage level, another drug, or placebo (Weingartner, 1978) (Table 17-2).

Two biological response patterns associated with the level of motivation are the fight–flight and the conservation–withdrawal patterns (Cannon, 1936; Engel, 1962). Kaufman (1977) considered these patterns (which are observable in the nonhuman primate) to be the biological analgen of anxious and depressive reactions, respectively. Unmodulated emotions (designated in Table 17-4 as concomitants of motivation) represent the transformations of displeasure into rage, terror, disgust and anguish; pleasure into ecstasy; startle into alarm; and alertness into excitement.

Emotional display at this level serves the function of enhancing an animal's chances of survival by signaling that the animal intends to fight or flee. For example, the expression of fight-threat behaviors communicates information that the animal is prepared to attack, which may disuade its antagonist from pressing the matter. Displays of courtship and mating, of greeting and recognition, of dominance and submission, and of warning and alarm are other examples of social signaling that play crucial roles in adaptation.

Sustained Activity and Social Communication

Reliance on physiological states and/or environmental cues may put an animal at a disadvantage in rapidly changing situations that have not been previously associated with such endogenous or exogenous cues. The success of human adaptation may be based on elaboration of the neocortex, which was able to launch information processing past its moorings in either physiology or situational context. Representations at the level of appositional consciousness (hypothetically in the nondominant cerebral hemisphere) involve the encoding of a gestalt, a patterning of stimuli that includes a distinctive perceptual quality of the particular emotional state associated with that pattern. Because the emotional state, speculatively, is activated by neurotransmitters rather than by the slower acting neuroendocrine system, the animal with affective state–labeled memory (in contrast to physiological state–labeled memory) can access this experience more readily and then respond on the basis of it (Table 17-2).

Many theories of emotion emphasize the importance of negatively toned emotions in helping an animal adapt to survival-related emergencies, or in signaling an internal need to reduce tension. Lazarus (e.g., Lazarus et al., 1980), among others, has stressed that positively toned emotions are equally crucial in the evolutionary context. Play and exploration are usually accompanied by the positive emotion of interest, which sustains these activities. I hypothesize that this emotion is generated at the level of appositional consciousness. White (1963) posited that such positively toned emotions as curiosity, interest, and excitement are particularly characteristic of human adaptive processes. Certainly, an alert, exploratory orientation to the world allows animals to learn about their environments, increasing their behavioral repertoire, and thus their adaptive potential (Table 17-3).

Emotional expression at the level of appositional consciousness enhances more complex social communication and maintains social bonding across time. The latter capacity is especially important in primates such as humans, who are dependent upon caretakers for up to two decades. Bowlby (1969) analyzed the social signal function of emotional behavior in infants. It is likely that a "mothering instinct," if it exists, would not be enough in itself to ensure persistent mother–infant attachment. The emotional responses of the infant to the mother elicit further emotional reactions in the mother that cement the bond (Emde et al., 1976).

Abstract Verbal Representation

In propositional consciousness, it is hypothesized that verbal, conceptual functions emerge from the visual articulation of relatively stable patterns that are subjectively felt in appositional consciousness as gestalten (Langer, 1942). A discursive, linear codification system using word-symbols is not dependent upon preexisting internal configurations, whether biological or mental in representation, to interpret stimuli. Thus, at the level of propositional consciousness, more information can be imported from external systems and then transformed and represented as a potentially infinite number of codes.

It is the freedom from direct experiential contact with the world that gives propositional consciousness some of its evolutionary advantages. Linguistic rather than spatiotemporal representations make long-term memory storage more efficient for both quick and complex manipulations. Semantic memory (Quillian, 1968) represents knowledge about words, their meanings and referents, and their relations organized into manageable units such as abstractions or generalizations (Table 17-2). Freedom from the here and now allows propositional consciousness to make long-range plans based upon symbols stored in memory. Instead of

constructing a plan according to an innately tried and true blueprint, propositional consciousness has a metaperspective on many possible combinations and recombinations of materials and construction plans. It facilitates the solution of problems by generating multiple alternative images of causes and effects in various combinations. This capability enables propositional consciousness to take an "overseer" or trouble shooter role when automatic operations hit a snag (Mandler, 1975). When automatic operations (e.g., habits) are interrupted, propositional consciousness provides a means whereby thoughts and behaviors may be selected purposively, opening up new directions for adaptation.

Another important function of verbal representation in propositional consciousness is that communication via language underlies the capacity for humans to work together at particular moments as a common information system, extending individual boundaries. Often, individual needs or goals can be more effectively met by taking into account the goals of others and then working together to reach these goals. At lower levels of organization, emotion recruited changes in the immediate internal and external subsystems; at the level of propositional consciousness, language is able to recruit changes that are spatially and temporally removed.

Behavioral concomitants at the level of propositional consciousness have reached an apogee of controllability by mental, as distinct from biological, structures. The habits, impulsive actions, and more automatic behaviors characteristic of appositional consciousness become *voluntary intended actions* and *goal-directed behaviors*. At this level, habitual actions and many biological programs can be modified. In terms of emotion-related behavior, the spontaneous facial expressions of appositional consciousness are capable of being voluntarily altered. (See Ekman, 1980), and Ekman et al., 1980, on the differences between spontaneous and nonspontaneous facial expressions). (Refer to Table 17-4.)

Continuity in emotional states across time is made possible by the emergence of propositional consciousness. It is hypothesized that the self is a crucial adaptation in human evolution. It is adaptive because it evaluates information and assigns meaning in a centralized, situationally flexible manner. For example, what is meaningful to one when one feels afraid is different from what is meaningful when one feels sexually excited. If these meanings were conferred only by biology, then one's actions subsequent to these feelings would be buffeted by the whims of environmental events within the constraints imposed by survival needs. If there were no organizational principle at the level of propositional consciousness, then an infinite amount of information would permeate the boundary between exogenous and endogenous systems. An open system cannot indiscriminatively incorporate information. Consistency as well as change is critical for the continued existence and modulated growth of living systems. It is proposed that the self system is the means by which consistency is achieved at the level of propositional consciousness.

Emotional Modulation, Amplification, and Reflexiveness

It is often assumed that the engagement of higher cortical systems can dampen responses. In my theory, as well, the transformation of information from neural and neuroendocrine representation in the limbic system—particularly in the amygdala and the hypothalamus (MacLean's 1969, paleomammalian brain; see also Mueller, in this volume, Chapter 10)—to symbolic spatiotemporal patterned representations in the nondominant cerebral hemisphere (MacLean's neomammalian brain) modulates the primal emotions and their associated behaviors. As emotional phenomena are transformed from the subsystem of Motivation to Appositional Consciousness, one difference may be intensity: rage becomes anger, terror turns to fear, anguish to sadness, ecstasy to joy, alarm to surprise, and curiosity to interest. Another basis for differences across transformational levels may be attributed to emotion elicitors. For example, the emotion of disgust results from an evaluation of the failure of an exogenous object or event to meet an expectation related to an internal need, drive, or drive-related affect. While the behavioral reflex of disgust occurs at very primitive subsystem levels (in the form of rejection at the level of sensation, or avoidance behaviors at the level of perception) where it is associated with noxious *physical* stimuli, at the level of Appositional Consciousness, the elicitors of disgust are presumed to include social stimuli, as well.

The emotions indicated above that hypothetically emerge at the level of Appositional Counsciousness are nearly identical to the list of what some emotion theorists (e.g., Tomkins, 1962, 1963, 1979; Ekman, Friesen and Ellsworth, 1972; Izard, 1971; and Pluchik, 1980) have called the "primary emotions." This list includes: anger, fear, sadness, joy, interest, surprise, disgust, and shame.

A remaining problem is to explain shame, which in the current theory, has no representative at prior transformational levels. It is proposed that shame is a precursor of the *affective judgements* that are the hallmark of emotionality at the level of Propositional Consciousness. Shame results from a reflexive evaluation of some failure to control an internal need, drive, or drive-related affect. Shame is also a precursor of self-consciousness in that it entails a heightened sense of the self that has motivational value for developing self-identity and self-esteem (Izard, 1979). The reflexiveness involved in shame also serves a basic self-monitoring function for an animal existing in a social group, with all its requirements for impulse control. It is proposed that at the level of Propositional Consciousness, in which cognitive judgment is in full blush, and self-reflexiveness is potentially complete, shame may be transformed into guilt.

The following explanation is proposed for the increasing modulation of emotion at hierarchically more complex subsystems of consciousness. In Tomkins' theory (1962, 1963, modified in 1979), affect lends its power to other systems such as drives via *analogic amplification*. A drive does not inspire humans to act; what motivates is drive transformed into emotion. Amplification (Tomkins' term) plus transformation culminates in the dawn of consciousness through the following process: A stimulus is amplified through its transformations across the subsystems of sensation, perception, and appraisal to acquire the urgency it possesses at the level of motivation. Metaphorically, further amplification in the dimension of loudness would only render that stimulus deafening. It is logical to propose that given further processing, the next transformation would involve a reflexiveness of this forward amplified transformation back onto itself. This reflexiveness then results in awareness of affects related to internal bodily states, which have been amplified up to this level (e.g., the feeling of thirst). The adaptive value of this reflexiveness is to direct the organism to correct the problem, or to meet the original biological need that gave rise to a drive state. It is hypothesized that amplification of emotional information above a certain level results in its *repression* when it is transformed to the level of appositional consciousness.

The process of reflexiveness culminates in the affective–cognitive operations that comprise propositional consciousness. At this level, subjectivity is expanded beyond awareness of endogenous states (e.g., recognizing thirst) to awareness of exogenous objects and events that affect the subject but are separate from him or her (e.g., "I am angry at her"), to self-awareness and awareness of this state (e.g., "I think, therefore I am").

STRESS AND STYLES OF COPING

Conceptualizing Stress

The concept of stress is perhaps the most talked about, most researched, but the least clearly understood in the psychological literature today. Reviews are abundant in the literature and the main concepts are well summarized in Chapters 4, 16, and 18.

For the purposes of forging a critical link in my information transformation theory of disease, a conceptualization of stress is elaborated in terms of environmental or situational events ("stressors") that have particular significance for the individual. This concept is a variation on the transactional theme proposed by Lazarus and his colleagues (e.g., Lazarus, 1980; Lazarus & Launier, 1978). It is likely that the relation between a stressor and a physiological or psychological disorder is not a simple linear one, and that mediators of the stressor-disorder connection probably include physiological predispositions, early childhood experiences, social resources, and personality variables (Kobasa, 1979). How a person appraises an environmental event as a stressor, and subsequently tries to deal with it (e.g., whether one feels in control, challenged, imbued with a sense of meaning in confronting the stressor, or the converse), rather than the nature of the stressor itself probably determines whether stress and stress-related disorders result. Depending on an individual's physiological and psychological predispositions, and current appraisals of the situation, a stress event or stressor induces or highlights reactions (such as depression or anxiety) within the individual. Stress reactions, then, are syndromes characterized by the appearance of certain affective states. Stress as a stimulus or a stressor is this differentiated from a stress response, which is not stress per se, but a reaction to a stressor. Of course, the term "stressor" itself implies a transaction between the environmental stimulus and the individual; that is, something within the individual determines what in the environment is a stressor and what is just another occurrence.

In this transactional perspective, stress is a psychosocial phenomenon that is neither an external stimulus nor an organismic response, but rather, a transactional process. Stress may be most usefully conceptualized as a state of adaptive commerce between an organism and its environment, a state that is characterized by uncertainty and results from a loss of structure (and hence, a gain in entropy) in the organism. The problem of adaptation becomes one of evolving, supplying, or supporting internal and/or external structure ("negentropy") in the face of change.

Internalizing and Externalizing Transactions

It is proposed that organisms undergo a continual dynamic dialectic between two kinds of transactions with their environments: environment-to-organism, and organism-to-environment. The first set of processes can be thought of as *internalization*, or the representation of aspects of the environment (for example, visual stimuli) in the organism as perceptions. The second process can be considered *externalization*, or the manifestation in the environment of some aspect of an organism's informational state in terms of action, or as an expression of a thought or an emotion. This discussion is congruent with the extensive psychological literature on cognitive style, in which internalizing and externalizing may be interpreted as the two major and contrasting modes of adapting (e.g., automatization versus perceptual restructuring, Broverman et al., 1964; external versus internal locus of control, Rotter, 1966; stimulus-bound versus non–stimulus-bound individuals, Schachter & Rodin, 1974; field dependence versus independence, Witkin et al., 1962; see discussion in Nisbett & Temoshok, 1976).

The dialectic between the tendency of the human mind to be open to new experience, and then to be selective about internalizing this experience appears to be a fragile one. Boundary regulations serve the adaptive function of maintaining a balance between integrity and identity, on the one hand, and growth and change on the other. If one process predominates, then the integrity of the mind, which is maintained by the mind–environment boundary, would be threatened; either the boundary could become too permeable to environmental influence, or it could inappropriately expand the realm of the mind into that of the environment. Externalizing and internalizing tendencies are viewed as transformational styles in the sense that they represent the individual's proclivity, when stressed, to transform organism–environment transactions along a certain trajectory. According to this theory, when too great a demand is placed on the system to adapt, one or the other of these two main adaptive processes may go awry. This could happen when the demand or stressor is intense or acute, and/or when adaptation is blocked or otherwise not possible. When this stressful situation emerges, then either internalization or externalization processes may become exaggerated.

Maladaptive externalization involves the extension of organismic boundaries into the environment, or the misplacing of one's properties onto the environment, where these properties are not recognized as one's own. Examples of inappropriate externalization include such intrusions of one's boundaries into another's as burglary, rape, or murder in the activity sphere, or communicative intrusions such as shouting in anger in the emotional sphere. A more familiar kind of externalization is the paranoid individual's projection of his or her impulses, expectations, desires, or intentions onto the environment.

Inappropriate internalization involves boundary penetration, i.e., being affected or influenced by the environment in such a way that one represents internally an aspect of the environment that is alien to or unintegrated with the internal order or structure. Examples include being influenced by another person to do something "alienated," such as committing murder for Charles Manson or suicide for Jim Jones, in the activity realm; or in the somatic realm, being negatively affected by noxious environmental agents such as bacteria and viruses. Another example is that of the person suffering bereavement who becomes depressed as a result of internalizing some aspect of that negative event or as a function of introjecting perceived negative characteristics of the lost loved one.

It is hypothesized that an internalizing or externalizing style of coping influences the direction of attempts to deal with a stressor, and ultimately influences the nature of the pathological processes that may result in disease when stress is not dealt with successfully.

Information Transforming Processes Under Stress

Speculatively, pathological processes are also influenced by information transformation. Earlier in this chapter an information processing theory of adaptation was described whereby information and meaning become increasingly elaborated across hierarchically organized levels from sensation to propositional consciousness. Information entering this transformational pathway is processed to the extent that is necessary to keep the organism in dynamic equilibrium with its environment. Thus, a very familiar stimulus may be processed through only a few levels and responded to in a reflexlike or habitual manner, while a more unfamiliar stimulus may be processed all the way up through propositional consciousness, which has a wide range of options for dealing with this problematic information.

If the information is too problematic (too intense, too much, too complex) to be processed at the level of propositional consciousness, then equilibrium has to be achieved by some other means. It is hypothesized that this is accomplished by a *reverse transformation* of the information across a subsystem boundary into the neighboring subsystem, or if it cannot be accommodated here, the next subsystem below that, and so on. Reverse transformation is a continuation of the process of information amplification, reflexiveness, and self-reflexiveness discussed earlier. In order to be accommodated at lower levels, information needs to be organized differently than it was in the forward transformation sequence. The necessity of a reorganization is apparent if one considers that in forward transformations there is generally an increasing amplification of information (which in appositional consciousness becomes reflexive, and in propositional consciousness becomes self-reflexive).

The hypothesis is that in order to accommodate complex, transformed information within less complex subsystems, the information is split into two sublevels. The splitting is accomplished such that a new transformational boundary is created between the two sublevels. The boundary separates the meaning of the information from its content. There is theoretical contiguity between this notion of information splitting and "repression."

In psychoanalytic theory, *repression* is an active process of keeping out of conscious awareness unacceptable or painful ideas or impulses. This is accomplished by first breaking such ideas or impulses into their basic affective and cognitive components, and then "repressing" one of these into subconsciousness. Speculatively, the more automatic and primitive defense mechanisms related to repression (e.g., denial) are elaborated in propositional consciousness into *suppression*, the conscious inhibition of an impulse, affect, or idea (Hinsie & Campbell, 1970). There may be precursors of repression at previous levels of information processing.[1]

Earlier in this chapter it was argued that appositional consciousness is organized around operations that serve the social communication system and function to maintain social order. To the extent that anxious and depressed states disrupt this order, and the place of the anxious or depressed individual in that order, it will be functional to repress them. I speculate further that repression serves the function of maintaining the "order," that is, the integrity, of the individual. Self-confrontation may elicit both physiological arousal, and increased anxiety and negative affect (Sackheim & Gur, 1978). Repression is used to avoid recognizing the often painful necessity of changing long-standing patterns of thinking, feeling, and/or behaving. These speculations on repression are consistent with Davidson's (1980) hypothesis that negative affective information processed in the right hemisphere does not get complete access to verbal centers in the left hemisphere. In this sense, there may be a functional disconnection between right hemispheric regions (from which appositional consciousness is proposed to emerge) involved in processing negative affect, and the verbal centers of the left hemisphere (from which propositional consciousness is proposed to emerge).

Repressed or retransformed information may be expressed at the level of its accommodation as a symptom. A *symptom* is any sign, physical or mental, that stands for something else (Hinsie & Campbell, 1970). In forward transformations, meaning is unitary, but the essence of a symptom as a maladaptive expression of information is the simultaneous existence of two forms of the original information. Symptoms are produced when these two forms are uneasily combined and expressed at a retransformed level as "compromise formations" (in psychoanalytic theory, a substitutive idea or act representing a repressed conflict; Hinsie & Campbell, 1970). The split-off meaning may also be kept from becoming conscious, and thus disruptive by its physiological, emotional, and/or behavioral expression. In Figure 17-2 the differences between forward and reverse transformations are represented in terms of information amplification or accommodation, respectively, and the concomitant expression of nonsymptomatic or symptomatic behavior, respectively, at each transformational level.

It is hypothesized that internalizing and externalizing styles express split-off meaning in different ways: the symptom is somatic for internalizers and psychological or behavioral for externalizers. In Figure 17-3 a mainly externalizing style under stress is depicted as exhibiting mainly psychological but some somatic symptoms, while a mainly internalizing style is shown as manifesting some psychological pathology along with the more prominent dysfunctional somatization. Internalizers mainly express symptomatology in terms of somatic disease. They may have some psychological manifestations, but these most likely will be less severe than the expressions of their externalizing equivalents. Externalizers mainly express psychological symptomatology, although they may express somatic pathology at a level less intense than their internalizing equivalents.

INFORMATION TRANSFORMATION THEORY APPLIED TO AN UNDERSTANDING OF DISEASE

Three-Dimensional Model of Maladaptive Transformations

Within a certain range of stimulus intensity and/or acuteness or chronicity, the organism may be strained but adapting—a state characterized by the engagement of certain processes of adaptation. These processes may include reflexes (e.g., pupilary dilation), attention, habituation, tolerance, felt emotion, coping efforts (including trial-and-error attempts), problem-solving strategies, and marshaling of resources. When the capacities of these adaptive processes are exceeded by an especially intense, acute, or chronic stressor, or when the organism cannot adapt within this normative range (perhaps because of preexisting organismic stress,

---

[1]For example, Gray (1976) postulated a behavioral inhibition system that mediates passive avoidance (the inhibition of behavior) in response to either punishing or extinctive situations. This system is hypothesized to respond to threatening stimuli by producing anxiety, but it *inhibits* motor behavior. There is evidence that the orienting response to novel stimuli is mediated by the behavioral inhibition system. At the level of motivation, exogenous feedback, which includes very basic social rules on the order of "do not express," shapes behavioral expression.

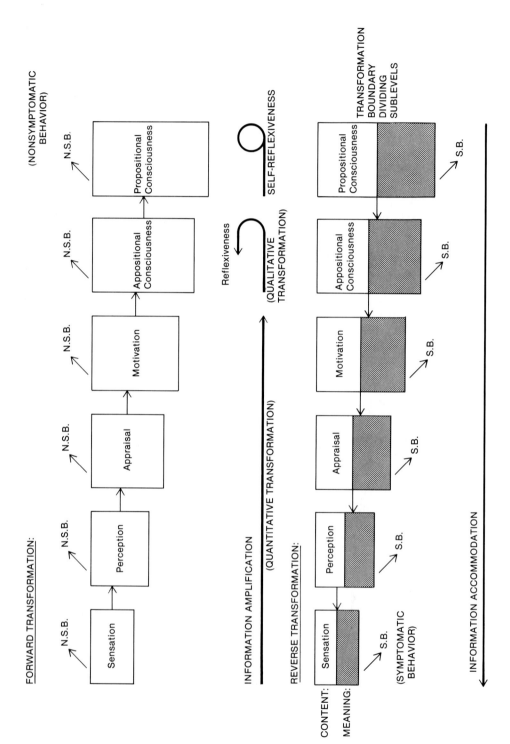

Figure 17-2. Comparison of forward and reverse information transformation.

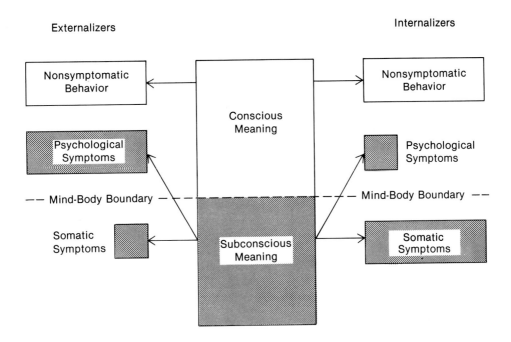

Figure 17-3.   Expression of symptomatic and nonsymptomatic behaviors by externalizers and internalizers.

limited coping ability, or vulnerability), then stress-related disorders may occur.

The theoretical distinction between acute and chronic stress must be emphasized. DSM-III (American Psychiatric Association, 1980) specifies as "conditions not attributable to a mental disorder" such acute stress-related phenomena as academic or occupational problems, "uncomplicated" bereavement, phase of life or other life circumstance problems, and parent–child problems. This view is compatible with my theory that conscious awareness arose in human beings as a system capable of more responsive adaptation. Acute stimuli evoke attention and emotion, which in turn mobilize conscious plans (intentions) to resolve the inequilibrium. Chronic stressors are less likely to be consciously noticed, and thus they are more likely to be handled by phylogenetically older systems of adaptation that handle stress by physiological reactions (e.g., fight, flight, or freeze behaviors and their endocrine-/immunologic concomitants). For these reasons, the remainder of this chapter is devoted to manifestations of chronic stress and chronically maladaptive coping.

It is hypothesized that for situations of chronic stress, the nature of the expressed symptom is a function of three factors: coping style (internalizing or externalizing), severity of the stressor (slight to extreme), and coping abilities (including intelligence, education, flexibility, experience, psychological and physical health, social support, money, and so forth). These three factors are thought to determine the transformational level at which stressful information can be accommodated. The manifestations of chronic psychological or somatric expressions at each transformational level are the disorders depicted in Figure 17-4. The specific disorders generated along the internalizing or externalizing trajectories are intended to be suggestive and illustrative, but certainly not comprehensive. No attempt is made to classify nor include behavioral disorders, such as malingering, antisocial or criminal behavior, psychosexual disorders, substance use disorders, or disorders of impulse control, (nor a great number of physical diseases). This conceptualization is structurally similar to Bahnson's (1969) model (reproduced in Figure 17-5) of complementarity of behavioral and somatic symptoms under increasing depth of repression. Bahnson's model presents somatic and psychological symptom formation as alternative attempted solutions to the basic need to express conflictual drive states. The differences between Figure 17-4 and 17-5 may be largely semantic, but they have implications for conceptualizing relationships among the principal terms in the two models. *Coping styles* in my model

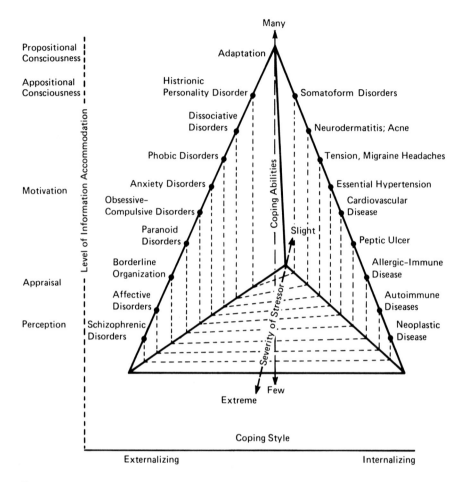

Figure 17-4. Maladaptive transformations: effects of stressor severity, coping effectiveness, and coping style on disease.

and *defense mechanisms* in Bahnson's model may be viewed as alternative ways of expressing the same function. The discrepancies in terminology which describe somatic and psychological behavioral symptoms are probably not significant, and reflect changes from 1969 to 1983 in the Diagnostic and Statistical Manual of Mental Disorders from earlier (DSM-I to DSM-II) to the latest (DSM-III) editions. For example, in DSM-III, phobias, anxiety states or neuroses, and obsessive-compulsive disorders are grouped together under the rubric of anxiety disorders, a proximity I try to maintain in my model.

A major difference between the models is that my transactional theory incorporates psychobiologic stress as a situational-environmental dimension, while Bahnson's theory implies psychobiologic stress

as a factor, but only depicts the organismic (psychologic and somatic) perspective in his model. Thus, instead of viewing symptom formation as the expression of conflictual drive states, I view symptoms as manifestations of maladaptive coping with stressors, whether internal or external in origin, as well as of coping abilities/resources.

Finally, Figure 17-4 incorporates my hypothesis that coping style, coping abilities and stressor severity enter into the adaptive equation to yield psychic and somatic disorders via maladaptive information transformation. These disorders are hypothesized to result from repressed, re-transformed information that is finally accommodated at a certain level (from perception to appositional consciousness). This process occurs when the organism is unable to deal with information either because

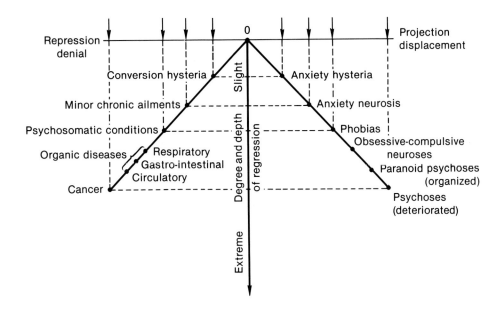

Figure 17-5. Bahnson and Bahnson's model of complementary behavioral and somatic symptoms under increasing depth of regression. (Reprinted from Bahnson CB (1969): Psychophysiological complementarity in malignancies: Past work and future vistas. Ann NY Acad Sci 164:319–334.)

of the uncertainty and/or complexity of the information (which makes it a stressor) and/or the lack of appropriate coping abilities to handle it. When information processing is chronically blocked at a certain level (e.g., endocrine, immune, hormone system responses) are first taxed and ultimately depleted. The particular symptom or disorder manifested in this set of circumstances is hypothesized to be a function of coping style and the physiological processes engaged at the level of transformation at which information is chronically accommodated.

For the remainder of Section III, the evidence that supports the particular placement of psychic and somatic disorders in Figure 17-4 is reviewed. Again, it should be noted that this effort will not be comprehensive: neither all the disorders in Figure 17-4, nor all the evidence for their hypothesized arrangement will be elaborated.

Histrionic Personality and Somatoform Disorders

What happens when propositional consciousness cannot represent a certain piece of information as a conscious intention? First, the recognition of intention is repressed or denied. One outcome

might be that more information is represented in imagination as a symbolic rather than a realistic enactment of an intention. The disorder corresponding to this hypothetical state is 'histrionic (formerly "hysterical") personality disorder.'

The exaggerated expression of emotion, the craving for activity and excitement, the overreaction to minor events, and the superficial level of interpersonal relationships are diagnostic criteria for the disorder that are congruent with the concept of splitting of content and meaning at the level of propositional consciousness, and the subsequent accommodation at the level of appositional consciousness. Emotion is expressed in an exaggerated, rather undifferentiated form. The meaningful aspects of interpersonal relationships are repressed such that only the superficial aspects of relations remain in consciousness and are behaviorally enacted (Temoshok & Heller, 1983).

The internalizing equivalent of a histrionic personality disorder is the transformation of intention into conversion symptomatology, that is, the symbolic representation of psychic conflict in terms of motor or sensory manifestations. (APA, 1980, p. 244). This process results in the somatoform disorders: somatization disorder, conversion disorder, psychogenic pain disorder, and hypo-chondriasis (APA, 1980). The attitude of *la belle indifference* that such patients often (or at least classically) take toward their conversion symptoms could be interpreted as the outward (psychic) expressions of the split-off awareness of the real origin of the symptoms.

The speculative model of the bifurcating pathways (internalizing and externalizing) of maladaptive expression could account for the striking parallels but puzzling low correlations betweeen personality types and psychophysiological disorders. In Figure 17-4, psychic disorders on the left slope of the triangle are comparable with, but not equal to nor coincident with somatic disease manifestations on the other slope. For example, patients with his-trionic personality and conversion disorder both transform information symbolically, deny or repress intention regarding this information, and dissociate the true meaning of the information. It is hypoth-esized, however, that the symbolic expressions are achieved through different transformational styles—internalizing for the individual with histrionic personality disorder, and externalizing for the individual who develops a somatization disorder. In partial support of this theory, many studies have shown only modest correlations, if any, between conversion and histrionic personality disorders. Ziegler et al. (1960) found that less than one-half of their conversion patients could be considered histrionic personalities. Two-thirds of the patients with conversion reaction in McKegney's (1967) study did not show serious character pathology.

Temoshok and Attkisson (1977) hypothesized that the histrionic mode of expression of psycho-somatic stress depends upon what biological, psychological, or cultural influence processes or "release valves" exist for and affect an individual or group. For example, under stress, men may be more likely than women to become sociopathic because such behavior is an extreme of acceptable male behaviors; whereas histrionic personality traits exhi-bited by women may be interpreted as an exaggera-tion or a "caricature of femininity" (Chodoff & Lyons, 1958). In terms of the present discussion, these release valves can be seen as alternative trans-formational pathways for processing potentially stressful information.

Anxiety and Hypertension

Although phobic disorders (i.e., agoraphobia with and without panic attacks, social phobia, and simple phobia) are categorized with the anxiety disorders in DSM-III, they have been linked historically with hysteria (i.e., anxiety-hysteria, a primitive reaction type and the most frequent neurosis of childhood; Hinsie & Campbell, 1970); thus, in Figure 17-4 they are located betwen histrionic and anxiety disorders.

In terms of this theory, information that is in some way conflictual or overwhelming is split into content (that which is frightening) and meaning (the emotion of fear). The marked fear that accompanies phobias is then displaced onto situations that are not the source of the fear and expressed. In anxiety states (e.g., panic attacks), there is a transformation of the split-off meaning into the acute physiological expression of some of the following symptoms: dyspnea, palpitations, chest pain or discomfort, dizziness or vertigo, choking or smothering sen-sations, paresthesias, hot and cold flashes, sweating, fainting, or trembling and shaking (APA, 1980). These autonomic nervous system–implicated symptoms are the hallmarks of the flight–fight biological response patterns, which are categorized under motivation in Tables 17-3 and 17-4. It should be emphasized that while these symptoms are phy-siological in nature, anxiety is still seen as a psychic rather than a somatic disorder in that these symptoms are acutely expressed rather than chroni-cally internalized.

It is hypothesized that the chronic internalizing equivalent of anxiety disorders is hypertension. There is some interesting evidence from animal studies (Dworkin et al., 1979) that the cortical and behavioral inhibitition produced by baroreceptor stimulation may reinforce the learning of elevations in blood pressure.

Alexander (1950) was among the first to formulate the psychological processes presumed to be active in the illnesses he defined as psychosomatic. He de-scribed the hypertensive as withdrawn, noncom-municative, inhibited in terms of behavioral and emotional expression, and, especially, unable to confront others in the expression of anger. Interna-lized anger may result in stimulation of the auto-nomic nervous system, and the release of large amounts of norepinephrine, which is associated with acute, and ultimately, with chronic hypertension. Brod (1970) concluded from a review of various psychiatric studies that persons with essential hypertension live under the burden of permanent life stress and responsibility, and the anxiety that they will not be able to shoulder that stress. Noyes et al. (1978) summarized data relating hypertension and anxiety neurosis which suggested that anxiety neurotics are more susceptible to the development of hypertension after anxiety symptoms have persisted for a number of years. This finding substantiates the idea that anxiety disorder, with its concomitant physiological expression, is an acute, externalizing expression that could become more chronic and internalized over time.

Obsessive-Compulsive Disorder and Coronory Heart Disease

Obsessive-compulsive disorders are also seen as involving a dissociation of information at the level of motivation. In anxiety disorders, however, emotion is expressed as thought (content) is repressed; while the reverse holds true for the obsessive-compulsive, who represses emotion and emphasizes thought. The obsessive-compulsive's conflict between obedience and defiance is kept out of conscious awareness, often by the use of rationalization or intellectualization. Theories, concepts, and words are discussed at a level detached from emotion and action in the real world. Intense and constant competition with others in work, sexual, and athletic arenas may reflect—although dimly and with the real emotion obscured—the original underlying struggle against (parental) authority. The obsessive-compulsive may engage in even less adaptive compulsive activities or obsessive thoughts that are substitutes for the repressed rage and the unresolved conflict between the desire for autonomy versus shame and doubt (Erikson, 1968). These thoughts and actions are divorced from their true emotional significance, which is repressed and contained at the subconscious sublevel. They may, however, be charged with other emotions. This emotional charge keeps intruding them into consciousness, where they may be repeated endlessly without resolution or understanding.

The type of psychosomatic disorder that corresponds to the obsessive-compulsive psychic expression is hypothesized to be coronary heart disease. The presumed dynamic is that chronically repressed rage that is not transformed into maladaptive obsessive thoughts or compulsive actions may find somatic expression. The so-called Type A behavior pattern is characterized by extremes of hostility, competitiveness, striving for achievement, aggressiveness, impatience, restlessness, hyperalertness, and feeling constantly under pressure (Friedman & Rosenman, 1959). While the strong and independent association between the Type A pattern and coronary heart disease has been repeatedly demonstrated in many retrospective studies, the most convincing evidence implicating

this behavior as an important risk factor for coronary heart disease has been the results of several large prospective studies (Haynes et al., 1978; Jenkins, 1976; Rosenman et al., 1975). Dongier (1974) reported that obsessive tendencies and overcontrol of emotions are rather strongly related to myocardial infarction, whereas patients with angina pectoris may be more reactive to their environment and more irritable (Jenkins, 1976). The pathophysiological mechanisms that may underlie the transformation of Type A behavior into coronary heart disease are currently being investigated (Dembroski et al., this volume, Chapter 7).

The question may be raised as to why some persons develop a psychic rather than a somatic pathology, or vice versa, under stress. Let us set aside the large contribution of risk factors, (e.g., genetic predisposition, smoking and eating habits, elevated blood pressure and serum cholesterol) and concentrate solely on the variance attributable to psychosocial factors—their influence on the commonly accepted risk factors, as well as their solitary contributions. Consider the personality description of the Type A individual: competitive, time conscious, striving for achievement, and so forth. This individual obviously cares a great deal about, or in psychoanalytic terms, strongly cathects certain contents concerned with ambition.

If the psychoanalytically presumed original impulses—craving for autonomy, fear of retaliation, and subsequent rage at submission to authority—have been repressed, then the Type A individual's ambitious and competitive behavior may be interpreted as reaction formation ("the development in the ego of conscious, socialized attitudes and interests which are the antithesis of certain infantile unsocialized trends which continue to persist in the unconscious"; Healy et al., 1930), or as the more mature defense mechanism of sublimation (a function of the normal ego that modifies an instinctive impulse in such a way as to conform to the demands of society while expressing the infantile struggle in a socially appropriate form; Hinsie & Campbell, 1970). Thus, the Type A person is seen as having an outwardly and consciously "normal," appropriate, and approved pattern of behavior. When stressed, this individual cannot afford to disrupt this highly valued and functional facade; thus, disequilibrating transactions are transformed into internal representations, which may culminate (through the pathopsychophysiological processes described above) in the somatic condition of coronary heart disease. This configuration of stress response contrasts with what I hypothesize occurs with the stylistically externalizing obsessive-compulsive neurotic, who tends to manifest symptoms that are less socially acceptable than are Type A behaviors.

Borderline Personality Organization and Allergic-Immune Disease

In this theory, personality disorders of greater structural deficit (i.e., paranoid, borderline, schizoid, narcissistic; APA, 1980) are the externalized manifestations of dissociated information at the level of appraisal. This kind of split usually results in a distortion of reality that is more extreme than the neurotic splitting of meaning at the levels of appositional consciousness or motivation, but less severe than the psychotic's withdrawal from interpersonal relations, collapse of ego boundaries, and massive deterioration of reality testing. To use an optical analogy, the neurotic views reality through a colored lens, the borderline through a distorted lens, and the psychotic through a shattered lens.

According to the DSM-III (APA, 1980), the borderline personality disorder is marked by an instability in a variety of areas, including interpersonal relations, mood, emotional expression, and self-image or identity, and by frequent impulsive, unpredictable, or physically self-damaging behaviors. In Kernberg's (1975) theory, the borderline personality organization is a disorder based on a personality arrest at the developmental stage, during which self-image and object-image are differentiated within the core "good" undifferentiated self-object image. The borderline individual is not able to synthesize positive and negative introjections and identifications. Thus, internal representations of other people or objects are either originally pleasurable and subsequently idealized "all good," or originally painful and subsequently "all bad." Aspects of external reality that do not conform to these internal representations are kept out of conscious awareness, or appear as contradictory perceptions: the resulting interpretations of reality are apt to be shallow, flat, and impoverished (Kernberg, 1977). Furthermore, while perception of other people and objects is confused for the borderline individual, identity is diffused because of the nonintegration of good and bad aspects of self-representations. The normal adaptive processes of problem solving are difficult for the borderline individual because thought is entwined with inappropriate and undifferentiated emotion (e.g., intense anger), which distorts reality testing.

In Figure 17-4, the somatic condition that is parallel to borderline personality disorder is allergic-immune disease. Just as the borderline individual has extreme difficulty in maintaining stable and appropriate boundaries between the self and the environment, so the individual suffering an allergic-immune disorder has an adaptive imbalance in the physiological regulation of lung function, and a major somatic difficulty in recognizing "appropriate" antigens. According to Knapp (1975), severe asthmatics have "borderline" or "narcissistic" personality organization; that observation is congruent with the placement of the disorder in Figure 17-4, although these problems may be masked by many effective areas of functioning. This "split" between more outwardly adaptive and internally maladaptive organization parallels the previous discussion of the Type A individual.

Bronchial asthma is a hypersensitive state of enhanced reactivity to a foreign substance, acquired by previous exposure to the same or to a similar substance (Movat, 1971). In the asthma attack itself, small airways are temporarily obstructed, presumably resulting from smooth muscle spasms, edema of bronchiolar mucosa, and/or hypersecretion. This results in the characteristic attacks of asthmatic wheezing, which occurs mainly during expiration. Immunological-allergic reactions can lead to an asthmatic response via a broncoobstructive process. This is the case for "extrinsic" asthma, in which predisposed individuals have a specific antibody in their blood serum and bronchial tissue. This is probably not the sole cause of asthma, however, since many chronic asthmatics do not manifest extrinsic allergy. One hypothesis discussed by Knapp (1975) is that there is a balance between sympathetic (bronchodilating) and parasympathetic (bronchoconstrictive) influences, both having links to the brain, and that asthma may represent an acute or a chronic imbalance between the two. The hypothalamus may be the mediator of this balance in autonomic activity, since lesions in or malfunctioning of certain hypothalamic regions may affect the autonomic balance and, subsequently, the immunological response.

Affective Disorders and Autoimmune Disease

The essential feature of affective disorders, according to DSM-III (APA, 1980), is a disturbance of mood, accompanied by a full or partial manic or depressive syndrome. The symptoms of manic episodes include hyperactivity, pressured speech, flight of ideas, inflated self-esteem, decreased need for sleep, distractibility, involvement in potentially self-destructive activities, and lability of mood with rapid shifts to anger or depression. In a major depressive episode, the essential feature is either a dysphoric mood, usually depression, or loss of interest and enjoyment in most usual activities. There may be disturbances of essential functions such as appetite, sleep, and psychomotor activity (agitation or retardation).

Loss of a parent in childhood could predispose an individual to adult depression. Sandler and Joffee (1965) believe that what is lost is not a specific love-object but the state of integration, which is biological for the young infant and psychological for the adult. Another way to think about the depression-prone individual is to consider the premorbid character style as revolving around certain depressive features. Such features would be mainly cognitive, rather than emotional or behavioral. In terms of my scheme, a depressive character style would be organized around very early internalized negative expectations (attitudes or schemata) about the world, which then become enduring and central psychic structures. A child whose early relations with significant others were precarious and characterized by prolonged and/or frequent abandonments would grow up with a vulnerable sense of self-esteem, which is the internalized transactional equivalent of the sense that relations with others are uncertain and vulnerable. There is a shaky stability of the organization of self and object representations on the intrapsychic side of the self-environment boundary because real interpersonal objects were not stable enough to be internally represented. Many psychoanalytic and nonpsychoanalytic writers have postulated a loss or nonestablishment of self-esteem as basic to all psychopathology, but what distinguishes depressive loss, in my view, is that it occurs early in development and at the basic information processing level of appraisal.

Along similar lines, Arieti and Bemporad (1978) suggested that a "preceding ideology" serves an integrating function in the patient's life, but paves the path toward depression by providing a special meaning to events encountered later in life, which are subsequently dealt with in characteristic ways. In depressive character (Bemporad, 1976), depression is a ubiquitous cognitive set applied to the world, the self, and the future (Beck, 1967), and accompanied by a constant dissatisfaction or boredom which may be exacerbated after a current frustration. In the depressed individual's system of ideas, the self is devalued and felt as deprived, so that others may be clung to in a desperate attempt to reinstate a childhood role of secure gratification and direction. Autonomous gratification—any pleasure or meaning in life—is basically feared and consciously considered impossible because all prior attempts at meaningful communication and activity were undermined by guilt and shame (Arieti & Bemporad, 1978). Thus, cognition is centrally implicated in depression, which cannot then be solely considered an affective disorder. The essential problem in depression is not the dysphoric affect, but structural determinants (information transforming proclivities): the depression-prone individual has a distorted cognitive set on self and others, which engenders negative affect when this set transacts with the world.

Metaphorically, there is a parallel between the self-destructive complexion of the affective disorders—the turning of anger and aggression against the self, resulting in ego deficiency—and the turning of protective immune mechanisms against host tissue and the concomitant immunological deficiency that are definitive of autoimmune diseases. Antibodies usually develop against substances that are foreign to a specific organism. Autoimmune diseases involve autoantibodies or sensitive lymphocytes formed against "host tissue," that is, cells that are antigenic in the organism from which they arise. Diseases generally considered to be autoimmune include, among others, rheumatoid arthritis, systemic lupus erythematosus, and polymyositis; and autoimmunity may play a role in multiple sclerosis, ulcerative colitis, diabetes, and Addison's disease (Solomon, 1981).

Rheumatoid arthritis is discussed in more detail here because it is the autoimmune disease most frequently researched (see Solomon & Amkraut, this volume, Chapter 14). The disease appears to be associated with states of relative immunological incompetence. Fudenberg (1971) hypothesized that a state of immunological deficiency arises when a latent virus or bacterium becomes pathogenic and alters the immunological mechanism such that the organism produces autoantibodies in a "misguided" attempt to protect itself. Solomon (1970) proposed that the immune deficient state may result when emotional influences activate the adrenal cortical system. In this view, the central nervous system plays a critical role in mediating the influence of psychological factors in autoimmune diseases.

In a series of studies, Moos and Solomon (1965a, 1965b) showed that healthy relatives of rheumatoid patients who had rheumatoid factor in their sera were particularly healthy psychologically, implying that their psychological stress resistance also provided resistance against the immunological predisposition. Solomon (1970) hypothesized that both an immune factor, which may itself have personality correlates, and the failure of psychological defenses in the fact of distress may be necessary to produce overt rheumatoid arthritis.

The general personality configuration of the arthritic patient which emerges from a number of studies is that of perfectionistic, self-conscious, introverted, and relatively inhibited individual. While these characteristics have an obsessive-compulsive flavor, they express more of a masochistic and self-sacrificing (depressive) essence (Moos & Solomon, 1965a, 1965b) than the externalizing, aggressive Type A individual who is prone to coronary heart disease.

Perhaps midway between these two disorders, in terms of characteristic obsessive-compulsive style, is the patient with ulcerative colitis, an inflammatory bowel disease in which anticolon antibodies are implicated (Solomon, 1970). Shorter et al. (1972) proposed that, in patients who early in life established a hypersensitivity to antigens of bacteria normally present in the gastrointestinal tract, factors including "psychic insult" may trigger the breakdown that results in a cell-mediated hypersensitive reaction to the bowel wall, which is characteristic of the disease. Engel (1975) described the association of disease onset and acute or chronic psychological stress, which is apt to consist of real or threatened interruptions of a key relationship, demands for performance the individual feels incapable of meeting, and overwhelming threat or disapproval by parental figures. Engel (1968) observed that the disease becomes active when the patient begins to feel unable to cope with the current circumstances, whatever their nature, and psychologically "gives up."

Schizophrenic and Neoplastic Disorders

In Figure 17-4, schizophrenic disorders are depicted as the most severe manifestation of an internalizing transformational style, equivalent to cancer in terms of the extent of disorganization. According to DSM-III (APA, 1980), this group of disorders involves disturbance of multiple psychological processes in several of the following domains: perception (various forms of hallucinations), affect (blunted, flattened, or inappropriate), form of

thought (loosening of associations, incoherent speech), content of thought (fragmented or bizarre delusions), relation to the external world (withdrawal, fantasy substitutions), psychomotor behavior (e.g., catatonic stupor, posturing, or negativism), volition (disturbance in goal-directed activity), and sense of self (loss of ego boundaries). These disorders are similar to the neoplastic disorders in the breakdown of the boundary between self and environment such that self and nonself cannot be distinguished. The difference is that, in the case of cancer, the failure to distinguish self from nonself is at the somatic, cellular level, and may be related to a failure of immunological defenses; whereas in the case of schizophrenic disorders, the failure occurs at the mental level and appears to be related to failure of the psychic defensive system.

If both cancer and schizophrenic disorders are the outcomes of unsuccessful attempts to adapt to extremely stressful conditions, each manifestation representing a different transformation mode, then we might expect that maladaptive transformation along one pathway precludes transformation along the other. To elaborate this idea: if, as some studies show, schizophrenics are protected from rheumatoid arthritis and possibly cancer, then it is likely that psychiatric conditions have immunological concomitants (see Solomon & Amkraut, this volume, Chapter 14). Solomon and his colleagues have reviewed the evidence on the relation of immunological abnormalities and the presence of autoantibodies in mental disorders. One study (Solomon et al., 1969) found a relative elevation of immunoglobulins among accutely ill schizophrenics, compared with psychiatric patients in general. However, Soloman and Amkraut (this volume, Chapter 14) found no convincing body of evidence for altered immunological *responsivity* in schizophrenics. Sacher (1963) found an elevation of corticosteroid secretion of to two to three times the normal levels during acute schizophrenic reactions, and related this to the failure of psychological defenses, which also results in the disintegrative anxiety characteristic of the beginning phases of acute schizophrenic reactions.

One way to integrate the various findings on immunological reactions in cancer and schizophrenic patients is to suppose that both are vulnerable to environmental threat, but the cancer-prone individual maintains psychological defenses at the expense of immunological ones, while the schizophrenia-prone individual may have adequate immunological responsivity but succombs on the psychological front. This etiological (psychosomatic) hypothesis probably does not extend to patients who already suffer from cancer; that is, the somatopsychic effects of cancer on an individual are probably so great that various mental disorders could well *result* from cancer. Similarly, more chronic forms of schizophrenia or other severe mental disorders could be associated with increased risk of cancer because of generalized boundary breakdown across several systems, physical as well as mental. The hypothesis that cancer patients should have a lower *premorbid* prevalence of mental disorder than the rest of the population is obviously testable. Previous studies relevant to this hypothesis are both methodologically problematic and contradictory, and thus are inconclusive (Fox, 1978).

There are, however, a number of methodologically adequate studies that examine the influence of emotional factors on cancer. Bahnson and Bahnson (1969) observed that cancer patients repressed and denied such unpleasant affects as anxiety, hostility, and guilt to a higher degree than matched controls. Greer and Morris (1974) found that women with malignant tumors suppressed anger and other emotions more than matched controls with benign tumors. In an ongoing prospective study, Thomas (1976) reported a relationship between premorbid indicators of denial (i.e., little overt depression, anxiety, or anger) and later cancer incidence. Derogatis et al. (1979) administered a battery of baseline psychological tests to 35 women with metastatic breast cancer. Patients who died within 1 year from baseline had significantly lower levels of hostility and higher levels of positive mood (measured by several instruments) than patients who lived longer than 1 year. The latter group demonstrated more psychiatric symptomatology, and higher levels of depression, anxiety, hostility, and negative attitudes toward their physicians. (This finding may be interpreted as confirmation for the hypothesis that cancer patients—or at least the ones with the worse prognoses—do not have evident psychiatric symptomatology.

Rogentine et al. (1979) found that malignant melanoma patients who minimized the amount of personal adjustment needed to cope with having melanoma and surgery for it were more likely to suffer relapse within 1 year. Using this measure of denial as a criterion, these researchers were then able to predict accurately relapse in 76 percent of a second group of melanoma patients with Stage I and Stage II disease. Temoshok et al. (in press c) obtained follow-up medical reports on 100 of 106 melanoma patients who were previously interviewed (mean of 18 months earlier) and given several psychological tests. Patients with no evidence of disease at follow-up were compared with those who died or had disease progression, recurrence, or metastases. Results showed the latter group had scored significantly *lower* on 4 scales from the Profile of Mood States, administered at the time of the initial interview: Tension-Anxiety, Depression-Dejection, Anger-Hostility, and Confusion. These findings suggest a repression of dysphoric emotions, denial of generally less socially acceptable feelings, or suppression of their behavioral expression.

It is not clear how "repression," "denial," or "suppression" of affect play a role in cancer induction and/or growth. These behaviors, when used to cope with the stress of having cancer, could contribute to poor medical prognosis by facilitating patients' delay in seeking necessary medical attention or noncompliance with medical recommendations. In this regard, Temoshok et al. (in press a, b) found that delay in seeking medical attention for suspicious lesions was strongly correlated with tumor thickness, which is the best medical indicator of melanoma prognosis.

An alternative suggestion is that certain types of coping responses may be associated with hormonal, neuroendocrine, and/or immune system responses that may exacerbate tumor growth and metastasis, and/or weaken the body's resistance to the malignant process. The extensive literature accumulating or the relationship between behavioral factors and cancer (Fox, 1978) is currently being enhanced by studies relating stress and behavioral factors to immune response (Ader & Cohen, 1982; Levy, 1981). Studies linking stress, behavior, physiology, and cancer growth in an integrated series of experiments need to be conducted. One emerging hypothesis is that stress mobilizes a characteristic pattern of coping that is manifested in certain behaviors. The literature also suggests that a complex set of central nervous system, neurotransmitter, endocrine, and other biological processes may be involved in the mediation of behavioral influences on immune function. Animal models may be useful in exploring the physiological mechanisms by which certain behaviors may mediate tumor growth, and whether there are stress–behavior interactions in this process. If studies using animal models are suggestive, then studies with patients could be mounted that incorporate the more complex emotional, cognitive, and transformation system variables discussed in this chapter.

CONCLUDING COMMENTS

In this chapter a multidimensional theory of emotion and adaptation has been proposed that addresses some of the observed and postulated relations between stress and psychological/somatic disorders. While stress has been related to the etiology of mental and physical disorders, the transition from stimulus, or from organism-environment transaction to psychosomatic disturbance has not been documented, but only presumed. If stressors can engender both physical and mental disorders, then how can we understand these differential outcomes? The more traditional explanations posit different categories of prior stressors: e.g., viruses and bacteria "cause" physical disease, while social stressors such as family conflicts "cause" mental disorders, perhaps via mediating or predispositional variables.

One conclusion to be reached from all the material and constructions presented in this chapter is that all disorders have psychosomatic–somatopsychic implications that result from strained or failed adaptive efforts. The assumption is that mind and body are holistically integrated. This holism, which represents a state of healthy adaptation, may then be disrupted by certain internal or external events that cannot be integrated into the sytemic whole as it has functioned previously.

Certain physical and/or psychological proclivities or vulnerabilities may predispose an individual to transform stressful transactions along a route that culminates in somatic disorder, or along another route that leads to varieties of psychic disorder. In this view, the difference between psychic and somatic disorder is not so much a matter of outcome—for although they are different, they are both expressions of stressful transactions—but stems from two main transformational styles that eventuate in differential outcomes. When organism–environment transactions are within the organism's coping range, the two basic transformational tendencies—internalizing and externalizing — are in balance, and the organism is in a state of dynamic equilibrium with its environment. When transactions are strained, either by extreme environmental conditions or events, or because of an organismic incapacity to adapt to these conditions, then transformational tendencies become

unbalanced, and the organism may be viewed as under stress or in a maladaptive state. The degree of uncertainty inherent in the original organism-environment transaction (which is affected by both organismic and situational variables) ultimately determines the extremity of expression and the degree of imbalance between internalizing and externalizing transformational modes. The degree of uncertainty also influences the imbalance between perceived environmental demands and the organism's response capabilities. These imbalances may implicate physiological and immunological processes that contribute to disease as an outcome of continued stress and maladaptive transformation.

The value of this theory lies in its generation of questions and testable hypotheses that go beyond the boundaries of this chapter, but focus on the following questions: (1) To what extent, under which conditions, and in which individuals are psychosocial factors and/or stress implicated in somatic and mental disorders? (2) What are the mechanisms by which psychosocial factors and/or stress produce or exacerberate somatic and mental disorders? (3) What interventions may be mounted to reduce the vulnerability, or to improve the coping capacities of individuals in order to reduce the likelihood of their susceptiblity to disease or psychiatric disorder? (4) If breakdown of either somatic or psychic boundaries is related to the organization of information, then how can we reduce the uncertainty, randomness, or lack of meaning in situations in order to increase the individual's opportunities for adaptive transactions with situations?

While I hope that the theory posed here proves to be a sturdy one, investigators are encouraged to test its durability and flexibility across many real-world examples, to expose its weakest links, to replace these with stronger ones, and to add empirical substance to its theoretical framework.

REFERENCES

Ader R, & Cohen N (1982): Behaviorally conditioned immunosuppression and murine systemic lupus erythematosus. Science 215:1534–1536.

Alexander F (1950): *Psychosomatic Medicine, its Principles and Applications*. New York, Norton.

American Psychiatric Association (1980): *Diagnostic and Statistical Manual of Mental Disorders* (ed. 3). Washington, DC.

Arieti S, & Bemporad J (1978): *Severe and Mild Depression*. New York, Basic Books.

Arnold MB (1960): *Emotion and Personality*, vols. I, II. New York, Columbia University Press.

Bahnson CB (1969): Psychophysiological complementarity in malignancies: Past work and future vistas. Ann NY Acad Sci 164:319–334.

Bahnson CB, & Bahnson MB (1964): Cancer as an alternative to psychosis: A theoretical model of somatic and psychological regression. Kissen DM, & LeShan L (Eds.). In *Psychosomatic Aspects of Neoplastic Disease*. London, Pitman.

Bahnson CB, & Bahnson MB (1969): Ego defenses in cancer patients. Ann NY Acad Sci 164:546–559.

Bakan P (1978): Two streams of consciousness: A typological approach. Pope KS, & Singer JL (Eds.). In *The Stream of Consciousness: Scientific Investigations into the Flow of Human Experience*. New York, Plenum Press.

Barash DP (1977): *Sociobiology and Behavior*. New York, Elsevier/North Holland.

Bateson G (1972): *Steps to an Ecology of Mind: Collected Essays in Anthropology, Psychiatry, Evolution, and Epistemology*. San Francisco, Chandler.

Battista JB (1978): The science of consciousness. Pope KS, & Singer JL (Eds.). In *The Stream of Consciousness: Scientific Investigations into the Flow of Human Experience*. New York, Plenum Press.

Beck A (1967): *Depression: Clinical, Experimental, and Theoretical Aspects*. New York, Hoeber.

Bemporad JR (1976): Psychotherapy of the depressive character. J Am Acad Psychoanal 4:347–372.

Bertalanffy von L (1968): *General System Theory*. New York, Braziller.

Bogen JE (1973): The other side of the brain: An appositional mind. Ornstein RE (Ed.). In *The Nature of Human Consciousness: A Book of Readings*. San Francisco, Freeman.

Bowlby J (1969): *Attachment and Loss*, vol. 1. New York, Basic Books.

Brod J (1970): Haemodynamics, an emotional stress. Koster M, Mushaph H, & Visser P (Eds.). In *Psychosomatics in Essential Hypertension*. New York, Karger, Basic Books.

Broverman DM, Broverman IK, Vogel W, Palmer RD, & Klaiber EL (1964): The automatization cognitive style and physical development. Child Dev 35:1343–1359.

Buckley W (1967): *Sociology and Modern Systems Theory*. Englewood Cliffs NJ, Prentice Hall.

Cannon WB (1936): The role of emotion in disease. Ann Intern Med 9:1453–1456.

Chodoff P, & Lyons H (1958): Hysteria, the hysterical personality and "hysterical" conversion. Am J Psychiatry 114:734–740.

Davidson RJ (1980): Consciousness and information processing: A biocognitive perspective. Davidson JM, & Davidson RJ (Eds.). In *The Psychobiology of Consciousness*. New York, Plenum Press.

Derogatis L, Abeloff M, & Melisaratos N (1979): Psychobiological coping mechanisms and survival time in metastatic breast cancer. JAMA 242:1504–1508.

Dongier M (1974): Psychosomatic aspects in myocardial infarction in comparison with angina pectoris. Psychother Psychosom 23:123–131.

Dworkin BR, Filewich RM, Miller NE, & Craigmyle N (1979): Baroreceptor activation reducer reactivity to noxious stimulation: Implications for hypertension. Science 205:299–301.

Ekman P (1980): Asymmetry in facial expression. Science 204: 832–834.

Ekman P, Friesen WV, & Ellsworth P (1972): *Emotion in the Human Face: Guidelines for Research and an Integration of Findings*. New York, Pergamon Press.

Ekman P, Hager JC, & Friesen WV (1981): The symmetry of emotional and deliberate facial actions. Psychophysiology 18:101–106.

Ekman P, Friesen WV, & Simons RC (in press): Behavioral criteria for distinguishing emotion: An examination of the startle reaction.

Emde RN, Gaensbauer T, & Harmon R (1976): *Emotional Expression in Infancy: A Biobehavioral Study*. New York, International University Press.

Engel GL (1962): *Psychological Development in Health and Disease*. Philadelphia, Saunders.

Engel GL (1968): A life setting conducive to illness: The giving-up–given-up complex. Bull Menninger Clin 32:355–365.

Engel GL (1975): Psychological aspects of gastrointestinal disorders. Reiser MF (Ed.). In *American Handbook of Psychiatry: Organic Disorders and Psychosomatic Medicine*, vol. IV. New York, Basic Books.

Erikson EH (1968): *Identity: Youth and Crisis*. New York, Norton.

Fox BH (1978): Premorbid psychological factors as related to cancer incidence. J Behav Med 1:45–133.

Frankenhaeuser M (1979): Psychoneuroendocrine approaches to the study of emotion as related to stress and coping. Dienstbier RA (Ed.). In *Human Emotion: Nebraska Symposium on Motivation 1978*. Lincoln, University of Nebraska Press.

Freud S (1946): *Collected Papers*, vol IV. London, Hogarth Press.

Friedman M, & Rosenman RH (1959): Association of specific overt behavior patterns of blood and cardiovascular findings. JAMA 169:1289–1296.

Fudenberg HH (1971): Are autoimmune diseases immunological deficiency states. Good RA, & Fisher RW (Eds.). In *Immunology*. Stamford, Conn, Sinauer.

Galin D (1974): Implications for psychiatry of left and right cerebral specialization. Arch Gen Psychiatry 31:572–583.

Graham FK (1973): Habituation and dishabituation of responses innervated by the autonomic nervous system. Peeke HVS, & Herz M (Eds.). In *Habituation: Behavioral Studies and Physiological Substrates*, vol 1. New York, Academic Press.

Graham FK, & Clifton RK (1966): Heart-rate change as a component of the orienting response. Psychol Bull 65:305–320.

Gray JA (1976): The behavioral inhibition system: A possible substrate for anxiety. Feldman MP, & Broadhurst AM (Eds.). In *Theoretical and Experimental Bases of Behaviour Modifiers*. New York, Wiley.

Greer S, & Morris T (1974): Psychological attributes of women who develop breast cancer: A controlled study. J Psychosom Res 19:147–153.

Grings WA, & Dawson ME (1978): *Emotions and Bodily Responses*. New York, Academic Press.

Groves PM, Thompson R (1970): Habituation: A dual process theory. Psychol Rev 77:419–450.

Haynes SG, Levine S, Scotch N, Feinlieb M, & Kannel WB (1978): The relationship of psychosocial factors to coronary heart disease in the Framingham Study. Am J Epidemiol 107:362–383.

Healy W, Bronner AP, & Bowers AM (1930): *The Structure and Meaning of Psychoanalysis*. New York, Knopf.

Heller BW (1978): *The holistic paradigm, general system theory and system properties*. Unpublished manuscript, University of California, Davis.

Hinsie LE, & Campbell RJ (1970): *Psychiatric Dictionary*, (ed. 4). New York, Oxford University Press.

Izard CE (1971): *The Face of Emotions*. New York, Appleton-Century-Crofts.

Izard CE (1979): Emotions as motivations: An evolutionary-developmental perspective. Dienstbier RA (Ed.). In *Human Emotion: Nebraska Symposium on Motivation, 1978*. Lincoln, University of Nebraska Press.

Jenkins CD (1976): Recent evidence supporting psychologic and social risk factors for coronary disease. N Eng J Med 294:1033–1038.

John ER (1976): A model of consciousness. Schwartz GE, Shapiro D (Eds.). In *Consciousness and Self-Regulation: Advances in Research*, vol. 1. New York, Plenum Press.

Kaufman IC (1977): Developmental considerations of anxiety and depression: Psychobiological studies in monkeys. Shapiro T (Ed.). In *Psychoanalysis and Contemporary Science*. New York, International Universities Press.

Kernberg O (1975): *Borderline Conditions and Pathological Narcissism*. New York, Aronson.

Kernberg O (1977): The structural diagnosis of borderline personality organization. Hartocollis P (Ed.). In *Borderline Personality Disorders: The Concept, the Syndrome, the Patient*. New York, International Universities Press.

Knapp PH (1975): Psychosomatic aspects of bronchial asthma. Arieti S (Ed.). In *Handbook of Psychiatry: Organic Disorders and Psychosomatic Disease*, vol. 40. New York, Basic Books.

Kobasa SC (1979): Stressful life events, personality, and health: An inquiry into hardiness. J Pers Soc Psychol 37:1:–11.

Krieger DT, & Liotta AS (1979): Pituitary hormones in brain: Where, how and why. Science 205:366–372.

Kuhn, A (1977): Dualism reconstructed. Gen Syst 22:91–98.

Langer S (1942): *Philosophy in a New Key: A Study in the Symbolism of Reason, Rite, and Art*. New York, Mentor Books.

Lazarus RS (1980): The stress and coping paradigm. Bond LA, & Rosen JC (Eds.). In *Competence and Coping During Adulthood*. Hanover, NH, University of New England.

Lazarus RS, Kanner AD, & Folkman S (1980): Emotions: A cognitive-phenomenological analysis. Kellerman H, Plutchik R (Eds.). In *Theories of Emotion*. New York, Academic Press.

Lazarus RS, & Launier R (1978): Stress-related transactions between person and environment. Lewis M, Pervin LA (Eds.). In *Perspectives in Interactional Psychology*. New York, Plenum Press.

Leeper RW (1948): A motivational theory of emotion to replace "Emotion as a disorganized response." Psychol Rev 55:5–21.

Levy SM (Ed.) (1981): *Biological Mediators of Disease: Neoplasia*. New York, Elsevier Biomedical.

MacLean PD (1969): *A Triune Concept of Brain and Behavior*. Toronto, University of Toronto Press.

Mandler G (1975): *Mind and Emotion*. New York, Wiley.

McGeer PL, & McGeer EG (1980): Chemistry of mood and emotion. Ann Rev Psychol 31:273–307.

McKegney FP (1967): The incidence and characteristics of patients with conversion reactions. I: A general hospital consultation service sample. Am J Psychiatry 124:542–545.

Miller EJ (1959): Technology, territory, and time: The internal differentiation of complex production systems. Hum Relations 12:243–272.

Miller GA, Galantner E, & Pribram KH (1960): *Plans and the Organization of Behavior*. New York, Holt, Rinehart, Winston.

Moos RH, & Solomon GF (1965a): Psychologic comparisons between women with rheumatoid arthritis and their non-arthritic sisters: I. Personality test and interview rating data. Psychosom Med 27:135–149.

Moos RH, & Solomon GH (1965b): Psychologic comparisons between women with rheumatoid arthritis and their non-arthritic sisters: II. Content analysis of interviews. Psychosom Med 27:150–164.

Moreland RL, & Zajonc RB (1977): Is stimulus recognition a necessary condition for the occurrence of the exposure effect? J Pers Soc Psychol 35:191–199.

Moreland RL, & Zajonc RB (1979): Exposure effects may not depend on stimulus recognition. J Pers Soc Psychol 37:1055–1089.

Movat HZ (1971): *Inflammation, Immunity, and Hypersensitivity*. New York, Harper & Row.

Nisbett RE, & Temoshok L (1976): Is there an "externalizing" cognitive style? J Pers Psychol 33:36–47.

Noyes R, Clancy J, Hoenk PR, & Slymen DJ (1978): Anxiety neurosis and physical illness. Comprehensive Psychiatry 19:407–413.

Piaget J (1952): *The Origins of Intelligence in Children*. New York, International Universities Press.

Plutchik R (1980): *Emotion: A Psychoevolutionary Synthesis*. New York, Harper & Row.

Quillian MR (1968): Semantic memory. Minsky M (Ed.). In *Semantic Information Processing*. Cambridge, Mass, MIT Press.

Stein J (Ed.) (1967): *Random House Dictionary of the English Language*. New York, Random House.

Reus VI, Weingartner H, & Post RM (1979): Clinical implications of state-dependent learning. Am J Psychiatry 136:927–931.

Rogentine S, Boyd S, Bunney W, Doherty J, Fox B, Rosenblatt J, & Van Kammen D (1979): Psychological factors in the prognosis of malignant melanoma. Psychosom Med 41:647–658.

Rosenman RH, Brand RH, Jenkins CD, Friedman M, Strauss R, & Wurm M (1975): Coronary heart disease in the Western Collaborative Group Study: Final follow-up experience of 8 1/2 years. JAMA 233:872–877.

Rotter JB (1966): Generalized expectancies for internal vs. external control of reinforcement. Psychol Monogr 38 (1, Whole No. 609).

Sacher EJ (1963): Psychoendocrine aspects of acute schizophrenic reactions. Psychosom Med 25:510–537.

Sackheim HA, & Gur RC (1978): Self-deception, self-confrontation, and consciousness. Schwartz GE, & Shapiro D (Eds.). In *Consciousness and Self-Regulation*, vol. 2. New York, Plenum Press.

Sandler J, & Joffee WG (1965): Notes on childhood depression. Int J Psychoanal 46: 88–96.

Schachter S, & Rodin J (1974): *Obese Humans and Rats*. Potomac Md, Erlbaum.

Schwartz GE (1975): Biofeedback, self-regulation, and the patterning of physiological processes. Am Sci 63:314–324.

Shorter RG, Hinzenga KH, & Spencer RJ (1972): A working hypothesis for the etiology and pathogenesis of nonspecific inflammatory bowel disease. Am J Dig Dis 17:1024–1032.

Simon HA (1967): Motivational and emotional controls of cognition. Psychol Rev 74:29–39.

Sokolov EN (1960): Neuronal models and the orienting reflex. Brazier MA (Ed.). In *The Central Nervous System and Behavior*. New York, Macy.

Solomon GF (1970): Psychophysiological aspects of rheumatoid arthritic and auto-immune disease. Hill OW (Ed.). In *Modern Trends in Psychosomatic Medicine*. New York, Appleton-Century-Crofts.

Solomon GF (1981): Emotional and personality factors in the onset and cause of auto-immune disease, particularly rheumatoid arthritis. Ader R (Ed.). In *Psychoneuroimmunology*. New York, Academic Press.

Solomon GF, Allansmith M, McClellan B, & Amkraut AA (1969): Immunoglobulins in psychiatric patients. Arch Gen Psychiatry 20:272–277.

Sperry R (1969): A modified concept of consciousness. Psychol Rev 76:532–536.

Sperry R (1976): Mental phenomena as causal determinants in brain function. Globus G (Ed.). In *Brain and Conscious Experience*. New York, Plenum Press.

Spinelli DN, & Pribram KH (1967): Changes in visual recovery function and unit activity produced by frontal cortex stimulation. Electroencephalogr Clin Neurophysiol 22:143–149.

Tart CT (1975): *States of Consciousness*. New York, Dutton.

Temoshok L (1983): Outline of a theory of information transformation for understanding mental and physical maladaptation. Gray W, Battista J, & Fidler J (Eds.). In *General System Theory and the Psychological Sciences*. San Francisco, Intersystem Press.

Temoshok L, & Attkisson CC (1977): Hysterical phenomena: Epidemiology and evidence for a psychosocial theory. Horowitz MJ (Ed.). In *Hysterical Personality*. New York, Aronson.

Temoshok L, DiClemente RJ, Sweet DM, Blois MS, & Sagebiel RW (in press a): Factors related to patient delay in seeking medical attention for cutaneous malignant melanoma.

Temoshok L, & Heller BW (1983): Hysteria. Daitzman RJ (Ed.). In *Diagnosis and Intervention in Behavior Therapy and Behavioral Medicine*. New York, Springer.

Temoshok L, Sweet DM, Blois MS, Sagebiel RW, & Heller BW (in press b): Medical and psychosocial factors in melanoma progression at 18-month followup.

Temoshok L, Sweet DM, Sagebiel RW, Blois MS, Heller BW, DiClemente RJ, & Gold ML (in press c): The relationship of psychosocial factors to prognosis in cutaneous malignant melanoma.

Thomas CB (1976): Precursors of premature disease and death: The predictive potential of habits and family attributes. Ann Intern Med 85:653–658.

Tomkins SS (1962): *Affect Imagery Consciousness: The Positive Affects*, vol. 1. New York, Springer.

Tomkins SS (1963): *Affect Imagery Consciousness: The Negative Affects*, vol. 2. New York, Springer.

Tomkins SS (1979): Script theory: Differential magnification of affects. Dienstbier RA (Ed.). In *Human Emotion: Nebraska Symposium on Motivation 1978*. Lincoln, University of Nebraska Press.

Tulving E (1972): Episodic and semantic memory. Tulving E, & Donaldson W (Eds.). In *Organization of Memory*. New York, Academic Press.

Weingartner H (1978): Human state-dependent learning. Ho BT (Ed.). In *Drug Discrimination and State-Dependent Learning*. New York, Academic Press.

White RW (1963): Ego and reality in psychoanalytic theory: A proposal regarding independent ego energies. Psychol Issues, vol. 3 (Monograph 11).

Witkin HA, Dyk RB, Faterson HF, Goodenough DR, & Karp SA (1962): *Psychological Differentiation: Studies of Development*. New York, Wiley.

Wolman BB (1973): *Dictionary of Behavioral Sciences*. New York, Van Nostrand Reinhold.

Zajonc RB (1968): Attitudinal effects of mere exposure. J Pers Soc Psychol Monogr 9 (2, Pt 2):1–28.

Ziegler FF, Imboden JB, & Meyer E (1960): Contemporary conversion reactions: A clinical study. Am J Psychiatry 116:901–910.

18

Emotions in Health and Illness: An Attempt at Integration

Leonard S. Zegans

In this book we have explored a topic both very familiar and yet quite contemporary in medicine, the relationship between emotions, health, and illness. The authors have speculated about the limbic system, epidemiological studies, brain peptides, T lymphocytes, bereaved spouses, and Navajo healing rites. At first glance this may appear like a melange of ideas; and yet, a set of central themes and concepts emerges.

The important issues that stitched the diverse of chapters into a coherent if somewhat quilt-like fabric are the following:

- A reconsideration of the old mind–body dichotomy.
- An attempt to conceptualize what is meant by the biopsychosocial model in contemporary medicine, and its implications for training practitioners.
- An approach to refining the concept of emotion in light of new biological and cognitive research.
- An attempt to understand how the brain processes and elaborates stimuli dealing with emotion and how these pathways interdigitate with neural structures controlling autonomic, endocrine, and immune processes.
- A consideration of the concepts of stress and coping and their role in influencing the balance between health and illness.
- A reconsideration of earlier concepts of psychosomatic medicine in light of recent findings in the behavioral sciences and clinical medicine.

THE MIND-BODY QUESTION

Several of the authors in this volume have made the assumption that thoughts and feelings can alter physiological processes (even to the extent of leading to disease), just as changes in organs and tissues can affect our moods. In philosophy the notion of a mutual influence of mind and body has been called *interactionism* (Popper & Eccles, 1981). Most classical concepts of psychosomatic medicine depend upon the belief that mental processes exist and are capable of impinging on the workings of the body. In everyday life we take interactionism for granted when we say, "The thought of spending the weekend with him made my stomach churn," or "When I opened the letter from the Internal Revenue Service my heart skipped a beat." The impact of emotions on the body has been long noted by physicians, poets, and philosophers. The effects of anger, grief and joy on the functioning of the heart are particularly familiar poetical themes.

The discussion of anger and hypertension by Appel et al. (Chapter 8), Van Dyke and Kaufman's speculations concerning bereavement and illness (Chapter 5), and Mandler's concept that stress can arise from a positive emotion (Chapter 16) are more clinically sophisticated than earlier literary and philosophical observations. Nevertheless, they all share the perception that a seemingly incorporeal feeling state can alter the function (and structure) of a material body organ. Although the effects of emotions on the body may seem evident, critical thought in philosophy and medicine has often denied the unity of the psychophysiological processes. This is important because the way science conceptualizes the mind–body issue will influence biobehavioral research priorities and the conduct of clinical practice. In the past, medicine has tended to minimize or ignore emotions or social stimuli, concentrating its search for the "cause" of illness on discrete organic factors.

In the past 200 years the tenets of materialism have dominated Western medicine (Popper & Eccles, 1981). Usually theorists have either given primacy to the mind or to the body as the dominating element of the human organism. Materialism, as a perspective, has been linked with the growth of mathematics and the improvement of technology for scientific measurement. It denies the reality and importance of entities that lack quantitative properties (mass, weight, velocity) and that cannot be reduced to more fundamental particles (molecules, atoms, electrons). As a philosophy it has either completely invalidated the reality of mental processes or viewed them as phenomena totally dependent upon physiochemical processes. Even Freud, who grew up professionally in the materialist tradition, found the clinical evidence that mental processes could provoke physical changes remarkable; he called it "the mysterious leap from mind to body" (Deutsch, 1959).

Traditionally, constructs such as "ego," "self," "symbol formation," and "affect" have not been favored subjects of scientific inquiry. Scientists have often scoffed at the notion that feelings, fantasies, or memories have a significant role to play in altering physiological reactions. Indeed "mind" began to fade as a subject of biological thought when Descartes separated out the "thinking" substance from corporality, making it possible to despiritualize the body and render it acceptable as an object for scientific inquiry (Descartes, 1637). Later in the 18th century, the French physician de la Mettrie (1748) wrote a *L'Homme Machine* in which he described the human body as a collection of machine-like parts (see discussion in Cohen, 1966; Weiner, 1973). His work, he felt, would free human biology from those spiritualist and unscientific superstitions that had retarded the development of a rational and effective medicine. No soul or psyche was expected to be found which activated the material body or motivated its behavior. The ghost was exorcised from the machine, spurring the emergence of the biomedical model which quickly developed reductionistic, physicalistic strategies in its search for specific causes of disease.

Despite the success of materialism as a theoretical attitude advancing biomedical research, this tradition has been criticized by many as an inadequate approach to understanding vital questions of human health and illness. Materialism has regarded emotion as a physiological state that results from some alteration of internal organic processes; it does not explain how or whether emotions can be affected by changing interactions with persons and things in the environment. It leaves out *meaning* as a biological event. Such dissatisfaction with monistic theories spurred the rise of "double-aspect" models. To Spinoza, mind and body were merely different aspects of an underlying unity that admits of varying representations. This is somewhat analogous to modern theories of light, which from one scientific perspective is viewed as a wave, and from another is regarded as a bundle of particles. The nature of light permits it to be experienced in two entirely different forms reflective of some (as yet unknown) underlying unity. The "self" has been similarly described by the philosopher P. F. Strawson (1959) as "a type of entity such that both predicates ascribing states of consciousness and predicates ascribing corporeal characteristics . . . are equally applicable to a single individual . . . "

Most dualistic theories, however, hold that the mentalistic and physicalistic statements are not only different in mode of expression, but actually reflect a referential nonidentity. In some ways thought events and physical events really differ; they represent either different substances or properties, relations, and events. Classical psychosomatic theory is based upon a tacit dualistic interactionist model.

Perhaps the most interesting of dualistic theories is a contemporary one, that of the neuroscientist Sir John Eccles. Based on his review of recent neuroanatomical and neurophysiological research, he proposed a theory in which the self-conscious mind is conceived of as "an independent unity that is actively engaged in reading out from the multitude of active centers in the modules of the liaison areas of the dominant cerebral hemisphere." (Eccles, 1981, p. 356). According to Eccles the self-conscious mind selects from the cerebral centers information in accord with its attention and interests, and "integrates its selection to give the unity of conscious experience from moment to moment." The self-conscious mind also has the ability to act back on the neural machinery. This mechanism, called "downward causation" by Popper, is the opposite of reductionism (Popper & Eccles, 1981). It occurs when the macrostructure as a whole acts on and alters the more elementary constituting particles. Popper, who collaborated with Eccles in a reconsideration of the mind–body issue, believes that "Besides the physical objects and states, there are mental states, and that these states are real since they interact with our bodies" (Popper & Eccles, 1981). Many behavioral scientists today are reconsidering the interactionist solution as the most likely explanation of current research and clinical findings which suggest that emotional states can alter autonomic, endocrine, and immunological functions.

For Eccles and Popper, biobehavioral events— including thoughts, feelings, memories, and their impact on the body—cannot be reduced to or explained by reference only to alterations of enzymes, molecules, or ions. A complete human biology must be able to generate a formal system that takes into account the complexity of the rules of social behavior, providing a language that describes patterns of life events and their meanings. For many years the most critical questions concerning the transactions of human experience were ignored in medicine because events involving symbolic meaning could not be reduced to classical mathematic equations. Emmanual Kant understood that perception and thought were activities that we perform rather than responses produced in us by molecular or environmental stimuli. He argued that human beings have interests that can be stated in rules and plans from which they act (Kant, 1978): "Actions are mediated by meanings; that is, considerations that arise from an understanding of connections that actions have with one another, and with their consequences in complex patterns of social life."

The goals, strategies, aversions, and fantasies of man are relevant information that biomedical researchers are beginning to study in order to understand the workings and malfunctions of the human body. Behavior is a critical biological event supporting species evolution and individual survival. The pioneering work of ethologists such as Lorenz or Tinbergen has demonstrated that animals elaborate behavioral programs to subserve the functions of mating, predation, aggression, social bonding, infant care, and territorial defense. Social stimuli related to these functions alter an animal's perceptions and motor behavior, while also influencing their autonomic, endocrine, and immune systems (Lorenz, 1965; Tinbergen, 1953). Patterned social communication and ritualized symbols have their substrate in the genetic coding of animal species, but often can be modified by later learning. Social behavior involves not only the use of sound and movement, but also changes in skin color, body temperature, respiration, and a host of other physiological alterations. Seeing or hearing a predator, losing a nestling, witnessing the sexual dance of a potential mate, all recruit and change a variety of body processes.

In humans there is no set of rigid genetic imperatives similar to those that exist in lower animals; we do not have fixed action patterns or innate releasing mechanisms (Zegans, 1967). We do, however, experience stress which may lead to psychological and physiological damage when we perceive threats to our achieving security, bonding, status, meaning, intimacy, and pleasurable arousal. The anticipation of loss of one or more of these basic needs often activates primitive physiological mechanisms as well as coping strategies. Behavioral scientists are now discovering (as many authors in this volume have discussed) possible mechanisms linking stressful events and changes in organ and tissue functions. (Frankenhaeuser, 1978; Glass, 1977; Hofer, 1981; Krohne, 1978; Mason et al., 1976; Stellar, 1976; Weich et al., 1980; Weiner, 1977; Wolf, 1981).

BIOPSYCHOSOCIAL MODEL

Although the traditional biomedical model, by denying the importance of behavioral events in the course of an illness, is an incomplete guide for the current practice of medicine, many physicians are reluctant to alter their approach to practice because of the stunning advances in our understanding of pathology and therapeutics which the traditional model has made possible. Since Pasteur, the biomedical model has emphasized the search for discrete etiological causes of illness which, through their toxic, invasive, or degenerative properties, can induce distinctive pathological changes. That model, by drawing heavily from the precepts of materialism, reduced consciousness and emotions to the status of derivatives of molecular processes; it could not then deal adequately with man as a symbol-producing, socially communicative being. The traditional biomedical approach went virtually unchallenged as long as medicine was engaged in studying and developing cures for acute infectious processes. With a shift of clinical and research concern toward more chronic ailments such as cancer and heart disease, a greater appreciation for the interplay of multiple factors involved in the onset and prolongation of illness emerged. Such an approach has been called the "biopsychosocial model" by Engel (1977). This model encourages the clinician to observe both morphological and biochemical changes in the patient while also attending to the patient's social environment, attitudes toward illness, life goals, intrapsychic conflicts, and emotional patterns.

The biopsychosocial model seeks to identify those various elements, whether invasive, genetic, or behavioral, which might alter the internal milieu and foster pathology. It asks professionals and the public to become increasingly concerned with the impact of occupational, familial, and economic tensions on our health. Bereavement, retirement, personality styles, and neuroses are being recognized as psychobiological factors that can affect how our bodies function. As Shakespeare wrote in *Henry IV* (part II), "We are all diseased and with our surfeiting and wanton hours have brought ourselves into a burning fever and must bleed for it."

Today the biopsychosocial model represents more of a change in perspective, attitude, and emphasis than a well-articulated scientific paradigm. It is built on the conviction that the brain and peripheral organs are linked in complex, mutually adjusting relationships, tuned to changes in social as well as physical stimuli. From this perspective, it is understood that disease is as much a result of the adaptive responses of the organism as it is a consequence of the destructive impact of pathogenic agents. The biopsychosocial model regards environmental stress or intrapsychic conflict as having pathological potential for the individual. The emotions may serve as the organism's bridge between the meaning (or significance) of stressful events and changes in physiological function. Freud's "mysterious leap" may occur on the wings of emotional responses to stress.

A biopsychosocial model is thus emerging and evolving. In this book certain ideas have been developed that contribute to the principles upon which this model is based. Among them are the following:

Psychological factors—including responses to environmental stressors, changes in developmental functioning, intrapsychic conflict, learning deficits, inadequate coping mechanisms, and lack of social support—may all make a contribution to the onset, response to, and recovery and recuperation from medical illness. An appropriate understanding of an organic illness must include the cognitive and emotional patterns of an individual in order to interpret changes in his or her environment and body states. Moreover, an illness alters the social, emotional, and occupational relationships of a patient. Such changes have meaning that may affect the duration, character, or intensity of an illness. Techniques are needed to understand these social changes that provide additional stress or favor the continuation of the sick role. Furthermore, psychosocial stress is an organismic state that can contribute to changes in body function which, if intense or chronic, lead to disease.

Neurotic or maladaptive characterological traits may directly affect physiological processes and contribute to the development of pathological changes in organs or lower the capacity of the body to respond adaptively to stress, thus creating greater vulnerability to illness. Certain profiles of personality traits may be identified which predict specific vulnerabilities to organic illness.

Processes of communication between health care providers and patients may significantly affect the quality of a response to medical care. A variety of difficulties in communication may occur that may either directly alter the pathophysiological processes or affect the quality of medical judgment and performance of diagnosis and treatment. Likewise, the structure and quality of the social environment from which a patient came and to which he or she will return after illness may either facilitate the recuperative process or exacerbate stress. The assessment of the patient's home and work environment is important to the total assessment.

Certain techniques of psychosocial intervention may be effective in changing pathophysiological processes either directly or mediated through stress-reducing mechanisms; these may include psychotherapy, relaxation techniques, behavioral modification, biofeedback, hypnosis, controlled imagery, etc. Different techniques may prove to be more effective for different types of pathological processes or different personality constellations.

Just as psychological factors can contribute to alterations of biological function, changes in nutrition, organ functioning, cerebral brain flow, endocrine status, renal filtration, and a host of other somatic variations also can produce profound effects in an individual's cognitive function, affective state, memory, attention and motivational performance.

The biopsychosocial model embraces an epidemiological perspective in understanding disease processes. (In Chapter 6, Weissman et al., in particular, have stressed that an epidemiological approach that assumes variations in risk factors for illness can generate new ideas about etiology, pathogenesis, treatment, and prevention.) Unlike older models of disease, this perspective assesses the individuated weight of genetic, nutritional, emotional, environmental, and invasive factors in codetermining the vulnerability to and expression of illness.

The Biopsychosocial Model and Behavioral Medicine

During the past 5 years there has been a growing interest in developing and integrating the behavioral and biomedical sciences in order to generate new knowledge and techniques relevant to health and illness. Researchers in behavioral medicine are interested in investigating those basic mechanisms "whereby behavioral phenomena influence the epidemiology, etiology, pathogenesis, prevention, diagnosis, treatment and rehabilitation of physical disorders." (Schwartz & Weiss, 1978). Behavioral medicine embraces a variety of disciplines, including psychology, sociology, anthropology, education, epidemiology, biostatistics, and psychiatry. A considerable overlap exists between behavioral medicine and the biopsychosocial model. One might regard the former as a broad-based field of investigation contributing to our basic knowledge of disease processes. The latter is a clinical approach to the assessment and treatment of a patient coming from a specific sociocultural environment, who presents with a set of organic and or psychological problems.

The development of the biopsychosocial model has implications for physicians and other health care professionals. Psychiatric residency programs are beginning to encourage young physicians to acquire certain skills and attitudes that this model embodies. They are designed to assist physicians to understand the health care delivery setting as a social system, emphasizing how the social structure of a ward or clinic enhances or interferes with diagnosis and treatment, affects the emotional well-being of patients, and influences relationships and communication among staff. Another goal is to make the physicians more aware of emotional and social factors that contribute to the onset and prolongation of medical illness. This involves understanding the meaning that medical illness carries for the patient and the emotional significance of diseased body parts, the social impact of illness and its significance to the family, and those emotional and social factors important in a successful adaptation to a changing physical function. Physicians are encouraged to become skilled in listening to and organizing psychosocial information necessary to make an accurate diagnosis and formulate appropriate treatment plan (Zegans et al., 1977).

At a more personal level, these programs facilitate the physician's understanding of those social and emotional stresses and conflicts that may impair his or her effective performance, and encourage the physician to consider in this context his or her personal ethical values relating to pain, death, prolongation of life, and allocation of medical resources. The young physician is also helped to accept the responsibility for the care of ill people, including the burden of making decisions of great consequence that cannot be avoided or shifted to another. Such responsibility includes developing intimate knowledge of, comfort with, and respect for another person's body in the face of disfigurement, decay, or intolerable behavior (Cooper, 1977).

PSYCHOSOMATIC APPROACH

For psychiatrists who entered the field at the time of World War II, the current enthusiasm concerning the biopsychosocial model and behavioral medicine may seem like the reemergence of familiar psychosomatic ideas under new labels. The term "psychosomatic" was first used in the early 19th century by Heinroth in reference to cases of insomnia. Its modern usage reflects the need for a term that would indicate how emotions and personality difficulties affect physiological functions such that they might lead to illness. Classical psychosomatic theory differs from contemporary concepts in behavioral medicine, in the following respects: Traditionally, it has dealt with a number of organic illnesses involving the autonomic nervous system (peptic ulcers, essential hypertension, ulcerative colitis, bronchial asthma). Cancer, autoimmune illnesses, and infectious processes have tended to fall generally outside the scope of its interests.

More basically, the classical theory has tended to search for "single-cause" psychodynamic explanations for specific illnesses rather than regarding psychological factors as part of a complex of influences, each of which contributes a portion to the risk of pathology. Alexander introduced a more multidimensional conception when he suggested that in psychosomatic conditions, patients experience intrapsychic conflicts, utilize immature psychological defenses, and activate primitive physiological reactions that were associated with these conflicts in childhood. He postulated an onset situation (current threat), a reaction of old conflicts, and a constitutional vulnerability of a specific tissue, organ, or system that would express the conflict by a disregulation of its function (Alexander, 1950). This was an advance over the theories of Freud's early disciples (Ferenczi, Garma), who believed that organic symptoms were symbolic representations (through a form of body communications) of a patient's repressed intrapsychic conflicts (Reiser, 1975).

Classical psychosomatic theory relied almost exclusively on psychoanalytic concepts to provide it with an explanatory framework. It tended to ignore environmental and cultural factors as contributing to the onset and exacerbation of disease. In contrast, modern behavioral medicine draws heavily upon the social sciences to provide it with ideas such as "life events," "coping style," "role theory," "social support systems," and "communicative styles," to help enhance an understanding of illness and its social and psychological consequences.

Early psychosomatic approaches tended to pay more attention to unconscious conflicts and attitudes of patients rather than explore characterological and cognitive styles. An exception was the work of Dunbar, who attempted to account for the specificity of symptoms based on a theory of personality types. Her early studies on the coronary-prone personality anticipated the more recent work on Type A and Type B behavior styles and coronary illness. Her approach, however, lacked the rigorous concern with design of current research, which attempts to isolate the most salient risk factors within the ensemble of personality traits. Dunbar (1943) believed that there was a direct causal link between personality types and physiological pathology. Reiser (1975) pointed out that it is questionable whether specific psychological factors alone constitute both the necessary and sufficient elements to determine the affected organ system and the nature of disease.

Classical psychosomatic theories placed more emphasis than behavioral medicine on those developmental factors in a patient's early life that might set the stage for later pathology. Early childhood trauma, fixations and conflicts were seen as contributing to the alteration of the individual's responsiveness to stressful stimuli and basic physiological regulatory patterns. Some theorists (e.g., Schur, 1955) believed that psychosomatic illness is accompanied by the reemergence of physiological patterns that are primitive, historical vestiges of childhood defensive reactions.

The role of early influences has been reexamined by Hamburg et al. (1975), who speculate that environmental and psychological factors early in a child's life may influence both the nature of adult emotional responses and the setting of adaptive brain mechanisms. Early experiences may alter neuroendocrine bioregulatory systems in such a manner that the organism's response to stress is modified for a long time, perhaps even permanently. For example, experiments with young mice confronted with chronic stress have shown that the enzymes tyrosine hydroxylase and phenylethanolamine N-methyl transferase (PNMT) which are crucial in the synthesis of catecholamines, are hyperactivated. These mice develop hypertension. Such findings may help us pinpoint the exact manner in which emotional factors change the body's basic chemistry and prepare the way for illness.

Early psychosomatic investigators were chiefly concerned with the relationship between intra-

psychic issues and alterations of the peripheral autonomic nervous system. The basic mediating role of the central nervous system in transducing symbolic meanings into alterations of physiological events, both within the brain and throughout the body, was not significantly appreciated. Of course, until recently the role of the brain in secreting neurohormones was not fully recognized and the cascade of knowledge concerning neurotransmitters, neuromodulators, T lymphocyte receptor sites, brain peptides, circadian rhythms, and the conditionability of immune responses was inaccessible to the pioneers of the field. Whereas early investigations linked defects of mature ego function of the adult with more primitive modes of autonomic reaction, the emphasis is gradually shifting to examining the relationship of psychological stress and inadequate coping responses with alterations of endocrine–autonomic–immunological control.

WHAT ARE EMOTIONS?

If emotions are a possible link between psychosocial meaning structures and physiological responses, then it is important to be clear how the term is used as a scientific construct. There are at least three types of experiences that we usually call "emotion:" (1) primary undifferentiated feelings of short duration; (2) differentiated feelings with accompanying autonomic and cognitive components of intermediate duration; and (3) mood states, or feelings lasting over a long period of time.

Function

Emotion appears to be a complex perceptual and physiological phenomena that subserves the functions of appraisal, motivation, and social communication in animals and man. The word "emotion" comes from the Latin verb *emovere*, which means "to move out." De Rivera (1977) says, "the word captures an important feature of emotion—that we experience ourselves or the other as being moved."

Ethologists have done extensive work describing and analyzing emotional behaviors and their functions in a variety of species. Emotions are regarded as a biological inheritance, essential for the adaptation and survival of species. Let us examine each of the three areas mentioned above in which emotion plays a vital role.

Appraisal

It is important for mammals to be able to evaluate information that might affect their security or reproductive success. Stimuli that can evoke emotion come from cospecies members, other aspects of the environment, or from within the organism itself (body cues). Some stimuli are invariably linked with specific affective responses in certain animals, and have been called *innate releasing mechanisms* (Lorenz, 1965). They involve both the preferential perception of cetain biologically significant stimuli and the mobilization of certain feeling states (rage, fright, sexual attraction). Predators, sexual displays, calls of immature young, and prey can release these genetically coded affective responses which trigger specialized patterns of defensive or adaptive behavior. Neurophysiological evidence suggests that parts of the paleocortex (septal region, amygdala, hippocampus, fornex) contain nuceli that mediate affective reactions in mammals (Brady, 1960; Brodal, 1981; Gloor, 1960; Green, 1960). Affective responses can also be learned in response to stimuli that are not genetically programed. Thus, memory is important in relating emotional responses to learned stimuli.

Penfield's work points to the medial temporal cortex as a key site of storage for the engrams of affective experience (Penfield & Jasper, 1954). It is obviously important for an animal to have an affect memory bank containing the engrams of emotion-related past experiences concerned with its safety, pleasure, and access to vital resources which it can match against current inputs.

Motivation

A second function of emotion in animals is to motivate certain behaviors. A frightened deer may freeze or run, an angry bull attack, and a sexually excited animal may engage in courting rituals. There is an important connection between affect and action. In certain lower animals the evocation of a certain feeling state results in a *fixed action pattern*; i.e., defensive, attack, or mating behaviors of a stereotyped nature. When there is no genetic linkage between emotions and fixed behaviors, there can be very strong learned patterns of response. Such a relationship assumes anatomical ties between the paleocortex and neocortex (see Mueller, this volume, Chapter 10).

There is also ample anatomical evidence of rich connections between the paleocortix and the volun-

tary motor system, the autonomic nervous system, and the expressive muscles of the face. Ablation experiments in animals suggest that emotion-linked behaviors are more easily evoked in the absence of neocortical influence (Brady, 1960). This indicates an important neocortical inhibitory role over emotion-mediated behaviors. Stimulation of portions of the paleocortex can cause a reciprocal inhibition of neocortical activity, causing a shift from fast beta waves to theta and delta activity more commonly observed in sleep. Thus, mechanisms exist to override the tonic neocortical control of certain emotion-related behaviors in situations of stress or crisis when immediate motor and expressive behaviors are adaptively necessary.

This effect appears to take place by a dampening of those reticular activating system fibers that activate the neocortex. Reticular activating system fibers originate in the brain stem, and some travel through the neocortex. In man, when the cortex becomes less arousable through the mediation of alcohol, drugs, infection, or injury, affect-motivated behaviors ordinarily under neocortical control can "escape." The opposite may also occur in humans, particularly in obsessives, in whom the strength of cortical inhibition (reinforced by learning) cannot be appropriately overcome even by a potent affect signal (learned passivity, sexual impotence).

Social Communication

Through various expressive channels, the motivational intentions of organisms are conveyed to others both within and outside the species (Argyle, 1973). The reading of the affective state of one animal by another gives it a good clue regarding the other's immediate behavioral intentions. Lorenz (1965), in his study of gray lag geese, made an elaborate set of predictions about the internal readiness of ganders during their "triumph ceremony" to flee or fight a rival by analyzing his neck and head movements. Therapists and lovers often infer both the meaning of a stimulus to an individual (appraisal) and that person's motivational intentions by "reading" his or her expressive signals. Emotional cues may not only convey information to another, but actually disrupt or control the other's behavior. Thus, the perception of a strong anger signal may lead an animal to freeze, fight, flee, or appease.

Sources of Stimulation

Having looked at what emotions do for the organism, let us examine more closely the sources of those stimuli that can evoke them. Signal-related stimuli are social stimuli (object relations), environmental changes (atmospheric, climatic, spatial, etc.), and changes in body schema and organ functioning (alterations in the observable parts of the body). Another class of stimuli are those that are drive related; these involve changes in endogenous levels of peripheral hormones and/or alterations in central neurohormones, neuromodulators, or neurotransmitters due to developmental, diurnal, pharmacological, and metabolic influences. Finally, there are idiosyncratic central nervous system changes that can stimulate emotions. These spontaneous rhythmic changes in firing patterns in paleocortical nuceli may be due to unknown causes or may be secondary to infections, injuries, or tumors of the central nervous system.

Primary Affects

We have seen that emotions can serve certain functions related to the survival interests of an organism and that affect-provoking stimuli can arise from other persons, the environment, the body, or the central nervous system. To some extent it is easier to define what emotions do and where they come from than what they are. Many theorists have tried to enumerate the basic human emotions. Many words express modulations or variations on what probably is a smaller core of fundamental emotional states. The word *anger*, for example, can be modulated into *chagrin, annoyance, irritation, peevishness, vexation, rage,* etc. It is unlikely that each of these words describes a different basic emotion. More likely, cognitive and situational variables both quantatatively and qualitatively modify the essential anger experience. My own list of primary affects present in most mammals includes the following:

1. Anger-rage
2. Fright-fear
3. Anticipation-surprise
4. Sadness
5. Sexual interest–erotic pleasure
6. Comfort-satisfaction (nutrient, kinesthetic pleasure)
7. Perplexity-uncertainty
8. Frustration-irritation
9. Disgust
10. Exploratory interest-curiosity.

Each of these primary affects may be elaborated in a specialized paleocortical site or center. A variety of studies have suggested that the septal area, amyg-dala, hippocampus, etc., are sites involved in the instigation of particular affects. Olds' work on the septal region as a location mediating "pleasure" is a classic of this type of work (Olds & Milner, 1954). Generally, research interest has focused more on stimulating or abating focal anatomical locations than on studying the contribution of more diverse neurotransmitter pathways. It may be productive in the future to think of affect circuits or systems, rather than describe anatomical centers, although paleocortical or limbic nuclei would be critical components in any such pathways. The elaboration of differentiated affective messages must involve the interplay of neurochemical substances.

Affect Systems

When we look at those behaviors called emotional and the words used to describe them it appears that two interlocking affect systems exist in humans. The first, which is a part of our early mammalian heritage, subserves critical survival and reproductive needs. Mediated through paleocortical circuits, it operates rapidly to appraise stimuli and motivate adaptive behaviors. As an emergency system, it can bypass cognitive elaboration and quickly trigger those physiological reactions necessary to prepare for appropriate action. We can assume that for every basic emotional state there exists a unique combination of facilitating expressive, autonomic, and hormonal responses. When the proper consummatory action is not achieved and the evoking emotion is unterminated, then the prevailing physiological reactions remain active. For convenience, we will call this the *basic emotional system.*

Occasionally, such basic emotions may be evoked in the absence of any obvious provoking situation. We can see this in certain pathological states, such as temporal lobe epilepsy, dementia, or some of the major psychiatric affective disorders. Sometimes during certain developmental phases such as adolescence or old age, minimal or inappropriate stimuli trigger strong basic emotional states.

The second system involves the more complex and conscious intervention of cognition. It is designed to facilitate social communication and secure the long-range goals of the individual. Physiological and expressive systems are modulated to take into account social and cultural conventions and necessities. Each society has its own expressive rituals and rules that regulate the way emotions are exposed and internally perceived (Eibl-Eibesfeldt, 1972). Social learning teaches most children how to modify, inhibit, or disguise the perception and communication of strong feeling states. This process results in the development of the second system, which we will call the *social emotional system.*

Within this system, emotions can be consciously modulated or inhibited; often such changes occur as a result of long-ingrained unconscious dictates. Regulatory control over the expression of basic emotions and the actions that they motivate is an important superego function. When an emotion is blocked or in some way altered, the physiological responses that usually accompany it may remain activated. An astute observer can often decipher a blocked emotional state that lies outside the conscious awareness of an individual by observing subtle changes in his or her skin color, breathing rate, pupillary dilation, and muscle tone (Ekman & Friesen, 1969).

Because physiological states are a necessary and inevitable feature of both emotional systems, it follows that any disorder of these systems is likely to be reflected in changes in organic functioning. Both emotional systems can be disturbed by developmental, environmental or learned stresses. Studies have shown that disorders of early mothering can affect the emotional responses of offspring, often leading to more anxious responses (Hofer, 1981; Yarrow, 1964). Rigid early disciplinary training can cause a child to develop patterns of inhibiting or distorting the perception and communication of certain emotions (Becker, 1964). Extreme environmental stresses, by repeatedly provoking strong emotional reactions, may lead to the disorganization or exhaustion of accompanying physiological responses (Zegans, 1982).

Emotion, as described in the preceding pages, is a set of complex processes that involves: orienting-alerting mechanisms, cognitive and memory functions, physiological responses, and expressive mechanisms. Although highly oversimplified, we can represent the major pathways that lead to a conscious, differentiated emotional state upon the reception of an environmental stimulus as shown in Figure 18-1.

Investigators have popularized a variety of theories about the nature of emotion. Some of these perspectives have already been mentioned in Chapters 15–17. In part, I believe that the proliferation of theories has occurred because of the existence in man of the two different but interlocking affective systems, the basic biological and the social. Most theories have focused on the role of emotions subserving either instinctive, biological needs or social-communicative functions.

The relationship of physiological measures to changes in emotion is of critical interest. There have been suggestions that certain kinds of alterations of emotion or mood may lead to changes in physical functioning. Alterations in physiology occur when there is suppression of certain emotions, exaggerated or intense emotions, inappropriate emotions, primitive or immature emotions, or prolongation or persistence of emotions.

The linkage of body changes to external stress or intrapsychic conflict through the mediation of emotion has generated much speculation but little solid research evidence. The concept of stress and its relation to emotion and illness is briefly reviewed next.

STRESS, EMOTIONS, AND ILLNESS

What is stress? How do the emotions play a role in stress reactions? Is there a direct relationship among stress, changes in physiology, and the onset of disease processes? These are vital questions that have been cautiously approached in this volume. Stress, as a psychosocial construct (Appley & Trumbull, 1977; Selye, 1966), has been very popular as an explanation of certain statistical correlations between critical life events and the appearance of illness (Rahe, 1968; Rahe et al., 1964). However, as the concept has been more carefully examined, questions about its explanatory power have been raised (Rabkin & Struening, 1976).

We must be careful not to cast stress into the role played earlier by bacteria, as a single-cause explanation for the triggering of pathophysiology. Hinkle (1973) pointed out that the meaning of this word has changed with the times and culture. In the 17th century it was associated with states of hardship, adversity, or affliction, whereas in the 18th and 19th centuries, the term denoted force, pressure, strain, or strong effort acting upon a material object. As in physics, the concept carried the connotation of an object being acted upon by forces while trying to maintain its integrity. Cannon (1932) used the term in a similar fashion, emphasizing the tendency of the living organism to bound back and restore its original state when impinged upon by an external force or disturbing agency.

More recently, Lazarus (1966) emphasized that there have been three main psychological variations on the meaning of the term. The most usual approach has been to see stress as a *stimulus,* a condition that produces turbulence or some kind of

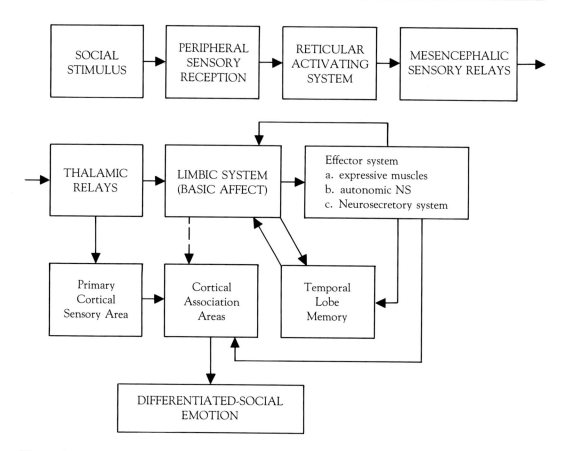

Figure 18-1. Signal related pathway leading to a differentiated emotional state.

reactive change in an object or person. Another way of thinking about stress is to emphasize the *response* side, the nature of the disturbance itself. Stress can also be seen as a relational or *transactional* concept describing the nature of adaptive interchange between a system and its environment.

If we look at stress as a stimulus, there are several kinds of events or situations that place unusual demand or strain on a person: (1) threats to physical security of safety; (2) stimuli that are new, intense, rapidly changing, sudden, or unexpected; (3) over- or understimulation or stimulus ambiguity; (4) deprivation of threat of loss of significant persons or objects; (5) loss or threat of loss of physical, cognitive, or affective functions; (6) frustration in attainment of anticipated rewards or goals; (7) changes in expectation concerning social or work performance; and (8) changes in social rules, values, or feedback mechanisms.

The "stress as stimulus" concept has catalyzed active research in the realm of stress and bodily illness as illustrated by the work of Holmes and Masuda (1974). These investigators equated the accumulation of a variety of stressful life events with the increased likeliness of physical illness.

However, viewing stress only from the perspective of the stimulus denies the importance of the mediation of psychological variables. There is a tendency to disregard the function of the interpretive meaning of the event. Situations in themselves are not inherently stressful, except in the most severe crises. The meaning or interpretation of an event is what Hamburg and Elliott (1981) called a "mediator," something that converts a potential stressor into a threat or noxious stimulus for the organism. It is clear that certain life events do place unusual demands upon an individual which may lead to stress and perhaps to illness. Often the only way to discover their impact is to study a person in depth, analyzing the meaning of the event, the person's attempts to cope, the emotions evoked, and the physical consequences that ensue. There have been a number of studies that have implemented such a comprehensive strategy, particularly in the area of bereavement (see Chapter 5).

There are many life occurrences that appear to be naturally stressful. Holmes and Rahe's (1967) list of critical life events includes the death of a child or spouse, going to jail, moving to a new location, losing one's job, etc. However, with the exception of certain major life-threatening occurrences, no raw stimulus serves as a universal stressor for everyone; a great deal depends upon the context within which the event takes place and the past history and coping skills of the person experiencing it.

While some stimuli may cause immediate, direct contact damage, the major impact of stress arises from the way in which the individual tries to adapt to the threat. The emotional and physiological reactions of the person are often taken as indicators of the presence and extent of stress. Research studies have tried to single out specific bodily responses that are reliable reflections of the scope of the stress. Some investigators have concentrated on autonomic fluctuations such as heart rate, galvanic skin responses, or respiration, while others have looked at cortisol or adrenalin excretion, changes in muscle tension, or EEG (Ackenheil, 1980; Christie et al., 1980; Frankenhaeuser, 1975; Lader, 1980; Pribram & McGuiness, 1975). Just as it appears that there are no universal stressors, it also seems that each person has a different way of expressing his or her stress through emotional and bodily channels.

If stress is a response to a noxious or threatening stimulus, it appears as the result of a complex, structured series of perceptions, appraisals, and adaptive responses. We can think of the progression of those events leading to the stress as occurring in the following stages (Zegans, 1982):

1. *Stage of alerting-alarm:* A potential stressor is perceived that triggers central nervous system arousal, orientation toward the stimulus, and cessation of extraneous ongoing activities.

2. *Stage of appraisal:* The nature of the stimulus is assessed through examining its content, the context within which it occurs, and past experience with similar situations. The appraisal incorporates the nature of the potential stressor, its possible consequences for the individual, and whether it should be

ignored or investigated further. No simple linear relationship exists between the immediate recognition of a stressor and the resulting emotional response. A number of tentative emotions may be elicited during this stage until some final judgment is made about the meaning of the event and its consequences.

3. *Stage of developing a coping strategy:* When unpleasant, dysphoric emotions are provoked by a stimulus, a search is made to find some means of terminating those affects. A stressor is dealt with either by altering or eliminating its danger or revising its meaning for the individual; this is called *coping.* Negative emotions and accompanying expressive and physiological states can be modulated when the individual anticipates control or mastery of the situation through the implementation of a successful coping strategy (Levine et al., 1978).

4. *Stage of the stress response:* When the coping strategy proves to be inadequate, inappropriate, or excessively long, a number of dysphoric emotional states may be instigated (grief, anxiety, anger, panic). These may be accompanied by inadequate ego defenses, poor cognitive organization, and the activation of altered autonomic and neuroendocrine patterns. This stage may end in a state of either mental and physical exhaustion or an episode of disorganization and discoordination of psychic and bodily processes.

Each of these stages of stress is accompanied by some alterations of organic processes. They are usually transient and adjusted to the demands of the situation. More extreme changes may occur with prolonged alerting, poor appraisal, inadequate coping, disorganization and exhaustion.

Stress as a response occurs even when an organism is confronted with a demand that it interprets as requiring serious adaptive adjustment, but that exceeds its coping capacities. There are many factors that may buffer or mediate the impact of a potential stressor: the individual's psychological and physical characteristics, social network and cultural assumptions, and available repertoire of coping skills (Bastiaans, 1978; Krohne, 1978; Pearlin & Schooler, 1978; Tache & Selye, 1978).

Emotions come into play at a number of points in the sequence just outlined; they are vital links bridging the appraisal and action processes, acting by triggering those physiological events necessary to carry out coping decisions. The complete stress response occurs when the coping strategy fails.

Emotions evoked at that juncture release physiological responses that can play a vital role in the transition from stress to possible illness.

STRESS, COPING, AND BODY CHANGES

Neither medical nor behavioral science has identified the exact mechanisms through which stress leads to specific changes in bodily function. There are, however, certain factors that seem to influence whether responses to a stressor will lead to significant changes in physiology (see Figure 18.2). Among the variables that seem particularly important are the following: (1) the nature of the stressor (influences the intensity and quality of the emotions provoked and the action set of motor, autonomic, and hormonal responses activated); (2) the severity of the stressor (how intense a demand is made on the organism); (3) the predictability of the onset of the provoking stressor (one can assume that a more predictable stress situation gives the organism an opportunity to adapt to it with greater control without triggering extreme emergency responses); (4) the nature of the coping repertoire of the individual, including control over the onset and termination of the stressor; (5) the individual's preparedness in dealing with the stress, including general state of health, mental alertness, and cognitive capacities; (6) previous experience in dealing with similar types of stress situations; (7) genetic and constitutional parameters; and (8) developmentally learned physiological reactions previously utilized to deal with similar situations or emotions.

There is no simple relationship between a stress situation and a physiological response; individuals have a set of genetic, experiential, and situational mediators that influence the final linkage between the demands placed on them and how they will respond. (Hamburg et al., 1975). The body's reaction to stress occurs on a tissue and organ level as well as on the more discrete plane of neuronal and biochemical change. Research has shown that chronic stress will decrease the brain's available norepinephrine (NE) level (Anisman, 1978). The recovery time for the NE levels to return to baseline appears to be a function of both the type and severity of the stressor. Mild stress promotes the increased utilization of NE, which then is compensated for by the neurons working to increase its synthesis. With a more intense or prolonged

stress a decline in the endogenous levels of NE is observed. The mechanism responsible for this effect is thought to be the disinhibition of tyrosine hydroxylase, which results in the increase of NE synthesis. Upon the restoration of the transmitter pools, tyrosine hydroxylase is once more inhibited. Under a severe or protracted stress, however, the synthesis of NE does not keep pace with its utilization.

A similar reaction occurs with serotonin synthesis and exhaustion. Dopamine does not appear to be as markedly affected as these other two neurotransmitters. Mild stress also has the effect of inhibiting monoamine oxidase, which preserves NE and serotonin, permitting the organism's immediate needs for these transmitters to be met.

An important observation concerning stress and the turnover rate of central nervous system catecholamines is that the intensity and duration of the stimulus is not the only factor controlling transmitter levels. Alterations in the levels and turnover rates of these neurochemicals are also related to the degree of control the organism has upon the occurrence of the stressor and its termination. Coping capacity also affects the release of acetylcholine and corticosterone under conditions of stress. Both of these substances show a rise during stress, but under circumstances when the animal has some control over the stimulus, the level of these substances remains constant.

The effects of coping abilities on physiological responses to stress are seen also in peripheral endocrine measures. Frankenhaeuser (1976) has demonstrated that adrenalin is regularly increased in subjects exposed to a stressful or threatening situation, characterized by uncertainty and unpredictability. Rises in adrenalin secretion are related to the intensity of emotional reactions under such conditions. As the uncertainty diminishes and the subject experiences better control, however, the adrenalin response decreases. Noradenalin release does not show the same relationship to coping as does adrenalin.

Coping skills have also been shown to be important in the regulation of such body compounds as cortisol, growth hormone, and free fatty acids. In experiments on trainees practicing parachute jumps, there was a high correlation between "internal locus of control" and high levels of fatty acids. Conversely, cortisol and growth hormone activation were related to poor performance and low coping skills. Based upon these studies, Baade and his co-workers (1978) concluded that stress causes a

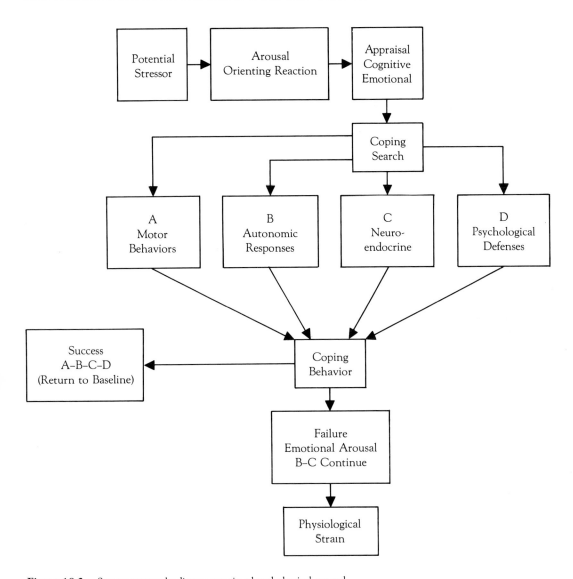

Figure 18-2. Stress response leading to emotional and physical arousal.

psychophysiological response activating autonomic and hormonal processes; when coping is established, this activation is reduced.

Coping abilities also play a central role in experimental work linking stress and cardiovascular pathology. In a National Institutes of Health report on coronary-prone behavior, it was concluded that

> In contrast to the pattern of cardiovascular responses that occur when an animal is able to exert control over its environment, a different pattern of cardiovascular changes seem to occur when an animal lacks control. Thus, during a procedure in which irregularly scheduled electric shocks are presented, after inescapable water stress, or when a submissive animal has no escape from a victor, a pattern is seen in which bradycardia may be followed by death, but evidence of structural pathology is not apparent. (*Proceedings of the Forum on Coronary Prone Behavior, 1978*)

Animals that have adequate coping skills in the face of prolonged, predictable stress exhibit a broad range of pathophysiological phenomena, including an increased cholesterol level, elevated arterial pressure, decreased clotting times, and myofibrillar degeneration. Severe or prolonged stress causes organic damage despite appropriate coping responses, but the physiological processes recruited are different than when the organism experiences passivity and helplessness.

The importance of stress in depleting NE and serotonin reserves is significant because of the role that these transmitters play in regulating the hypo-thalamic–pituitary–adrenal axis (Krieger, 1979). Stress appears to activate this central adaptational system. Serotonin exerts an inhibitory influence on this axis, while hypothalamic NE tonically inhibits ACTH and corticotropin-releasing factor secretion. When NE levels decrease, the anterior pituitary is disinhibited, resulting in ACTH release and a rise in corticosterone. Negative feedback from the pitui-tary–adrenal axis results in NE restimulation and subsequent ACTH inhibition. The corticosterone activation that results from reduced NE control over ACTH may help account for the decline in immun-ological competence that often follows prolonged or intense stress. The relationship among emotions, stress, limbic system activity changes in hypo-thalamic neurotransmitters, and alternations of the pituitary–adrenal axis are most critical to our understanding of how psychosocial events influenc bodily function.

EMOTIONS AND THE HYPOTHALAMIC–PITUITARY–ADRENAL AXIS

Some of the most exciting research in the neuro-sciences in the past few years has taken place in clarifying the role of the brain as a neuroendocrine organ (Ellendorf & Parvizi, 1980; Palkovits, 1980; Pelletier et al., 1979). This work helps us understand how emotional reactions can also be responsible for widespread physiological alterations in the following systems: hypothalamic–pituitary–adrenal cortical axis; autonomic nervous system–adrenal medullary system; immune system; reticular-activating system; voluntary muscular system; attentional and memory storage system in the central nervous system; and circadian rhythms. A number of important dis-coveries concerning the brain neuroendocrine function have led to our present understanding (Brownstein, 1980; Krieger, 1979; Lal & Martin, 1980; Pelletier et al., 1979).

As early as 1933, the idea that nerve cells could have a secretory function was proposed by Harris, based on structural peculiarities of the supraoptic and paraventricular nuclear cells. In 1955 a Noble Prize was given to Du Vignaud for having isolated

the structure of oxytocin and vasopressin, identifying them as brain hormones and peptides.

Guillemin and Schally instigated research to determine the chemical structure of those hypo-thalamic hormones that regulate the secretions of the anterior pituitary gland. In 1969 thyrotropin-releasing hormone (TRH) was isolated and analyzed, as were luteinizing hormone–releasing hormone (LHRH) in 1971 and growth hormone-release-inhibiting hormone (somatostatin) in 1973. Hor-mones have been identified in neuronal secretory granules in the median eminence, near the portal vessels that empty into the pituitary. The hypophyseal–portal blood supply carries hormones from the hypothalamus to the pituitary and in a retrograde direction from the pituitary to the hypothalamus.

The neurohormones act far from their site of production. They may reach their ultimate target organ through axons, blood vessels, or cerebrospinal fluid. Substances that act as hormones when trans-ported by the blood stream to distant targets can also be liberated at the axon terminals of the producing neurons and alter the function of another neuron. When the chemical substance acts in this way it is considered to be a neurotransmitter. Neurohormones have been found to be present in most brain areas. The hypothalamus, and especially the median eminence (which links it to the pituitary through a vascular portal system), contains neuro-hormones in the highest concentrations.

Neurophysiological studies have shown that a number of extrahypothalamic regions, such as the amygdala, hippocampus, and cingulate gyrus, and involved in the mediation of pituitary hormone release. Electrical stimulation of these regions can induce or inhibit the production of hypophyseal endocrines, raising the possibility that these sites are involved in emotional and stress-induced mech-anisms of hormone regulation.

Dopamine and NE receptors have been shown to exist on tuberoinfundibular neurons, indicating the existence of dopaminergic and adrenergic pathways to these cells. Some neurotransmitter effects on hor-mones have been demonstrated. NE, for example, is involved in the tonic and cyclic release of gonado-tropins, it also plays a stimulating role in growth hormone release via a still hypothetical growth hormone–releasing factor. Some evidence exists that ACTH may be inhibited by NE. Dopamine appears to have a definite stimulatory role in the control of thyrotropin secretion. The administration of pimozide, a specific dopaminergic receptor blocker, has been shown to decrease the circulating level of thyrotropin. Prolactin is inhibited by dopamine, which acts on both pituitary and hypothalamic levels. Serotonin has been cited as a major factor in the control of growth hormone secretion and plays an inhibitory role in the release of gonadal hormones. ACTH release also is influenced by serotonin, which exerts a tonic stimulatory effect at the hypothalamic level and an inhibitory control at the level of the limbic system that modulates ACTH release during stress.

It is clear that the catecholamines and serotonin (there is some evidence of a cholinergic tuberoinfundiluber pathway similar to the dopaminergic one) exert a major regulatory control over anterior pituitary function (Collu, 1977; Ellendorf & Parvizi, 1980). They can modulate the secretion of several hormones either through influence over hypothalamic–hypophysiotropic factors, or through direct action on the pituitary function during stress or emotional episodes. Links can thus be established between the following:

1. A potential stressor and its cognitive elaboration as a threatening stimulus.

2. The development of an emotional response and changes in limbic discharge that can alter neurotransmitter influence on hypothalamic peptidergic neurons.

3. Alteration of hypophyseal endocrine release and physiological change in function at target organ site (thyroid, adrenal gland, etc.).

The link between the brain catecholamines and peptide hormones is essential to our understanding of the relationship between emotions and bodily changes. It has been suggested that the catecholamines play a critical role in the neural integration of drives, aversive responses, arousal, and reinforcement. Serotonin, dopamine, NE, and the peptide hormones all utilize the same "second messenger" system (cyclic adenosine 3', 5'-monophosphate). This may imply a relationship in which a peptide mediates a drive state and the catecholamines subserve the reward mechanism. Catecholamines may thus be crucial in regulating the organism's response to stress. In the normal individual the relationship between drive and reinforcement is well regulated, arousal and emotion are kept within adaptive bounds, and reward and aversive events serve to reinforce new adaptive behavior in successful learning (Stellar, 1976).

In psychopathological conditions or when coping responses to stress fail, something goes awry with this regulatory balance (Carroll & Mendels, 1976). The arousing stimulation may be too strong or the responding neural system too sensitive or too refractory, possibly as a result of a depletion of catecholamines. Under these conditions, the emotional responses are extreme, labile, or inappropriate and adaptation fails. This failure may be reflected not only in affective and cognitive disturbances, but also in disregulation of the hypophyseal–adrenal–neurodocrine axis, the autonomic nervous system; and possibly the immune system.

In addition to oxytocin, vasopressin, TRH, LHRH, and somatostatin, there is evidence for at least six other hypothalamic hormones involved in pituitary regulation (Reichlin, 1979): corticotropin-releasing factor (CRF), growth hormone-releasing factor, prolactin release–inhibiting factor, melanocyte-stimulating hormone release–inhibiting factor, and melanocyte-stimulating hormone-releasing factor.

Several of the hypothalamic hormones have properties that are important for our understanding of emotions and behavior. A description of some of these hormones or factors follows.

Corticotropin-Releasing Factor

Schally, who won a Noble Prize for his work on hypothalamic hormones, has written that, "The central nervous system and the hypothalamus, in particular, mediate the classical response to 'stress.' Physical and emotional stimuli which interfere with the body's ability to maintain homeostasis can result in the liberation of corticotropin-releasing factor (CRF) which stimulates the release of ACTH from the pituitary" (Schally & Arimura, 1977). In turn, ACTH augments the secretion of glucocorticoids necessary for survival.

It has been demonstrated that there is a periodicity for cortisol and ACTH secretion that is well established in early childhood and remains fairly constant throughout life (Sachar, 1980; Weitzman, 1980). Circulating cortisol levels rise to a maximum between 6:00 and 8:00 a.m. and fall during the day, with ACTH secretion changing in a parallel fashion. The periodicity of CRF secretion by the hypothalamus is closely related to the ACTH circadian cycle. Psychiatric studies have indicated that the production or secretion rate of cortisol is consistently elevated in most patients with depression. During clinical recovery the values for the hormone return to normal. A relationship has also been observed among cortisol production, levels of anxiety, and psychotic disorganization.

Serotonin apparently also plays an important role in ACTH release. Diurnal rhythms of serotonin in the limbic system coincide with those of plasma corticosterone in rats. The neuroendocrine system, which regulates ACTH, responds quickly to stress situations. Many different stressful physical and social stimuli, including fear, fever, noise, pain, and hypoglycemia, can cause rapid ACTH release. They can all override the circadian and feedback systems that usually control ACTH secretion. The CRF circuit demonstrates how limbic–hypothalamic–pituitary–adrenal relations can affect both emotional and physical states (de Wied et al., 1976; van Wimersma Greidanus, 1979).

Growth Hormone Release-Inhibiting Hormone (Somatostatin)

A tetradecapeptide identical in structure to somatostatin has been isolated from the hypothalami of both sheep and pigs (Palkovits, 1980). High concentrations of somatostatin have also been found in the pancreas, stomach, and duodenum of rats. Somatostatin possesses inhibitory effects on the secretion of pituitary growth hormone and thyrotropin in mammals and humans. It also suppresses the secretion of glucagon and insulin in a variety of species. The hormone affects gastric function in man; it inhibits gastric acid and pepsin secretion, exerting a direct effect on both parietal and peptic cells, while inhibiting the production and secretion of cholescystokinin, the duodenal mucosa and pancreatic fluid. The hormone thus has important functions in digestive physiology.

Work with primates indicates that growth hormone may inhibit platelet aggregation. Somatostatin may also be important in immunological reactions, since growth hormone has been implicated in the activation of T lymphocytes (Comsa et al., 1975). Somatostatin is found in highest concentration in the hypothalamus, but has also been found in other parts of the brain, suggesting that it functions also as a neurotransmitter.

Melanocyte-Stimulating Hormone Release-Inhibiting Factor

Hypothalamic extracts cause an inhibition of the pituitary release of melanocyte-stimulating hormone (MSH), suggesting the existence of an MSH-releasing factor. Dopaminergic mechanisms are involved in tonic MSH inhibition; alpha-adrenergic mechanisms also have an inhibitory effect, and stimulatory beta-adrenergic mechanisms have been identified. MSH has some behavioral effects on the central nervous system. Studies indicate that it has a role in improving attentional processes. It may raise the threshold for stimuli and serve as a filtering mechanism to protect the organism from distracting perceptual noise. Processing of patterned information may also be enhanced by MSH (Sandman et al., 1977). It has been demonstrated to rise significantly in response to stress. When given to normal volunteers, MSH triggers a significant decrease in moment-to-moment anxiety.

MSH has been observed to rise and fall along with ACTH. Both hormones have been found to be contained within a larger common percursor, referred to as 31K ACTH endorphin or "pro-opiocortin." This molecule also contains β-lipotropic hormone, which can be broken down into the smaller peptide β-endorphin. It is of considerable interest that concentrations of MSH, ACTH, and β-endorphin, as well as prolactin, thyrotropin, growth hormone, and other peptides have been found in the central nervous system after hypophysectomy (Krieger, 1979). These findings suggest that the central nervous system can synthesize these peptide hormones.

The presence of pituitary hormones in the brain suggests that they play different roles within the central nervous system than when they are released into the peripheral circulation. Peptidergic neurons produce not only vasopressin and the hypophysiotropic hormones, but also a whole class of other peptides (substance P, endorphins, enkephalins). These peptides may function as neuromodulators by altering the effect of the neurotransmitter on its receptors. The role of pituitary and hypothalamic peptides on brain function promises to be an exciting area of future research (Lipton & Breese, 1976; Prange et al., 1979; Rostogi, 1979).

Of equal interest is the distribution of peptides found in such organs as the lungs, stomach, and intestines. For example, the control of the trache-obronchial tree has traditionally been held by excitatory cholinergic nerves and inhibitory (smooth muscle–relaxing) adrenergic nerves. Current work indicates, however, that there is also a nonadrenergic inhibitory system of innervation, possibly related to the vasoactive intestinal peptide. This substance seems to relax bronchial smooth muscle independently of adrenergic or cholinergic receptors (Bitar & Makhlouf, 1982). It is widely distributed in organs containing smooth muscle, especially in sphincters, independently of adrenergic or cholinergic receptors. A deficiency of this system has been postulated as an explanation for hyperactivity of the bronchial airways during asthma (Matsuzaki et al., 1980). The nature of control of these peripheral peptides by central processes is currently uncertain. Their presence provides a potential link between the brain and a set of organs characterized by smooth muscle function that have historically been implicated in several psychosomatic diseases.

Vasopressin

It has been established that vasopressin is synthesized in the medial hypothalamus, transported to the posterior pituitary, and released into the systemic circulation to regulate renal water clearance. It has also been shown to be transported from the hypothalamus to the third ventricle. It is distributed by the cerebrospinal fluid to the brain and mediates a number of central nervous system effects (Edwards, 1977). These are related to information processing and include an influence on learning and memory (Weingartner et al., 1981). Vasopressin has been administered experimentally to improve learning and recall in patients with progressive idiopathic dementia (Alzheimer's disease) with evidence of definite increases in cognitive ability, particularly in memory recall.

The neurosecretory functions of the brain thus involve control of both classical endocrine target organs, such as the thyroid or adrenal glands, and portions of the central nervous system itself (McKenzie, 1979). The hypothalamic–pituitary–adrenal axis can be seen as a critical regulatory system of the body influencing autonomic, renal, smooth muscle, cognitive, affective, and memory functions.

STRESS AND HYPOTHALAMIC REGULATION OF IMMUNE AND AUTONOMIC PROCESSES

The hypothalamus serves as an integrative center linking the limbic system which is important in the coordination of emotions and motivated behavior, the autonomic nervous system which controls the cardiorespiratory and visceral activities of the body, the endocrine system which regulates metabolic,

fluid electrolyte, and reproductive functions, and the immune system which is critical in maintaining the cellular integrity of the body. This close relationship between neural and vegatative systems provides a mechanism through which emotional events can affect physiological activities and, in turn, be influenced by them.

Autonomic Nervous System

The pioneering experiments of Karplus and Kriedl demonstrated that electrical stimulation of the hypothalamus could elicit a variety of autonomic responses, and Bard demonstrated that brain stem transections caudal to the posterior hypothalamic area could abolish sympathetic "sham rage." These findings provided convincing evidence that the hypothalamus contains a system of cells, normally under cortical inhibition, that is capable of causing a coordinated autonomic activation (Saper, 1979).

The hypothalamus directly projects to preganglionic cells of the spinal cord and also is involved in polysynaptic pathways through the brain stem reticular formation to establish its control of the autonomic nervous system. There is evidence that at least some hypothalamoautonomic axons are collaterals of neurons that project to the neurohypophysis and that they may utilize oxytocin as their transmitter agent. Research also indicates that the hypothalamoautonomic neurons not only have direct projections to, but also may receive direct inputs from the primary autonomic nuclei, thus establishing a regulatory feedback loop. Of great interest to the study of emotion and its influence on the body are recent findings that implicate the amygdala and septum in modulating the hypothalamic control of the nervous system (Polosa et al., 1979).

Although much psychophysiological research has focused on rapid changes of the autonomic nervous system in response to behavioral inputs, there is growing attention to the tonic activity of this neural network. Functionally, autonomic tone contributes to the maintenance of required levels of activity in autonomic effector cells. Arterial pressure is thus maintained at a level greater than that determined by intrinsic properties of the blood vessels due to the contraction of vascular smooth muscle evoked by tonically active sympathetic postganglionic cells. The tonic activity provides effector cells with the potential for bimodal responses that either increase or decrease activity. Such a capacity is vital for maintaining homeostasis in the face of variable adaptational demands on the organism by increasing the system's responsiveness to changing conditions.

The system also gains flexibilty when the effector units can combine tone from the sympathetic and parasympathetic components of the autonomic nervous system. Systems with such dual antagonistic innervation remain inherently more stable, showing minimal effects from widespread perturbations of neuronal activity that alter the activity of the two components in the same direction. Conversely, such tonic control system makes the affected cells more highly sensitive to any factor that increases the difference between levels of sympathetic and parasympathetic interaction. The existence of such tonic control activity is important in understanding how chronic stress may alter the function of organs innervated by the autonomic nervous system.

Recent studies have implicated both serotonin and norepinephrine as being involved in the maintenance of the tonic activity of the autonomic nervous system. Serotonin apparently mediates those excitatory processes underlying tonic activity, while NE may serve as the mediator of tonic inhibition (Polosa et al., 1979). This relationship, while still tentative, points to the possibility that disruption of the levels of these neurotransmitters (which may occur in affective disorders) may also alter those homeostatic physiological functions that depend upon tonic innervation of the autonomic nervous system. A difference in the tone of the autonomic nervous system may account for the "hot" reactors alluded by Dembrowski et al. in Chapter 7.

Research on the tonic innervation of the autonomic nervous system and its relationship to personality factors may prove a fruitful area of future investigation, particularly in patients with cardiovascular problems. Recent research by Iriuchijima (1979) has clearly identified a tonic neurogenic influence in rats with spontaneous hypertension. This condition appears to be maintained principally by an increase in sympathetic nerve tone originating from the medullary cardiovascular centers (possibly under hypothalamic control). The importance of such central nervous system control over the autonomic nervous system visceromotor system has been recognized by the experimental physiologists. Lisander (1979) remarked,

This important part of the nervous system is strongly influenced by cortico-hypothalamic levels and what characterizes these particular autonomic effects is their very close linkage to behavioral and endocrine changes.

Thus, the highest brain levels responsible for "cognitive and affective" functions involve, in their expressions, all three efferent systems of the body, forming patterns that are designed to cope with the various environmental challenges that the organism has to face in daily life (page 385).*

The concept of *patterned responses* to stressful situations is important to our understanding of emotions and illness. Lisander believes that although the somatomotor expressions of emotional behavior vary considerably among species, the autonomic and hormonal adjustments mediated by the hypothalamus remain more constant. MacLean (1970) developed the concept of a "triune brain" that increases in complexity with evolutionary advance, permitting higher mammals a more varied and differentiated set of responses to challenging situations. The *protoreptilian* brain provides stereotyped, species-typical behavior for animals living in narrow ecological niches confronted with predictable adaptive demands. The later *paleomamalian brain* (related to the limbic system) permits more complex sets of behaviors associated with instincts and their accompanying patterns of emotional reaction. The most advanced brain development, the human *neocortex*, interacts with the older forebrain components to permit more individualized, finely tuned behaviors responsive to learned social cues and predicted consequences of potential actions.

The neocortex can modify the perception of the evoked emotions and completely suppress the somatomotor components of emotional expression. What it cannot do is entirely extinguish the patterned autonomic and hormonal responses elaborated by the hypothalamus in response to signals from the more primitive parts of the brain. A dissociation may occur between the action-oriented "goals" of behavior and the vegetative adjustments necessary to effectively realize them. Lisander commented that several hypothalamic areas have been identified where topical stimulation brings about drastic and quite specific autonomic changes linked to hormonal and somatomotor adjustments in an "integrated fashion." These response patterns occur in reaction to specific environmental stimuli in the intact organism and are termed "push-button patterns." Mentioned specifically are the well-

*From Lisander B (1979): Somato-autonomic reactions and their higher control. In Brooks C, Koizumi K, & Sato A (Eds.): *Integrative Functions of the Autonomic Nervous System.* New York, Elsevier, p. 385.

known defense reaction, the so-called pressor response, which causes increased sympathetic discharge but without any activation of cholinergic sympathetic vasodilator fibers, and the withdrawal reaction which is activated when flight or attack are impossible.

Mason, (1975; Mason et al., 1976), in studying endocrine responses to stress, also discovered typical hormonal response patterns or profiles that reflect extraordinary sensitivity to psychological stimuli. A variety of autonomic, emotionally charged patterns exist that are available to an organism in reaction to stereotyped stress situations. The limbic system may organize the message to the hypothalamus, designating which of the available repetoire of patterned responses is appropriate in a given circumstance. (Isaacson, 1974). Different stress prototypes (loss, pain, threat, overstimulation) may each recruit a specific autonomic–hormonal pattern intended to facilitate an adaptive somatomotor response (Ellendorf & Parvizi, 1980). This may place continuing vegetative demands upon the body because of possible divergent neocortical and limbic-hypothalamic strategies of response. Such a situation may, if prolonged, set the stage for structural organ insult and, ultimately, disease (Weiner, 1977; Wolf, 1981; Wolff, 1950).

The central nervous system influence over immune processes has been thoroughly reviewed in Chapters 12 and 14. The role of the hypothalamus in influencing a variety of immunological responses has been repeatedly demonstrated (Stein et al., 1981). The integration of immune, endocrine, and autonomic reactions to stress is vital to maintaining the health of the organism (Riley, 1981; Rogers et al., 1979). The anatomical and neurophysiological relationships among the neocortex, limbic system, and hypothalamus is being carefully analyzed in laboratories throughout the world. The significance of psychosocial events and their emotional elaboration by these networks has been the focus of this volume. By bringing together various basic and clinical disciplines to share their ideas and techniques, we may come closer to understanding how feelings and meaning can change molecules and our health.

CONCLUDING REMARKS

Most of us who have been educated in the Western scientific tradition usually feel uncomfortable with things that seem too complicated and undefined. We like to believe (despite outward appearances) in a system of rational explanations for events in which things ultimately cohere. Medical researchers dealing with phenomena that are tractable to those quantitative methods that have proven successful in the empirical sciences. We prefer whenever possible to bring things under the reign of causal or statistical laws. Unfortunately, human illnesses often have a way of confounding our attempts at predictability and order. They tend to be complex events that involve change in both physical organs and our social relations and self-esteem. In different ways the authors in this volume have argued that expectations, feelings, and conflicts are biological events having relevance not only for the way in which we externally behave, but also for those three vital internal systems of adaptation—the neuroendocrine, immune, and autonomic systems. We do not yet know how a symbolic image, a sad thought, or an angry intention becomes transformed into an enzymatic change or axonal discharge. However, exciting discoveries are being made each day that confirm the ancient wisdom that man is a psychophysiological unity and whatever affects the "self" also alters, sometimes pathologically, the body (Sperry, 1982).

REFERENCES

Ackenheil M (1980): Hormonal response to stress in mental illness. Van Praag H (Ed.). In *Handbook of Biological Psychiatry*, Part III. New York, Dekker, pp. 195–215.

Alexander F (1950): *Psychosomatic Medicine*. New York, Norton.

Anisman H (1978): Neurochemical changes elicited by stress. Anisman H (Ed.). In *Psychopharmacology of Aversely Motivated Behavior*. New York, Plenum Press, pp. 119–172.

Appley MJ, & Trumbull R (1977): The concept of psychological stress. Lazarus M, & Monat A (Eds.). In *Stress and Coping*. New York, Columbia University Press.

Argyle M (1973): *Social Encounters: Readings in Social Interaction*. Harmondsworth, England, Penguin Books.

Baade E, Ellertsen B, Johnson TB, & Ursin U (1978): Physiology, psychology and performance. Baade E, Levine S, & Ursin H (Eds.). In *Psychobiology of Stress*. New York, Academic Press.

Bastiaans J (1978): The optimal use of anxiety in the struggle for adaptation. Sarason IG, & Spelberger CD (Eds.). In *Stress and Anxiety*, vol. 5. Washington, D.C., Hemisphere, pp. 219–231.

Becker W (1964): Consequences of different kinds of parental discipline. Hoffman L, & Hoffman M (Eds.). In *Review of Child Development Research*. New York, Russel Sage Foundation, pp. 169–208.

Bitar KN, & Makhlouf GM (1982): Relaxation of isolated gastric smooth muscle cells by vasoactive intestinal peptide. Science 30:216:531-535.

Brady J (1960): Emotional behavior. Field J (Ed.). In *Handbook of Physiology*, Sect. I: *Neurophysiology*, vol. III. Washington, D.C., American Physiological Society, pp. 1529-1552.

Brodal A (1981): The amygdala, the hippocampus, the "limbic system." Motta M (Ed.). In *Neurological Anatomy*. New York, Raven Press, pp. 143-154.

Brownstein MJ (1980): Distribution of hypothalamic hormones. Motta M (Ed.). In *The Endocrine Functions of the Brain*. New York, Raven Press, pp. 143-154.

Cannon W (1932): *The Wisdom of the Body*. New York, Norton.

Carroll BJ, & Mendels J (1976): Neuroendocrine regulations in affective disorders. Sachara EJ (Ed.). In *Hormones, Behavior and Psychopathology*. New York, Raven Press, pp. 193-224.

Christie M, Little BC, & Gordon A (1980): Peripheral indices of depressive states. Van Praag H (Ed.). In *Handbook of Biological Psychiatry*, Part II. New York, Dekker, pp. 145-182.

Cohen J (1966): *Human Robots in Myth and Science*. London, Allen and Unwin.

Collu R (1977): Role of central cholinergic and aminergic neurotransmitters in the control of anterior pituitary hormone secretion. Besser GM, & Martini L (Eds.). In *Clinical Neuroendocrinology*. New York, Academic Press, pp. 43-65.

Comsa J, Leonhardt T, & Schwarz JA (1975): Influence of the thymus-corticotropin-growth hormone interaction on the rat. Friedman H (Ed.). In *Thymus Factors in Immunity*. New York, New York Academy of Sciences, pp. 387-401.

Cooper A (1977): *The internship and issues of educational quality*. Paper presented at American Psychiatric Association panel: The internship experience: Prospects and problems. Toronto, Canada, May.

de la Mettrie (1748): *L' Homme Machine*, reprinted. Wiener P (Ed.). In *Dictionary of the History of Ideas*, vol. III. New York, Schribner, 1973, p. 139.

De Rivera J (1977): A structural theory of emotions. Psychol Issues (Monograph 40) 10(4).

Descartes R (1637): Meditations on the first philosophy. Rand B (Ed.). In *Modern Classical Philosophers*. Cambridge, Mass., Houghton Mifflin.

Deutsch F (1959): *On the Mysterious Leap from the Mind ɔ the Body*. New York, International University Press.

de Wied D, Bohus B, Gispen WH, & Urban I et al (1976): Hormonal influence on motivational, learning and memory processes. Sachar E (Ed.). In *Hormones, Behavior and Psychopathology*. New York, Raven Press.

Dunbar HF (1943): *Psychosomatic Diagnosis*. New York, Hoeber.

Eccles JC (1981): Eccles JC, & Popper KR. In *the Self and Its Brain*. New York, Springer International.

Edwards CRW (1977): Vasopressin. Besser GM, & Martini L (Eds.). In *Clinical Neuroendocrinology*. New York, Academic Press, pp. 527-567.

Eibl-Eibesfeldt I (1972): Similarities and differences between cultures in expressive movements. Hinde RA (Ed.). In *Non-Verbal Communication*. New York, Cambridge University Press, pp. 297-312.

Ekman P, & Friesen W (1969): The repertoire of nonverbal behavior: Categories, origins, usage and coping. Semiotica (1):49-98.

Ellendorf F, Parvizi N (1980): The endocrine function of the brain. Motta M (Ed.). In *Role of Extrahypothalamic Centers in Neuroendocrine Integration*. New York, Raven Press, pp. 297-325.

Engel GL (1977): The need for a new medical model: A challenge for biomedicine. Science 196:129-136.

Frankenhaeuser M (1975): Experimental approaches to the study of catecholamines and emotion. Levi L (Ed.). In *Emotions: Their Parameters and Measurement*. New York, Raven Press, pp. 22-35.

Frankenhaeuser M (1976): The role of peripheral catecholamines in adaptation to understimulation and overstimulation. Serban G (Ed.). In *Psychopathology of Human Adaptation*. New York, Plenum Press, pp. 173-191.

Frankenhaeuser M (1976): The role of peripheral catecholamines in adaptation to understimulation, (in chapter: Psychopathology of Adaptive Learning: Motivation, Anxiety and Stress). Serban G (Ed.). In *Psychopathology of Human Adaptation*. New York, Plenum Press, pp. 173-191.

Frankenhaeuser M (1978): Psychoneuroendocrine approaches to the study of emotion as related to stress and coping. Howe H (Ed.). In *Nebraska Symposium on Motivation*, vol. 26. Lincoln, University of Nebraska Press, pp. 123-161.

Glass D (1977): *Behavior Patterns, Stress and Coronary Disease*. Hillsdale, NJ, Erlbaum.

Gloor P (1960): Amygdala. Field J (Ed.). In *Handbook of Physiology*, Sect. 1: *Neurophysiology*, vol. II. Washington, D.C., American Physiological Society, pp. 1395-1420.

Green J (1960): The hippocampus. Field J (Ed.). In *Handbook of Physiology*, Sect. 1: *Neurophysiology*, vol. II. Washington, D.C., American Physiological Society.

Hamburg D, & Elliott G (1981): Biobehavioral sciences: An emerging research agenda. Psychiatr Clin North Am 407-421.

Hamburg D, Hamburg B, & Barchas J (1975): Anger, depression in perspective of behavioral biology. Levi L (Ed.). In *Emotions: Their Parameters and Measurement*. New York, Raven Press.

Hinkle L (1973): The concept of stress in the biological and social sciences. In *Sciences, Medicine and Man*, vol. I. New York, Pergamon Press, pp. 31-48.

Hofer MA (1981): Toward a developmental basis for disease predisposition: The effects of early maternal separation on brain, behavior and cardiovascular system. Myron H, Stunkard A, & Weiner H (Eds.). In *Brain, Behavior and Bodily Disease*, vol. 59. New York, Raven Press.

Holmes T, & Masuda M (1974): Life change and illness susceptibility. In *Stressful Life Events*. New York, Wiley, pp. 45–72.

Holmes T, & Rahe RH (1967): The social readjustment rating scale. J Psychosom Res 2:213–218.

Iriuchijima J (1979): Origins of tonic activity in hypertension. Brooks C, Koizuma K, & Sata A (Eds.). In *Integrative Functions of the Autonomic Nervous System*. New York, Elsevier/North-Holland, pp. 355–359.

Isaacson RL (1974): *The Limbic System*. New York, Plenum Press.

Kant I (1798): Anthropology from a pragmatic point of view. Quote reprinted. Harre H, & Secord PF (Eds.). In *The Explanation of Social Behavior*, Chap. 2. Adams, Totawa, Littlefield, 1973.

Krohne HW (1978): Individual differences in coping with stress and anxiety. Spielberger CD, & Sarason IG (Eds.). In *Stress and Anxiety*, vol. 5. Washington, D.C., Hemisphere, pp. 233–260.

Lader M (1980): The psychophysiology of anxiety. Friedman H (Ed.). In *Thymus Factors in Immunity*, Part II: *Brain Mechanisms*. New York, New York Academy of Sciences.

Lal S, & Martin J (1980): Neuroanatomy and neuropharmacological regulation of neuroendocrine function. Van Praag HM (Ed.). In *Handbook of Biological Psychiatry*. New York, Dekker, pp. 101–167.

Lazarus R (1966): *Psychological Stress and the Coping Process*. New York, McGraw-Hill.

Levine S, Weinberg J, & Ursin H (1978): Definition of the coping process and statement of the problem. Ursin H (Ed.). In *Psychobiology of Stress*. New York, Academic Press.

Lipton MA, & Breese GR (1976): Behavioral effects of hypothalamic polypeptide hormones in animals and man. Sachar E (Ed.). In *Hormones, Behavior and Psychopathology*. New York, Raven Press, pp. 15–24.

Lisander B (1979): Somato-autonomic reactions and their higher control. Brooks C, Koizuma K, & Sato A (Eds.). In *Integrative Functions of the Autonomic Nervous System*. New York, Elsevier, pp. 385–395.

Lorenz K (1965): *Evolution and Modification of Behavior*. Chicago, University of Chicago Press.

MacLean PD (1970): The triune brain, emotion and scientific bias. Schmitt FO (Ed.). In *The Neurosciences Second Study Program*. New York, University Press, pp. 336–349.

Mason JW (1975): Emotions as reflected in patterns of endocrine integration. Levi L (Ed.). In *Emotions: Their Parameters and Measurement*. New York, Raven Press.

Mason J, Maher J, Hartley LH, Mougey E, Perlow M, & Jones L (1976): Selectivity of corticosteroid and catecholamine responses to various natural stimuli. Serban G (Ed.). In *Psychopathology of Human Adaptation*. London, Plenum Press, pp. 147–171.

Matsuzaki Y, Hamasaki Y, & Said SI (1980): Vasoactive intestinal peptide: A possible transmitter of nonadrenergic relaxation of guinea pig airways. Science 210:1252–1253.

Mckenzie JM (1979): Stress and thyroid function. Tolis G (Ed.). In *Clinical Neuroendocrinology: A Pathophysiological Approach*. New York, Raven Press, pp. 319–328.

Mckenzie JM, Pelletier G, Lecleric R, & Dube D (1979): Labrie F, Martin JB, Naftolin F, & Tolis G (Eds.). In *Clinical Neuroendocrinology: A Pathophysiological Approach*.

Olds J, & Milner P (1954): Positive reinforcement produced by electrical stimulation of septal area and other regions of the brain. J Comp Physiol Psychol 47:419–427.

Palkovits M (1980): Functional anatomy of the "endocrine" brain. Motta M (Ed.). In *The Endocrine Functions of the Brain*. New York, Raven Press, pp. 1–19.

Pearlin LI, & Schooler C (1978): The structure of coping. Health Soc Behav 19:2–21.

Pelletier G, Leclerc R, & Dube D (1979): Morphologic basis of neuroendocrine functions in the hypothalamus. Tolis G et al. (Ed.). In *Clinical Neuroendocrinology: A Pathophysiological Approach*. New York, Raven Press, pp. 15–27.

Penfield W, & Jasper H (1954): *Epilepsy and the Functional Anatomy of the Brain*. Boston, Little.

Polosa C, Mannard A, & Laskey W (1979): Tonic activity of the autonomic nervous system: Functions, properties, origins. Brooks C, Koizuma K, & Sata A (Eds.). In *Integrative Functions of the Autonomic Nervous System*. New York, Elsevier/North-Holland, pp. 342–354.

Prange A, Nemeroff C, & Loosen P (1979): Collu R, Ducharme JR, Barbeau A, & Rochefort JG (Eds.). In *Central Nervous System Effects of Hypothalamic Hormones*. New York, Elsevier, pp. 342–354.

Popper K, & Eccles J (1981): *The Self and its Brain*. New York, Springer International.

Pribram K, & McGuiness D (1975): Arousal, activation and effort in the control of attention. Psychol Rev 82:116–149.

Proceedings of the Forum on Coronary Prone Behavior (1978). DHEW Publ (NIH) 78-1451, p. 162.

Rabkin JG, & Struening EL (1976): Life events, stress and illness. Science 194:1013–1020.

Rahe RH (1968): Life-change measurement as a predictor of illness. Proc R Soc Med 61:1124–1126.

Rahe RH, Meyer M, Smith M, Kjaerg G, & Holmes T (1964): Social stress and illness onset. J Psychosom Res 8:35–44.

Reichlin S (1979): An overview of the anatomical and physiological basis of anterior-pituitary regulation. Labire F, Martin J, Naftolin N, & Tolis G (Eds.). In *Clinical Neuroendocrinology: A Pathophysiological Approach*. New York, Raven Press.

Reiser M (1975): Changing theoretical concepts of psychosomatic medicine. Arieti S (Ed.). In *American Handbook of Psychiatry*, vol. 4. New York, Basic Books.

Riley V (1981): Psychoneuroendocrine influences on immunocompetence and neoplasia. Science 212: 1100–1109.

Rogers MP, Dubey D, & Reich P (1979): The influence of the psyche and the brain on immunity and disease susceptibility: A critical review. Psychosom Med 41:147–164.

Rostogi R (1979): Thyrotropin-releasing hormone influences on behavior: Possible involvement of brain monoaminergic systems. Barbeau A, Colly R, Ducharme JR, &

Rochefort JG (Eds.). In *Central Nervous System Effects on Hypothalamic Hormones and Other Peptides.* New York, Raven Press, pp. 123–140.

Sachar E (1980): Neuroendocrine approaches to psychoneuropharmacologic research. Van Praag HM (Ed.). In *Handbook of Biological Psychiatry,* Part III. New York, Dekker, pp. 169–177.

Sandman C, Kastin A, & Miller L (1977): Central nervous system actions of MSH and related pituitary peptides. Besser GM, & Martini L (Eds.). In *Clinical Neuroendocrinology.* New York, Academic Press, pp. 443–469.

Saper C (1979): Anatomical substrates for the hypothalamic control of the autonomic nervous system. Brooks C, Koizumi K, & Sata A (Eds.). In *Integrative Functions of the Autonomic Nervous System.* New York, Elsevier/North-Holland, pp. 333–341.

Schally A, & Arimura A (1977): Physiology and nature of hypothalamic regulatory hormones. Besser GM, & Martini L (Eds.). In *Clinical Neuroendocrinology.* New York, Academic Press, pp. 1–41.

Schur M (1955): Comments on the metapsychology of somatization. Psychoanal Study Child 10:119–164.

Schwartz G, & Weiss S (Eds.). (1978): *Proceedings of the Yale Conference on Behavioral Medicine.* DHEW Publ. No. (NIH) 78–1424.

Selye H (1966): *The Stress of life.* New York, McGraw-Hill.

Sperry R (1982): Some effects of disconnecting the cerebral hemispheres. Science 217:1223–1226.

Stein M, Keller S, & Schleifer S (1981): The hypothalamus and the immune responses. Deweine H, Hofer M, & Stunkard A (Eds.). In *Brain, Behavior and Bodily Disease,* vol. 59. New York, Raven Press, pp. 1059–1094.

Stellar E (1976): Neurophysiological mechanisms of adaptive behavior. Serban G (Ed.). In *Psychopathology of Human Adaptation.* New York, Plenum Press, pp. 125–134.

Strawson P (1959): *Individuals.* London, Methuen.

Tache J, & Selye H (1978): On stress and coping mechanisims. Sarason IG, & Spielberger CD (Eds.). In *Stress and Anxiety,* vol. 5. Washington, D.C., Hemisphere, pp. 3–24.

Tinbergen N (1953): *Social Behavior in Animals.* London, Methuen.

van Wimersma Greidans TjB (1979): Neuropeptides and avoidance behavior; with special reference to the effects of vasopressin, ACTH and MSH on memory processes. In *Central Nervous System Effects of Hypothalamic Hormones and Other Peptides.* New York, Raven Press, pp. 177–187.

Weich B, Ritter S, & Ritter R (1980): Plasma catecholamines: Exaggerated elevation is associated with stress susceptibility. Physiol Behav 24:864–874.

Weingartner H, Gold P, Ballenger J, Smallbeg S, Rubinow D, Post R, & Goodwin F (1981): Effects of vasopressin on human memory functions. Science 211:601–607.

Weiner H (1977): Psychobiological contributions to human disease. Weiner H (Ed.). In *Psychobiology and Human Disease,* pp. 579–651. New York, Elsevier.

Weiner P (Ed.). (1973): *Dictionary of the History of Ideas,* vol. III. New York, Scribner, pp. 131–146.

Weitzman E (1980): Neuroendocrine rhythms and the sleep cycle. Van Praag HM (Ed.). In *Handbook of Biological Psychiatry.* New York, Dekker, pp. 319–341.

Wolf S (1981): The role of the brain in bodily disease. Myron H, Stunkard A, & Weiner H (Eds.). In *Brain, Behavior and Bodily Disease,* vol. 59. New York, Raven Press, pp. 1–9.

Wolff HG (1950): Life stress and bodily disease: A formulation. In *Life Stress and Bodily Disease.* Baltimore, Williams & Wilkins, pp. 1059–1094.

Yarrow L (1964): Separation from parents during early childhood. Hoffman L, & Hoffman M (Eds.). In *Review of Child Development Research.* New York, Russell Sage Foundation, pp. 89–136.

Zegans LS (1967): An appraisal of ethological contributions to psychiatric theory and research. Am J Psychiatry 124:729–744.

Zegans LS (1982): The relationship of stress to the development of somatic disorders. Goldberger L, & Shlomo B (Eds.). In *Handbook of Stress.* New York, Free Press.

Zegans, LS, Sledge W, & Thompson T (1977): *Reintroduction of the internship into a department of psychiatry.* Paper presented at the American Psychiatric Association panel: The internship experience: Prospects and problems. Toronto, Canada, May.

INDEX

Page numbers in *italics* indicate illustrations.
Page numbers followed by t indicate tables.